THE PAPERS OF
THOMAS JEFFERSON

THE PAPERS OF
Thomas Jefferson

Volume 17
6 July to 3 November 1790

JULIAN P. BOYD, EDITOR

CONSULTING EDITOR

LUCIUS WILMERDING, JR.

PRINCETON, NEW JERSEY

PRINCETON UNIVERSITY PRESS

1965

In common with other editorial enterprises,
THE PAPERS OF THOMAS JEFFERSON
is a continuing beneficiary of the good offices
of The National Historical Publications Commission,
through its Chairman, Wayne C. Grover,
its Executive Director, Oliver W. Holmes, and its staff.

FOREWORD

Owing to space and other considerations—chief among which was the dislocation in the present volume resulting from the group of documents on the Anglo-Spanish war crisis of 1790 and the editorial problems posed thereby—the Appendix concerning the opinions of Hamilton and Jefferson on the question of arrearages of soldiers' pay as announced in Volume 16, page 462, will not appear in this but instead in the next volume. The documents on the war crisis, together with other editorial comment and some additional texts, have been made available in separate form by the Princeton University Press under the title *Number 7: Alexander Hamilton's Secret Attempts to Control American Foreign Policy.*

Since the appearance of the last volume a little over three years ago two events of enduring significance concerning historical source materials have taken place. The first was the enactment into law by the Congress of the United States of enabling legislation in support of the program of the National Historical Publications Commission for collecting, describing, editing, and publishing (including microfilming and other forms of reproduction) of documentary sources significant to the history of the United States. The second was the grant by the Ford Foundation to the National Archives Trust Fund Board of $2,000,000 to be administered for a ten-year period in support of certain major editorial enterprises and for the training of scholars in methods of documentary editing. Both of these events took place in 1964. *The Papers of Thomas Jefferson*, in common with other enterprises for the publication of the sources of American history, has benefited greatly from the cooperation and good offices of the National Historical Publications Commission and from the financial assistance made available to the Commission by the Ford Foundation. It is with a sense of gratitude commensurate with the promise held forth by these two significant events that, on behalf of the Editorial Advisory Committee and of all others connected with this enterprise, I record our deep appreciation of these indispensable benefits.

It is also appropriate at this time to renew our profound expressions of gratitude for the original and continued grant from The New York Times Company that made it possible for *The Papers of Thomas Jefferson* to become a reality. Other benefactions from the Charlotte Palmer Phillips Foundation, the John Simon Guggen-

FOREWORD

heim Memorial Foundation, and loyal friends of the work such as Mr. J. R. Wiggins and Ambassador David Bruce have provided not only material aids of an essential character but, like the generous cooperation of librarians, archivists, collectors, and others, have brought immeasurable encouragement and inspiration.

JULIAN P. BOYD
Editor

10 February 1965

GUIDE TO EDITORIAL APPARATUS

1. TEXTUAL DEVICES

The following devices are employed throughout the work to clarify the presentation of the text.

[. . .], [. . . .]	One or two words missing and not conjecturable.
[. . .][1], [. . . .][1]	More than two words missing and not conjecturable; subjoined footnote estimates number of words missing.
[ ]	Number or part of a number missing or illegible.
[roman]	Conjectural reading for missing or illegible matter. A question mark follows when the reading is doubtful.
[*italic*]	Editorial comment inserted in the text.
⟨*italic*⟩	Matter deleted in the MS but restored in our text.
⟦ ⟧	Record entry for letters not found.

2. DESCRIPTIVE SYMBOLS

The following symbols are employed throughout the work to describe the various kinds of manuscript originals. When a series of versions is recorded, *the first to be recorded is the version used for the printed text.*

Dft	draft (usually a composition or rough draft; later drafts, when identifiable as such, are designated "2 Dft," &c.)
Dupl	duplicate
MS	manuscript (arbitrarily applied to most documents other than letters)
N	note, notes (memoranda, fragments, &c.)
PoC	polygraph copy
PrC	press copy
RC	recipient's copy
SC	stylograph copy
Tripl	triplicate

All manuscripts of the above types are assumed to be in the hand of the author of the document to which the descriptive symbol pertains. If not, that fact is stated. On the other hand, the follow-

[ix]

ing types of manuscripts are assumed *not* to be in the hand of the author, and exceptions will be noted:

FC   file copy (applied to all forms of retained copies, such as letter-book copies, clerk's copies, &c.)

Tr   transcript (applied to both contemporary and later copies; period of transcription, unless clear by implication, will be given when known)

3. LOCATION SYMBOLS

The locations of documents printed in this edition from originals in private hands, from originals held by institutions outside the United States, and from printed sources are recorded in self-explanatory form in the descriptive note following each document. The locations of documents printed from originals held by public institutions in the United States are recorded by means of the symbols used in the National Union Catalog in the Library of Congress; and explanation of how these symbols are formed is given above, Vol. 1: xl. The list of symbols appearing in each volume is limited to the institutions represented by documents printed or referred to in that and previous volumes.

CLSU	University of Southern California Library, Los Angeles
CLU	William Andrews Clark Memorial Library, University of California at Los Angeles
CSmH	Henry E. Huntington Library, San Marino, California
Ct	Connecticut State Library, Hartford, Connecticut
CtY	Yale University Library
DeHi	Historical Society of Delaware, Wilmington, Delaware
DLC	Library of Congress
DNA	The National Archives, with identifications of series (preceded by record group number) as follows:

           CD   Consular Dispatches
           DCI   Diplomatic and Consular Instructions
           DD   Diplomatic Dispatches
           FL   Foreign Letters

MLR	Miscellaneous Letters Received
MTA	Miscellaneous Treasury Accounts (cited as M235 [microfilm series], with the number of the reel)
NL	Notes from Legations
PCC	Papers of the Continental Congress
SDC	State Department Correspondence
G-Ar	Georgia Department of Archives and History, Atlanta
ICHi	Chicago Historical Society, Chicago
IHi	Illinois State Historical Library, Springfield
IMunS	St. Mary of the Lake Seminary, Mundelein, Illinois
MB	Boston Public Library, Boston
MBAt	Boston Athenæum, Boston
MH	Harvard University Library
MHi	Massachusetts Historical Society, Boston
MHi:AM	Adams Manuscripts, presented by the Adams Manuscript Trust to the Massachusetts Historical Society
MdAA	Maryland Hall of Records, Annapolis
MdAN	U.S. Naval Academy Library
MeHi	Maine Historical Society, Portland
MiU-C	William L. Clements Library, University of Michigan
MoSHi	Missouri Historical Society, St. Louis
MWA	American Antiquarian Society, Worcester
NA	New York State Library, Albany
NBu	Buffalo Public Library, Buffalo, New York
NcD	Duke University Library
NcU	University of North Carolina Library
NhD	Dartmouth College Library, Hanover, New Hampshire
NHi	New-York Historical Society, New York City
NK-Iselin	Letters to and from John Jay bearing this symbol are used by permission of the Estate of Eleanor Jay Iselin.
NN	New York Public Library, New York City
NNC	Columbia University Libraries
NNP	Pierpont Morgan Library, New York City

NNS	New York Society Library, New York City
NjP	Princeton University Library
NjMoW	Washington Headquarters Library, Morristown, N.J.
PBL	Lehigh University Library
PHC	Haverford College Library
PHi	Historical Society of Pennsylvania, Philadelphia
PP	Free Library, Philadelphia
PPAP	American Philosophical Society, Philadelphia
PPL-R	Library Company of Philadelphia, Ridgway Branch
PU	University of Pennsylvania Library
PWW	Washington and Jefferson College, Washington, Pennsylvania
RPA	Rhode Island Department of State, Providence
RPAB	Annmary Brown Memorial Library, Providence
RPB	Brown University Library
Vi	Virginia State Library, Richmond
Vi:USCC	Ended Cases, United States Circuit Court, Virginia State Library
ViHi	Virginia Historical Society, Richmond
ViRVal	Valentine Museum Library, Richmond
ViU	University of Virginia Library
ViU:McG	McGregor Library, University of Virginia
ViU:TJMF	Manuscripts deposited by the Thomas Jefferson Memorial Foundation in the Alderman Library, University of Virginia
ViW	College of William and Mary Library
ViWC	Colonial Williamsburg, Inc.
VtMC	Middlebury College Library, Middlebury, Vermont
VtMS	Secretary of State, Montpelier, Vermont
WHi	State Historical Society of Wisconsin, Madison

4. OTHER SYMBOLS AND ABBREVIATIONS

The following symbols and abbreviations are commonly employed in the annotation throughout the work.

Second Series   The topical series to be published at the end of this edition, comprising those materials which are best suited to a classified rather than a chronological arrangement (see Vol. 1: xv-xvi)

TJ   Thomas Jefferson

TJ Editorial Files   Photoduplicates and other editorial materials in the office of *The Papers of Thomas Jefferson*, Princeton University Library

TJ Papers   Jefferson Papers (applied to a collection of manuscripts when the precise location of a given document must be furnished, and always preceded by the symbol for the institutional repository; thus "DLC: TJ Papers, 4:628-9" represents a document in the Library of Congress, Jefferson Papers, volume 4, pages 628 and 629)

RG   Record Group (used in designating the location of documents in the National Archives)

SJL   Jefferson's "Summary Journal of letters" written and received (in DLC: TJ Papers)

SJPL   "Summary Journal of Public Letters," an incomplete list of letters written by TJ from 16 Apr. 1784 to 31 Dec. 1793, with brief summaries, in an amanuensis' hand except for six pages in TJ's hand listing and summarizing official reports and communications by him as Secretary of State, 11 Oct. 1789 to 31 Dec. 1789 (in DLC: TJ Papers, at end of SJL)

V   Ecu

ƒ   Florin

£   Pound sterling or livre, depending upon context (in doubtful cases, a clarifying note will be given)

s   Shilling or sou. (Also expressed as /)

d   Penny or denier

₶   Livre Tournois

⅌   Per (occasionally used for pro, pre)

5. SHORT TITLES

The following list includes only those short titles of works cited with great frequency, and therefore in very abbreviated form, throughout this edition. Their expanded forms are given here only in the degree of fullness needed for unmistakable identification. Since it is impossible to anticipate all the works to be cited in such very abbreviated form, the list is appropriately revised from volume to volume.

Adams, *Works*   Charles Francis Adams, ed., *The Works of John Adams*, Boston, 1850-56, 10 vols.

Adams, *Diary*   *Diary and Autobiography of John Adams*, ed. L. H. Butterfield and others, Cambridge, 1961, 4 vols.

AHR   *American Historical Review*, 1895-

Annals   *Annals of the Congress of the United States: The Debates and Proceedings in the Congress of the United States . . . Compiled from Authentic Materials by Joseph Gales, Senior*, Washington, Gales & Seaton, 1834-56, 42 vols. The edition employed here is that which contains the running heads on verso and recto pages respectively: "Gales & Seatons History" and "of Debates in Congress." Another printing, with the same title-page but with running heads on both recto and verso pages reading "History of Congress," has a different pagination, so that pages cited in the edition employed here should be converted by subtracting approximately fifty-two from the number given in the citation. All editions are undependable.

ASP   *American State Papers: Documents, Legislative and Executive, of the Congress of the United States*, Washington, Gales & Seaton, 1832-61, 38 vols.

Atlas of Amer. Hist., Scribner, 1943   James Truslow Adams and R. V. Coleman, eds., *Atlas of American History*, N.Y., 1943

Bemis, *Jay's Treaty*   Samuel Flagg Bemis, *Jay's Treaty: A Study in Commerce and Diplomacy*, New Haven, 1962, revised edn.

Betts, *Farm Book*   Edwin M. Betts, ed., *Thomas Jefferson's Farm Book*, Princeton, 1953

Betts, *Garden Book*   Edwin M. Betts, ed., *Thomas Jefferson's Garden Book*, Philadelphia, 1944

Biog. Dir. Cong.   *Biographical Directory of the American Congress, 1774-1949*, Washington, 1950

B.M. Cat.   British Museum, *General Catalogue of Printed Books*, London, 1931-; also *The British Museum Catalogue of Printed Books, 1881-1900*, Ann Arbor, 1946

B.N. Cat.   Bibliothèque Nationale, *Catalogue général des livres imprimés. . . .Auteurs*, Paris, 1897-1955

Brant, *Madison*, I   Irving Brant, *James Madison: The Virginia Revolutionist*, Indianapolis, 1941

Brant, *Madison*, II   Irving Brant, *James Madison: The Nationalist, 1780-1787*, Indianapolis, 1948

Brant, *Madison*, III   Irving Brant, *James Madison: Father of the Constitution, 1787-1800*, Indianapolis, 1950

Brant, *Madison*, IV   Irving Brant, *James Madison: Secretary of State, 1800-1809*, Indianapolis, 1953

Brant, *Madison*, V   Irving Brant, *James Madison: The President, 1809-1812*, Indianapolis, 1956

Burnett, *Letters of Members*   Edwin C. Burnett, ed., *Letters of Members of the Continental Congress*, Washington, 1921-1936, 8 vols.

Butterfield, *Rush*   *Letters of Benjamin Rush*, ed. L. H. Butterfield, Princeton, 1951, 2 vols.

Cal. Franklin Papers   I. Minis Hays, ed., *Calendar of the Papers of Benjamin Franklin in the Library of the American Philosophical Society*, Philadelphia, 1908, 6 vols.

Carter, *Terr. Papers*   *The Territorial Papers of the United States*, ed. Clarence E. Carter, Washington, 1934-62, 26 vols.

CVSP   William P. Palmer and others, eds., *Calendar of Virginia State Papers . . . Preserved in the Capitol at Richmond*, Richmond, 1875-1893

DAB   Allen Johnson and Dumas Malone, eds., *Dictionary of American Biography*, N.Y., 1928-1936

DAE   Sir William A. Craigie and James Hulbert, eds., *A Dictionary of American English*, Chicago, 1938-1944

DAH   James Truslow Adams, ed., *Dictionary of American History*, N.Y., 1940, 5 vols., and index

DNB   Leslie Stephen and Sidney Lee, eds., *Dictionary of National Biography*, 2d ed., N.Y., 1908-1909

Dumbauld, *Tourist*   Edward Dumbauld, *Thomas Jefferson American Tourist*, Norman, Oklahoma, 1946

Elliot's *Debates*   Jonathan Elliot, ed., *The Debates of the Several State Conventions on the Adoption of the Federal Constitution . . . together with the Journal of the Federal Convention*, 2d ed., Philadelphia, 1901, 5 vols.

Evans   Charles Evans, comp., *American Bibliography*, Chicago, 1903-1955

Ford   Paul Leicester Ford, ed., *The Writings of Thomas Jefferson*, Letterpress Edition, N.Y., 1892-1899, 10 vols.

Freeman, *Washington*   Douglas Southall Freeman, *George Washington*, N.Y., 1948-1957, 6 vols.; 7th volume by J. A. Carroll and M. W. Ashworth, New York, 1957

Fry-Jefferson Map   Dumas Malone, ed., *The Fry & Jefferson Map of Virginia and Maryland: a Facsimile of the First Edition*, Princeton, 1950

Greely, *Public Documents*   Adolphus Washington Greely, ed., *Public Documents of the First Fourteen Congresses, 1789-1817: Papers Relating to Early Congressional Documents*, Washington, 1900

HAW   Henry A. Washington, ed., *The Writings of Thomas Jefferson*, N.Y., 1853-1854, 9 vols.

Hening   William Waller Hening, ed., *The Statutes at Large; Being a Collection of All the Laws of Virginia*, Richmond, 1809-1823, 13 vols.

Henry, *Henry*   William Wirt Henry, *Patrick Henry, Life, Correspondence and Speeches*, N.Y., 1891, 3 vols.

Humphreys, *Humphreys*   F. L. Humphreys, *Life and Times of David Humphreys*, New York, 1917, 2 vols.

JCC   Worthington C. Ford and others, eds., *Journals of the Continental Congress, 1774-1789*, Washington, 1904-1937, 34 vols.

JEP   *Journal of the Executive Proceedings of the Senate of the United States . . . to the Termination of the Nineteenth Congress*, Washington, 1828

JHD   *Journal of the House of Delegates of the Commonwealth of Virginia* (cited by session and date of publication)

JHR   *Journal of the House of Representatives of the United States*, Washington, Gales & Seaton, 1826-

Jefferson Correspondence, Bixby   Worthington C. Ford, ed., *Thomas Jefferson Correspondence Printed from the Originals in the Collections of William K. Bixby*, Boston, 1916

JS   *Journal of the Senate of the United States*, Washington, Gales, 1820-21, 5 vols.

Kimball, *Jefferson*, I   Marie Kimball, *Jefferson the Road to Glory 1743 to 1776*, New York, 1943

Kimball, *Jefferson*, II   Marie Kimball, *Jefferson War and Peace 1776 to 1784*, New York, 1947

Kimball, *Jefferson*, III   Marie Kimball, *Jefferson the Scene of Europe 1784 to 1789*, New York, 1950

King, *King*   C. R. King, ed., *The Life and Correspondence of Rufus King, Comprising His Letters, Private and Official, His Public Documents, and His Speeches, 1755-1827*, New York, 1894-1900, 6 vols.

L & B   Andrew A. Lipscomb and Albert E. Bergh, eds., *The Writings of Thomas Jefferson*, Washington, 1903-1904, 20 vols.

L.C. *Cat.*   *A Catalogue of Books Represented by the Library of Congress Printed Cards*, Ann Arbor, 1942-1946; also *Supplement*, 1948-

Library Catalogue, 1783   Jefferson's MS list of books owned or wanted in 1783 (original in Massachusetts Historical Society)

Library Catalogue, 1815   *Catalogue of the Library of the United States*, Washington, 1815

Library Catalogue, 1829   *Catalogue: President Jefferson's Library*, Washington, 1829

Loubat, *Medallic history*   J. F. Loubat, *The Medallic History of the United States of America, 1776-1876*, New York, 1878, 2 vols.

Maclay, *Journal*, ed. Maclay   Edgar S. Maclay, ed., *Journal of William Maclay, United States Senator from Pennsylvania, 1789-1791*, New York, 1890

Madison, *Letters and Other Writings*   James Madison, *Letters and Other Writings of James Madison*, Philadelphia, 1865

Malone, *Jefferson*, I   Dumas Malone, *Jefferson the Virginian*, Boston, 1948

Malone, *Jefferson*, II   Dumas Malone, *Jefferson and the Rights of Man*, Boston, 1951

Malone, *Jefferson*, III   Dumas Malone, *Jefferson and the Ordeal of Liberty*, New York, 1962

Miller, *Hamilton*   John C. Miller, *Alexander Hamilton Portrait in Paradox*, New York, 1959

Mitchell, *Hamilton*   Broadus Mitchell, *Alexander Hamilton*, New York, 1957, 1962, 2 vols.

MVHR   *Mississippi Valley Historical Review*, 1914-

OED   Sir James Murray and others, eds., *A New English Dictionary on Historical Principles*, Oxford, 1888-1933

PMHB   *Pennsylvania Magazine of History and Biography,*
1877-

Randall, *Life*   Henry S. Randall, *The Life of Thomas Jefferson*, N.Y., 1858, 3 vols.

Randolph, *Domestic Life*   Sarah N. Randolph, *The Domestic Life of Thomas Jefferson, Compiled from Family Letters and Reminiscences by His Great-Granddaughter*, Cambridge, Mass., 1939

Sabin   Joseph Sabin and others, comps., *Bibliotheca Americana. A Dictionary of Books Relating to America*, N.Y., 1868-1936

Sowerby   E. Millicent Sowerby, comp., *Catalogue of the Library of Thomas Jefferson*, 1952-1959, 5 vols.

Sparks, *Morris*   Jared Sparks, *Life of Gouverneur Morris*, Boston, 1832, 3 vols.

Swem, *Index*   Earl G. Swem, comp., *Virginia Historical Index*, Roanoke, 1934-1936

Swem, "Va. Bibliog."   Earl G. Swem, comp., "A Bibliography of Virginia History," Virginia State Library, *Bulletin*, VIII (1915), X (1917), and XII (1919)

Syrett, *Hamilton*   *The Papers of Alexander Hamilton*, ed. Harold C. Syrett and others, New York, 1961—, 7 vols.

TJR   Thomas Jefferson Randolph, ed., *Memoir, Correspondence, and Miscellanies, from the Papers of Thomas Jefferson*, Charlottesville, 1829, 4 vols.

Tucker, *Life*   George Tucker, *The Life of Thomas Jefferson*, Philadelphia, 1837, 2 vols.

U.S. Statutes at Large   *The Public Statutes at Large of the United States of America, from the Organization of the Government in 1789, to March 3, 1845. . . . Edited by Richard Peters* (and others). Second edition. Boston: Little, Brown, and Company, 1856-1873. 17 volumes.

Van Doren, *Secret History*   Carl Van Doren, *Secret History of the American Revolution*, New York, 1941

VMHB   *Virginia Magazine of History and Biography*, 1893-

WMQ   *William and Mary Quarterly*, 1892-

CONTENTS

CONTENTS

CONTENTS

CONTENTS

CONTENTS

CONTENTS

CONTENTS

CONTENTS

CONTENTS

ILLUSTRATIONS

See pages 218, 394, 427

See pages 218, 394, 427

CREEK INDIAN CHIEFS WHOM JEFFERSON MET AT THE
TREATY OF 1790

In July, 1790, when John Trumbull finished his full-length portrait
of Washington for the Common Council of New York City, the President was curious to know what effect this realistic delineation would
have on the deputation of Creek Indians who accompanied McGillivray
northward to negotiate the Treaty of 1790. He therefore directed
Trumbull to place the picture in an advantageous light facing the
entrance to the painting-room. Washington on this occasion, as in
the portrait, was in full uniform. He invited several of the principal
chiefs to dine with him and after dinner proposed a walk. When the
door to the painting-room was thrown open, the Indians, according
to Trumbull, were struck mute with astonishment and even more with
perplexity on seeing before them another and identical White Father
transfixed on thin fabric. "I had been desirous of obtaining portraits of
some of these principal men, who possessed a dignity of manner, form,
countenance, and expression, worthy of Roman senators," Trumbull
wrote, "but after this I found it impracticable; they had received the
impression, that there must be magic in an art which could render a
smooth flat surface so like to a real man; I however succeeded in
obtaining drawings of several by stealth" (John Trumbull, *Autobiography* [New York, 1841], p. 165; see also Trumbull, *Autobiography*,
ed. Theodore Sizer, p. 166-7). The two pencil sketches here illustrated
are among those reproduced between p. 164 and 165 in the 1841
edition of the *Autobiography* and bear these captions: "John—a Creek—
N. York—July 1790. J. T." and "Tuskatche Mico, or the Birdtail
King of the Cusitahs. N. York July 1790—J. T."

Since these likenesses were done by stealth, it is probable that
Trumbull sketched them during one of several gatherings between the
time the Indians arrived in the city on the 21st of July and the formal
ratification ceremonies in Federal Hall on the 13th of August. One
such event was the "Complimentary conference" in the great Wigwam
of the Society of St. Tammany with the members of that organization
in full Indian dress. Speeches, songs, and toasts marked the occasion.
Jefferson was present, smoked the calumet of peace, and joined in
the "*shake-hands*" conducted in the Indian manner (*New-York Journal*, 3 and 10 Aug. 1790; *Daily Advertiser*, 4 Aug. 1790; see note,
TJ to Knox, 12 Aug. 1790). Jefferson, always zealous in gathering
information about the American natives, took care to note on a slip
of paper that an "Account of the Creek Nation" had appeared in
Fenno's *Gazette of the United States* of 14 Aug. 1790 (DLC: TJ
Papers, 59: 10012). Few indeed could have had a deeper interest in
the language, the manners, and the individuals of this tribe than he.

In 1786 Benjamin Hawkins had described both McGillivray and the Creeks and had sent to Jefferson copies of the treaties of Hopewell that he now employed under a liberal construction of the treaty power as a means of enforcing the secret article of the Treaty of 1790 (see Hawkins to TJ, 14 June 1786; see notes to TJ's opinion on McGillivray's monopoly, 29 July 1790, and to Randolph to TJ, 14 Aug. 1790).

INDIAN FIGURE PRESENTED TO JEFFERSON

On 8 July 1790 Harry Innes transmitted to Jefferson an "Image carved of Stone of a naked Woman kneeling . . . about nine or ten Inches high" and in 1791 Jefferson presented this object to the American Philosophical Society (Innes to TJ, 8 July 1790, note). In the latter part of the 19th century many of the Society's botanical and mineralogical specimens, Indian artifacts, and other antiquities were deposited with the Academy of Natural Sciences of Philadelphia. This figure of a woman is now in the Fitzhugh collection of the Heye Foundation with "accompanying data of provenience" identifying it as from the Cumberland river, Kentucky (Frederick J. Dockstader, Director, Museum of the American Indian, to the Editors, 27 Oct. 1960). This figure measures 9¾ inches in height. (*Courtesy of the Museum of the American Indian*)

MARKET STREET, PHILADELPHIA, LOOKING EAST TOWARD OFFICES OF DEPARTMENT OF STATE AND RESIDENCE OF SECRETARY OF STATE

The print here reproduced was "Drawn Engraved & Published by W. Birch & Son" and "Sold by R. Campbell & Co. No. 30 Chestnut Street Philada. 1799," the caption of which reads: "HIGH STREET, from Ninth Street. PHILADELPHIA." The offices of the Department of State cannot be certainly identified in the illustration, though if the suggestion of a street on the north side just beyond the sentry box is 8th, then 274 High (or, as it was commonly called, Market) street is on that corner. Diagonally across on the south side of the street stood the "very large four story house" that Jefferson occupied as his residence, the fourth house west from 8th street. If the view represented in the print actually was taken from 9th street, then this house, owned by Thomas Leiper, must be one of those in the immediate foreground on the south side. For a description of the house, see Dumbauld, *Tourist*, p. 163-7. (*Courtesy of the Historical Society of Pennsylvania*)

THE OFFICES OF THE DEPARTMENT OF STATE IN PHILADELPHIA, 1790

This three-story brick house on the northwest corner of Market at 7th street housed the offices of the Department of State after the removal of the government to Philadelphia in the autumn of 1790. For a description of the building and the offices, see notes to Document

VII in the group of documents relating to departmental personnel and services, p. 377-80. This representation of the building was drawn by David J. Kennedy in 1836 and is a detail of a water color showing two other houses: (1) the home of Jacob Hiltzheimer on the southeast corner of Market at 7th street, below which on 7th Hiltzheimer built the continental stables, and (2) the large two-story house on the southwest corner of Market at 7th in which Jefferson drafted the Declaration of Independence (the drawing of this house shows that it bore on its roof a large sign extending the full width of the structure and reading: "JEFFERSON HOUSE"). This drawing is accompanied by explanatory notes made by Kennedy after 1891 (Kennedy Collection, PHi; for a note on Kennedy and his work, see PMHB, LX (1936), 67-71). The building housing the offices of the Department of State in 1790 was No. 307 High street. (*Courtesy of the Historical Society of Pennsylvania*)

JEFFERSON'S CHART OF NATIONAL DIPLOMATIC ESTABLISHMENTS

A tabular summary of "the Diplomatic establishments of the principal courts" appears on the verso of the chart here illustrated and is printed below, p. 221, note 20 (MS and its PrC are in DLC: TJ Papers 232: 41620-1; Tr in DNA: RG 59, SDC; the Dupl of the chart, also entirely in TJ's hand, that TJ submitted to the President is in DNA: RG 59, MLR). As explained in the Editorial Note to the group of plans and estimates that Jefferson drew up for the diplomatic establishment, this conspectus was characteristic of his method (see p. 216-31). In addition to the various materials gathered by Jefferson for this purpose and described in note to Document III of that group, there exist various lists of diplomatic representatives sent and received by the courts of Great Britain, Portugal, and Spain that were used by him in compiling the chart illustrated (MSS in DLC: TJ Papers, 236: 42314, 42315, 42352, 42353, 42354, 42355; those for Great Britain and Portugal are in the hand of Lucy Ludwell Paradise).

"PLAN OF A FORTIFICATION ON THE SOUTH FORK OF ELKHORN"

This chart with its accompanying description is "the Plan of an old Fortification" that Harry Innes enclosed in his letter to Jefferson of 8 July 1779. It is not in Innes' hand and perhaps was drawn by some military officer, as was the case with the comparable plan of an Indian site on the Muskingum that was sent by Ezra Stiles to Jefferson on 8 May 1786 (see Vol. 9: xxix, 419, 477-8; Stiles seemed to think that plan was drawn by General Samuel Holden Parsons who transmitted it to him, but actually it was a "Plan of the Remains of Some Ancient Works on the Muskingum by Jona. Heart Captn. 1st. Amera. Regt." and an engraving of it with accompanying essay by Heart was published in the May, 1787, issue of *Columbian Magazine*, p. 425-7). The plan here illustrated is dated "January 26th. 1790." Its unidentified author did not share Innes' view that the fortification was the work of aborigines, for he thought it appeared to be "above the power and abilities of Indians to perform" and asked: "Could Ferdinand de Soto have encampt at this place?" Jefferson retained the drawing among his papers though he gave the Indian artifact that accompanied it to the American Philosophical Society (MS in DLC: TJ Papers, 56: 9076-7, now separated from Innes' covering letter). (*Courtesy of the Library of Congress*)

WILLIAM LOUGHTON SMITH

At the time this miniature was painted by John Trumbull (1792), William Smith had not adopted his middle name, which he did later in order to avoid confusion with another political figure of the same name from South Carolina. For a statement of the reasons for identifying Smith as the author of the public letter to the President signed by *Junius Americanus* and calling for the veto of the Residence Bill as being unconstitutional, see Editorial Note, Opinions on the Constitutionality of the Residence Bill, p. 178-82, and notes to Documents I and IX in that group of documents. The miniature is signed and dated on the back (Theodore Sizer, *The Works of Colonel John Trumbull* [New Haven, 1950], p. 51). (*Courtesy of Yale University Art Gallery*)

ARTHUR ST. CLAIR

This pencil sketch by John Trumbull was drawn in New York in 1790 (Theodore Sizer, *The Works of Colonel John Trumbull* [New Haven, 1950], p. 48). Since St. Clair made his remarkable journey from Pittsburgh to New York late in August, arriving on the evening of the 20th and leaving presumably on the 24th, it follows that the delineation was made during the extraordinarily busy weekend when Knox, Hamilton, and St. Clair were planning and arranging the details for the expedition against Indians in the Northwest Territory and when the Secretary of the Treasury, in a confidential conversation with George Beckwith, revealed its object (see notes to Document XI in the group of documents pertaining to the war crisis, p. 131-4). The portrait, therefore, is that of a field officer caught at an exhausting and anxious moment. (*Courtesy of the Metropolitan Museum of Art*)

MEDAL AWARDED HENRY LEE

On 24 Sep. 1779 the Continental Congress resolved that "the thanks of Congress be given to Major Lee, for the remarkable prudence, address and bravery displayed by him" at the attack on the British fort at Paulus Hook; that "they approve the humanity shewn in circumstances prompting to severity, as honourable to the arms of the United States, and correspondent to the noble principles on which they were assumed"; and that "a medal of gold, emblematical of this affair, be struck . . . and presented to Major Lee" (JCC, xv, 1099-1100). But this resolution was overlooked in the list of "honorary Rewards to Officers . . . still due" that Robert Morris transmitted to David Humphreys in 1784 with directions to have the swords and medals commemorative of Saratoga, Stony Point, Cowpens, and other events of the Revolution "executed agreeably to the Resolutions of Congress" (see Vol. 16: 59). In 1789 Jefferson completed Humphreys' unfinished task and brought the medals back to the United States. It was presumably soon thereafter that he learned of the oversight when Henry Lee himself informed him of it and presented a copy of the resolution of Congress. Jefferson thereupon "put it in hand with [Joseph] Wright to be executed in Philadelphia." In an undated memorandum Jefferson wrote: "Wright, as well as I recollect, would not agree to warrant against the quality of the steel. His dies broke after they were executed, so that this matter was not concluded when I left Philadelphia" (Vol. 16: 78). The sequel is revealed in Treasury accounts. On 13 Jan. 1795 Joseph Stretch, administrator of the estate of Joseph Wright, submitted a statement of account for $233.33 due Wright "For modelling the likeness and cuting two dies for a model of Henry Lee Esq. as certified by the Secretary of State." Accompanying this account are the following documents: (1) a copy of the last will of Joseph Wright, "Miniture Painter and Engraver"; (2) a statement by Edmund Randolph, dated 10 Oct. 1794, reading: "The above account was produced to my predecessor in office, Mr. Jefferson. He told me that it was reasonable, and left a memorandum to that effect. As this was a transaction of his, I certify upon these premises, that the account is reasonable" (TJ's memorandum not found); (3) a statement by Moid Wetherill, 11 Sep. 1793, reading: "Joseph Wright being very ill [of yellow fever] and not expecting to recover, requested the Subscriber to make a memorandum as follows.—That the said Joseph Wright had presented an account against the United States for cuting a medal amount 50 Guineas.—Two Essays of a Quarter Dollar, cut by direction of David Rittenhouse Esqr. and presented to him (broke in hardening) value about 40 Guineas" (MS in DNA: M 235/19; Wright's invoice bears no date but is endorsed by TJ: "Wright Joseph"; on verso of Randolph's statement is a certificate signed by him to the effect that this service was performed under the direction of TJ by order of the President and in conformity to the resolution of 24 Sep. 1779).

The obverse of the example of this relatively rare medal that is here reproduced shows "a very distinct crack in the obverse die" (Henry Grunthal, Acting Chief Curator, American Numismatic Society, to the Editors, 24 Feb. 1961). Obverse, legend: HENRICO LEE LEGIONIS EQUIT. PRÆFECTO. Exergue: COMITIA AMERICANA. On the truncation: J. WRIGHT. Reverse, inscription (ten lines): NON OBSTANTIB. | FLUMINIBUS VALLIS | ASTUTIA & VIRTUTE BELLICA | PARVA MANU HOSTES VICIT | VICTOSQ. | ARMIS HUMANITATE | DEVINXIT. | IN MEM PUGN AD PAULUS | HOOK DIE XIX. | AUG. 1779. Betts, *American colonial history illustrated by contemporary medals* (New York, 1894), p. 266n., states that the original obverse die is in the United States Mint but that that of the reverse "has been lost" and another cut by William Barber. (*Courtesy of The American Numismatic Society*)

ROBERT MORRIS

This silhouette of the man who received most of the public condemnation for the bargain by which the seat of government was transferred to Philadelphia is one of Joseph Sansom's "Physiognomical Sketches . . . designed to preserve the characteristic features, personally, mentally, or officially [of] Remarkable Characters." That Sansom achieved his multiple object with astonishing penetration and clarity for such a medium is demonstrated both in this likeness of the financier and in the profiles of Washington, Franklin, Madison, and other figures reproduced in Charles Coleman Sellers' "Joseph Sansom, Philadelphia Silhouettist," PMHB, LXXXVIII (1964), 395-438, from the originals in the Perot Collection, The Historical Society of Pennsylvania. It is regrettable that, so far as known, Sansom did not execute a silhouette of Jefferson. (*Courtesy of The Historical Society of Pennsylvania*)

ROBERT MORRIS MOVES THE SEAT OF GOVERNMENT TO PHILADELPHIA

Although the controversial Assumption and Residence Acts resulted from an accommodation of interests arranged by Alexander Hamilton and Thomas Jefferson, these chief negotiators of the legislative bargain were at the time screened from public obloquy. It was instead Robert Morris, a prominent but not principal figure in the arrangement, who became almost the sole target of the squibs, satires, caricatures, and other manifestations of popular indignation that filled the press during and after passage of the two measures. "Your delegates and your city," wrote a New Yorker (or more likely one posing as a New Yorker) to a Pennsylvanian, "have been roughly handled in the course of the debates. The abuse of Mr. Morris has been both indecent and unmerited, for every part of his conduct of this business has been fair and candid" ([N.Y.] *Daily Advertiser*, 15 July 1790, quoting extract of letter of 9 July written from New York as published in Philadelphia). Morris himself, sensing victory at last and no doubt sharing the prevalent view in the north that a ten-year removal to Philadelphia would doom the Potomac site forever, bore the abuse with cheerful equanimity. "The Yorkers," he wrote to his wife, ". . . lay all the blame of this measure on me, and abuse me most unmercifully, both in the Public Prints, private conversations, and even in the streets; and yesterday I was nearly engaged in a serious quarrel with one of them.— However, I don't mind all they can do, and if I carry the point, I will, like a good Christian, forgive them all" (Morris to his wife, 2 July 1790, quoted in Frank M. Etting, *An historical account of the old State House or Independence Hall* [Boston, 1876] p. 139-40).

The possibility of a bargain was suspected almost as soon as the residence question came up during the stalemate over assumption and the barrage of ridicule began at once. "As I was walking up Wall-street," declared *A Country Correspondent* early in June, "I heard a man say, as how Congress were about making a great *balloon* out of *continental certificates* and *public securities*; that they were filling of it as fast as they could with *inflammable air*; that in about a fortnight it would be nearly inflated; and that the great *hall*, which cost you *Yorkers* about £30,000, was to be then suspended to the balloon, with all its animate and inanimate contents, and set down near the new gaol in the city of Philadelphia" (*New-York Journal*, 4 June 1790). The prediction that the phenomenon would take place "in about a fort-night" proved to be quite accurate and the idea of transporting the seat of government by air may have inspired the anonymous cartoonist to place Federal Hall on the shoulders of Robert Morris. It seems almost certain that the engraving appeared before passage of the Residence Act. The anxiety expressed by some of the members of Congress, the words of encouragement by that almost obligatory con-vention of political cartoonists of the period—the devil, the presence of a procuress and another of "the Girls" among the devil's proffered inducements, the divided comments of the onlookers and retainers, the roughness of the road Morris is traveling on, and his own exhorta-tion to his followers to have confidence in him—all seem to point to an object not yet achieved. If this conjecture is well founded, the carica-ture must have appeared late in June or early in July (William Murrell, *A History of American Graphic Humor* [New York, 1933], p. xiii, 45-6, assigns the year 1798 both to this and to the two cartoons of Morris described below, but all three unquestionably belong to 1790).

Two examples of this rare engraving are known: (1) the fine impression in the American Antiquarian Society here reproduced, having contemporary coloring in red, yellow, blue, and green; and (2) a plain copy in Independence Hall which bears on its face this caption in a contemporary and unidentified hand: "1790 | Carricature of ROBERT MORRIS by the New Yorkers in Consequence of the removal | of the Seat of Government through his instrumentality from their City to the city of | Philadelphia." A redrawn engraving of the latter with its caption appears in Frank M. Etting, *An Historical Account of the old State House or Independence Hall* (Boston, 1876), p. 139, and a facsimile is in William Murrell, *A History of American Graphic Humor* (New York, 1933), p. 45 (though its location is erroneously assigned, p. xiii, to the New-York Historical Society).

This engraving is unsigned, but R. W. G. Vail, "A Rare Robert Morris Caricature," PMHB (1936), p. 184-6, attributes it to Henry G. Jenks of Boston on three grounds: (1) that the draftsmanship of the front elevation of Federal Hall in the caricature bears a "very similar if not identical" relationship to that of a larger engraving of the struc-ture which appears in Isaiah Thomas' *Massachusetts Magazine* for June 1789; (2) that the original drawing for this latter engraving was described by I. N. Phelps Stokes, *Iconography of Manhattan Island*, III (New York, 1918), p. 904, as being signed by Jenks;

and (3) that the example of the caricature in the American Antiquarian Society was purchased in 1934 among the effects of Henry G. Jenks.

There is no doubt that Stokes' authority is impressive and that the circumstance of finding this caricature among Jenks' effects must be given due weight. But, aside from the fact that the pen-and-ink sketch described by Stokes has not been located for comparison, the following considerations must be noted: (1) Stokes only identified the drawing as "an early unfinished sketch made by Henry G. Jenks," not as one signed by him, and in consequence the attribution may possibly have been that of the gallery in which he examined it; (2) he went no further than to say that this was "probably the original of the plate" that appeared in the *Massachusetts Magazine*; and (3) he identified the engraver of that plate not as Jenks but as S. Hill. Further a comparison of Hill's "View of the Federal Edifice in New York" with the crudely drawn representation of that structure as carried by Robert Morris seems to reveal only striking inequalities. The former (also engraved for the Columbian *Magazine*, Aug. 1789) bears favorable comparison with the Peter Lacour-Amos Doolittle engraving of Washington's inauguration of 30 Apr. 1789 and even with the drawing of Federal Hall by Archibald Robertson (I. N. Phelps Stokes and Daniel C. Haskell, *American Historical Prints* [New York, 1932], frontispiece; see Vol. 16, following p. 52). The latter is faulty in its perspective and in its imperfect proportions. In any case the comparison of the craftsmanship of the two engravings is between work known to be by Hill and work by an unidentified person. The attribution of this caricature to Henry G. Jenks must, therefore, be regarded as inconclusive. (*Courtesy of the American Antiquarian Society*)

THE RESIDENCE BARGAIN SATIRIZED

I. "View of C-o-n-ss on the road to Philadelphia." This satirical engraving shows Robert Morris carrying on his back a majority acquired—as the caricaturist suggests none too subtly—by means of the financier's money bags, with the minority bound by leading strings and obliged to follow along. The division between a solid majority and an overpowered "Manority" indicates that the print was executed after the voting on the Residence Bill had revealed the tendency of the voting but before the bill had been enacted. The remark by one of the minority that "It is bad to have a gouty Constitution" and the reply by another that "I am affraid bobby's dance will not mend it" also suggest that the print may have been published about the time that the constitutional issue was being discussed (see Opinions on the Constitutionality of the Residence Bill, p. 163-208). The engraver signed the cartoon with the obviously pseudonymous initials "Y. Z." (*Courtesy of the New-York Historical Society*)

II. "Cong-ss Embark'd on board the Ship Constitution of America bound to Conogocheque by way of Philadelphia." The use of a ship as symbol of the Constitution and of Robert Morris as her commander grew naturally out of the public debate over the Assumption and Residence bills. Late in June a writer in the *New-York Journal*, pretending to correct the ship news that had appeared in Fenno's *Gazette of the United States*, described *Congress* as "a new ship, on her second voyage—a heavy and lubberly sailor—her cabin fitted up with French decorations." *Assumption*, he wrote, was also a new ship, fitted out by "an eastern company of insolvents," and *Residence*, still another new vessel, was owned by a declining merchant. The voyage of the latter had been temporarily postponed, but the writer added: "It is expected she will sail in company with the Assumption" (*New-York Journal*, 29 June 1790). A few days later J.P. and R.H.L. signed this satirical advertisement: "Six d-----s a day will be given for good caulkers to repair and caulk the new ship C--------., R[obert] M[orris] commander. The seams of her bottom having never been properly squared, and the plank [being] of green stuff, it is proposed to give her a thorough repair before she is properly fitted for the great and important voyage to Philadelphia" (same, 2 July 1790). This may have been intended as a warning that the constitutional issue was about to be raised, but in any event it was quite natural that from such materials as these the unknown engraver of this cartoon should have developed his derisory "Cong-ss Embark'd"—the ship *Constitution* with her figurehead of a goose instead of an eagle, her commander Robert Morris at the helm, the devil beckoning him on to the rapids, the figure below crying to his companions "If we can catch the cargo never mind the ship"—the cargo being identified as the Treasury—and the minority towed along in the painter, whose helmsman calls out to one in the bow "Cut the Painter as soon as you see the ship in danger," to which the bowman, knife in hand and voicing a clear threat of disunion, cries: "Ay, Ay. I had best do it now, for I believe she is going to the devil."

It is obvious, too, that this caricature appeared after the Residence Act became law on 16 July 1790. For when one of the men in the painter remarks to a companion "I wonder what could have induced the Controller [President Washington] to sign our clearance"—that is, to decline to veto the measure as *Junius Americanus* and others urged— he is answered in a manner typical of the feelings of resentment against Washington for his silent but influential part in the controversial proceedings: "Self gratification, I suppose, for it cannot be any advantage to the owners"—that is, to the people of the country. (*Courtesy of the Historical Society of Pennsylvania*)

Volume 17

6 July 1790 to 3 November 1790

JEFFERSON CHRONOLOGY
1743 · 1826

1743.	Born at Shadwell, 13 Apr. (New Style).
1772.	Married Martha Wayles Skelton, 1 Jan.
1775-76.	In Continental Congress.
1776.	Drafted Declaration of Independence.
1776-79.	In Virginia House of Delegates.
1779.	Submitted Bill for Establishing Religious Freedom.
1779-81.	Governor of Virginia.
1782.	His wife died, 6 Sep.
1783-84.	In Continental Congress.
1784-89.	In France as commissioner to negotiate commercial treaties and as minister plenipotentiary at Versailles.
1790-93.	U.S. Secretary of State.
1797-1801.	Vice President of the United States.
1801-09.	President of the United States.
1814-26.	Established the University of Virginia.
1826.	Died at Monticello, 4 July.

VOLUME 17
6 July 1790 to 3 Nov. 1790

12 July	Advises policy of neutrality in Anglo-Spanish war crisis, with exactions from belligerents
15 July	Renders opinion on constitutionality of Residence Bill
17 July	Reports to President on diplomatic establishment
21 July	Reports on candidates for consular vacancies
25 July	Engages house in Philadelphia from Thomas Leiper
29 July	Renders opinion on monopoly of trade with Creek Indians, upholding supremacy of treaties over laws
Early Aug.	Recurrence of illness
2-12 Aug.	Prepares Humphreys' mission to Spain
12 Aug.	Inaugurates inquiry into violations of Treaty of Peace by states
15 Aug.	Departs with President for Rhode Island
21 Aug.	Returns from Rhode Island
26 Aug.	Prepares "rule of office" for consuls
26 Aug.	Renders opinion on fiscal policy
29 Aug.	Prepares agenda for President on seat of government
1 Sep.	Leaves New York with Madison
13 Sep.	Confers with landowners at Georgetown about seat of government
15 Sep.	Reports to Washington at Mount Vernon about conference
19 Sep.	Arrives at Monticello
27 Sep.	Departs for Richmond on business affairs
5 Oct.	Arranges for sale of Elk Hill lands
7 Oct.	Proposes that Virginia build private dwellings at seat of government

THE PAPERS OF
THOMAS JEFFERSON

·《══════》·

From Peter Carr

DEAR SIR   Spring-forest July. 6. 1790.

In my letter of April. 30th. I mentioned in what manner my time had been imployed to that date; And as in the study of the law, there is no great variety (the mind being in pursuit of a single and fixed object) you must only suppose me to have gone on constantly and regularly in the course you have pointed out. Coke's first Institute I have read thrice; And am now ingaged with the second. Concurrent with these, the smaller books—Dalrymple, Hale, and Gilbert have claimed my attention.

Political writings have had but a small share in my course, though I acknowledge it is a kind of Reading, of which I am fond; if you think proper, and will mention the books in that branch, I shall find time to Read them. Dabney has received all the books he will want for some time, from me, when he wants those, which I have not, you shall be informed. Mr. Randolph and Patsy were at Eppington, a few days since, in good health. My mother has been persecuted for some time with the ague and fever, and talks of going to the Mountains to recover her health. Your friends here, expect the pleasure of seeing you in Autumn—Among whom Believe me none will receive more satisfaction than your affectionate friend & Servt.,   PETER CARR

RC (ViU); endorsed as received 17 July 1790 and so recorded in SJL. FC (ViU); in Carr's hand, docketed: "Copy of letter to Thos. Jefferson written July 6. 1790"; varies slightly in phraseology.

From Nathaniel Cutting

SIR   St. Marc, Island of St. Domingue July 6th. 1790.

I took the liberty of writing you, dated at Sea, 5th. March ulto. A few days after that period, at Cape Mount on the Windward

Coast of Africa, I had the pleasure of receiving the Letter where-with you honor'd me under date 21st. Novr. ulto. Under March 30th. I acknowledged the receipt of that welcome notice of your arrival in Virginia. I dispatch'd my Letters for New York via the West Indies; so that it is very possible you may not have known till this moment that I have been engaged on a voyage of observation during the last eight months. In my Letter of March 5th. I stated some of my reasons for quitting my residence at Havre. Permit me now to acquaint you that I am on the point of returning thither again; and allow me to repeat the assurance that nothing can give me so much pleasure as to meet any of your commands there.

I recollect to have heard you say that you wish'd to obtain some of the *true upland Rice*. While I was on the Coast of Africa I made enquiry of several residentiary Traders concerning the different kinds of Rice cultivated on the Windward Coast. A Mr. Cleveland at the Island of Bananoes in the Latt. 8.° North, inform'd me that the natives sow their Rice in the months of May, June and July; it comes to maturity in the months of August, September and October.

There are three species of this Rice, so that if all three of them were sown at the same period, there would be nearly a month difference in the time of their arriving at maturity:—This is what most of the Cultivators aim at, with a double view; that of making the labour come lighter, and of guarding against the ravages of Birds and other animals who are very mischievous at particular times. I enquired whether they ever cultivate low, marshy lands? Mr. Cleveland replied that the Natives have a distinct species of Rice which they sometimes sow in such grounds; but they do not like it. It does not possess half the nutriment of the upland Rice, being very watery; and, like that of Carolina, frequently causes violent fluxes.

From the *time* at which they sow their upland Rice, it may be observed that though it yields well in a high, and we may suppose a naturally dry soil, yet it requires much water; for the latter part of May, which is the beginning of their seed time, is likewise the commencement of the Rainy Season. The Rain generally continues to fall almost incessantly till September; from hence it may be naturally inferred that though the Red Rice, as this kind is some-times call'd, is a distinct species, and that the Fields do not require to be laid under water, yet a great quantity of moisture's necessary to its producing a good Crop. During my short stay at the Island of Bananoes, it was found impossible to procure me a sample of the different species of Rice in their natural state. Before I left the Coast, however, a Mr. Holman, who for many years has held a Factory for his own account in the River Denby, about the Latt. 9.° 30′ North, procured me a ten gallon Keg of that Rice which he calls *the heavy upland Rice.*

I have the pleasure to forward it to you herewith under care of Mr. Samuel Clark, formerly of New-Jersey, who goes Passenger from hence for Philadelphia in the ship call'd the Vanderweeke.

I am made very happy by intelligence that Peace and Good Government shed their benign influences over the extensive Domains of the Thirteen United States. In this Island the Case is widely different. The French Colonists, suddenly and unexpectly emancipated from the galling fetters of a despotic Government, entertain some very excentric ideas of Laws and the Administration of them. They have not yet learnt to sacrifice private opinion to public utility. They cannot all think alike respecting some points proposed to them by the National Assembly of France. In consequence of this difference in Political sentiments, Anarchy has begun to unfurl her hateful Banner, and Commerce already languishes beneath its malignant influence.

I am confident you know, much better than I do, the extent and importance of the French Colony of St. Domingue; but allow me to acquaint you with what I have recently learnt respecting the present State of its Police. Soon after the Commencement of the late Revolution in France, the French Inhabitants of this Island became sensible of their consequence and determin'd to assert the natural rights of men. They voluntarily divided the Colony into three great Districts, term'd the Southern, Western and Northern. Each of these *Districts* include a number of *Parishes.* Each of these Districts appointed a Kind of *Convention,* consisting of Deputies from each Parish. These different *assemblies* were to correspond with each other and to direct such regulations as might be thought conducive to the general Good. The National Assembly of France, it seems lately directed the Inhabitants to chuse Delegates for a General Assembly of the Colony, who should have authority to regulate and superintend the Internal Police, and to make Laws adapted to its particular situation and exigencies; subject, however, to the revision, and not to be in force without the sanction of the National Assembly of France. The Inhabitants of the Colony at large accordingly chose Representatives, who conven'd at this place in the month of March ult.

In course of their deliberations certain opinions were advanced which gave offence to some of the Inhabitants of the Northern *District*, which includes Cape François, the most important Town of the Colony. The Assembly of that District (which it seems is not annihilated though a General Assembly of the Colony certainly supercedes its powers) was sitting at the Cape, and took upon itself to recall the Delegates which the Northern District had previously sent to the General Assembly. Most of the Northern members, considering that they had been constituted by the People, refused to recognize the authority of the Assembly at the Cape, and continued at St. Marc. The Delegates from the Southern and Western Districts applied to their constituents to know whether the previous resolves of the General Assembly should be confirm'd, whether they should still continue their sittings, or whether they should dissolve themselves and make way for another General Election.

The Electors were unanimously for confirming all previous trans- actions of the assembly and for its continuance. The Delegates accordingly hold their meetings every day in the Church of this place which is fitted up for their accommodation.

Wishing to conciliate their northern Brethren, the General As- sembly sometime since appointed four Commissioners to repair to Cape François and negociate between the Parties that cause this unhappy division in this Colony. This amicable overture on the part of the General assembly did not meet with the desir'd success.

We are told that it is with the Petit Assembly at the Cape that the Governor corresponds, affecting to consider it as a Body of Delegates legally appointed. It is also asserted that the Petit Assembly has been guilty of intercepting several important com- munications from the General Assembly that were intended for the Municipalities of the Cape and for the information of People at large, Communications calculated to dissipate those groundless Jealousies and unhappy dissentions that wicked and designing men had disseminated among the Inhabitants of the Northern District.

I am inform'd that there are in Cape François from 5 à 6000 White Inhabitants: and as in the appointment of Delegates, regard is had to the *number* of Constituents as well as to their *property*, that Town has twenty-four Members in the District-Assembly. It is said that when the Commissioners of the General Assembly before-mention'd discover'd at the Cape the villainy of some Persons who had intercepted those communications intended for the Public, they publish'd the purport of them. One consequence of this judicious proceeding was that seventeen of the twenty-four members from the Cape receded from the principles they had previously supported in the Assembly.

It is reported that the President of that Assembly and several other members who through Party views had been violently opposed to the General assembly, and of course disobey'd its requisitions, have since absconded.

The advocates for harmony and good government entertain hopes that all Party differences will soon be amicably adjusted and that Union of sentiment, that great source of Political felicity, will very soon be firmly established.

The General Assembly lately past a Decree for establishing Municipalities in all the Towns of the Colony: but it seems the Governor has refused to give it his sanction; whether this salutary regulation will be carried into effect without waiting new directions from France, is at present uncertain. I have the honor to be, with the greatest respect, Sir, Your most obedt. & very huml. Servt.,

NAT. CUTTING

RC (DLC). Recorded in SJL as received 6 Sep. 1790.

On 8 July 1790 Cutting wrote TJ that he had met there Samuel Wall who "proposes to offer himself a Candidate for the office of American Consul in the French Part of St. Domingue. Many impositions have been practised upon the Americans whom Commerce has attracted to this Island; even the Public Bureaux have, either actively or passively, authorized the exaction of much higher Port-Charges on American Vessels than the Law directs. Though private Complaints respecting this abuse have never been attended to, yet redress might probably have been obtain'd by a Person invested with the authority of a Consul. . . . Mr. Wall had the honor to serve his Country, both by Land and Sea, in course of the late War, in a respectable capacity. He was a Brigade Major in the Continental service, and was afterward captured in the ship Queen of France of Charlestown So. Carolina, when that City unfortunately fell into the hands of the British Forces. He afterwards visited France for the purpose of acquiring the Language. By means of that Tour, and his long residence in this Colony, he is become exceedingly well acquainted with the Language, Customs and manners of its Inhabitants; and from his known abilities and attachment to America, I am confident would discharge all the Duties of the station to which he aspires, with much honor to himself, and great advantage to his Country" (DLC: Applications for Office under Washington; recorded in SJL as received 15 Dec. 1791).

From David Howell

DEAR SIR   Providence, July 6, 1790.

Your favour of the 23d. ult. came duly to hand.—I thank you for your polite attention to the business with which I reluctantly charged you, and hope I have the honour of standing, by your means, *rectus in Curia.*

Having been informed that a Printer is to be Selected in each of the States, for promulgating the laws of the United States, the immediate object of this letter is to recommend for that Employment John Carter, Esq; who has for 20 years past kept the Post-Office here. His Printing-Office was the first established in this town. He is the Senior Printer of our State, and circulates a much greater number of Papers than any other Typographer Therein.

Mr. Carter was taught "the Art which preserves all other Arts" under the late Dr. Franklin, is uncontrovertibly the most accurate Printer in the State, and is himself *a good Writer* also. He has many Claims to the Notice of the Public, has a numerous Family to provide for, is a worthy Citizen, and a Friend to good Government. I am, with great Esteem, dear Sir, Your most obedient humble Servant,   DAVID HOWELL

RC (DLC); addressed; endorsed as received 14 July 1790 and so recorded in SJL.

From Madame de Tessé

a Reuchenette près Bienne en suisse ce 6 juillet 1790.

Jai beaucoup desiré mais bien peu esperé votre Retour, Monsieur, comment se refuser a être utile et heureux! Nous ne vous meritons pas. Et si vous eties assis parmi nos legislateurs vous seriés meconnu ou persecuté. J'estime, autant que mes foibles lumieres le comportent votre païs a ce periode ou les hommes de votre trempe commencent a pouvoir beaucoup pour le bien general qui ne s'opere jamais que difficilement et imparfaitement sous leffervescence de la liberté. Vous apprendrés quon a detruit la Noblesse en France. Lorsque j'en ai reçu la nouvelle en suisse ou je suis venue chercher un peu de santé, jai eprouvé un sentiment de joie tant soit peu condamnable puisqu'il etoit le resultat d'un esprit de vengeance contre la vanité qui s'opposoit a la liberté a l'ouverture de notre assemblée et qui m'a degoutée par sa sotte arrogance depuis que j'existe. Des personnes qui pensent bien et plus sagement que moi pretendent que ma joie est indiscrete et que notre peuple qui respectoit un peu la noblesse par habitude va la regarder comme un troc parcequelle est detruite, et que sa destruction lui donnera moins de jouissances que de colere. Cela peut arriver, mais je veux encore esperer qu'on pourra rire de quelques figures tout a fait ridicules lorsquelles voudront dissimuler le grand chagrin que leur donne une si petite privation.

Mr. Mounier dont le sort ne peut manquer de vous interesser a ete forcé de venir en suisse pour epargner un crime a ses concitoyens et a ses amis le danger de le defendre. Je ne lai point vu parceque nous habitons a une grande distance l'un de l'autre. Je sais seulement quil a ete reçu et traité a Genêve ou il demeure, avec beaucoup de distinction. J'attends impatiemment les nouvelles qui doivent decider du sort de Mr. Short dont je desire le succès plus ardemment que personne. Ma santé qui netoit pas bonne a reçu un coup terrible durant le massacre de versailles. La fievre qui me prit alors et m'a duré longtems m'a considerablement affoiblie. J'aurois succombé si je ne me fusse vouée a la solitude la plus complette. Je ne laisse pas de m'occuper de mon jardin et de ma pepiniere dans les rochers ou je me suis retirée et j'entretiens avec mon jardinier une correspondance tres suivie. Il est déja instruit de la prochaine arrivée de vos dons. Il en a reçu la liste, il est prêt a en jouir. Les logemens et la nourriture sont preparés pour les nouveaux hôtes. Si vous nous gratifies de quelques dons l'année prochaine nous vous conjurons d'être plus liberal en graines qu'en plans. Nous vous recommandons surtout les glands qui demandent a être embarqués au moment de la Recolte et être semés promptement. Me. de Tott penetree dattachement et de veneration pour vous est bien touchée de votre souvenir et regrette bien de ne vous avoir pas prié d'accepter quelques uns de ses ouvrages qui le perpetuent a Monticello. Daignés nous permettre a toute deux de vous offrir quelquefois l'hommage de ces sentimens profonds avec lesquels jai l'honneur dêtre, Monsieur, votre tres humble et tres obeissant servante,

NOAILLES DE TESSÉ

RC (DLC); endorsed as received 23 Nov. 1790 and so recorded in SJL.

From John Garland Jefferson

HONOURED SIR   Hanover (Virginia) 7th July 1790.

Your favour of the 11th June by my uncle Garland afforded me the most agreeable sensations, and demands my most grateful acknowledgements. Heaven was pleased in my infancy to deprive me of the best, and most indulgent of fathers, and nature still prompts the tribute of a tear, to his memory: but altho the dispensation seemed very afflictive I think I receive the most ample compensation for the loss in being taken under your most respectable patronage. My uncle has hitherto supplyed the place of a father to me. He has kept me at Washington Henry Academy in this County for several years at which I have endeavoured to lay such a foundation in classical knowledge as I hope has prepared me for the further improvement under your kind protection. My inclination led me to the study of the law, and you Sir, have removed every difficulty that was in the way of my design. For this be pleased to accept the poor return of my most cordial thanks and permit me to assure you that I shall make it my most constant study to requite your unbounded generosity, by the most diligent improvement of your favours, and as, you have raised my humble hopes, it shall become my ambition through life to acquire such a reputation in my profession as will show I have had the benefit of your instructions.

I expect to set off for Albemarle in a few days, where I shall diligently apply to the studies you have prescribed as the first instance of that gratitude which warms my heart. In the mean time I shall await with anxious hopes a letter from your friendly hand, with advice and instructions for my inexperienced youth. I have the honour to be with the most grateful respect, Dear Sir, Your most obliged humble Servant,   JOHN G. JEFFERSON

RC (ViU); endorsed as received 17 July 1790 and so recorded in SJL.

From William Short

DEAR SIR   Paris July the 7th. 1790

The intelligence of your long and painful indisposition has given me, in common with all your friends here a real concern. They join me in solliciting you not to allow too intense an application to business to expose you again to an attack which by repetition must necessarily become dangerous. The account of the President's narrow escape affected sincerely all the friends to America here. His re-establishment gives great pleasure. At present I have recieved either the originals or copies of all the letters you mention in yours of May the 27th. except—that of March the 28th and April 7th. My private letters since I have recieved from you the information of your remaining at New-York, have been June the 14th. and 29th. Of the first I sent a duplicate.

Petit and the packers are going on with the greatest expedition possible. I foresee no delay unless the fever of going to work at the Champ de Mars should take possession of the packers. They think that every thing will be ready in seven or eight days.—Petit still continues his determination not to go to America, unless he should hear farther from you. I suppose the truth is that he counts on being employed by your successor. Should he fail there and not be able to find any other suitable place, which is highly probable under the present circumstances of this country, then I think he would be easily induced to go to America, though he says that his plan in that case is to return to his province, where he has some land which he will attend to the cultivation of.—The old chariot and cabriolet are sold for 300.ᵗᵗ It was the most that could be got. The horses are not sold because the highest price was twenty five guineas. I did not send them to the market because I feared they would not sell for so much. I have thought it would be best to keep them for your successor who will certainly be glad to give much more for them. Should it fall to my lot, of which however I am far from entertaining hopes I should be glad to have them and I judge of others by myself. Still if a tolerable price is offered for them they shall be sold.

Since my last I have heard nothing either from Langeac, who is in Switzerland, or his brother who is his attorney here. There is no doubt however that you are obliged by the expressions of the lease to keep the house three years from the day of its renewal, and I suppose as little doubt that Langeac will insist on that interpretation of it.—Still he may be certainly engaged to relinquish his claim for a small sacrifice and particularly as he is in treaty and has hopes of selling his house. There will be no difficulty in making the house rent paid since your departure, enter into Mr. Grand's accounts and it shall be done.

Tolozan spoke to me again a few days ago and told me he knew that by the Constitution you could accept the present with the consent of Congress, which he knew also could be easily obtained. I told him that as yet there had been no instance of it, and that I supposed you did not chuse to be the first to sollicit it. Our conversation ended there, and he seemed well enough satisfied.

It has been understood that the Corps diplomatique are to be invited to the ceremony of the 14th. The Imperial, Spanish and Neapolitan Ambassadors not chusing to be present, and not liking either to refuse an invitation of the sort, are endeavouring to prevent the invitation. The Sardinian is going to visit the Bishop of Liege, it is supposed either that he may be absent on the 14th. or because a Mr. Cordon mistaken for him on the confines of Savoy has been arrested and insulted.—The English Ambassador and Ambassadress seem to please here very generally. They are still lodged in a hotel garni. She enquired of me very particularly about you some days ago, and told me she knew you here last year.

The Marquis de la fayette is running through his fortune and I fear will get to the end of it. He refuses to accept any salary which has been repeatedly offered to him by the municipality. He has a large tent spread in his garden which holds a table of an hundred plates. He intends that it shall be filled every day as long as the deputies of the gardes nationales continue here. Mde. de la fayette's life has been despaired of; but she is now quite out of danger. Mde. de Tessé has been very ill also. She is still in Switzerland. I have sent her the letter you inclosed me. Pio, I am told has entered the service as one of the garde soldée. It has been a long time since I have seen him, but I suppose he has some expectation of promotion, as he begun by being a private soldier. He is considered as the most violent enragé, and lives now in the district of the Cordeliers as I am told, which is the maddest of all Paris.

I have just recieved a letter from London which informs me that the Queen of Portugal has appointed M. Friere her minister there as minister to America. There may be and probably is some mistake as to the name and rank of the person in question. The Ambassador of Portugal certainly knew nothing of it three days ago.

I hope I shall not be much longer without knowing something as to the foreign establishment which Congress shall decide on. In the present uncertainty I know not what steps to take and although I endeavour as much as possible to keep this situation out of my sight still it presents itself too often and with too much force to be resisted. I am sorry you did not say who were those veterans in office who were on the public list, for it is the only list you speak of. I enter very readily into your situation with respect to myself. I know your respect for public opinion and easily concieve that whatever might be your opinion as to my fitness for this place, if you concieved that the public would attribute my appointment to partiality in you, that you would be averse to taking such a degree of responsability on yourself. You my dear Sir are certainly the best and only judge how far that should weigh, and whether such an opinion would have existed in public. It certainly however could not have existed as to the appointment of chargé des affaires, and I think your opinion sometimes was that that grade was not an improper one. Certainly no inconvenience could have arisen for its being preserved for some time, and particularly during the absence and uncertain return of the French Minister. After having exercised that grade during that time, I should have shewn either that I was not proper to be appointed as Minister, or that I might be appointed with propriety even in the public opinion. This was what I had supposed would be the case. Others thought I should be appointed Minister immediately because they knew your opinion of me. I supposed it would be mediately because I knew better than they how those matters stood in America. I desired to be appointed for several reasons, and if I do not mistake one of them and the strongest was because I had allowed myself to be persuaded that I was more fit for it than another, and because I did not doubt I could be useful. I still hope that if by accident I should be continued here, I shall give no reason to repent of it. Adieu. Yr friend & servant,

W: SHORT

RC (DLC); at head of text: "*Private*"; endorsed as received 25 Oct. 1790 and so recorded in SJL. PrC (DLC: Short Papers).

This letter was enclosed in one from St. John de Crèvecoeur to TJ, L'Orient, 10 July 1790, who wrote: "It no doubt contains ample Informations of the Extraordinary Event which is to Take place in Paris on the 14th. Instant; I Tremble lest the Good Marquis shou'd not be able to maintain Peace and Good Order among so Great a concourse of People as will Flock there from every Part of the Kingdom. Messrs. Otto and de la Forest will send you the Gazette nationale for the Month of June. Few Instances Excepted in the Southern Provinces where the Sparks of the old Fanaticism have been Kindled by the Priests, Peace and Tranquillity every where Prevail. The Immense Crops which covers the Surface of the Kingdom, Promise Plenty. God Grant it may be Gathered without Rain" (RC in DLC; endorsed as received 14 Oct. 1790 and so recorded in SJL—a puzzling circumstance since both Short's private and public letters of 7 July 1790 were received on 25 Oct. 1790 and these were the only ones that Crèvecoeur's could have covered).

Only three days before writing the above letter Short, learning from Crèvecoeur's son that his father had landed in France, wrote in some agitation: "He tells me you left New York on the 20th of May, and as I recieved the day before yesterday a letter from Mr. Jefferson by the Packet, I suppose you have crossed the Atlantic in it. . . . I take the liberty of writing to ask if you came by the French Packet and if you can tell me how it happens that I get letters dated early in April by a vessel which sailed late in May. My latest letters from Mr. Jefferson are of the 30th of April. I am much surprized that he should not have made use of your good offices in forwarding me letters and gazettes as late as the day of your sailing. If you know any thing also relative to the intended foreign arrangements you will satisfy my impatience and render me a very acceptable service in communicating it. By Mr. Jefferson's letter I learned only that this arrangement was awaiting the passage of a bill—that many were talked of in public and desired to come as minister to France—so that it is doubtful whether I should be appointed. He did not say who were the persons talked of in public. I will thank you to let me know who they are—as you come from New-York you must necessarily be in the way of knowing. Ever since the 10th of June, when these letters arrived, I have been in this state of uncertainty. Until then I had considered myself as fixed at Paris for some years. . . . As a state of suspense of uncertainty is of all others the most disagreeable I will thank you to be so obliging as to let me know how these matters stood at the time of your leaving New-York as far as you may be able to judge" (Short to Crèvecoeur, 4 July 1790; RC owned by Louis Saint-John de Crèvecoeur,

Montesquieu-sur-Losse, France; PrC in DLC: Short Papers). This letter crossed one of 2 July 1790 that Crèvecoeur dispatched to Paris with TJ's letters for Short: it had been delayed because, on landing at L'Orient, Crèvecoeur has been "harrased, fatigued, and taken up with looking for a decent Lodgings in this Dirty City." He said that he had seen TJ the day before he left New York, "and he repeatedly declared He had not the Least Idea of the Person Intended to replace him at Paris; the Bill Empowering the President To appoint Ministers and Consuls was past the Lower house but had not been Taken up by the Senate; I make no doubt Mr. Jefferson as a friend and peculiar confident of the President must have a Great Influence in the appointment of his Successor, if a Successor is as yet Sent. I have often mentioned your name without being able to form any Jugement of his Intentions; I did more. I assured him that Mr. Maddison was the Person pitched upon by the Public. 'I have not heard the Least Syllable about it'—was his answer;—I hope and pray you May be continued and have an opportunity of Seeing the conclusion of this Grand and Interesting Scene which is ennacting under your Immediate Inspection" (Crèvecoeur to Short, [ca. 15] July 1790; endorsed as received on the 18th; DLC: Short Papers).

From William Short

DEAR SIR   Paris July the 7th. 1790

I have just recieved your letter of the 27th of May, which has been sent here from L'Orient by Mr. de Crevecoeur. [My last letters will have informed you of the present situation of the business relative to the American captives at Algiers. You will have seen there that nothing has been done, or possible to be done, for their redemption. This I know will not surprize you when you recollect the circumstances attending it. Still I shall leave nothing untried and will write you regularly as you desire respecting it.][1]— Some days ago a person who has resided many years at Algiers, called on me in company with M. Volney whom you know, to speak of a means of procuring peace with that Regency on advantageous terms. It was for Congress to equip some frigates themselves, or to authorize a company to do it, and to cruise in the Mediterranean, particularly on the coast of Egypt against the Turkish merchant vessels. He said it was unquestionable that the Porte could force Algiers to conclude a treaty with any power whatever, that finding their commerce harassed, the Turks would gladly exchange their interposition at Algiers for its security, and that thus the United States who would be sure of failing so long as they should address the Algerines by embassies or entreaties, would be as sure of succeeding whenever they should speak to the fears and interest of the Turks.—This is the leading idea of his plan, which he seems to have considered under all its circumstances. He went into several details respecting it, which he is to communicate to me in writing. He has reasons for not chusing to be named; but wishes his ideas to be communicated to Congress. His calculation is that three frigates manned by two hundred men each would suffice. He does not propose their cruising off Algiers because a greater number would then be necessary, because a much longer time would be requisite for making an impression on the Algerines by this means, and consequently the success much less certain. He proposes cruising against the Turkish merchantmen because the prizes would much more than indemnify for the expences of equipment, and because it is much the most expeditious and certain mode of effecting the business at Algiers.—His favorite idea is that the affair should be mercantile, viz. that all the expences should be furnished by individuals on the condition of their having all the profits, and he desires to be interested in the enterprize by placing a part of his fortune in it. He wishes that Congress should give the letters of marque for reasons that are obvious.—There are several objections which occur at first view, to this plan: still as it may lead to something towards the business with Algiers I thought it my duty to communicate it. This person's long residence at Constantinople and at Algiers gives him an opportunity of being fully acquainted with the relations which subsist between those two countries. He says there are several instances where the Regency has not complied with the requisitions of the Porte; but that they are cases where the Porte makes requisitions for form sake, and where a private agreement takes place for exempting the Regency from obedience. He affirms that the Regency never disobeys the decided will of the Porte. It is from thence he concludes that the United States should make use of the Porte in order to effect their peace. The Turkish interest being more exposed to the attacks of the United States than that of Algiers, is an additional motive, as it is interest alone which will weigh with them.

It has been said in the national assembly lately that the last peace with Algiers cost France 1,400,000.ᵗᵗ instead of 800,000.ᵗᵗ as I mentioned in a former letter. I have been since assured that the additional 600,000.ᵗᵗ were occasioned by the after charges and unexpected exactions of the Regency. You will remember they did the same with respect to Spain. It is apprehended that some un-authorized violence lately offered by the inhabitants of the French coast of the Mediterranean to a number of Algerines, will force France to renew the humiliation and expences of another treaty.

You express a wish that I should be able to obtain the free introduction of our salted provisions into France.—My letters will have shewn that I have not lost sight of this important subject, and in my No. 33. I inclosed you a letter which Mr. Lambert the comptroller general had written me relative to it. Mr. Necker has since told me he would give orders for a contract for a small supply merely as an experiment. He wished me to recommend some American merchant for this purpose. I knew of none except Parker who is in London, and I have written to him on the subject, but do not know whether he will give himself the trouble for a small contract. Mr. Necker doubts much whether the people of Paris will be brought to make use of salted provisions at any price however moderate, for some time to come. The only duties to which salted provisions from America are subjected as you will have seen by Mr. Lambert's letter, are those which are paid on French provisions passing from one part of France to another. I have no doubt that even those duties will be taken off as soon as the new regulations of commerce take place. At present however the ministry cannot take it on themselves, and in fact do nothing of the kind. It shall however be fully attended to; and the exception as to tonnage not forgotten, as soon as I shall know that it has passed.

I communicated to Mr. Necker the Resolve which you inclosed me in a former letter. He received with pleasure that proof of the attention of Congress to their foreign engagements. He is very anxious to know their decision relative to the loan lately made at Amsterdam.—I still think as formerly that a person properly authorized by Congress might make that loan the basis of others so as to effect on advantageous and sure terms such as they will judge proper probably to have made for the discharge of their debts due this country, and which it is so essential to attend to without delay, from a variety of considerations.

The subject of the Duke of Orleans's return was brought before the assembly yesterday by a letter which he wrote to his Chancellor to be communicated to them. He said that he was preparing to leave London when the Ambassador of France called on him with an aide de camp of M. de la fayette, who told him that the general conjured him not to return to Paris. He wished the national assembly to be consulted and added that if they declared *qu'il n'y avoit point lieu à deliberer*, he should consider it as permission to return.—M. de la fayette in answer to this letter observed to the assembly that he had informed the Duke of Orleans that the reasons for his absenting himself still continued. He took that opportunity however of assuring the assembly that the more the 14th. approaches the less grounds he saw for the alarms which were circulated as to the event of that day.—The assembly proceeded to the order of the day without taking the letter into consideration, but at the same time avoiding the expression *qu'il n'y avoit pas lieu à deliberer*. It is therefore still uncertain whether the Duke will return. The King has written to him also to engage him to defer it for the present. In the mean time he has published what he calls an '*exposé de sa conduite dans la revolution de france*.' This was probably intended as his precursor. It is a narrative of facts known to every body, and neither proves or disproves any thing.

The deputies are arriving from all parts of France for the 14th. Besides those who are deputed a great number of others come as spectators. It began to be feared that the works of the Champ de Mars would not be finished in time. Some volunteers went to assist the workmen employed. This spread like a flame through Paris and people of both sexes and all ranks and descriptions flock there to work. This carries others as spectators so that the Champ de Mars would not be finished in time. Some volunteers went to assist carting of the earth and other operations of the sort which are going on there.—Many legs and arms have already been broken in the confusion. These crowds going and returning give the streets of Paris the appearance they had last year as to numbers, but very different as to humour. As yet they are all gaiety. Still it is impossible to say what impulsion they may take, if they are to be acted on as is suspected by foreign gold. The enthusiasm has extended beyond the limits of Paris. At this instant large numbers of peasantry from the neighbouring villages are formed in a line of march which extends from the new grille to a considerable distance beyond M. de Richelieu's, and are going to work at the Champ de Mars.

The committee of constitution are preparing a decree by the direction of the assembly in order to explain that of the 19th. They propose to allow every person to retain the name he is accustomed to, the titles however to be abolished, i.e. all public acts where they are used to be void. Some other alterations also will be made as to the article concerning liveries and coats of arms. One of the members of the assembly, the Baron de Menon, proposed some time ago that all orders should be abolished such as *cordons bleus, rouge* &c. The order of the day however was brought on without the motion being then taken up. Still one of the leading members of the committee of constitution is for rendering it a constitutional decree should it be proposed by that committee, which however is not certain, it will unquestionably pass.

Some time ago one of the members of the assembly was arrested by the orders of a municipality on suspicion of trying to debauch a regiment. The question of inviolability being taken up on account of this affair, it was decreed that it extended even to criminal cases, that is, that no member should be arrested unless the accusation were previously laid before the assembly, who should decide whether there were grounds for arrest.—To-day a creditor of one of their members has written to them that he has obtained judgment; and desired to know if he was authorized to proceed to arrest him. It was decided that he could. Thus the inviolability of the members is for criminal and not for civil cases. These contradictions must necessarily arise so long as the assembly proceed as at present in passing laws on a single reading.

A letter has just arrived here from Bilbao written by a well known merchant, which says the Spanish ministry had sent to inform them there that an arrangement had taken place with England, in consequence of which all vessels might follow their destination with safety. M. Bourgoin tells me that he knows the writer of the letter and is persuaded of its veracity. He has no doubt that arrangements are made for continuing the peace between Spain and England. He remains, however, and so does M. Montmorin, astonished that the first intelligence should come by a private and circuitous chanel. There is no doubt that the terms of accomodation must be disadvantageous to Spain. More certain intelligence is hourly expected. The last accounts of the British fleet are that it was still at Torbay, their destination therefore still as uncertain as when they left port.

You will no doubt have learned that several American sailors were impressed in London, and that they were rescued by the zealous exertions and activity of Mr. Cutting. Since then one other has been impressed whom Mr. Cutting has been unable to get released. He is on board of the fleet and will probably be forced to serve so long as they have any occasion for him. You will certainly have received from Mr. Cutting the particulars of this affair which seems to deserve the earliest attention of Congress, and points out the necessity of some arrangement being made for preventing such cases in future.

[I omitted mentioning above that the number of our prisoners at Algiers is now reduced to fourteen. A Scotch boy who was among them having been redeemed by the intervention of English Consul. The price was somewhat more than 7000.^{tt} but additional and unavoidable expences raised it on the whole to about 8000.^{tt} The person of whom I spoke in the beginning of this letter, told me that he thought the remaining captives might be redeemed at the same price for the common sailors and about 12,000.^{tt} for each of the Captains. He added that the Spanish Consul was at present in the greatest favor with the Regency, and would be the most proper person for being charged with such a commission. The same person told me that he had understood the present Emperor of Morocco had begun his reign by shewing dispositions to observe the treaties made by his predecessor. He thought it probable that ours would be continued. In general however I have understood that we should be obliged to renew it. This is the opinion also of Carmichael,][1] from whom you will certainly first learn the result. I mention to you in the case of his letters being longer on their way, that he has received your despatches of the 11th. of April, and been presented in consequence of the new letter of credence.

I beg you to be assured of the sentiments of respect and attachment with which I am, Dear Sir Your most obedient humble

W. SHORT

P.S. The Leyden gazettes will be inclosed in this letter. The journals of the assembly and other papers shall be forwarded to Havre by the diligence to be sent by the first vessel sailing for New York.

PrC (DLC: Short Papers); at head of text: "No. 36." Tr (DNA: RG 59, DD). Recorded in SJL as received 25 Oct. 1790. Tr of Extract (see note 1 below) in DLC and another in DNA: RG 59, MLR; see report on Algerine captives, 28 Dec. 1790.

1 The matter within brackets (sup-

plied) comprises the text of the extract referred to above and employed in the report on Algerine captives, 28 Dec. 1790.

From Harry Innes

SIR   Kentucky Danville July 8th. 1790

After an interval of about nine years I have ventured to renew our slight acquaintance by presenting you with a curiosity lately found by one of the Settlers on the Cumberland River. It is the Image carved of Stone of a naked Woman kneeling; it is roughly executed, but from the coarseness of the Stone the instrument with which it was probably carved and its antiquity I think shews the maker to have had some talent in that way, the design being good.

I am informed that the Image which is about nine or ten Inches high was found by a Farmer as he was ploughing his Corn field. He supposed it to have been about five or six Inches under the Surface, the Land was well timbered and lay several miles from the River; I have desired my Informer to examine the place and see if he can discover any appearances of a Settlement having been made there, and if so to cut down a Tree and ascertain the age thereof.

You will also recieve the Plan of an old Fortification herein inclosed, which I have viewed and which is accurately laid down; from the great number which are discovered in this Western Country I am clearly of opinion they were by Inhabitants and not by European Adventurers as some writers have suggested; I am the more confirmed in this opinion from the Burying Grounds which are large and contiguous to some of these Fortifications.

In another Letter I propose to state to you Sir some matters relative to this Western Country in the Political Line. At this time I am prevented by business. I am with very great respect Sir your mo. ob. Servt.,   HARRY INNES

RC (DLC). Recorded in SJL as received 30 Nov. 1790. For the enclosed PLAN OF AN OLD FORTIFICATION, see illustration in this volume.

TJ was greatly impressed by the IMAGE . . . OF STONE, and at once conjectured that the creator had, if not intentionally, "very happily hit on the representation of a woman in the first moments of parturition" (TJ to Innes,

7 Mch. 1791). This conjecture became an accepted fact when, on 19 Aug. 1791, TJ presented to the American Philosophical Society a "curious piece of Indian sculpture representing an Indian woman in labor, found near Cumberland, Va." (Procs., XXII, pt. 3 [1885], p. 196). This object was borrowed by Benjamin S. Barton in 1802 and returned a few months later (same, p. 329). See illustration in this volume.

To Alexander Hamilton

DEAR SIR   New York [July] 9. 1790.

You were so kind as to say you would write to our bankers in Holland to answer my draught for a part of the balance due me for salary &c. I suppose in fact it will be necessary to clear their minds on the subject, for tho' they know that the diplomatic expences in Europe were paid on the funds in their hands, yet as I am here they will naturally expect your instructions should accompany my draught. It will be for £350. sterling, expressed in gilders; I do not know as yet how many gilders exactly, nor in whose favor I shall draw. Messrs. Leroy and Bayard are to negociate the matter so that it may be finished in the morning before the packet sails and also before we set out on our party which I understand is to be at 9. oclock. It will suffice I presume if you say in general terms that I shall make the draught and that it will be for about £350 sterl. expressed in gilders. I apprehend a duplicate also of your letter will be necessary. I shall accompany them with a letter of advice naming the drawee and sum in gilders exactly. I will take the liberty of sending to you at 8. oclock in the morning for the letters; and am with great & sincere esteem Dear Sir Your most obedt. humble servt.,   TH: JEFFERSON

PrC (DLC).
TJ did not receive the LETTERS the next morning: Hamilton's letter was not written until 31 July 1790. For an explanation of the delay, see TJ to Fitzhugh, 21 July 1790; see also note, TJ to Willink & Van Staphorst, 4 Aug. 1790.

From Charles Bellini

Williamsburg, 10 July 1790. "L'Eminentissimo Nostro Monsignor Arcivescovo Madison" who hoped to be consecrated in America will probably have forwarded the answer to TJ's most kind letter of 13 June.—The word *impotent*, which Bellini's evil genius let drop at the end of TJ's letter, would have been more than enough to discourage the strongest spirit: the effect of that unexpected thunderbolt on his, already crushed by so many travails, may be imagined, but in that most violent shock, upsetting to his whole mechanism and the weak springs that sustain it, he recalled an ancient anecdote not at all inappropriate to his own case.

Giovan Gastone, last Grand Duke of Tuscany of the Medici family, was perpetually annoyed by a priest who kept asking him, in the most insolent manner, for all the vacant benefices—which in that territory are most numerous and highly lucrative—without having ever obtained one because of his importunings; at last the Grand Duke, though a most patient man, was unable any longer to bear the petulant, petitioning priest, and with a solemn decree forbade him, under severest penalties, ever to request another thing so long as he should live. Within a few hours of the publication of this edict, the priest presented to his sovereign a petition no less impertinent than just, praying for the power to petition. Whereupon the Grand Duke, knowing that the priest's action—called by jurists "Oris Aperitio" was just and that the priest was not an ignorant man, at once conferred on him the best benefice then vacant. TJ is the sovereign in the sense that he is patient and a benefactor; Bellini is the petitioner, doubtless indiscreet and perhaps impertinent, but not a priest.

A *cause célèbre* in the Virginia admiralty court, at which he had the honor to serve as interpreter and translator of numerous Spanish documents "in lingua Americana," impressed many gentlemen, particularly Col. Innes, with the utility of having a sworn interpreter for all cases. Innes told Bellini that he would like to write to TJ and Madison on the subject, but Bellini thinks that, as he has many important matters on his hands, he may not remember, and therefore begs TJ to intercede directly or indirectly in his favor. He has imitated the petitioning priest only too well, but he knows what he did not and could not know: that TJ's natural inclination to assist wretched humanity is much greater than all the troublesome annoyances that might be produced upon TJ by all men, and his confidence in TJ is such that it can only be inadequately expressed in the saying of the poet king: "In te, Domine, speravi, non confundar in eternum."—He asks pardon for an insipidly prolix letter, and begs TJ himself not to forget that his patience is infinite: he remembers how and to what extent it was tried, there in that earthly paradise mistakenly called Monticello ("nel Paradiso Terrestre abusivamente chiamato Monticello"), by the most efficaceous and indefatigable Mazzei, and also the motives that once, at Elk-Hill, drew from the depths of TJ's heart that stupendous "I AM DEAD" ("e dei motivi che una volta a Elk-hill estrassero dal più profondo del suo cuore quello stupendo: 'SON MORTO'"). All the waters of the river Lethe could not make him forget that.—His poor crippled wife thanks TJ for the affection with which he honors her.

RC (DLC: Application for Office under Washington); in Italian; endorsed by TJ as received 20 July 1790 and so recorded in SJL.

Bellini's answer that presumably was carried to New York by the Rev. James Madison has not been found and is not recorded in SJL. The allusion to the incident at ELK-HILL unfortunately cannot be clarified. But for evidence of the fact that Mazzei could put even TJ's patience to the test, see TJ to Madison, 16 Mch. 1784, wherein he expressed alarm at the idea of Mazzei's coming to Annapolis and said it would be worse for him than a return of his "double quotidian head-ach."

From Beverley Randolph

DEAR SIR   Richmond July 10th. 1790.

Mr. Stephen Austin one of the Proprietors of the lead mines in this State proposes to make application to the Congress of the United States for some encouragement in order to enable them to furnish this Country with manufactured Lead in all its various Forms. He also wishes to contract with the general government to supply such Quantity of Lead as may be wanted for their Magazines & caet: In order to give every aid to his application I take the Liberty to introduce Mr. Austin to you and to request the Favour of you to assist him by your advice and Recommendation to those who may have Power to forward his views.

I believe you are well acquainted with the Fertility of these Mines. From the Information which I have received I conceive they are capable of producing such a Quantity of Lead as will intitle them to the Countenance of Government. The inclosed certificate speaks fully of their present Situation and future Prospects. I am Dear Sir Yrs. sincerely,   BEVERLEY RANDOLPH

RC (DLC). Recorded in SJL as received 23 July 1790. Enclosure: Certificate signed by Arthur Campbell, R. Sayers, and William Migomry, dated at the lead mines, 23 June 1790, and addressed to the governor and council of Virginia, reading: "We, professing ourselves friends to the promotion of American Manufactures, especially those of necessary Articles, and being requested by Mr. Stephen Austin to view the present state of the Works now carrying on at the Lead Mines, Do certify, that there are between fifty and sixty men employed as miners, Artificers and labourers, that there are seven pits sunk of about seventy feet in depth, which are so productive, that from six to eight tons of Ore, may be raised in a day; that the appearances give confidence to conclude, that the bodies of Ore, that may be found in the Hill is inexhaustible; that at present a very simple but improved manner of beating and Washing the Ore are adopted; that there are in forwardness materials for erecting a New furnace which may be ready for use in less than two Months, but that built by the late Colonel Chiswell is now so repaired that above one ton and an half of Lead may be smelted every day while it stands.—From these beginnings and from the activity and professed Views of the Owners, we are sanguine enough to believe, that with a small encouragement from the general Government, so as to compensate in a degree for so distant a land Carriage, that Lead will be produced and Manufactured in the Course of the ensuing year, Sufficient for the Consumption of the United States.—It has been mentioned to us that a duty of one Cent per pound on all foreign Lead imported will operate as an ample encouragement to bring about a completion of their Views. We are not so well acquainted with the Commercial Interests of the United States as to urge the adoption of such a proposition; but wish to remind our Rulers, that the time has been, that much depended on the preservation and success of this same Manufacture: That similar Occasions may happen in the Course of future events, that will show the good policy of being independent of all the World for so necessary an Article" (Tr in DLC; also DNA: RG 59, MLR). Randolph also wrote to Washington on 10 July 1790 enclosing a copy of this certificate, introducing Stephen Austin, and stating that he wished to make a contract with the government (same). The certificate was published in the (N.Y.) *Daily Advertiser* for 23 July 1790 as from the "Virginia Chronicle"—presumably the *Norfolk and Portsmouth Chronicle*—and was signed "A Friend to American Manufactures."

TJ was indeed familiar with the LEAD MINES of southwestern Virginia that had been formerly operated by Col. John Chiswell: it was he who drafted on 15 July 1776 a recommendation that these mines be developed by the state; during his governorship and until 1782 they were so managed and operated; their productivity was of crucial importance in the campaigns of 1781; and no one in Virginia during the war years was more concerned with the output of the mines than he (see, for example, Ross to TJ, 4 May 1781, commenting on the "great anxiety . . . expressed" by TJ in his missing letter of 3 May 1781 about the mines). See also, Hening, IX, 237-8; X, 193-4; CVSP, III, 390; VMHB, IV, 359. On 12 July 1790 John Harvie also wrote TJ: "Mr. Moses Austin, a Merchant in this City and his Brothers have leas'd the Lead Mines in this State formerly Chiswells and propose working them extensively if they can Obtain some small Encouragement from the General Government. They have Established at this place a factory of Sheet Lead and Shott, which is Carry'd on with diligence and I believe good Success. No one can be better Acquainted with the Situation of these Mines in respect to Land Carriage and

Navigation than yourself and any remark of mine relative to the proposition of these Gentlemen would be Superfluous, as their Views and Wishes can be best explain'd by themselves" (RC in DLC; endorsed as received 23 July 1790 and so recorded in SJL). TJ's reply to Harvie must be interpreted in the light of his disposition at this time to show friendship (see TJ to Martha Jefferson Randolph, 17 July 1790, note) and of his fear that encouragement of private ventures by the general government might set a dangerous precedent (TJ to Harvie, 25 July 1790). There is no evidence that he replied to Gov. Randolph's letter and his fear may have influenced the casual response that Washington gave to the Virginia governor: Washington on 25 Aug. 1790 wrote that it had not required any "particular answer" and hence he had deferred acknowledging it (*Writings*, ed. Fitzpatrick, XXXI, 95).

In *Notes on Virginia* TJ gave the best contemporary description of the lead mines and suggested means of shortening the land transportation from the mines to Richmond: this road led from the mines "130 miles along a good road, leading through the peaks of Otter to Lynch's ferry, or Winston's, on James river"—thus passing near his own place at Poplar Forest (*Notes on Virginia*, ed. William Peden, Chapel Hill, 1955, p. 27).

Pig lead was admitted free of duty under the revenue act of 1789. But within a month after Moses and Stephen Austin appeared in New York, bearing letters of introduction to TJ, Madison, and doubtless to others, Congress levied a duty of "one cent per pound on bar and all other lead imported"; the resolution was introduced by John Brown (1757-1837), TJ's former law student who was then representing the Kentucky District of Virginia in Congress. (See *Annals*, II, 1740; *Statutes at Large*, I, 26, 180; Victor S. Clark, *History of Manufactures in the United States*, 1929 edn., I, 288). John Walker wrote Randolph that his letter had arrived in good time, that the duty of one cent per pound on all imported lead was readily agreed to, and that he hoped this would be "a sufficient protection for our infant Manufacture of this article" (Walker to Beverley Randolph, July 1790, PHi: Dreer Collection).

To James Monroe

Dear Sir New York July 11. 1790.

I wrote you last on the 20th. of June. The bill for removing the federal government to Philadelphia for 10. years and then to Georgetown has at length past both houses. The offices are to be removed before the 1st. of December. I presume it will be done during the President's trip to Virginia, which will be in September and October. I hope to set out for Virginia about the 1st. of September and to pass three or four weeks at Monticello.—Congress will now probably proceed in better humour to funding the public debt. This measure will secure to us the credit we now hold at Amsterdam, where our European paper is above par, which is the case of no other nation. Our business is to have great credit and to use it little. Whatever enables us to go to war, secures our peace. At present it is essential to let both Spain and England see that we are in a condition for war, for a number of collateral circumstances now render it probable that they will be in that condition. Our object is to feed, and theirs to fight. If we are not forced by England, we shall have a gainful time of it.—A vessel from Gibraltar of the 10th. of June tells us O'Hara was busily fortifying and providing there, and that the English Consuls in the Spanish ports on the Mediterranean had recieved orders to dispatch all their vessels from those ports immediately. The Captain saw 15. Spanish ships of war going to Cadiz. It is said that Arnold is at Detroit reviewing the militia there. Other symptoms indicate a general design on all Louisiana and the two Floridas. What a tremendous position would success in these objects place us in! Embraced from the St. Croix to the St. Mary's on one side by their possessions, on the other by their fleet, we need not hesitate to say that they would soon find means to unite to them all the territory covered by the ramifications of the Missisipi.—Mrs. Monroe's friends were well three or four days ago. We are all disappointed at her not coming here. Present me to her affectionately and accept yourself assurances of the sincere esteem of Dr. Sir Your friend & servt.,

Th: Jefferson

RC (NN); addressed: Colo. James Monroe at Charlottesville to be put into the Richmond mail, and sent thence by the private post of Charlottesville"; franked; postmarked: "NEW-YORK * july 11" and "FREE." PrC (DLC).

To Thomas Mann Randolph, Jr.

DEAR SIR   New York July 11. 1790.

Your last favor was of May 25. Mine was of June 20. having written regularly every third week to you, and the intermediate ones to Patsy or Polly. The bill for the removal of the federal government to Philadelphia for 10. years and then to Georgetown has at length past both houses, so that our removal is now certain: and I think it tolerably certain that the President will leave this place on a visit to Mount Vernon about the last of August or first of September. That will fix my visit to Monticello to the same time. I am in hopes yourself and the girls may take your arrangements to pass three or four weeks there with me, suppose from the middle of Sep. to the middle of Octob.—We are in hopes Congress will now proceed quietly to the funding the public debt; and by that measure fix the credit which we at present possess in Amsterdam, where all our European paper is above par, which is not the case with that even of England. This is the more interesting to us, as whatever puts us in a condition to go to war, secures our peace. Abundance of little circumstances induce a belief that England means to force Spain into a war. Her orders to her different dominions shew she expects to be at war. A vessel from Gibraltar the 10th. of June brings news that they were busy in fortifying and laying in stores there, and that the English Consuls in all the Spanish ports on the Mediterranean had received orders to dispatch all their vessels immediately. The captain saw 15. Spanish ships of war going to Cadiz. We shall have a difficult task to steer between these two nations. Peace is our business. Produce of all kinds will assuredly keep high for years to come, and especially bread. Wheat is now at a dollar and a quarter at Philadelphia. We cannot push that culture too boldly. I will thank you if in all your letters you will be so good as to give me a particular account of the seasonableness of the weather and the state and prospect of crops of wheat, corn and tobacco as these things are very interesting. Mr. Donald writes me the crop of wheat is abundant and of good quality. Present my warm affections to my dear Martha and to Maria if you are together. I am with sincerity Dear Sir Your's affectionately,

TH: JEFFERSON

RC (DLC); addressed: "Thomas Mann Randolph junr. esq. Richmond"; franked; postmarked: "NEW-YORK * july 11" and "FREE."

From William Short

DEAR SIR   Paris July the 11th. 1790

I wrote to you on the 7th. of this month in answer to your's of the 27th. of May. That letter was sent by the way of Havre. This will be sent to L'Orient to go by the packet in the case of its sailing. But that you know is a conveyance too uncertain to be counted on and therefore I consider this letter as an adventure.—The intelligence which I mentioned in my last as coming from Bilbao, and in such a direction as to leave little doubt of a pacific arrangement having taken place between England and Spain has not been yet confirmed. What is still more extraordinary, neither M. de Montmorin, the Spanish, or English Ambassador have received any courier since that time, and the Spanish post expected the day before yesterday has not yet arrived. Everybody seems in a state of uncertainty respecting this matter and M. Bourgoin told me yesterday morning he began to suspect the letter was a forgery, probably for the purpose of stock-jobbing. Still I apprehend that the English cabinet have hopes that this business will end soon and in a treaty at least commercial with Spain.

I saw the Duke of Orleans's reception this morning at court. He arrived late last night. He was recieved cooly by the King, graciously by the Queen, and most contemptuously by the courtiers, particularly the female part. The time he passed in the Queen's antechamber waiting until she was ready, which you know is not short, he appeared quite insulated. Nobody spoke to him, but the glances of the eye and frowns of the women of the court were such as were really indecent and remarked by every body. From the court he went to the assembly and took his seat. I am told he was very well received there. It is not yet possible to know what impression his arrival will make on the people. He has certainly a strong party among them: and should he desire to make use of them and have the means which is supposed, he will certainly find them ready. From his writings and late conduct however one would think he would wish to remain quiet if his partisans would allow him.

The works in the champ de Mars are much advanced and it is not now doubted that they will be ready for the 14th. Three sides of the field are raised in a kind of Amphitheatre by earth that has been brought there. In the middle a monticule of earth is raised on which the altar is to be erected where the King is to take the following oath, after the deputies of the Gardes nationales and of the assembly shall have taken that adopted the 4th. of February.—"Moi Roi des Francois, je jure à la nation d'employer tout le pouvoir qui m'est delegué par la loi constitutionelle de l'Etat, à maintenir la constitution decretée par l'Assemblée nationale et acceptée par moi, and à faire executer les loix." The Committee of constitution had proposed, 'Moi, premier citoyen &c.'—but these two words were left out by the assembly on the principle that the oath was taken as King and not as a citizen.

The corps diplomatique determined this morning on the requisition of the Spanish and Neopolitan Ambassadors that they could not accept of the intended invitation of the municipality. This will be made known to M. Bailli and probably no invitation will be sent. The minority consider themselves bound by the decision of the majority and therefore will go and place themselves as they can. Some of the Ambassadors are of this class. As the day approaches apprehensions of danger seem to diminish. The deputies are nearly all arrived. Besides them great numbers of amateurs have arrived with their families from the distant provinces. The deputies are lodged in private houses, that is such as chose to recieve them. The private soldiers are treated with the greatest marks of civility and attention even by the Marechals of France who lodge them. In short it is impossible to concieve a more equalising system than that which prevails at present.

A Person called here whilst I was out this morning and left a packet of newspapers and the report of the Secretary of Treasury. They are directed to me in your hand writing, and marked as having been recieved at Bordeaux the 25th. of June. The same person said he had letters also which he would bring to-morrow morning; but my letter will be gone before the reciept of them. They are certainly duplicates of those I have already received, which you mention having sent by the way of Bordeaux.

I recieved a letter yesterday from London which informed me of Rhode Island having adopted the federal constitution, and the very great probability of Congress adjourning to Philadelphia. Should I learn that this is realized before your furniture leaves Havre, I shall have it sent there. I learned at the same time, I believe the intelligence comes by the English June Packet, that the bill concerning the foreign establishment is lost. [If I thought that would retard any decision being taken relative to your successor until the arrival of my letter, I should be emboldened to trouble you on the subject more perhaps than I am authorized to do. But I have always considered what I should write as so much too late, that my pen has refused to follow the dictates of my mind or followed them not in the manner I wished. Several of the members of the corps diplomatique have read a paper which mentioned two or three days ago your having taken the oath of office. This brought on the subject of my appointment again this morning. They consider it a matter so certain, and so natural now that you are at the head of the department of foreign affairs, that they will be sure if it does not take place it can be owing to nothing but entire incapacity on my part. The same conclusion or something very much like it will be formed by a great many people in America also. They will not know that it proceeds from an aversion in you perhaps to take so great a degree of responsibility on yourself and to be exposed at the same time to the suspicion of being partial. I had intended to have written this letter without saying a word of myself, but I have been surprized into this observation. I beg pardon for it.][1] The packing of your furniture will not be finished I fear for the fifteenth. I am hurrying them however as much as possible as I wait only for that in order to go and pass eight or ten days at La Rocheguyon. Accept my most ardent wishes my dear Sir for your health and happiness, and believe me unalterably your friend & servant,   W. Short

RC (DLC); at head of text: "*Private*"; part of text carefully obliterated by short diagonal marks drawn through each letter in the whole of the passage indicated in note 1 below, but not deleted in PrC (DLC: Short Papers); endorsed as received 14 Oct. 1790 and so recorded in SJL.

[1] The matter enclosed in brackets (supplied) comprises the part of the text obliterated as indicated above. It is possible that TJ himself made this deletion, perhaps because of a desire to protect Short against the too-often reiterated expression of his ambition. A similar deletion occurs in Short to TJ, 16 July 1790. The fact that in neither case was the deletion made in the press copy suggests that Short was not the one who made it.

From Richard O'Bryen

Esteemed Sir   City of Algiers July 12th. 1790

We the fourteen unfortunate Americans in Algiers, were informed by Mr. Abraham Bushara and Dininio, capital Jew merchants of this City, that they had received orders from America, by way of London and Lisbon, to make application to this Regency, to ascertain and fix the ransom of the American captives, after their surmounting many difficulties, at last on the 7th. instant prevailed on the Dey and Ministry to agree and fix the price of the said fourteen Americans at Seventeen thousand two hundred and twenty five Algerine Sequins. I have often explained relative to the purport of Mr. Lamb's audiences when in Algiers; at present I shall only mention to you that Mr. Lamb had five audiences with the Dey and Ministry, and he agreed for the ransom or release of the American captives agreeable to the price then asked. The ransom of the fourteen Americans at present in Algiers, amounted to 17.500 Algerine Sequins.

At that period there were nearly 3,000 Slaves in Algiers; but the Spaniards, Neapolitans and other Nations redeeming their people, and the Pest in 1787-88 carrying off 780 slaves (among this number were six Americans) the number of Slaves is reduced to 700. The major part of these are deserters from the Spanish garrison of Oran. Since that period the Dey has raised the price on Slaves, and is but little inclinable to admit of Slaves being redeemed, they being much wanted to do the public work, which be assured, Sir, is very laborious. The price asked for the Americans is by no means exorbitant, considering the present want of Slaves, and the terms of release of captives of other Nations.

Mr. Bushara and Dininio having a great knowledge of these people, were thereby very fortunate in prevailing on the Dey and Ministry, to fix the release of the Americans at 17.225 Sequins. Our greatest fears were, that the Dey would not permit us to be redeemed on any terms. The Dey asked 27.000 sequins, but was prevailed on by the prime Minister to let our ransom be on the terms mentioned.

The Dey and Ministry signified that the ransom of the Americans was fixed and agreed on with Mr. Lamb, the american Ambassador, in 1786; and that he promised to return with the Money in four months, but that he broke his word and agreement. The Ministry observed, that if the Americans did not keep their word on so small an affair as the sum asked for our release, that there was no dependence to be put in them in Affairs of more importance. Indeed, Sir, I hope for the honor and interests of the United States of America, that the price now fixed for our release will be immediately agreed to: and be assured, Sir, if this opportunity in our behalf is not embraced, that we shall be the most miserable slaves in the World, for we shall be doomed to perpetual Slavery.

After the price was fixed, the prime Minister observed that he could not conceive what ideas the Americans had of the Algerines, by first sending an ambassador, who making a regular bargain or agreement for our release and promising to return in four months, had not kept his word. We said that at that time our country was forming a Government, and that we did not suppose the Ambassador had informed Congress of the agreement he made. The prime Minister said the ambassador did not act right. We answered, that perhaps he did not understand that he made a regular bargain, or that all was badly interpreted. Much passed on this subject. The present Causendal or Lord chamberlain to the Dey, said he was present when Mr. Lamb agreed for our release.

On the 8th. instant the prime Minister sent privately to me, and desired that when I wrote to mention all he said, and make it known to my Country. Indeed we are much indebted to the prime Minister; for depend, Sir, he is a friend to America. He was so when Mr. Lamb was in Algiers; and even at that period, had matters been well managed, the foundation of a peace might have been laid.

Should any change happen in this Government, we apprehend it would be very prejudicial to our release; or should the Portuguese, Neapolitans or Genoese redeem their people on higher terms, than is at present asked for the Americans, depend upon it, Sir, that to get us clear would be attended with much difficulty.

You will please to consider, Sir, what our sufferings must have been in this country, during the trying period of five years captivity, twice surrounded with the pest and other contagious distempers, far distant from our country, families, friends and connections.

Depend upon it, Sir, that it is prejudicial to any nation that leaves it's Subjects in slavery; for in no respect can it answer any public benefit, or be any advantage to the Country they belong to. The longer the time they are in slavery, the greater the difficulty is there in releasing them: and it is well known that the price of the slaves is rising on every application, owing to the decrease of slaves, as the Algerines find they cannot carry on the public work without slaves.

Since our redemption has been ascertained and fixed, several applications have been made to the Dey and Ministry to permit captives of other Nations to be redeemed on the same terms as fixed on for the Americans, but the Dey answered, that he wanted Slaves. These applications were for certain persons, but not for any general or national redemption.

[31]

On the 7th. day of April 1786 Mr. Lamb agreed with the Dey
on these terms for the release of the Americans.
For each Master 3000 Sequins.
For each Mariner 750 Sequins.
For each Mate 2000 Sequins.
At present there are in Algiers, at the Dey's price with Mr. Lamb,

2 Masters at 3000 Sequins each, is	6000
2 Mates at 2000 Sequins each, is	4000
10 Mariners at 750 Sequins each, is	7500

Sequins	17.500

Duties and fees on the ransom of slaves,⎫
   amounting to 15 or 18 per Cent ⎬

On the 7th. July 1790 our ransom was ascertained and fixed
by Bushara and Dininio with the Dey and Ministry, at, vizt.—

2 Masters, OBryen and Stephens, at 2000 Sequins each, is	4000
2 Mates, Alexander Forsyth and Andrew Montgomery, at 1500 Sequins each, is	3000
Jacobus Jysanier a young lad aged 22 years and page to the dey	2000
William Patterson a smart seaman at	1500
James Cathcart a young lad understanding navigation	1500
George Smith a young lad and page to the Dey at	900
Philip Sloan at	700
John Robertson at	700
Peleg Lorin at	700
James Harnet at	700
James Hull at	700
John Gregory Billings at	700

First cost	17.100
Extra fees	125

N.B. a sequin is equal to 8s. Sterling. Sequins	17.225

   A duty of 15 or 18 per Cent to be
added, being fees on the redemption
of slaves

Indeed, Sir, there is no alternative. We are at the lowest price
that any public Slaves will be redeemed whilst the present Government stands; and I am shure our Country will see, by our ransom,
the fatal and bad consequence of being at War with the Barbary

States, particularly so commercial a Nation as the American is. All other commercial Nations have experienced the bad policy of a War with the Barbary States.

Who could have thought that the haughty Spanish Nation would have given such vast sums for making and keeping peace with the Barbary States, and changed their national flag. But the Spaniards saw they were made a sort of political tool by all the other commercial Nations.

The Regency, some time past, wanted three of the young Americans to embrace the Mahometan religion, but they would not. This I suppose may account for the motives of their price being something extra.

Two months past one of my crew, Charles Colvill, was redeemed by charitable contributions raised by his friends. His ransom cost 1700 dollars. I believe he returns to America. He is capable of giving much information on Barbary affairs.

Three Algerine gallies have taken a polacre with sixteen greeks, with a pass from the deceased Grand Seignior. They are enslaved by the Algerines by their having been under Jerusalem colours. They also took a Neapolitan Brig, the crew of which escaped; and a Genoese vessel, but an armed Tartan of Genoa retook this vessel with 20 moors and turks on board. The Algerine Galley took another Neapolitan Vessel near Toulon. The neapolitan seamen in that port manned their boats, and went out of Toulon and retook the vessel. This is likely to be a serious affair. Depend upon it, Sir, that the Chamber of Commerce of Marseilles must pay all damages.

I have now the pleasure of informing you, that the Court of Portugal has dropped their idea of making a peace with this Regency. I believe all their propositions were rejected by the Algerines. Indeed, Sir, this is very fortunate for the Americans, for if the Algerines were at peace with Portugal, the cruisers of this Regency would meet with no obstruction in their cruising in the Atlantic, which of course would be very prejudicial to the commerce of America.

The Minister for Foreign Affairs being further sounded relative to a peace with America, asked if we had wrote to our Country the purport of what he said on the subject. He was answered, that I had wrote on the subject to the American ambassadors in Europe.

He answered and said that he would do all he had promised, and not deviate or withdraw his word. This answer was about the 4th.

of June. Indeed as the present Minister for foreign Affairs has expressed himself so friendly in behalf of America, I hope there will be a lasting friendship between them and him, who, you may depend Sir, is well inclined to serve the Americans.

My brother sufferers and I, Sir, return you our sincere thanks for befriending us so much in the cause of liberty, being convinced that you have done all in your power with the Congress, to redeem this unfortunate and faithful remnant of Americans; and we make not the least doubt, that our Country will immediately see the necessity of agreeing to pay the sum for our release, as has been ascertained. Our dependence is on a generous and humane Country, whom that God may prosper is the sincere wish of, Esteemed Sir Your most obt. most h'ble. Servt.,

RICHARD OBRYEN in behalf of myself and
brother Captives.

P.S. We are much indebted to the Spanish Consul and other gentlemen for many favors, rendered in times of impending danger.

Tr (DLC); at head of text: "Copy." FC (DNA: RG 59, SDR). Recorded in SJL as received 12 Jan. 1791. TJ forwarded a copy of this letter, together with copies of letters from O'Bryen to Carmichael of 17 May and 24 June 1790, to the senate on 20 Jan. 1791.

The War Crisis of 1790

EDITORIAL NOTE

On 1 May 1790 Gouverneur Morris reported to Washington his most recent discussion with the British Secretary for Foreign Affairs. He was as unaware at the time as any Londoner that in the crucial cabinet meeting the night before William Pitt boldly took the risk of general war by seizing upon the Nootka Sound incident to deliver the first effective challenge to Spanish claims to exclusive rights of sovereignty and commerce in the Pacific since the origin of those claims in the forgotten Treaty of Tordesillas of 1494.[1] Morris' report, accompanied by private letters describing the excitement of the 6th of May when the issue was disclosed to a shocked nation, arrived in New York late in June. For the next four months war seemed inevitable, with the issue hanging on the question whether France would honor the Family Compact by supporting Spain. Despite debt and mounting taxes, England under Pitt's leadership seemed to embrace the danger eagerly: "a mad Credulity prevails here," one observer in London wrote as late as November, "just as it did at the Commencement of the American War, we despise our Enemy, and dream of nought but Victory, and the capture of Spanish Wealth, the Mines of Mexico and Peru are already ideally in our Possession."[2] Simultaneously with the arrival of Morris' report in New York, the Governor General of Canada, Lord Dorchester, received important secret dispatches reflecting the concern of the ministry at the part the United States might play in a conflict between two powers possessing territories that encircled it.[3]

Dorchester at once sent his aide-de-camp, Major George Beckwith, hurrying down from Quebec on his fifth and final mission to the United States as confidential agent. In New York on the morning of the 8th of July Beckwith was closeted with the Secretary of the Treasury. At noon the latter reported to the President about the conversation with Dorchester's emissary, the Secretary of State also being present. Jeffer-

[1] Morris to Washington, 1 May 1790, Vol. 16: 532-5; a dramatic account of the beginning of the crisis is in Rutledge to TJ, 6 May 1790. For the general background, see W. R. Manning, "The Nootka Sound Controversy," Am. Hist. Assn., *Ann.Rept.*, 1904, p. 363-87; Bemis, *Jay's Treaty*, p. 70-85. Sparks, *Morris*, II, 4-56, contains the whole of Morris' correspondence with Leeds and of his reports to Washington. See also TJ's report on Morris' correspondence, 15 Dec. 1790.

Morris did guess that something was going on behind the scenes, possibly indicating war. He wrote Washington after his first conference with the Duke of Leeds: "from his Countenance and Manner on the Perusal of your Letter, he seemed to derive from it that Sort of Pleasure which a Man feels at the Removal of Something which every now and then brings to his Mind disagreeable Ideas. I do not exactly see from what Cause this Emotion was produced. By the Eagerness of his subsequent Expressions I conjectured that the critical Situation of Europe had excited some Disquietude respecting the Part which the United States might take in Case of a general War. What strengthened that Idea, and perhaps led me to form it was that in a Chamber to which I was introduced previous to the Audience there was a large Book of Maps open at that of Poland. But the Silence since observed leads to a suspicion that his Satisfaction was derived from another Source. I am told that in a late Debate the Ministers committed themselves by throwing out in pretty clear Terms the Idea that some sort of Treaty was on the Carpet with America; and if so, the Opening now given must have relieved them from the fear of future Contradiction" (Gouverneur Morris to George Washington, 13 Apr. 1790; RC in DLC: Washington Papers). The atlas in the antechamber open at the map of Poland may have been an intentional miscue for visitors to the Foreign Office, but there is no doubt that Washington's letter brought a sense of relief to the cabinet.

[2] John Barker Church to Alexander Hamilton, 3 Nov. 1790, Syrett, *Hamilton*, VII, 136-7.

[3] Grenville to Dorchester, Dispatches Nos. 22-24, all dated 6 May 1790 and all marked "Secret"; PRO: CO 42/67, f. 87-9, 91-2, 93-102; texts printed in Brymner, *Report*, 1890, p. 131-3.

son's preferences on commercial relations with England, on the unsettled issues of the Treaty of Peace, on preserving good neighborhood to the north and south, on binding the "men on the western waters" to the union, and on the paramount necessity of opening the navigation of the Mississippi were clear and had long been known. But the threat of a general European war brought into conjunction at mid-summer of his first year in office a complex set of forces that made it virtually impossible for the administration to speak with a coherent voice on foreign policy. All came to agree that this should be one of neutrality and Washington firmly supported Jefferson in defining that policy. But the extent to which the surface unity was undermined by the countervailing efforts of the Secretary of the Treasury was wholly unknown at the time to the President and the Secretary of State and has since been obscured by misconceptions of Beckwith's role in the United States between 1787 and 1792. This fact has unavoidably affected interpretations of matters of far greater moment than the missions of the able and respected officer whom Jefferson called, without derision, "the poor Major." That role must therefore be defined with some precision, particularly as it related to the initial appointment of Gouverneur Morris as the President's personal agent in London and also to the events set in motion by the war crisis of 1790. This becomes obligatory in view of the fact that the documents tracing the evolution of Jefferson's policy cannot be understood unless the validity of those to which in some degree they are a response is assessed.

I

When the Archivist of Canada, Douglas Brymner, first published some of Beckwith's reports in 1890, he stated that the agent was employed by Dorchester "in the absence of any resident recognized diplomatic agent from Great Britain" and that he was regarded by Washington's administration as "a real, although unofficial diplomatic agent, acting on behalf of the British government."[4] This estimate has been accepted as accurate and indeed has been confirmed by emphasis and amplification.[5] Beckwith himself added to misconceptions of his role

[4] Brymner, *Report*, 1890, p. xxxvi, xli.

[5] For example, in "The United States and the Abortive Armed Neutrality of 1794," AHR, XXIV (Oct. 1918), 29, Bemis states: "Alexander Hamilton . . . had for five years been in confidential communication with the British Minister, George Hammond, and with Major George Beckwith, in an informal sense his predecessor." In 1940 Mayo stated that Beckwith "had been employed in the United States by Dorchester as confidential agent, and later by the Foreign Office itself as Great Britain's informal representative, from 1787 to the arrival of Hammond in October of 1791"; "Instructions to British Ministers, 1791-1812," ed. Bernard Mayo, Am. Hist. Assn., *Ann.Rept.*, 1936, III, 21n. Bemis, *Jay's Treaty*, p. 57-9, 96-8, has the fullest and best account of Beckwith's role, but he goes so far as to suggest that Washington, after consulting members of the cabinet as well as Adams and Jay, made the "decision of the government not to extend any official recognition to Dorchester's aide, who carried no proper credentials." In this and in other respects Bemis' account differs from the interpretation set forth in the present analysis. See also Bemis, "Thomas Jefferson," in *American Secretaries of State and Their Diplomacy*, ed. Bemis, II, 27-9; Malone, *Jefferson*, II, 273, 309; Miller, *Hamilton*, p. 367-8; Freeman, *Washington*, VI, 269-70; Syrett, *Hamilton*, V, 482.

by stating three years after the event that in 1789 he bore a message from Grenville "to The Executive Government of the United States, on the subject of a discrimination of duties" and that this "led to certain overtures on the part of their Government . . . communicated by Lord Dorchester."[6] Both assertions are in error. Beckwith's mission was not to the government but to those individuals in and out of office known to support views friendly to Great Britain. While such persons expressed their opinions freely to Beckwith and these were promptly reported to Quebec and London, no overtures "on the part of their Government" were ever made in consequence of his missions. At no time from 1787 to 1792 was the agent clothed with public authority, informal or otherwise, either by Dorchester or by the British ministry, in such a way as to authorize him to speak for one government to another government. When Beckwith's agency was brought into the open in July 1790, Washington and Jefferson at once grasped the true status of the emissary without suspecting the full extent of his confidential role.[7] The subject of recognition or even of direct negotiation never arose because, as Hamilton himself said he told Beckwith, it was "out of question." Jefferson never held any conversation with the agent until his final mission had closed.[8] That Beckwith should have been led to mistake the nature of his role is quite natural. He had access to men of influence in all branches of the government who at times spoke of themselves as the governing majority. It is particularly understandable that he should have regarded himself as dealing with the "Executive Government of the United States" when he held discussions with the Secretary of the Treasury. Hamilton said nothing at all to avoid creating such an impression, much to deepen it.

[6] George Beckwith to Henry Dundas, 20 June 1792, PRO: FO 4/12; text printed in Bemis, *Jay's Treaty*, p. 377-80.

[7] Washington, *Diaries*, ed. Fitzpatrick, IV, 139; TJ to Morris, 12 Aug. 1790, Document VIII below.

[8] Early in 1792 TJ wrote the following memorandum which he deposited in the files of the Department of State: "Colo. Beckwith called on me and informed me that tho' not publicly commissioned he had been sent here on the part of his government, that arriving before I came into office *he had been put into the hands of another department*, not indeed by the Chief Magistrate directly as he had never had any direct communications with him, but informally, and had never been transferred to my department: that on commencing his correspondence with the Secretary of State of Gr. Britain he had thought it his duty to make that circumstance known to us: that Mr. Hammond's arrival had now rendered his longer continuance here unnecessary, as his residence hitherto had been only preparatory to Mr. Hammond's reception, that he had received orders by the last packet from the Secretary of State to return to England by the next, and that he should accordingly do so. He acknoleged the personal civility with which he had been treated generally, and his entire satisfaction. [Note this was the first conversation I ever had with him but merely as a private gentleman. I note it's purport because he was sent here by Ld. Dorchester from Quebec, which consequently authorises us to send such a character to Quebec]"; MS in TJ's hand, dated 12 Feb. 1792, in DNA: RG 59, MLR; not recorded in SJL or SJPL (brackets in MS, but emphasis supplied). It is possible that by 1792 Beckwith had persuaded himself that he had been sent to New York by his government and that this was done preparatory to the sending of a minister. It is also possible—such being the state of party animosities at the time—that he was urged by Hamilton to give such an account of his presence in New York and Philadelphia.

EDITORIAL NOTE

Major George Beckwith (1753-1823) came from a very distinguished military family of Yorkshire. His father was Major-General John Beckwith, who commanded the 20th regiment at Minden and who later served under Frederick II of Prussia. George Beckwith's rise in rank and his subsequent career prove him a man of talent and integrity. He was commissioned an ensign of the 37th regiment in 1771 and embarked the same year for America. He distinguished himself with that unit in active service throughout the war. He was made lieutenant of the 37th in 1775, captain in 1777, major in 1781, lieutenant-colonel in 1790, and colonel in 1795, the last two grades being partly in recognition of his missions in America between 1787 and 1792. In 1779 he served as aide to General Wilhelm von Knyphausen, perhaps because as a youth he had acquired a knowledge of the German language during his father's service in Prussia.[9] At the end of the Revolution he was appointed aide to Sir Guy Carleton. When the latter returned to Canada in 1786 as Lord Dorchester, young Beckwith—he was about two years older than the Secretary of the Treasury—went with him. In 1787 Dorchester sent him on the first of his missions to the United States.

The nature of Beckwith's role cannot be properly understood unless a distinction is made between the two periods into which his activities fall. The first period covered the four missions that he undertook between the spring of 1787 and the spring of 1790. The second covered his residence of nineteen months in New York and Philadelphia that began with the interview of the morning of the 8th of July with the Secretary of the Treasury.

In the three years from 1787 to 1790 Beckwith's role in the United States was that of secret agent serving under Lord Dorchester as Governor General of Canada. Like John Connolly whom Dorchester sent into the Northwest Territory early in 1788, Beckwith was part of an extended system of intelligence activity in America that was supplied with funds by the British government and received orders from it or from Dorchester. The object of that activity, of course, was the acquisition of information, the establishment of connections with influential Americans, and the cultivation of sentiments favorable to the interests of Great Britain. Its presence was manifested in such sensitive areas as Vermont, Kentucky, the borders of Florida and Louisiana, and the principal cities of the Atlantic seaboard. Those engaged in it operated covertly and often effectively, being aided by Tory refugees in

9 Beckwith achieved rank as a major-general in 1798 and as lieutenant-general in 1805. He served as governor of Bermuda (1797), St. Vincent (1804), and Barbadoes (1808), commanding the British forces in the West Indies and South America. For his conquest of Martinique in 1809 he was voted the thanks of both houses of Parliament and the same year he was created a knight of the Bath; DNB; MAH, X (1883), 330; Van Doren, *Secret History*, p. 260-3, 278-9, 321-2, 410-3; Bemis, *Jay's Treaty*, p. 58-9. Beckwith's father, after serving in the Prussian army, visited Paris in 1779 and offered his services to Franklin in the Continental army. Franklin declined on the ground that he had no authority to make such appointments (Beckwith to Franklin, undated, Franklin Papers, PPAP; Franklin to John Beckwith, 17 May 1779; Franklin, *Writings*, VII, 315). Franklin had known General John Beckwith in London (PMHB, LX [1936], 470-1).

London, by the United Empire Loyalists of Canada, and by their adherents in the United States who, in varying degrees of loyalty or disloyalty to the young republic, were friendly to or identified with "the British interest." The unifying bonds of friendship, family, and commerce, strengthened by preferences for monarchical over republican government, naturally did not terminate at the borders of the United States or cease with the Treaty of Peace. Their existence indeed provided the sinews of party division on the great issues that the nation faced in its formative years. As one of Beckwith's informants told him, there were at the beginning of the Revolution many Americans "who opposed Great Britain in certain points, who had no views of a separation and who were drawn on step by step into the measure of Independence; and many others much against their inclination, and without the power of looking back." There was not a gentleman from New Hampshire to Georgia, he added, "who does not view the present government [under the Articles of Confederation] with contempt, who is not convinced of its inefficiency, and who is not desirous of changing it for a Monarchy."[10]

Intelligence agents such as Beckwith found that these natural and powerful bonds of interest, consanguinity, and political principle opened up sources of information that in Europe would have required the outlay of vast sums of money. From 1790 to 1801 Lord Grenville in the Home and Foreign Offices disbursed the very considerable sum of £841,902 sterling for secret service operations in the diplomatic field alone, including £100,597 for the same period expended by George Hammond, who served as minister to the United States from 1791 to 1794.[11] No evidence is available to indicate what portion of this sum was devoted to intelligence activity in America, but it is very unlikely that more than a minute fraction, if any, could have been so employed. There was little need to purchase influence or information when friends, connections, and sympathizers, often in high place, made their services freely available as a quite natural consequence of the bitter divisions of civil war. Those who remained skeptical of the equalitarian principles of republicanism and who had not the power of looking back possessed nevertheless the means and the will to support those principles still claiming a residual allegiance. There were also the motives of ambition for position and power that prompted some not merely to serve Dorchester's emissary but also to make use of him.

Though the circumstances were as different as those of war and peace, Beckwith's role in this first period was in reality a resumption of the secret service operations he had carried on in the closing years

10 Beckwith's report, enclosed in Dorchester to Sydney, 10 Apr. 1787, PRO: CO 42/50, f. 92, 94-9. William Samuel Johnson was almost certainly the person who made this statement.

11 Declaration of Account, 20 Feb. 1790 to 20 Feb. 1801, PRO: AO 1/ Bundle 2121; another account for the same period gives the total as £837,342, as stated "on protestation of honor" 31 Mch. 1801, PRO: AO 3/949. Neither of these accounts provides a detailed analysis of times, places, or purposes of disbursement; many letters between Hammond and Grenville in 1801 discuss secret service accounts, but none in America; Grenville Papers, Boconnoc, bundle marked "Hammond."

of the war. As aide to Knyphausen while Sir Henry Clinton was absent on expeditions against Charleston and Newport in the spring and summer of 1780, Beckwith had handled the correspondence with Benedict Arnold as the treason plot unfolded, being addressed on one occasion as "G[eorge] B[eckwith] Ring [two rings were employed, one kept by Beckwith and one sent to Arnold to prove authenticity of messages] Executor to the late John Anderson, Esq. [Major John André] in care of James Osborne [the Rev. Jonathan Odell]." He was almost certainly the "officer in the department of the adjutant general" of the British commander-in-chief who made it possible for William Heron, the American double spy, "frequently to obtain important and very interesting intelligence" for General Samuel Holden Parsons, thus keeping this channel open for Clinton's intelligence service.[12] When Major Oliver DeLancey of the prominent Loyalist family of New York succeeded Major André in the office of adjutant general, Beckwith was his assistant along with Major Thomas MacKenzie.[13] These officers, aided also by Col. Beverley Robinson, a Loyalist, drew up in 1781 "Proposals for a Plan of Gaining Intelligence" that had for its object the opening of correspondence "with persons of consequence in different parts of the country." As one of the most experienced of these officers in intelligence work, Beckwith was probably the principal author of this scheme, as he was certainly the one most actively engaged in putting it into operation. All intelligence received was systematically recorded in a manuscript volume entitled "Private Intelligence . . . For Sir Henry Clinton," accompanied by another volume labelled "Information of Deserters and others not included in Private Intelligence," being almost entirely in Beckwith's hand.[14] These records of letters, conversations, and reports from deserters, Loyalists, and spies were continued until 19 July 1782 when the volume called "Private Intelligence" was closed. The next day Beckwith alone assumed responsibility for secret service duties as aide to Sir Guy Carleton, who had succeeded Clinton as commander of the British forces. He continued to direct this intelligence activity up until the moment of Carleton's evacuation of New York late in 1783. If anything, his espionage work in this period of relative peace at the close of the war was heavier than during the period when the issue of the contest was still in doubt. For in the sixteen months between 20 July 1782 and 18 Nov. 1783 Beckwith's expenditures for secret service operations amounted almost to a fifth of the total spent by Sir Henry Clinton for such purposes during the critical years from 1778 to 1782, Beckwith's being £4,495 sterling and Clinton's £24,878 sterling.[15]

Thus for at least three years before the end of the war Beckwith had been stationed in New York with important responsibilities at the

[12] Parsons to Washington, 6 Apr. 1782, DLC: Washington Papers.
[13] MAH, X (1883), 330.
[14] Originals of both are in Emmett Collection, NN, and some extensive selections from the first are printed in MAH, X (1883)-XII (1884); Van Doren, *Secret History*, p. 406; texts of the André-Arnold correspondence in which Beckwith figures are conveniently accessible in same, p. 439-81.
[15] Beckwith's Declaration of Account, 4 July 1785, PRO: AO 1/Bundle 2121; Account of Paymaster John Smith, 20 Dec. 1782, PRO: AO 3/118.

[41]

center of intelligence activities. He had become familiar with the leading Loyalist families of the city and with refugees of similar leanings from Pennsylvania, New Jersey, and New England. When he returned to Canada with Dorchester in 1786, therefore, he was the logical choice as a confidential agent to re-establish connections in the city where he had gained such an intimate knowledge of the attitudes of leading personages. Dorchester later made it clear that this, in fact, was the reason for his being chosen for the role—thus providing also the tribute of Beckwith's commanding officer to the competence with which he had discharged his secret service duties in wartime.[16] When he arrived in New York early in 1787, Beckwith was once again among friends, having ready access to homes and positions of influence.

This very fact has helped to obscure the true nature of his role as a secret agent. Such consular and commercial agents as Sir John Temple, Phineas Bond, George Miller, and John Hamilton regularly dispatched reports to Whitehall that duplicated some of the information sent by Beckwith. Indeed, in respect to commerce and economic conditions their reports, especially those of Bond, possessed much greater value than his. Dorchester was well aware of the fact that the ministry received intelligence from such sources and his initial purpose in sending his aide to New York was to satisfy himself about American affairs as these affected his own situation in Canada. But Beckwith opened up sources of information on matters of policy of such great importance as to give his reports a value in this respect greater than that of all intelligence gathered by others. Beckwith, Dorchester, and Grenville must have been astonished to find their recent enemies so fully and freely communicating their views and aims—even their cabinet secrets—to the confidential agent of a foreign power. The very success of the mission produced a natural and obvious change in the character of Beckwith's role, a change reflected even in the sums of money spent by him.

As a military intelligence officer in wartime, as noted above, Beckwith had spent £4,495 sterling. In the three years from 1787 to 1790 his four missions cost a total of £224 5s. 11d. In the year and a half from 1790 to early 1792 his disbursements totalled £1,156 3s 4d.[17] The conclusion suggested by these figures is clear. During the war, Beckwith was obliged to employ informers, reward deserters, and pay for intelligence; in the first period of his peacetime services in New York he operated covertly and his expenses were such as a British army officer on his travels might have had; in the second period his activities were more open though still largely hidden from the government, his costs being amplified by the need to maintain a residence and to offer hospitality to friends and persons of influence; and in neither of these periods were the sums large enough to indicate that information or influence was procured by rewards in the classic European sense. Success

[16] Dorchester to Grenville, 7 July 1790, referring to his private letter to Sydney of 24 Oct. 1788 in which a similar view was expressed, PRO: CO 42/68, f. 252-3.
[17] "Extraordinaries abroad from 1784 to 1791," Quebec, PRO: PMG 14/73, f. 170, 217, 274, 332, 338, 341; PMG 14/74, f. 1,2.

of remarkable proportions transformed the secret agent into a means of communication, not between two powers in any diplomatic sense but between Great Britain and those friendly to her policy. Nor did the change wholly remove the element of secrecy.

Beckwith's changing role is further shown in the changing nature of his reports. The first report of March 1787 revealed how strong a monarchical sentiment prevailed in New York and showed what little expectations some Federalists had for the forthcoming Federal Convention except as a means of advancing further toward the English form of government. Dorchester was so impressed by this report that he at once sent it to the Secretary for Home Affairs, thinking it contained matters of importance that might "not all readily find their way into a more direct channel"—that is, by the reports of Bond, Temple, Miller, and others.[18] There were no further reports until Beckwith returned to New York in the autumn of 1788. He found the same monarchical attitudes prevalent there, though subdued. The adoption of the Constitution had forced some who held such views to conclude that "the re-union of the empire" was not then practicable.[19] He was also told that there was "a growing British interest in the United States" and that it would be "good policy to hold a friendly language to that Country, and to show a disposition to form a treaty of commerce with them." This report revealed such a range of important sources and contained such highly significant matter that it may have prompted Dorchester to suggest that Beckwith report his findings in person to the British cabinet. In any event, Beckwith did return to England and in the spring and summer of 1789 held various conversations with Lord Hawkesbury, Lord Sydney, and Lord Grenville. He was in London when reports of debates in the House of Representatives on the tariff and tonnage bills arrived from consular and secret agents. Grenville, who had succeeded Sydney as Secretary for Home Affairs, authorized Beckwith on his return to New York to sound warnings of commercial retaliation should Madison's "discriminating clauses" be adopted.[20]

The report of October 1789, which Beckwith delivered in person to Dorchester after having transmitted Grenville's message to those in New York for whom it was intended, was by far the most important intelligence gathered by the agent up to that point, for it was the first to be made after the successful launching of the new government. This fact gave new significance to Beckwith's role and, above all, to the

[18] Dorchester to Sydney, 10 Apr. 1787, PRO: CO 42/50, f. 92; Beckwith's report, same, f. 94-9. Reports of Bond, Temple, and Miller are in the FO 4 series in PRO; most of those of Bond, with important omissions of enclosures, are in Am. Hist. Assn., *Ann. Rept.*, 1896, I, 513-659; same, 1897, p. 454-568.

[19] Dorchester to Sydney, 14 Oct. 1788, PRO: CO 42/61, f. 104; Beckwith's report, same, f. 106-17. In this period of Beckwith's absence in England, Peter Allaire, who went to Quebec in the summer of 1788 to arrange a means of communication, kept Dorchester informed of events in New York. On Allaire, see below, note 121.

[20] Bemis, *Jay's Treaty*, p. 56, 59. There is no other authority for the responsibility given Beckwith by Grenville than Beckwith's own statement (see note 6), but since this was an assertion easily verifiable by Henry Dundas to whom it was made, it must for this and other reasons be given full credit.

meaning of the part played by those upon whom he relied. Some of the latter were now no longer private individuals free to voice their political preferences at will. They were clothed with public responsibility as members of the executive, legislative, and judicial branches of government, a fact that should have limited the freedom with which they could discuss the policy of government with the secret agent of a foreign power. It was also in the autumn of 1789 that the Secretary of the Treasury entered into these discussions, becoming thenceforth the most important public character upon whom Dorchester's agent depended. In this opening interview Hamilton manifested his aim to influence foreign policy, thereby initiating the long divisive struggle in the cabinet—a struggle culminating five years later in the settlement that, in the words of the leading authority, more "aptly . . . might be called Hamilton's Treaty."[21]

In brief, while the significance of Beckwith's role had been greatly augmented by the newly assumed public character of his sources of information and less so by the British ministry's use of him as a direct channel of influence with friends in positions of influence, its clandestine character had not been altered in any degree. He was still the covert agent of an alien power, a fact given fresh emphasis at this time by his beginning the use of a cipher to protect the names and rank of his informants while disclosing their identity to the ministry.[22] His presence in New York was known to Washington, of course, and doubtless to many others in government who were not aware of the nature of his mission. Washington had known Beckwith in 1783 as the officer who brought Carleton's dispatches when preparations were being made for the evacuation of New York.[23] When he saw Dorchester's aide there

21 Bemis, *Jay's Treaty*, p. 373.

22 The cipher key for the discussions in the autumn of 1789 was transmitted in Dorchester to Grenville, 28 Oct. 1789, marked "*Private*," PRO: CO 42/66, f. 245, 247. The most important individuals in this list, excepting Washington with whom Beckwith exchanged two unimportant remarks, were William Samuel Johnson (No. 1), Philip Schuyler (No. 2), "A Gentleman in Office of the United States," who can only have been Henry Knox (No. 4), and Alexander Hamilton (No. 7). The cipher key for seven additional names of persons consulted in the spring of 1790 was enclosed in Dorchester to Grenville, 7 June 1790, marked "*Private*," PRO: CO 42/68, f. 229, 231. The principal persons in this group were William Paterson, Senator from New Jersey (No. 10), John Jay (No. 12), and Thomas Scott, "Member of House of Representatives from Counties West of Allegheny Mountains" (No. 14). The cipher key for six further names was transmitted in Dorchester to Grenville, 25 Sep. 1790, marked "*Private*," PRO: CO 42/46, f. 384, 385. The principal informants of Beckwith in this group were Fisher Ames (No. 17), Richard Henry Lee (No. 18), and Isaac Sherman (No. 21). The entire list is printed in Brymner, *Report*, 1890, p. xli, xlii, consisting of twenty-three names. Of these David Humphreys (No. 20) and Gouverneur Morris (No. 23) were alluded to in the reports but were not among Beckwith's informants.

23 Washington to Carleton, 14 Nov. 1783, *Writings*, ed. Fitzpatrick, xxvii, 240. John Hamilton, British consul at Norfolk, saw Beckwith at Philadelphia early in 1791 and reported to Leeds: "He assumes no official Character, but attends all Levées, which occasions some uneasiness and suspicions, but he is generally very much respected" (Hamilton to Leeds, 10 Apr. 1791, PRO, FO 4/9, f. 225). Sir John Temple also reported to Leeds about the same time: "Lord Dorchester has had one of his aids de Camp here and at Philadelphia, for the year past! The

again in 1789 he may have considered him merely as an officer on his travels—such, for example, as Lieutenant John Enys, who had come down from Montreal in 1784, had met leading figures in New York and Philadelphia, and had been entertained by Washington at Mount Vernon.[24] More likely the President, wise in the ways of intelligence work, guessed that Beckwith had returned from England by way of New York in order to gather what information he could about American affairs.

But Washington certainly could not have known that his Secretary of the Treasury had requested an interview with the secret agent and had advanced the "certain overtures" that were to be transmitted to Dorchester and to the ministry. For the fact is that, while Hamilton was willing to give Dorchester blanket authority to use his communication "in whatever Manner" he should judge proper, he did not "chuse to have this go any further in America."[25] Hamilton and Beckwith might reassure themselves time and again, as each did, that theirs was only "a private conversation," and each might flatter the other's sense of delicacy in respecting divergent loyalties, but this was in truth nothing less than a penetration of the highest councils of the nation by the confidential agent of another power. Beckwith's astonishing success had indeed justified Dorchester's confidence that "the advantages which this gentleman derived from his employments [in secret service activities in New York] during the war . . . rendered his being employed on those occasions the more eligible."[26] This greatly understated the case, yet, able and experienced though he was, Beckwith could scarcely have accomplished this remarkable result had he not been so warmly embraced by men in office eager to share in the covert shaping of foreign policy. His timely appearance in the autumn of 1789 bearing Grenville's warning provided a convenient instrument that was immediately and boldly grasped by the Secretary of the Treasury. As the events of the summer of 1790 proved, this was a two-edged tool, for it involved the brilliant but unpredictable Gouverneur Morris and his appointment

---

status of this Person about Congress hath indeed disgusted not a few who heretofore leaned towards Great Britain. An Envoy, say they, from a Colony Governor, to a Sovereign power is a business heretofore unheard of! He can be considered in no other light than as a petty Spy! What the purposes of Major Beckwith's being sent here, or By What Authority he is here,—or, of what his Powers may be (if he has any in the Diplomatic line,) I am totally ignorant! I have however shown him all the Countenance and respect, due from me, to any Officers of His Majestys army, and heartily wish that his Mission, if any he has from Authority, may not turn out fruitless, or detrimental to His Majesty's General Service in the States" (Temple to Leeds, 23 May 1791, PRO, FO 4/10, f. 62). That Temple—vain, garrulous, indiscreet, and lavish with exclamation points—should have known so little of Beckwith's purpose or mission is itself an eloquent tribute to the prudence and trustworthiness of Dorchester's agent.

[24] MS journals of John Enys, 1783-1787, originals in possession of Miss E. D. Enys, The Cottage, Enys, Penryn, Cornwall; microfilm in NjP.

[25] Beckwith's report, enclosed in Dorchester to Grenville, 25 Oct. 1789, PRO: CO 42/66, f. 278, 280-310; that part of the report quoting the conversation with Hamilton is conveniently accessible in Syrett, *Hamilton*, v, 482-90.

[26] Dorchester to Sydney, 7 July 1790, reiterating an opinion stated in his private letter to Sydney of 24 Oct. 1788 (not found); PRO: CO 42/68, f. 252-3.

as Washington's informal but official agent in London. The fact that such an appointment was made at that precise moment is no less surprising than that the influences prompting it have never been examined.

The decision to appoint Morris as agent came just after Washington had signed Jefferson's commission as Secretary of State. Hamilton learned of the intention to name Jefferson only the day before the nomination was sent to the Senate, though Madison had known for some weeks that this would be done.[27] At this juncture in 1789 Congress was on the point of adjourning, Washington was preparing to set off on a tour of New England, the French minister and the Spanish *encargado de negocios* were about to depart for home, the debate over Madison's "discriminating clauses" and the residence question—the two most serious threats to legislative harmony—had been stilled for the time being, and relations with Canada were so tranquil that Dorchester had just asked leave to return to England on private affairs.[28] One ardent Federalist assured Beckwith after Congress adjourned that the session on the whole had been a smooth one and that a foundation had been laid "for much future good."[29] It was at this quiet moment, in fact, that Dorchester received the first official communication from the United States since his appointment as Governor General in 1786— a request that Andrew Ellicott be permitted to make astronomical observations at Niagara to define the limit of the New York cession of 1781. Dorchester was so impressed by American "assurances of a friendly disposition towards Great Britain" that he promptly sent the letter to Grenville so that the ministry might read these sentiments of the President as transmitted by John Jay, then acting as Secretary for Foreign Affairs: "It gives me Pleasure, my Lord, to be instructed, to assure you of the President's Disposition to promote an Interchange of friendly Offices between the two Nations, and particularly to protect and maintain between their bordering Territories, the Right of Hospitality and good Neighbourhood."[30] Dorchester, always remembering the "surprize . . . done at Tyconderoga" in 1775, keenly aware of the weakness of his own far-flung defenses, and disturbed by the steady march of the American line of frontier settlements, was by no means disposed to welcome visitors from the United States. But in this instance the friendly attitude of the American government won his consent, though the civility was accompanied by orders to the military escort for Ellicott's party to be on guard "to prevent the King's interest being injured . . . by any surveys or reconnoitering of the country foreign to the ostensible object."[31]

[27] Brant, *Madison*, III, 285; Syrett, *Hamilton*, V, 409.

[28] Freeman, *Washington*, VI, 234-9; Dorchester to Sydney, 22 Aug. 1789, and to Grenville, 8 Feb. 1790, PRO: CO 42/65, f. 77; CO 42/67, f. 25.

[29] Beckwith's report, enclosed in Dorchester to Grenville, 25 Oct. 1789, PRO: CO 42/66, f. 278, 281.

[30] Dorchester to Grenville, 30 Sep. 1789, enclosing copies of Jay to Dorchester, 4 Sep. 1789, Henry Motz to Jay, 24 Sep. 1789, and related documents, PRO: CO 42/65, f. 199-207; Washington to Knox, 5 Sep. 1789, *Writings*, ed. Fitzpatrick, XXX, 394-5.

[31] The orders are among the related documents indicated in the preceding note; the weak condition of Canadian defenses is a constant theme in Dorchester's dis-

In brief, in the autumn of 1789 no domestic or foreign urgency existed that required the immediate appointment of an agent in London to manifest friendly dispositions or to ascertain the attitude of the British ministry on such questions as treaty obligations and commerce. Not only was the general situation of affairs tranquil—there were also powerful arguments that counseled delay in the making of such an appointment. The ablest and best informed American diplomat abroad, whose advice could presumably have been useful both as to the decision to make the appointment and as to the person to be chosen, was known to be on his way home and was expected to arrive in the United States at any moment. Indeed, under the circumstances Jefferson could have expected to be consulted on such an important move—his commission as Secretary of State had just been signed. Washington himself conceded as much both by his scrupulous regard for proper procedure on other occasions and by the instructions given to Morris. "This Communication," he wrote, "ought regularly to be made to you by the Secretary of State, but that Office not being at present filled, my Desire of avoiding Delays induces me to make it under my own Hand."[32] A few months earlier the President had expressed his general policy to De Moustier. "I have . . . been taught to believe, that there is, in most polished nations, a system established, with regard to the foreign as well as the other great Departments, which, from the utility, the necessity, and the reason of the thing, provides that business should be digested and prepared by the Heads of those departments."[33] On the matter of subsequent diplomatic and consular appointments the President usually consulted Jefferson and depended largely upon his recommendations—with the significant and notable exception of the appointment of Gouverneur Morris in 1791 as minister to France.

There were even more cogent reasons for delay, as Washington was soon reminded by the one who up to this point had been his principal adviser, James Madison. It was not Madison, however, but John Jay with whom Washington first discussed the propriety of taking "informal means of ascertaining the views of the British Court with respect to our Western Posts . . . and to a Commercial treaty." This was on the 7th of October and Jay had just given Washington the substance of the British ministry's inquiries about American trade, productions, tonnage duties, manufactures, population, debts to British merchants, and other matters—information that he had obtained from Sir John Temple. Jay thought the move advisable and recommended as agent Dr. Edward Bancroft, "a man in whom entire confidence might be placed."[34] That same day Washington consulted Hamilton, who

patches during this period; the allusion to Ticonderoga is in Dorchester to Gordon, 9 May 1791, PRO: CO 42/72, f. 155.

[32] Washington to Morris, 13 Oct. 1789, *Writings*, ed. Fitzpatrick, XXX, 440.

[33] Washington to De Moustier, 25 May 1789, same, XXX, 333-5.

[34] Washington, *Diaries*, ed. Fitzpatrick, IV, 16. Jay's recommendation is plausible and understandable. Bancroft was a native American, he was in London, he was respected in scientific circles as a member of the Royal Society, he was friendly with Lord Sydney and others in the ministry, and he enjoyed the esteem of Franklin, Jefferson, and other Americans. It was not until a century later that

"highly approved of the measure, but thought Gouv'r Morris well qualified."[35] The fact that Temple had seen fit to reveal to Jay, and the latter
to the President, the important and comprehensive inquiries reflecting
the ministry's interest in matters about which the informal agent in
London would concern himself suggests that this may have been the
means by which the question of an appointment was raised in Washington's mind. This may have occurred to Washington himself on reading the ministry's inquiries about comparative duties on imports, tonnage fees, and port charges as between English vessels and those of
other countries—inquiries that were given added significance in light
of the debate over Madison's "discriminating clauses."[36] Since Jay was
acting as Secretary for Foreign Affairs, it would have been quite proper
for him to have opened the subject in this manner and to have suggested the important step of appointing an informal agent in London.
Washington on this day noted in his diary that he had consulted Jay
on the propriety of taking the New England trip, but on the topic of
the appointment of an agent stated only that he had "had conversation"
with him. The difference in phraseology may or may not have significance, but the former suggests that Washington himself initiated the
subject while the latter leaves the question open.

The next day Washington sought the opinion of Madison, who was
just setting out for Virginia. The response was immediate, emphatic,
and negative. The President carefully recorded in his diary the three
cogent reasons advanced against making the appointment at that time—
"if the necessity did not press." In the first place, Madison pointed out,
it "would be better to wait the arrival of Mr. Jefferson, who might be
able to give the information wanted on this head." Second, if Morris
were appointed agent—a supposition indicating that Washington had
already accepted Hamilton's recommendation as to the person to be
named—it "would be a commitment for his appointment as Minister,
if one should be sent to that Court, or wanted at Versailles in place of
Mr. Jefferson." Finally, if Morris wished either of these diplomatic appointments, his reports on the views of the British ministry "might . . .
be made with an eye to it."[37] Washington was undoubtedly given
pause by these arguments. He passed over the first in silence, so far
as the diary reveals, but conceded the force of the last two by agreeing with them. To the weight of all of these opposing factors he paid
the tribute of delaying his decision almost a week.

A significant omission occurring in this interval must be noted. On
important matters Washington was accustomed to ask the opinions

his remarkable role as a double-spy came to light. Arthur Lee and George III
were among the few of his contemporaries who distrusted him; see articles by the
Editor in WMQ, XVI (Apr., July, Oct. 1959), 166-87, 319-42, 515-50.

[35] Washington, *Diaries*, ed. Fitzpatrick, IV, 16.

[36] Washington made extensive notes of Jay's communication; same, IV, 15-16.
On the general scope of the inquiries from the ministry, see note to TJ to Harison
and others, 12 Aug. 1790.

[37] Madison had come to take leave of Washington when the subject of the
appointment was broached; Washington, *Diaries*, ed. Fitzpatrick, IV, 17, under
8 Oct. 1790.

of the Chief Justice and the Vice-President as well as the heads of departments. Under the circumstances it would seem that John Adams would have been the logical if not indeed the first person to be sought out for advice. He was the second officer in the administration, he had been American minister at London, he had proposed in 1785 an exchange of ministers as well as a commercial treaty, and the next year he and Jefferson had in fact submitted the projet of such a treaty to the British Secretary for Foreign Affairs. During this interval between the discussion with Madison and the appointment of Morris, Washington saw Adams at least twice. One of the occasions was at dinner and the other was on an all-day excursion by presidential barge to the gardens of William Prince at Flushing. On the return from that expedition the party stopped at the seat of Gouverneur Morris in order to see a barn of which Washington had often heard its owner speak. The question still unresolved surely could not have been far from the President's mind that October day in the barn at Morrisania. Yet it was not until the war crisis of the summer of 1790 that Washington placed in Adams' hands the correspondence between Morris and Leeds, informed him of the decision that had been taken months before, and asked for his opinion under the circumstances then existing. It is revealing that, though Adams naturally was not asked to approve the decision after the fact, Washington recorded in his diary that the Vice-President "expressed his approbation that this step had been taken."[38]

The conclusion suggested by this seems inescapable. Having already encountered Madison's forceful arguments, Washington must have intentionally avoided the risk of meeting with another negative vote—indeed less risk than certainty. Adams was not only firmly fixed in the opinion that Great Britain, having ignored American overtures, should make the first move toward an exchange of ministers. He also had no very high opinion of Gouverneur Morris, thinking him a man of wit who "made pretty verses—but of a Character trés legere."[39] The significant point is not that Adams in all probability would have agreed with Madison but that Washington seemed to avoid opposition to a decision toward which he was evidently inclined either for his own reasons or for others suggested to him.

There is no doubt that Washington felt strongly about the importance of executing the provisions of the Treaty of Peace and of removing the source of friction in the continued British occupation of the posts. Some Americans were already demanding removal by force rather than by diplomacy.[40] There is also no doubt that he was equally

38 Same, IV, 132, under 1 July 1790. It is worth noting, as possibly indicating the President's state of mind, that at Prince's famous gardens Washington found the "shrubs . . . trifling, and the flowers not numerous" and at Morrisania he thought the barn expensive and not of a construction to suit him. The Adamses were at dinner with the President on the day that the conversation with Madison took place; same, IV, 17, 18, 19.

39 Butterfield, *Adams Diary*, II, 390, under 22 June 1779.

40 For example, a Connecticut friend of Dr. Edward Bancroft wrote in 1786 reporting a conversation with one of the latter's former friends in New England: "You know his disposition, sanguine, turbulent, avaricious, and fond of troubled waters. He has however considerable influence in our councils. From what he said

troubled by the closing of the West Indies to American trade and by the long-standing threat of commercial retaliation most recently expressed in the form of Madison's resolutions. Both of these concerns were given emphasis in the instructions to Morris, which Washington evidently drafted himself. On the first problem the agent was directed to note that the establishment of the new government and a federal judiciary removed the objections theretofore made by the ministry for retaining the posts. Washington had no need to refer to the problem of debts or to explain the implications of this bare statement to one who had also sat in the Convention of 1787. He shared the general expectation that the federal courts would uphold the treaty provisions over any state laws tending to impede British merchants in the collection of debts owed them by Americans.[41] On the second source of danger, Washington pointed out that "a very respectable number of both houses were inclined to a discrimination of duties unfavorable to Britain, and that it would have taken place but for conciliatory considerations, and the probability that the late change in our government and circumstances would lead to more satisfactory arrangements." Morris was therefore to inquire whether the ministry contemplated a treaty of commerce with the United States and on what general principles. Then came the point of greatest emphasis: "In treating this subject, let it be strongly impressed on your mind, that the privilege of carrying our productions in our vessels to their Islands, and of bringing in return the productions of those Islands to our own ports and markets, is regarded here as of the highest importance; and you will be careful not to countenance any idea of our dispensing with it in a treaty."[42]

These were powerful motives but they provide no satisfactory answer to Madison's arguments. Both sources of friction had existed for some years and the need to remove them at this moment did not press with any urgency. Washington explained to Morris that he made the decision in order to avoid delay—and had delayed the making of it for some days because of divided councils. Yet he was unwilling to postpone it longer to await the arrival, momentarily expected, of the man he had just appointed Secretary of State. This, Washington's first significant act in foreign affairs, had ramifications and results that

---

ought to be done I confess I have my fears of what is *intended* to be done. He said that the Forts on the Frontiers held by G. Britain contrary to treaty should be demanded at the head of an Army, and if refused to be delivered up, taken by Force." The friend added: "It is not an acquisition of territory I want . . . it is their Floating riches"—that is, the opportunity for privateering ("Extract from Connecticut," 1 Apr. 1786, PRO: FO 4/4, f. 79-80). Bancroft at once sent the extract of this letter to the Foreign Office.

[41] See note, TJ to Temple, 11 Aug. 1790.

[42] Washington to Morris, 13 Oct. 1789 (letter of instructions), of which there is no retained file copy in the Washington Papers; Washington, *Writings*, ed. Fitzpatrick, xxx, 440-2. Fitzpatrick printed the text "from Ford, who took it from Sparks" (see Sparks, *Gouverneur Morris*, ii, 4-5). The text is also printed in Morris, *Diary*, ed. Davenport, i, 462-4. Washington wrote two other letters to Morris on the same date: (1) a private letter (text in *Writings*, ed. Fitzpatrick, xxx, 442-5); and (2) the letter of credence (same, xxx, 439-40; RC in Washington's hand in NNC: Gouverneur Morris Papers).

affected many things, among them the ultimate designation of Morris as minister to France, the resultant disappointment of William Short, the silence that Jefferson was forced to maintain towards his mortified friend on this subject, the inability of the Secretary of State to press Short's appointment or to oppose that of Morris, and, most significant of all, the declining influence of Madison and the rising power of Hamilton in the administration. Why, then, was the decision made?

Madison obviously guessed at once that some influences in the background were at work. On the day Washington asked his advice, he wrote a letter to await Jefferson's arrival that was expressed in such urgency its relevance to the consultation cannot be doubted. He was about to depart for Philadelphia and would welcome the opportunity to make the journey to Virginia with Jefferson. He then added: "I wish on a public account to see you as soon as possible after you become informed of the new destination provided for you. It is of infinite importance that you should not disappoint the public wish on this subject. Be persuaded of this truth, with proper opportunity it can be demonstrated to you."[43] When he wrote this, Madison did not know what the ultimate decision would be. But he knew, as Jefferson did, that to press a matter too far with the President was to undo its effect. He could thus guess at the strength of the demand for Morris' appointment from the power of the argument he had dared mobilize against it. Like Jefferson, Madison preferred amicable to adversary relations in commerce, yet both dared to act on the belief that, as Jefferson expressed it in his outline of policy in 1790, "the latter would be infallible, and in our own power." From this Washington shrank back, preferring to see whether conciliation could be brought about. But even at the moment the President was making his troubled decision, a Federalist Senator was saying to Dorchester's secret agent: "To suppose Great Britain should in any shape sollicit our Commercial Friendship is idle, and absurd; there are individuals who profess such opinions, but the more enlighten'd part of the Senate hold them to be ridiculous."[44] In the long fight that was just beginning, Washington in this troubled week chose not to align himself with the views on commercial policy that Madison and Jefferson had long supported. The mission of Gouverneur Morris ended in failure, but this was of less importance than the fact that Washington's underlying purpose was thwarted in the very act in which it was stated. "It is in my opinion very important," he wrote Morris, "that we avoid errors in our system of policy respecting Great Britain; and this can only be done by forming a right judgment of their disposition and views."[45]

In making the appointment Jay and Hamilton had recommended, Washington unwittingly committed his administration to a course in

43 Madison to TJ, 8 Oct. 1789.
44 William Samuel Johnson, as quoted in Beckwith's report of "Conversations with different persons," enclosed in Dorchester to Grenville, 25 Oct. 1789, PRO: CO 42/66, f. 278, 280-310; text in Brymner, *Report*, 1890, p. 121-9. Johnson added: "were this to be done I should be sorry for it."
45 Washington to Morris, 13 Oct. 1789 (see note 42 above).

which, despite the fidelity Morris gave to the charge placed in his hands, the disposition and views of the British government were obscured by the worst fate that could befall the Chief Executive in his conduct of public affairs—that of deliberate misrepresentation on the part of a trusted member of his cabinet.

II

It has been generally assumed that Major George Beckwith arrived in New York only in October of 1789 and that this was after the appointment of Gouverneur Morris had been made. This assumption is based upon Beckwith's statement three years later that "in the month of August . . . he was the bearer of a message from" Grenville which he delivered "in the October following."[46] It is very likely that Beckwith left for America in the August packet that arrived late in September. Whether he came by that vessel or not, he was definitely in New York and in consultation with those upon whom he depended at least as early as the 30th of September, the day after Congress adjourned.[47] For on the 30th Beckwith was closeted with Dr. William Samuel Johnson, president of Columbia College and Senator from Connecticut. This eminent lawyer, who made no attempt to hide his distaste for republican principles or his disapproval of Jefferson, was evidently the first person to whom Beckwith addressed himself on this third mission. In the cipher key that he began at this time Beckwith assigned to Johnson the symbol Number 1—a designation well deserved until Alexander Hamilton entered the discussions a few days later as Number 7.

Johnson had long been useful to Beckwith and to Sir John Temple. "I have since my Residence here found him undeviating in his attachment to the interests of our nation," the latter had written in 1788, "and I have had some usefull information from him. Though much courted and solicited by the people, he would have nothing to do with public affairs during the late contest, nor until his Majesty had granted independence to the states. After that he took a seat in Congress and had a great share in framing the new Constitution, and would now probably be sent Minister to London if the states were not fearful of his being too much attached to the interests and government of Great Britain."[48] Johnson was almost certainly the man whom Beckwith had consulted in the spring of 1787 and who informed him that even "the Presbyterian Clergy are become Advocates for Monarchy, the community in general finding from experience, that a Republican System however beautiful in theory, is not calculated for an extensive country."[49] He

---

[46] George Beckwith to Henry Dundas, 20 June 1792, PRO: FO 4/12. On the basis of this statement, Bemis and others have assumed that "Beckwith reached New York . . . in October, 1789" and that when he arrived the decision to send a person to the British court had already been made; Bemis, *Jay's Treaty*, 61, 65.

[47] This is proved by the assertion made to him by William Samuel Johnson that Congress had "adjourned yesterday"—that is, on 29 Sep. 1789 (see note 44).

[48] Temple to Sneyd, 2 Oct. 1788, PRO: FO 4/6.

[49] Dorchester to Sydney, 10 Apr. 1787, enclosing "Certain Communications of

was beyond question the Senator who told Beckwith the day after Congress adjourned in 1789: "I am naturally well disposed to the Country, in which I live, and however I may lament and condemn the dismemberment of a great Empire, to the government and principles of which I have ever been strongly attached, in the present posture of affairs I certainly cannot have any views or motives unconnected with the general good, but I do think that, in the hands of able and dispassionate men, a system might be formed to the advantage of both countries." Johnson was very clear as to where the general good lay.

It was absurd, he said, to suppose Great Britain would solicit commercial friendship with America in any form. Madison, "an eleve of Mr. Jefferson's," had with great warmth and spirit pressed his "discriminating clauses" in the late session. But when the measure came before the Senate, the majority were too enlightened and too moderate to approve measures "they viewed . . . as a declaration of commercial war, which it was neither wise nor just to commence against a powerful nation." Johnson coupled this with a warning that Beckwith underscored in his report. The advocates of discrimination had brought in a quick report which had in view "the *not permitting your shipping to clear out from our ports, either for your West India Islands, or for your Provinces upon this Continent, but the Senate thought it prudent to let the matter lay over until next session.*" With this hint at the means that Jefferson a year later thought "infallible, and in our own power," Johnson underscored the point that Washington had emphasized so strongly. He could not tell whether the President was "perfectly free from a French bias or not, but the moderate and thinking party" wished greatly for a commercial treaty and "nothing would facilitate this more than the admission of small vessels" into the British West Indies under certain regulations. He could assure Beckwith that a majority of the Senate were disposed to enter upon the consideration of such a subject dispassionately, but he was not certain about the attitude of the House of Representatives. Further, no minister would be sent to London. Indeed, if one had gone "he would not have been a person of a disposition to promote those views of harmony and friendship between the two countries" that Johnson had at heart: he "would have been a second edition of Mr. Adams." The Senate, therefore, had struck from the appropriation bill clauses enabling the President to send ministers abroad if he should "judge it necessary to send any to Europe, prior to [Congress'] next meeting in January."[50]

Such was the reply that Johnson gave to the secret agent after the latter had delivered Grenville's unveiled warning: "I am authorized to acquaint you, and the gentlemen in public office here, that had the Bill in question passed as sent up from your House of Representatives with those discriminating clauses, which appeared in your public papers, we were prepared to meet it; a discretionary power is by an annual Act of Parliament, vested in the King and Council for such purposes,

a very interesting nature" received from Beckwith, PRO: CO 42/50, f. 92-9; text in Brymner, *Report*, 1890, p. 97-9.

[50] Beckwith's report of "Conversations with different persons"; see note 44.

and the continuance of the indulgencies shewn to your shipping in our ports in Europe, depends upon your own Conduct."[51] This was blunt talk straight from Whitehall. Fisher Ames a few years later in denying the charge of British influence, defined such influence as "political power . . . exerted to modify or control, or prevent the public measures of the American nation."[52] Other powers pressed the young republic also by bringing similar influences to bear, but, by the definition of one of the highest of Federalists, the message brought by Beckwith was in fact an effort to prevent public measures. There can be no better proof than this of the secrecy of the interviews. Knowledge of foreign influence thus operating within the legislature would have given unity and strength to the system of commercial reciprocity of which Jefferson's "infallible means" was a last resort.

Beckwith next consulted Senator Philip Schuyler, father-in-law of Alexander Hamilton and one of those who, in the biting words of William Maclay, were "amazingly fond of the old leaven" of monarchism.[53] Again the agent sounded the warning to a Senator whose disposition of friendliness to Great Britain could not be doubted: "Whilst you were without an efficient Government, and some of the local Legislatures adopted such measures, we did not take any steps whatever, trusting that the formation of a strong government here would lead to their repeal, but if one of the first measures of the present government had such objects in view, the case was materially altered, and certainly, if the States chose to mark commercial hostility to us, we were to lose no time in changing our system."

Schuyler echoed in his reply the sentiments Johnson had expressed. He shared the general regret in the Senate that treaties with France did not permit the United States to give "a decided preference to Great Britain" in matters of trade, declared that he thought a firm connection with England "to be preferred to that of all the powers of Europe besides," and stated that "the President wishes well to this principle." He also said the funds for sending ministers abroad during the recess had been withheld because "the extent of those appointments ought to depend upon the character of the men employed, and the nature of the objects." Schuyler then asked Beckwith two blunt questions. Would England send a minister to the United States if one were sent there? Would Beckwith permit him to mention the conversation—that is, the warning from Grenville about commercial retaliation—to the Secretary of the Treasury? The agent could not answer the first, but to the second he gave an emphatic "by all means," indicating that Hamilton was the person whom he was most "pleased to communicate it to."

It was natural that he should have been pleased. Hamilton stood high in "The Executive Government of the United States" and this was as far as Beckwith dared go with the ministry's warning. The agent could report only an exchange of two sentences with the President.

[51] Same, text in Brymner, *Report*, 1890, p. 121.
[52] Essays of *Phocion* (Apr. 1801) in Fisher Ames, *Works*, ed. Seth Ames, II, 152.
[53] Maclay, *Journal*, ed. Maclay, p. 167.

Washington hoped the application for permission allowing Andrew Ellicott's surveying party to enter Canadian territory would be granted. "Sir," the agent replied, "I am persuaded of Lord Dorchester's general disposition to promote mutual harmony and the extension of science." That was all. The brief, formal, and polite exchange perhaps took place at a levée, certainly not in private. If any serious discussion of matters of public business had taken place, Beckwith would surely have reported it to his commanding officer. If conveyed at all, the message from the ministry had to reach the President by indirection.

Beckwith next gathered some gleanings of little consequence from a New York merchant and from John Trumbull. From "A Gentleman in Office of the United States" who can only have been the Secretary of War, Henry Knox, he learned something of Indian affairs and the situation of the army. He was also told that the "very favourite object" of obtaining the posts was obstructed solely by lack of resources in the hands of those "men in office in the States, who in their hearts aim at no less than the subversion of the British Power in North America." He was pointedly made aware of the fact that the activities of the secret agent John Connolly were well known to the government. "These things cause jealousy," Knox added.[54]

The seventh interview was with Hamilton. "I have requested to see you," the latter remarked at the opening of the talk, ". . . from a wish to explain certain points relative to our situation, and from a desire to suggest a measure, which I conceive to be both for the interest of Great Britain and of this Country to adopt. We have lately established a Government upon principles, that in my opinion render it safe for any nation to enter into Treaties with us, either Commercial or Political, which has not hitherto been the case; I have always preferred a connexion with you, to that of any other country, *we think in English*, and have a similarity of prejudices and of predilections. . . . We wish to form a commercial treaty with you to every extent, to which you may think it for your interest to go." The broad plan of this nature that Lansdowne had contemplated at the close of the war was not now attainable, *"considering the spirit of* [Great Britain's] *late navigation and regulating Acts, as well as from various publications by persons of considerable weight in England."* Yet a treaty might be formed *"upon terms advantageous to both countries."*

Specifically Hamilton suggested what William Samuel Johnson had urged: admission of small vessels into the British West Indies so as to enable Americans to carry their produce there "and to bring from thence the productions of those Islands to [American] ports" under such restrictions as to prevent the possibility of interference with the British carrying trade in Europe. This would be better, Hamilton told Beckwith, than "by *a rigid adherence to your present plan to produce a system of warfare in Commercial matters*" such as France had encouraged during the late session of Congress and such as he had always regretted "as being directly opposed to that system, which upon mature

[54] Beckwith's report of "Conversations with different persons"; see note 44.

[55]

reflexion, I have thought it most eligible for us to pursue."[55] This was very close to saying that the rigid mercantilist policy advocated by Sheffield and Hawkesbury had initiated the chain of events productive of commercial warfare, though such was far from the language used to defeat Madison's system of reciprocity, so closely allied to that of Shelburne in principle.[56]

Again Hamilton echoed what Johnson had said: "The present moment I view as particularly favorable for a plan of this nature. We are now so circumstanced as to be free to enter into a discussion of this sort, from our condition with regard to the other maritime powers: this may not be the case hereafter." The navigation of the Mississippi was "a matter of great importance to settle with Spain." The western territories, he added, "must have that outlet" or be lost to the union. The United States had no interest in extending her territories to the northward. If the United States were forced to rely on the House of Bourbon, such a connection might "become important to [British] West India possessions." But this, Hamilton implied, was a necessity to which the United States could only be driven: "connected with you, by strong ties of commercial, perhaps of political, friendships, our naval exertions, in future wars, may in your scale be greatly important, and decisive. These are my opinions, they are the sentiments, which I have long entertained, on which I have acted, and I think them suited to the welfare of both countries. I am not sufficiently authorized to say so, it is not in my department, but I am inclined to think a *person will soon be sent to England to sound the disposition of your court upon it.*" Beckwith said in response that he had told Schuyler what would have resulted if the "discriminating clauses" of the tariff bill had been adopted and asked if the conversation arose from Schuyler's request for permission to communicate this to Hamilton. Hamilton replied: "It does." He went on to say—as each assured the other this was "merely a private conversation" —that the "ideas . . . thrown out, may be depended upon as the sentiments of the most enlightened men in this country." More pointedly, he added: "they are those of General Washington, I can confidently assure you, as well as of a majority in the Senate."

Thus with a single voice the close-knit majority of the Senate and the Secretary of the Treasury tried to commit the government to a policy through covert consultations of which, so far as the records and the plausibilities indicate, the President was wholly unaware. Even Hamilton with all of his daring could scarcely have done this had he not been confident that the pledge would be met. Beckwith thought he clearly understood the scope of Hamilton's communication, but the implications must have shaken him, for he asked bluntly: "Pray what use do you intend me to make of it? Is it with a view to my mentioning it to Lord Dorchester?" Hamilton replied: "Yes, and by Lord Dorchester to your Ministry, in whatever manner His Lordship shall judge proper;

[55] Same; emphasis supplied in the last two of the italicized passages, the first being underscored in Beckwith's report.

[56] For a discussion of the liberal principles of Shelburne, see Gerald S. Graham, *British Policy and Canada 1774-1791* (London, 1930), p. 56-7.

but I should not chuse to have this go any further in America." There was much else in this extraordinary consultation, but Hamilton reinforced his insistent emphasis on the idea that that moment was particularly favorable for a commercial treaty by stating two points. The first, again echoing William Samuel Johnson, was that the "advocates for discrimination . . . had in view *a much stronger measure*." Beckwith correctly interpreted this to mean an embargo on British shipping in American ports for the Canadian provinces or the West Indies—a recourse to the harsh measures of 1770 and a precursor to those of 1807. The second point concerned Washington's emissary, who Beckwith had feared might frustrate the object if "his mind should have any bias towards any other foreign power." On this Hamilton reassured him by saying that "these nominations originate with General Washington, who is a good judge of men, and the gentleman, to be employed in this business, is perfectly master of the subject, and if he leans in his bias towards any foreign country, it is decidedly to you."

These discussions offer the most plausible explanation for the puzzling fact that Washington rejected Madison's plea for a brief delay in the appointment of an agent to London when no apparent urgency existed calling for haste. The threat of renewal of Madison's proposals in the next session, the danger even of resort to the drastic weapon of an embargo, the desire for a lowering of barriers to trade with the West Indies, Beckwith's timely arrival, his repetitive warnings of more rather than less restrictions on commerce with England and her possessions, the withholding of authority from the President to send ministers abroad, the wish of the Senate to have a voice in the choosing of such a person as would promote harmony between the two countries—all of these factors revealed in the conversations could have prompted those who thought of themselves as the governing majority to believe that this was an auspicious moment for a bold stroke. If so, and if a single factor towering above all others was needed as a catalyzing force, it was provided by the President about the time of Beckwith's arrival late in September.

On 25 Sep. 1789 Washington asked Hamilton to consult with John Jay about the names of thirty-five persons he had culled from the mass of applicants for office and to advise him if one could be found who was, "under all circumstances . . . more eligible for the Post Office than Col O[sgood]." He then added: "And, that you may have the matter *fully* before you, I shall add that, it is my *present* intention to nominate Mr. Jefferson for Secretary of State, and Mr. Edmd. Randolph as Attorney Genl; though their acceptance is problematical, especially the latter."[57] The next day the Senate confirmed the nomination of Jefferson and forty-seven others with so perfunctory a voice that Senator William Maclay did not even bother to note the proceedings in his diary.[58] But

[57] Washington to Hamilton, 25 Sep. 1789; Syrett, *Hamilton*, v, 409; Washington, *Writings*, ed. Fitzpatrick, xxx, 413, contains the full list of names.

[58] JEP, I, 29-33. Most of the nominees were those of the Chief Justice, the Justices of the Supreme Court, and the judges, attorneys, and marshals of the

there can scarcely be room for doubt as to the feelings of some as they cast their votes for the Secretary of State. William Samuel Johnson four days later told Beckwith plainly that he regretted Jay's removal from the Office of Foreign Affairs. And a few months later he said to him even more bluntly: "Mr. Jefferson . . . is greatly too democratic for us at present, *he left us in that way*, but we are infinitely changed, and he must alter his principles.—I think this Gentleman's ideas are not friendly to the formation of a commercial treaty with you. . . . Mr. Jefferson is a republican and a frenchman."[59] New Englanders in the Senate could be grateful for what Jefferson had done in France for the whale fishery and yet be far from sympathetic to Jefferson's use of it as a political institution to draw the United States closer to France by commercial ties that would aid "in maintaining the field against the common adversary." John Jay as Secretary for Foreign Affairs did not need to read between the lines of Jefferson's *Observations on the Whale-Fishery* to understand why he had been warned against letting such a document become public.[60] Neither Jay nor the Federalist majority in the Senate could be expected to look with enthusiasm upon a Secretary of State who, merely as a diplomat abroad, had devised such a retaliatory stroke of policy against the commercial and naval power of England. His advanced principles of commercial reciprocity were set forth in treaties of commerce that he had been sent abroad to negotiate with Adams and Franklin, and his disposition to use trade as an instrument of national policy was equally apparent, making it certain that during the ensuing session of Congress his sympathies would be on the side of Madison's hated proposals. A Secretary of State hostile to the idea of a commercial treaty with Great Britain—as one able and upright Senator genuinely believed Jefferson to be—could be expected to advise the President either that no minister be sent to London or that the one chosen should be only "a second edition of Mr. Adams." Those Federalists who could discern this possibility so clearly could also grasp the idea quite as readily as Washington and Madison did that a personal agent sent between sessions of Congress would involve something like a commitment to name him as minister should one be appointed. Viewing all the circumstances surrounding this surprising action taken by the President at so tranquil a moment, against Madison's strong argu-

---

Federal District Courts that had been submitted by Washington on 24 Sep. 1789. The President's letter transmitting the names of TJ, Randolph, Osgood, and others was dated on the same day as his letter to Hamilton, 25 Sep. 1789.

59 Beckwith's report of "Conversations with different persons" (italics supplied; see note 44). It is significant that Johnson was aware that TJ's principles were already formed and known before he departed for France in 1784. The two men could have had few opportunities to know each other before 1790, for Johnson had declined to serve in the Continental Congress before the Revolution and his service afterward began in 1785 when Jefferson was in Europe. But in the autumn of 1789 there were some among the Federalists in the Senate—Robert Morris, for example—who could have very easily acquainted Johnson with the general views of the new Secretary of State. Johnson's strong comments to Beckwith about a man he may not even have met up to that time must, therefore, reflect attitudes and comments prevalent among the governing majority of the Senate.

60 See Documents Concerning the Whale Fishery, Vol. 14: 217-69.

ment, and at a time Jefferson was momentarily expected, it is difficult to avoid the conclusion that the designation of a Secretary of State so unsympathetic to the views of the governing majority of the Senate produced in this situation a sense of urgency that was otherwise wholly lacking. Did the impetus for the appointment of an agent come out of such fears or originate with Washington? The answer must remain conjectural.

But Washington could not have shared the apprehensions about Jefferson that Johnson and others had. To suppose that he would have initiated Morris' appointment out of the same sort of distrust felt by the Federalists for the man he had just named Secretary of State is to suppose an act on his part that would have been not merely uncharacteristic but incredible. Nor could Washington have done this because of Beckwith's warnings of commercial retaliation, about which he had no knowledge. Had he known of these warnings there would undoubtedly have been aroused in him precisely those feelings of national honor and dignity that Beckwith had said Pitt and the ministry would feel should Madison's proposals be adopted. "Upon such minds," Beckwith said, "[the tendency of compulsory measures] must be diametrically opposite. The purposes of national glory are best attained by a close adherence to national honour, alike prepared to meet foreign friendships, and to repel foreign hostility."[61] Hamilton, engaged in a course that belied his words, told Beckwith that these sentiments did honor to any nation. Few could have known better than he that, however little the President might employ such declamatory expressions, Washington was the very embodiment of such concepts of national dignity.

Further, if direct disclosure of the hint of stern measures by the ministry was imprudent, means were readily available for the use of indirection. Sir John Temple had just received the ministry's extensive inquiries, reflecting among many interests a concern over possible discrimination in tariff and tonnage duties. If Temple required data and thus disclosed his circular for that purpose, presumably he would have turned first to the Treasury, where some of the information, if available, might be found. But why should he have made the inquiries known to Jay or Jay have given the substance of them to the President? The fact that Washington took pains to record the headings of the document suggests that the purpose for which these were disclosed to him was that of providing a hint of the attitudes of the ministry— a hint in which the connection with Madison's "discriminating clauses" was immediately apparent.[62] Jay and Hamilton a few days earlier had been consulted by the President on appointments to office. Then fol-

[61] Beckwith's report of "Conversations with different persons" (see note 44 above); text in Brymner, *Report*, 1890, p. 127-8.

[62] Under 7 Oct. 1789 Washington noted that "Mr. Jay communicated the purport of the Instructions received by Sir John Temple, British Consul, from the Duke of Leeds, Secretary for Foreign Affairs, viz. . . . What tonnage—whether any and what difference between *British* and others—what on *American*. What *Port charges* on foreign vessels—whether any and what difference etca. . . ."; Washington, *Diaries*, ed. Fitzpatrick, IV, 15-16.

lowed Jefferson's appointment and Beckwith's arrival. As acting Secretary for Foreign Affairs it was both proper and appropriate for Jay to have suggested—on the basis of the hint in Temple's circular of the ministry's disposition toward the United States—that an informal agent be appointed to ascertain this more precisely. The mere hint of a hardening attitude on the part of the ministry, coupled with the threatened revival of harsher measures of discrimination in the next session of Congress, would have been sufficient to indicate the need of prompt action. Hamilton's recommendation of Gouverneur Morris was as obvious and as natural a choice as that suggested by Jay on the same day. The supposition that the appointment was thus brought about by indirection and by the agency of such prompting influences must perhaps remain without the support of direct evidence. There is abundant proof, however, that such members of the Senate as Johnson, Schuyler, and Morris shared with the Secretary of the Treasury a confidence in Gouverneur Morris that they could not extend to the incoming Secretary of State. Hamilton had good reason to tell Washington that he "highly approved of the measure" and perhaps better reason to feel gratified that the person he thought leaning in his bias toward England had been chosen.

The question naturally arises whether Hamilton made his proposal to Beckwith before or after he recommended the appointment of Morris. It has been assumed that he did so afterwards, but the possibility that this assumption is unwarranted cannot be dismissed. Fully eight days intervened between Beckwith's opening interview with Johnson and Hamilton's recommendation of Morris. In view of Schuyler's intermediation and Hamilton's request—in neither of which can the note of urgency fail to be observed—it does not seem likely that Hamilton would have long delayed his solicitation of the interview. Hamilton's words to Beckwith—"I am not sufficiently authorized to say so, it is not in my department, but I am inclined to think *a person will soon be sent to England to sound the disposition of your Court*"—have been interpreted as if spoken even after the decision to appoint Morris had been made. But this interpretation was grounded on the assumption, now known to be untenable, that Beckwith had not arrived in New York at the time that decision was arrived at.[63] This would have placed the interview a full two weeks after Beckwith talked with William Samuel Johnson, an interval scarcely compatible with the sense of urgency that all participants save Madison seemed to feel. The words are equally applicable to the situation existing prior to Hamilton's suggestion of the name of Morris to Washington on the 7th of October.[64] For Hamilton to have

[63] See note 46 above.

[64] Two further points should be noted: (1) Hamilton advanced substantially the same observation to Beckwith that Washington made to Morris in his letter of instructions—that the establishment of the new government and its judiciary removed the objections theretofore advanced by the ministry for putting the United States in possession of the frontier posts; and (2) Beckwith referred to Hamilton's disclosure as "*its being your intention* to send a person to learn our disposition" (emphasis supplied), as if perhaps the object at this stage were no more than an intent. Both of these points seemed to lend strength to the assumption made above.

disclosed the intent to Beckwith before that date would have represented an even less daring risk than the one he took the following spring in virtually identifying Washington with his own proposal of a closer connection with Great Britain, for on this occasion he spoke tentatively, on the other with assurance. Such an interpretation gains force in view of Hamilton's confident statement to Beckwith in the autumn of 1789 that the ideas he threw out about "strong ties of commercial, perhaps of political, friendships" were "those of General Washington . . . as well as of a great majority in the Senate." It was Hamilton's nature to speak and act boldly, as if in fact he spoke for the administration. The supposition that the plan originated with him seems more plausible than that assumption which preceded it and which can no longer be given the status it once enjoyed. Since Beckwith first revealed his warning on the 30th, it is scarcely plausible to suppose that so bold an administrator as Hamilton would allow eight days to elapse before seeking an interview with the agent who brought the warning. As devious as he was bold, Hamilton could have seen at once the advantage of initiating such a move through John Jay as acting Secretary for Foreign Affairs, using as a reason for the manoeuver the circular that Sir John Temple had just received from the Secretary for Home Affairs. Such a move would have been far less disingenuous than that for which the Secretary of the Treasury was indubitably responsible during the war crisis of 1790. Both actions were characteristic of the man.

Beckwith returned to Quebec by way of Vermont presumably about the time that Washington left New York on his New England tour. When the latter departed on the morning of the 15th, Hamilton, Jay, and Knox rode a little way out of the city with him. The weather was cheerless, but the two Secretaries and the Chief Justice had cause for satisfaction. The government had been safely launched, all departments had been created, no urgent problems pressed, they were clearly of the majority in both cabinet and Congress, and two separate lines of communication with the British ministry had been established. The President, having left with Jay the letters of credence and instructions for Morris, could share all of these satisfactions save one. He could not have known two channels of communication with the ministry had been set up and that the one officially authorized by him as head of state was the one of lesser importance. The other, arranged in secret and now guided by the Secretary of the Treasury, was undoubtedly intended to prepare the way for a cordial reception of the President's agent.

But the report carried back by Beckwith nullified this intent by its evidence of an almost unanimous acquiescence under the warning brought by him from London. Dorchester at once forwarded the astonishing communication about those aligned with or friendly to the British interest—indeed so promptly that the ministry knew its contents a full month before Morris received Washington's instructions. The next spring, as the war crisis was developing behind the scenes, the Secretary for Foreign Affairs found it "necessary in the first instance . . . to hold a language of firmness" with Morris and to "point out the non execution of the Treaty on the part of America, and the inadequate return made for the liberal manner in which they [had] been treated in point of commerce."[65] This was a natural and logical position for Leeds to take. Morris could reply that he knew of no liberality save that the United States could easily dispense with—the impressment of seamen—but the attempted pleasantry fell flat. His position had been weakened by those most anxious to make it secure. In their anxiety to shape foreign policy, Hamilton, Schuyler, and Johnson had damaged their cause by placing themselves and their nation not in the posture of negotiators but in that of petitioners, the exact opposite of those principles that Hamilton told Beckwith reflected honor on any nation. The language held out to Morris was indeed less harsh than the admonition conveyed by Beckwith in 1789. But the two lines of communication, aside from becoming thus entangled in England, produced another unanticipated result in America in the summer of 1790. This arose from their differing auspices: being a public agent, Morris was obliged to report his discussions to the President.

Before this came about, another British secret agent in February 1790 sent an express to Dorchester from New York with alarming news of impending military preparations. "The pretence to the public," Dorchester reported in a secret dispatch to Grenville, "is to repel the Indians, but those, who must know better, and see that an Indian warfare does not require so great a force, nor that very large proportion of artillery, are given to understand, that part of these forces are to take possession of the frontier as settled by treaty, to seize the posts, and secure the fur trade; a more secret motive perhaps is to reduce the State Governments, and crush all internal opposition. . . . The United States should bring forward a frontier treaty, settling all past infractions, together with a treaty of commerce. This, as mentioned in [Hamilton's communication by Beckwith] is their true interest; their present politics I apprehend will lead to something less solid, but more brilliant; to what may captivate the people, and prepare their submission to new authorities, to what will strengthen that connection, which I think has great influence at present *as it may better answer personal views.* I send Major Beckwith to thank [Hamilton] for some complimentary declarations, and to inform him I have sent home his communications, that *I approve of the general idea, and think something might be formed on that plan to the advantage of both countries.*"[66]

Beckwith arrived in New York late in March and immediately consulted Hamilton. Jefferson had assumed office the day before, but Beckwith's informant already knew that the Secretary of State thought the struggle in France would be successful, that the outcome would mean great commercial benefits to the United States, and that this

[65] Grenville to Dorchester, 6 May 1790, No. 24, "*Secret,*" PRO: CO 42/67, f. 93-102; text in Brymner, *Report*, 1890, p. 89.

[66] Emphasis supplied in both passages. Dorchester to Grenville, 8 Mch. 1790, No. 18; PRO: CO 42/67, f. 116-23. The allusion to personal views, immediately followed by that to Hamilton, seems to make it clear that both Beckwith and Dorchester had formed a surmise that Hamilton was prompted in making his proposals by a desire to enhance his own power and influence in the administration.

would be brought about, in Hamilton's words, by "the influence of the Marquis de la Fayette . . . as well as from that general bias, which those who guide that party" had always shown to America. Hamilton then revealed to the agent what effect this had had upon himself. "I am the more strongly disposed," he declared, "to view the present time as particularly favorable for the consideration of a Commercial Treaty." On the question of exchanging ministers, Hamilton, responding to a direct question as to whether he had "any further communications to Lord Dorchester," said: "I cannot at this moment determine whether it may be proper to communicate further with Lord Dorchester, or to carry it forward through a regular channel.—Mr. Jefferson arrived last night, and these matters are in his department." He thought it might be possible to say something on this head before Beckwith returned to Quebec. Later he assured the agent that nothing had happened to change the views expressed in the former conversation. A treaty of commerce was generally wished, the full consideration of the subject was desirable, the reciprocal appointment of ministers was also agreeable, and the particular rank was a matter of secondary consideration.

Beckwith had long conversations with William Samuel Johnson who spoke in almost identical terms about Jefferson's views and about the subject of a treaty and the matter of exchanging ministers. The astute politician put his finger on the heart of the matter. The great difficulty in the way of amicable commercial relationships, he said to Beckwith, is that "your Navigation Act is so very important to your naval greatness, that you will not be disposed to break through so essential a part of it, as to give us a share in your West India trade." In a late discussion of the problem in the Senate, he added, some had preferred to negotiate an amicable adjustment of differences "by a reciprocal appointment of Arbitrators, or in any other equitable manner, or if this [should] not be thought eligible, by the Appointment of Commissioners in Europe." Johnson, who had been one of the Connecticut counsel in the notable and impressively successful arbitration of the dispute between Pennsylvania and his native state, came nearer to an endorsement of republican principles than he may have realized in making this suggestion. But neither he nor the Senate had changed attitudes. In the Southern states, Beckwith was told by diminutive William Paterson, Senator from New Jersey, "peculiar as it may seem a more democratic opinion prevails . . . than in the middle and eastern States, where the science of government is better understood.—Mr. Jefferson is proof of this, he is a man of some acquirements . . . but his opinions upon Government are the result of fine spun theoretic systems, drawn from the ingenious writings of Locke, Sydney and others of their cast, which can never be realized."

Just before returning in mid-April, Beckwith sought another interview with Alexander Hamilton in order to ask what he felt to be a necessary but hoped was not an improper question. "I take it for granted," he said, "the different communications you have been pleased to make to me, flow from that source, which under your present Government, is alone competent to make them." A direct answer could scarcely have been avoided. The response proved how little Washington knew of these secret discussions that went so far towards committing his administration. "I am not authorized to say to you in so many words," Hamilton replied, "that such is the language of the President of the United States; to a gentleman, who has no public character such a declaration cannot be made, but my honor and character stand implicated in the fulfilment of these assurances."[67]

Early in April Beckwith reported to Grenville on the subject that had caused him to be sent to New York. The military plans on foot, he thought, had three objects: to meet the threat of an Indian war, to strengthen "the general government of the Union, by an increase in the military establishment," and to establish a force in the Northwest Territory that would be sufficient to overawe the Indian tribes and, ultimately, to undertake offensive war. The last he regarded as being no immediate aim: "on the contrary," he added, "I have ground to believe there is a wish to cultivate a connexion, infinitely important in my humble apprehension to the genuine interest and future prosperity of this country." On his way back to Quebec Beckwith was confirmed in this view by the sheriff of Clinton county, who saw something mysterious in the military preparations: at first a "very considerable body of Troops" had been proposed, then there was much secret discussion, and then a greater degree of moderation prevailed.[68] Grenville received the dispatch just four days after Leeds and Pitt, under the changed circumstances induced by the war crisis, had greatly softened the language held out to Gouverneur Morris. He concluded on the basis of that dispatch that there was "no probability of an immediate attack in the course of the present Year upon our posts from the United States."[69] There was no further softening of the language.

Beckwith arrived in Quebec just as the war crisis broke in London. This not only sent him hurrying back to New York in July but, through circumstances that compelled a removal of some of the secrecy shrouding his missions theretofore, brought to a close the first period of his activity as Dorchester's agent.

III

If war "does happen," Gouverneur Morris reported to Washington after his conference with Leeds and Pitt on the 21st of May, "then they

[67] Beckwith's report of conversations, Mch.-Apr. 1790, enclosed in Dorchester to Grenville, 27 May 1790, PRO: CO 42/67, f. 235, 237-63. The text of Beckwith's report is printed in Brymner, *Report*, 1890, p. 134-43, but with a very serious error. Brymner identified the first part of Beckwith's report of his conversations with the figure 1 (William Samuel Johnson) whereas the report itself as received by Grenville has the figure 7 (Hamilton) in the margin. Hamilton's remarks are those set forth by Brymner at p. 134-6, whereas Johnson's statements begin at the bottom of p. 136 where the figure 1 is repeated. The confusion of 1 and 7 was an easy error to make but it has had most unfortunate consequences, misleading even such thorough scholars as Bemis and Syrett (see Bemis, *Jay's Treaty*, p. 91).

[68] Beckwith to Grenville, 7 Apr. 1790, PRO: CO 42/72, f. 180-3; duplicate, f. 359-66, both endorsed as received 25 May 1790.

[69] Grenville to Dorchester, 5 June 1790, draft, Secret, PRO: CO 42/67, f. 160-2.

will give us a good Price for our Neutrality, and Spain I think will do so too, wherefore this appears to be a favorable Moment for treating with that Court about the Mississippi." The two ministers had assured him that he had misunderstood Leeds' letter respecting a treaty of commerce. "I answered coolly," Morris reported, "that it was easy to rectify the Mistake, but it appeared idle to form a new Treaty untill the Parties should be thoroughly satisfied with that already existing."[70] This brought on a discussion of violations of the Treaty of Peace by both nations. When Pitt stated that national honor required the retention of the posts as a guarantee of compliance by the United States, Morris replied with warmth: "the Conduct you have pursued naturally excites Resentment in every American Bosom. We do not think it worth while to go to War with you for these Posts, but *we know our Rights, and will avail ourselves of them when Time and Circumstances may suit.*" In response to Pitt's question as to whether he had powers to treat, Morris gave the answer that had already been hinted at more delicately to Beckwith in America—that since the United States had sent one minister to London, no other could be sent as long as England neglected to do the same. Pitt then asked Morris what Philip Schuyler had asked Beckwith nine months earlier. Would a minister be sent in return for one dispatched? Morris replied that he could "almost promise" that one would be sent, but had no authority to offer positive assurances. He proposed that a minister be appointed by England and offered himself to remain in London until informed of a similar appointment by the United States. The inconclusive exchange brought nothing save a promise that Leeds and Pitt would consult and inform Morris of the result.[71]

The language of the ministry had softened only to the extent of trying to avoid giving offense—not altogether successfully—at a time when the disposition of the American government was a matter of some concern. That of Morris, however, offered a striking contrast to the position taken by his sponsor in the discussions with Beckwith. Hamilton's pledge of honor to the commitment he had assumed for the administration and Beckwith's reassuring news about developing military plans came to Grenville a few days after Morris' interview with Leeds and Pitt. But the ministry had not needed this reassurance to decide in what manner to counteract any inducements Spain might hold out to the United States as the price of alliance against England. Its decision was not to communicate directly with Washington's official agent. To have done that would have brought on all the risks of negotiation—offers, counter-offers, perhaps pledges—and it would not have enabled the ministry to pursue its growing interest in Vermont and Kentucky. The discussion would not be held with the agent of a sovereign power close at hand but rather with "the British interest" in America.

Two weeks before Morris' interview with Leeds and Pitt, Grenville

[70] Morris to Washington, 29 May 1790 (RC in DLC: Washington Papers).
[71] The whole of Morris' correspondence with Leeds and his reports to Washington is to be found in Sparks, *Gouverneur Morris*, II, 3-56; see also TJ's report to Washington, 15 Dec. 1790.

sent three urgent and secret dispatches to Dorchester, all written the day Pitt disclosed the war crisis to the nation. The first announced the danger of conflict, expressed fear the Americans might seize the opportunity to demand the forts, and asked Dorchester to remain in Canada to direct defense preparations. The second was devoted to the importance of preserving friendly relations with Vermont. If it could be the means of "attaching the people of Vermont sincerely to the British interest," a concession to export flour into Quebec might be justified. The third dispatch, dealing directly with American relations, stands as a tribute to the strength of the British interest in the United States that Beckwith's reports had disclosed. In this Grenville admitted that Washington's letter of credence to Morris indicated "some disposition on the part of the United States to cultivate a closer connection." Even though the ministry had been obliged to hold out a firm language to Morris in the beginning, Grenville explained, "it will certainly be our object to establish, if possible, a greater degree of interest than we have hitherto had in that country." He thought it by no means impossible "to turn the tide of opinion and wishes of America" in favor of Great Britain by holding up to their view—particularly those in Kentucky and the western territories—the possibility of British aid in obtaining free navigation of the Mississippi, an "object . . . at least as important [to them] as the possession of the Forts." The instruments by which this desirable result might be achieved were precisely the same as those that had been employed in recent years. To cultivate the British interest in the United States and to increase it if possible, Dorchester was directed to "find the means of sending proper persons" to promote this object "and at the same time . . . to give . . . the earliest information of hostile designs, if any such should be meditated against the forts or against Canada itself." Such emissaries, Grenville explicitly stipulated, were *not* to be clothed with authority under any public commission. They would have no status equivalent to that of Gouverneur Morris.

Thus the ministry, holding Washington's agent at arm's length, appealed to its friends in America who could not know that the heart of its policy lay in a report just submitted by the Lords of the Committee of the Privy Council for Trade, presided over by the arch-mercantilist Lord Hawkesbury. Grenville's dispatches were grounded on that report: "The Lords are of opinion that, in a commercial view, it will be for the benefit of this country to prevent Vermont and Kentucky and all the other Settlements now forming in the interior parts of the great Continent of North America from becoming dependent on the Government of the United States, or on that of any other foreign country, and to preserve them on the contrary in a state of Independence and to induce them to form Treaties of Commerce and Friendship with Great Britain."[72] The British interest in America, unaware of the rising ascendancy of Hawkesbury's principles of exclusion, was also being held at

[72] Report of the Committee, 17 Apr. 1790, PRO: Chatham Papers, 363; Grenville to Dorchester, Dispatches Nos. 22-24, all dated 6 May 1790 and all marked "*Secret*"; PRO: CO 42/67, f. 87-9, 91-2, 93-102; texts printed in Brymner, *Report*, 1890, p. 131-3.

arm's length. However much it might be courted through Dorchester and Beckwith, that interest had no ground to expect access to the West Indies or a commercial treaty such as the ministry was prepared to accord to independent settlements on the borders of the United States.

The moment he received Grenville's dispatches, Dorchester sent Beckwith off to New York on his fifth and final mission, hoping he would arrive there in time to take advantage of the July packet for England. He furnished the agent with two sets of instructions. The first restated the arguments set forth by Grenville and authorized him —as the occasion might require or his discretion direct—to express Dorchester's hope that the threat of war or even war itself would not "make any alterations in the good disposition of the United States to establish a firm friendship and Alliance with Great Britain to the Mutual advantage of both countries." Dorchester explained to Grenville that these instructions to Beckwith were intended to "clothe him with consequence, and authorize him to speak generally on certain public topics," but it is quite incorrect to speak of them as being public instructions or as being intended for the President of the United States.[73] They were merely, as Dorchester himself said, "of a less secret nature" than those accompanying them. They were in no sense comparable to the letter of credence that Washington as head of state had given to Morris, but were only instructions to a secret agent setting forth the hopes of the Governor General of Canada, to be disclosed to such persons as the occasion and Beckwith's discretion authorized.[74] If intended for anyone, they were presumably to be shown to the one to whom Beckwith actually disclosed them on arrival in New York, the Secretary of the Treasury.

The second letter of instructions was marked "*Secret*," thus to be hidden even from those who had proven themselves so friendly to Great Britain. These instructions directed Beckwith to try to discover the American attitude "towards peace or war, separately, and unconnected with the affairs of Spain . . . and whether they expect any assistance from France in her present situation"; to pay particular attention to the characters of military men and to all military arrangements; and, while being cautious in saying anything specific on the subject of the navigation of the Mississippi, to try to "ascertain the extent and importance of the adherents of each particular system." The agent was directed to remain in New York as long as he found his presence there to be "of advantage to the King's services."[75] It was the last instruction that altered the character of Beckwith's role and led to the unwarranted assumption that the emissary functioned as an unaccredited minister in

[73] Fitzpatrick, for example, states that Beckwith "had presented a memorandum to the President"; Washington, *Writings*, ed. Fitzpatrick, XXXI, 102n.; see also, Syrett, *Hamilton*, VI, 486, note 8; Bemis, *Jay's Treaty*, p. 92.

[74] Dorchester to Beckwith, 27 June 1790, PRO: CO 42/68, f. 255, enclosed in Dorchester to Grenville, 7 July 1790, same, f. 252-3; both the covering letter and these "less secret" instructions are printed in Brymner, *Report*, 1890, p. 133, 143.

[75] Dorchester to Beckwith, 27 June 1790, "*Secret*," PRO: CO 42/68, f. 258-60, enclosed in Dorchester to Grenville, 7 July 1790 (see note 75); text of instructions in Brymner, *Report*, 1890, p. 144.

residence. Neither the authority granted him nor the explanation made by Dorchester to Grenville justifies such an inference. Owing "to the shortness of his occasional visits to that country," Dorchester explained, "he can only procure such desultory information, as happens to fall in his way, without being able to follow the chain of events, or attend to the different changes, which that government is still liable to."[76] Beckwith's information on four previous missions had been far from desultory or accidentally come by, but it was natural for Dorchester to assume that, having achieved such extraordinary results on flying visits, Beckwith would be able to give added value both to his connections and his communications by a continuous residence. Far from interrupting or changing the nature of his role as a confidential agent, this order had the effect of strengthening it. The disclosure of that role to public view resulted from other factors than the instructions of the Governor General. The ministry, of course, had nothing to do with the choice of Beckwith. Grenville had only authorized Dorchester to "find the means of sending proper persons" to cultivate the British interest and to act as secret agents. Dorchester authorized Beckwith on occasion to communicate directly with Grenville only because the risk of delay by way of Quebec might be harmful to public affairs.

The journey from Quebec to New York normally required at least a fortnight. Since Beckwith's instructions were dated 27 June and since he disclosed these to Hamilton on the morning of 8 July, it is clear that the trip was uncommonly hurried and that the disclosure was made immediately on arrival.[77] At noon of that day Hamilton reported the conversation to Washington and Jefferson, thus for the first time bringing the role of the confidential agent into public view. There would appear to have been less reason for this sudden revelation in 1790 than there had been in 1789. On the former occasion Beckwith had brought an authoritative message directly from Grenville, while on this he was only Dorchester's agent having private instructions that showed no discernible authority from Whitehall. He brought no offers or proposals, only Dorchester's hope that the threat of war had made no alteration in the disposition previously manifested by Hamilton. Further, the price attached to disclosure was the certainty of closer scrutiny, of aroused suspicions, and of diminished effectiveness—a price both Beckwith and Hamilton might have to pay. Both apparently had much to risk and little to gain by the ending of secrecy. Why, then, was Dorchester's vague and noncommittal expression of hope reported immediately to the President when Grenville's unequivocal warning of 1789 had not

[76] Dorchester to Grenville, 7 July 1790, PRO: CO 42/68, f. 252-3.

[77] Beckwith's remarkable journey could not have taken more than ten days. In 1787 the secret agent Peter Allaire traversed the distance "in Twenty three days of Tedious Journey . . . riding 643 miles of Roads unknow[n] of in Europe," though on learning the route he stated that he could make the trip in fifteen days. Christopher Colles' *Survey of the Roads of the United States* that had appeared in 1789 extended only to Albany. Between that and Quebec lay great stretches of wilderness. This, Allaire stated, interposed such a barrier to communication that Canadians knew less of affairs in the United States than Englishmen knew of events in China (Peter Allaire to Sir George Yonge, 16 Aug. 1787, with enclosed report of "Occurrences," PRO: FO 4/5, f. 313, 323).

been? There is no doubt that it was Hamilton who, with characteristic boldness, chose disclosure and that he did so under the compulsion of untoward circumstances. This, as well as the motive that prompted it, is indicated by the manner in which the disclosure was made.

Under 8 July 1790 Washington made this entry in his diary: "About noon the Secretaries of State, and of the Treasury called upon me—the last of whom reported a communication made to him by Majr. Beckwith . . . which he reduced to writing." It has been assumed that Hamilton first reported the conversation to Jefferson and then to the President.[78] Other than the ambiguous allusion in Washington's diary, there is no evidence to support this assumption, though it is possible that it is well grounded and equally so that it is not. Nor is it clear from the entry whether Hamilton had already reduced the interview to writing or did so after first making an oral report to the President. Again either is possible, though the latter seems more plausible. The haste of Beckwith's journey from Quebec, the retrospective tone given to the title of Hamilton's memorandum, the "recollected" contents of Dorchester's letter, the delicate situation that brought about disclosure, the studied care with which the report was prepared—all tend to support this assumption.[79] Even so, Hamilton must have reduced the interview to writing with some haste, for Washington recorded the memorandum in full in his diary under the same date. That report can only be understood by a close comparison of Grenville's dispatch to Dorchester, the latter's instructions to Beckwith, and Hamilton's version of the conversation. Perhaps significantly, Beckwith made no report of what transpired that morning.

It is indicative but unimportant that Hamilton represented the agent's communication as having been made to him "by direction of Lord Dorchester," whereas Beckwith's instructions about disclosure were permissive and discretionary, not mandatory. But there are numerous discrepancies of substance between the instructions and the memorandum and two of these are of such importance that they must be particularly examined. The first concerns the mission of Gouverneur Morris. Grenville in his secret dispatch had sent Dorchester a copy of Washington's letter of credence to Morris of 13 Oct. 1789, together with a communication from Morris to Leeds and the latter's response. Grenville noted the good dispositions Washington's letter revealed, gave full value to the fact that it came from the President, and qualified this only by saying that it was "vague and inexplicit." Dorchester's instructions reflected Grenville's comments in this as in other respects. He had learned with satisfaction, Dorchester wrote, "that some steps towards an amicable System have been commenced at home, through the Agency of Mr. Morris, though not yet so explicit and formal as the case may require."

[78] Washington, *Diaries*, ed. Fitzpatrick, IV, 137; Freeman, *Washington*, VI, 269-70.

[79] "Memorandum of a Communication made on Thursday the Eighth of July to the Subscriber by Major Beckwith *as by direction of Lord Dorchester*" (emphasis supplied); MS in Hamilton's hand in DLC: Washington Papers; text printed in Syrett, *Hamilton*, VI, 484-6. Washington transcribed the entire document in his diary under 8 July 1790; *Diaries*, ed. Fitzpatrick, IV, 137-8.

He made no hint of any lack of cordiality on either side in such negotiations. This, however, is what Hamilton reported to Washington: "Major Beckwith . . . next proceeded to observe that Lord Dorchester had been informed of a negociation commenced on the other side of the water through the Agency of Mr. Morris; mentioning the Subscriber understood principally by way of proof of Ld. Dorchesters knowlege of the transaction that Mr. Morris had not produced any regular credentials, but merely a letter from the President directed to himself, that some delays had intervened partly on account of Mr. Morris's absence on a trip to Holland as was understood and that it was not improbable those delays and some other circumstances may have impressed Mr. Morris with an idea of backwardness on the part of the British ministry. That his Lordship however had directed him to say that an inference of this sort would not in his opinion be well founded as he had reason to believe that the Cabinet of Great Britain entertained a disposition not only towards a friendly intercourse but towards an alliance with the United States."

The first substantive discrepancy in the opening remarks of Hamilton's memorandum presents a puzzle. Why was it necessary to produce proof of Dorchester's knowledge of the negotiations? If proof were necessary and cordiality the aim, why the disparagement of Morris' credentials as "merely a letter from the President"? The British Secretary for Foreign Affairs had expressed himself as pleased with that letter, had given it due credit, and had proceeded to hold conversations with the agent it authorized. Nor had the Governor General of Canada made any such disparagement in his instructions to Beckwith. If proof were necessary in order to explain delays and to counter inferences, why was not that evidence used in which delay was mentioned and explained—that is, the letters between Morris and Leeds? These as well as a copy of Washington's letter of credence had been enclosed in Grenville's secret dispatch to Dorchester. If Dorchester had shown any of these secret documents to Beckwith—a supposition plausible enough but perhaps not provable—the agent could have known that Morris had mentioned his expectation "of hearing from his Grace at an early period" and that Leeds had explained the delay on the ground of Morris' absence in Holland, his own illness, and "a Multiplicity of Engagements."[80] Or, if these were not shown, Dorchester could have told Beckwith of these facts and prepared him against unwarranted inferences. But if this were to be done at all, why was it not done in the written instructions where the emphasis was upon cordiality rather than in an oral instruction where—according to Hamilton's memorandum—the emphasis was upon the untoward aspect of the negotiation and its purpose to dispose of ill-found inferences? The answer to such questions can only be deduced. But the fact is that Morris' first reports of his correspondence

[80] The texts of Leeds' letter to Morris of 28 [i.e. 29] Apr. 1790 and of Morris' reply of 30 Apr. 1790, together with Washington's letter of credence to Morris of 13 Oct. 1790, were enclosed in Grenville's secret dispatch No. 24 to Dorchester of 6 May 1790; texts of all are printed in Brymner, *Report*, 1890, p. 129-31, 133. See also Vol. 16: 531-6.

with Leeds had arrived in New York only a short while before Beck-with appeared. Hamilton knew well enough what inferences were being drawn from these reports by the President and particularly by the Secretary of State. Washington in fact had shown the correspondence to John Adams on the 1st of July and the Vice-President had immedi-ately declared the result to be "of a piece with their conduct towards him whilst Minister at that Court" and "just what he expected."[81] These inferences, as the event proved, were essentially the same as those drawn by Morris himself—that the delays were evasive, that a com-mercial treaty was thought by the ministry to be unnecessary.

Was it Dorchester who instructed his agent to anticipate these in-ferences? It is quite implausible to suppose that he did, not only because his instructions carry no such allusions but also because of the simple fact that he had no reason to suppose anything untoward affected the negotiations. The exchange of letters between Morris and Leeds that Grenville sent him was polite, formal, and candid, but Dorchester on reading these letters alone can have had no such feeling for the tone of the negotiations as to have instructed his agent to counter its ill effect. Both the letters and the instructions convey at that point the impression that the discussions in London were proceeding amicably and normally. Grenville's secret dispatch had the effect of confirming this impression, containing nothing to offset it. Some months later Dorchester indeed stated that he had had no accounts of the progress of the negotiation and that he thought it natural enough the discussions with Spain "should have occasioned some delay."[82] But this was occasioned by Beckwith's report of the surprise felt by Hamilton at a "certain reserve" exhibited by the ministry to Morris. Here Dorchester was responding to an in-ference in a very different manner from that attributed to him in the summer of 1790. All evidence points to the fact that when he drafted

81 Washington, *Diaries*, ed. Fitzpatrick, IV, 132, under 1 July 1790. It is ob-vious that Washington had shown Morris' report of the interview with Leeds and Pitt to Hamilton as well as to Adams and TJ (Beckwith's report, enclosed in Dorchester to Grenville, 10 Nov. 1790, PRO: CO 42/72, f. 61-8, 69-72; see Syrett, *Hamilton*, VII, 70).

82 Henry Motz, secretary to Dorchester, to George Beckwith, 10 Feb. 1791, PRO: CO 42/73, f. 133-5; text in Brymner, *Report*, 1890, p. 168-9. This remark was in response to Beckwith's report that Hamilton seemed surprised at the re-serve shown by the ministry toward Morris. In addition to the reason given, Motz added: "There is indeed another cause, from the influence of which it is to be hoped Mr. M[orris] is free, but which his Lordship is inclined to think has oper-ated ever since the peace against a connexion between the two countries. No doubt many gentlemen, and some of high and distinguished character, in the states, see through the clouds, that have been raised with so much industry to mislead that people, but the general spirit and language for some years after the peace have been by no means of a conciliating nature. This disposition appears of late to have in a great measure abated, particularly on the shores of the Atlantic, though there are still some indications of it; but in the western territory it would seem great pains are still taken to keep it up at its original height. As this spirit operated, it would naturally produce a corresponding reserve on the part of our government. And perhaps the wisest plan, that could be followed by Great Britain, under such circumstances, was, to leave the states time to reflect, and by their own good sense to find out that course which is most consonant to their true interest."

the instructions he gave Beckwith no authority to say more on the subject of the negotiations in London than these authorized.

But were the words attributed to him those of Beckwith? It is conceivable that he learned of Morris' report to Washington after he arrived in New York. If so, he could only have received the information from the person to whom he obviously addressed himself first, Alexander Hamilton. But it is scarcely in the realm of the possible that, having just learned of the inferences drawn from Morris' report, the agent would then have repeated this to his informant as his own; that he would have stated in the next breath that Dorchester had "directed him to say that an inference of this sort" was ill-founded; and that Hamilton, accepting such an absurd repetition at face value, would have solemnly passed the representation on to the President as coming from Dorchester through Beckwith. The implication is clear. Beckwith could not have said what Hamilton quoted him as saying about the London negotiations. These were words put in the mouth of the agent by Hamilton, who had every reason for doing so.

The second substantive discrepancy between Dorchester's instructions and Hamilton's memorandum involves a far graver matter, for it distorted the expressed intent of a foreign power and therefore was an act of deception on the administration in its conduct of foreign policy. According to Hamilton's memorandum, Beckwith quoted Dorchester as saying that "*he had reason to believe* that the Cabinet of Great Britain entertained a disposition not only towards a friendly intercourse but towards an alliance with the United States."[83] This is a gross misrepresentation of what Grenville had authorized and what Dorchester had actually said, committing both to a position neither had occupied. Dorchester's carefully drawn and less secret instructions to Beckwith said: "You will at the same time express my hope, that neither the appearance of a War with Spain nor its actually taking place, will make any alterations in the good disposition *of the United States* to establish a firm friendship and Alliance with Great Britain to the Mutual advantage of both Countries; I am persuaded it can make none on the part of Great Britain, whose liberal treatment of the United States in point of Commerce sufficiently evinces her friendly disposition, notwithstanding the non execution of the treaty on their part, which, and various misrepresentations, I have always attributed to an unsettled state of their government, and of the minds of the multitude, influenced perhaps by a power not very cordial even to the United States.[84] The instructions and the memorandum could scarcely be more contradictory on the central point involved.

In drafting the instructions Dorchester no doubt intended only to follow the line adopted by Leeds of holding out a firm language to Morris. But there were at least three forceful reasons why the Secretary of the Treasury should not have wished these expressions to be transmitted undiluted to the President or the Secretary of State. First, the innuendo about the influence of France, the implied reflection on "the minds of the multitude," and the charges about various misrepresenta-

[83] Italics supplied.　　　[84] Italics supplied.

tions made presumably by the leaders of an unsettled government were little calculated to promote friendly dispositions, especially on the part of the Secretary of State. Second, Dorchester had in fact made no other assurances about British intent than that, despite the failure of the American government to live up to its treaty obligations, the threat of war would cause no alteration in her previous attitude of leniency in matters of commerce. This was to have been expected. It approximated the position taken by the ministry with Morris. It reflected also much of what Beckwith had said to Johnson, Schuyler, and Hamilton in 1789. The gist of the passage was that the threat of war would not cause any alteration in the previous "friendly disposition" of the ministry. Even this was set forth only as Dorchester's opinion, with much of its amicable intent being effaced by the claim of British liberality and the charges of American delinquency in which the opinion was imbedded. There was nothing in the passage conveying an authoritative expression of the ministry's intent. There could not have been, for Grenville expressly forbade Dorchester to clothe his agent with authority to speak under a public commission. The disposition of the British ministry was far more hidden in this passage than that of the President had been in the letter of credence to Morris that Grenville found so vague and inexplicit. Third, and most important of all, the Secretary of the Treasury could not have revealed the exact words of Dorchester's instructions without exposing himself to the President as having committed the administration on his own authority to a position it had not assumed and of having done this in secret negotiations, pledging in support of the commitment his own honor and character.

Far from manifesting a desire on the part of Great Britain to effect a "firm friendship and Alliance," Dorchester had merely authorized Beckwith to express his hope that the threat of war would not cause "any alterations in the good disposition *of the United States*" to establish such a connection.[85] The government of the United States had expressed no such desire for an alliance. But the Secretary of the Treasury had gone very far toward declaring this aim for the administration. In employing such an expression as "firm friendship and Alliance," Dorchester in effect was only paraphrasing Hamilton's proposed plan of 1789 for "strong ties of commercial, perhaps of political, friendships" between the two countries; his assurance that it was then safe for any nation to "enter into Treaties . . . either Commercial or Political" with the United States; and his flat declaration to Beckwith: "We wish to form a commercial treaty with you to every extent, to which you may think it for your interest to go." The paraphrasing could not have gone to the President in Dorchester's own words without immediately raising delicate and searching questions. The risk of exposing to view the secret discussions of the preceding year and with it the commitment he had gone so far in making was one that Hamilton dared not take except on his own terms. In addition to the motives that had compelled secrecy up to that point, Thomas Jefferson was now a counterpoise in the administration.

[85] Italics supplied.

The glaring discrepancy between what Beckwith was authorized to say and what Hamilton quoted him as saying forces the question of responsibility to be raised. Could Beckwith have so misrepresented his superior or Hamilton have so misunderstood the agent that this contradiction came about through mere mistake or defect in communication? Neither man theretofore or afterwards seems to have exhibited in their exchanges any lack of clarity or precision without taking pains at once to remove all ambiguity. Beckwith was especially careful to do this. The nature of the exchange placed this responsibility upon him particularly, for it was Hamilton's ideas about a closer connection that were being transmitted, not the reverse. There is no evidence to show that his reports in these five years ever failed to represent both his informants and his superior with fidelity and accuracy. He was an experienced intelligence officer, trusted by Dorchester on the basis of more than a decade of close association and knowledge of character. On a matter affecting the national interest so deeply, at so critical a juncture, it is implausible to suppose that either Beckwith or Hamilton could have permitted so gross a discrepancy between the agent's instructions and his alleged remarks to have occurred through mere inadvertence. Clearly the contradiction can only have resulted from deliberate choice, not from accident or failure of communication. Was this deliberate choice made by Beckwith or by Hamilton, the only two in the chain of communication who could have created the contradiction?

The effect of Hamilton's memorandum is to place the responsibility squarely upon Beckwith. According to this, Beckwith at the conclusion of his lengthy statement produced a letter signed by Dorchester containing "ideas similar to those he had expressed though in more guarded terms and without any allusion to instructions from the British Cabinet." Hamilton added: "This letter *it is now recollected* hints at the non execution of the treaty of peace on our part." The memorandum concluded with the statement that, on Hamilton's noting that the letter seemed to speak only the sentiments of Dorchester, Beckwith replied: "it was to be presumed . . . his Lordship knew too well the consequence of such a step to have taken it without a previous knowledge of the intentions of the Cabinet."[86] Thus, according to this memorandum, full responsibility for committing Dorchester to a step he had not taken rests upon his agent. But this cannot be made to accord with the facts or with reason.

The letter supposedly introduced at the conclusion of the interview can only have been Dorchester's less secret instructions. The first point to be noted is that, assuming so experienced an officer as Beckwith actually had quoted his superior as saying he "had reason to believe that the Cabinet of Great Britain entertained a disposition" toward a friendly intercourse and even an alliance, it is scarcely conceivable that he would thereupon have been so imprudent as to bring forth the instructions and thus wholly discredit what he had just said. Further, this was the first time in all of his missions that, so far as the documents reveal, Beckwith carried written instructions with him. The critical

[86] Italics supplied.

situation justified this. Dorchester, carrying out Grenville's instructions to cultivate and strengthen the "growing British interest," must have intended the letter to be presented to Hamilton—as in fact it was, immediately on Beckwith's arrival. The agent thus could have disclosed the instructions at the beginning of the interview, permitting Dorchester to speak for himself and saving himself from the charge of going far beyond what his instructions authorized. Even if Beckwith had failed to follow this prudent course, Hamilton still had at hand infallible means of measuring the exact dimensions of the discrepancy between what the agent—according to his account—had attributed to Dorchester and what the latter had expressed for himself. In so important a matter it was his duty to do this with some precision in order to provide his own government with the most reliable representation possible of Dorchester's statements. Beckwith was authorized to reveal the instructions as the occasion and his discretion suggested. Hamilton could have insisted, in fact, upon transmitting the letter itself or a careful précis of its contents, just as Gouverneur Morris had done for his correspondence with Leeds. Beckwith in April had not hesitated to pin the Secretary of the Treasury down with a very blunt though politely-phrased question about his authority to speak for the government on the measure he had proposed the preceding autumn. But Hamilton, to judge from his own memorandum, did not insist upon defining Beckwith's spoken and written communications in a way that would have truly reflected their conflict. On the contrary, his report tended to erase all evidence of that conflict that could be removed. More than four-fifths of the memorandum focused on Beckwith's alleged words, while the contents of Dorchester's letter were noted in an almost off-hand manner. In effect, Hamilton asked the administration to attend the oral testimony of the agent rather than the written message of the principal. Dorchester's language was much firmer than that Leeds had held out to Morris, but no trace of this remained in Hamilton's memorandum save the vague recollection about neglect of treaty obligations. All stern admonitions, all innuendoes about the influence of France on the minds of the multitude, all charges of misrepresentation by the leaders of an unsettled government, all claims of British indulgence in matters of trade, all reference to the declared disposition of the government of the United States for a closer connection—indeed all offensive statements of whatever sort were screened from Dorchester's instructions by Hamilton's memorandum.

This much was only negative, a failure to report Dorchester in a full and accurate manner. But Hamilton went further. He declared unequivocally that the letter contained ideas similar to those expressed by Beckwith. Yet on the central question—the declaration that the British ministry desired friendly intercourse *and an alliance*—there was no similarity, only irreconcilable contradiction. Asserting the similarity, Hamilton compounded the misrepresentation by his supposed comment to Beckwith that the letter contained no evidence of instructions from the cabinet but only Dorchester's opinion. So far as the memorandum indicates, he thereupon accepted without comment Beckwith's reply that

Dorchester knew the consequences of such a step too well to have taken it without a previous knowledge of the disposition of the ministry. But, having read the letter, Hamilton knew that Dorchester had *not* taken any step beyond the noncommittal response Leeds had given to Morris, that in fact there was nothing in the letter to warrant in any degree the asserted similarity on this central point. Neither the ministry nor Dorchester had given any evidence whatever of wishing to seek an alliance so far as the letter from Grenville or the letter of instructions to Beckwith revealed. Thus in asserting a similarity where none existed, Hamilton destroyed the credibility of his memorandum. On the basis of this single statement he exposed himself to two charges. Either he failed to detect the glaring discrepancy or he made a deliberate effort to conceal that discrepancy. There can be no doubt that Hamilton deliberately chose concealment. It seems likely that he had Dorchester's letter before him while preparing his own memorandum, and the nature of the latter certainly cannot have been revealed to Beckwith.[87] Hamilton alone must bear responsibility for the words that he attributed both to the agent and to the Governor General. The memorandum cannot be accepted as other than a deliberate and gross distortion. The question indeed is not whether Hamilton did this but what purposes moved him.

Beckwith could have had no apparent reason for wishing to misrepresent his superior, while Hamilton had every inducement to soften the impact of Dorchester's words. If he had disclosed the exact terms or even the substance of Dorchester's instructions, several results would have been certain to follow. The President and the Secretary of State would have been affronted by a language even harsher than that exhibited by Leeds to Morris. Questions of responsibility for creating in the mind of Dorchester any impression of the government's disposition for an alliance would have arisen, and with them the risk of exposing the secret discussions and Hamilton as the one who had made proposals leading to such an impression. Gouverneur Morris would have been confirmed in his belief that the ministry intended to retain possession of the posts and considered "a Treaty of Commerce with America as being absolutely unnecessary."[88] Advocates of Madison's "discriminating clauses" would have been given renewed strength. The *rapprochement* toward which Hamilton had labored so long and for which he had risked so much would have been correspondingly endangered. Madison, in fact, had revived his plan for commercial reciprocity immediately

[87] Hamilton might also have shown his account of the conversation to Beckwith for verification if he had wished to report an accurate précis, but he only told the agent later that he had made the proper use of what was communicated. The supposition that he had Dorchester's letter before him as he wrote is supported not only by the circumstances that make it most plausible but also by the fact that (1) both Dorchester's instructions and his own memorandum parallel each other in the order in which the topics are taken up and that (2) Hamilton was able to remember the names and spelling of such obscure persons as Hart and Wemble, yet on the direct charge of delinquency as to treaty obligations he could only present this as a vague hint not categorically set forth but "as . . . now recollected."

[88] Morris to Washington, 1 May 1790; Vol. 16: 533.

after news had arrived of the threat of war.[89] Simultaneously General Irvine's report that Benedict Arnold was in Detroit training the Canadian militia inflamed old passions and instilled in Washington the fear that a descent on Louisiana across American territory was being planned.[90] There was the possibility that other influences would drive the administration toward Spain. John Adams, agreeing with Morris' analysis of the ministry's attitude and believing war almost inevitable, went so far as to tell the President that he thought it good policy and to the interest of the United States to take sides against England in the conflict.[91] Hamilton could assume with certainty that the Secretary of State, aided by James Madison, John Brown, and other members of Congress from the South, would set about doing what he had so long been concerned about and what in fact he was about to do—to seize the war crisis as a means of bargaining with Spain over the opening of the Mississippi. The situation was indeed a critical one, threatening with defeat the carefully developed plans of the Secretary of the Treasury. Its urgency is reflected in the note that Hamilton sent on the day after his interview with Beckwith to John Jay, who was then in attendance on his dying father-in-law, William Livingston: "Certain circumstances of a delicate nature have occurred, concerning which the President would wish to consult you. *They press.* Can you consistently with the Governor's situation afford us your presence here? I cannot say the President directly asks it, lest you should be embarrassed; but he has expressed a strong wish for it."[92]

In this critical situation when war was considered almost inevitable, it is understandable that Hamilton should have made use of Dorchester's communication both to conceal its import and to offset the damaging effect of Morris' report. A measure of Hamilton's concern is to be seen in the fact that the price attached to a disclosure of Beckwith's role was a high one. Nor could his anxiety for his policy and his acute discomfort in the hard-pressing circumstances have been lessened by his own knowledge of the delicate circumstances. Placing Leeds' letter to Morris beside that of Dorchester to Beckwith, he alone in the administration knew that neither contradicted the other.

The two documents spoke the same noncommittal tones. Nowhere in them could be found a trace of a British proposal for "an alliance with the United States" or even for a commercial treaty. Hamilton was aware, too, that the responsibility could not be placed upon Gouverneur Morris. Only Dorchester had expressed approval of the "general idea" advanced by the Secretary of the Treasury, while the British cabinet had revealed its coolness to the suggested *rapprochement* by ignoring it.[93] Having done as much as possible to pave the way for a cordial reception of Morris, Hamilton might have been justified in feeling that

[89] See Documents on American Commercial Policy, 1790, Vol. 16: 513-34.
[90] This report was brought to Washington by Irvine on Sunday, 4 July 1790; Washington, *Diaries*, IV, 136.
[91] This was on 1 July 1790; same, IV, 132.
[92] Hamilton to Jay, 9 July 1790; Syrett, *Hamilton*, VI, 488. Livingston died on 25 July 1790.
[93] Dorchester to Grenville, 8 Mch. 1790, "*Secret*," PRO: CO 42/67, f. 116-23.

he had been betrayed in the house of friends. If so, he gave no further expression of this than the pained surprise he expressed to Beckwith over "a certain reserve" shown by Leeds to Morris.[94] His response to the critical situation was not one of dismay or bitterness but of bold and characteristic action. In reshaping and concealing the true meaning of Dorchester's message, Hamilton measured his devotion to the policy he had promoted by these secret and circuitous means. While the treaty that should have been called Hamilton's was still years in the future, this first step towards it closed with an act of deception on the President and the Secretary of State in their conduct of foreign policy. This desperate act to salvage the policy at a critical moment was indeed one in which, as Hamilton had said to Beckwith in April, his own honor and character were implicated.

Desperate as the gamble was, it failed to convince. Jefferson saw at once—though he was obliged to accept Hamilton's version at face value—that no change had occurred to invalidate Morris' reports. He wrote to Morris a statement of policy in words of simple dignity: an honorable neutrality to be given in exchange for a pledge to execute the Treaty of Peace and to attempt no territorial conquests adjacent to the United States. As for the communications through Dorchester, these were mere "tamperings" by the ministry. "Besides what they are saying to you," Jefferson wrote Morris, "they are talking to us through Quebec; but so informally that they may disavow it when they please; it would only oblige them to make the fortune of the poor Major whom they would pretend to sacrifice; through him they talk of a Minister, a treaty of commerce, *and alliance*. If the object of the latter be honorable, it is useless; if dishonorable, inadmissible."[95] The emphasis given and the comment made on the words *"and alliance"* reflect Jefferson's disbelief of the ministry's intent as communicated by Hamilton. But in suspecting a dishonorable and deceptive act, the Secretary of State clearly focused his gaze in the wrong direction.

Nor was the President misled, though he, too, evidently accepted without question Hamilton's assertion that Beckwith had spoken of the ministry's desire for an alliance. Contrary to his usual caution in such matters and without waiting for advice,[96] Washington grasped the true nature of "this business in the moment of its communication," as he expressed it in his diary that day. Accepting the memorandum at face value, he thought the purported declaration from the ministry "appears simply, and no other than this;—We did not incline to give any satisfactory answer to Mr. Morris, who was *officially* commissioned to ascertain our intentions with respect to the evacuation of the Western Posts within the territory of the United States and other matters into

[94] See note 82 above. On 6 May 1791 Motz wrote Beckwith in further explanation: "The contexture of [Morris'] communications is easily accounted for from his personal views. It is rather surprizing that this effect should have escaped the discernment of those, who were acquainted with the nature and extent of his private pursuits in France. Such channels naturally tinge whatever they convey"; Brymner, *Report*, 1890, p. 169-70.

[95] Jefferson to Morris, 12 Aug. 1790, Document VIII below.

[96] Freeman, *Washington*, VI, 369.

which he was empowered to enquire until by this unauthenticated mode we can discover whether you will enter into an alliance with us and make Common cause against Spain. In that case we will enter into a Commercial Treaty with you and *promise perhaps* to fulfil what [we] already stand engaged to perform." The President decided, nevertheless, to ask Jefferson and Hamilton, as well as Adams, Jay, and Knox to "resolve this matter in all its relations in their minds" that they might be prepared to give their opinions in two or three days.[97]

Jefferson's opinion, delivered two days after it was requested, went further than anyone in the administration was prepared to go in stating the position of the government with precision and in tones both friendly and admonitory. He would have authorized Hamilton to say to Beckwith that nothing could be done about the supposed offer of alliance "till it's object be shewn" and even then unacceptable if inconsistent with existing engagements; that the United States had never desired a commercial treaty except on terms of "perfect reciprocity" and these provided its own price; that in matters of commerce the government preferred "amicable to adversary arrangements, *tho the latter would be infallible" and in the nation's power*—an ominous allusion to Madison's "discriminating clauses" and to the stronger threat of an embargo against British ships in American ports carrying produce to and from the West Indies; and that, in the event of war, the government was disposed to be neutral but would view with extreme uneasiness any attempts of either power to seize the possessions of the other" on the American frontiers.[98]

Two days after this opinion was submitted Washington conferred with Hamilton and Jay. There is no evidence that Jefferson was present at this conference and presumably he was not. The Chief Justice and the Secretary of the Treasury apparently did not prepare written opinions and Washington made no record of the discussion except to summarize its result. This stated the attitude of the government toward Beckwith and the message Hamilton said he had brought from Dorchester: "Had some further conversations . . . with respect to the business on which Majr. Beckwith was come on. The result—To treat his communications very civilly—to intimate, delicately, that they carried no marks official or authentic, nor in speaking of Alliance, did they convey any definite meaning by which the precise object of the British Cabinet could be discovered. In a word, that the Secretary of the Treasury was to extract as much as he could from Major Beckwith and *to report to me*, without committing, by any assurances whatever, the Government of the U. States, leaving it entirely free to pursue, unreproached, such a line of conduct in the dispute as her interest (and

[97] This comment appears in Washington's *Diaries*, ed. Fitzpatrick, IV, 139, under 8 July 1790 immediately following the transcription of Hamilton's memorandum. Washington apparently made the request of TJ and Hamilton for their opinions on that day. He probably informed them also of his intention to ask similar advice of Adams, Jay, and Knox, for in his urgent letter to Jay on the next day Hamilton intimated as much; see note 92.

[98] See Document I below, enclosure (italics supplied).

honour) shall dictate."[99] From this it is clear that the recommendations of the Secretary of State—which must have been shown by the President to Hamilton and Jay—were unacceptable. There was no question of extending recognition to Beckwith or even of carrying on formal conversations with him, for he had no status comparable to that of Gouverneur Morris. Possibly it was this obvious fact that enabled the President's advisers to persuade him that the policy suggested by the Secretary of State should not be stated to the agent. Even so, it is surprising that Washington did not insist on an expression of the concern voiced in that statement about attempts of conquest on American borders. For his alarm over the possibility that the British had a design on the Spanish settlements, "and of course to surround these United States," grew so vigorously that by the end of summer it had become a certainty in his mind—despite the fact that Dorchester on his part had fears just as strong about the danger of American aggression and, so far as the evidence discloses, neither he nor the ministry contemplated any attack on Louisiana by land.[100] Hamilton was aware of the President's concern, a fact that may have affected one aspect of his report of the next interview.

Thus the course to which Hamilton had pledged his honor collided with that Washington was determined to follow in maintaining the dignity of the nation. But this embarrassing dilemma gave him no pause. Having proved himself a faulty channel of communication from Beckwith to the administration, Hamilton now demonstrated equal unreliability in the reverse direction. Whatever the arguments employed in the consultation with Washington, the conversations with Beckwith were precisely on the ground on which Hamilton could have most desired them to be. All warnings of commercial retaliation and admonitory tones against aggression had been eliminated from the message he was to take back. He could not produce administrative proposals for a commercial treaty, much less for an alliance, but for the moment danger to the coveted *rapprochement* had been averted. Most important of all, the conversations were in his hands. The crisis had presented a serious threat to his plan, but this had been momentary. Hamilton moved boldly forward.

According to his version of what took place at the second interview, the Secretary of the Treasury told Beckwith that he had made "proper use" of what had been communicated at the first meeting. "As to what regards the objects of a general nature mentioned by you," Hamilton told Washington he said to Beckwith, "though your authority for the purpose from Lord Dorchester is out of question, and though I presume from his Lordship's station and character and the knowlege he appears to have of what is passing on the other side of the water with regard to Mr. Morris, that the Step he has taken through you is conformable to the views of your Cabinet and not without its sanction; yet you are no

[99] Washington, *Diaries*, ed. Fitzpatrick, IV, 143, under 14 July 1790 (italics supplied).

[100] Bemis, *Jay's Treaty*, 98. As indicated below, however, suggestions for such an overland attack were advanced by Americans and these were given close attention by the British government.

doubt sensible that the business presents itself in a shape, which does not give the proper authenticity to that fact, and is wholly without formality. You must also be sensible that there is a material difference between your situation and that of Mr. Morris. His Credentials though not formal proceed from the proper source. Your's are neither formal nor authoritative."[101]

There is nothing in this that conflicts with Hamilton's first memorandum. On the contrary, its polite tone suggests that only formal credentials were needed to support the fact that the step taken by Dorchester was indeed sanctioned by the ministry. Dorchester had taken no such step, but Beckwith did not know that this had been asserted in Hamilton's first memorandum. Thus the actual words Hamilton said he used would have meant far less to him than they did to Washington or to anyone who had read the memorandum. Even so, these are not the words Hamilton expressed to Beckwith—if we may judge from the latter's testimony. This, according to Beckwith, is what Hamilton said to him: "however authoritative [the subjects communicated] may be on your part, in so far as respects Lord Dorchester, and however evident it is to me that His Lordship is apprized by your Cabinet of Mr. Morris's Agency, yet you must be sensible, that official formality is wanting, but it is conceived that his Lordship would not have gone the lengths he has, without being acquainted with the general views of your administration, as they respect this Country."[102] The two reports, understandably different in phraseology, had a subtle difference of substance that could have been detected only by one standing in Hamilton's position. Fortunately for the Secretary of the Treasury, no one else was able to do this. As Hamilton struggled to move the administration toward the position that he and the ruling majority of the Senate had already assumed, and at the same time to conceal the embarrassing conflict from Beckwith, he seemed as little conscious of the danger of destruction as Washington had been at Long Island in 1776. On the central question his performance—as he himself reported it to Washington—even had a touch of the dramatic:

> As to Alliance [he said he told Beckwith] this opens a wide field. The thing is susceptible of a vast variety of forms. 'Tis not possible to judge what would be proper or what could be done unless points

[101] Undated memorandum in Hamilton's hand, DLC: Washington Papers; text in Syrett, *Hamilton*, VI, 493-5. In the memorandum itself Hamilton indicated that this interview took place on "Thursday the 22d. instant"; Beckwith early in August referred to the same interview as taking place "on the 15th. of last month," that is, on the day after Washington had consulted with Jay and Hamilton and had directed the latter what to say to the agent. Syrett points out the impossibility of proving which of the two men is in error, but concludes that Hamilton would not likely have waited eight days before carrying out Washington's instructions. This plausible conjecture is supported by the fact that Beckwith's report arrived in Quebec on 5 Aug. 1790, that the interview with Hamilton occupied first place in it, and that subsequent conversations with other persons took place just after Alexander McGillivray had arrived in New York, which was on 20 July, N.Y. *Daily Advertiser*, 22 July 1790; see two following notes.

[102] Beckwith's report, undated, enclosed in Dorchester to Grenville, 25 Sep. 1790, in which he stated that he had received the communication on 5 Aug.; PRO: CO 42/69, f. 14, 16-25; text in Brymner, *Report*, 1890, 145-9.

were brought into view. If you are in condition to mention particulars, it may afford better ground of conversation.

I stopped here for an answer.

Major Beckwith replied that he could say nothing more particular than he had already done.

That being the case (continued I) I can only say that the thing is in too general a form to admit of a judgment of what may be eventually admissible or practicable. If the subject shall hereafter present itself to discussion in an authentic and proper shape, I have no doubt we shall be ready to converse freely upon it: And you will naturally conclude that we shall be disposed to pursue whatever shall appear under all circumstances to be our interest as far as may consist with our honor. At present I would not mean either to raise or repress expectation.

Major Beckwith seemed to admit that as things were circumstanced nothing explicit could be expected.

The pause for an answer was an imaginative touch, but the conversation could not have occurred in the sense in which Hamilton wished it to be understood by Washington. Since Beckwith had brought no general proposition about alliance, or indeed any proposal, he naturally was in no "condition to mention particulars." Beckwith's account of the conversation was much more prosaic. This, according to his usually reliable reporting, is what Hamilton said to him on the central point: "In the present stage of this business it is difficult to say much on the subject of a Treaty of Alliance; Your rupture with Spain, if it shall take place, opens a very wide political field; thus much I can say, we are perfectly unconnected with Spain, have even some points unadjusted with that Court, and are prepared to go into the consideration of the subject."[103] In his own account, Hamilton had placed Beckwith on the defensive as the messenger proffering alliance. In Beckwith's report, the roles were reversed, naturally enough, since the idea had been initiated by the Secretary of the Treasury.

On the draft of the memorandum reporting this second interview, Hamilton noted: "Mr. Jefferson was privy to this transaction." But the Secretary of State, like the President, was privy only to what Hamilton said of it. This concealed far more than it revealed and, most important of all, gave the false impression that the proposal of an alliance had come from the ministry by way of Dorchester. The bold deception was maintained with skill. At this second interview Hamilton even held the door open for future discussion should "the thing" thereafter "*present itself* to discussion in an authentic and proper shape."[104] He could

103 The last statement also tends to support the date of the interview as taking place on the 15th of July, for it was on the 12th that TJ submitted his outline of policy to the President; see Document I below.

104 Italics supplied. In his note on the draft (DLC: Hamilton Papers) Hamilton also stated: "The views of the Government were to discard suspision that any engagements with Spain or intentions hostile to Great Britain existed—to leave the ground in other respects vague and open, so as that in case of Rupture between G B and S—the U States might be in the best situation to turn it to account in reference to the Disputes between them and G B on the one hand and Spain on

have had no expectation that this would come about of itself or be initiated by the ministry. The Governor General had indeed authorized Beckwith to say for him: "I think the interests of the United States, in case of a war, may be more effectually served by a junction with Great Britain, than otherwise."[105] But this was very far from suggesting or proposing an alliance. Hamilton's reports of the interviews thus left him free in the widening field of the war crisis to continue pursuit of the object he had sought so perseveringly thus far. Beckwith and Dorchester understood him to mean this, however little they knew of the misrepresentations made of them to the President. Thus the course of secret intrigue could be pursued as before. The previous discussions between Beckwith and the Secretary of the Treasury evidently had not been suspected and certainly had not been disclosed. The secret line of communication nevertheless had failed to bring the desired object on for "discussion in an authentic and proper shape." This could be done only through an exchange of ministers and Hamilton at once turned his attention to this aspect of the problem. He did so at the same interview at which he was required to state the attitude of the government and to report back to Washington what had transpired.

"The rest of our conversation," Hamilton said in his memorandum to Washington, "consisted chiefly of assurance on my part" that the threats against the posts were unauthorized by the government and of a repetition by Beckwith of the assurances he had given of Dorchester's disposition to discourage Indian outrages.[106] He thus led the President mistakenly to believe that the conversation had ended at this point. In requiring his Secretary of the Treasury to report what was said at the interview, Washington naturally expected both an accurate and a full account. He received neither, but the significant omission in Hamilton's report was set forth in detail in the report by Beckwith to his principal.

"It appears to me," Beckwith quoted Hamilton as saying, "that, from the nature of our Government, it would be mutually advantageous if this negociation could be carried on at our seat of government, as it

---

the other." This attributes to the administration views which, so far as the record discloses, Washington had not expressed. If the President had wished Hamilton to say—as Beckwith was led to understand was the case—that the United States was "perfectly unconnected" with Spain, it is strange that he failed to record so important an instruction in his otherwise explicit directions. The manner in which Hamilton explained the occasion for his own version of a milder assurance confirms the silence in the documents: it is a justification for a communication to Beckwith that Hamilton made on his own initiative, not one executed under orders. The conclusion suggested by this is clear: that the endorsement on the draft was made at a later date and that its purpose, like that of the explanation in the memorandum, was to justify. Washington certainly could not have authorized Hamilton to state to Beckwith that the administration was "prepared to go into the consideration" of matters unadjusted with Spain. This was a subject just unfolded in TJ's memorandum of 12 July 1790 (Document I, below) which inaugurated discussion of a plan surrounded from the beginning in the utmost secrecy.

[105] Dorchester to Beckwith, 27 June 1790, "*Secret,*" PRO: CO 42/68, f. 258-60; text in Brymner, *Report*, 1890, p. 144.

[106] Memorandum in DLC: Washington Papers; text printed in Syrett, *Hamilton*, VI, 494-5.

would produce dispatch and obviate misconception."[107] This hint was supported by Beckwith's later conversation with William Samuel Johnson, who told the agent that Madison continued indefatigable in his pursuit of commercial discrimination; that in fact the advocates of discrimination were gaining ground because of what they considered "as the commencement of a commercial warfare" on the part of Great Britain; that Jefferson, "a decided republican and perfectly devoted to a French interest," had been greatly instrumental "in promoting the removal of the Legislature from a city which he considers as being perfectly in an English interest"; that indeed his occupying the office of Secretary of State was "unfortunate in the idea of forming any close connection with [Great Britain] as he [could not] be confided in"; that Jefferson was thought to be "in great favor with the President"; but that the Secretary of the Treasury had more favorable sentiments, possessed "a solid understanding, great candor and sincerity in his dealings, and a manly mind, which [would] not be restrained from a free declaration of its principles." This from a distinguished lawyer, president of Columbia College, framer of the Constitution, and United States Senator could have been intended to allay any doubts about the pledge of honor given by Hamilton in April, a pledge that had resulted thus far only in a vague and noncommittal response.

Hamilton, who began the conversation with Beckwith "as from one gentleman to an other" because he thought he might not have the possibility of making such an explanation thereafter, moved on to the next step as if no shadow had been cast over the pledge:

> If it shall be judged proper to proceed in this business by the sending or appointing a proper person to come to this country to negotiate on the spot, [he told Beckwith] whoever shall then be our Secretary of State, will be the person in whose department such negotiation must originate, and he will be the channel of communication with the President; in the turn of such affairs the most minute circumstances, mere trifles, give a favorable bias or otherwise to the whole. The President's mind I can declare to be perfectly dispassionate on this subject. Mr. Jefferson our present Secretary of State is I am persuaded a gentleman of honor, and zealously desirous of promoting those objects, which the nature of his duty calls for, and the interests of his country may require, but from some opinions which he has given respecting Your government, and possible predilections elsewhere, there may be difficulties which may possibly frustrate the whole, and which might be readily explained away. I shall certainly know the progress of the negotiation from the president from day to day, but what I come to the present explanation for is this, that in case any such difficulties should occur, I should wish to know them, in order that I may be sure they are clearly understood, and candidly examined, if none takes place the business will of course go on in the regular official channel.

[107] Beckwith's report, enclosed in Dorchester to Grenville, 25 Sep. 1790, PRO: CO 42/69, f. 14, 16-25.

Beckwith replied that he could not say what his government might do about this, that—"You may depend on it"—he would make proper use of what had been said, and that this would never be revealed by him in a way to create "an impression different from the causes which occasioned it."[108] None of this, of course, was reported to Washington.

Thus the pledge from one gentleman to another, meeting on the middle ground between their respective obligations. The meaning of this extraordinary exchange between a high official of one nation and the secret envoy of another has been assessed by one of the most sympathetic biographers of Alexander Hamilton, quite accurately, in these words: "In effect, Hamilton was proposing to aid the representative of a foreign power in counteracting the policies of the Secretary of State."[109] This was no new or sudden proposal. It was implicit in every move that the Secretary of the Treasury had made since he entered the discussions with Beckwith in the autumn of 1789. It was also far from being the last of such efforts.

IV

The first and most essential requirement of a foreign policy is that it be coherent and consistent. For in discourse between one nation and and another, that speaking with a forked tongue—to employ the metaphor arising out of the simple wisdom of the American Indians in their forest diplomacy—inevitably discounts its own credibility. The cabinet of England, though marked differences of opinion existed within it, nevertheless spoke with a single voice in its relations with the United States. The American Secretary of State in his conduct of foreign policy stood on wholly different ground. He possessed no such system of intelligence as that available to the British ministry, had no funds available for the procurement of information or influence, and was unsustained by any trans-Atlantic bonds of interest, consanguinity, and loyalty reaching into the executive and legislative branches of the British government. Worse, he suffered the crippling handicap of the secret discussions that would continue long beyond that one forced momentarily into the open by the threat of war. It was not until the appoint-

---

[108] Beckwith's report, marked "Secret," undated, enclosed in Dorchester to Grenville, 25 Sep. 1789, PRO: CO 42/69, f. 14, 27-8. While this is a separate enclosure added to the longer report of conversations with Hamilton and others as described in notes 102, 104, and 107, there is no reason to suppose that it took place at a date other than that on which Hamilton had suggested the transfer of negotiations to America. Syrett, *Hamilton*, VI, 497, assigns the date 15 July 1790 to this separate memorandum and there can be little doubt that, as the opening sentence indicates, this was a continuation of the remarks that Hamilton failed to report to Washington. Beckwith's separating this part of the interview from that in the main body of his report can be explained on three grounds. First, its great importance: as a means of protecting British interests in case formal negotiations took place, this would have given the British minister to the United States a powerful advantage over the Secretary of State. Second, the substance was entirely confidential, hence the designation "Secret," not ordinarily given to other dispatches. Third, in assuring Hamilton he might depend upon proper use being made of this astonishing request, Beckwith may have meant he would make a separate report so that Grenville in the Home Office might at once forward it to Leeds in the Foreign Office, within whose jurisdiction such a matter lay.

[109] Miller, *Hamilton*, p. 368.

ment of George Hammond as minister that Jefferson, through formal negotiation, possessed the means of verification and thus could begin to guess with some accuracy—but never with full knowledge—at the extent to which cabinet councils were placed at the disposal of those with whom it was his duty to negotiate. He could not even guess at the degree to which his own policies were in similar manner discounted by his colleague. The British minister, who promptly became the confidant that Hamilton desired him to be, felt some annoyance because the Secretary of State insisted on conducting the discussions in writing. But the betrayal of secrets began long before Jefferson suspected that written diplomatic discourse—for him a natural mode of doing any business— was also a necessary precaution. The most profound secret of the administration and the first to be violated was that involving Jefferson's overture to Spain.

If, as Jefferson and many others believed at the time, war was almost inevitable, there was no question but that neutrality was to be the policy of the United States. Jefferson himself was the first to hint at such a policy, doing so in a manner to insure its being communicated to the British ministry.[110] But this was far from being a mere passive position as he conceived it. In his formal proposal of the policy he looked to the possible independence of Louisiana and the Floridas, suggested the approach to Madrid, and gave an intimation of how close to war he was prepared to go in order to achieve two paramount objectives, the preservation of a balance of power among neighbors and the opening of the Mississippi to navigation—an intimation that Jefferson thought prudent to make much softer in the final than in the first draft.[111] By the beginning of August it was clear that the President had given full support to the course suggested by Jefferson. Washington's letters to Rochambeau, La Luzerne, and others that David Humphreys carried with him when he departed on the mission to Spain made no allusion to that purpose, but the one to Lafayette was a perfect reflection of sentiments Jefferson had expressed long before the war crisis arose:[112]

It seems to be our policy to keep in the situation in which nature has placed us, to observe a strict neutrality, and to furnish others with those good things of subsistence, which they may want, and which our fertile land abundantly produces, if circumstances and events will permit us to do so. This letter is committed to Colonel Humphreys to carry to London, whither he is going. Should he, by any accident be in France, he will be able to give you a full state of our affairs and prospects. Gradually recovering from the distresses in which the war left us, patiently advancing in our task of civil government, unentangled in the crooked politics of Europe, wanting scarcely any thing but the free navigation of the Mississipi (which we must have and as certainly shall have as we remain a Nation) I have supposed, that, with the undeviating exercise of a just, steady, and

[110] TJ to Benjamin Vaughan, 27 June 1790, note.
[111] See Document I, below.
[112] Washington to Lafayette, 11 Aug. 1790; *Writings*, ed. Fitzpatrick, XXXI, 85-8. On the letters carried by Humphreys, see notes to Document VII below.

prudent national policy, we shall be the gainers, whether the powers of the old world may be in peace or war, but more especially in the latter case. In that case our importance will certainly increase, and our friendship be courted. Our dispositions would not be indifferent to Britain or Spain. Why will not Spain be wise and liberal at once? It would be easy to annihilate all causes of quarrels between that Nation and the United States at this time. At a future period that may be far from being a fact. Should a war take place between Great Britain and Spain, I conceive from a great variety of concurring circumstances there is the highest probability that the Floridas will soon be in the possession of the former. . . . P.S. Not for the value of the thing, my dear Marquis, but as a memorial and because they are the manufacture of the City, I send you herewith a pair of shoe buckles.

There can be no doubt that on all essential points Washington and Jefferson were in firm agreement. Even the language, the use of Lafayette as a channel of communication, the hint at the progress of local manufactures—all reflect views and methods of the Secretary of State. William Samuel Johnson told Beckwith about this time that Jefferson was "thought to be in great favor with the President," but neither he nor Hamilton could have looked with enthusiasm upon Jefferson's approach to Spain. The annihilation of all quarrels with that power would have been a serious blow to Hamilton's efforts of the preceding year.

This aspect of the policy was shrouded in profound secrecy. The selection of Humphreys was clearly that of the President, who had a confidence in the young aide that the Secretary of State could not have fully shared. Only five persons in the government were supposed to be privy to the mission to Madrid aside from the envoy himself—the President, the Secretary of State, the Secretary of the Treasury, and two members of Congress long active in the Mississippi problem: James Madison of Virginia and John Brown of Kentucky. Even Gouverneur Morris and William Short, the two representatives abroad, were not informed of it in the instructions given them. Humphreys' letter to Jefferson late in July shows that the need for keeping this secrecy inviolate had been impressed upon him:[113]

Upon finding that the Packet would sail sooner than I had expected, I hastened to make the necessary arrangements for my departure. Apprehensive, however, that I may be too much pressed for time, to have opportunities of acquiring, in conversation, as much information as could have been desired on the different subjects which will claim attention, I shall be extremely happy to have the deficiency supplied by such written Notes as Mr. Madison, Mr. Brown and yourself may think proper to give. The best possible care will be taken of all secret papers, as well as of the Cyphers which shall be committed to me for my use, and for the Consul or Agent who may be

[113] Humphreys to TJ, dated at "Mrs. Haviland's Tavern," Rye, 31 July 1790; RC in DNA: RG 59, DD, endorsed by TJ as received 1 Aug. 1790 and so recorded in SJL; on the treaty with Portugal, signed but not ratified, see Vol. 9: 410-33.

employed in London.—I beg leave to suggest whether a Copy of the Treaty as signed on our part with Portugal, together with any observations which may have since occurred, will not be requisite for me.—It is my intention to be in New York on Tuesday night if practicable.

The language of this letter suggests that Humphreys must have regarded himself as the personal representative of the President, somewhat in the capacity of aide-de-camp in which he had so long served, and that he therefore considered himself free to discuss the mission with all who knew of it. But Humphreys' instructions, which ignored the suggestions while urging secrecy, came from the Secretary of State, as was proper. While Jefferson had directed him to depart by the first convenient vessel, the knowledge that he intended to go in the English packet must have raised some doubts about security. Whether this was the cause or not, passage was engaged for him on another vessel, said to be a swift sailer but "not . . . a very safe one." That vessel was also British-owned, and before embarking Humphreys consulted both "the Secretaries of the States and the Treasury in order to learn what they would wish to have done" with their secret papers in case of war and capture.[114] Benjamin Walker, another close friend and former aide of the President, was the person consulted about the vessel and the fact that he also embarked at this time suggests that Washington—who was well experienced in the methods of secret intelligence—may have urged him to make the trip as protective cover for Humphreys' mission. For it is remarkable that Walker suddenly chose this moment to ask his superior, the Secretary of the Treasury, for leave of absence from his post as naval officer of the district of New York in order that he might go to England. Whether intended or not, this move and the personal reason advanced for its being undertaken became known at once to Beckwith and were promptly reported to Dorchester: "Colonel Walker who was an Aid de Camp to General Washington during the war, has lately sailed from hence to London; this gentleman . . . is by birth an Englishman, although he has been many years here, and his father, who is a brewer near Knight's bridge has pressed him greatly for some years to pay him a visit, to which he has at length consented; whether Mr. Walker has any thing in charge of a public nature I do not know, but he has always been on the best terms with the President."[115] There is no evidence to show how Beckwith became possessed of these details, but Walker had stated his reasons to his superior in asking leave, Hamilton had referred them to the President for his decision, knowing that such absences were contrary to general policy,

[114] Humphreys to Washington, 1 Sep. 1790, Humphreys, *Humphreys*, II, 25-7.
[115] Beckwith's reports, received at Quebec 27 and 30 Oct. 1790, enclosed in Dorchester to Grenville, 10 Nov. 1790, PRO: CO 42/72, f. 59-60, 61-8, 69-72; Hamilton to Washington, 28 Aug. 1790, and Lear's response, same date, Syrett, *Hamilton*, VI, 575, 577-8. It later developed that, in addition to the personal reasons of the nature stated, Walker was engaged by William Duer to look into the affairs of the Scioto Company in England; Walker to Hamilton, 28 Dec. 1790, same, VII, 388-9.

and Washington had referred them back to the Secretary of the Treasury.

The extraordinary precautions taken to protect the secrecy of Humphreys' mission are also reflected in the arrangements for the necessary funds. On 14 Aug. 1790 Jefferson wrote Hamilton:[116]

Colonel Humphreys will be entitled to draw from the Treasury of the United States from about this date till further order, at the rate of two thousand two hundred and fifty dollars, a year, and in addition to this a sum for postage of letters, the amount of which cannot be known beforehand, and will not be considerable. This is to be charged to the fund of the foreign department. I must ask the favour of you to let him know in what manner he can receive this money in the several situations he will be in. I think he ought to receive the full sum, and to have nothing to do with the loss or gain of exchange, charges of negociating &c.

Hamilton replied the same day:[117]

I enclose you a warrant for 500 Dollars for Col. Humphreys use; and shall for the present take arrangements for paying his salary or allowance by a Credit on our Commissioners in Holland. Hereafter we will endeavour to put this matter upon some more convenient footing.—I draw in your favour to avoid introducing Col. Humphreys into the books of the Treasury, which would excite more conjecture than is perhaps desireable in the outset considering the nature of his mission. I hope this will be agreeable to you.

On obtaining this sum, Jefferson made the following note in his personal Account Book: "received by warrant from the Treasury 500 Dollars, which I paid immediately to Colo. Humphreys for a public purpose known to the President, Colo. Hamilton, Mr. Madison and Mr. Brown, not to be entered in my private account as it no ways concerns me but as minister for the foreign department."[118]

Such precautions are understandable and Hamilton's expressed desire to avoid public conjecture could be accepted as genuine were it not belied by an extraordinary move that he made just before Humphreys departed. That move, unknown to the President and the Secretary of State, would have had the effect almost of a guarantee that the public character if not the nature of Humphrey's mission would become known to the British ministry. It was, however, only one more characteristic step in the studied invasion of the domain of the Secretary of State that had begun with Jefferson's appointment. It can best be understood against

[116] FC in DNA: RG 59, PCC No. 120.

[117] RC in DLC, endorsed as received 14 Aug. 1790 and so recorded in SJL. The warrant was actually received by Remsen in TJ's name and converted into money, which Remsen gave to TJ and he in turn issued a receipt for it; MS in TJ's hand, DLC: TJ Papers, 57: 9707, dated 14 Aug. 1790; the letter of credit for $2,500 per year drawn on Wilhem & Jan Willink, N. & J. Van Staphorst & Hubbard was sent by Hamilton to Humphreys the same day; Syrett, *Hamilton*, VI, 557-8.

[118] Account Book under 14 Aug. 1790, MHi.

the background of public attitudes which seemed to make Jefferson's proposed policy of neutrality virtually impossible of fulfillment in the event of war between England and Spain.

Beckwith, other secret agents, and the British consuls in America were almost unanimous in their reports of the national mood. "In as far as I can judge at present of the general disposition of this country," Beckwith reported, "it is by no means favorable to a Spanish interest. The bias of mercantile and seafaring men, both here and to the east-ward, appears to me to be evidently in our scale, and there are symp-toms of a privateering spirit, which may be readily brought forward in the event of a Spanish war." From a member of Congress Beckwith learned that many in the West looked to the "probable dismemberment of the Spanish Monarchy" as hastening forward an event theretofore considered as remote. "Your possessing New Orleans," this representa-tive from Western Pennsylvania declared, "we think an object of great consequence both to You and to Us, and we feel deeply interested in the event. . . . We think the present moment peculiarly favorable for you, and we are capable of great exertions at this time, from the military spirit, which every country possesses at the close of a civil war, and from the number of officers, who, having acquired military habits, are anxiously desirous of service; of these there are some of high rank, and I am strongly inclined to think, that General Knox, our Secretary at War, would be eager to promote any system of national friendship with you, both from his general turn of thinking, and from his passion for military command. If such a plan should be followed up he would be a proper man to command a body of troops to clear away the Spanish Posts on the upper part of the Mississippi, whilst you should attack New Orleans, and this effected, to conduct an Army, to be formed in the Western country, by land from thence into Spanish America; we think such an undertaking very practicable."[119]

This remarkable language was similar to what had been coming to Dorchester from Kentucky for the past year or two, coupled with re-ports of a growing inclination among the people of that region "to de-clare Independence of the Federal Union, take possession at New Or-leans, and look to Great Britain for such assistance as might enable them to accomplish these designs."[120] Such language had made a deep im-pression on Grenville and now during the summer and fall of 1790 a succession of dispatches came from the secret agent Peter Allaire, por-traying Louisiana and the Floridas as a vast granary filled with resources that would make it a new and greater East Indies, ripe for the harvest. From five to seven thousand men on the Western waters, he declared,

[119] Beckwith's report, enclosed in Dorchester to Grenville, 25 Sep. 1790, PRO: CO 42/69, f. 14, 16-25. The member of Congress is identified in Beckwith's cipher key as "14. Mr. Scott, Member of House of Representatives from Counties West of Allegheny Mountains." This was Thomas Scott (1739-1796) of Wash-ington county, Pennsylvania, a lawyer and member of the Pennsylvania ratifying convention of 1787 (*Biog. Dir. Cong.*).

[120] Dorchester to Sydney, 11 Apr. 1789, PRO: CO 42/64, f. 152-5; same to same, 7 June 1789, CO 42/65, f. 10-13, "Secret"; Grenville to Dorchester, 20 Oct. 1789, CO 42/65, f. 193-6, "Secret."

"would assist any nation" to dispossess the Spaniards on condition of being given free navigation of the Mississippi. "It is now in your power," Allaire wrote to the ministry at the height of the war crisis, ". . . to bind us in Adamantine Chains of Friendship and Alliance with you. Take the Floridas, Open a free Navigation of the Mississippi for the Western Inhabitants, and you bind that Country and its inhabitants for Ever in spite of Congress and all the world."[121] The men from the West would join in the enterprise to recover the Floridas, he wrote in another dispatch, "not by Order consent or Approbation of the United States, but by those who Acknowledge Allegiance to NONE. Men hardy, inured to fatigue and danger, expert woodsmen, who live by hunting and who . . . Above all . . . Want Employ being most of them destitute of Clothes and Money."[122] The prospect was a tempting one, for by this

[121] "Occurrences" (the form in which Allaire sent his reports) from 5 July to 3 Aug. 1790, PRO: FO 4/8, f. 284. In this dispatch Allaire also reported: "You may Rest Assured nothing can be done with this Government at present. No Offer would tempt them at present to Enter into a War."

The identity of Peter Allaire has been confused even by such able scholars as Frederick Jackson Turner and Samuel Flagg Bemis, both of whom regarded the name as a pseudonym for an unknown secret agent and the former thought that the initials "R.D." were also pseudonymous (Turner, AHR, VII, 716; Bemis, *Jay's Treaty*, p. 98, n. 20). The fact is that Peter Allaire (1740-1820) was a respected New York merchant who belonged to the well-known Huguenot family of that name and whose ancestor, Alexander Allaire, had settled at New Rochelle late in the 17th century. Allaire was employed by the British secret intelligence during the Revolution but, while he was known to Franklin in Paris, he failed to gain Franklin's confidence in the way that Edward Bancroft had. After the war he engaged in trade in New York City, and on occasion accepted members of Congress as boarders —among them David Ramsay and Richard Henry Lee. He was also involved in trade with the West Indies. He was a friend of Sir George Yonge and it was through Yonge's influence that Allaire was engaged to report American intelligence, for which he was paid £200 sterling per annum. There is no mystery about the manner in which his reports of "Occurrences" came to the attention of Grenville and Pitt. All save a few reports to Dorchester were sent to the Foreign Office through Yonge, with whom Allaire was engaged in land speculation in the Champlain valley, and were delivered by the agent himself to the captain of the British packet boats. Communications to him were received in the same manner and were addressed to "P. Arlington"—the only pseudonym Allaire is known to have used (the initials that Turner read as "R. D." were Allaire's monogram "PA"). The agent's best guarantee of security was his own respected name. He knew, and often commented upon, Sir John Temple, Phineas Bond, and Beckwith, but he did not disclose himself as an intelligence agent to any of these. The identity of Allaire is derived from the following sources and from a comparison of the distinctive handwriting in the dispatches with his own authentic letters, though most of the facts about him are to be drawn from his own reports: Robert Bolton, *History . . . of the County of Westchester* (New York, 1905), I, 677-9; "The Narrative of Peter Allaire written in the Bastile," George G. Wood, ed., *Now and Then* (Muncy, Pennsylvania), VIII (April, 1948), p. 297-305; letters to Franklin concerning the imprisonment in the Bastile are in the Franklin Papers in the American Philosophical Society.

A more extended account of Allaire, to be published in a volume containing the texts of his important dispatches as well as those of Edward Bancroft and George Beckwith, is in preparation by the Editor.

[122] "Occurrences" from 6 Aug. to 1 Sep. 1790, PRO: FO 4/8, f. 307; same 4 Sep. to 7 Oct. 1790, FO 4/8, f. 409; same 1 Dec. 1790 to 6 Jan. 1791, FO 4/9, f. 50-3. Some of the principal people in North Carolina later authorized John Hamilton, British consul at Norfolk and formerly a wealthy Loyalist of that state,

one stroke the ministry could look to the encirclement of the Atlantic states by unbroken possessions running from the Gulf of St. Lawrence to the tip of Florida and could behold the promise of lumber and provisions for the British West Indies, that source of clamorous cries to Parliament and the ultimate target of American statesmen who spoke of infallible instruments of commercial retaliation.[123] Pitt, like Grenville the year before, was deeply impressed and gave orders that Allaire be encouraged to continue his reports on the possibility of repossessing the "*Southern Farms.*"

It is not surprising, therefore, that when the member of Congress from western Pennsylvania unfolded the object of great consequence both for Britain and the United States, Beckwith should have decided that the time had come to make use of the discretionary power given him in Dorchester's secret instructions. "In case of a war with Spain," he replied, "I see no reason, why we should not assist in forwarding whatever your interests may require."[124] In this climate Jefferson's policy seemed all but reversed. He had urged that Beckwith be given a warning on the supposition that, if British councils were divided as to whether to mount an attack against Spanish territory adjacent to the United States, this might tip the scales by the "prospect of having an enemy the more or less, according to the object" the ministry should select. This was an essential element of the policy of making an overture to Spain, but it was almost cancelled out by the western Congressman who in effect altered it to mean "an ally the more or less"; by men in shipping and trade in the eastern states who caught visions of commerce opening up with South America; and by the continuing efforts on the part of Hamilton and members of the Senate to achieve a closer connection with England. With Washington's support and in the total absence of a Spanish interest except for purposes of bargaining, the policy of neutrality was not difficult to endorse by those who leaned toward Great Britain. Even William Samuel Johnson told Beckwith that he thought the United States should remain neutral, but, he added, "whether this will be our conduct I really do not know."[125]

Hamilton did not openly oppose the approach to Madrid, but he used the opportunity to allay Washington's fears of a British overland expedition against Spanish possessions—and also to reassure Beckwith. In the report that Washington required him to make of the second interview with the British agent, Hamilton stated that "Something was said respecting the probable course of military operations in case of war between Britain and Spain" and that "Major Beckwith supposed

to say to Leeds "that if Hostilities had, or should commence between Great Britain and Spain . . . Twenty thousand men could be easily raised in the service of Great Britain to act against the Spaniards, under proper Authority and encouragement from the Court of Great Britain"; Hamilton to Leeds, 25 May 1791, PRO: FO 4/10, f. 63-6.

[123] See enclosure, Document I, concluding section.

[124] Dorchester to Beckwith, 27 June 1790, "*Secret,*" PRO: CO 42/68, f. 258-60; text in Brymner, *Report*, 1890, p. 144.

[125] Beckwith's report, enclosed in Dorchester to Grenville, 25 Sep. 1790, PRO: CO 42/69, f. 14, 16-25.

[these] would be directed towards South America alleging however that this was mere conjecture on his part." There are valid reasons for concluding that Beckwith did not make this conjecture, quite aside from the fact that, having proved himself an unreliable reporter on the central object of the discussions, Hamilton thereby drew a veil of doubt over all unverifiable matters in his account. First, he knew that Beckwith's opinion about strategy could not be discounted as the supposition of a junior officer: it would be assessed by Washington as the view of one who had served through years of confidential relationship with the commander-in-chief of the British forces in America—of a commander who, on the authority of Hamilton's own reports, was assumed to be privy to the aims of the ministry as these had been shaped by the crisis. Second, Beckwith scarcely needed the ideas advanced by the member of Congress from western Pennsylvania to be aware that, whatever else might be contemplated, an overland expedition was assuredly in the realm of probability. Third, it is scarcely plausible to assume that so seasoned an officer of military intelligence would have volunteered his opinion of future military objectives to an official of a recent and potential enemy of his nation—unless to mislead. Finally, there is no mention in Beckwith's reports of his discussion of military strategy with Hamilton. It seems safe to conclude that, knowing how deeply the President feared a British attack on New Orleans, Hamilton could not have been unaware that a supposition of operations directed at South America, coming from a source so close to Dorchester, was one calculated to allay apprehensions and that he included it in the report for that reason.

In the same vein Hamilton said that he "hinted cautiously our dislike of an enterprise on New Orleans." This assertion is also suspect. If uttered at all, it was very far indeed from being the grave warning suggested by Jefferson that England might have an enemy the more or less according to the object chosen for attack. If expressed at all, the hint found its place in the following summation made by Beckwith of American attitudes:[126]

In case of a rupture with Spain the probable effect, which such an event may produce upon the navigation of the Mississippi attracts the very particular attention of this government, and excites the notice of all orders of people; our power to take possession of New Orleans, and to retain it, is not doubted, but the consequences of this measure are considered to be of the first importance. If the fate of war should give us possession of New Orleans, its vicinity to the West India Islands, the immense resources of the countries on the Western waters in lumber, naval stores, hemp, flour, tobacco, and other exports are contemplated as forming a competition with the Atlantic States, as having a direct tendency to accelerate the population and wealth of the former at the expense of the latter, and as the laying an immediate foundation for a rivalship.

The "consequences . . . of the first importance" comport with the ideas

[126] Same.

of the western member of Congress and with the plan of Allaire for repossessing the *"Southern Farms"* quite as well as they do with a supposed hint of dislike conveyed by Hamilton. It is possible, however, that Hamilton did hint at the danger of dismemberment of the union for fear a hostile move against Spanish possessions would drive the administration closer to an accommodation with Spain and thus endanger his long-laid plans for a commercial treaty with England. But this was far more than a cautious softening of the position advocated by the Secretary of State.

It must be noted in this passage that someone in office had informed Beckwith of the "very particular attention" being given by government to the Mississippi Question. This, in the context, could scarcely relate to the interest excited in "all orders of people" or to the expressions of the member of Congress: it must have alluded to the concern of the administration, not of the Congress that was about to adjourn. If so, the statement could only refer to the cabinet discussions late in July leading up to the decision to send Humphreys to Spain, and in that case the information must have come from one of the five persons who were privy to the profound secret. Four of these—Washington, Jefferson, Madison, and Brown—may be dismissed at once as the probable source of Beckwith's information. None had ever had an interview with the agent except for the President's brief exchange of pleasantries with him. Even so, it is implausible to suppose that the Secretary of State who originated the plan, or the President and the two members of Congress who supported it, would have unveiled the discussions to that nation against which it had been thought necessary to erect a barrier of utmost secrecy and of which Beckwith was a known agent. The supposition that it was Hamilton who must have revealed the direction in which the attention of the administration was being focused is supported by Hamilton's later conversations with Beckwith and by the latter's comment on the attitude of the administration.

In July Hamilton had assured the British agent that the United States was "perfectly unconnected with Spain," had some points unadjusted with that nation, and was "prepared to go into the consideration of the subject."[127] By late September, after Humphreys had departed, Beckwith again summarized American attitudes and found his previous report confirmed:[128]

> The inhabitants of the Western country wish New Orleans to be in our possession, as the best means of getting a good price for their productions.—The Atlantic people in general wish the navigation to remain closed, from the dread of a rivalship, especially in the West India market.—The Executive Government are anxious to possess it themselves, in order to connect and consolidate both sides of the Allegany Mountains, knowing that although the western exports must issue from the Mississippi, their imports will to a certainty

[127] Same.
[128] Beckwith's report, before 30 Sep. 1790, enclosed in Dorchester to Grenville, 10 Nov. 1790, PRO: CO 42/72, f. 61-8, 69-72.

be conveyed through the Atlantic States. The free navigation of this river, whether to have been secured by the possession of New Orleans, or by the erection of a post in a preferable situation, was I am convinced the boon of all others the most likely to have induced the States to have taken an active part against Spain. They do not wish for a West India island at this time, sensible that they have no marine to protect it; these remarks apply to the executive government.

There can be no doubt that these remarks about administration views came from Hamilton. In the same memorandum in which they are recorded Beckwith quoted the Secretary of the Treasury as saying:[129]

We look forward to procuring the means of an export for our western country, and we must have it. We cannot suffer the navigation of the Mississippi to remain long in its present state. That country is at this moment ready to open it if they met with the smallest encouragement, and undoubtedly we look forward to the possession of New Orleans.

This was said after Hamilton had assured Beckwith the United States had no desire for a West India island and had no wish to extend its territories in the north beyond the existing boundaries, *"with an exception to the Forts."* In an interview taking place presumably soon thereafter, Hamilton returned to the theme:[130]

You have considerable American and West India possessions, our friendship or enmity may soon become important with respect to their security, and I cannot foresee any solid grounds of national difference, between us; I do not think the posts are to be considered in this light, and we have no desire to possess any thing to the northward of our present boundaries as regulated by the peace; but the navigation of the river Mississippi we must have, and shortly, and I do not think the bare navigation will be sufficient, we must be able to secure it by having a post at the mouth of the river, either at New Orleans, or some where near it; there are reports, that the Spanish Government are disposed to change their system, but this I doubt, for it is so different from their national character.

You know we have two parties with us; there are gentlemen, who think we ought to be connected with France in the most intimate terms, and that the Bourbon compact furnishes an example for us to follow; there are others who are at least as numerous, and influential, who decidedly prefer an English connexion, but *the present condition of Great Britain and the States is favorable to the former party*, and they are zealous to improve it; the present therefore is the moment to take up the matter seriously and dispassionately, and I wish it done without loss of time.

We consider ourselves perfectly at liberty to act with respect to Spain in any way most conducive to our interests, even to the going to war with that power, if we shall think it advisable to join You.

Thus did Hamilton seize upon Jefferson's idea, including that of

[129] Italics supplied.   [130] Italics supplied.

having a post at the mouth of the Mississippi to keep navigation open, in order to move as expeditiously as the Secretary of State was moving —but in the opposite direction and for different purposes, offering not an honorable neutrality in exchange for a pledge against aggression but a hint of alliance in order to achieve this great national interest. This was more delicately phrased than the language held out by the member of Congress from western Pennsylvania but its substance was the same. Accompanied by a glowing picture of the way in which English commercial capital and American agricultural production could operate in a harmonious and mutually advantageous exchange of produce and manufactures, this suggestion of a policy that would counterbalance conditions favorable to those who wished to move the United States to a closer connection with France was also accompanied by a subtle intimation: the nation was perfectly free to come to any arrangement with Spain that its interests—the sole guide for the intercourse of nations, Hamilton had told Beckwith—might suggest. In brief, the example furnished by the Bourbon compact might be followed. Outwardly identical with the effort of the administration to obtain free navigation of the Mississippi, Hamilton's clandestine manoeuver was in fact aimed at the defeat of the Spanish mission. None of this was disclosed, naturally enough, in a letter written by Hamilton to the President about this interview. That letter, besides misrepresenting the conversation, was intended to discredit the man whom Hamilton had recommended as the President's envoy to London.

According to Beckwith, Hamilton opened their interview late in September with an expression of disapproval of Gouverneur Morris' conduct. He confessed that the Duke of Leeds' reply to Morris' first application had not led him to think favorably of the prospect. But the June packet had brought news of the interview with Pitt. "From [Morris'] own detail of what passed," Hamilton said, "there was something in his conduct on that occasion, which I confess I do not altogether approve." Beckwith then asked if Morris had been out of England, perhaps to France. To this Hamilton replied:[131]

> Not that I know of, and if [Morris] has cultivated an intimacy with the Ministers of any other power in Europe, or has caused suspicion on that ground with respect to France, or elsewhere, he has had no authority, for so doing; it occurs to me, that he was very intimate with Monsr. de La Luzerne the Ambassador of France now in London, when he was Minister in this country, possibly from that circumstance he may have been more frequently there, than prudence ought to have dictated, and the knowledge of this circumstance may have produced a greater reserve on the part of Your administration; *these ideas strike me, although I have no grounds to go upon.*

The conversation then turned to the navigation of the Mississippi, after which Beckwith, pointing out that he had always preserved the

131 Italics supplied. Beckwith's report, ca. 25-30 Sep. 1790, enclosed in Dorchester to Grenville, 10 Nov. 1790, PRO: CO 42/72, f. 61-8, 69-72; see Syrett, *Hamilton*, VII, 70.

strictest silence respecting Morris, said that he had heard it said among Morris' relations and others that he had been frequently with La Luzerne and with Charles James Fox. Hamilton admitted that this had been reported and that he believed it in some measure to be true, the more so from extracts he had seen of Morris' letters. He added: "I do not question this gentleman's sincerity in following up those objects committed to his charge, but to deal frankly with You, I have some doubts of his prudence; this is the point in which he is deficient, for in other respects he is a man of great genius, liable however to be occasionally influenced by his fancy, which sometimes outruns his discretion." Beckwith then reported himself as paying tribute to La Luzerne and Fox, after which he added: "it is for Your consideration, how far a gentleman in [Morris'] situation ought to form intimacies with persons in public political situations, excepting they are in administration." Far from taking umbrage at a suggestion about a relationship much less improper than the one in which he and Beckwith were engaged, Hamilton responded: "I am quite of Your opinion, and this amongst other causes led me to remark, that it is greatly desirable, that this negotiation should be transferred to our seat of Government."

Hamilton's letter to Washington about this interview stands in flat contradiction to what Beckwith reported, both as to the nature of the conversation and as to its object. He had lately had a visit "from a *certain Gentleman*," Hamilton wrote, "the sole object of which was to make some observations of a delicate nature, concerning *another Gentleman* employed on a *particular errand*; which, as they were doubtless intended for your ear, and (such as they are) ought to be known to you, it is of course my duty to communicate."[132] Hamilton added:

He began (in a manner somewhat embarrassed which betrayed rather more than he seemed to intend to discover) by telling me that in *different companies* where he had happened to be, *in this City* (a circumstance by the way very unlikely) he had heared it mentioned that that *other Gentleman* was upon terms of very great intimacy with the representative of a certain Court at the one where *he* was employed and with the head of the party opposed to the Minister; and he proceeded to say, that if there were any symptoms of backwardness or coolness in the Minister, it had occurred to him that they might possibly be occasioned by such *an intimacy*; that he had no intimation however of this being the case, and that the idea suggested by him was mere matter of conjecture; that he did not even know it as a fact that the intimacy subsisted. But if this should be the case (said he) you will readily imagine that it cannot be calculated to inspire confidence or facilitate free communication. It would not be surprising, if a very close connection with the representative of another power should beget doubts and reserves; or if a very familiar intercourse with the head of the opposition should occasion prejudice and distance. Man, after all, is but man; and though the

---

[132] Hamilton to Washington, 30 Sep. 1790, Syrett, *Hamilton*, VII, 84-5.

Minister has a great mind, and is as little likely as most men to entertain distrusts or jealousies; yet there is no saying what might be the effect of such conduct upon him. It is hardly possible not to have some diffidence of those, who seem to be very closely united with our political or personal enemies or rivals. At any rate, such an intimacy, if it exists, can do no good, may do some harm.

Such, Hamilton reported to the President, was the substance of what Beckwith had laid before him as "the sole object" of the visit. To this he told Washington that he had replied: "I have never heared a syllable, Sir, about the matter you mention. It appears to me however very possible that an intimacy with both persons you mention may exist." He explained, he said, that Morris and La Luzerne had been drawn by their situations into an intimacy while both were in America. To have avoided this in London "would not have been without difficulty, on the score of politeness, and would have worn an extraordinary and mysterious aspect." As for Morris' association with Charles James Fox, this was equally natural, arising "from a similarity of dispositions and characters; both brilliant men, men of wit and genius; both fond of the pleasures of society." According to his report, Hamilton then added: "It is to be hoped that appearances, which admit of so easy a solution will not prove an obstacle to any thing which mutual interest dictates. It is impossible that there can be any thing wrong.—He replied that he certainly had no idea there could be any thing wrong; but that as trifles often mar great affairs he thought it best to impart to me his conjecture, that such use might be made of it as should be thought adviseable."

These two accounts of the interview stand in such marked contrast and contradiction to each other that the discrepancy cannot be dismissed as the natural result of misconceptions, misunderstandings, or varying degrees of emphasis on the part of two different reporters, both interested. Clearly, one version or the other is a contrived and deliberate misrepresentation. There can be no doubt that Hamilton's report to Washington is unreliable and calculated to mislead both in its details and in its aim. It falls inexorably into the pattern of his secret relations with Beckwith of the preceding year. In effect what Hamilton did in this letter was exactly what he had done in misrepresenting the interview of the 8th of July: he put words in Beckwith's mouth in order to defend and support his own object. In both instances his aim was to offset the coolness that Washington and Jefferson—as well as Hamilton himself, of course—saw in the posture of the British cabinet. But in this most recent attempt he sought to place the blame for the ministry's aloofness upon Gouverneur Morris' supposed lack of tact and discretion, attributing to Beckwith sole responsibility for a charge that in reality was his own. Again, as in the July episode, he did so by basing this upon a supposed conjecture advanced by the British agent. Further, "the sole object" of the interview, far from being that attributed by Hamilton to Beckwith, was his own and was twofold: (1) to seize the moment of crisis as one in which to take up "seriously and dispassionately, and . . . without loss of time" the matter of a closer connection with England because circumstances favored those who thought the Bourbon compact an example to follow and these circumstances required a counterpoise; and (2) to transfer the negotiations to America where the Secretary of the Treasury himself could keep a close eye on them and have a hand in shaping them. It is scarcely necessary to add that both of these objects were fully disclosed to Beckwith and were withheld from the President, who was led to believe that the agent had sought the interview for the sole purpose of making delicate hints about Gouverneur Morris' conduct. Hamilton's letter can only be regarded as a contrived effort to discredit the agent of the President.

This misrepresentation gave rise to the generally accepted belief that the coolness of the ministry was in fact due in part to Gouverneur Morris' lack of tact and discretion.[133] But this supposition is grounded upon the assumption that Beckwith complained of Morris' friendly relations with the French ambassador and with the leader of the opposition, a complaint far less Beckwith's than Hamilton's and one arising from feelings of resentment in New York, not in London. In raising the question in the delicate manner he did, Beckwith was merely responding to Hamilton's observations and his report was not one of a complaint that he had registered but rather one of disappointment that had been expressed to him. There is no evidence that Dorchester or the ministry were affected in their attitudes by anything that Morris did or said, much less that they requested their agent to make observations about his conduct. That Hamilton made so much of so implausible and trivial a factor is an indication of the strength of his desire to counteract the mission to Spain.

Gouverneur Morris, brilliant and self-assured, possessed manners— as Madison had warned the President before the appointment was made —that produced unfavorable opinions of himself both "before . . . known, and where known." Like most foreign envoys, he also rendered accounts in his diplomatic dispatches that did no discredit to his own powers as a negotiator. Leeds and Pitt may well have been offended by some of his blunt rejoinders—if those rejoinders were in fact as blunt as Morris reported them to be. Even so, the general tenor of the negotiation was polite and amicable. The fact is that Morris was not enjoined to secrecy and he was not forbidden to reveal his mission to the French ambassador. It was quite natural that the latter should have made use of the information so as to suggest that France had prompted the move by Washington. This could scarcely have caused surprise either to Morris or to Leeds. Morris himself, indeed, had similar and no higher motives for making the disclosure, though his action has been called honorable but imprudent. Like La Luzerne, he was only engaged in gaining credit on flimsy grounds. He saw the French ambassador before he saw Leeds, though he called on the latter immediately on arrival in London and found him absent. "I communicated to the french Embassador *in Confidence*," Morris reported to Washington, "that you had directed me to call for a performance of the Treaty. He told me at once that they would not give up the Posts. Perhaps he may be right. I thought it best

---

[133] Bemis, *Jay's Treaty*, p. 68, 80, 84.

to make such Communication because the Thing itself cannot remain a Secret and by mentioning it to him we are enabled to say with Truth that in every Step relating to the Treaty of Peace we have acted confidentially in Regard to our Ally."[134] Morris at times may have been lacking in tact, but he was too much a man of the world, too experienced in Parisian court and diplomatic circles, to be naive. To reveal in the strictest confidence what he knew could not be kept secret was only an effort to enhance the value of a gesture toward an ally. La Luzerne no doubt penetrated the motive as clearly as he perceived the attitude of the ministry respecting the western posts.

As for Charles James Fox, there seems to be no more substance than this to the report being spread in New York and made pointed in Hamilton's letter to Washington. When Morris later learned of the allegation that the negotiations had been damaged by his indiscretions, he denied this and said that, having deliberately avoided opposition circles, he had dined with Fox only once. There is no reason to doubt this. He reported one of these meetings to Washington in words that could have given Hamilton concern if he had seen them. Morris stated that he dined in company with Fox on the 17th of April and then added:[135]

[134] Morris to Washington, 7 Apr. 1790; RC in DLC: Washington Papers. La Luzerne undoubtedly knew this even before Morris told him, for the latter had informed Montmorin of his mission "in the most perfect Confidence" before leaving Paris; Morris, *Diary*, ed. Davenport, I, 374, under 22 Jan. 1790—that is, immediately on receiving Washington's letter of 13 Oct. 1789.

[135] Morris to Washington, 2 May 1790, "Private"; RC in DLC: Washington Papers. Morris gave substantially the account that appears in his diary, though he omitted the response that he made to Fox about trade with the West Indies: "I tell him that [his] is a solid Principle of Policy, for that our Position renders the Islands so materially dependent on us that they should make it our Interest to keep them in Possession. That further, if we chuse to lay them under Disadvantages in our Ports we can materially injure their Navigation, whereas the Admission of our Vessels into their Islands can do them no Harm in that Respect. All this is true, but I suspect that we shall be obliged in America to give them the Conviction of their Senses"; Morris, *Diary*, ed. Davenport, I, 485-6. Morris learned of the rumors being spread about his mission from Washington himself in an extremely frank letter written two years later: "That in England you indiscreetly communicated the purport of your Mission in the first instance, to the Minister of France, at that Court, who availing himself in the same moment of the occasion, gave it the appearance of a movement through his Court. This, and other circumstances of a similar nature, added to a close intercourse with the opposition Members, occasioned distrust, and gave displeasure to the Ministry; *which was the cause, it is said, of that reserve which you experienced in negotiating the business which had been intrusted to you*"; Washington to Morris, 28 Jan. 1792, "(Private)," *Writings*, ed. Fitzpatrick, XXXI, 469 (emphasis supplied). These comments Washington presented as "the ideas of [Morris'] political adversaries." Since the letter in which they were couched was drafted by Jefferson himself, it is possible he may have suspected they were the result of rumors spread by Hamilton and perhaps others. Robert Morris was also informed that La Luzerne had rushed to tell Leeds what Gouverneur Morris had told him. The latter indignantly denied the charge, repeating to Robert Morris the substance of what he had said to Fox: "Seriously, my friend, the Obstacle to a Treaty was in the British Cabinet. . . . If you mean to make a good Treaty with Britain, support your pretensions with Spirit *and they will respect you for it*. You must give them *visible Reasons* because they will have *to justify their Conduct*: and it will not do to say to a House of Commons *the American Minister was such a charming Fellow that we could not resist him*. I rather think

The state of french Politics formed of course a large **Part of the** Conversation. The situation of other Countries was then passed in Review, and it became a Question how far Britain might be engaged in the Affairs of the Continent. At length I took an Opportunity to ask what System the Administration had adopted respecting America. He told me that he could not tell but believed they had none, and would in all Probability be governed by Events. That he did not believe Mr. Pitt would trouble his Head about the Matter, but would probably leave it to Lord Hawksbury and Mr. Grenville who are both of them indisposed to us whereas Pitt himself is he supposes rather friendly than otherwise. Mr. Fox said farther that he and Burke are now almost alone in their Opinion that we should be permitted to trade in our own Bottoms to their Islands, and that this Opinion loses Ground daily tho for his own Part he persists in it.— I find that the Ministers apply for Information respecting America, and particularly American Commerce to a Mr. Irwin who long resided in America and is now here in the Customs. A mighty Sour Sort of Creature and one who seems to have a mortal Aversion for us. I met him at Dinner one Day and he took Pains to let me know that he was doing all he could to prevent any Encouragement from being given to our Exports by the Corn Bill which is now on the Carpet. He declared that he would by the force of Starvation oblige the People of Britain to raise Corn enough for their own Consumption, and that even the Supply of the West India Islands ought to be provided in this Country.—You will readily perceive Sir from this rude sketch of influential Characters, that there is but little Disposition for treating with us at present.

Presumably Washington did not reveal this private letter to Hamilton, but the meeting with Fox was known in New York and given

---

it would be at least as good Ground to say *The American Legislature would have greatly injured our Navigation and Commerce if we had not by this Treaty have induced them to repeal their Laws, and there was Reason also to apprehend that the United States would connect themselves still more intimately with France, who for the Sake of such Connection would doubtless support them in their Claims as soon as the State of her domestic Affairs would permit her to look abroad"*; undated letter, Gouverneur Morris to Robert Morris, in Morris, *Diary,* ed. Davenport, I, 615-16 (italics in the original). Morris rarely found himself in agreement with Jefferson and Madison, but on this occasion he both negotiated and defended his conduct on precisely the principles that the Secretary of State had advocated.

It is a curious fact that the one time Morris dined with Charles James Fox was at the home of Alexander Hamilton's brother-in-law, John Barker Church. Indeed, as soon as Morris arrived in London, Church went off to seek Fox to have him meet Morris. A few days later Morris dined at Church's and noted that Fox could not be there that day. A week later he again dined at Church's and *promised* to meet Fox there at dinner the following Saturday. He did so on the 17th—the occasion he reported to Washington; Morris, *Diary,* I, 469, 472, 480, 485. Morris, denying the allegations as "totally false," later told Washington that he avoided going to Church's home solely because he wished to avoid meeting Fox; Morris to Washington, 10 Apr. 1792, same, I, 614-15. There can be no doubt that the allegations that Morris disposed of in these two brilliant letters arose from rumors employed if not originated by the man who had nominated him for the office, that is, the Secretary of the Treasury.

an interpretation by the Secretary of the Treasury that, so far as the evidence discloses, was never given it by the ministry. The growing restrictions of the British customs, the rising influence in the ministry of Grenville and particularly of Hawkesbury, the apparent justification of strict mercantilist doctrine by its fruits, the assurances received from America that a closer connection was desired by the British interest, that indeed an alliance might be sought to dispossess the Spaniards from New Orleans—these and other factors were the motivating forces of British policy, not the trivial one of Gouverneur Morris' diplomatic manners. In any case, the alleged protest by Beckwith came at the close of the mission, was made three thousand miles away, and could have had no effect whatever upon its outcome. Washington was no more deceived in September than he had been in July, though again he looked in the wrong direction for hidden motives. His reply of dismissal to the subject raised by Hamilton was one whose irony even the President himself could not have perceived. "The motives . . . by which the Author of the communication to you was actuated," he wrote Hamilton, "although they may have been pure and in that case praiseworthy, do also (but it may be uncharitable to harbour the suspicion) admit of a different interpretation and that by an easy and pretty direct clew."[136] Washington let the matter drop there, leaving Hamilton perhaps to speculate in some anxiety as to the nature of the clue to motives not pure or praiseworthy. The next clue came to the President shortly after this exchange, though the action initiating it took place some weeks earlier. It was indeed an "easy and pretty direct clew" and it should have caused Washington to search for motives in the right and unmistakable direction.

V

Jefferson's instructions to Gouverneur Morris of 12 Aug. 1790 were explicit. The offer of neutrality in return for pledges was not to be disclosed except in the event of war and after hostilities had begun. The instructions also included expressions approving Morris' conduct of the negotiations. The President had not only sanctioned the instructions thus drafted but, in replying to Morris' dispatches of April and May, he had said: "as far as your intercourse with the british ministry had then gone [permit me] to assure you of my entire approbation of your conduct."[137] An interval of more than three weeks elapsed between

---

[136] Washington to Hamilton, 10 Oct. 1790, "Private," *Writings*, ed. Fitzpatrick, XXXI, 131-2; Syrett, *Hamilton*, VII, 107-8. Conclusive proof that Hamilton opened the subject of Morris' alleged misconduct lies in the fact that, some months later, Beckwith himself reported this to Grenville as information presumably not known to the minister: "Without wishing to lessen in any shape, the consideration due to a gentleman in Mr. Morris's situation," he wrote, "it becomes my duty to apprize your Lordship, that an intimacy has long subsisted between him and Monsieur de la Luzerne, the French Ambassador, and it has been suggested to me from a respectable quarter here, that Mr. Morris at an early period disclosed to that Minister, the nature of his objects in England; in this undoubtedly I am liable to be misled, but I believe it to be true" (Beckwith to Grenville, 6 Apr. 1791, PRO: FO 4/12, f. 86-7).

[137] Washington to Morris, 7 July 1790, *Writings*, ed. Fitzpatrick, XXXI, 68. See Document VIII, below.

the date of these instructions and the time of Humphreys' departure during which Hamilton might have registered his disapproval of Morris' conduct had he chosen to do so. For a part of this time Jefferson and Humphreys were absent with Washington on the tour to Rhode Island, while Hamilton remained in New York. Even so, more than a week remained after their return in which Hamilton might have expressed his disagreement with the administration's position. That he did not do this is clear from his later report of what he supposedly said to Beckwith. For that report is flatly contradicted not only by Beckwith's statements but also by Hamilton's own act at this time. Instead of taking advantage of the interval available to him, Hamilton waited until both the President and the Secretary of State had left New York for Virginia. Both departed on the morning of the 30th of August. The very next day Humphreys was sought out by the Secretary of the Treasury. The envoy to Madrid simultaneously revealed this fact and his own ineptitude as a diplomat in a farewell letter to Washington:[138]

> Yesterday, I had two pretty long conversations with the Secretary of the Treasury, in the course of which the general interests of the U.S. were discussed, and the several contingencies that might take place between them and the different European Powers. I was glad to have an opportunity of becoming acquainted with his sentiments, and to have it in my power to compare his reasoning on some important points with that of other political Characters.

If Washington had any doubt about the meaning of the allusion to the discussion about the national interest and the comparison of Hamilton's views with those of other political characters, all ambiguity was removed by the astonishing revelation in Humphreys' next communication, written from London:[139]

> The night after you left New York Col. Hamilton in a very confidential conversation, expressed himself (though still he mentioned his high opinion of the talents and honor of the gentleman in question) not perfectly satisfied with the manner in which Mr. G[ouverneur] M[orris] had conducted the business entrusted to him with the Duke of Leeds, and he desired me, upon investigating the temper of the British administration with regard to the points in agitation between the United States and Great Britain to write you, or him, the result of my Information. This, in the absence of Mr. M[orris] and in the private character it is necesary for me to preserve I have found in a manner impossible, without exposing myself to be considered as a person at least some way or another, employed in political affairs.

What Beckwith quoted Hamilton as saying to him about Morris a few weeks after Humphreys sailed thus stands confirmed and Hamilton's report of that interview discredited by the innocent revelations of an inexperienced envoy. Not the least of the charges to which the Secretary of the Treasury exposed himself in this further act of decep-

---

[138] Humphreys to Washington, 1 Sep. 1790, Humphreys, *Humphreys*, II, 25-7.
[139] Humphreys to Washington, 31 Oct. 1790, same, II, 50-4, "(*Secret*)."

tion on the President and the Secretary of State is that of misjudging the instrument he had chosen—unless, as is possible, he deliberately made the secret approach to Humphreys because he knew him to be pliable, impressionable, and inept as the envoy of an administration whose policy and instructions to him left no ground whatever for ambiguity. Washington, who had already penetrated the effort to discredit Morris though without guessing its true origin in Hamilton's distortion of Beckwith's words and purpose, took the news of this attempt in characteristic silence.[140]

In urging Humphreys to undertake what Morris was officially authorized to do, Hamilton set in motion an operation that he must have known would result in the disclosure of the public character if not the exact nature of the mission to Spain, as even Humphreys himself belatedly realized. But there is no evidence that he otherwise violated the secrecy to which he was bound. In the same interview with Beckwith in which Hamilton urged so strongly that arrangements for a commercial treaty be pressed at that moment, the former reported to Dorchester: "It has been asserted here, that Colonel Humphries is gone to Europe to negotiate [the Holland loan]; it is on the other hand supposed that his objects are in England." Sir John Temple learned of the mission by accident or otherwise. "Since I finished my letter," he wrote to Leeds on 2 Sep. 1790, "I have casually learn'd that Colonel Humphreys (a distinguished favorite of General Washington) has taken passage in . . . a Merchant Ship bound for London in two or three days! His going it seems was intended to be a profound secret. This Gentleman was, first, Secretary to the Minister from these States to France . . . it is more than probable that he goes in some Diplomatic Character, if not to our Court, to France, Spain, or some other."[141] The "profound secret" was also known to French as well as British agents, as Humphreys found to his discomfort soon after arriving in London:[142]

---

[140] Washington to Humphreys, 16 Mch. 1791, *Writings*, ed. Fitzpatrick, XXXI, 241-2. Humphreys had said that Count Andriani had written things "monstrously absurd and ill founded—that the United States are divided into two factions, Mr. Jefferson and the northern [thus in MS] States in favour of France, the southern [thus in MS] States and New York in favour of Britain . . . that there was no man in Congress but Mr. Madison who argued in a gentlemanlike and solid manner—nor, in short, any man out of it in America, but Col. Hamilton, who possessed abilities." To this Washington replied: "The remarks of a foreign Count are such as do no credit to his judgment and as little to his heart. They are the superficial observations of a few months' residence, and an insult to the inhabitants of a country, where he has received much more attention and civility than he seems to merit." But the idle tales and the insult, so far as these touched upon the relations of the two key figures in the cabinet, were given ample proof in the very communication in which Humphreys reported the differing sentiments of "political Characters."

[141] Temple to Leeds, 2 Sep. 1790, PRO: FO 4/8, f. 327.

[142] Humphreys to Washington, 31 Oct. 1790, Humphreys, *Humphreys*, II, 50-4, "(Secret)." Humphreys, who had known La Luzerne in America, conveyed Washington's letter of 10 Aug. 1790 to the minister. "As you know fully the manner in which that Gentleman has been in my family and connected with me for many years," Washington wrote La Luzerne, "I will say nothing more on his subject, than that he expects to travel in several parts of Europe; and that, if it should be convenient to your excellency to give him letters to any characters of your nation

I have not even once mentioned the subject to the Marq. de la Luzerne [Humphreys wrote to Washington]. On the contrary, I have judged it expedient to use all the discretion in my power, equally avoiding all appearances of curious enquiry or mysterious reserve, in order to pass for a meer common traveller. Yet somebody has written to Paris, describing a person, once a Colonel, in the American Army, as now employed here in intrigues relative to the Spanish War. This must be absolutely the effect of conjecture, without any ostensible grounds; for I have never opened my lips to any Creature in existence on any matter that led to it since my arrival. I have hitherto escaped all observations in the News Papers here. With this object in sight, I have carefully avoided seeing the Spanish Ambassador, and when I was asked by the Marquis de la Luzerne, if I had come to Europe on public business I answered, as I might with veracity, in the negative.

La Luzerne had reason to believe that the answer was not in fact veracious, but whether the conjectures and reports that arrived simultaneously with Humphreys arose from his own indiscretions before departure, from accident, or from intentional disclosure in New York is not known. Nor could that disclosure have been significant except as it underscored the point made by Hamilton to Beckwith—that he was displeased with Morris' conduct, that the time was ripe for establishing a closer connection between England and the United States, that there was no understanding with Spain, that the navigation of the Mississippi was a national interest so vital to the United States as to justify war against Spain as an ally of England to obtain it, and that, most particularly, the negotiations needed to be pressed at that time and to be carried forward in America as a counterpoise to those who leaned toward the house of Bourbon.

The last point Hamilton drove home repeatedly. "I have already mentioned my wish," he told Beckwith, "that when matters shall be brought to a point, and a serious discussion takes place between Great Britain and us, pains may be taken to guard against any jealousies in the manner of it; we are a new people, which may occasion a coyness. Some of us possibly may entertain doubts of your wanting to Mark a Superiority, and such an idea may give a turn to the whole negotiation."[143] Here, at bottom, lies the explanation of the long months of clandestine discussions with a secret agent, the repeated deceptions practised on the administration, the attempt by indirection to thwart the policy agreed upon with respect to Spain. The belief in the possibility of a close and harmonious commercial connection with Great Britain was the paramount object, but the spring of action was an overarching self-confidence, matched by the fear that this great end

---

in the Countries or Courts which he may happen to visit, I shall consider the interest you take on his behalf in a very acceptable and obliging point of light"; Washington, *Writings*, ed. Fitzpatrick, XXXI, 85.

[143] Beckwith's report of conversations (ca. 12 Aug. 1790), enclosed in Dorchester to Grenville, 25 Sep. 1790, No. 49, PRO: CO 42/69, f. 28, 30-48.

might be endangered by the imprudent responses of a Gouverneur Morris or by the manners of a new people as embodied in the Secretary of State. The belief at that period was illusory, but the fear was well grounded. Jefferson, however, did not call it coyness: "with those who respect their own dignity so much," he wrote Morris, "ours must not be counted at nought." On this the President agreed. The government of the United States, he instructed Hamilton to remember in his consultation with Beckwith, should be left "entirely free to pursue, unreproached, such a line of conduct in the dispute as her interest (and honor)" should dictate. But neither Washington nor Jefferson ever knew to what extent both the national dignity and the national interest as pursued by the administration had been compromised by Hamilton who had said in the course of the secret discussions: "foreign nations in common are guided solely by their respective interests in whatever concerns their intercourse." In forgetting the national dignity, Hamilton also sacrificed his own honor and official character.

The failure of the house of Bourbon to respect the family compact doomed Jefferson's approach to Spain. But even Hamilton learned in a short time that a proposal to exchange ministers between the United States and Great Britain, whether proceeding from the coyness of a new people or from a sense of national dignity, would have to come first from that power that had ignored the initial advance of the other. Even so, he cannot have realized how greatly he contributed to the decision of the British cabinet to appoint a minister to the United States. For that decision resulted not at all from the proposals and suggestions made so insistently by him through Beckwith and Dorchester for over a year and a half before the appointment was made. It came rather from the fear instilled by the weapon he had unintentionally put in the hands of the member of the cabinet against whom his moves were directed from the beginning. The fear was well justified. When at the opening of the ensuing session of Congress the President asked the Secretary of State to study and report upon the correspondence of Gouverneur Morris, the conclusion arrived at was one that both men had reached months earlier.[144] When this was disclosed to the Senate, whose proceedings were hidden from the public, both the fact and the documents were immediately made available to George Beckwith. "These papers," a Senator told the secret agent, "were submitted to us yesterday at the instigation I believe of Mr. Jefferson, and in order to induce us to favor a French interest, from a certain coldness which runs through Mr. Morris's communications, as they regard the dispositions of your Minis-

[144] See report, 15 Dec. 1790, and Washington's message of 14 Feb. 1791 transmitting Morris' correspondence. That message, as no doubt TJ intended, prompted the revival of Madison's proposals of the preceding summer. "For the moment," writes Setser, "it appeared that Jefferson's star was in the ascendant and that his policy of resistance to Great Britain was to become the avowed policy of the United States Government.—That a navigation law was not enacted early in 1791 was due to the decision of the British government to send a minister to Philadelphia" (Vernon G. Setser, *The Commercial Reciprocity Policy of the United States 1774-1829*, p. 110).

try towards us.—I am very explicit with you on this subject, and I wish to impress you with its being my conviction, that there is an absolute necessity of following up this business during the summer; a delay, I do assure you will at least be dangerous, and may throw us into a French interest."[145] Worse, the application of the French chargé d'affaires on the matter of tonnage duties, combined with Jefferson's use of the Morris correspondence, so Beckwith reported, gave "the French party . . . an accession of strength" in the House of Representatives. But Madison and his followers did not force the issue. Had a vote been compelled in the evenly-divided House, Beckwith reported, the opposition were determined "not only to debate the validity and propriety of Mr. Morris's proceedings, arising from his conversations with Mr. Pitt, but to investigate at large, in how far his opinions supported the inference drawn from them by the Executive in this Country, and whether all circumstances considered, they ought to have been made the basis of a legislative procedure; this would have produced a very delicate discussion indeed, as it respected the President personally, rather than have suffered any strong measure to have taken place at this time."[146] The President's message and the response had sounded warning signals that the ministry clearly heard. Beckwith's report arrived late in May. Within a week Lord Grenville directed George Hammond to return as speedily as possible from Madrid. His next mission would be that of minister to the United States.

Thus, ironically, by a course of deception begun when he recommended Gouverneur Morris for appointment in 1789, Hamilton had succeeded only in furnishing the Secretary of State with a powerful instrument that came very close to bringing success to his and Madison's commercial policy. No advance toward a *rapprochement* had been made but the ministry had been filled with apprehension. Back of their fear lay the possibility that the Secretary of State, preferring amicable to adversary relations in commerce, might be able to employ the means that he considered both available and infallible. The West India planters doubtless would have agreed, and the swiftness with which the ministry responded to the mere threat indicates how clearly they grasped the reality of the danger. Hamilton's duplicity had in fact come very near wrecking his own policy. But when the exchange of ministers ultimately came about, he moved on undaunted along the same course, saying one thing to the administration and another to the envoy of Great Britain.

"The worst Evil that can happen in any Government," wrote John Adams, "is a divided executive."[147] After the experience of his first term Washington grimly declared that he would never knowingly bring into office any man whose tenets were averse to those of the government—

---

[145] Beckwith to Grenville, 14 Mch. 1791, enclosing statement from "a Member of the Senate" (probably William Samuel Johnson), PRO: FO 95/1; the quotation is from the enclosure.

[146] Beckwith to Grenville, 14 Mch. 1791, PRO: FO 95/1.

[147] Adams to Pickering, 31 Oct. 1797, MHi: AM; text in Adams, *Works*, ed. C. F. Adams, VIII, 560.

that, he said, "would be a sort of political Suicide."[148] Both men spoke from bitter experience. Alexander Hamilton voiced the same opinion before coming into office. "Energy in the Executive," he declared in *The Federalist*, "is a leading character in the definition of good government." He then placed first in importance among all of the elements requisite for an energetic executive that of "unity." The principle of administration was elementary and no doubt the Secretary of the Treasury uttered the words with conviction. But the unity that he professed to place at the apex of his system of administrative conduct was a principle that he himself, hailed as one of the greatest of administrators, was the first to violate, not as an isolated example in the summer of 1790 but as a consistent and studied pattern of behavior. The manoeuver that had begun immediately on the signing of Jefferson's commission as Secretary of State was repeated in one form or another in almost every aspect of foreign affairs for the next four years, foredooming the major objectives of Jefferson's policy to failure and making his continuance in office intolerable once the President shifted the immense weight of his influence to the other side of the scales. The calculated and continuing use of deception by the Secretary of the Treasury is thus a major factor that must be reckoned with in the assessment of foreign policy in the first administration and beyond.

[148] Washington to Pickering, 27 Sep. 1795, MHi: Pickering Papers; text in Washington, *Writings*, ed. Fitzpatrick, XXXIV, 314-16.

I. Secretary of State to the President, enclosing Opinion

July 12. 1790.

Th: Jefferson had a conference yesterday with Mr. Madison on the subject recommended by the President. He has the honor of inclosing him some considerations thereon, in all of which he believes Mr. Madison concurred. He has sketched the heads only, as the President's mind will readily furnish the developement of each. He will wait on the president at one aclock on some other business, and then and at all other times be ready to enter more into the details of any part of the subject the president may chuse.

RC (DNA: RG 59, MLR); addressed: "The President of the United States"; endorsed by Washington: "From Thoms. Jefferson Esqr. 12th July 1790 on the Subject of the War between Great Britain and Spain. Opinion." Entry in SJPL reads: "Opn. Th: J. on conduct of U.S. in War between Spain & Gr. Br."

Jefferson's Outline of Policy Contingent on War between England and Spain

Heads of consideration on the conduct we are to observe in the war between Spain and Gr. Britain and particularly should the latter attempt the conquest of Louisiana and the Floridas.

The dangers to us should Great Britain possess herself of those countries.

She will[1] possess a territory equal to half ours, beyond the Missisipi[2]

She will seduce that half of ours which is on this side the Missisipi[3]

by her language, laws, religion, manners, government, commerce, capital.

by the possession of N. Orleans, which draws to it the dependance of all the waters of Misspi

by the markets she can offer them in the gulph of Mexico and elsewhere.

She will take from the remaining part of our States the markets they now have for their produce by furnishing those markets cheaper with the same articles. Tobacco, rice, indigo, bread, lumber, naval stores, furs.

She will have then possessions double the size of ours, as good in soil and climate.

She will encircle us compleatly, by these possessions on our land-board, and her fleets on our sea-board.

Instead of two neighbors balancing each other, we shall have one, with more than the strength of both.

Would the prevention of this be worth a war?

Consider our abilities to take part in a war.

Our operations would be by land only.

How many men should we need to employ?—Their cost?

Our resources of taxation and credit equal to this.

Weigh the evil of this new accumulation of debt

Against the loss of markets, and eternal expence and danger from so overgrown a neighbor.

But this is on supposition that France as well as Spain shall be engaged in the war. For with Spain alone, the war would be unsuccessful, and our situation rendered worse.[4]

No need to take a part in the war as yet. We may chuse our own time.

Delay gives us many chances to avoid it altogether.

In such a choice of objects, Gr. Britain may not single out Louisiana and the Floridas.

She may fail in her attempt on them.

France and Spain may recover them.

If all these chances fail, we should have to re-take them.[4]

The difference between retaking, and preventing, overbalanced by the benefits of delay.

Delay enables us to be better prepared:

To obtain from the allies a price for our assistance.[5]

Suppose these our ultimate views. What is to be done at this time?
1. As to Spain?
>If she be as sensible as we are that she cannot save Louisiana and the Floridas,
>>Might she not prefer their Independance to their Subjection to Grt. Britain?
>>Does not the proposition of the Ct. d'Estaing furnish us an opening to communicate our ideas on this subject to the court of France, and thro them to that of Madrid? And our readiness to join them in guaranteeing the independance of those countries?
>This might save us from a war, if Gr. Britain respects our weight in a war.
>And if she does not, the object would place the war on popular ground with us.[6]

2. As to England? Say to Beckwith
>'that as to a Treaty of commerce, we would prefer amicable, to adversary arrangements, tho the latter would be infallible, and in our own power:[7]
>That our ideas are that such a treaty should be founded in perfect reciprocity; and would therefore be it's own price:
>That as to an Alliance, we can say nothing till it's object be shewn, and that it is not to be inconsistent with existing engagements:[8]
>That in the event of war between Gr. Brit. and Spain we are disposed to be strictly neutral:[9]
>That however, we should view with extreme uneasiness any attempts of either power to seize the possessions of the other on our frontier, as we consider our own safety interested in a due balance between our neighbors.' [It might be advantageous to express this latter sentiment, because if there be any difference of opinion in their councils, whether to bend their force against North or South America, or the islands, (and certainly there is room for difference) and if these opinions be nearly balanced, that balance might be determined by the prospect of having an enemy the more or less, according to the object they should select.]

Th: Jefferson
July. 12. 1790.

MS (DNA: RG 59, MLR); in TJ's hand; endorsed by Washington: "The Secretary of State 12th July 1790"; brackets in MS. Dft (DLC); in TJ's hand; text varies from that above, principally in phraseology, but some of more important differences are noted below (full text printed, though not with complete accuracy, in Ford, v, 199-203; e.g. "reduce" instead of "seduce"). FC (DNA: RG 59, SDC).

[1] In this and the succeeding four heads, Dft reads: "She would."

[2] This head in Dft reads: "Beyond the Missi. a territory equal to half ours."

[3] This head in Dft reads: "She would seduce ⟨draw to it⟩ our Cis-Missi. possessions."

[4] This head not in Dft.

[5] This head in Dft reads: "To stipulate with Spain and France advantages for our assistance."

[6] Preceding two words not in Dft.

[7] This head takes on a more expanded form in Dft: "That as to a treaty of

commerce, we had never desired it but on terms of perfect reciprocity.—That therefore we never thought to give any price for it but itself.—That we had wished for it to avoid giving mutual wounds to the commerce of both nations.—But that we have the measures in our own power which may save us from loss."

8 In Dft this head reads: "⟨That no considerations⟩ ⟨France as well as Spain will be involved⟩ That as to the Alliance they propose, it would involve us against France and Spain and considered even in a moral view, no price could repay such an abandonment of character."

9 In Dft this head reads: "That we are truly disposed to remain neutral."

II. Secretary of State to William Carmichael, enclosing Outline of Policy

DEAR SIR   New York August 2d. 1790.

This letter will be delivered you by Colo. Humphreys, whose character is so well known to you as to need no recommendations from me. [The present appearances of war between our two neighbours, Spain and England, cannot but excite all our attention. The part we are to act is uncertain, and will be difficult. The unsettled state of our dispute with Spain may give a turn to it very different from what we would wish. As it is important that you should be fully apprised of our way of thinking on this subject, I have sketched, in the enclosed paper, general heads of consideration arising from present circumstances; these will be readily developed by your own reflections]¹ and in conversations with Col. Humphreys, who possessing the sentiments of the Executive on this subject, being well acquainted with the circumstances of the Western Country in particular, and of the State of our affairs in general, comes to Madrid expressly for the purpose of giving you a thorough communication of them: he will therefore remain there as many days, or weeks, as may be necessary for this purpose. [With this information,]¹ written and oral, [you will be enabled to meet the minister in conversations on the subject of the navigation of the Missisippi to which we wish you to lead his attention immediately. Impress him thoroughly with the necessity of an early and even an immediate settlement of this matter, and of a return to the field of negociation for this purpose: and though it must be done delicately, yet he must be made to understand unequivocally that a resumption of the negociation is not desired on our part, unless he can determine, in the first opening of it, to yield the immediate and full enjoyment of that navigation. (I say nothing of the claims of Spain to our Territory north of the 31st. degree, and east of the Missisippi: they never merited the respect of an answer; and you know it has been admitted at Madrid that they were not to be maintained.) It may be asked what need of negociation, if the navigation is to be ceded at all events? You know that the navigation cannot be practised without a port where the sea and river vessels may meet and exchange loads, and where those employed about them may be safe and unmolested. The right to use a thing comprehends a right to the means necessary to it's use, and without which it would be useless: the fixing on a proper port, and the degree of freedom it is to enjoy in it's operations, will require negociation, and be governed by events. There is danger indeed that even the unavoidable delay of sending a negociator here, may render the mission too late for the preservation of peace: it is impossible to answer for the forbearance of our western citizens. We endeavor to quiet them with the expectation of an attainment of their rights by peaceable means, but should they, in a moment of impatience, hazard others, there is no saying how far we may be led: for neither themselves nor their rights will ever be abandoned by us.

You will be pleased to observe that we press these matters warmly and firmly under this idea, that the war between Spain and Great Britain will be begun before you receive this; and such a moment must not be lost. But should an accommodation take place, we retain indeed the same object, and the same resolutions unalterably; but your discretion will suggest that, in that event, they must be pressed more softly; and that patience and persuasion must temper your conferences, till either these may prevail, or some other circumstance turn up which may enable us to use other means for the attainment of an object, which we are determined in the end to obtain at every risk.][1] I have the honor to be with great esteem Dear Sir &c.

FC (DNA: RG 59, PCC No. 121); at foot of text: "(signed) Thomas Jefferson." Entry in sjl designates this letter as "(secret)." Tr of Extract (CLU); in TJ's hand, with the following caption: "Extracts from a letter to Mr. Carmichael dated Aug. 2. 1790" (see note 1 below).

[1] This and other passages enclosed in brackets (supplied) comprise the text of the continuous document described above as Tr of Extract. It is to be noted that, aside from the complimentary close, the only passages not included in the text of the extract are those alluding to David Humphreys' mission. This extract was sent by TJ to Short, 10 Aug. 1790, after Washington had given his approval. See TJ to Washington, 8 Aug. 1790 (Document V).

ENCLOSURE

Jefferson's Outline of Policy on the Mississippi Question

Heads of consideration on the Navigation of the
Missisipi for Mr. Carmichael.
We have a *right* to the navigation of the Missisipi   1. by Nature:
                                               2. by Treaty.
It is *necessary* to us.

More than half the territory of the U.S. is on the waters of that river.
200,000 of our citizens are settled on them, of whom 40,000 bear
arms.[1]

These have no other Out-let for their tobacco, rice, corn, hemp,
lumber, house timber, ship timber.

We have hitherto respected[2] the indecision of Spain, because we wish
peace: because our Western citizens have had vent at home for
their productions.

A surplus of production begins now to demand foreign markets.

Whenever they shall say 'We cannot, we will not, be longer shut up'
The U.S. will be reduced to the following dilemma:
1. To force them to acquiescence:
2. To separate from them, rather than take part in a war
against Spain:
3. Or to preserve them in our union, by joining them in the
war.

The 1st. is neither in our principles, nor in our power:
2. A multitude of reasons decide against the 2ᵈ.

It may suffice to speak out one: were we to give up half
our territory rather than engage in a just war to preserve it, we should not keep the other half long.[3]

3. The 3ᵈ. is the[4] alternative we must necessarily adopt.

How are we to obtain that navigation?[5]
(A) By *Force*
1. Acting *separately*.

That we can effect this with certainty and promptitude,
circumstances decide.

Objection. We cannot retain New Orleans, for instance,
were we to take it.

Answer. A moderate force may be so secured, as to hold
out till succoured.

Our succours can be prompt and effectual

Suppose, after taking it, we withdraw our force.

If Spain retakes it by an expedition, we can recover
it by a counter-expedition and so as often as the case
shall happen. Their expeditions will be slow, expensive, and lead to catastrophes: Ours sudden, economical, and a check have no consequences.[6]

We should associate the country to our union.

The inhabitants wish this.

They are not disposed to be of the Spanish government.

It is idle in Spain to suppose our Western inhabitants will unite with them.[7]

They could be quiet but a short time under a government so repugnant to their feelings.

Were they to come under it for present purposes, it would be with a view to throw it off soon.[8]

Should they remain, they would communicate a spirit of Independence to those with whom they should be mixed.

II. Acting in *conjunction* with Great Britain, and with a view to partition.

The Floridas and island of New Orleans[9] would be assigned to us.

Louisiana (or all the Western waters of the Missisipi) to them.

We confess that such an Alliance is not what we would wish.

Because it may eventually lead us into embarrassing situations with our best friend.

And put the power of two neighbors into the hands of one.

Ld. Lansdowne has declared he gave the Floridas to Spain rather than the U. S. as a bone of discord with the House of Bourbon, and of reunion[10] with Gr. Britain.

Connolly's attempt (as well as other facts) proves they keep it in view.

(B.) By *Negociation.*

1. What must Spain do[15] of *Necessity*?[11]

The conduct of Spain has proved that the occlusion of the Missisipi is system with her.

If she opens it now, it will be because forced by imperious circumstances.

She will consequently shut it again when these circumstances cease.

Treaty will be no obstacle.

Irregularities, real or pretended, in our navigators, will furnish colour enough.

Perpetual broils, and finally war will ensue.

Prudence, and even necessity, imposes on us the law of settling the matter now *finally*, and not by *halves.*

With experience of the past, and prospect of the future, it would be imbecility in us to accept the naked navigation.

With that, we must have what is necessary 1. to it's use, and without which it would be useless: 2. to secure it's continuance.[12]

[114]

That is, a port near the mouth to recieve our vessels,
and protect the navigation. So well separated in jurisdiction and fact as to avoid the danger of broils.[13]

But even this will not secure the Floridas, and Louisiana
against Great Britain.
If we are neutral, she will wrest those possessions from
Spain.
The inhabitants (French, English, Scotch, American)[14]
would prefer England to Spain.
II. What then had Spain better do[15] of *choice*?
Cede to us all territory on our side of the Missisipi:[16]
On condition that we guarantee all her possessions on
the Western waters of that river:
She agreeing further, to subsidize us, if the guarantee
brings us into the war.
Should Gr. Britain possess herself of the Floridas and
Louisiana,   -
Her governing principles are Conquest, Colonization,
Commerce, Monopoly.
She will establish powerful colonies in them.
These can be poured into the gulph of Mexico, for any
sudden enterprize there.
Or invade Mexico, their next neighbor, by land.
Whilst a fleet co-operates along shore, and cuts off
relief.
And proceed successively from colony to colony.
With respect to us, if Gr. Britain establishes herself on
our whole land-board
Our lot will be bloody and eternal war; or indissoluble
confederacy.
Which ought we to chuse?
what will be the lot of the Spanish colonies, in the jaws
of such a confederacy?
What will secure the Ocean against Monopoly?
Safer for Spain that we should be her neighbor, than
England.
Conquest not in our principles: inconsistent with our
government.
Not our interest to cross the Missisipi for ages.
And will never be our interest to remain united with
those who do.
Intermediate chances save the trouble of calculating so
far forward.
Consequences of this Cession, and Guarantee.[17]
1. Every subject of difference will be removed from be-
tween Spain and the U. S.

2. Our interest will be strongly engaged in her retaining her American possessions.

3. Spain will be quieted as to Louisiana, and her territories West of that.

4. She may employ her whole force in defence of her islands and Southern possessions.

5. If we preserve our neutrality, it will be a very partial one to her.

6. If we are forced into the war, it will be, as we wish, on the side of the H. of Bourbon.

7. Our privateers will commit formidable depredations on the Brit. trade, and occupy much of their force.

8. By withholding supplies of provision, as well as by concurring in expeditions, the British islands will be in imminent danger.

9. Their expences of precaution, both for their continental and insular possessions will be so augmented as to give a hope of running their credit down.

In fine, for a narrow slip of barren, detached, and expensive country, Spain secures the rest of her territory, and makes an Ally, where she might have a dangerous enemy.   TH: JEFFERSON
Aug. 2. 1790

PrC (CLU); in TJ's hand, being a fair copy of texts indicated below as Dft and MS, but having important variations which are indicated in the textual notes. Tr (DNA: RG 59, DD); filed with Humphreys' letter to TJ, 17 Aug. 1791; in clerk's hand. Dft (DLC); with numerous alterations, some of which are indicated in notes below; at head of text: "Aug. 2. 1790." MS (MHi); in TJ's hand. FC (DNA: RG 59, SDC). Internal evidence in Dft shows that TJ copied it from some previous text, but with alterations being made in the course of transcription, and it is plain that he utilized the draft of the statement of policy transmitted to Washington on 12 July 1790 in preparing this outline for Carmichael. In his letter to Washington of 8 Aug. 1790 TJ stated that the text drawn up earlier that had been left with the president contained "two or three small differences" from that then enclosed. A collation of the various texts shows clearly that Dft, MS, and FC represent the earlier state and that PrC and Tr represent the state enclosed in the letter to Washington on 8 Aug. 1790. The missing RC from which PrC was executed was evidently the text sent to Carmichael.

1 The words ". . . of whom 40,000 bear arms" are not in Dft, MS, or FC.

2 Instead of "respected," Dft, MS, and FC read "borne."

3 Dft reads: "One only shall be spoken out. The Nation that gives up half it's territory, rather than engage in a just war to preserve it, will not keep the other half long." All other texts read as above.

4 In Dft TJ first wrote, and then deleted, "only."

5 In Dft TJ first wrote ". . . obtain the enjoyment of our right of navigation," and then altered the passage to read as above.

6 Dft and MS both read originally: ". . . a check of little consequences," and in the course of transcribing the latter from the former TJ altered the text in both to read as above.

7 This passage in Dft reads: "⟨unite with them⟩ submit to their government." TJ thus restored the earlier reading in PrC.

8 Dft originally read: ". . . with a view soon to set up for themse[lves],"

and TJ altered the text to read as above.

⁹ All texts save PrC read: "The Floridas (including N. Orleans)," &c.

¹⁰ This word interlined in Dft in substitution for "coalition," deleted.

¹¹ Dft originally read: "What are the lowest terms we could admit?" TJ then altered the query to read as above.

¹² Dft, MS, and FC read: "We must have what will secure it's continuance: That is a port near the mouth, to recieve our vessels, and protect the navigation."

¹³ This sentence not in Dft, MS, or

FC.

¹⁴ Tr alone of all texts reads "German" for "American," clearly a clerk's error.

¹⁵ This word interlined in Dft in substitution for "yield," deleted.

¹⁶ Dft originally read: "cede to us the Floridas, i.e. all her possessions East of the Missisipi," and then TJ altered the passage to read as above.

¹⁷ Dft originally read: "Consequences of this cession of the Floridas to us, and guarantee of Louisiana to Spain," and then TJ altered the passage to read as above.

III. Thomas Jefferson to Luis Pinto de Souza

SIR   New York August 7th. 1790.

Under cover of the acquaintance I had the honor of contracting with you, during the negociations we transacted together in London, I take the liberty of addressing you the present letter. The friendly dispositions you were then pleased to express towards this Country, which were sincerely and reciprocally felt on my part towards yours, flatter me with the hope you will assist in maturing a subject for their common good. As yet we have not the information necessary to present it to you formally, as the Minister of her most faithful Majesty; I beg therefore that this letter may be considered as between two individual friends of their respective Countries, preliminary to a formal proposition, and meant to give an acceptable shape to that.

It is unnecessary, with your Excellency, to go through the history of our first experiment in Government, the result of which was a want of such tone in the governing powers, as might effect the good of those committed to their care: the nation became sensible of this, have changed it's organization, made a better distribution of it's powers, and given to them more energy and independence. The new Government has now for some time been under way, and so far gives a confidence that it will answer it's purposes: abuses under the old forms have led us to lay the basis of the new in a rigorous economy of the public contributions. This principle will shew itself in our diplomatic establishments, and the rather as, at such a distance from Europe, and with such an ocean between us, we hope to meddle little in it's quarrels or combinations: it's peace and it's commerce are what we shall court; and to cultivate these, we propose to place at the Courts of Europe most interesting to us, diplomatic characters of economical grade, and shall be glad to receive like ones in exchange. The important commerce carried on between your Country and ours, and the proofs of friendly disposition towards us which her Majesty has manifested, induce us to wish for such an exchange with her, to express our sensibility at the intimations heretofore received of her readiness to meet our wish in this point, and our regret at the delay which has proceeded from the circumstances before touched on. The grade to be exchanged is the present question, and that on which I ask a friendly and informal consultation with you: that of Chargé des affaires is the one we would prefer; it is that we employ at the Court of Madrid. But it has been said that, by the etiquette of your Court, that grade cannot be received there under a favorable countenance. Something like this existed at the Court of Madrid but his most Catholic Majesty, in consideration of our peculiar circumstances, dispensed with a general rule, in our favor, and in our particular case; and our Chargé des affaires there enjoys at Court the privileges, the respect and favor due to a friendly nation, to a nation whom distance and difference of circumstances liberate in some degree from an etiquette to which it is a stranger at home as well as abroad. The representative of her Majesty here, under whatever name mutual convenience may designate him, shall be received in the plenitude of friendship and favor. May we not ask a reciprocal treatment of ours with you? The nations of Europe have already seen the necessity of distinguishing America from Europe, even in their Treaties: and a difference of commerce, of government, of condition and character must every day evince, more and more, the impracticability of involving them under common regulations. Nor ought a difference of arrangement with respect to us to excite claims from others whose circumstances bear no similitude to ours.

I beg leave to submit these considerations to your Excellency's wisdom and goodness. You will see them to be such as could not be offered formally. They must shield themselves under the protection of those sentiments of veneration and esteem with which your character heretofore inspired me, and which I flattered myself were not merely indifferent to you. Be so good as to honor, with a conference hereon, the bearer Col. Humphreys (who was known to you in London) a gentleman who has long been of the President's family, and whose worth has acquired so much of our confidence that whatever shall be arranged with him, on this subject, may be considered as settled. Presuming on a continuance of her Majesty's dispositions, accept this private assurance that a proper person shall be appointed in due form to reside with you, as soon as we shall know the result of your deliberations with Colonel Humphreys, who I beg leave to present to your notice; adding the homage of those sentiments of respect and attachment, with which I have the honor to be your Excellency's most obedient and most humble servant,

THOMAS JEFFERSON

FC (DNA: RG 59, PCC No. 121).
On its face this was a private letter. But the text is recorded in the files of the Department of State; it was sent to the President for his approval; and it had the same secret status as other dispatches carried by Humphreys on his urgent mission—facts which give it an official character while stamping it as a typical example of TJ's flexible and indirect diplomacy. While negotiating with De Pinto for a treaty of

commerce in 1786, TJ had formed the opinion that the minister from Portugal was "sensible, candid," and favorably disposed toward America. He had also supposed that De Pinto might be promoted to the post of foreign minister at Lisbon and that this would be favorable for the adoption of the treaty and for the admission of American flour into Portugal (Vol. 9: 410-33; 10: 242). The sanguine attitude was characteristic, but the hopes were disappointed.

IV. Secretary of State to Joshua Johnson

SIR New York Aug. 7. 1790.

The President of the United States, desirous of availing his country of the talents of it's best citizens in their respective lines, has thought proper to nominate you Consul for the U.S. at the port of London. The extent of our commercial and political connections with that country marks the importance of the trust he confides to you, and the more as we have no diplomatic character at that court. I shall say more to you in a future letter on the extent of the Consular functions, which are in general to be confined to the superintendance and patronage of commerce, and navigation; but in your position we must desire somewhat more. Political intelligence from that country is interesting to us in a high degree. We must therefore ask you to furnish us with this as far as you shall be able; to send us moreover the gazette of the court, Woodfall's parliamentary paper, Debrett's parliamentary register: to serve sometimes as a center for our correspondencies [with] other parts of Europe, by receiving and forwarding letters sent to your care. It is desireable that we be annually informed of the extent to which the British fisheries are carried on within each year, stating the number and tonnage of the vessels and the number of men employed in the respective fisheries: to-wit the Northern, and Southern whale fisheries, and the Cod-fishery. I have as yet no statement of them for the year 1789. with which therefore I will thank you to begin.— While the press of seamen continues, our seamen in ports nearer to you than to Liverpool (where Mr. Maury is Consul) will need your protection. The liberation of those impressed should be desired of the proper authority, with due firmness, yet always in temperate and respectful terms, in which way indeed all applications to government should be made.

The public papers herein desired may come regularly once a month by the British packet, and intermediately by any vessels bound directly either to Philadelphia or New York. All expences incurred for papers, and postages shall be paid at such intervals as you chuse either here on your order, or by bill on London whenever you transmit to me an account.

There was a bill brought into the legislature for the establishment of some regulations in the Consular offices: but it is postponed to the next session. That bill proposed some particular fees for particular services. They were however so small as to be no object. As there will be little or no legal emolument annexed to the office of Consul, it is of course not expected that it shall render any expence incumbent on him. I have the honor to be with great esteem, Sir Your most obedient & most humble servant,

TH: JEFFERSON

RC (DNA: RG 59, CD); slightly mutilated, with loss of one or two words being supplied from FC; addressed: "Mr. Joshua Johnson Merchant London"; endorsed as "Received 14 October Answerd 2 November. [1790] ℗ the Two Brothers Capt. Sely." FC and Tr (DNA: RG 59, PCC No. 121).

V. Secretary of State to the President

Aug. 8. 1790.

Th: Jefferson has the honor to inclose to the President the following papers.

1. The secret letter and paper of Aug. 2. for Mr. Carmichael.
2. The secret letter for the Chevalr. de Pinto.
3. A letter for Mr. Joshua Johnson.

on supposition that, delivering them himself to Colo. Humphreys, he might wish to comment to him on their contents, and particularly as to the 1st. to qualify such of the considerations as he may think need qualification, and to enlarge such as are too restrained. He will observe two or three small differences between the considerations of Aug. 2. now inclosed, and the first copy left with the President which are submitted to him.

The letter of Aug. 7.[1] to Mr. Carmichael and the cyphers, are all that will remain of the dispatches necessary for Colo. Humphreys for London, Lisbon, and Madrid, as Th: J. supposes.

Will the President be pleased to consider, at his leisure, how far it might be safe and useful to communicate the letter and considerations of Aug. 2. to Mr. Short, or the M. de la Fayette?

RC (NjP); endorsed. PrC (DLC). Enclosures: (1) TJ to Carmichael, 2 Aug. 1790 and its enclosure. (2) TJ to De Pinto, 7 Aug. 1790. (3) TJ to Johnson, 7 Aug. 1790.
On the TWO OR THREE SMALL DIF-

FERENCES, see notes to TJ's outline of policy on the Mississippi Question, enclosed in TJ to Carmichael, 2 Aug. 1790 (Document II, enclosure).

[1] I.e., 6 Aug.

VI. Secretary of State to William Short

DEAR SIR   New York Aug. 10. 1790.

This letter, with the very confidential papers it incloses, will be delivered you by Mr. Barrett with his own hands. If there be no war between Spain and England, they need be known to yourself alone. But if that war be begun, or whenever it shall begin, we wish you to communicate them to the Marquis de la Fayette, on whose assistance we know we can count in matters which interest both our countries. He and you will consider how far the contents of these papers may be communicated to the Count de Montmorin, and his influence be asked with the court of Madrid. France will be called into the war, as an ally, and not on any pretence of the quarrel being in any degree her own. She may reasonably require then that Spain should do every thing which depends on her to lessen the number of her enemies. She cannot doubt that we shall be of that number, if she does not yield our right to the common use of the Missisipi, and the means of using and securing it. You will observe we state in general the necessity, not only of our having a port near the mouth of the river (without which we could make no use of the navigation at all) but of it's being so well separated from the territories of Spain and her jurisdiction, as not to engender daily disputes and broils between us. It is certain that if Spain were to retain any jurisdiction over our entrepot her officers would abuse that jurisdiction, and our people would abuse their privileges in it. Both parties must foresee this, and that it will end in war. Hence the necessity of a well defined separation. Nature has decided what shall be the geography of that in the end, whatever it might be in the beginning, by cutting off from the adjacent countries of Florida and Louisiana, and inclosing between two of it's channels, a long and narrow slip of land, called the island of New Orleans. The idea of ceding this could not be hazarded to Spain, in the first step; it would be too disagreeable at first view: because this island, with it's town, constitutes at present their principal settlement in that part of their dominions, containing about 10,000 white inhabitants of every age and sex. Reason and events however, may, by little and little, familiarize them to it. That we have a right to some spot as an entrepot for our commerce, may be at once affirmed. The expediency too may be expressed of so locating it as to cut off the source of future quarrels and wars. A disinterested eye, looking on a map, will remark how conveniently this tongue of land is formed for the purpose; the Ibberville and Amit channel offering a good boundary and convenient outlet on the one side for Florida, and the main channel an equally good boundary and outlet on the other side for Louisiana; while the slip of land between is almost entirely morass or sand-bank; the whole of it lower than the water of the river, in it's highest floods, and only it's Western margin (which is the highest ground) secured by banks and inhabited. I suppose this idea too much even for the Count de Montmorin at first, and that therefore you will find it prudent to urge, and get him to recommend to the Spanish court only in general terms 'a port near the mouth of the river, with a circumjacent territory sufficient for it's support, well defined, and extraterritorial to Spain,' leaving the idea to future growth.

I inclose you the copy of a paper distributed by the Spanish commandant on the West side of the Missisipi, which may justify us to M. de Montmorin for pushing this matter to an immediate conclusion. It cannot be expected we shall give Spain time, to be used by her for dismembering us.

It is proper to apprise you of a circumstance which may shew the expediency of being in some degree on your guard even in your communications to the court of France. It is believed here that the Count de Moustier, during his residence with us, concieved a project of again engaging France in a colony upon our continent, and that he directed his views to some of the country on the Missisipi, and obtained and communicated a good deal of matter on the subject to his court. He saw the immediate advantage of selling some yards of French cloths and silks to the inhabitants of N. Orleans. But he did not take into account what it would cost France to nurse and protect a colony there till it should be able to join it's neighbors, or to stand by itself; and then what it would cost her to get rid of it. I hardly suspect that the court of France could be seduced by so partial a view of the subject as was presented to them; and I suspect it the less since the National assembly has constitutionally excluded conquest from the objects of their government. It may be added too that, the place being ours, their yards of cloth and silk would be as freely sold as if it were theirs.

You will perceive by this letter, and the papers it incloses, what part of the ideas of the Count d'Estain coincide with our views. The answer to him must be a compound of civility and reserve, expressing our thankfulness for his attentions; that we consider them as proofs of the continuance of his friendly dispositions, and that tho' it might be out of our system to implicate ourselves in trans-Atlantic guarantees, yet other parts of his plans are capable of being improved to the common benefit of the parties. Be so good as to say to him something of this kind, verbally, and so as that the matter may be ended as between him and us.

On the whole, in the event of war, it is left to the judgment of the Marquis de la Fayette and yourself how far you will develope the ideas now communicated to the Count de Montmorin, and how far you will suffer them to be developed to the Spanish court.

I inclose you a pamphlet by Hutchins for your further information on the subject of the Missisipi, and am with sentiments of perfect esteem & attachment Dr. Sir Your most obedient & most humble servt.,   TH: JEFFERSON

RC (CLU). FC (DNA: RG 59, PCC No. 121). Enclosures: (1) TJ to Carmichael, 2 Aug. 1790 (the text enclosed is the item there described as Tr of Extract, which omitted the references to Humphreys' mission). (2) TJ's outline of policy on the Mississippi Question, enclosed in the foregoing (the text sent Short is presumably that approved by Washington: for its identity, see notes to enclosure, TJ to Carmichael, 2 Aug. 1790). (3) Thomas Hutchins, *An historical and topographical description of Louisiana, and West-Florida* (Philadelphia, 1784). This pamphlet had excited TJ's attention since 1784 when he corresponded with Hutchins about it and pointed out errors in its map (see Hutchins to TJ, 11 Feb. 1784, where the pamphlet is erroneously conjectured to be Hutchins' *Topographical Description of Virginia, Pennsylvania*, &c. [London, 1778; see Sowerby, No. 525]). TJ was undoubtedly influenced at that time by Hutchins' perception of the strategic importance of the Mississippi: "The safety and commercial prosperity which may be secured to the United States by the definitive treaty of peace, will chiefly depend upon the share of the navigation which shall be allowed to them. Is it not amazing, true as it is, that few amongst us know this to be the key to the northern part of the western continent? . . . To expect the free navigation of the Mississippi is absurd, whilst the Spaniards are in possession of New Orleans" (Hutchins, *An historical and topographical description of Louisiana*, p. 23). TJ's description of the "long and narrow slip of land, called the island of New Orleans" is based on that of Hutchins, though he makes the population of the city 10,000 instead of the 7,000 that Hutchins estimated (same, p. 25-8). (4) The "copy of a paper distributed by the Spanish commandant" has not been identified, but Washington and TJ were well informed of Spanish-American intrigues in the Southwest. The President had received from Gov. Beverley Robinson of Virginia a copy of a letter from "the Spanish Governor of New Orleans to a respectable Gentleman in Kentucky" (Esteban Miró to Benjamin Sebastian) continuing the correspondence of the previous year in which Miró gave Sebastian and others "liberty to settle in any part of Louisiana, or any where on the east side of the Mississippi below the Yazou river," offering as inducements grants of land up to 3000 acres, exemption from taxation, freedom of religion, and trading privileges (Randolph to Washington, 30 May 1790; Miró to Sebastian, 16 Sep. 1789, both under the former date in DNA: RG 59, MLR; Washington to Randolph, 14 June 1790, *Writings*, ed. Fitzpatrick, XXXI, 49n.). The Anglo-Spanish war crisis produced in the Southwest precisely the same sort of intrigues threatening dismemberment of the United States that were taking place in Vermont. James O'Fallon, representing the South Carolina Yazoo Company, equalled in secret negotiations, in grandiose schemes, and in fanciful rhetoric what Ethan Allen had proposed to Dorchester in 1789. In taking advantage of the crisis to convert the enterprise of the company he represented to that of an independent buffer colony with close links to Spain, he definitely saw himself as the leader of a Southwestern Vermont—the embodiment of the spirit against which TJ's policy was directed. He offered to Miró to bring from three to five thousand well-armed men to a location on the Yazoo "clear of the old Line of West Florida, but on its Mar-

gin; so that, should any attack be made upon them, in that acknowledged Spot of *rightful* possession; the three most Southern States, from whence the Colonists have come, and in which the Gentlemen of the three Company's bear greatest sway) must insist on *federal aid and protection*. This the Congress *dare* not, from the terms of the constitution, refuse them, *in such circumstance*. In such circumstances, the old claims about *territorial boundaries*, and the diplomatic right of *freely navigating the Mississippi* must again be ushered into view . . . and the *Kentucky men, and the Frankliners* now galled under the pressure of Commercial regulations, at New Orleans, would most cheerfully conspire, to bring all those ancient disputes to an issue, on principles of *Self-interest*. . . . But if, on the other hand, the terms of *union* now ofered by the South Carolina Yazou Company be *properly* embraced and acceded to—; all this trouble will be everlastingly precluded—; Louisiana will have a robust Ally of Americans, independent among themselves, like *Vermont*, or *Rhode Island* for its Barrier; and . . . the people of *Kentucky, Franklin and Cumberland* must, in their own defence, be induced, to have followed their example, and the whole to confederate among themselves . . . under the protection of his Majesty. It is a fact well known, and acknowledged throughout the whole of the *Western Country* (and Nations, like Individuals, are always, eventually, led by their Interests): that the Inhabitants thereof, can derive no *Commercial* or *political* advantage whatever, by their being subjected to *Congressional Supremacy* placed in the *Atlantic States*; and that their last hope of ever rising into any consequence, as a people, must be founded, on confederating, independently, among themselves, on the basis of a *Separate* Sovereignty from that of the present Congress and, on the Stipulation of a general Market or *free trade* at New Orleans, for their productions, firmly to coalesce, as sincere Allies, with that European power, who shall hold it" (O'Fallon to Miró, 16 July 1790, Lexington, Lawrence Kinnaird, ed., "*Spain in* the Mississippi Valley, 1765-1794," *Am. Hist. Assn.*, *Ann. Rept., 1945*, III, p. II, 359-60; O'Fallon even surpassed in flattery what Ethan Allen had said to Dorchester; on the overtures made by O'Fallon and their failure, see Kinnaird, same, xxvii-x, and Whitaker, *Spanish-American* Frontier, p. 140-4).

On the ideas proposed by D'ESTAIN[G], see D'Estaing to Washington, 20 Mch. 1790, Vol. 16: 555-9.

VII. Secretary of State to David Humphreys

SIR   New York Aug. 11. 1790.

The President having thought proper to confide several special matters in Europe to your care, it will be expedient that you take your passage in the first convenient vessel bound to the port of London.

When there you will be pleased to deliver to Mr. G. Morris and to Mr. Johnson the letters and papers you will have in charge for them, to communicate to us from thence any interesting public intelligence you may be able to obtain, and then take as early a passage as possible to Lisbon.

At Lisbon you will deliver the letter with which you are charged for the Chevalier Pinto, putting on it the address proper to his present situation. You know the contents of this letter, and will make it the subject of such conferences with him as may be necessary to obtain our point of establishing there the diplomatic grade which alone coincides with our system, and of ensuring it's reception and treatment with the requisite respect. Communicate to us the result of your conferences, and then proceed to Madrid.

There you will deliver the letters and papers which you have in charge for Mr. Carmichael, the contents of all which are known to you. Be so good as to multiply as much as possible your conferences with him in order to possess him fully of the special matters sketched out in those papers, and of the state of our affairs in general.

Your stay there will be as long as it's objects may require, only taking care to be returned to Lisbon by the time you may reasonably expect that our answers to your letters to be written from Lisbon may reach that place. This cannot be earlier than the first or second week of January. These answers will convey to you the President's further pleasure.

Thro' the whole of this business it will be best that you avoid all suspicion of being on any public business. This need be known only to the Chevalier Pinto and Mr. Carmichael. The former need not know of your journey to Madrid, or if it be necessary, he may be made to understand that it is a journey of curiosity to fill up the interval between writing your letters and recieving the answers. To every other person it will be best that you appear as a private traveller.

The President of the United States allows you from this date at the rate of two thousand two hundred and fifty dollars a year for your services and expences, and moreover what you may incur for the postage of letters; until he shall otherwise order.

TH: JEFFERSON

RC (NjP); at head of text: "To Colonel David Humphreys"; endorsed. FC (DNA: RG 59, PCC No. 121). It is possible that some or all of the letters and papers carried by Humphreys were enclosed with the above, but it is also possible that Washington himself handed the more important ones to the envoy (see TJ to Washington, 8 Aug. 1790). In addition to ciphers, newspapers, &c. these included: (1) TJ to Carmichael, 2 and 6 Aug. 1790 and their enclosures. (2) TJ to De Pinto, 7 Aug. 1790. (3) TJ to Johnson, 7 Aug. 1790. (4) TJ to Morris, 12 Aug. 1790. (All of the foregoing are printed in the present series.) (5) Circular of Secretary of State to American Consuls in Europe, 25 Aug. 1790. (6) Secretary of the Treasury to Wilhem & Jan Willink, N. & J. Van Staphorst & Hubbard, 28 Aug. 1790, enclosing a commission of the same date ratifying and confirming the provisional loan of 3,000,000 florins notified in their letter of 25 Jan. 1790 and informing them that half of this sum was destined as a payment on the American Debt to France and to be applied by direction of William Short as chargé d'affaires (text of letter and enclosure in Syrett, Hamilton, VI, 580-5). (7) Secretary of the Treasury to William Short, 29 Aug. 1790 (printed in same, VI, 585-6; Short was by this letter referred to the Secretary of State "for instructions with regard to the timing of the intended payment" to France). Humphreys also carried various letters written by Washington (see below).

TJ took pains to see that his own secret dispatches to Short did not go by way of London with Humphreys. His public and private letters to Short of 9, 10, 12, 25, 26, and 31 Aug. 1790 were carried by a trusted individual, Nathaniel Barrett, with instructions that they

were to be "delivered . . . with his own hands" to Short in Paris (TJ to Short, 10 Aug. 1790, Document VI in present series). Hamilton, on the other hand, instructed Humphreys to place his dispatches for Short in the custody of his brother-in-law, John Barker Church, a member of Parliament. Shortly after arriving in London, Humphreys wrote Short a letter revealing this fact and giving a hint of the effect Hamilton's confidential conversations had had upon him: "To get the public debt into manageable way, if I may so express myself, seems now to be the great desideratum with our wisest and best political characters. On this subject you will be more particularly informed from some dispatches addressed to you by the Secretary of the Treasury, and which by his direction I am going to put into the hands of Mr. Church in order to be forwarded by a safe conveyance" (Humphreys to Short, 14 Oct. 1790, Humphreys, II, 31-2). It was rumored in New York before Humphreys departed that he had gone to Europe to "negotiate [the Holland loan]" (see above, p. 75).

In his capacity as a private traveler, which the administration took exceptional precautions to establish in order to conceal the public nature of his mission, Humphreys carried letters written by Washington on 10 and 11 Aug. 1790 to Paine, D'Estaing, Gardoqui, Rochambeau, La Luzerne, Lafayette, and (on personal matters) Gouverneur Morris (texts in Washington, Writings, ed. Fitzpatrick, XXXI, 80-8, 92-3). The longest and most carefully composed of these letters—that to Lafayette—bears almost unmistakable evidence of TJ's influence if not indeed of his hand. Washington touched first on affairs in France and the leadership manifested by Lafayette, revealing both in this letter and in that to Rochambeau that TJ had given a corrective to accounts of the progress of the Revolution in English newspapers both by his own testimony and by calling attention to the accounts in the *Gazette de Leide*. He then adverted to American affairs, reported them on the whole to be satisfactory, and asserted that the treaty with the Creeks would "leave us in peace from one end of our borders to the other," except for a small "banditti" of Shawnee and Cherokee that could easily be punished or destroyed. He then came to the main point—the threat of war, the policy of neutrality, the relations with Spain, and the mission of Humphreys. In France TJ had unquestionably influenced Lafayette's letters to Washington and there can be little doubt that he exercised a similar influence in the reverse direction as Secretary of State.

VIII. Secretary of State to Gouverneur Morris

DEAR SIR   New York August 12th. 1790.

Your letter of May 29th. to the President of the United States has been duly received. You have placed their proposition of exchanging a Minister on proper ground. It must certainly come from them, and come in unequivocal form; with those who respect their own dignity so much, ours must not be counted at nought. On their own proposal formerly to exchange a Minister, we sent them one; they have taken no notice of that, and talk of agreeing to exchange one now, as if the idea were new. Besides what they are saying to you, they are talking to us through Quebec; but so informally that they may disavow it when they please; it would only oblige them to make the fortune of the poor Major whom they would pretend to sacrifice; through him they talk of a Minister, a treaty of commerce *and alliance*. If the object of the latter be honorable, it is useless; if dishonorable, inadmissible. These tamperings prove they view a war as very possible; and some symptoms indicate designs against the Spanish possessions adjoining us. The consequences of their acquiring all the country on our frontier from the St. Croix to the St. Mary's are too obvious to you to need developement. You will readily see the dangers which would then environ us. We wish you therefore to intimate to them that we cannot be indifferent to enterprizes of this kind, that we should contemplate a change of neighbours with extreme uneasiness; and that a due balance on our borders is not less desireable to us, than a balance of power in Europe has always appeared to them. We wish to be neutral, and we will be so, *if they will execute the treaty fairly*, and *attempt no conquests adjoining us*. The first condition is just; the second imposes no hardship on them; they cannot complain that the other dominions of Spain would be so narrow as not to leave them room enough for conquest. If the war takes place, we would really wish to be quieted on these two points, offering in return an honorable neutrality; more than this they are not to expect. It will be proper that these ideas be conveyed in delicate and friendly terms; but that they be conveyed, if the war takes place; for it is in that case alone, and not till it be begun, that we would wish our dispositions to be known; but in no case need they think of our accepting any equivalent for the posts. I have the honor to be with great respect and esteem Dear Sir &c.

TH: JEFFERSON

FC (DNA: RG 59, PCC No. 121).
For note on Morris' LETTER OF MAY 29TH and other reports by him, see TJ's memorandum to Washington, 15 Dec. 1790. The dispatch of 29 May 1790 came by the June packet which arrived late in July—that is, after Hamilton's interview with Beckwith on the 8th. The above dispatch, it is to be noted, does not refer to the mission of David Humphreys, by whom it was conveyed. This was an intended omission, for Humphreys' instructions permitted him to reveal his object only to "the Chevalier Pinto and Mr. Carmichael" (TJ to Humphreys, 11 Aug. 1790). Morris had left for the continent before Humphreys arrived and so did not receive the dispatch until 23 Dec. 1790 on his return (Morris to TJ, 24 Dec. 1790).

IX. Queries from the President to Members of the Cabinet

(*Secret*)

United States August 27th. 1790

Provided the dispute between Great Britain and Spain should come to the decision of Arms, from a variety of circumstances (individually unimportant and inconclusive, but very much the reverse when compared and combined) there is no doubt in my mind, that New Orleans and the Spanish Posts above it on the Mississippi will be among the first attempts of the former, and that the reduction of them will be undertaken by a combined operation from Detroit.

The *Consequences* of having so formidable and enterprizing a people as the British on both our flanks and rear, with their navy in front, as they respect our Western Settlements which may be seduced thereby, as they regard the Security of the Union and its commerce with the West Indies, are too obvious to need enumeration.

What then should be the Answer of the Executive of the United States to Lord Dorchester, in case he should apply for permission to march Troops through the Territory of the said States from Detroit to the Mississippi?

What notice ought to be taken of the measure, if it should be undertaken without leave, which is the most probable proceeding of the two?

The Opinion of the Secretary of State is requested in writing upon the above statement.

GO: WASHINGTON

RC (DLC); in Lear's hand, signed by Washington. Recorded in SJPL but not in SJL. Another RC (DLC: Hamilton Papers). Dft (DLC: Washington Papers); in Humphreys' hand, with space left blank for designation of officer addressed and with following note at foot of text: "(Addressed thus separately to the Secretary of State, the Secy. of the Treasury, and the Secretary of War. Addressed to Mr. Jay thus: 'Mr. Jay will oblige the Presidt. of the United States by giving his opinion in writing on the above Statement' "; accompanied by wrapper docketed by Lear: "Quaeries to and Opinions of the Vice-President, the heads of the Departments and Chief Justice of the U.S. of what Answer should be given if a Request should be made to March troops from the British territory to the Mississippi. 27th Augt. 1790."

X. First Opinion of the Secretary of State

Opinion on the Questions stated in the President's note of August 27. 1790.

I am so deeply impressed with the magnitude of the dangers which will attend our government if Louisiana and the Floridas be added to the British empire, that in my opinion we ought to make ourselves parties in the *general war* expected to take place, should this be the only means of preventing the calamity.

But I think we should defer this step as long as possible; because war is full of chances which may relieve us from the necessity of interfering; and if necessary, still the later we interfere the better we shall be prepared.

It is often indeed more easy to prevent the capture of a place, than to retake it. Should it be so, in the case in question, the difference between the two operations of preventing, and retaking, will not be so costly, as two, three or four years more of war.

So that I am for preserving neutrality as long, and entering into the war as late, as possible.

If this be the best course, it decides, in a good degree, which should be our conduct, if the British ask leave to march troops thro' our territory, or march them without leave.

It is well enough agreed, in the Law of Nations, that for a Neutral power to give or refuse permission to the troops of either belligerent party to pass through their territory, is no breach of neutrality, provided the same refusal or permission be extended to the other party.

If we give leave of passage then to the British troops, Spain will have no just cause of complaint against us, provided we extend the same leave to her when demanded.

If we refuse (as indeed we have a right to do) and the troops should pass notwithstanding, of which there can be little doubt, we shall stand committed. For either we must enter immediately into the war, or pocket an acknowledged insult in the face of the world: and one insult pocketed soon produces another.

There is indeed a middle course, which I should be inclined to prefer. That is, to avoid giving any answer. They will proceed notwithstanding. But to do this under our silence, will admit of palliation, and produce apologies, from military necessity; and will leave us free to pass it over without dishonor, or to make it a handle of quarrel hereafter, if we should have use for it as such.—But if we are obliged to give an answer, I think the occasion not such as should induce us to hazard that answer which might commit us to the war at so early a stage of it; and therefore that the passage should be permitted.

If they should pass without having asked leave, I should be for expressing our dissatisfaction to the British court, and keeping alive an altercation on the subject, till events should decide whether it is most expedient to accept their apologies, or profit of the aggression as a cause of war.

TH: JEFFERSON
Aug. 28. 1790.

RC (DLC: Washington Papers); endorsed by Washington: "The Secretary of State 27th. Augt. 1790." Recorded in SJPL but not in SJL. PrC (DLC).

At the time he wrote this opinion TJ's expectation of a general war was stronger than here indicated—he thought that war was "almost a certain event" and viewed it as tolerably certain that France would join in as an ally of Spain (TJ to Randolph, 29 Aug. 1790). In view of this and of Hamilton's extended argument against allowing such sentiments as gratitude to influence decisions in foreign affairs—an argument that could only have been aimed at the position he assumed TJ would adopt— the strength of his attachment to the policy of neutrality and of his counsel to avoid involvement except as a last recourse against a calamitous encirclement becomes all the clearer. The essential difference between the two men on this and other issues in foreign affairs is that the Secretary of State followed the policy of neutrality consistently and out of profound conviction, whereas the Secretary of the Treasury supported the doctrine outwardly but endeavored steadily and unceasingly to insinuate a pro-British policy into almost all measures of the government.

XI. Second Opinion of the Secretary of State

On considering more fully the question Whether it will be expedien[t] to Notify to Ld. Dorchester the real object of the expedition preparing by Governor St. Clair, I still think it will not be expedient. For

If the Notification be early, he will get the Indians out of the way, and defeat our object.

If it be so late, as not to leave him time to withdraw them before our stroke be struck, it will then be so late also, as not to leave him time to withdraw any secret aids he may have sent them. And the Notification will betray to him that he may go on without fear in his expedition against the Spaniard[s] and for which he may yet have sufficient time after our expedition is over.

On the other hand, if he should suspect our preparations are to prevent his passing our territory, these suspicions may induce him to decline his expedition; as, even should he think he could either force or steal a passage, he would not divide his troops, leaving (as he would suppose) an enemy between them able to take those he should leave, and cut off the return of those he should carry.

These suspicions too would mislead both him and the Indians; and so enable us to take the latter more completely by surprise; and prevent him from sending secret aid to those whom he would not suppose the objects of the enterprise, thus effecting a double purpose of preventing his enterprize, and securing our own.

Might it not even be expedient, with a view to deter his enterprize, to instruct Gov. St. Clair either to continue his pursuit of the Indians till the season be too far advanced for Ld. Dorchester to move, or, on disbanding his militia, to give them general orders (which might reach the ears of Ld. Dorchester) to be ready to assemble at a moment's warning, tho' no such assembly be really intended? Always taking care neither to say nor do, against their passage, what might directly commit either our Peace, or Honour.

TH: JEFFERSON
Aug. 29. 1790.

FC (DNA: RG 59, SDC). PrC (DLC); in TJ's hand, and arranged in heads as in the case of the original opinion. Not recorded in SJL but entry in SJPL for this and preceding two documents reads: "[1790. Aug.] 27. GW. his Qu? if British wish to march thro' our territory to attack Spain. 28.

Th:J.'s answer to that Question. 29. P.S. to do."

Although Washington had sought the opinions of Adams, Jay, and members of the administration on the stand to be taken if British troops moved across American territory against Spanish possessions, there is no evidence that he asked anyone except TJ whether the object of the expedition against the Shawnee and Miami Indians should be disclosed to Lord Dorchester. This may be significant, and the fact that Harmar's stroke at harvest time was intended to be both punitive and a calculated surprise is certainly so. "While, on the one hand, your movements and execution should be so rapid and decisive as to astonish your enemy," Secretary of War Knox wrote General Harmar, "so, on the other, every possible precaution in the power of human foresight should be used to prevent surprise" (Henry Knox to Josiah Harmar, 24 Aug. 1790, *ASP, Indian Affairs*, I, 99). TJ's emphasis on this point in the above opinion obviously coincided with Washington's desire for an expeditious and hidden move. Yet, as historians have long known, the request for the opinion and TJ's response had already been rendered needless by the fact that, in a secret interview with Beckwith, the Secretary of the Treasury gave the agent in confidence what TJ here strongly urged the President to withhold. Naturally neither Washington nor TJ knew that Hamilton had done this or that Dorchester would be in possession of the information less than a fortnight after the Secretary of State urged that he be kept in the dark. While the fact of Hamilton's disclosure has been known, some of its most serious implications have been obscured because the date of the secret interview has not been established with precision. The chronology of the episode sheds some light on this but also raises disturbing questions.

At Pittsburgh on 16 Aug. 1790, Governor Arthur St. Clair, on his way to New York for consultation and approval of his plans, urged the militia of Virginia and Pennsylvania to rendezvous early in September for a sixty-day tour of duty. The governor travelled in such urgency both going and returning that he was back in Marietta just thirty days from the date of these instructions. He must, in fact, have left Pittsburgh that day, for he arrived in New York on Friday, 20 Aug. 1790—an astonishing feat for a man of fifty-four, surpassing that of the much younger Beckwith on his journey from Quebec in July (*New-York Journal*, 24 Aug. 1790). When he arrived, both the President and the Secretary of State were in Rhode Island, the Secretary of War and the Secretary of the Treasury in New York. There

can be no doubt that St. Clair saw both Knox and Hamilton immediately.

On Saturday the 21st, about sundown, the President and his party returned to the city. On the 23d St. Clair wrote the Secretary of War outlining his plans for the expedition, enclosing the journal of Antoine Gamelin who had carried his fruitless messages of peace to the Indians the preceding April. Two facts in Gamelin's journal are significant. At the Miami village he saw five Potawatomi bring in two Negro prisoners whom they sold as indentured servants to Indian traders. On the 25th of April Blue Jacket of the Shawnee returned the two proffered pieces of wampum and said to him: "we can not give an answer without hearing from our father, at Detroit"; three days later Le Gris, chief of the Miami, told him: "we can not give a definitive answer without consulting the commandant of Detroit" (Arthur St. Clair to Henry Knox, 23 Aug. 1790, with Gamelin's journal, *ASP, Indian Affairs*, I, 92-4). Knox transmitted these documents to the President, Washington immediately gave his approval and his views concerning the expedition, and Knox furnished St. Clair with his instructions. All of this took place on Monday, the 23rd. Further, on that same day Knox gave Hamilton an estimate of the cost of maintaining 1700 militia and 400 troops in the field for three months ($100,000); procured an advance from the Treasury for the contractors in order to enable them to obtain provisions and quartermaster's supplies; wrote to Samuel Hodgdon, commissary of military stores at Philadelphia, instructing him to send forward to the Northwest Territory, immediately, two tons of rifle and musket powder, four tons of lead bullets, and artillery shot; and gave orders for the transportation of these articles from Pittsburgh (Knox to St. Clair, 23 Aug. 1790, *ASP, Indian Affairs*, I, 98-9). Thus two days after the President's return the whole object of St. Clair's urgent journey had been accomplished. There was no need for him to remain longer in the city save perhaps to receive for Harmar the instructions that Knox wrote on the 24th. Beckwith later reported that the governor's stay in the city was "very short" (Dorchester to Grenville, 10 Nov. 1790, enclosing Beckwith's undated report, received at Quebec 27 Oct. 1790, PRO: CO 42/72, f.59, 61). There can be little doubt that St. Clair left New York on the 24th.

It is this brief chronology between the 20th and the 24th that fixes the time of Hamilton's interview with Beckwith, for it is clear that this took place while St. Clair was still in the city and before the expedition had been approved. Obviously, therefore, Beckwith sought out Hamilton on Saturday the 21st or on Sunday the 22d. The former seems more plausible. For Beckwith told Hamilton that he had heard "that very morning" an "officer attached to the person of the President" quote St. Clair in the presence of witnesses to the effect that traders under British protection at Detroit were encouraging Indian hostilities by purchasing prisoners as indentured servants. Beckwith admitted that he had heard instances of this, but stated that he had sought out Hamilton to give an explanation. Such transactions, he declared, were not only "done upon principles honourable to the parties, and to the general feeling of humanity," but "a procedure of the nature suggested" by St. Clair's information was contrary both to Dorchester's dispositions and to the spirit of his instructions to officers at the upper posts. To this Hamilton replied that St. Clair had brought information of many "excesses committed by the Savages, to which the Government had previously been strangers" and that, while nothing hostile to the United States had been expressed in the talks with the Indians "they indeed had said when proposals were made to them, that they must consult their father at Detroit, but nothing further." Then Hamilton added "that circumstances rendered it probable, measures would shortly be taken for an Expedition into the Indian Country in that quarter." Beckwith concluded with this information to Dorchester: "he mentioned it to prevent any alarm at our posts, *although he relied on my not speaking of it here*; but he did not say against which of the nations beyond the Ohio this expedition was intended to be directed." The dispatch was received in Quebec on 11 Sep. 1790 (Dorchester to Grenville, 25 Sep. 1790, PRO: CO 42/69, f. 28, 30-48; italics supplied; this conversation is the last recorded in a lengthy report covering interviews with various persons, beginning about 8 Aug. 1790; endorsed as received 4 Nov. 1790).

From this it is to be noted first of all that Hamilton anticipated action by the government just as he may have done

when he discussed the appointment of an agent to London in the fall of 1789. Second, it is clear that he was privy to the information St. Clair brought in Gamelin's journal. This was natural, for Hamilton, Knox, and St. Clair all had official responsibilities connected with the proposed expedition. Consultation among them in the President's absence was essential. Third, it seems equally certain that from the moment Hamilton gave his voluntary assurance to Beckwith about the limited object of the campaign, he endeavored to have this assurance made official by the government. In this he succeeded with the Secretary of War but not, as the above opinion indicates, with the Secretary of State.

It is sometimes assumed that Washington learned of St. Clair's letter to the commandant at Detroit notifying him of the object of the expedition only after it was written (Freeman, *Washington*, VI, 284). This is in error. The fact is that Knox gave authority for this notification in his instructions to St. Clair: "There are existing jealousies in the minds of the British officers in Canada," he wrote, "of the designs of the United States respecting the posts to have been relinquished by the last peace. It will be a point, therefore, of delicacy, that you should take measures, by sending some officer or messenger, at a proper time, to assure the commanding officer of the real object of the expedition. That the Shawanese, and some others joined with them, have committed such enormous offences against the citizens of the United States, as are any longer insupportable; but, to assure him of the entire pacific disposition of the United States towards Great Britain and its possessions" (Knox to St. Clair, 23 Aug. 1790, *ASP, Indian Affairs*, I, 98). St. Clair wrote to the commandant on 19 Sep. 1790, stating that he was commanded to do so by the President. He sent a copy of this letter to Knox and Knox in turn forwarded the covering letter and presumably its enclosure to Washington (St. Clair to Knox, 19 Sep. 1790, enclosing his of the same date to the commandant at Detroit, same, I, 95-6). It is certain, therefore, that Washington gave the authorization to St. Clair to say to the commandant what Hamilton had already said to Beckwith. When he learned that the governor had done this with so little regard for the central element in the instructions, he was filled with apprehension. The instructions had stipulated that the notification be made "at a proper time," and Washington thought that St. Clair's revelation had been "unseasonable"— that it "was certainly premature to announce the operation intended until the troops were ready to move; since the Indians, through that channel, might receive such information as would frustrate the expedition" (Washington to Knox, 4 Nov. 1790, *Writings*, ed. Fitzpatrick, XXXI, 144). What Washington was concerned about was the timing of the notification to Major Murray at Detroit. This also was the basic reason for the above opinion by TJ. And it was this fundamental requirement of successful strategy that Hamilton blandly disregarded in his clandestine conference with Dorchester's agent.

The news of the expedition, of course, was spread throughout the Northwest Territory. Major Murray replied to St. Clair's letter on 14 Oct. 1790. Three days later a private letter from Detroit described the effects of the projected expedition on British merchants engaged in the Indian trade. And soon St. Clair's letter of 8 Sep. to the Seneca and that of 19 Sep. 1790 to the Wyandots were in Dorchester's hands along with other reports from the upper posts (Dorchester to Grenville, 10 Nov. 1790, PRO: CO 42/72, f. 73, 75-88, with seven enclosures; endorsed as received 18 Dec. 1790). The military preparations on such a scale could not have been concealed in any event, but what British officers in the upper posts now knew with certainty because of St. Clair's premature disclosure and because of Hamilton's voluntary assurance to Beckwith was precise. An expedition

of considerable force was imminent and its objective was the group of Indians who had been troublesome, who had struck no major blow against the Americans, but who looked to Detroit for protection.

The ill-fated force under General Harmar produced a noteworthy series of coincidences on the 4th of November 1790. On that day Washington at Mount Vernon learned with apprehension of St. Clair's premature disclosure, fearing the surprise which Harmar had been so solemnly warned to avoid. On that day at Whitehall the Secretary for Home Affairs learned that the Secretary of the Treasury had told a British agent in confidence that the expedition was about to be undertaken and that its object was only the Indian nations. And on that day at Fort Washington General Harmar tabulated the list of officers and men killed in the engagements against the Miami towns. The total was 183, far more than anyone expected and approximately twice what he had calculated on 22 Oct. 1790 at the camp on the night after the destruction of the Indian harvests and towns. This he lamented but added on that day of battle: "it is the fortune of war" (*ASP, Indian Affairs*, I, 106; Washington to Knox, 4 Nov. 1790, *Writings*, ed. Fitzpatrick, XXXI, 144; Dorchester to Grenville, 25 Sep. 1790, enclosing Beckwith's dispatch containing the conversation with Hamilton of 21 or 22 Aug. 1790, endorsed as received 4 Nov. 1790; PRO: CO 42/69, f. 28, 30-48). There had been three ambushes. The chain of coincidence closed exactly a year later, 4 Nov. 1791, when St. Clair suffered his crushing defeat—caused by surprise.

XII. Opinion of the Chief Justice

SIR   New York 28 Augt. 1790

The Case which I had Yesterday the Honor of recieving from you gave occasion to the following Remarks and Reflections.

Whether the Issue of the Negociations depending between the british and spanish Courts be Peace or War, it certainly is prudent to anticipate and be prepared for the consequences of either Event. In the present State of Things it would doubtless militate against the Interests of the U.S. that the spanish Territories in question should be reduced, and remain under the Government of his B. Majesty; and probably that circumstances would strongly unite with those others which must naturally lead him to regard the Possession of those countries as a desireable object.

If permission to march Troops for that Purpose, thro' the Territories of the U.S. should be requested, it will be necessary to consider

1. Whether the Laws of Nations entitle a *belligerent* Power to a free Passage for Troops thro' the Territories of a *Neutral* Nation? and

2. In Case the Right to such Passage be not a *perfect* one, whether circumstances render a Refusal or a compliance most adviseable on the present occasion?

The Right of Dominion involves that of excluding (under the Restrictions imposed by Humanity) all Foreigners. This Right is very rigidly exercised by some States, particularly the Empire of China. European Nations consider this as a general Right or Rule, and as subject to Exceptions in favor not only of Nations at *Peace*, but also of Nations at *War*. The Exceptions which respect the *former* do not touch the present question. Those which relate to the *latter*, seem to be comprized within *two* Classes vizt. cases of *urgent necessity*, and Cases of *Convenience*. The present case belongs to the latter. Vattel, who well understood the subject, says in the 7th: chapter of his 3d. Book:

That an *innocent* Passage is due to all Nations with whom a State is at Peace, and that this comprehends Troops equally with Individuals—That the Sovereign of the country is to judge whether this Passage be *innocent*—That his Permission must be asked—and that an Entry into his Territories without his consent, is a violation of the Rights of Dominion—That if the neutral Sovereign has *good* Reasons for refusing a Passage, he is not bound to grant it; but that if his Refusal be evidently unjust (the Passage requested being *unquestionably innocent*) a nation may do itself Justice, and take by force, what it was unjustly denied; so that such Requests may be refused in all Cases, except in those rare Instances, where it may be most evidently shewn that the Passage required is absolutely without Danger or Inconvenience.

If the Passage in contemplation should appear to be of this Complection, a Refusal would generally be deemed improper, unless the united States should declare and make it an invariable maxim in their Policy, *never to permit the Troops of any nation to pass thro' their country*. Such a measure *might* be wise, in Case the U.S. were in capacity to act accordingly; but that not being as yet the Case, it would perhaps in the present moment be unseasonable.

I say "such a measure *might* be wise." Whether it would or not, is a question that involves others, both legal and political of great Magnitude. Nations have *perfect* Rights. Regard to mutual Convenience may and often does induce Relaxations in the Exercise of them; and those Relaxations, from Time and usage, gradually assume to a certain Degree the Nature of Rights. I think it would appear on a full Investigation of the Subject, that the United States, being a new nation, are not bound to yield the same Relaxations, which in Europe from long Practice and acquiescence amount almost to an implied Cession; and therefore, that they may justly exercise rigorously the Right of denying free Passage to foreign Troops. It is also to be observed, that if they deny this Priviledge to others, it will also be denied to them; but this leads to political consequences and Considerations not necessary now to develope or investigate.

If a Passage should be requested and insisted upon, on the Ground of its being perfectly *innocent*, and accompanied with such Terms and Precautions, as that a Refusal, altho justifiable, would not appear to be more than barely so; then it will be adviseable to calculate the Probability of their being restrained by such a Refusal.

If the Probability should be, that they would nevertheless proceed; then it would become important to consider whether it would not be better to grant Permission, than by a Refusal to hazard one of two enevitable Inconveniences vizt. that of opposing their Progress by Force of arms, and thereby risque being involved in the War; or of submitting to the Disgrace and Humiliation of permitting them to proceed with Impunity. In my opinion it would in such a Case be most prudent, considering the actual State of our affairs, to consent to the Passage. The answer therefore to be given to Lord Dorchester, in Case he should apply for Permission to march Troops thro' the Territory of the U.S. from Detroit to the Missisippi, will I think necessarily depend on the nature of the Propositions contained in the application, compared with the before mentioned Principles and Probabilities.

As to the notice proper to be taken of the Measure, if it should be under taken *without* Leave? There appears to me to be no choice.

Such a Measure would then be so manifest a Departure from the Usage of civilized nations, so flagrant and wanton a Violation of the Rights of Sovereignty, and so strong and indecent a mark of Disrespect and Defiance, that their March (if after Prohibition persisted in) should I think be opposed and prevented at every Risque and Hazard.

But these Remarks in my Judgment retain but little Force, when applied to the leading of Troops from Posts in their actual Possession, thro' Territories under their actual Jurisdiction, altho' both the Posts and the Territories of right belong to the U.S. If therefore they should march their Troops from such posts, thro' such Territories, that measure would not appear to me to afford *particular* cause of complaint. On their arrival by such a Route at the Missisippi, they may in Virtue of the 8th article of the Treaty navigate it up to its source, or down to the ocean.

This subject naturally brings into View a Question both difficult and important vizt. whether as the Possession of the Floridas would afford G. Britain additional means and Facilities of annoying the U.S. the latter would for that Reason be justifiable in endeavouring to prevent it by direct and hostile opposition? The Danger of permitting any nation so to preponderate, as to endanger the Security of others, introduced into the Politics of Europe the Idea of preserving a Ballance of Power. How far the Principles which have thence been inferred, are applicable to the present Case, would merit serious Inquiry, if the U.S. had only to consider what might be right and just on the occasion. But as the State of their affairs strongly recommends Peace, and as there is much Reason to presume that it would be more prudent for them *at present* to permit Britain to conquer and hold the Floridas, than engage in a War to prevent it, such Inquiries would be premature.—With the most perfect Respect and Esteem I have the Honor to be Sir, Your most obt. & most humble Servant

John Jay

RC (DLC: Washington Papers).

XIII. Opinion of the Vice-President

Sir New York August 29¹ 1790

That New Orleans, and the Spanish Posts on the Missisippi, will be among the first attempts of the English, in case of a war with Spain, appears very probable: and that a combined operation from Detroit, would be convenient to that end cannot be doubted.

The Consequences, on the western Settlements, on the commerce with the West Indies, and on the general Security and tranquility of the American confederation, of having them in our rear, and on both our flanks, with their navy in front, are very obvious.

The interest of the United States duely weighed, and their Duty conscientiously considered, point out to them, in the Case of Such a War, a neutrality, as long as it may be practicable. The People of these States would not willingly Support a War, and the present government has not Strength to command, nor enough of the general Confidence of the nation to draw the men or money necessary, untill the Grounds, causes and Necessity of it Should become generally known, and universally approved. A pacific Character, in opposition to a warlike temper, a Spirit of Conquest, or a disposition to military Enterprize, is of great importance to us to preserve in Europe: and therefore We Should not engage even in defensive War, untill the Necessity of it, should become apparent, or at least untill We have it in our Power to make it manifest, in Europe as well as at home.

In order to preserve an honest Neutrality, or even the Reputation of a disposition to it, the United States must avoid as much as possible, every real Wrong, and even every appearance of Injury to either Party. To grant to Lord Dorchester in case he Should request it, permission to march troops through the territory of the United States, from Detroit to the Missisippi, would not only have an appearance offensive to the Spaniards, of partiality to the English, but would be a real Injury to Spain. The Answer therefore to his Lordship Should be a refusal, in terms clear and decided, but guarded and dignified, in a manner, which no Power has more at command than the President of the United States.

If a measure so daring offensive and hostile, as the march of Troops through our Territory to Attack a Friend, Should be hazarded by the English, without leave, or especially after a refusal, it is not so easy to answer the Question, what notice ought to be taken of it.

The Situation of our Country is not like that of most of the nations in Europe. They have generally large numbers of Inhabitants in narrow territories: We have Small numbers Scattered over vast regions. The Country through which the Brittons must pass from Detroit to the Missisippi, is, I Suppose, so thinly inhabited, and at such a distance from all the populous Settlements, that it would be impossible for the President of the United States to collect Militia or march troops Sufficient to resist the Enterprize. After the Step shall have been taken there are but two Ways for Us to proceed one is War and the other negotiations. Spain would probably remonstrate to the President of the United States but whether she should or not, the President of the United States should remonstrate to the King of Great Britain. It would not be expected I suppose by our Friends or Ennemies that the United States should declare War at once. Nations are not obliged to declare War for every Injury or even Hostility. A tacit Acquiescence under Such an Outrage, would be misinterpreted on all hands; by Spain as inimical to her and by Brittain, as the effect of Weakness, Disunion and Pusillanimity. Negotiation then is the only other Alternative.

Negotiation in the present State of Things is attended with peculiar difficulties. As the King of Great Britain, twice proposed to the United States, an Exchange of Ministers, once through Mr. Hartley and once through the Duke of Dorsett, and when the United States agreed to the Proposition, flew from it: to Send a Minister again to St James's till that Court explicitly promises to send one to America is an humiliation to which the United States ought never to Submit. A Remonstrance from Sovereign to Sovereign cannot be Sent, but by an Ambassador of some order or other: from Minister of State to Minister of State, it might be transmitted in many other Ways: A Remonstrance in the form of a Letter from the American Minister of State to the Duke of Leeds, or whoever may be Secretary of State for foreign affairs, might be transmitted, through an Envoy, Minister Plenipotentiary, or Ambassador of the President of the United States, at Paris, Madrid or the Hague and through the British Ambassador at either of those Courts. The Utmost length, that can be now gone, with Dignity would be to send a Minister to the Court of London, with Instructions to present his Credentials, demand an Audience, make his Remonstrance, but to make no Establishment and demand his audience of leave and quit the Kingdom in one, two or three Months if a Minister of equal degree were not appointed and actually sent to the President of the United States, from the King of Great Britain.

It is a Misfortune, that in these critical moments and Circumstances, the United States have not a Minister of large Views, mature Age Information and Judgment, and Strict Integrity, at the

Court of France Spain London and the Hague. Early and authentick Intelligence from those Courts may be of more importance than the Expence: but as the Representatives of the People, as well as of the Legislatures, are of a different opinion they have made a very Scanty Provision for but a part of such a system. As it is, God knows where the Men are to be found who are qualified for such Missions and would undertake them. By an Experience of ten years which made me too unhappy at the time to be ever forgotten, I know, that every Artifice which can deceive, every temptation which can operate on hope or fear, Ambition or Avarice, Pride or Vanity, the Love of Society Pleasure or Amusement will be employed to divert and warp them from the true line of their Duty and the impartial honour and interest of their Country.

To the Superior Lights and Information derived from office; the more Serene temper and profound Judgment of the President of the United States, these crude and hasty thoughts concerning the Points proposed, are humbly Submitted, with every Sentiment of respect and Sincere Attachment, by his most obedient and most humble Servant JOHN ADAMS

RC (DLC: Washington Papers); at foot of text: "The President of the United States."

1 Adams first wrote "28" and then altered it to read as above.

XIV. Opinion of the Secretary of War

SIR   War office 29th August 1790

In answer to your secret communication of the 27th instant, and the questions stated therein I humbly beg leave to observe,

That the United States, by not being under the obligation of any treaty, either with Spain or England, are in a situation, to grant, or deny, the passage of troops, through their territory, as they shall judge fit.

The granting or refusing therefore the expected demand of a free passage to the troops of England, through the territory of the United States, in order to attack the dominions of Spain upon the Mississippi, will depend upon a due estimation of the consequences arising from either alternative.

The United States are too well aware, of the great and permanent evils, which would result from Englands becoming possessed of the Mississippi and West Florida, to concur in any arrangements to facilitate that event.

The law of Nations establish the principle, that every neutral nation may, refuse the passage of troops through its territory, when such passage may tend to its injury.

In the present case, the passage of the British troops, would be to effect an object directly contrary to the interests and welfare of the United States. If therefore the demand should be made, it may be refused, consistently with the principles of self preservation, and the law of Nations.

But there are two modes of refusal—a denial, unaccompanied by any other act; and a denial accompanied by force to oppose the passage, if it should be attempted after having been refused.

The first mode is all that can with propriety be done under the present state of things. If after the denial, the british troops should proceed, they become the aggressors, and establish a just cause of War, whenever the interests of the United States shall dictate the measure. Although a denial, unaccompanied by any other act, might be unpleasant to great Britain, yet she would not probably think it, of itself, a sufficient cause for waging war against the United States. But if a force should be actually opposed to the passage of the troops, a war with great Britain would appear to be the inevitable and immediate consequence.

The true interests of the United States dictate a state of neutrality in the affair between Spain and England. Should the United States be dragged into the war in the present moment, the loss of their commerce might justly be expected; The Source of their revenue would be cut off, and the proposed system of public credit fatally postponed if not entirely blasted. These are serious evils and to be avoided if possible.

It is however to be remarked that it is highly improbable that Spain would enter into the War, unless she expected to be supported by France—Nor does there appear any solid objections to this expectation, but the present debilitated and convulsed state of France. The family compact and other treaties between the two Kingdoms will continue to exist, notwithstanding the situation of France, until formally renounced. This has not been the case. The probability therefore is that France will be combined with Spain.

If this should be the case, every effort on the part of France will be employed to associate America in the War. And it is a question of great moment whether the United States could strictly comply with the treaty of friendship and Commerce entered into with France on the 6th of February,[1] and observe an exact neutrality.

Although it would seem hardly possible that either England, or France and Spain combined, would make such Offers to the United States as to counterbalance the advantages of Neutrality, yet the case may be otherwise, or the United States may be obliged to enter into the War in order to avert a greater evil.

These considerations with their several extensive relations unite in dictating an answer to Lord Dorchester in terms as little exceptionable as possible.

That the United States had recently manifested their sincere desires, not only to continue at peace with Great Britain but to cement the same by commercial arrangements which might be reciprocally beneficial.

But that the real causes of dispute between England and Spain were too little understood at present by the United States for the President to consent to a measure which would seem to be inconsistent with that strict neutrality the United States would desire to observe.

But if notwithstanding this answer, or if no request should be made for the purpose, and the troops march through the territory of the United States, to attack the dominions of Spain it might be proper for the President of the United States to convene immediately the legislature if the occasion should be so urgent as to require their meeting at an earlier day than the adjournment, and to lay the whole affair before them, with his opinion of the measures proper to be pursued. For the Congress are vested with the right of providing for the common defence, and of declaring war, and of consequence they should possess the information of all facts and circumstances thereunto appertaining.

In the mean time the dispositions and designs of the contending parties will unfold themselves, The terms of each side be known and estimated, and the United States better able than at present, to judge of the exact line of conduct they ought to pursue.—I have the honor with perfect Respect to be Sir Your humble Servant

H Knox

RC (DLC: Washington Papers); at foot of text: "The President of the United States"; endorsed by Washington: "From The Secry. of War 29th. Augt. 1790."

Knox' allusion to the recent manifestation of a desire to effect COMMER-CIAL ARRANGEMENTS with Great Britain can only refer to the letter of credence given by Washington to Morris on 13 Oct. 1789; Washington, *Writings*, ed. Fitzpatrick, xxx, 439-40.

1 Thus in MS, the date 1778 being omitted.

XV. Opinion of the Secretary of the Treasury

New York September 15. 1790

Answers to Questions proposed by The President of the United States to the Secretary of the Treasury

Question the first

"What should be the answer of the Executive of the United States to Lord Dorchester, in case he should apply for permission to march troops through the territory of said States from Detroit to the Mississippi?

Answer

In order to a right judgment of what ought to be done in such case, it may be of use previously to consider the following points.

First, whether there be a right to *refuse* or *consent*, as shall be thought most for the interest of the United States.

Secondly, The consequences to be expected from *refusal* or *consent*.

Thirdly, The motives to the one or to the other.

As to the first point, if it were to be determined upon principle only, without regard to precedents, or opinions, there would seem to be no room for hesitation about the right to refuse. The exclusive jurisdiction, which every independent Nation has over its own territory appears to involve in it the right of prohibiting to all others the use of that territory in any way disagreeable to itself, and more especially for any purpose of war, which always implies a degree of danger and inconvenience: with the exception only of cases of necessity.

And if the United States were in a condition to do it, without material hazard, there would be strong inducements to their adopting it as a general rule never to grant a passage for a voluntary expedition of one power against another, unless obliged to it by treaty.

But the present situation of the United States is too little favourable to encountering hazards, to authorise attempts to establish rules, however eligible in themselves, which are repugnant to the received maxims or usages of Nations.

It is therefore necessary to inquire what those maxims or usages enjoin in the case suggested.

With regard to usage it has been far from uniform. There are various instances in ancient and modern times of similar permis-sions being demanded; many in which they have been granted; others in which they have been refused and the refusal acquiesced in; but perhaps more in which, when refused, a passage has been forced, and the doing it has often been deemed justifiable.

Opinions are not more harmonious. Among those who may be considered as authorities on such subjects, Puffendorf and Barbeyrac confine within narrow limits *the right of passage* through neutral territories; while Grotius and Vatel, particularly the former, allow to it greater latitude. Puffendorff treats it not as a natural right but as derived from compact or concession; especially when the enemy of a neighbouring state desires leave to march troops through a neutral Country against its neighbour. For it seems (says he) to be a part of *the duty which we owe to our neighbours*, especially such as have been kind and friendly, not to suffer any hostile power to march through our Country to their prejudice; *provided we can hinder the design with no great inconvenience to ourselves.* And as it may have a tendency to make our own Country the theatre of the war, (since the power intended to be attacked may justifiably march within our limits to meet the approaching enemy) he concludes that it is the safest way of acting in such case, *if we can do it, without any considerable prejudice to our own affairs* to deny the enemy passage, and *actually to oppose him*, if he endeavour to force it without our consent. But if we are either too weak to hinder his progress or must on this score engage in a dangerous war, he admits, that the plea of necessity will fairly justify us to our neighbour.

Examples, he adds, have little force in the decision of this question. For, generally, as people have been stronger or weaker, they have required passage with modesty or with confidence, and have in like manner granted or refused it to others.*

Barbeyrac in his commentary on Grotius is still stronger against the right of passage.† He affirms that even though we have nothing to apprehend from those who desire a passage, we are not therefore obliged in rigour to grant it. It necessarily follows (says he) from the right of property, that the proprietor may refuse another the use of his goods. Humanity indeed requires that he should grant that use to those who stand in need of it, when it can be done without any considerable inconvenience to himself; but if he even then refuses it, though he transgresses his duty, he does them no

* Puffendorffs Law of Nature and Nations pages 239, 240.
† Note I on Book II Chapt II § xiii.

wrong, properly so called; *except they are in extreme necessity*, which is superior to all ordinary rules. Thus far and no further extends the reserve with which it is supposed the establishment of property is accompanied.

Grotius on the other hand, expresses himself thus: ‡ A free passage ought to be granted to persons where *just occasion* shall require, over any lands or rivers, or such parts of the sea as belong to any nation; and after enumerating several examples in support of his position, he concludes that the *middle opinion* is left; to wit, that the liberty of passing ought first to be demanded, and if denied may be claimed by force. Neither (says he) can it be reasonably objected that there may be suspicion of danger from the passing of a multitude; for one man's right is not diminished by another man's fear. Nor is the fear of provoking that prince against whom he that desires to pass is engaged in a *just* war, a sufficient reason for refusing him passage. Nor is it any more an excuse that he may pass another way, for this is what every body may equally allege, and so this right of passing would be entirely destroyed. But 'tis enough that the passage be requested without any fraud or ill design, by the nearest and most convenient way. *If* indeed, he who desires to pass undertakes an *unjust* war, or *if* he brings people who are my enemies along with him, I *may* deny him a passage; *for in this case* I have a right to meet and oppose him, even in his own land, and to intercept his march. Thus it would seem to be the opinion of Grotius that a party engaged in a just war has a right, of course, to a passage through a neutral territory, which can scarcely, if at all, be denied him, even on the score of danger or inconvenience to the party required to grant it.

But Vatel, perhaps the most accurate and approved of the writers on the laws of Nations, preserves a mean between these different opinions. This is the sum of what he advances: * That an *innocent passage* is *due* to all nations, with whom a state is at peace, for troops equally with individuals, and to annoy as well as to avoid an enemy. That the party asking and the party asked are both, in different degrees, judges of the question *when innocent?* That where the party asked has *good reasons* for refusing, he is not under any obligation to grant, and in *doubtful* cases his judgment ought to be definitive; but in evident ones, or those in which the harmlessness of the passage is manifest,

‡ Rights of War and Peace Book II Chap II § xiii No. 1.2.3.4.
* Book III Chap: VII § 119. 120. 121. 122. 123.

the party asking may, in the last resort, judge for himself, and after *demand* and *refusal* may force his way. That, nevertheless, as it is very difficult for the passage of a powerful army to be absolutely innocent, and still more difficult for its innocence to be apparent, a refusal ought to be submitted to, *except* in those *very rare* cases, when it can be shewn in the most palpable manner, that the passage required is absolutely without danger or inconvenience. And lastly that this right of passage is only *due* in a war *not manifestly unjust.*

Perhaps the only inference to be drawn from all this is, that there exists in the practice of nations and the dogmas of political writers a certain vague pretension to a right of passage in particular cases, and according to circumstances, which is sufficient to afford to the strong a pretext for claiming and exercising it, when it suits their interests, and to render it always dangerous to the weak to refuse, and, sometimes not less so, to grant it.

It is, nevertheless, a proper inquiry, whether a refusal could be placed on such ground as would give no reasonable cause of umbrage to the party refused, and as in the eye of the world would justify it.

Against the propriety of a refusal are the following circumstances; that there is no connection between us and Spain, which obliges us to it: That the passage asked will be down rivers, and for the most part through an uninhabited wilderness; whence no injury to our citizens or settlements will be to be apprehended: And that the number of troops to be marched, especially considering the route, will probably not be such as on their own account, to be a serious cause of alarm. These circumstances may give our refusal the complexion of partiality to Spain and of indisposition towards Britain, which may be represented as a deviation from the spirit of exact neutrality.

In support of the propriety of a refusal, the following is the only assignable reason: That it is safer for us, to have two powerful, but *rival* nations, bordering upon our two extremities, than to have one powerful nation pressing us on both sides and in capacity, hereafter, by posts and settlements, to invelop our whole interior frontier.

The good offices of Spain in the late war; the danger of the seduction of our Western inhabitants; the probable consequences to the trade of the Atlantic States; are considerations rather to be contemplated, as motives, than alleged, as reasons.

The first reason, however, is of a nature to satisfy the mind of the justice of a refusal; admitting the authority of the more moderate opinions, which have been cited. And the danger, too, upon the supposition of which it is founded, appears to be obvious enough to vindicate it in the opinion of the disinterested part of Mankind; little likely as it may be to engage the acquiescence of the party whose wishes would be thwarted by the refusal. It deserves notwithstanding to be noticed on this point, that the ground of dissent would not result from the thing itself, that is the *mere passage*, but from the nature of the *acquisition*, to which it would give facility. This circumstance may somewhat obscure the clearness of the conclusion that there is a perfect right to refuse.

But upon the whole there does not appear to be room enough for a scruple about the right, to deter from refusal, if upon examination it shall be found expedient.

Does the right of consenting to the passage stand upon ground equally unexceptionable?

This question *Vatel* answers in the following manner:* "When I have no reason to refuse the passage, the party against whom it is granted has *no room for complaint,* much less for making it a pretence for war; since I did no more than what the law of nations enjoins. Neither has he any right to require, that I should deny the passage, because he is not to hinder me from doing what I think is agreeable to my duty, and *even* on occasion *when I might with justice deny the passage*, it is *allowable* in me *not to make use of* my right; *especially when I should be obliged to support my refusal by my sword.* Who will take upon him to complain of my having permitted the war to be carried into his own country rather than draw it on myself? It cannot be expected, that I should take up arms in his favour, unless obliged to it by a Treaty." And Puffendorff admits, as has been before noted, that if we are either *too weak* to hinder his progress or must on that score engage in a *dangerous* war, the plea of necessity will fairly justify us to our neighbour.

Nothing need be added to reasoning so perspicuous and convincing. It does not admit of a moment's doubt as a general rule that a neutral state, unfettered by any stipulation, is not bound to expose itself to a war, merely to shelter a neighbor from the approaches of its enemy. It remains to examine, if there are any circumstances, in our particular case, capable of forming an exception to that rule.

It is not to be forgotten that we received from France, in our late

* Vattel Book III Chap VII Section 127.

revolution, essential succour, and from Spain valuable countenance and some direct aid. It is also to be remembered that France is the intimate ally of Spain, and that there subsists a connection by treaty between the former power and the United States.

It might thence be alleged that obligations of Gratitude towards those powers require that we should run some risk, rather than concur in a thing prejudicial to either of them, and particularly in favour of that very nation against which they assisted us. And the natural impulse of every good heart will second the proposition, 'till reason has taught it, that refinements of this kind are to be indulged with caution, in the affairs of Nations.

Gratitude is a word the very sound of which imposes something like respect. Where there is even an appearance upon which the claim to it can be founded, it can seldom be a pleasing task to dispute that claim. But where a word may become the basis of a political system, affecting the essential interests of the state, it is incumbent upon those who have any concern in the future administration, to appreciate its true import and application.

It is necessary then to reflect, however painful the reflection, that gratitude is a duty or sentiment which between nations can rarely have any solid foundation. Gratitude is only due to a kindness or service, the predominant object of which is the interest or benefit of the party to whom it is performed. Where the interest or benefit of the party performing is the predominant cause of it, however there may result a debt, in cases in which there is not an immediate adequate and reciprocal advantage, there can be no room for the sentiment of gratitude. Where there is such an advantage there is then not even a debt. If the motive to the act, instead of being the benefit of the party to whom it is done, should be a compound of the interest of the party doing it and of detriment to some other, of whom he is the enemy or the rival, there is still less room for so noble and refined a sentiment. This analysis will serve as a test of our true situation, in regard both to France and Spain.

It is not to be doubted that the part which the Courts of France and Spain took in our quarrel with Great Britain is to be attributed, not to an attachment to our independence or liberty, but to a desire of diminishing the power of Great Britain by severing the British empire. This they considered as an interest of very great magnitude to them. In this their calculations and their passions conspired. For this, they united their arms with ours and encountered the expences and perils of war. This has been accomplished; the advantages of it are mutual; and so far the account is ballanced.

In the progress of the war* they lent us money, as necessary to its success, and during our inability to pay they have foreborn to press us for it. The money we ought to exert ourselves to repay with interest, and as well for the loan of it, as for the forbearance to urge the repayment of the sums, which have become due, we ought always to be ready to make proportionate acknowlege- ments, and, when opportunities shall offer, returns answerable to the nature of the service.

Let it be added to this, that the conduct of France in the manner affording her aid bore the marks of a liberal policy. She did not endeavour to extort from us, as the price of it, any disadvantageous or humiliating concessions. In this respect, however she may have been influenced by an enlightened view of her own interest, she intitled herself to our esteem and good will. These dispositions towards her ought to be cherished and cultivated but they are very distinct from a spirit of romantic gratitude calling for sacrifices of our substantial interests; preferences inconsistent with sound policy; or complaisances incompatible with our safety.

The conduct of Spain towards us presents a picture far less favourable. The direct aid we received from her during the war was inconsiderable in itself, and still more inconsiderable compared with her faculty of aiding us. She refrained from acknowleging our independence, has never acceded to the Treaty of Commerce made with France, though a right of doing it was reserved to her, nor made any other Treaty with us. She has maintained possessions within our acknowleged limits without our consent. She persever- ingly obstructs our sharing in the navigation of the Mississippi; though it is a privilege essential to us, and to which we consider ourselves as having an indisputable title. And perhaps it might be added upon good ground that she has not scrupled to intrigue with leading individuals in the Western County to seduce them from our interests and to attach them to her own.

Spain therefore must be regarded, upon the whole, as having slender claims to peculiar good will from us. There is certainly nothing that authorises her to expect we should expose ourselves to any extraordinary jeopardy for her sake. And to conceive that any considerations relative to France ought to be extended to her would be to set up a doctrine altogether new in politics. The ally

* France has made us one loan since the peace.

of our ally has no claim, as such, to our friendship. We may have substantial grounds of dissatisfaction against him, and act in consequence of them, even to open hostility, without derogating in any degree from what we owe to our ally.

This is so true, that if a war should really ensue between Great Britain and Spain, and if the latter should persist in excluding us from the Mississippi (taking it for granted our claim to share in its navigation is well founded) there can be no reasonable ground of doubt that we should be at liberty, if we thought it our interest, consistently with our present engagements with France, to join Britain against Spain.

How far it might be expedient to place ourselves in a situation, which in case France should eventually become a party in the war, might entangle us in opposite duties on the score of the stipulated guarantee of her West India possessions, or might have a tendency to embroil us with her would be a mere question of prudential and liberal calculation, which would have nothing to do with the right of taking side against Spain.

These are truths necessary to be contemplated with freedom, because it is impossible to foresee what events may spring up, or whither our interests may point; and it is very important to distinguish with accuracy, how far we are bound, and where we are free.

However vague the obligations of gratitude may be between Nations, those of good faith are precise and determinate. Within their true limits, they can hardly be held too sacred. But by exagerating them, or giving them a fanciful extension, they would be in danger of losing their just force. This would be converting them into fetters, which a nation would ere long become impatient to break, as consistent neither with its prosperity, nor its safety. Hence while it is desireable to maintain with fidelity our engagements to France, it is adviseable on all occasions to be aware, that they oblige us to nothing towards Spain.

From this view of the subject there does not appear any circumstance in our case capable of forming an exception to the general rule; and as it is certain that there can hardly be a situation less adapted to war than that in which we now find ourselves, we can with the greatest sincerity offer the most satisfactory excuse to Spain for not withholding our consent, if our own interests do not decide us to a contrary course. The conclusion from what has been said is that there is a right either to refuse or consent as shall be judged for the Interest of the United States; though the right to consent is less questionable than that to refuse.

The consequences to be expected from refusal or consent present themselves next to consideration. Those of consent shall be first examined.

An increase of the means of annoying us, in the same hands is a certain ill consequence of the acquisition of the Floridas and Louisiana by the British. This will result not only from contiguity to a greater part of our territory but from the increased facility of acquiring an undivided influence over all the Indian tribes inhabiting within the borders of the United States.

Additional danger of the dismemberment of the Western Country is another ill consequence to be apprehended from that acquisition. This will arise as well from the greater power of annoying us, as from the different policy, which it is likely would be pursued by that nation, if in possession of the key to the only outlet for the productions of that Country. Instead of shutting, they would probably open the door to its inhabitants and by conciliating their good will on the one hand, and making them sensible on the other of their dependence on them for the continuance of so essential an advantage they might hold out to them the most powerful temptation to a desertion of their connection with the rest of the United States. The avarice and ambition of individuals may be made to cooperate in favour of those views.

A third ill consequence of that acquisition would be material injury in time to come to the Commerce of the Atlantic states. By rendering New Orleans the emporium of the products of the Western Country, Britain would at a period, not *very* distant have little occasion for supplies of provisions for their Islands from the Atlantic States; and for their European Market they would derive from the same source copious supplies of Tobacco and other articles now furnished by the Southern States: whence a great diminution of the motives to establish liberal terms of Commercial Intercourse with the United States collectively.

These consequences are all expressed or implied in the form of the Question stated by the President. And as far as our consent can be supposed likely to have influence upon the event they constitute powerful objections to giving it.

If even it should be taken for granted that our consent or refusal would have no influence either way, it would not even then cease to be disagreeable to concur in a thing apparently so inauspicious to our interests. And it deserves attention, that our concurrency might expose us to the imputation either of want of foresight to discover a danger or of vigour to withstand it.

But there is almost always in such cases a comparison of evils; and the point of prudence is to make choice of that course which threatens the fewest or the least, or sometimes the least certain. The consequences of refusal are therefore to be weighted against those of consent.

It seems to be a matter taken for granted by the writers upon the subject, that a refusal ought to be accompanied with a resolution to support it if necessary by the sword; or in other words, to oppose the passage, if attempted to be forced, or to resent the injury, if circumstances should not permit an effectual opposition. This indeed is implied in the nature of the thing; for to what purpose refuse, unless it be intended to make good the refusal? Or how avoid disgrace, if our territories are suffered to be violated with impunity, after a formal and deliberate prohibition of passage?

These are cases in which a nation may without ignominy wink at infractions of its rights; but this does not appear to be one of them. After having been asked its permission and having refused it, the presumption will be that it has estimated the consequences, calculated its means, and is prepared to assert and uphold its rights. If the contrary of this should turn out to be its conduct, it must bring itself into contempt for inviting insult which it was unable to resist, and manifesting ill will towards a power whom it durst not resist. As on the one hand, there cannot be conceived to be a greater outrage than to pass through our country, in defiance of our *declared* disapprobation, so on the other there cannot be a greater humiliation than to submit to it.

The consequence therefore of refusal if not effectual must be absolute disgrace or immediate war. This *appears* at least to be the alternative.

Whether a refusal would have the desired effect is at best problematical. The presumption, perhaps, is, that Great Britain will have adverted to the possibility of it; and if under the uncertainty of what would be our conduct she should still have resolved on prosecuting the enterprise through our territory, that she will at the same time have resolved, either to ask no questions or to disregard our dissent. It is not unlikely, that the reasoning of the British Cabinet will have been to this effect. If the United States have no predilection for Spain, or if their views of their own interest are not opposed to the acquisition we meditate, they will not withold their consent; if either the one, or the other be the case, it ought to be determined before hand, whether their enmity be a greater evil, than the projected acquisition, a good; and if we do not choose to renounce the one, we must be prepared to meet the other.

A further ill-consequence of the refusal, if ineffectual, not *wholly* destitute of weight, is this, that Great Britain would then think herself under less obligation to keep measures with us and would feel herself more at liberty to employ every engine in her power to make her acquisition as prejudicial to us as possible; whereas, if no impediment should be thrown in the way by us, more good humour may beget greater moderation, and in the progress of things, concessions securing us, may be made, as the price of our future neutrality. An explicit recognition of our right to navigate the Mississippi to and from the Ocean, with the possession of New Orleans, would greatly mitigate the causes of apprehension from the conquest of the Floridas by the British.

The consequences of refusal or consent constitute leading motives to the one or to the other; which now claim a more particular discussion.

It has been seen that the ill effects to be apprehended from the conquest of the Spanish territories in our neighbourhood, are an increase of the means, whereby we may be hereafter annoyed, and of the danger of the separation of the Western Country from the rest of the Union, and a future interference with the trade of the Atlantic States, in a manner too not conducive to the general weal.

As far as there is a prospect that a refusal would be an impediment to the enterprize, the considerations which have been mentioned afford the strongest inducements to it. But if *that* effect of it be doubtful, the force of these inducements is proportionably diminished; if improbable, it nearly ceases. The prospect in this case, would be that a refusal would aggravate instead of preventing the evil, it was intended to obviate. And it must be acknowleged that the success of it is at least *very doubtful*.

The consideration that our assent may be construed into want of foresight or want of vigour, though not to be disregarded, would not be sufficient to justify our risking a war in our present situation. The cogent reasons we have to avoid a war are too obvious and intelligible; not to furnish an explanation of and an apology for our conduct in this respect.

Whatever may be the calculations with regard to the probable effect of a refusal, it ought to be predicated upon the supposition, that it may not be regarded, and accompanied with a determination to act as a proper attention to national dignity would in such an event dictate. This would be to make war.

For it is a *sound maxim*, that a state had better hazard any calamities than submit tamely to absolute disgrace.

Now it is manifest, that a Government scarcely ever had stronger motives to avoid war, than that of the United States, at the present juncture. They have much to dread from war; much to expect from peace; something to hope from negotiation, in case of a rupture between Britain and Spain.

We are but just recovering from the effects of a long arduous and exhausting war. The people but just begin to realise the sweets of repose. We are vulnerable both by water and land without either fleet or army. We have a considerable debt in proportion to the resources which the state of things permits the government to command. Measures have been recently entered upon for the restoration of Credit, which a war could hardly fail to disconcert, and which if disturbed would be fatal to the means of prosecuting it. Our national government is in its infancy. The habits and dispositions of our people are ill suited to those liberal contributions to the treasury, which a war would necessarily exact. There are causes which render war in this country more expensive, and consequently more difficult to be carried on than in any other. There is a general disinclination to it in all classes. The theories of the speculative and the feelings of all are opposed to it. The support of public opinion (perhaps more essential to our government than to any other) could only be looked for in a war evidently resulting from necessity.

These are general reasons against going into war. There are others of a more particular kind. To the people at large the quarrel would be apt to have the appearance of having originated in a desire of shielding Spain from the arms of Britain. There are several classes of men to whom this idea would not be agreeable, especially if the Dutch were understood to be in conjunction with the British. All those who were not friendly to our late revolution would certainly dislike it. Most of the descendants of the Dutch would be unfriendly to it. And let it not be overlooked, that there is still a considerable proportion of those who were firm friends to the Revolution who retain prepossessions in favour of Englishmen, and prejudices against Spaniards.

In a popular government especially, however prejudices like these may be regretted, they are not to be excluded from political calculations.

It ought also to be taken into the account, that by placing ourselves at this time in a situation to go to war against Great Britain we embark with the weakest party, with a total uncertainty what accession of strength may be gained, and without making any terms, with regard either to succour, indemnity or compensation.

France is the only weight which can be thrown into the scale capable of producing an equilibrium. But her accession however probable ought not to be deemed absolutely certain. The predominant party there may choose to avoid war as dangerous to their own power. And if even obstacles should not arise from that quarter, it cannot be foreseen to what extent France will be in condition to make efforts. The great body of malcontents comprehending a large proportion of the most wealthy and formerly the most influential class; the prodigious innovations which have been made, the general and excessive fermentation which has been excited in the minds of the people, the character of the Prince, or the nature of the government likely to be instituted, as far as can be judged prior to an experiment, does not prognosticate much order or vigour in the affairs of that country for a considerable period to come.

It is possible indeed that the enthusiasm which the transition from Slavery to Liberty may inspire, may be a substitute for the energy of a good administration, and the spring of great exertions. But the ebullitions of enthusiasm must ever be a precarious reliance. And it is quite as possible that the greatness, and perhaps immaturity, of that transition may prolong licentiousness and disorder. Calculations of what may happen in France must be unusually fallible; not merely from the yet unsettled state of things in that kingdom, but from the extreme violence of the change which has been wrought in the situation of the people.

These considerations are additional admonitions to avoid as far as possible any step that may embroil us with Great Britain. It seems evidently our true policy to cultivate neutrality. This at least is the ground on which we ought to stand, until we can see more of the scene, and can have secured the means of changing it with advantage.

We have objects which in such a conjuncture are not to be neglected. The Western posts, on one side, and the navigation of the Mississippi, on the other, call for a vigilant attention to what is going on. They are both of importance. The securing of the latter may be regarded in its consequences as essential to the unity of the Empire.

But it is not impossible if war takes place, that by a judicious attention to favourable moments we may accomplish both, by negotiation. The moment however we became committed on either side the advantages of our position for negotiation would be gone. They would even be gone in respect to the party, with whom we were in cooperation; for being once in the war we could not make terms as the condition of entering into it.

Though it may be uncertain how long we shall be permitted to preserve our neutrality; that is not a sufficient reason for departing from it voluntarily. It is possible we may be permitted to persist in it throughout. And if we must renounce it, it is better it should be from necessity than choice; at least till we see a prospect of renouncing, with safety and profit. If the government is forced into a war the chearful support of the people may be counted upon. If it brings it upon itself, it will have to struggle with their displeasure and reluctance. This difference alone is immense.

The desire of manifesting amity to Spain, from the supposition, that our permanent interest is concerned in cementing an intimate connection with France and Spain ought to have no influence in the case. Admitting the existence of such an interest, it ought not to hurry us into premature hazards. If it should finally induce us to become a party, it will be time enough, when France has become such and after we shall have adjusted the conditions, upon which we are to engage.

But the reality of such an interest is a thing about which the best and the ablest men of this country are far from being agreed. There are of this number, who, if the United States were at perfect liberty, would prefer an intimate connection between them and Great Britain as most conducive to their security and advantage; and who are of opinion, that it will be wise to cultivate friendship between that country and this, to the utmost extent which is reconcileable with the faith of existing engagements: While the most general opinion is, that it is our true policy, to steer as clear as possible of all foreign connection, other than commercial, and in this respect to cultivate intercourse with all the world on the broadest bases of reciprocal privilege.

An attentive consideration of the vicissitudes which have attended the friendships of nations, except in a very few instances, from very peculiar circumstances, gives little countenance to systems which proceed on the supposition of a permanent interest to prefer a particular connection. The position of the United States, detached as they are from Europe admonishes them to unusual circumspection on that point. The same position, as far as it has relation to the possessions of European powers in their Vicinity, strengthens the admonition.

Let it be supposed that Spain retains her possessions on our right and persists in the policy she has hitherto pursued without the slightest symptom of relaxation of barring the Mississippi against us, where must this end, and at a period not very distant? Infallibly in a War with Spain, or separation of the Western Country. This Country must have an outlet for its commodities. This is essential to its prosperity, and if not procured to it by the United States must be had at the expence of the Connection with them. A war with Spain, when our affairs will have acquired greater consistency and order, will certainly be preferred to such an alternative. In an event of this sort we should naturally seek aid from Great Britain. This would probably involve France on the opposite side, and effect a revolution in the state of our foreign politics.

In regard to the possessions of Great Britain on our left, it is at least problematical, whether the acquisition of them will ever be desireable to the United States. It is certain that they are in no shape essential to our prosperity. Except therefore the detention of our Western posts (an object too of far less consequence than the navigation of the Mississippi) there appears no necessary source of future collission with that power.

This view of the subject manifests, that we may have a more urgent interest to differ with Spain, than with Britain. And that conclusion will become the stronger, if it be admitted, that when we are able to make good our pretensions, we ought not to leave in the possession of any foreign power, the *territories* at the mouth of the Mississippi, which are to be regarded as the key to it.

While considerations of this nature ought not to weaken the sense, which our Government ought to have of any obligations which good faith shall fairly impose, they ought to inspire caution in adopting a system, which may approximate us too nearly to certain powers, and place us at too great a distance from others. Indeed every system of this kind is liable to the objection, that it has a tendency to give a wrong biass to the councils of a Nation, and sometimes to make its own interest subservient to that of another.

If the immediate cause of the impending war between Britain and Spain be considered, there cannot be drawn from thence any inducements for our favouring Spain. It is difficult to admit the reasonableness or justice of the pretensions on her part, which occasioned the transaction complained of by Great Britain, and certainly the monopoly, at which those pretensions aim, is intitled to no partiality from any maritime or trading people. Hence considerations, neither of justice nor policy, as they respect the immediate cause of the quarrel, incline us towards Spain.

Putting therefore all considerations of peculiar good will to Spain or of predilection to any particular connection out of the Question, the argument respecting refusal or consent, in the case supposed, seems to stand thus.

The acquisition of the Spanish territories, bordering upon the U States, by Britain would be dangerous to us. And if there were a good prospect, that our refusal would prevent it, without exposing us to a greater evil, we ought to refuse. But if there be a considerable probability that our refusal would be ineffectual, and if being so, it would involve us in war or disgrace, and if positive disgrace is worse than war, and war, in our present situation, worse, than the chances of the evils, which may befal us, from that acquisition, then the conclusion would be that we ought not to refuse. And this appears to be the true conclusion to be drawn from a comprehensive and accurate view of the subject; though first impressions are on the other side.

These reflections also may be allowed to come in aid of it. Good or evil is seldom as great, in the reality, as in the prospect. The mischiefs we apprehend may not take place. The enterprise, notwithstanding our consent, may fail. The acquisition, if made, may in the progress of things be wrested from its possessors. These if pressed hereafter (and we are willing to accept it) may deem it evident to purchase our neutrality by a cession to us of that part of the territory in question, which borders on the Mississippi accompanied with a guarantee of the navigation of that river. If nothing of this sort should happen, still the war will necessarily have added millions to the debt of Britain, while we shall be recruiting and increasing our resources and our strength. In such a situation, she will have motives of no inconsiderable force for not provoking our resentment. And a reasonable confidence ought to be reposed in the fidelity of the inhabitants of the Western County; in their attachment to the Union; in their real interest to remain a part of it, and in their sense of danger from the attempt to separate, which *at every hazard* ought to be resisted by the United States.

It is also to be kept in view, that the *same* danger, if not to the *same* extent, will exist, should the territories in question *remain in the hands of Spain.*

Besides all this, if a war should ever be deemed a less evil than the neighbourhood of the British in the quarter meditated, good policy would still seem to require as before intimated, that we should avoid putting ourselves in a situation to enter into it, till we had stipulated adequate indemnities and considerations for doing so; that we should see a little further into the unravellment of the plot, and be able to estimate what prospect there would be by our interference of obviating the evil. It deserves a reflection, that if those territories have been once wrested from Spain, she will be more tractable to our wishes, and more disposed to make the concessions, which our interests require, than if they never passed into other hands.

A question occurs here whether there be not a middle course between refusal and consent; to wit, the waving an answer by referring the matter to further consideration. But to this there appear to be decisive objections. An evasive conduct in similar cases is never dignified, seldom politic. It would be likely to give satisfaction to neither party, to effect no good, to prevent no ill. By Great Britain, it would probably be considered as equivalent to a refusal, as amounting to connivance by Spain, as an indication of timidity by all the world.

It happens that we have a post on the Wabash, down which River the expedition, it is presumeable, must go. If the Commanding Officer at that post has no orders to the contrary, it will be his duty to interrupt the passage of the British troops; if he does, it would seem necessary for them in order to the safe passage of their boats, with their artillery stores, provisions and baggage to take that post. Here then would be a passage through our territory, not only without our permission, but with the capture of a post of ours; which would be in effect making war upon us. And thus silence, with less dignity, would produce the same ill consequence, as refusal.

If to avoid this private orders were to be sent to the commanding officer of that post not to interrupt the passage, his not being punished for his delinquency would betray the fact and afford proof of connivance.

The true alternative seems to be to refuse or consent: And if the first be preferred, to accompany it with an intimation, in terms as free from offense as possible, that dispositions will be made to oppose the passage if attempted to be forced; and, accordingly, as far as practicable to make and execute such dispositions.

If on the contrary consent should be given it may deserve consideration whether it would not be expedient to accompany it with a candid intimation that the expedition is not agreeable to us, but that thinking it expedient to avoid an occasion of controversy, it has been concluded not to withold assent. There are however objections to this mode. In case of consent an early and frank *explanation should be given* to Spain.

Question the *Second*.

What notice ought to be taken of the measure, if it should be undertaken without leave, which is the most probable proceeding of the two?

If *leave* should be *asked* and *refused* and the enterprise should be prosecuted without it, the manner of treating it has been anticipated, that is the passage if practicable should be opposed, and if not practicable, the outrage should be resented by recourse to arms.

But if the enterprise should be undertaken without *asking* leave, which is presumed to be the import of the question, then the proper conduct to be observed will depend on the circumstances.

As the passage contemplated would be by water, and almost wholly through an uninhabited part of the Country, over which we have no *actual* jurisdiction, if it were unaccompanied with any violence to our citizens or posts, it would seem sufficient to be content with remonstrating against it, but in a tone that would not commit us to the necessity of going to war: the objections to which apply with full force here.

But, if as is to be feared will necessarily be the case, our post on the Wabash should be *forced*, to make good their passage, there seems to be no alternative but to go to war with them; unwelcome as it may be. It seems to be this, or absolute and unqualified humiliation: which, as has been already noticed, is in almost every situation a greater evil than war.

In such an event, it would appear advisable immediately to convene the Legislature; to take the most vigorous measures for war; to make a formal demand of satisfaction; to commence negotiations for alliances; and if satisfaction should be refused to endeavour to punish the aggression by the sword.

ALEXANDER HAMILTON
Secretary of the Treasury

MS (DLC: Washington Papers).

Hamilton enclosed the above opinion in his letter to Washington of 15 Sep. 1790 and explained its delay as follows: "The urgent avocations, in which I have been engaged, towards putting, in a train of execution, the laws of the last session, affecting my department, and a desire of reflecting, maturely, and giving the reasons for the result of my reflections, fully, have caused me to delay, longer than I wished, the answers to the questions . . . and I hope will excuse the delay.—The judgments formed, in particular cases, are almost always connected with a general train of ideas, in respect to some more comprehensive principles or relations; and I have thought it adviseable to lay that train before you, for the better explanation of the grounds of the opinion, I now give, or may hereafter have occasion to give on the like subjects, in obedience to your commands" (DLC: Washington Papers; full text in Syrett, *Hamilton*, VII, 36-7). Neither the delay nor the substance of the opinion, however, can be separated from the context of the discussions that Hamilton was engaged in with Beckwith and Humphreys at the time this document was being prepared.

On the arguments urged by Hamilton for a position of neutrality, of negotiation, and of seeking commercial "intercourse with all the world on the broadest bases of reciprocal privilege," Hamilton seemed to stand with TJ. So, too, on the matter of a realistic assessment of the national interest. But the whole drift of the argument, like that of Hamilton's negotiations with Beckwith, was calculated to lead to another position—that of some of the "best and the ablest men" who were of opinion that it would be wise to cultivate friendship between the United States and Great Britain "to the utmost extent which is reconcileable with the faith of existing engagements." These were almost the exact words that Hamilton had spoken to Beckwith. In neither case could he reveal to the President that this, in a peculiar sense, was his own view of policy, not just that of some of the best and the ablest men. The discourse on the irrelevance of a sentiment such as gratitude in the conduct of foreign policy was itself irrelevant, for the realities affecting the national interest were assumed in all of the other opinions to be determinative. But the irrelevancy served two purposes. It laid the foundation for such opinions as Hamilton might thereafter "have to give on the like subjects" and it concealed the predilections—whether arising from a comparable sentiment or from a regard for the national interest—that led Hamilton away from the position of neutrality and of commercial reciprocity that he professed. The true nature of Hamilton's position cannot be found in the convolutions of this involved and belated opinion, but must be sought in the clear tendency of his actions and his communications to Beckwith during the preceding year.

To C. W. F. Dumas

DR. SIR   New York July 13th. 1790

I wrote you last on the 23d. of June, since which I have received yours of March 24th. to 31st. Your Letters are long on their Passage, as you will observe by the following Statement.

Date of letters.	*When received.*	*Time of Passage.*
December 2d. to January 26th.	May 3d.	97 Days
February 28th.	June 10th.	102 "
March 24th. to 31st.	July 2d.	93 "

Could we receive them quicker, their Contents would be more interesting. Our Communications from London are from thirty to forty Days only; but these are mixed with such large Doses of Falsehood as to render it extremely desirable that we should receive authentic intelligence with the same Quickness. I cannot therefore but press on you to effect the certain Transmission of the Leyden Gazette by the English Packet.

Congress have passed a Bill for removing the federal Government to Philadelphia for ten Years, and after that to George Town. Be pleased therefore to direct your future Dispatches to me at Philadelphia. The English Packet will still come to New York, and their Dispatches will come from thence by Post to Philadelphia in two Days.

Congress are still engaged in their funding Bills. The foreign Debts did not admit of any Difference of Opinion: they were settled by a single and unanimous Vote; but the domestic Debt requiring Modifications and Settlements, these produce great Difference of Opinion, and consequently retard the passage of the funding Bill. The States had individually contracted considerable Debts for their particular Defence, in Addition to what was done by Congress. Some of the States have so exerted themselves since the war as to have paid off near the half of their individual Debts; others have done nothing. The State Creditors urge that these Debts were as much for general Purposes as those contracted by Congress, and insist that Congress shall assume and pay such of them, as have not been yet paid by their own States. The States who have exerted themselves most, find that notwithstanding the great Payments they have made, they shall by this Assumption still have nearly as much to pay as if they had never paid any Thing; they are therefore opposed to it. I am in Hopes a compromise will be effected by a proportional Assumption, which may reach a great part of the Debts, and leave still a part of them to be paid by those States who have paid few or none of their Creditors. This being once settled, Congress will probably adjourn and meet again in December at Philadelphia. The appearance of War between our two Neighbours, Spain and England, would render a longer Adjournment inexpedient. I have the honor to be with great Esteem &c:,

FC (DNA: RG 59, PCC No. 121). Tr (Lloyd W. Smith, Madison, N.J., 1946).

Opinions on the Constitutionality
of the Residence Bill

EDITORIAL NOTE

Probably the most celebrated and most controverted coalition in American history is that by which Thomas Jefferson and James Madison came to the aid of Alexander Hamilton's plan to assume the states' war debts and thus insured its adoption. It is a remarkable fact that one aspect of the opposition that they encountered, involving legislative construction of the constitution and an effort to focus public attention on this argument at the moment that final decision lay with the president, has remained unexplored. There is little doubt that Washington was disturbed by the tone and force of arguments by *Junius Americanus*. The questions that he addressed to Jefferson when he read these arguments in the *Daily Advertiser* of 13 July 1790 show that he suspected the enemies of the Potomac site for the seat of government of holding in reserve a powerful legal and moral assault that would, in effect, place the decision in the context of Washington's devotion to constitutional government. There is also no doubt that Washington's questions betrayed his desire to learn who was back of this attempt to break the coalition on the rock of his own integrity. Thus, because *Junius Americanus* addressed himself to a serious inconsistency in Madison's position on the question, the President's searching questions were in effect directed to both men. Their collaboration in the rebuttal of *Junius Americanus*' arguments proves that they so interpreted these questions. In their handling of the thorny constitutional predicament in which their coalition effort had placed them, they were in effect engaged with *Junius Americanus* in a contest in which the decisive influence of the President was the goal.

Early in 1790 the French chargé d'affaires expressed the belief that the eternal discussions about fixing the seat of government, fanned into a new flame by Virginia's offer of land on the Potomac, by her plans to improve the navigation of the river, by her pledge of $120,000 for the construction of buildings in the federal district, and by her invitation to Maryland to join in the gesture, would give a more perceptible shock to the union than the problems of reorganization had done in the first session. The prophecy was accurate. The debate on residence reached its peak six months later in an atmosphere in which the threat of disunion was clear and ominous. But the old flames had never been extinguished. The issue had become intermingled with many important measures of the national government from the very beginning of the union, exacerbating sectional feelings and arousing personal and local interests. Jefferson and Madison had collaborated six years earlier in the effort to move the capital away from an eastern city and to a position central to the extreme northern and southern states and accessible to the western regions by improved navigation.[1] In 1789 Madison and other Southerners, by the narrowest of margins, had stood off the combination arranged between Robert Morris and Rufus King whereby the Pennsylvania delegation signed a pledge and engaged its honor—Senator Maclay abstaining—to keep the government in New York until 1793 on condition that a bill should pass Congress that session fixing the permanent seat at Germantown.[2] Now in 1790 Jefferson and Madison were participants in another and successful bargain that removed the troublesome issue forever from American politics.

On Sunday, 13 June 1790, Jefferson informed several friends in Virginia that the old issue of the residence would come on in that session. To George Mason, whose favorable disposition towards the administration it was important to cultivate, he said that the proposal for assuming the debts of the states, then quiescent because of the bitter animosities that had been aroused, would be revived in some form. "My duties preventing me for mingling in these questions," he added, "I do not pretend to be very competent to their decision."[3] To another friend that same day he also wrote: "I am only a passenger in their voyages, and therefore meddle not."[4] But in letters to Virginia, written on the following Sunday, no such note of aloofness can be detected. In these he explained that Congress was faced with "two of the most irritating questions that ever can be raised among them," assumption and residence. Unless "some plan of compromise" could be agreed upon, no funding bill would be adopted, American credit at Amsterdam would "burst and vanish, and the states separate to take care everyone of itself." In the face of this situation, he said, efforts were being made

[1] See Vol. 6: 361-70; see also, TJ to Monroe, 17 June 1785: "It is evident that when a sufficient number of the Western states come in, they will remove [Congress] to George Town." For the comment by Otto, see translation of some of his dispatches by Margaret M. O'Dwyer, "A French Diplomat's View of Congress, 1790," WMQ, 3rd Ser., XXI (July 1964), 415.

[2] King, King, I, 374; the agreement is dated 23 Sep. 1789, just before Congress adjourned.

[3] TJ to William Hunter, Jr., to Nicholas Lewis, to George Mason, and to George Wythe, 13 June 1790.

[4] TJ to Francis Hopkinson, 13 June 1790.

to bring about a disposition for "some mutual sacrifices." He admitted that he himself saw the need to listen "to the cries of the creditors in certain parts of the union, for the sake of union, and to save us from the greatest of all calamities, the total extinction of our credit in Europe." The proposed ground of accommodation was a modification of the assumption bill to allow each state a fixed sum in proportion to its census, with a temporary residence at Philadelphia for twelve or fifteen years and a permanent location thereafter at Georgetown. In this way, Jefferson concluded, there would be "something to displease and something to soothe every part of the Union, but New York, which must be contented with what she has had." On this ground the Pennsylvania and Virginia delegations had conducted themselves honorably and with fixed determination not to yield to "insidious propositions made to divide and defeat them." They had done this by recognizing their concurrent interests, without stipulations and without "descending to talk about bargains."[5] Obviously, the process by which the assumption and residence measures were blended was one that came to a point of crystallization sometime during the six days that separated these two stints of Sunday letter-writing.

In view of the exacerbated feelings aroused by the proposal to assume the state debts, with the Massachusetts delegation leading the fight for adoption and, so Abigail Adams thought, with the Virginia representatives following Madison like a flock of sheep in his effort to defeat the measure, a composition of interests was a natural and perhaps inevitable plan that no doubt occurred to many.[6] Having arranged a similar combination in 1789, Robert Morris lost no time in making delicate hints of his objectives even to the President in the new session.[7] But there can be no doubt that the Secretary of the Treasury, whether he originated the move to connect the two measures or not, was the key figure in this maneuver to save the assumption bill as an integral part of his funding system. Jefferson may have overdrawn the picture of Hamilton's uncharacteristic despondency as they met before the President's house that fateful morning, but Hamilton was indubitably caught in the coils of those ligaments of interest with which he had sought to bind men of substance to the federal government. Their clamors, thought Senator Maclay, were as insistent as Shylock's cry for his bond. "The nonAssumption of the state debts," wrote Henry Jackson to the Secretary of War in a typical outburst coming from New England at this time, "has thrown the people into the greatest confusion, and will be the means of weakening the Federal government more than any other measure they could have pursued. Its best and most *substantial friends* are shagreen'd, mortified and disappointed, and ap-

[5] TJ to Monroe, 20 June 1790; TJ to Randolph, 20 June 1790.
[6] Abigail Adams to ———, 30 May 1790 (MHi: AM).
[7] Robert Morris to Mrs. Morris, 28 Apr. 1790: "I was at Court yesterday to see the President who has been riding on Long Island all last week and he has regained his looks, his appetite and his Health. I tell him we must remove him to Philada. where he will have room enough to Ride as far as he pleased without Crossing to any Island for the purpose" (CSmH: Morris Papers).

pear ready to say or do anything to release themselves from a government that are not disposed to do them common justice. From the present temper of the *People* I am clear in it that unless this measure is obtained in the present session of Congress very serious consequences will take place. I assure you the minds of the people are more agitated than I ever knew them."[8]

Madison, disliking assumption from the beginning but willing to accept it under some modification as being what Jefferson called it, "a choice of evils," was given pause by the threat of disunion. "The Eastern members talk a strange language on the subject," he wrote James Monroe. "They avow, some of them at least, a determination to oppose all provision for the public debt which does not include this, and intimate danger to the Union from a refusal to Assume. We shall risk their prophetic menaces if we should continue to have a majority."[9] Jefferson noted the danger as well and his contemporary comments reinforce the assertion made in his history of the episode—that assumption was "acquiesced in merely from a fear of disunion."[10] The ligaments of interest were indeed powerful, but they were at this time threatening to pull the government apart and with it the man who had done so much to create them.

It is therefore misleading to describe the accommodation of interests reached in mid-June as the result of a deadlock between champions of Hamilton's proposal to transfer the state debts and those determined to move the national capital southward.[11] Until late May the residence issue was not actively agitated. Madison in April was in command of the majority against assumption, but he had not much hope of moving the capital to the Potomac: that, he said, "seems pretty much out of sight."[12] Jefferson had been ill, was immersed in his report on weights and measures, and had formed a strict resolution to confine himself to his own department and not to intermeddle in legislative questions. Washington, deeply interested as everyone knew, was equally aloof. It was not a Virginian but Thomas FitzSimons of Pennsylvania who on 31 May 1790 called up the tabled motion for the next session of Congress to be held in Philadelphia.[13] Further, assumption was a sharply

[8] Henry Jackson to Henry Knox, Boston, 25 Apr. 1790; in another letter of 27 June 1790, Jackson asked Knox: "How stands assumption and Residence? The people here are damn mad and almost ripe for anything"; see also Jackson to Knox, 4 July 1790 (MHi: Knox Papers).

[9] Madison to Monroe, 17 Apr. 1790, *Writings*, ed. Hunt, vi, 13; TJ to Randolph, 18 Apr. 1790.

[10] TJ to Monroe, 20 June 1790; TJ to Randolph, 20 June 1790; Document x in the present group. After the agreement had been reached, Lee in the House spoke of the danger of disunion and called for "a national generous, and equal attention to the Southern and Northern interests." (*Annals*, 1661, 1663.)

[11] Mitchell, *Hamilton*, ii, 79.

[12] Madison to Henry Lee, 13 Apr. 1790, *Writings*, ed. Hunt, vi, 10.

[13] Vining, in supporting the motion, said that "no undue influence or combinations that he knew of existed"; White thought that there could be no difficulty in agreeing upon Philadelphia as a temporary residence in view of the majority in favor of Germantown the preceding session; Boudinot of New Jersey, an ardent supporter of assumption, introduced into the discussion the question of fixing a

defined sectional issue in a sense that the decision on locating the seat
of government was not. Maclay, who fought for the Susquehanna with
single-minded intransigence, and Robert Morris, who maneuvered for
the Delaware more adroitly but just as hard, were the first and the most
zealous promoters of the residence intrigues in the second session as
they had been in the first. Rufus King of New York was just as valiant
in mobilizing support from New England and elsewhere to keep Congress where it was. The advocates of the Hudson, the Delaware, the
Susquehanna, the Chesapeake, and the Potomac were representatives of
competing local interests and their maneuvers were perennial. When
Richard Peters heard that a resolution had been adopted to hold the
next session at Baltimore, he needed no more than the newspaper account to detect the feint. "The Transactions on that subject," he wrote
Jefferson, "cast a shade on the congressional Character. I had enough
of it when I was in the old Congress and I see it is the same Pack of
Cards shuffled and used for another game. An odd Trick is often won
I see by those who do not get the Rubber."[14] Far from arising out of a
deadlock between equally matched and determined forces, the accommodation grew naturally out of this perennial competition among
local interests over the seat of government.

The possibility of a bargain was sensed by assumption forces immediately on the adoption of FitzSimons' motion. *A Federalist* in the
Daily Advertiser of 3 June 1790 wrote:[15]

A report is circulated (for the honour of America may it be false)
that certain gentlemen, belonging to certain states, between New-
York and Florida, have made the following *bargain* with certain
other gentlemen who come from states directly opposite to the
west of New-York, viz. That the former will vote for the assumption
of the state debts, if the latter will support the motion for removing
to Philadelphia.—True or false, it is currently spread, and by some

permanent residence, to be located on the Delaware; Daniel Carroll saw no possibility of agreement on Baltimore and was therefore willing to vote for Philadelphia "as being nearer the center than any other situation he saw a prospect of
being agreed to"; *Annals*, II, 1678-82. FitzSimons' motion was adopted by a vote
of 38 to 22. The Pennsylvania and Virginia delegations voted in unison on the
various counter-motions, but it is clear at this stage that Madison and his fellow
delegates saw no possibility of obtaining more than a temporary residence at Philadelphia.

14 Peters to TJ, 20 June 1790. On 2 July 1790 the (N.Y.) *Daily Advertiser*
printed an extract of "a letter from a gentleman in New York to his friend in
Baltimore, June 20" saying that he had hoped to be able to congratulate him on
the fixing of the permanent residence "from the late almost unanimous vote in
favor of Baltimore, but the postponement of the question, by the Senate, has given
time for intrigues; and it is now confidently asserted that the Philadelphians have
outwitted your members by offering to vote for the Patowmac as the permanent
seat provided they vote for Congress remaining fifteen years in Philadelphia, which
bait has been greedily swallowed."

15 The communication from *A Federalist* was dated 1 June; it was on that day
that Senator John Langdon of New Hampshire asked William Maclay to assure
the two senators from Massachusetts that "there was no bargain with the Virginians" (Maclay, *Journal*, ed. Maclay, 279).

believed. If it be true, some gentlemen have brought themselves into a very awkward situation. If they really think that the assumption would injure the interests of the United States, base must be their principles if any consideration can induce them to vote for the measure. If they think that it would promote those interests, no less base is their conduct in waiting for a *bribe* to do their duty. The friends of America must, with indignation, execrate their caballing, which makes her most precious interests an article of *barter*. I am persuaded that the citizens of Philadelphia, would not esteem the residence of Congress a desireable acquisition, when they considered it as the fruit of *perfidy*.

A Federalist admitted this was strong language, but, he added, "the author loves his country." He sounded remarkably like Senator Maclay, a scribbler for the newspapers whose sensitivity to the whispers of bargaining was extraordinarily acute.

The first direct evidence of trading maneuvers came to Maclay on the morning of the 14th of June when he called at the Treasury on a matter of business. There Tench Coxe pushed aside the business, "so keen was he on the subject of proposing a bargain . . . Pennsylvania to have the permanent residence on the *Susquehanna*, and her delegation to vote for the assumption." Maclay restrained his "indignation at this proposal with much difficulty within the bounds of decency." He doubted the sincerity of the one he regarded as the principal, Alexander Hamilton. Later that day Robert Morris told him of a meeting on the 11th at the lodgings of Thomas FitzSimons and George Clymer, with the President's secretary, William Jackson, and Tench Coxe also being present. The object was the same bargain, save that the location of the permanent residence was to be "in Pennsylvania." Morris, distrusting the intermediaries, had sought out Hamilton himself, who stipulated one vote in the Senate and five in the House as the price for placing "the permanent residence . . . at Germantown or Falls of the Delaware." Morris agreed to sound the Pennsylvania delegation but stipulated temporary residence at Philadelphia as the price. "You need not consult me," Maclay bluntly interrupted. Morris went on to say that Hamilton had reported that morning that his friends would not hear of his negotiating about the temporary residence. He knew that the Secretary of the Treasury had been able to "manage the destruction of the Baltimore vote" without his aid but could not tell how. Morris added: "I think he has some other assurances."[16]

It was on the 14th that the Baltimore resolution was postponed, thus opening the way for the accommodation arranged by Hamilton and Madison with Jefferson's intermediation. As the Senate rose on the 15th, Morris told Maclay that "he had had a communication from Mr. Jefferson of a disposition of having the temporary residence fifteen years in Philadelphia and the permanent residence at Georgetown. Morris added that he had called a meeting of the delegation at six o'clock. All

16 Maclay, *Journal*, ed. Maclay, p. 291-3.

that transpired at that caucus was a repetition of the offer by Hamilton of the permanent residence in Pennsylvania. Maclay thought the offer mad and spoke with detestation of the "bargain proposed by Hamilton." Morris repeated the "communciation from Mr. Jefferson."[17]

Hamilton was enmeshed. The Pennsylvanians, knowing the impossibility of settling the question of a permanent site at that session without provoking a violent fight and thus endangering assumption, worked for the temporary residence in the hope that this would ultimately become the fixed seat. The Massachusetts advocates of assumption, impatient at the attempt to inject this disruptive problem into their drive for the funding system, promptly took advantage of the intrusion to press for decision on the permanent site. If, as Fisher Ames hoped, that bone of contention could be tossed to the bargainers, the champions of the funding system might be able to "dictate their own terms."[18] By this strategy Massachusetts balked the New Yorkers while frustrating Morris and the Pennsylvanians at the game they were playing. Rufus King made a desperate effort to influence Caleb Strong and other New England friends to stand by New York.[19] Hamilton afterward explained to King why Massachusetts did not: nothing but Philadelphia as the permanent residence or that place temporarily and the Potomac permanently, he said, would insure the assumption, which was the object of the Massachusetts delegation.[20] But before that time arrived, Hamilton had undergone the agony that Jefferson described.

The atmosphere of bargaining and intrigue is impenetrable, but both chronology and the known facts suggest that Jefferson's meeting with Hamilton and his offer of intermediation came earlier than is generally supposed. The day of confusion and irregularity in the Senate on the 8th of June perhaps reflected and certainly set the stage for the kind of strategy that Fisher Ames contemplated.[21] By the time of the meeting on the 11th at the lodgings of Clymer and FitzSimons, bargaining for votes at Hamilton's instigation was definitely under way. Morris and Hamilton must have had their meeting at the Battery on Saturday the 12th, for that night Henry Wynkoop of the Pennsylvania delegation—so earnest for assumption that in April Maclay had deemed him "all Secretary"—came to sound out the stubborn advocate of the Susquehanna and implacable enemy of the transfer of debts. Maclay gave him short shrift. The next day Morris and FitzSimons took George Read of Delaware into the country, seeking from him the vote that

[17] Same, p. 294. Maclay's entry is confused, perhaps because he was ill: "Mr. Morris repeated Mr. Jefferson's story, but I certainly had misunderstood Mr. Morris at the Hall, for Jefferson vouched for nothing."

[18] Quoted by Brant, *Madison*, III, 314.

[19] King, *King*, I, 381-3; Dft in NHi; King Papers; undated but perhaps about 8 June 1790.

[20] Same, I, 384-5; memorandum dated 30 June 1790; MS in NHi: King Papers.

[21] *Annals*, II, 1021-3; Maclay, *Journal*, ed. Maclay, p. 285-6; Maclay's account of the confusion, as well as his subsequent comments about efforts of the New York delegation, suggests that on this day the even division was brought about primarily by their influence and by the energetic cooperation of Izard and Butler of South Carolina. This seems confirmed by the voting.

Maclay would not give. Read joined the combination readily enough. Morris had no reason to doubt that he could rely on the Pennsylvania delegation to deliver the four or five votes needed in the House. Thus on the day that Jefferson wrote Virginia friends of his detachment from legislative proceedings, the bargain to give the temporary residence to Philadelphia seemed about to be sealed. But on the morning of the 14th Morris received the note from Hamilton that dashed these hopes. Misreading Hamilton's position for one of strength gained from "other assurances," Morris did not realize that the Secretary of the Treasury had far greater reason than he to be dismayed at the outcome of this promising arrangement.

It must have been on that day that Jefferson met Hamilton in front of the President's house. Both the urgency of the situation and the blow that Hamilton had been dealt by his supporters justify the assumption. On issues of such importance it would seem uncharacteristic of Hamilton to have delayed several days when he found himself blocked. Given the desperate circumstances surrounding the assumption measure and the attendant threat to the union which Hamilton delivered as a *sine qua non*, no other hypothesis about the date of the decisive meeting seems adequate. Jefferson stated that he wrote immediately to both Hamilton and Madison inviting them to dinner the next day. No such letters have been found, but the invitations could have been sent by messenger for delivery orally or in writing.[22] Unless it is assumed that the meeting took place on the 14th, Morris' report to Maclay on the 15th about Jefferson's agreement to a temporary residence in Philadelphia seems inexplicable.[23] The confused entry in Maclay's journal does not necessarily mean that Jefferson communicated directly with Morris. All it may mean is that, once Hamilton had found he could get votes from Virginia by sugar-coating the pill of assumption, he reported that fact to Morris. The financier, knowing Maclay's readiness to see Hamilton's hand in every move, may have found it expedient to conceal the source of the communication from this ardent foe of assumption.

The bargain seems to have been a well-kept secret, otherwise Hamilton would not have had to explain the acceptability of its terms to the Massachusetts delegation, as he did to Rufus King without, presumably, revealing the manner of arriving at those terms.[24] No one engaged in

[22] No such letters are recorded in SJL.

[23] On the various accounts of the episode, those by Brant, *Madison*, 312-8, and Malone, *Jefferson*, II, 299-306, are the most judicious. On the basis of Madison's letters, Malone concludes that the meeting took place between the 17th and the 22nd but interprets Morris' report to Maclay on the 15th about the temporary residence as indicating that Jefferson had made such a move independently of the bargain over assumption. This interpretation seems incompatible with TJ's letters of the 13th and also his account of the interview which Malone—correctly, in the Editor's opinion—accepts as accurate and dependable.

[24] Even Maclay failed to detect the arrangement. Blaming Washington for playing off New York against Philadelphia for the temporary residence, he said: "But I did not then see so clearly that the abominations of the funding system and the assumption were so intimately connected with it" (Maclay, *Journal*, ed. Maclay, p. 329, under 15 July 1790).

the deal left a record of the transaction save Jefferson, who explained his part in it on at least three occasions. His three accounts are: (1) the statement made to the President that the Secretary of the Treasury had duped and used him as a tool for forwarding his schemes; (2) the explanation made to the collection of memoranda called *Anas*; and (3) the undated document called "The Assumption" included in the present grouping and conjecturally assigned to 1792.[25] On essential points all three are in agreement. This is natural, Jefferson's systematic habits being what they were, for when he compiled one account late in life he used both his letter files and the earlier accounts to guide his recollections. This is demonstrable, though it is also true that the version written in 1818 was guided in its extreme expressions by Jefferson's resentment against Marshall's *Washington* and against the tendency of its author's Supreme Court decisions, both of which seemed to him to embody Hamiltonian doctrines.

It was in the last account that Jefferson asserted he had been duped "most ignorantly and innocently . . . to hold the candle" to Hamilton's schemes. Much has been made of this as an unworthy impugning of Hamilton's motives, as a pretension to innocence belied by the facts, as a belated attempt at justification dictated by partisan animosities, and as an expression of Jefferson's deep hunger for posthumous fame.[26] It is quite obvious, of course, that in the spring of 1790, despite his recent arrival, his preoccupation with the affairs of his own department, and his lengthy illness, Jefferson could not possibly have been unaware of the general nature of the funding and assumption proposals even if he had been less astute politically than he was. It is difficult to believe that he could have seriously intended or expected his words to mean an ignorance or innocence of the measures themselves. Significantly, so literal and restrictive an interpretation of his meaning is usually based upon the words that Jefferson wrote in 1818, not on those of similar purport he penned in 1792. But in the latter year when he told Washington that Hamilton had duped and made a tool of him to forward his schemes, the words were set in a context that made their meaning crystal clear to the President. What rendered Hamiltonian measures "not then sufficiently understood" was not their exact nature. It was, he said, their ultimate tendency as part of a system that "flowed from principles adverse to liberty, and was calculated to undermine and demolish the republic, by creating an influence of [Hamilton's] department over the members of the legislature." It was for his unwitting part in forwarding principles of administration so opposed to his own, not for aiding assumption as such, not certainly for satisfying a deep hunger for posthumous fame, that Jefferson said in this most private and candid letter to Washington: "of all the errors of my political life,

25 See TJ to Washington, 9 Sep. 1792; Document X in the present group, where the problem of the date is discussed; and the introduction to the *Anas*, 4 Feb. 1818; see first entry of *Anas*, 13 Aug. 1791.

26 See, for example, Mitchell, *Hamilton*, II, 76-85 (the most extreme interpretation), and Miller, *Hamilton*, p. 246-52; Brant, *Madison*, III, 315-6.

this has occasioned me the deepest regret."[27] The true meaning of Jefferson's agony over the matter was that he had lent himself, so he thought, to a betrayal of his own principles. A narrowed interpretation of his subsequent explanations obscures the equally important truth, fully verifiable by letters at the time, that his acquiescence in assumption was primarily to forestall a dissolution of the union threatened by those who were not bound to it, as he was, by ligaments of liberty.

When at last the residence bill passed the Senate, having survived a last-ditch struggle to keep the government in New York, Robert Morris announced the good news to his wife. He was cautious in predicting ultimate success, for he knew what a trial of fire awaited in the House. "I cannot help remembering," he said, "what happened the last year; we were nearer to our object then, than we are now, and yet we lost it, at the moment when we were most sure. The majority in the House of Representatives is so small, that . . . it is best not to be too sanguine." This was his only concern. "There is no room to fear the President's consent," he confidently asserted.[28] Such confidence was understandable, considering Washington's well-known wish to have the government on the Potomac. But in the preceding session when Maclay heard a false rumor that the House had passed the residence bill, he had concluded that the New Yorkers had "no resource but in the President."[29] The first warning that such a resource would now be employed came during the debate in the House.

The ordeal was as fiery as Morris anticipated. Madison and others of the Virginia and Maryland delegations argued against any amendment, lest the opportunity to take the government to the Potomac be lost forever. Gerry called the measure "a delusion, a deception, sanctioned by Congress itself."[30] Laurance charged that the issue had been "secretly settled" already and Smith and Burke repeated the allegation. Further, the moment the government left New York, faction and party would continue to affect all measures:[31]

> There will be one party endeavouring to carry the bill into effect, and another, and a very strong one too, that will exert themselves to oppose it. . . . The influence of these factions will go into every measure of government: it is expected that if a bill passes, a majority of the two houses will not be able to repeal it, because the dissent of another branch of government may make it necessary to have two thirds to repeal the bill. Sir, should this be the case, the exertions

27 TJ to Washington, 9 Sep. 1792.

28 Robert Morris to his wife, 2 July 1790; PMHB, LX (1936), 184-5. The bill passed the Senate 1 July 1790 by a vote of 14 to 12; *Annals*, I, 1039-40; Maclay, *Journal*, ed. Maclay, p. 312-4. Its text appeared in the (N.Y.) *Daily Advertiser*, 3 July 1790. *The New-York Journal*, 6 July 1790, declined to print the bill "till its fate be known" (but did so three days later).

29 Same, p. 168, under 28 Sep. 1789.

30 *Annals*, II, 1723-4.

31 (N.Y.) *Daily Advertiser*, 7, 8, and 9 July, 1790, giving the debates in the House on 6 July in a fuller version than that in *Annals*, II, 1716-25. See also *Cassius*, whose piece dated at New Haven, 8 June, was printed in the *Daily Advertiser* of 15 July 1790 from the *Connecticut Courant*.

of party will go into the election of the chief magistrate himself, and that great and good man now at the head of our government may feel the influence of it.

The dissent of the third branch of government was sought on the ground of constitutionality. This issue was evidently raised on the 7th of July, for on the 8th John Page of Virginia replied to such an argument. According to *Junius Americanus*, Madison also must have made a rebuttal.[32] But the report of the debates makes no mention of this or of the speech by the member who raised the issue. It is impossible, therefore, to assign responsibility for this turn of the argument, though it seems to have been employed as a last resort in the face of a disciplined coalition who time after time voted down every amendment proposed. This is precisely what happened in the preceding session when Madison and the advocates of the Potomac site found themselves facing an implacable combination intent on fixing the permanent residence in Pennsylvania.

On that occasion, after a prolonged debate devoted chiefly to the idea of centrality of territory and population, William Smith of South Carolina was the first to appeal to the constitution, but on other grounds. He opposed FitzSimons' resolution authorizing purchase of lands for the seat of government on the ground that the Constitution required a cession of the right of soil as well as jurisdiction. Fisher Ames thought the argument "more ingenious than solid, and hoped it was not intended to embarrass the business"—as doubtless it was.[33] The debate continued for three weeks of acrimonious exchange. Madison was certain that there was a "predetermined majority" ready to ride roughshod over all the arguments advanced by the advocates of the Potomac.[34] The blunt charge of bargaining was angrily reprobated, but there was no yielding. At last Madison rose in the final days of the session in apparent surrender. He would offer no further opposition to the bill were it not for his compelling belief that the provision for continuance of the temporary residence at New York was "irreconcilable with the spirit of the Constitution." He then declared:[35]

From the Constitution, it appeared that the concurrence of the two Houses of Congress was sufficient to enable them to adjourn from one place to another; nay, the legal consent of the President was, in some degree, prescribed in the 7th section of article 1st, where it is

---

[32] According to *Annals*, II, 1731, 1733, Page made his remarks on the 8th and, after the defeat of Burke's amendment, William Smith of South Carolina moved that the words "at which place the ensuing session of Congress shall be held" be deleted as unconstitutional. This caused further debate, but the motion was defeated. Since the debates as reported in *Annals* are so defective, it is possible that Page's remarks against the amendment came *after* Smith's motion as a part of the debate that ensued. It is also possible, and indeed more plausible, to assume that the entry of the 8th concerning Smith's motion actually referred to that of the 9th, for which *Annals* records a roll call vote, whereas none is recorded for Smith's supposed motion of the 8th. See also Document x, notes.

[33] *Annals*, I, 909, 910. [34] Same, I, 912.

[35] Same, I, 940-1.

declared, that every order, resolution, or vote, to which the concurrence of the Senate and House of Representatives may be necessary, (except on a question of adjournment,) shall be presented to the President of the United States, and approved by him, before the same shall take effect. Any attempt, therefore, to adjourn by law, is a violation of that part of the Constitution which gives the power, exclusively, to the two branches of the Legislature.

He therefore urged the rejection of this clause. The contention that New York was not central had been little valued, but he hoped members "would be guided by arguments springing from a superior source." Further, the two houses possessed the right to adjourn for more than three days and to any other place they thought proper. The President was constitutionally restrained from interfering. It would therefore "be dangerous to attempt to give to the President a power which the Constitution expressly denied him." He did not suppose that the attempt to vest such a power in the President would "absolutely convey" such power but he thought it wrong to make the experiment. He reminded the majority that an unconstitutional clause might bring on risks to their coveted bill in its passage through the Senate. He rejected the doctrine that the seat of government might be at a place different from that where Congress held its sessions and that, while the residence could be determined by law, Congress might nevertheless remove elsewhere:[36]

What is the Government of the United States for which a seat is to be provided? Will not the Government necessarily comprehend the Congress as a part? In arbitrary Governments, the residence of the monarch may be styled the seat of Government, because he is within himself the supreme Legislative, Executive, and Judicial power; the same may be said of the residence of a limited monarchy, where the efficiency of the Executive operates, in a great degree, to the exclusion of the Legislative authority; but in such a Government as ours, according to the legal and common acceptation of the term, Government must include the Legislative power. . . . There was another clause favorable to this opinion; it was, that giving Congress authority to exercise exclusive Legislation in all cases whatsoever over such district as may, by cession of particular States, and the acceptance of Congress, become the Seat of the Government of the United States; this was the only place where any thing respecting the seat of Government was mentioned; and would any gentleman contend that Congress might have a seat of government over which they are empowered to exercise exclusive Legislation, and yet reside at a distance of 2 or 300 miles from it? Such a construction would contradict the plain and evident meaning of the constitution, and as such was inadmissible.

Sherman conceded the force of the argument, but said that even if the seat of government were designated by law, Congress might still

[36] Same, I, 941.

adjourn to some other place. Page wondered why the clause was defended when obviously it had "no binding force as it related to its main object"—the continuance in New York. If the clause were unconstitutional, Laurance asked, why had the opponents of the bill voted for a temporary residence at New York or Wilmington without advancing the argument? Moreover, how could Madison insist that Congress have a right to adjourn by concurrence to such place as they choose and that their presence determines the seat of Government, yet at the same time advocate the fixing a permanent seat by law? If Congress fixed a permanent seat, they could still remove elsewhere. Hence, if they should remove from their permanent seat, there would become two seats of Government. Which of these would have legal operation with respect to departments obliged to transact business at the seat of government? Laurance concluded that Madison's arguments applied with equal force against both permanent and temporary residence. He also rejected the idea that the presence of the legislature was an absolute requisite for determining the seat of government. The more rational construction in his view was that the seat of government "was determined by the residence of the Executive, the great officers of Government, the Judges, and the foreign ministers, public archives, &c." Madison's construction, he concluded, was filled with dangers and inconveniences.

Madison denied the inconsistency. He could not "as an American, with an eye to the American constitution and the American language, separate the Legislative Power from that of the Government; it appeared to him, to be the most essential part of any free Government, but much the most extensive and essential in the Government of the United States." Fisher Ames agreed with Laurance in thinking Madison's objection equally valid against the permanent and temporary residence of Congress, paid tribute to Madison's role in the formation of the Constitution, and yet was not "disposed to pay implicit deference to that gentleman's expositions" of the instrument. He would take the Constitution as he found it and he could say with Madison: "as an American, with an eye to that constitution, the language of liberty in his mouth, and the love of it in his heart, he hoped it would never be considered . . . that the two Houses of Congress are the Government of the United States." The inconsistency of the doctrine was so apparent that he hoped it would be given up. Madison protested that he had made no such assertion, claiming only that the Congress was a part of the government. This, he argued, was also supported by the constitutional provision requiring the electoral votes to be transmitted to the seat of government and there opened by the President of the Senate in the presence of the two houses. But his rebuttal was in vain. Fisher Ames possessed both the eloquence and the votes. Madison's appeal to the Constitution as a last resort failed by a vote of 29 to 23.

The next day Daniel Carroll, with the engrossed bill before the House, arose in embarrassment. He had felt obliged to vote for location of the seat of government on the Susquehanna upon adoption of the clause making it obligatory upon Maryland and Pennsylvania to concur in opening the navigation. Nothing restrained him from agreeing to the bill save the constitutional argument advanced by Madison. "I have endeavored to remove this conviction from my mind," he declared, ". . . but as I am under the sacred obligation of an oath to support the constitution, as I cannot efface the conviction from my mind that it is contrary to the Constitution, and as we could not succeed in striking out the clause, I feel myself under the disagreeable necessity of giving my dissent to the bill." This made no difference. The measure was adopted by a vote of 31 to 17. Smith of South Carolina, who agreed that the seat of government should be fixed by law, thought that the bill was "perfectly constitutional."[37]

Now, in 1790, it fell to Madison to lead the "predetermined majority" and to others to hurl his constitutional arguments back at him. Smith of South Carolina, supporting the motion of his colleague Ædanus Burke to substitute Baltimore for Potomac, urged conciliation and warned against arrangements and combinations between two such powerful states as Virginia and Pennsylvania. He declared it a delusion to expect removal from Philadelphia at the end of ten years. New England would combine with Pennsylvania in forcing a repeal. Resorting to ridicule—a characteristic of his writings and speeches—he derided those who sought the enactment of a law that would only become operative in the next century. Madison, who had become the South Carolinian's bitter foe on assumption and navigation bills, exposed the diversionary nature of the amendment. If a law fixing the seat at Potomac could be repealed, why vote for Baltimore when it could obviously suffer the same fate? Any alteration, Madison declared, would only defeat the measure and prolong the agitation. Several amendments were offered, but the lines held firm. Ames, Gerry, Smith, Madison, White, and several others joined in the ensuing debate on the 7th. As indicated above, it must have been during this unreported discussion that the issue of constitutionality was brought forward.

The next day Burke's amendment to fix the seat of government in New York for two years and then in Philadelphia until 1800 was debated. John Page denied that New York had any claims whatever, repeated the argument that any alteration jeopardized the bill, and added:[38]

There is one argument indeed which deserves attention. I mean that which is founded on the supposition that the bill is unconstitutional, and that this was the opinion of my colleague on a former occasion. Sir, it was then my opinion also; but we were then overruled by this House, and now have the opinion of the Senate also against our construction of the Constitution. However, I rely not merely on this

[37] Same, I, 942-5.
[38] (N.Y.) *Daily Advertiser*, 10 July 1790; *Annals*, II, 1729-32. The names of those who joined in the debate after the exchange between Madison and Smith are given in the former but not in the latter.

circumstance, for I find, upon an examination of all that the Constitution says about an adjournment, that the clause in the bill is perfectly constitutional, as there are but two sentences in the Constitution respecting adjournments. The last clause of the fifth section of the first article, and the third section of the second article, the former of which runs thus: 'Neither House, during the session of Congress, shall, without the consent of the other, adjourn for more than three days, nor to any other place than that in which the two Houses shall be sitting.' Now, sir, to be inconsistent with this clause of the Constitution, the bill should direct that adjournments shall take place without the consent of the Senate; but the bill before us was framed by the Senate, and a perfect concurrence of the three branches of the Legislature is proposed to the adjournment now under consideration; how, then, can it be inconsistent with the third section of the second article of the Constitution, which gives the President a right to interfere in case of a disagreement respecting the time of an adjournment? It might, indeed, be said, upon a question concerning common adjournments, that the two Houses would do well to retain the right of adjourning without the consent of the President. But, sir, this is an extraordinary case, in which it will be happy for Congress and their constituents if the business of adjournment shall depend upon the joint consent of the three branches of the Legislature, and not on that of the two Houses alone. Without this check, after getting to Philadelphia on an adjournment, we might be brought back to New York, and then carried back again; and so on without end. I think, therefore, that the clause in the bill is not only constitutional but proper.

Page did the best he could, but the strategy of the opposition forced him to employ arguments he had repudiated in the previous session. The following day William Smith of South Carolina moved that the clause stipulating that Congress should hold its next session at Philadelphia be struck out. He contended "that it was unconstitutional to pass a law for the purpose; the constitution having provided that the two houses should adjourn by concurrent resolution, without the controul of the President." The motion was defeated by a majority almost as decisive as that of the previous year, 33 to 26. Smith, too, had abandoned the position he assumed in 1789. So, too, had Ames, Laurance, and others.[39] Evidently the question of constitutionality depended upon the predetermined majority to which one belonged, for in a situation in which there was no substantial distinction in the texts of the bills both minorities had appealed to the constitution as a last resort and both majorities had ridiculed the appeal. If Madison was inconsistent, so were those who made the allegation.

Yet the charge struck home with the greater force because this time the minority had been overridden. The constitutional arguments of

[39] (N.Y.) *Daily Advertiser*, 10 July 1790, giving the debates of 9 July. The quotation is not in *Annals*, II, 1736, where it is merely stated that Smith moved the deletion of the clause as being unconstitutional.

Junius Americanus, coming to Jefferson and Madison through the President, could not be voted down but had to be answered. Jefferson employed every device of rebuttal available. He repeated and amplified Page's claim that the charge of unconstitutionality had been overruled by majorities of both houses. Indeed, since Page was not a lawyer, it is possible that this was an argument Jefferson had advanced to the collegemate who remained as close as a brother to him for half a century. Certainly it is difficult to believe that Jefferson, Madison, Page, and others of the Virginia delegation were not in close consultation during the bill's ordeal of fire in the House. But *Junius Americanus* —or perhaps the fear that the seat of government might not be brought to the Potomac after all if every trace of doubt in the President's mind could not be removed—forced Jefferson onto higher ground. His ultimate argument was grounded on natural law. Though created by the Constitution, the two houses in his opinion held their right of adjournment "not from the constitution, but from nature."[40] The resort to such an argument is an emphatic testimonial to the strength of Jefferson's desire to sustain the dual object of the predetermined majority of 1790— the assumption whose advocates warned of disunion and the residence on the Potomac that he had long regarded as just. But he overlooked the fact that *Junius Americanus* had also recognized the right of adjournment as inherent—"a right which all legislative bodies possess, of reserving to themselves . . . the power of declaring at what place they will re-assemble."

Junius Americanus cannot be identified with absolute certainty, but there is little doubt that he was the arch-Federalist from South Carolina, William Smith. Jefferson may indeed have intended to point in his direction when he argued that the constitutional objection had been overruled by every state in the union, "South Carolina excepted." It would be surprising indeed if Madison did not detect the hand of his foe in the performance. Jefferson could have suspected his identity from Madison or from the report of debates in the newspapers showing that it was Smith who raised the constitutional issue. Both would surely have seen the evidence of the man in the address itself—in the style with its repeated characterization of opponents' arguments as "absurdity" and "folly"; in its attack on Madison for an inconsistency that Smith himself shared; in its narrowly legalistic and syllogistic forensics; and especially in its allusion to some members' holding their seats in the House of Representatives "under a resolution of that house alone." For, in addition to the four persons of the New Jersey delegation to whom this remark applied and whose votes on the issue were divided, the only member to whom it was also applicable was the South Carolinian who had moved to amend the bill by deleting the adjournment clause he regarded as unconstitutional.

William Smith, son of a wealthy merchant-planter of Charleston, had spent the years 1770 to 1783 mostly in England where he studied, traveled, and lived the life of a self-indulgent, undisciplined young man of fortune until late in 1779 when he began to keep term at the

[40] Document v in the present group.

Middle Temple. He arrived at Charleston only in 1783 on the wave of returning Loyalists and British merchants, being refused permission to land for ten days and evidently succeeding then only through family influence. Confining his practice mainly to the British merchant group, Smith had recouped his fortune and gained political prominence in the short space of five years. In 1788, at the age of thirty, he was elected to Congress against two opponents. One of them, David Ramsay, contested the election on the ground that the victorious candidate had not been seven years a citizen of the United States as required by the Constitution. Smith defended himself with a recital of his years spent abroad in which both the facts omitted and those supplied ran counter to his assertions on material matters, but he was seated.[41] A zealous advocate of assumption and perfectly at home in the city that was even more pro-British in sympathy than Charleston, Smith fought as stubbornly as his friends Schuyler, King, Wadsworth, Sedgwick, and others to keep the residence in New York. He was able, indefatigable, and aggressive. It is not likely that he could have raised the constitutional issue except on his own initiative or that he did so solely to obstruct. Smith revered the Constitution and regarded Washington almost as its embodiment. His concepts of fundamental law were imbibed in his youth from the fountainhead of Mansfieldianism. When he later became well known as the author of a text-book of American constitutionalism, he did not conceal his high-Federalist beliefs. He thought the Pennsylvania Constitution of 1790 excellent because modelled on that of the nation. But the democratic Constitution of 1776 which it supplanted he regarded as productive of many evils. Its "feeble and clogged Executive, a single uncontrouled and despotic" legislature, and a dependent judiciary, he thought, had kept the state in "a perpetual scene of faction and disorder." Even its excellent reformation, however, had not been perfect. Here and there in the Constitution of 1790 were sacrifices to old habits and popular prejudices. "The vesting the appointment of sheriffs in the people," he thought, ". . . is a striking deformity in their constitution."[42] The constitutionalism of Smith was the exact reverse of that of Jefferson.

[41] Compare Smith's statement before the House 22 May 1789, with the facts set forth in the thoroughly-documented biography by George Rogers, junior, *Evolution of a Federalist William Loughton Smith of Charleston (1758-1812)* (Columbia, S.C., 1962), especially p. 79-96, 104. Smith gave the House the impression that lack of funds interfered with his determination to return to America during the war. There is nothing in the record to sustain his claim of such an intention, much to refute it. He seems to have had no such concern for the fate of his country as, for example, did John Laurens, who returned early in 1777. Even his friend Gabriel Manigault, under a belated act of conscience or perhaps influenced as some others were by South Carolina's threat of confiscation of estates of absentee citizens, returned in time to undergo the siege of Charleston in 1780. —Smith assumed his middle name in 1804 to avoid confusion with another South Carolina political figure of the same name.

[42] William Smith, *A Comparative View of the Constitutions of the Several States with each other, and with that of the United States: Exhibiting in Tables the Prominent Features of each Constitution, and Classing together their most important Provisions under the Several Heads of Administration* (Philadelphia, 1796), p. 15, 16.

It was in this ardent constitutionalist's diatribe against Madison and Jefferson two years later—a pamphlet which designated the leader of the Virginia delegation as "the General" and the Secretary of State as "the Generalissimo"—that Smith virtually identified himself as *Junius Americanus* by recalling the debate on the residence bill. In this scathing attack he alluded in revealing terms to the constitutional objection that had been raised:[43]

> The Residence Bill [he wrote], which was the offspring of a political cohabitation (for it cannot be called a marriage) between Pennsylvania and Virginia, was passed this session; it was begotten in darkness and its Nurses were afraid of its being exposed to the light—having forced its way through the Senate (to which it was first introduced) by a bare majority, it was ushered into the house of Representatives, where it underwent the solemn farce of a discussion—a phalanx of well disciplined troops were placed to guard it, and their General was so barefaced as to declare in public debate that not a word of it should be altered; that it must not go back to the Senate, and that however absurd, it should go down just as it was, and so it did by a majority of two or three;—containing a clause, which he had in a former bill respecting the same subject, proved to be *unconstitutional*.

The concluding sentence states in summary a large part of the argument of *Junius Americanus*. The case for the identity of Smith as *Junius Americanus* must remain conjectural, but it seems very doubtful indeed whether any member of the minority who faced the phalanx of well-disciplined troops of 1790 would have remembered so long and so accurately the way the constitutional argument was overruled save the one who had raised the issue and had presumably continued to debate it before the public.

Junius Americanus must also have been *One of the Gallery* who repeated the substance of the constitutional argument on the day that Jefferson handed in his opinion to the President.[44] The unsigned rebuttal, coming almost a month later and after the issue was settled, is a silent acknowledgment of the storm that raged in cartoons, squibs, and denunciations of Congress for removing Congress to Philadelphia as the result of a presumed bargain. It bears all of the earmarks of origin in the Virginia delegation if not in a collaboration between its leader and the Secretary of State.[45] So, too, the sarcastic reply of *Truth*

[43] *The Politicks and Views of a Certain Party, Displayed* (Philadelphia? 1792) p. 12-13; elsewhere, p. 8-9, Smith had affected not to know whether the assumption bill "was made the medium of a Bargain with Pennsylvania, Meryland and Virginia for the Seat of Government Bill" and declared that he had "too much respect for the representatives of those States and for truth to assert such a fact without the clearest evidence." TJ evidently did not possess a copy of this pamphlet, though he had another by Smith attacking him with even greater ridicule and virulence (see Sowerby, No. 3174).

[44] See Document VII in the present group.
[45] See Document VIII in the present group.

that it evoked seems only attributable to the pen of *Junius Americanus*.[46]

These were not the only newspaper references to the constitutional issue. Long after the bill was signed by the President, the argument continued amid the squibs and paragraphs, many of them coarse and some evidently too much so even for that day.[47] *A Citizen of America*, remarkably similar to *Junius Americanus* in his flattery of Washington and in some of his phraseology, declared:[48]

> I can bestow a smile of contempt on the little intrigue of *a book worm*; I can bestow a sigh on the avarice of *a mercantile Senator*, who has distracted and convulsed the government of the Union for his own *personal accommodation*. The duplicity and avarice of these men, as individuals, may excite contempt—Charity may exercise a kind of *forgiveness*, which would hurt their feelings (if they have any) as the chiefs of a party, which have fabricated a law, which violates the constitution, and which contains *an insidious snare* for the virtue of the executive, by a Grecian gift. . . . If a faction can violate the constitution; this sacred charter of government, which they are sworn to support, may be considered as blank paper. The convention marked with precision the respective limits of legislative and executive powers, and concessions and encroachments should be viewed with alarm. . . . The *residence bill* was a political trap, set for the integrity and popularity of the executive.

On the day that Washington made the residence bill law, another squib stated that wagers were still being placed, though rumor had it that the President had signed on the 12th. The name of the bill did not need to be specified:[49]

> Whether the President of the United States has signed *the bill*— was *the question* in all companies yesterday, and on which many minds appeared to be much agitated. A certain female personage was heard to say, that she expected soon to leave the city—says one. Aye, says another—then the matter is all over—the bill is signed without a doubt!—You blockhead, says a third, do you really suppose the President will sign it—he never will—for an adjournment can be constitutionally effected without the agency of the President, and his feelings spared on so delicate a subject.

Junius Americanus had indeed raised a storm on the constitutional issue. From that point on the contributors were not so tender of the President's sensibilities. One took the Mayor and members of the Common Council to task for commissioning a portrait of Washington for the City Hall: "Is it," he asked, "for that *inflexible justice*, that *distinguished gratitude* to the city of New-York, in giving his sanction to the *unconstitutional residence bill*?" On the same subject *Vox Res*

46 See Document IX in the present group.
47 *New-York Journal*, 10 Aug. 1790.
48 *New-York Journal*, 27 July 1790. Madison, of course, was the intriguing bookworm and Morris the mercantile Senator.
49 Same, 16 July 1790.

Publica declared it to be "an inauspicious moment for the wise fathers of a republican city, to pay a prodigal compliment to the——[President] when the c-sti-ti-al propriety of his conduct is ambiguous, and divides the opinion of the wise."[50]

By the end of July when the debate on assumption took place, Timothy Bloodworth of North Carolina gave notice of his intention to move to repeal for a limited time the controversial fifth section of the residence Act. All of those members of the Virginia and Maryland delegation who were targets of *Junius Americanus* and all who were involved in the accommodation arranged by Jefferson—Madison, Page, Carroll, Lee, and White—voted against the motion and decisively defeated it.[51] It was just at this time that one newspaper correspondent announced the fate of the assumption bill in words that must have brought pain to Jefferson, Madison, and the President:[52]

> The true reason of the *removal of Congress* from this city will be explained to the people in the course of a very few days. To the lasting disgrace of the majority in both houses it will be seen, that the Pennsylvania and Patowmack interests have been purchased with *twenty one and an half millions of dollars*, and that the good people of this state will have to pay about one eighth part of that enormous assumption, merely to remove Congress from their capital.
>
> The debates upon the funding bill, as sent down by the Senate, will be well worth the attention of the citizens: it will be curious to see all the reasoning against the assumption done away: even the powers of Mr. M-----n are to be silent on the subject, but to preserve a consistency of character, he must vote against it, his mouth is to be shut, his silent negative is to satisfy his new friends, and he is to prove 'that every man may be purchased, if his price is offered;' his price is the Potowmack; he has accepted, and, no doubt, he is a man of too much honor not to perform his part of the bargain.

A member of the Virginia delegation—perhaps White or Lee—explained his vote on the assumption to a friend in Alexandria in terms similar to those Jefferson employed in letters at the time and in his retrospective accounts: "it appeared impractical to go on with the government without it in some shape or another. I was therefore among those who agreed to it under certain modifications, which have either removed, or greatly lessened, my original objections."[53] This was essentially the position of Jefferson and Madison. But the sugar coating of the pill of assumption was already affected by public censure and derision over bargains, disciplined phalanxes, and unconstitutional measures, with worse yet to come for Jefferson from the promptings of conscience over the unwitting aid he had given to Hamilton's principles of ad-

[50] *New-York Journal*, 13, 16, 23, 27 July and 20 Aug. 1790.
[51] *Annals*, II, 1755-6, 1760-1; (N.Y.) *Daily Advertiser*, 6 Aug. 1790.
[52] *B.K.* in *New-York Journal*, 27 July 1790.
[53] Extract of a letter from a member of Congress to a gentleman in Alexandria, 28 July 1790, quoted from an Alexandria dateline of 5 Aug. in (N.Y.) *Daily Advertiser*, 13 Aug. 1790.

ministration. Only William Smith seemed able to depart at the close of the session with a feeling of consistency and rectitude. This was not wholly deserved, but he had labored zealously both for assumption and for the letter of the Constitution, in each case out of deep conviction. If, as seems certain, he was *Junius Americanus*, it is ironic that Jefferson soon found himself cooped up with him for two days, for the President had invited Smith to be one of the party on the journey to Rhode Island. The sea was ordeal enough for the Secretary of State, without the enforced company of a young and aggressive Federalist of the highest tone. Washington extended the invitation to Smith on Friday the 13th, the day after Congress adjourned and the day the address of *Junius Americanus* appeared.[54]

[54] *Journal of William Loughton Smith 1790-1791*, ed. Albert Matthews (Cambridge, 1917), p. 35. Smith left the party at Providence and made a tour through Connecticut, western Massachusetts, and Vermont, thence down the Hudson. He was an experienced observer and made acute observations of the land and the inhabitants in an informative journal. He was also perfectly at home with his Federalist friends in New England, and his journey, like that undertaken by Jefferson and Madison the following year, revealed an obvious and natural tendency to seek out those of congenial political views. He visited Jeremiah Wadsworth, Theodore Sedgwick, the future father-in-law of Fisher Ames, and others of the Federalist persuasion, but passed by the home of Chancellor Livingston.

I. Address to the President, by

Junius Americanus

SIR   July 12. [1790]

With esteem for your person, and the sincerest reverence for your high public and private character, I humbly request your candid perusal of the following observations: They have been occasioned by a serious attention to the Bill which has recently passed the two Houses of Congress, and now waits your sanction: they spring from an affection for the constitution, and an anxious solicitude to guard it from invasion.

In the fifth section of the bill, is this clause, "*at which place the session of Congress, next ensuing the present shall be held:*" A doubt hath arisen, whether that clause be conformable to the constitution; in which it is declared, by the 3d clause of the 7th sec. art. 1st. that "every order, resolution or vote, to which the concurrence of the Senate and House of Representatives may be necessary, (*except on a question of adjournment,*) shall be presented to the President." From this *exception* it is obvious, that it was intended by the Constitution, to reserve *to the two Houses* the right of adjourning to such time and place as they should deem proper:

To relinquish that right is to betray their own privileges, and is a departure from that line of legislation which the constitution hath wisely chalked out.

An attentive inspection of that instrument, which we have all engaged to support, evinces that there are various modes by which the several component parts of the government are to manifest their will. In matters which relate to *each house* in its *separate capacity* a *single vote* of *each house* is alone sufficient to have the force of law; thus by the 5th section, "Each house shall be the judge of the elections, returns and qualifications of its own members, and may punish a member for disorderly behaviour, and even expel him."

In cases wherein the *two branches* of the legislature are concerned, a *joint vote* is prescribed; thus by the 4th clause of the 5th section, "it is inhibited to either house to adjourn, during the session of Congress, for more than three days, *without the consent of the other*, or to any other *place* than that in which the two houses shall be sitting:" Where the two houses disagree as to the *time* of adjournment, it is provided by the 3d sec. of the 2d art. That "the President may adjourn them to such time as he shal think proper;" where they differ as to the *place*, Congress must re-assemble at the *place* where they were last sitting: In this case the President has no agency, nor is it intended by the constitution that he should.

Such are the provisions established in matters which concern *each house separately* and the *two houses collectively*: in none of them is the President called upon to act, except in the *single* instance above mentioned, where he performs the part of an umpire, and where his interposition is necessary, because the *time* of meeting *must* be fixed; the *place* is unnecessary, because if none be appointed, they will of course return to the former place.

But in matters of a general nature which concern the public at large, the wisdom of the Constitution requires something more than the act of the two houses; the President must *approve* them; it is therefore declared that every *order, resolution or vote*, to which the concurrence of the Senate and House of Representatives may be necessary (*except on a question of adjournment*) shall be presented to the President.

Here are then *three* modes of passing orders, resolutions or votes: the *first* by each house; the *second* by the *two houses*; the third by the *two houses and the President*. The question now occurs, Is it consistent with the constitution to depart from the modes above prescribed?

If it be in one instance, it must be so in all. If it be constitutional to require the assent of the President in cases where the two houses, without such assent, are competent to decide, it must likewise be constitutional to require the assent of the Senate in cases where the House of Representatives are alone capable of determining: it would therefore be a constitutional act for the two houses to decide, by a *concurrent resolution*, on the *privileges of each house*. Some of the members of the House of Representatives hold their seats under a resolution of *that house alone*; did the idea ever suggest itself that there would be no impropriety in sending such resolution to the Senate for their concurrence? Would not such an idea have been severely reprobated? Why? Because each house is the judge of the qualifications of its own members; because, to have required the concurrence of the Senate, would have been a violation of the rights of the House of Representatives; and is less respect due to the rights of the two Houses:

If it be an infraction of the constitution to require the concurrence of the two houses where one house can decide, is it less an infraction to demand the approbation of the President, where the two houses can decide? Suppose the President should refuse his assent; the bill will then be lost, unless it be passed by *two thirds* of both houses, but a *majority* of the two houses have a *constitutional right* to adjourn to such place as they shall think proper; either then the two houses will have relinquished a power they possess by the constitution, and a majority will be insufficient to adjourn where they please, or, a *bare majority* of the two houses will give effect to a measure which has been formally *disapproved* by the President: whereas the constitution expressly declares in the 2d and 3d clause, 7th sect 1st art. that it shall be repassed by *two thirds* by the Senate and House of Representatives, before it can take effect.

In what absurdity will Congress be involved when the period of adjournment arrives? If the question respecting the place of adjournment be already determined by the bill, then the two houses have relinquished a right which all legislative bodies possess, of reserving to themselves to the very last day of adjournment, the power of declaring at what place they will re-assemble. When this point is settled by a concurrent vote of the two houses, they may at any time prior to the adjournment, rescind the resolution. At the last session Congress resolved to adjourn on the 22d of September; the vote was not sent to the President, such an absurdity was never thought of: when the 22d arrived, they saw the difficulty of adjourning on that day, and the vote was rescinded; had it been approved by the President, they must have had his approbation to the prolongation of the session, which he might have withheld; if there would have been an absurdity in requiring his assent to *the time*, there would have been a greater absurdity in requiring it to *the place*, for he has the power of interfering when the two houses disagree as to the *time*, none as to the *place*.

If the question be still unsettled, notwithstanding the clause in the bill, and this was admitted by its advocates, then this inconsistency occurs, that a clause is agreed to knowing it to be inoperative, and that its inefficacy results from its unconstitutionality. To make this more striking, place the argument in the shape of a syllogism; the constitution is violated when any law or part of a law is past, which is repugnant to it, but the friends of the bill admitted that the clause was *nugatory*, because it was repugnant to it, therefore in passing it they violated the constitution.

It is no answer to the argument to alledge that the clause will do no harm. If it be intended that it should be carried into effect, it controuls the will of the majority of the two houses, against the express words of the constitution; if it be nugatory, and the same thing must hereafter be determined, by a concurrent vote of the two houses, such inconsistency will expose Congress to public censure and derision. It will be asked why do Congress determine by a concurrent vote of the two houses that which they have already decided by law? If the public are told that the law was nugatory, and that Congress were apprized of it when they passed it, they will lose all respect for their proceedings; it will be said, if an act has already passed on the subject, a resolution can neither inforce or repeal it: If the act was void, it was because it deviated from the constitution, and it should not have been passed.

If laws are made which are unconstitutional, because they may do no harm, Congress will soon proceed to those which may and will do harm. The example is a dangerous one, and will be quoted on future occasions. Every law does not undergo the revision of the judiciary; this will certainly not; the President of the United States can alone arrest its progress. Having his sanction, the public will consider every part of the bill as valid, because they know he would not approve any bill that contained a syllable that was unconstitutional; the clause will then be deemed binding, because every part of the bill must have its operation, for words in a law which com-

mand a particular act to be done, cannot be viewed as mere surplusage: If the law remains unrepealed or invalidated by the judiciary, the thing commanded to be done must be carried into effect;
a bare resolution of the two houses, without the approbation of the
executive, cannot repeal a law, which has his approbation, because
it requires the same power to repeal a law as to pass it: The two
houses will then be precluded from exercising their constitutional
privilege.

A gentleman* who supported an objection to the bill of last session, on the ground that a law fixing the *temporary seat of government* was *unconstitutional*, attempted the other day to prove that it
is not unconstitutional to fix by law, even the *session of Congress*. If
there was any force in his arguments against fixing by law, the
temporary seat of government, the arguments against fixing, by law,
the *session of Congress*, must be conclusive: But he is reconciled to
the measure of this session, because his objection was overruled in
the last by a majority. When a member of his knowledge of, and attachment to the Constitution, suffers himself to be influenced by
a *precedent* which he must himself acknowledge to be a *bad one*,
it is time to apprehend danger from precedents, and to put a stop
to them. *No precedent can justify a wrong measure*; but the bill
of last session did not pass into a law. Where then is the precedent?
He has agreed to make one this session. It is remarkable too that
the objection last year was totally inapplicable, for it related to
fixing the seat of government, which must be done by law, whether
it be the permanent or temporary seat.

The constitution provides that a district of territory shall, by
the cession of a state and the acceptance of Congress, become *the
seat of government*; that acceptance must be declared by law; for
both houses must concur in the measure, and every vote in which
they both concur, must be sent to the President, except on a question
of adjournment, but the two houses may afterwards adjourn *from
that place to any other*. This is undeniable from the various clauses
already quoted. Congress may also declare, by law, prior to their
establishing the permanent seat of government, where the temporary seat shall be, that the public officers, foreign ministers, and
the judges of the supreme court, may know where to assemble; but
it does not follow that the two houses are to sit at that place.

This distinction between the seat of government and the seat of
Congress, has been however denied by that gentleman. He con-

* See 2d. vol. Cong. Reg. page 425, Mr. M[adison]'s Speech.

tended, that Congress being a part of the government, the seat of government must be *wherever they hold their session*. It would then follow, either that during the recess of Congress there would be no seat of government, or should they, by concurrent vote, adjourn to any other place than that fixed by law as the seat of government, there would be two seats of government.

The executive and judicial, and the officers of state, are component parts of the government; the judicial is as much a part of the government as the legislative, and yet it is declared by law, that the supreme court shall hold their sessions at the seat of government; the executive is also as much a part of the government as the legislative, and yet the President may reside where he pleases.

This, however, is clear, that the gentleman was *persuaded last session* that it was *an unconstitutional act to fix, by law, the place where Congress should hold their next session*; his words were these, "from the constitution it appeared, that the concurrence of the two houses was sufficient to enable them to adjourn from one place to another, nay the legal consent of the President was in some degree *proscribed*[1] in the 7th Sec. of Art. 1. where it is declared that every order, &c. to which the concurrence of the senate and house of representatives may be necessary (except on a question of adjournment) shall be presented to the President, &c. *any attempt therefore to adjourn by law*, is a violation of that part of the constitution which gives the power *exclusively* to the two branches of the legislature. By another clause in the constitution it is declared, that neither house, during the session of Congress, shall, without the consent of the other, adjourn for more than three days, nor to any other place than that in which the two houses shall be sitting; from hence he inferred, that the two houses by a concurrence, could adjourn for more than three days, and to any other place which they thought proper; by the other clause he had mentioned, the *executive power is restrained from any interference with the legislative on this subject*; hence he concluded it would be dangerous to attempt to give to the President *a power the constitution expressly denied him*. He did not suppose that the attempt to vest the executive with a power over the adjournments of the legislature would absolutely convey the power, but he conceived it wrong to make the experiment. He submitted it to those gentlemen who were attached to the success of the bill, how far an *unconstitutional* declaration may impede its passage through the other branch of the legislature."

[188]

On the same occasion, another member of the H. of Representatives addressed the House in these words, "the Susquehannah being agreeable to the wishes of a great part of my constituents, I felt myself under an obligation to vote for it, *and nothing would restrain me from giving my assent to the bill, but that clause which requires the concurrence of the President*, respecting the seat of government until Congress meet at their permanent seat. To this clause I have *strong constitutional objections*. I have endeavoured to remove this conviction from my mind, in order to give my assent to the bill, but as I am under the sacred obligation of an oath to support the constitution, as I cannot efface the conviction from my mind that *it is contrary to the constitution*, and as we could not succeed in striking out the clause, I feel myself under the disagreeable necessity of giving my dissent to the bill."

If the clause was unconstitutional last session, is it less so this? If it was an infraction of the constitution to fix by law the temporary seat of government, is it not a more palpable one to fix by law the place where Congress shall hold their next session: can the vote of last session render the measure constitutional? Admitting that some members had then violated the constitution, was not a greater obligation imposed on others to resist any further invasion? For what will become of the government if such encroachments are allowed to succeed, and its friends do not step forward and oppose them?

This is the moment when public measures should be narrowly watched; in the cool hour of calm discussion, when the subject is little interesting to the passions, there is no danger; on the slightest[2] suggestion of unconstitutionality, a clause would be struck out; but when the mind pursues a favorite object with passionate enthusiasm, men are too apt, in their eager embrace of it, to overlook the means by which it is attained. These are the melancholy occasions when the barriers of the government are broken down, and the boundaries of the Constitution defaced! There is danger in another respect; from the apparent unimportance of the clause objected to. In the eye of the law the offence is equally great; in the eye of reason and prudence it is greater, because the public are more inattentive to the incroachment, and *because the success of one step infallibly leads to another*. It is a wedge which having entered the gap, makes way for further progression. The Constitution is the rock of our political salvation; it is the palladium of our rights; it is the safeguard of the rights of States as well as individuals; it is our only bond of union; the smallest deviation from it is a mortal blow to those rights, and ought to be opposed by every citizen who wishes the preservation of the Union; nay, every citizen who has taken an oath to support the Constitution, *violates that oath* if he silently suffers any law to pass which appears to him, in the smallest degree, repugnant to it.

That the clause in question is repugnant to it is admitted, but it is justified on the principle that *it will be inoperative*; this is however a mistaken idea, for it will have an operation, unless formally annulled by the judiciary, and it is impossible the construction of it can ever go before the federal courts; it can't be alledged that it will be nugatory, and that a subsequent resolution of the two houses may adjourn to some other place, for then there would exist this solecism in politics, of *a smaller power rescinding the act of a larger*; there would also exist this *absurdity* of *one place being fixed by law* and *another by a simple resolution of the two houses*; if both the law and the resolution should name the same place, then there would exist *another absurdity* of a *resolution without* the President's approbation *enforcing a law* which *had received his sanction.* It cannot be justified on the ground that the two houses may, if they think proper, *waive* their *right* of determining for themselves, and request the concurrence of the President, because such a relinquishment of their privileges is not only *a departure from the plain words of the Constitution* which they have *sworn to support*, but is a transfer of rights which they enjoy *as members of the legislature*, not *as individuals*, as *trustees for the public*, not as their *own property*; they therefore *betray* the trust reposed in them, when they wantonly, and with their eyes open, *curtail or alienate those privileges.*

The circumstance of the clause being only a small part of the law, does not alter the case; the law ought not to pass, if there be any part of it inconsistent with the constitution; if the President signs it, he approves the whole; if he objects to any part, he must return it with his objections, and the two houses may expunge the exceptionable part, and then the President can give it his sanction. The bill may still pass with the *sound* part; if the *unsound* part should not be cut out, it will *contaminate* the whole, and be perpetually a good cause of repeal. There will always remain on the minds of *scrupulous* men, *conscientious doubts* respecting the efficacy of a law, which *contains within it an unconstitutional clause*, which may considerably *tend to defeat its operation.* Even the sanguine promoters of it, will look at it with different eyes from what they now do, when their ardent zeal shall have cooled; they reprobated it once themselves, as highly unconstitutional. What will not some men do to attain a favorite object? The reflection is mortifying and degrading!

Can there be a doubt, that, if the law consisted of only this one clause, that there would have been a general clamor at the absurdity of sending it to the President—even had the two houses been so ignorant of the constitution as to pass such a law would not the President have returned it with this answer, that *by the constitution he had nothing to do with it.* What would have been the consequence of such a measure? Either the two houses would discover what they ought to have known before, that they could do without his assent, or they must have repassed by *two thirds,* what by the constitution *a majority is competent to*: and does it make any difference, in point of constitutionality, whether the *objectionable clause* is a *whole law* or only *part of a law*? No man of common understanding will assert it.

Will not the public lose respect for the acts of Congress, when they see them blindly pursuing favorite measures, to the total disregard of the constitution? What appearance will it have to *pass laws* which are *admitted not to be binding*? What folly to require the assent of the President, when it would be as *effectual without it*?

Some of these arguments were stated. It was acknowledged that the clause was *nugatory, because it was unconstitutional,* but it was *retained*—why? Because the bill was *unalterable: sic volo, sic jubeo*; these things ought not to be. JUNIUS AMERICANUS

Text from (N.Y.) *Daily Advertiser,* 13 July 1790, where it occupies four full columns; at head of text: "To the PRESIDENT of the *United States.*"

The GENTLEMAN WHO SUPPORTED AN OBJECTION TO THE BILL OF LAST SESSION is identified both in the footnote citation to the *Congressional Register* and in the textual corrections in the next day's paper (see notes 1 and 2). Hence the President was well aware that the argument was aimed at James Madison. The other MEMBER whose speech was quoted from the first session's proceedings was Daniel Carroll. *The Congressional Register; or, History of the Proceedings and Debates of the First House of Representatives* used by

Junius Americanus was not an official publication, though the speeches there recorded were taken down in shorthand by David Lloyd. The quotations from the remarks of Madison and Carroll are also to be found in *Annals,* I, 940-1, 945-6 (see also Editorial Note). Neither in these quotations nor in those from the Constitution is the phraseology given with exactness.

A good example of Smith's polemical style for comparison with that of *Junius Americanus* may be seen in the facsimile reproduction of his broadside, "A Dose for the Doctor," addressed to David Ramsay on 25 Nov. 1788 (Rogers, *Evolution of a Federalist,* facing p. 211). A distinctive characteristic of his style in this broadside (as also in his pamphlet of 1792 against Madison and Jefferson, *The Politicks and Views of a Certain Party, Displayed*) is the unusual use of the colon instead of the period in punctuation. This, it will be noted, is a characteristic of *Junius Americanus*. So, too, the excessive use of italics distinguishes both the broadside and the above address. By 1792 when he wrote his first certainly identifiable pamphlet, Smith made less frequent use of italics, but if anything his peculiar use of the colon seems to have become more pronounced by that time.

Aside from these and other coincidences of phraseology and the factors pointed out in the Editorial Note as supporting the hypothesis that Smith was *Junius Americanus*, Smith's constitutional arguments in the first session in the debates on organizing the departments of government bear a striking resemblance to those of the author of the address to the President. On the question of the power of the President to remove heads of departments, Smith's belief in the sanctity of property collided with and overrode his strong advocacy of the importance of energy in the executive, causing him even to disagree with Hamilton's position as set forth in *The Federalist.* He argued that an incumbent had a vested right to his office of which he could be deprived only by a fair and impartial trial—impeachment. As the events of the 1790's caused the Federalists to emphasize more and more the prerogative of the executive, Smith acknowledged his error and reversed his opinion. But in 1789 he revealed himself to be quite as strict and literal a constitutionalist as *Junius Americanus*: "I would premise that one of these two ideas are just: either that the constitution has given the President the power of removal, and therefore it is nugatory [a word repeated by *Junius Americanus*] to make the declaration here; or it has not given the power to him, and therefore it is improper to make an attempt to confer it upon him. If it is not given to him by the constitution, but belongs conjointly to the President and Senate, we have no right to deprive the Senate of their constitutional prerogative; . . . I imagine, sir, we are declaring a power in the President which may hereafter be greatly abused; for we are not always to expect a Chief Magistrate in whom such entire confidence can be

placed as in the present. Perhaps gentlemen are so much dazzled with the splendor of the virtues of the present President, as not to be able to see into futurity. . . . To return to my argument, I have stated that if the power is given by the constitution, the declaration in the law is nugatory; and I will add, if it is not given, it will be nugatory also to attempt to vest the power. If the Senate participate, on any principle whatever, in the removal, they will never consent to transfer their power to another branch of the government; therefore, they will not pass a law with such a declaration in it" (*Annals*, I, 474-7). Then, in a remarkable passage that anticipated Marshall in *Marbury v. Madison*, Smith declared that the matter should be left to the judiciary: "It will be time enough to determine the question when the President shall remove an officer in this way. I conceive it can properly be brought before that tribunal; the officer will have a right to a mandamus to be restored to his office, and the judges would determine whether the President exercised a constitutional authority or not" (same, 477; see Rogers, *Evolution of a Federalist*, p. 172). *Junius Americanus*, it will be noted, also accepted the idea of judicial review as a matter of course.

Finally, a fact that should not be overlooked but may have no significance is that, as an impressionable youngster of twelve, William Smith arrived in London just after the letters of the English Junius had jarred the whole political world. At that time Arthur Lee, who preceded Smith at the Middle Temple by a decade, was "dipping his pen into the Junius bottle" and, in a series of letters addressed to the statesmen and people of England, was signing himself *Junius Americanus* (DAB). Smith certainly met Lee in Paris in 1778 if not earlier, and it is at least possible that his choice of a pseudonym in 1790—one tending to give respect and force to his communication—was influenced by his youthful recollections of the English Junius and his American imitator.

¹ This word substituted for *"prescribed."* In the issue of the *Daily Advertiser* for 14 July 1790 there appeared this correction: "Errata—In our last in the quotation from Mr. M----n's

speech, for *prescribed*, read *proscribed*. 3d col. 4th line, for *slighty* read *slightest*."

2 This word substituted for "slighty"; the correction was made in the newspaper of the next day (see note 1).

II. George Washington to Thomas Jefferson

DEAR SIR   Thursday 15th. July

Have you formed an opinion on the subject I submitted to you on Tuesday?—Have you heard whether the Bill[1] was disputed in both or either House of Congress on the ground of the Constitution, or whe[ther] this objection (in its full force) was held in petto for the last move, in the present stage of the business?—If it was debated, as above, whether the Arguments adduced by the Author of the Address to the P—— were made use of, and how treated? And What would be the consequence supposing such a case, as he states, should arise? Yours sincerely & affectionately

Go: WASHINGTON

RC (DLC); addressed: "Mr. Jefferson (Private)"; endorsed as received 15 July 1790 and so recorded in SJL.

1 Opposite this word TJ wrote in margin of RC, perhaps much later, the following: "for fixing the seat of the federal govmt."

III. Thomas Jefferson to George Washington

SIR   Thursday July 15. 1790.

I have formed an opinion, quite satisfactory to myself, that the adjournments of Congress may be by law, as well as by resolution, without touching the constitution. I am now copying fair what I had written yesterday on the subject and will have the honor of laying it before you by ten aclock.—The address to the President contains a very full digest of all the arguments urged against the bill on the point of unconstitutionality on the floor of Congress. It was fully combated on that ground, in the committee of the whole, and on the third reading. The majority (a Southern one) overruled the objection, as a majority (a Northern one) had overruled the same objection the last session on the Susquehanna residence bill. So that two majorities, in two different sessions, and from different ends of the Union have overruled the objection, and may be fairly supposed to have declared the sense of the whole union. I shall not lose a moment in laying before you my thoughts on the subject. I have the honor to be with the most respectful esteem Sir Your most obedient & most humble servt. TH: JEFFERSON

RC (DNA: RG 59, MLR); at foot of text: "The President of the United States"; signature cut away and supplied from PrC (DLC). FC (DNA: RG 59, SDC); at head of text: "Opinion of the Secretary of State on the constitutionality of the Residence Act."

IV. Thomas Jefferson to George Washington

July 15. 1790.

Th: Jefferson begs pardon of the President for being later in sending the inclosed than he had given him reason to expect. The sole cause has been that the act of copying took him longer than he had calculated. He will have the honor of waiting on the President to answer any thing which he may have omitted materially in these papers.

RC (DNA: RG 59, MLR); addressed: "The President of [the United States]"; endorsed by Washington, in part: "Opinion on the Constitutionality of the Residence Act." FC (DNA: RG 59, MLR). Enclosure: See following document.

V. Jefferson's Opinion on the Constitutionality of the Residence Bill

A Bill having passed the two houses of Congress, and being now before the President, declaring that the seat of the federal government shall be transferred to the Patowmac in the year 1790 [i.e. 1800], that the session of Congress next ensuing the present shall be held at Philadelphia, to which place the offices shall be transferred before the 1st. of December next, a writer in a public paper of July 13. has urged on the consideration of the President that the constitution has given to the two houses of Congress the exclusive right to adjourn themselves, that the will of the President mixed with theirs in a decision of this kind would be an inoperative[1] ingredient, repugnant to the constitution, and that he ought not to permit them to part, in a single instance, with their constitutional rights: consequently that he ought to negative the bill.

That is now to be considered.

Every man, and every body of men on earth, possesses the righ[t] of self-government: they recieve it with their being from the hand of nature.[2] Individuals exercise it by their single will:[3] collections of men, by that of their majority; for the law of the *majority* is the natural law of every society[4] of men. When a certain description of men are to transact together a particular business, the times and places of their meeting and separating depend on their own will; they make a part of the natural right of self-government.[5] This, like all other natural rights, may be abridged or modified in it's exercise, by their own consent, or by the law of those who depute them, if they meet in the right of others: but so far as it is not abridged or modified, they retain it as a natural right, and may exercise it in what form they please, either exclusively by themselves, or in association with others, or by others altogether, as they shall agree.

Each house of Congress possesses this natural right of governing itself, and consequently of fixing it's own times and places of meeting, so far as it has not been abridged by the law of those who employ them, that is to say, by the Constitution. This act manifestly considers them as possessing this right of course, and therefore has no where given it to them. In the several different passages where it touches this right, it treats it as an existing thing, not as one called into existence by them. To evince this, every passage of the constitution shall be quoted, where the right of adjournment is touched; and it will be seen that no one of them pretends to give that right; that on the contrary every one is evidently introduced[6] either to enlarge the right where it would be too narrow,[7] to restrain it where, in it's natural and full exercise, it might be too large and lead to inconvenience, to defend it from the latitude of it's own phrases, where these were not meant to comprehend it, or to provide for it's exercise by others where they cannot exercise it themselves.

'A majority of each house shall constitute a quorum to do business; but a *smaller number* may adjourn from day to day, and may be authorised to compel the attendance of absent members.' Art. 1. sect. 5. A majority of every collection of men being naturally necessary to constitute it's will, and it being frequently to happen that a majority is not assembled, it was necessary to enlarge the natural right, by giving to 'a *smaller number* than a majority' a right to compel the attendance of the absent members, and in the mean time to adjourn from day to day. This clause then does not pretend to give to a majority a right which it knew that majority would have of themselves, but to a number *less than a majority* a right which it knew that lesser number would not have of themselves.[8]

'Neither house, during the session of Congress, shall, without the consent of the other, adjourn for more than three days, nor to any other place than that in which the two houses shall be sitting.' Ibid. Each house exercising separately it's natural right to meet when and where it should think best, it might happen that the two houses would separate either in time or place, which would be inconvenient. It was necessary therefore to keep them together by restraining their natural right of deciding on separate times and places, and by requiring a concurrence of will.

But as it might happen that obstinacy, or a difference of object might prevent this concurrence, it goes on to take from them, in that instance, the right of adjournment altogether, and to transfer it to another, by declaring Art. 2. sect. 3. that 'in case of disagreement between the two houses with respect to the time of adjournment the President may adjourn them to such time as he shall think proper.'

These clauses then do not import a gift, to the two houses, of a general right of adjournment, which it was known they would have without that gift, but to restrain or abrogate the right it was known they would have, in an instance where, exercised in it's full extent, it might lead to inconvenience, and to give that right to another who would not naturally have had it. It also gives to the President a right, which he otherwise would not have had, 'to convene both houses, or either of them, on extraordinary occasions.' thus substituting the will of another, where they are not in a situation to exercise their own.

'Every order, resolution, or vote, to which the concurrence of the Senate and house of representatives may be necessary (except on a question of adjournment) shall be presented to the President for his approbation &c.' Art. 1. sect. 7. The latitude of the general words here used would have subjected the natural right of adjournment of the two houses to the will of the President,[9] which was not intended. They therefore expressly 'except questions of adjournment' out of their operation. They do not here give a right of adjournment, which it was known would exist[10] without their gift; but they defend the existing right against the latitude of their own phrases, in a case where there was no good reason to abridge it.

The exception admits they will have the right of adjournment, without pointing out the source from which they will derive it.[11]

These are all the passages of the constitution (one only excepted which shall be presently cited) where the right of adjournment is touched: and it is evident that none of these are introduced to give that right; but every one supposes it to be existing, and provides some specific modification for cases where either a defect in the natural right, or a too full use of it would[12] occasion inconvenience.

The right of adjournment then is not given by the constitution; and consequently it may be modified by law, without interfering with that instrument. It is a natural right, and, like all other natural rights, may be abridged or regulated in it's exercise by law; and the concurrence of the third branch in any law regulating it's exercise is so efficient an ingredient in that law,[13] that the right cannot be otherwise exercised, but after a repeal by a new law. The express terms of the constitution itself shew that this right may be modified *by law*, when, in Art. 1. sect. 4. (the only remaining passage on the subject not yet quoted) it sais 'the Congress shall assemble at least once in every year, and such meeting shall be on the 1st. Monday in December, unless they shall, *by law*, appoint a different day.' Then another day may be appointed, *by law*; and the President's assent is an efficient ingredient in that law. Nay further, they cannot adjourn over the 1st. Monday of December but by *a law*.[14] This is another constitutional abridgment of their natural right of adjournment: and completing our review of all the clauses in the constitution which touch that right, authorises us to say no part of that instrument gives it; and that the houses hold it, not from the constitution, but from nature.

A consequence of this is, that the houses may by a joint resolution remove themselves from place to place; because it is a part of their right of self-government: but that as the right of self-government does not comprehend the government of others, the two houses cannot, by a joint resolution of their majorities only, remove the executive, and judiciary from place to place. These branches possessing also the rights of self-government from nature, cannot be controuled in the exercise of them, but by a law, passed in the forms of the constitution. The clause of the bill in question therefore was necessary to be put into the form of a law, and to be submitted to the President, so far as it proposes to effect the removal of the Executive and Judiciary to Philadelphia. So far as respects the removal of the present houses of legislation thither, it was not necessary to be submitted to the president: but such a submission is not repugnant to the constitution. On the contrary, if he concurs, it will so far fix the next session of Congress at Philadelphia, that it cannot be changed but by a regular law.

The sense of Congress itself is always respectable authority. It has been given very remarkeably on the[15] present subject. The address to the President in the paper of the 13th.[16] is a complete digest of all the arguments urged on the floor of the Representatives against the constitutionality of the bill now before the President; and they were over-ruled by a majority of that house, comprehending the delegations of all the states South of the Hudson, except South Carolina. At the last session of Congress, when the bill for remaining a certain term at New York, and then removing to Susquehanna or Germantown was objected to on the same ground, the objection was overruled by a majority, comprehending the delegations of the Northern half of the union with that of South Carolina. So that the sense of every state in the union has been expressed, by it's delegation, against this objection, South Carolina excepted, and excepting also Rhode island which has never yet had a delegation in place to vote on the question. In both these instances the Senate concurred with the majority of the Representatives. The sense of the two houses is stronger authority in this case, as it is given against their own supposed privilege.[17]

It would be as tedious, as it is unnecessary, to take up and discuss one by one, the objections proposed in the paper of July 13. Every one of them is founded on the supposition that the two houses hold their right of adjournment from the constitution. This error being corrected, the objections founded on it fall of themselves.

It would also be work of mere supererogation to shew that, granting what this writer takes for granted (that the President's assent would be an inoperative ingredient, because excluded by the constitution, as he says) yet the particular views of the writer would be frustrated. For on every hypothesis of what the President may do, Congress must go to Philadelphia. 1. If he assents to the bill, that assent[18] makes good law of the part relative to the Patowmac, and the part for holding the next session at Philadelphia is good, either as an ordinance, or a vote of the two houses, containing a compleat declaration of their will, in a case where it is competent to the object, so that they must go to Philadelphia in that case. 2. If he dissents from the bill, it annuls the part relative to the Patowmac; but as to the clause for adjourning to Philadelphia, his dissent being as inefficient as his assent, it remains a good ordinance, or vote, of the two houses for going thither, and consequently they must go in this case also. 3. If the President witholds his will out of the bill altogether, by a ten days silence, then the part relative to the Patowmac becomes a good law without his will, and that relative to Philadelphia is good also, either as a law, or an ordinance, or a vote of the two houses, and consequently in this case also they go to Philadelphia. TH: JEFFERSON

July 15. 1790.

MS (DNA: RG 59, MLR); entirely in TJ's hand and signed by him. Tr (DNA: RG 59, SDC). Dft (DLC: TJ Papers, 56: 9610-4); differs from MS in some particulars (see notes below).

1 This word interlined in Dft in substitution for "inefficient," deleted.

2 In Dft TJ wrote: "they derive ⟨it⟩ ⟨this⟩ ⟨that right⟩ it from nature; it is inherent ⟨to⟩ in their being," and then altered the passage to read as above.

3 In Dft TJ wrote: ". . . this right by their own will," and then altered the text to read as above.

4 In Dft TJ wrote "collection" and then deleted the word.

5 In Dft TJ wrote: ". . . the rights of self-government" and then altered the text to read as above.

6 In Dft this word is interlined in substitution for "meant," deleted.

7 In Dft TJ first wrote: ". . . it would have been too contracted," and then altered the passage to read as above.

8 This paragraph in Dft ended with this sentence: "This clause goes to this and no other object." TJ then altered the text to read as above.

9 Dft reads: "President, in all cases";

the last three words are not deleted.

10 Dft reads: ". . . it was known they would possess," &c., and the passage was then altered to read as above.

11 In Dft this sentence is interlined.

12 This word is interlined in Dft in substitution for "might," deleted.

13 In Dft TJ first wrote: "and the will of the president is ⟨an⟩ so effective an ingredient in that law," and then altered the passage to read as above.

14 At this point in Dft TJ wrote: "⟨and that law⟩ and for this we have the evidence of the constitution itself unequivocally," and then deleted the clause.

15 In Dft at this point TJ wrote: ". . . Constitutionality of adjournments by law as well as by resolution," and then altered the passage to read as above.

16 TJ first wrote in Dft: "the very paper in question," and then altered the text to read as above.

17 This paragraph is written on a separate sheet and marked for insertion at this point.

18 In Dft TJ first wrote: "If he approves the bill, that approbation . . ." and then altered the text to read as above.

VI. James Madison's Concurring Opinion

[14 July 1790]

This reasoning is inforced by the clause (Art. 2. Sect. 1. ⟨cl. 3⟩) which says the list of votes of the electors shall be transmitted to the seat of Govt. directed to the President of the Senate who in presence of the Senate and H of Reps. shall open the certificates &c. The seat of *Congress* then must be at the seat of Govt.[1] It is admitted that the seat of Govt. can not be where the *Ex: part* of the Govt. does not sit. The three branches then must sit together and each having a will independent of the others, all must concur in saying where the common seat shall be, that is, a law ought to pass for the purpose.

MS (DLC: TJ Papers, 56: 9611); undated, pencilled memorandum in Madison's hand, attached to Dft of TJ's opinion (see preceding document); addressed "Mr. Madison." The date of this memorandum is established by the fact that the slip on which it is written, though mutilated, contains 9 of the names of 14 senators who voted for, and 6 of the 11 who voted against, a resolution proposing a loan of $21,000,000

to the United States. Underneath this tally, in the hand of Benjamin Hawkins, is the following: "14 Ays 11 nays. Gunn was absent." This tabulation and partial identification can only apply to the vote on this resolution, taken on 14 July 1790 (*Annals*, I, 1047).

1 At this point in MS Madison wrote, and then deleted: "otherwise the list of votes would be directed to a."

VII. *One of the Gallery* on the Conduct of Madison, Page, and Carroll

[15 July 1790]

What shall we say to those men who, *a few months ago*, declared most solemnly that it was an *unconstitutional act to fix by law the session of congress*, and now *give their votes for a cause which fixes by law the next session of congress*? Those who have read the speeches of Mr. M-----n, Mr. P--e, and Mr. C-----l, as recorded in the 2d. volume of the Congressional Register, pages 425, 427, and 432, must now see with an astonishment mingled with grief, the names of those gentlemen on the Journal giving sanction to a law which they think unconstitutional. Mr. P--e, in his speech published a few days ago says that the law to be inconsistent with the constitution, should direct the adjournment to take place *without the consent of the senate* because the constitution is, that 'neither house shall adjourn *without the consent of the other*:' ingenious quibble! Compare it with his speech of last session, Congressional Record, 2d. vol. page 427, where he asked, 'where was the necessity of adhering to a clause, which its warmest advocates must allow had *no binding force*, as it related to its main object, namely, the *continuance of the two houses to sit in this city*.' He says in the latter part of his speech 'that it might indeed be said upon a question concerning *common adjournments*, the two houses would do well to retain the right of adjourning *without the consent of the presi-dent*; but this is *an extraordinary case*.' (A very extraordinary case

—truly Mr. P! and so there must be an extraordinary deviation from the constitution to suit the case!) There are two sorts of adjournment, a *common* one and an *uncommon* one: the common one, when congress ought to fix by law that the temporary seat of government shall be at New-York is *not binding* and unconstitutional: the *uncommon* one when they are to adjourn to meet at Philadelphia, must be fixed by law and have the consent of the president; *without this check*, says this conscientious patriot, after getting to Philadelphia on an adjournment, they may be brought back to New-York; pray, Mr. P. will this check prevent congress adjourning back to New-York, if they are so disposed; if I remember right, the law only says the *next session* shall be at Philadelphia, and where is the check if the clause has *no binding force*, as was said by Mr. P. last session? It would be a prudent thing for some persons to think before they speak.—*litera scripta manet!*

What is become of another person's *oath* which stuck in his throat last session, and prevented his voting for the Susquehannah? Has he swallowed it since that time? Or is it so long since he took it that he has forgot it? Or have the waters of the *Patowmac* the virtue of the *Lethe*, that those who drink of them lose their memory?

ONE OF THE GALLERY

Text from (N.Y.) *Daily Advertiser*, 15 July 1790.

VIII. Reply to *Junius Americanus* and Others

Aug. 9.

The public attention having been drawn to the meaning of the constitution, as applied to two bills, one before the last, the other before the present session of Congress, the following candid view of this subject is submitted by one who has carefully attended to the whole discussion.

By the   article of the constitution the power of adjourning to *another* place is vested in the two houses,—whose joint vote for the purpose is not to be submitted to the President.

The bill at the last session for continuing the *seat of government* at New-York, for a term not exceeding four years, was a violation of the said article.

Because the seat of government included the seat of Congress, as being an essential part of the government; and as is proved by the clause requiring the votes of the electors to be sent to the *seat of government* to be opened *in the presence of the two houses.*

Because the bill of consequence imposed a restraint on the right of the two houses alone during the said term, to adjourn from New-York.

The clause in the late act fixing the temporary and permanent seat of government, which declares 'that the ensuing session of Congress shall be held at Philadelphia,' is not a violation of the said article of the constitution.

Because the article refers to an *adjournment.*

Because an adjournment refers to the *same Congress.*

Because a new election of representatives makes a new Congress, notwithstanding the *sameness* of the senate as a new house of commons makes a new Parliament, notwithstanding the *sameness* of the house of lords.

Because, therefore, as the ensuing session might have been that of a new Congress, by the intervening election of a new house of representatives, the approbation of the President would in that event have been operative, and even necessary.

Because even on a contrary event the clause attempts no restraint on a future Congress, but binds only the two existing houses, and that equally, whether the President approves or disapproves their joint vote of adjournment involved in the clause.

From this view of the subject it is evident, 1st. that those who objected to the constitutionality of the former bill, and concurred in that of the latter, voted consistently with the constitution, and with themselves.

2d. That those who concurred in the former and objected to the latter, voted inconsistently both with the constitution and with themselves.

3d. That the President in signing the latter added one more to the reiterated proofs given of a judgment not to be bewildered by false reasoning, and of a *patriotic* firmness not to be affected by *local* discontents.

Text from (N.Y.) *Daily Advertiser,* 11 Aug. 1790.

Among those who had CAREFULLY ATTENDED TO THE WHOLE DISCUSSION in the first and second sessions of Congress and in the newspaper attacks by *Junius Americanus* and others, James Madison seems by far the most logical and natural one to suspect of being the author of this statement. He had originated the constitutional argument in 1789, he had been singled out with particular emphasis by *Junius Americanus* for abandoning that position, and he had certainly been called upon to give close attention to the subject in framing a response to the President's queries. The terse, disciplined style also seems as indicative of Madison's hand as the logical ordering of the argument. Since the public indignation seemed to be growing rather than subsiding, it is possible that TJ and Madison concluded a public rebuttal was necessary and they may have called upon Page or Carroll to frame it. But Madison seems the most likely author.

IX. Response by *Truth* to the Foregoing

Aug. 11.

A paltry attempt in yesterday's paper to impose on the public requires some notice—the writer of it asserts that the bill of last session *for continuing the seat of government* at New-York was *unconstitutional* and the bill of this session for *adjourning to Philadelphia, constitutional*: the citizens of this country are too enlightened to be deceived by the flimsey reasoning which is employed to support these points. Let us examine them. Fixing the seat of government, says the author, at New-York for four years was a violation of the article of the constitution which vests the power of adjourning in the two houses alone, because the seat of government included the seat of Congress, and because the bill imposed a restraint on the right of the two houses alone during the said term to adjourn from New-York. Hence he infers that it was unconstitutional to fix by law the seat of government, because Congress is part of the government—how then does he pretend to justify the bill of this session which fixes the seat of government for ten years at Philadelphia? Will not Congress constitute a part of the government and be included therein as much at Philadelphia as at New-York, or does the difference between four years residence in the one bill and ten years in the other make one bill violate the constitution and the other conform to it? Where then is the proof of unerring judgment in approving a bill which, according to this sagacious writer, restrains Congress from adjourning for the space of ten years from Philadelphia.

It is then evident, that this author is mistaken in his first position, viz., that the seat of government cannot be fixed by law for a term of years; or that if he be right in his first position, he must be wrong in his second, viz. That the bill of this session is constitutional, because the said bill contains a clause similar to the one in the bill of last session, which he declares unconstitutional.

A slight attention to the subject, will also refute his second position; he says that the clause in question does not violate the constitution, because the article refers to an *adjournment*, and because an adjournment refers to the *same Congress*. The writers reasoning in this part, is so involved in confusion, that it is difficult to trace it. His distinction between the *same* and *another Congress*, is perfectly absurd as applicable to this question and unfounded from the very words of the constitution; nay, he refutes himself, for in the very outset of his remarks, he says, 'by the article of the Constitution the power of adjourning to another place is vested *in the two houses*, whose joint vote for the purpose is not to be submitted to the President.' Where does he find any distinction between an adjournment of the same Congress and meeting of the new one?—there is none in the constitution.—But here his own argument turns strongly against himself, for the clause in the bill declares that the *next session of Congress* shall be held at Philadelphia, and not the *session of the next Congress*; the law therefore binds the *same Congress* who had a right to adjourn themselves by concurrent resolution.

Would the assent of the President be *necessary* to a concurrent resolution of one Congress directing where another should assemble? No; because the constitution vests in the *two houses alone* the power of adjournment in every case.—If the old Congress should assign a place for the meeting of the new one, they would of course assemble at the place where the offices of state were held, and where the former Congress had held their session; if a place should be assigned, the new Congress would assemble there, but they would have the power by concurrent resolution to adjourn to any other place; the assent of the President therefore to the act would be nugatory, for it would not be binding on the new Congress, who would by virtue of the constitution possess the power of adjournment,—in any case then the assent of the President to a vote of adjournment is unconstitutional.

The author refutes himself in more than one place; he acknowledges that the clause *attempts no restraint on a future Congress*; then the assent of the President is *not valid*, quoad a new Congress; but says he, it *binds only the two existing houses* and that *equally* (wonderful conclusions from his premises!) *whether the President approves or disapproves their joint vote of adjournment* involved in the clause. So that tho' he in one paragraph insinuates that the *approbation of the President would have been very necessary*, as applicable to a *new Congress*, yet in a subsequent one he contends that the clause *attempts no restraint on a future Congress*; and tho he insists on the constitutionality of the clause, yet he admits that the signature of the President adds no validity to the vote of adjournment, but that it would be *equally binding without it*; and why? Because as he has above declared the *two houses alone possess the power of adjournment*. There is reason then to apprehend that false reasoning has been too successfully employed in bewildering a judgment that has hitherto given reiterated proofs of its soundness, and in subduing that patriotic firmness which should have rejected any impression arising from *local prejudices* which, upon this and another late occasion (the unnecessary detention of a very necessary bill) appear to have had far more influence than was proper.

TRUTH

Text from (N.Y.) *Daily Advertiser,* 12 Aug. 1790.

The style, the ridicule of an opponent, the forensics of the advocate, the strict and literal appeal to the text of the Constitution, the allusion to Washington's sound judgment and patriotic firmness, the remark about the unnecessary delay to the assumption—A VERY NECESSARY BILL—the use of such a favored word as "nugatory," and the logic of the situation all point to *Junius Americanus* (and to William Smith) as the author of this piece. It was his argument that had been rebutted and the responsibility for surrebuttal lay upon him. The challenge to find express authority in the Constitution echoes that made by William Smith in the first

session when he argued against vesting the power of removal in the President: "Examine the constitution; the powers of the several branches of Government are there defined; the President has particular powers assigned him; the Judiciary have in like manner powers assigned them; but you will find no such power as removing from office given to the President. I call upon gentlemen to show me where it is said that the President shall remove from office. I know they cannot do it. Now, I infer from this, that, as the constitution has not given the President the power of removability, it meant that he should not have that power" (*Annals,* I, 475). Unwearied repetition was also a characteristic of *Junius Americanus.*

X. Jefferson's Account of the Bargain on the Assumption and Residence Bills

[1792?]

The assumption of the state debts in 1790. was a supplementary measure in Hamilton's fiscal system. When attempted in the House of Representatives it failed. This threw Hamilton himself and a number of members into deep dismay. Going to the President's one day I met Hamilton as I approached the door. His look was sombre, haggard, and dejected beyond description. Even his dress uncouth and neglected. He asked to speak with me. We stood in the street near the door. He opened the subject of the assumption of the state debts, the necessity of it in the general fiscal arrangement and it's indispensible necessity towards a preservation of the union: and particularly of the New England states, who had made great expenditures during the war, on expeditions which tho' of their own undertaking were for the common cause: that they considered the assumption of these by the Union so just, and it's denial so palpably injurious, that they would make it a sine qua non of a continuance of the Union. That as to his own part, if he had not credit enough to carry such a measure as that, he could be of no use, and was determined to resign. He observed at the same time, that tho' our particular business laid in separate departments, yet the administration and it's success was a common concern, and that we should make common cause in supporting one another. He added his wish that I would interest my friends from the South, who were those most opposed to it. I answered that I had been so long absent from my country that I had lost a familiarity with it's affairs, and being but lately returned had not yet got into the train of them, that the fiscal system being out of my department, I had not yet undertaken to consider and understand it, that the assumption had struck me in an unfavorable light, but still not having considered it sufficiently I had not concerned in it, but that I would revolve what he had urged in my mind. It was a real fact that the Eastern and Southern members (S. Carolina however was with the former) had got into the most extreme ill humor with one another, this broke out on every question with the most alarming heat, the bitterest animosities seemed to be engendered, and tho' they met every day, little or nothing could be done from mutual distrust and antipathy. On considering the situation of things I thought the first step towards some conciliation of views would be to bring Mr. Madison and Colo. Hamilton to a friendly discussion of the subject. I immediately wrote to each to come and dine with me the next day, mentioning that we should be alone, that the object was to find some temperament for the present fever,[1] and that I was persuaded that men of sound heads and honest views needed nothing more than explanation and mutual understanding to enable them to unite in some measures which might enable us to get along. They came. I opened the subject to them, acknoleged that my situation had not permitted me[2] to understand it sufficiently but encouraged them to consider the thing together. They did so. It ended in Mr. Madison's acquiescence in a proposition that the question should be again brought before the house by way of amendment from the Senate, that tho' he would not vote for it, nor entirely withdraw his opposition, yet he should not be strenuous, but leave it to it's fate.[3] It was observed, I forget by which of them, that as the pill would be a bitter one to the Southern states, something should be done to soothe them; that the removal of the seat of government to the Patowmac was a just measure, and would probably be a popular one with them, and would be a proper one to follow the assumption. It was agreed[4] to speak to Mr. White and Mr. Lee, whose districts lay on the Patowmac and to refer to them to consider how far the interests of their particular districts might be a sufficient inducement to them to yield to the assumption. This was done.[5] Lee came into it without hesitation. Mr. White had some qualms, but finally agreed. The measure came down by way of amendment from the Senate and was finally carried by the change of White's and Lee's votes. But the removal to Patowmac could not be carried unless Pennsylvania could be engaged in it. This Hamilton took on himself, and chiefly, as I understood, through the agency of Robert Morris, obtained the vote of that state, on agreeing to an intermediate residence at Philadelphia. This is the real history of the assumption, about which many erroneous conjectures have been published. It was unjust,[6] in itself oppressive to the states, and was acquiesced in merely from a fear of disunion, while our government was still in it's most infant state. It enabled Hamilton so to strengthen himself by corrupt services to many, that he could afterwards carry his bank scheme, and every measure he proposed in defiance of all opposition: in fact it was a principal ground whereon was reared up that Speculating phalanx, in and out of Congress which has since been able to give laws and to change the political complexion of the government of the US.

MS (DLC: TJ Papers, 231: 41531); at head of text: "The Assumption"; entirely in TJ's hand except for the following notation at head of text made much later by George Tucker: "Slip 1st. in the order they were arranged"; undated, but perhaps set down in 1792. Ford, VI, 172-4, assigns the queried date "Feb.? 1793." Malone, *Jefferson*, II, 507, thinks it may have been written about the time TJ "left the administration, that is, late in 1793 or early in 1794." All that can be said with certainty is that the memorandum was set down after the establishment of the Bank of the United States in 1791. Tucker's notation on the text may mean that this was placed first in the three volumes of *Anas*, in which the initial entry as now ascertainable is under date of 13 Aug. 1791. But even if this assumption is valid, it does not necessarily follow that the text was composed before that time. It seems more likely that it was written sometime during 1792. In that year TJ had several conversations with the President about his increasing unhappiness over the tendency of the administration as reflected in Hamilton's system (see under 1 Mch. 1792, 10 July 1792, and 1 Oct. 1792). It was in this year, too, that TJ wrote the famous letter setting forth in brief form another account of the episode that agrees in substance with the above (TJ to Washington, 9 Sep. 1792). Further, entries in SJPL—in which TJ customarily recorded immediately the dated memoranda that later became known as the *Anas*—for items that appear to be missing may include the present document. The most significant of these is that of 6 Oct. 1792, which reads: "Notes. Hamilton." No identifiable document for that date and subject has been found, and it may be that this entry covered a number of memoranda of which that labelled "The Assumption" was one, perhaps being the first and thus perhaps explaining the notation by Tucker. Another entry in SJPL under 2 Feb. 1793 for which no document can be found is entitled "History of A. Hamilton." It is possible that these entries relate to those items of the *Anas* which in 1818 TJ "cut out from the rest, because . . . they were incorrect, or doubtful, or merely personal or private" (see under 13 Aug. 1791), but it is also possible that they allude to such a note or such a history as the above. Certainly at the time TJ made the entry of 6 Oct. 1792 his most profound concern was over the evident drift of the administration away from republican principles under the impact of Hamilton's methods and his system of finance. In mid-summer he had written a "Note of Agenda to reduce the government to true principles" (entry in SJPL for 11 July 1792); on his way northward, after giving Washington a full and frank account of his views and of his part in securing the transfer of state debts, he had stopped at Gunston Hall and discussed with George Mason Hamilton's fiscal system as well as his "maneuvres in the grand convention" of 1787; and the next day at Mount Vernon he had gone over the same familiar ground of discordant principles. Neither before nor after 1792 is TJ known to have spoken and written so often or so forcefully to Washington about Hamiltonian methods and their effect on the "principles of administration" that he had so much at heart. The date of the history of his part in a transaction that had become abhorrent

to him cannot be ascertained, but the year 1792 when he made such desperate efforts to swing the helm back on course—particularly the autumn of that year—seems the most plausible time of composition. The allusion to the "Speculating phalanx" in the final sentence, the tense employed, and the similarity of this to an allusion of the same import in the letter to Washington of 9 Sep. 1790 all seem to support this conjecture.

I IMMEDIATELY WROTE TO EACH: No letters to Hamilton and Madison during the week of 13-20 June 1790 have been found and none is recorded in SJL. MR. WHITE AND MR. LEE: Richard Bland Lee (1761-1827) and Alexander White (1738-1804). Both were re-elected. In addition to these, Daniel Carroll (1730-1796) also supported the agreement respecting assumption and the seat of government (of which his cousin Charles Carroll of Carrollton was one of the leaders in the Senate). Daniel Carroll resigned as representative from Maryland and on 22 Jan. 1791 was appointed by Washington one of the Commissioners of the District of Columbia. Alexander White was also made a Commissioner in 1795, the year that Carroll resigned because of ill health.

¹ This word substituted for "difference," deleted.
² TJ first phrased this passage as follows: "I . . . acknoleged my situation did not permit me . . ." and then altered it to read as above.
³ At this point TJ wrote and then deleted: "He observed."
⁴ Preceding three words interlined in substitution for "Mr. Madison undertook," deleted.
⁵ At this point TJ wrote and then deleted: "They agreed to vote for the m[easure?]."
⁶ At this point TJ wrote and then deleted: "impolitic."

From C. W. F. Dumas

The Hague, 14 July 1790. Since his last of 6 May—5 June European affairs have continued "en violente crise entre la paix ou la guerre générale.—Aujourd'hui est le grand jour d'où dépend le salut interne de la France et son influence externe." He will hold the dispatch until next week to learn the happy success of the celebration in Paris. "En attendant, je passe les intermédiaires avec tous les bons ici, en voeux les plus chauds pour le bonheur de la nation françoise, plus que jamais digne Soeur de la nôtre. D'autres ici ont leurs raisons d'envisager cela de tout un autre oeil, et de former des voeux contraires." He encloses the *Gazette de Leide* of 29 June containing an article from Paris of the 24th: some have expressed surprise that no Americans were among the representatives of various nations—English, Dutch, Prussians, Russians, Swedes, Poles, Germans, &c.—who took part in the solemn address to the National Assembly. To these he replied that no American could or would sign it. "Et pourquoi?—!—Parce qu'ils ne sont *ni opprimés, ni sous le joug*, comme ces gens se plaignent de l'être chez eux." This stops all questions. The French chargé d'affaires, a faithful disciple of the late Turgot, heartily applauds this retort.—He encloses under a flying seal, in order that the Department may see its contents, his letter to the "Académie des Arts et Sciences établie à Cambridge près Boston."— He went into mourning as soon as he learned of the death of Franklin and only left it off on 4 July, "en souhaitant que nos illustres Président, Vice-President, Ministres et tous les autres Sages qui ont coopéré avec ce Nestor au bonheur et à la gloire de l'Union américaine soient rassasiés comme lui d'années, avant d'aller à l'heureuse immortalité qui leur est destinée." Congratulates Congress on the accession of Rhode Island. [*In postscript*:] 20 July. "La journée du 14e. s'est passée heureuse- ment, Dieu Merci, à la satisfaction de l'aimable nation et de son bon Roi, à l'honneur de La Fayette à qui la sureté, l'ordre public, le salut du tout étoit confié, et à celui de la Capitale d'une Monarchie aujourd'hui la mieux constituée de la terre, qui l'a parfaitement secondé. Tous se réunissent ici à dire, mais chacun selon son inclination et systême, les uns bénissant, les autres maudissants, que les François copient les Américains et La Fayette leur Washington. Et moi, au milieu d'eux, je leur dis, vive la vérité, l'humanité et les constitutions qui naîtront comme l'Américaine, ou se régénereront comme la Françoise." [*In post- script*:] 23rd. The Swedes have been defeated in the Baltic. The kings of Hungary and Prussia are still bargaining, and in spite of the gazettes there is beter reason to believe in war than peace between them, but there is hope of peace between Spain and England. He thinks it necessary to warn TJ that the English have recently sent another reinforcement of troops to Canada.—"Pour revenir à la France, per- sonne ne doute que sa nouvelle Constitution ne fasse naître un nouvel ordre des choses dans toute l'Europe."

He had communicated to Luzac news of the honor done him by the American Academy of Arts and Sciences, leaving it up to him to pub- lish the announcement or not. He annexes a copy of Luzac's reply be- cause it gives a lively characterization of the "*crabroni*" that Luzac fears to irritate, whose rule "en bon Latin est l'*impotentia muliebriter tyrannica.*"

RC (DNA: RG 59, PCC No. 93); at head of text: "No. 66. Dupl. A Son Excellence Mr.   Ministre d'Etat pour les Aff. Etr. En Congrès genl. des Et. Un. d'Am."; endorsed by TJ as received 2 Nov. 1790 and so recorded in SJL. FC (Dumas Letter Book, Rijksar- chief, The Hague; photostats in DLC).

Enclosures: (1) Dumas' letter of acceptance of certificate of membership in the American Academy of Arts and Sciences, to which he had been elected on John Adams' recommendation. (2) Jean Luzac to Dumas, 10 July 1790, saying that he finds himself precisely in Dumas' situation, being spared no more than Dumas "les 'avanies' et les torts"; that he has been studiously "*evité*" during the whole course of the academic year at all of the dinners, even among his friends, where colleagues were invited to sup with "le jeune Prince" who had honored them with his presence; that he had suspected the cause, but now knows that his being excluded is the result "*d'Ordres exprès*"; that this odious exception is only a light mark of the rancor that they have for him and show at all times; that, to make the parallel more evident, he himself has just received from the Academy the same honor and with it "la Patente précisément dans le même temps, dans les mêmes termes, par la même voie et de la même façon," but that he would not announce it publicly and would mention it only to his friends. Luzac added: "Je ne cherche point à complaire; je ne fais ni ne ferai de ma vie des bassesses; *l'integer vita* est mon unique ambition. Cependant, je ne veux pas non plus *irritare crabrones*. Je sais que j'exciterois leur malignité, en même temps que leur envie et qu'à leurs yeux le choix que nos dignes Amis ont fait seroit une matiere pour gloser. Je ne crains donc pas la publicité, mais je ne la cherche pas non plus." (Tr in Dumas' hand, annexed to RC on separate leaf.)

From La Motte

Le Havre, 15 July 1790. He replies to TJ's letter of 11 Mch. in French because "vous entendés trop bien le françois et j'ecris trop mal l'Anglois." The plants have not arrived, and no notice of the shipment has come from Norfolk. He supposes the box went to Dunkerque, but will forward it as directed if it comes to Le Havre. Congratulates TJ on his "nouvelle dignité." Haviland Le Mesurier & Cie. learned of this from the superscription on Short's dispatches sent to them to be forwarded.—Of all the American ships which have come with flour, not one has wanted to take salt on the return, although the restriction on salt has been cancelled for three months and the price is only 20 sous per 60 ℔.: "Ils paroissent préférer se lester *with burr stones and plaster.*" The American harvest is reported to be "très belle": that in France "s'est presentée belle audelà de ce qu'on ait vû depuis longtems, mais nous avons depuis quinze Jours des pluyes abondantes accompagnées de vents violents; ce tems est général par toute la France et s'il continüe encore une huitaine, nous courons de gros risques de voir nos esperances frustrées."—Mr. [Nathaniel] Cutting, now "aux Isles de Los sur la Côte d'Afrique," asked before leaving whether La Motte would be vice consul at Le Havre if the American government offered the post: "Je repondis que Oui, et je vous confirme, Monsieur, que cela ou toute autre chose, proffitable ou non, qui en etendant nos liaisons dejà considerables avec les Americains, nous mette à même de montrer à la nation ou à ses individus notre estime, nous fera toujours, et à moi en particulier, grand plaisir.—Nous attendons avec impatience une décision sur la paix ou de la guerre entre l'Angleterre et l'Espagne. Des lettres d'Espagne, auxquelles on ne peut se refuser d'ajouter foi, disent que le gouvernement a donné dans les ports des ordres officiels de laisser partir les Navires marchands pour leur destination, parceque les

querelles avec l'Angleterre sont arrangées à l'Amiable. Notre gouvernement n'en sçait rien officiellement. Les Paquebots Anglois étant de-
montés de matelots par la presse, ne passent pas, pour nous confirmer
cette nouvelle. Dans ces Circonstances, nous supposons que l'Espagne,
piquée de la Necessité où nous met notre révolution de ne pas l'aider,
aura fait quelque traité avec l'Angleterre, qui nous sera défavorable."
[*In postscript:*] 17th. No more particulars on the question of war and
peace.

RC (DNA: RG 59, CD); addressed: "Thos. Jefferson Secretary of State New York"; postmarked: "Baltimore, Sep. 26" and docketed as forwarded from there on that date by S. Sterett & Co.; endorsed by TJ as received 25 Oct. 1790 and so recorded in SJL; endorsed by Remsen as received "Septr. 30th."

To William Temple Franklin

DEAR SIR   New York July 16. 1790.

On further reflection it appears to me that the houses you mentioned of Mrs. Buddin's would suit me so perfectly that I must
beg the favor of you to ensure me the refusal of two of them adjoining to each other, on the best terms you can. Houses will doubtless rise in the first moment, but as the residence of Congress really
calls for but a very few houses, such as those, (probably not a
dozen) I suppose there will be new buildings immediately erected
more than equal to the new demand. This ought to be a consideration with the proprietor to be moderate, in order to ensure the continuance of a tenant. My object in taking two houses is to assign
the lower floor of both to my public offices, and the first floor and
both gardens entirely to my own use. Perhaps the third floor of
one of them might also be necessary for dead office papers, machines
&c. I should wish for such a gallery on the back of the building as
I have had erected here. It might cost about £250 on which I would
pay the usual additional rent. This need only be spoken of so as
to prepare them for agreeing to make the addition.—A good neighbor is a very desireable thing. Mr. Randolph the Attorney General
is probably now in Philadelphia, and I think would like the same
part of the town. I wish the 3d. house (my two being secured)
could be proposed to him. I beg your pardon for giving you so
much trouble, but your kind offer brought it on you. I am with
sincere esteem Dr. Sir Your most obedt. humble servt.,

TH: JEFFERSON

RC (PPAP); addressed: "William Temple Franklin esq. Philadelphia"; franked. PrC (DLC). By MACHINES TJ probably meant models accompanying applications for patents. For the plan of a GALLERY see TJ to Franklin, 25 July 1790.

From William Short

Dear Sir   Paris July the 16th. 1790

I did not recieve until yesterday the letters which I mentioned, in my last to you of the 11th. inst., had been promised by a person who called here and left the newspapers. They were forwarded to me by M. Bondfield of Bordeaux. I had previously recieved duplicates of all of them except that of March the 30th. At present I have recieved all the letters which I know of your having written except that of March the 28th.—The several letters for your friends here which came inclosed in that recieved yesterday shall be safely conveyed to them. That for the Duke de la Rochefoucauld I have already given him, as well as the one for his mother who is in the country. I recieved yesterday also the model which you inclosed me for the copying press. It will be impossible to have it made so as to go with your furniture. I shall put immediately into the hands of Charpentier and hurry him as much as possible. When finished, it shall be forwarded in the most expeditious manner.—Petit and the packers had promised me that every thing should be ready for the 15th. (yesterday). But they have not kept their word; there are several things which are not yet packed. The paper hangings also have not been finished agreeably to Arthur's promise, nor is the clock ready. They lay the blame on the present situation of Paris relative to the ceremony of the 14th. which has turned the heads of all the workmen.

This great ceremony took place the day before yesterday in the midst of a storm of rain and wind which by intervals lasted the whole day. I inclose you the order of procession. It passed along the quai. Opposite the champ de Mars a bridge of boats was thrown across the river over which the procession passed and entered the Champ de Mars in passing under an Arc de triomphe. The alter was in the middle of the area, and joining to the Ecole militaire a covered gallery facing the altar was erected where was the throne. The ceremonies as described in the paper inclosed were performed. They ended a little after five o'clock in the evening. The national assembly was applauded moderately by the spectators on their arrival. But the King recieved acclamations of applause from all quarters which are without example. His presence and particularly the moment of his taking the oath produced a kind of intoxication which was unlike any thing I ever saw. In general it is observable that the deputies sent from the provinces to this federation are much more Royalist than the Parisians or national assembly. The most perfect harmony and concord have prevailed as yet. Should they return immediately to their several provinces there is no doubt they would carry with them good dispositions, and many of them I am told are preparing already to return.—The apprehensions of ill which were entertained respecting this federation are dissipated. The faction in the national assembly which was so much dreaded, remain quiet and seem to have had little communication with the *federés*. The Duke of Orleans seems studiously to have avoided any conspicuous conduct. He was in the procession as member of the assembly and was little applauded. His return has made scarcely any impression. The Marquis de la fayette has acquired the adoration of the *federés*. His popular manners have won them all. Besides he has kept open house for them. I told you he had prepared a table of an hundred plates for them to be filled every day. He augmented it to an hundred and fifty, and besides has every day additional tables in every room in his house below stairs; so that there are daily between two and three hundred persons who dine there.

I mentioned in my last that the corps diplomatique had determined not to go to the Champ de Mars. They afterwards on recieving a pointed invitation changed their mind. I got a letter from Tolozan on tuesday evening which informed me of it. He added that the rendezvous was at the Nuncio's and that he had obtained a cavalier d'ordonnance which would accompany each of the members of the corps diplomatique to the rendezvous, in order that they might go in their carriages. From thence we went in a body to the ecole militaire. All the Ambassadors were there except the Dutch who was sick. They were all so pleased with the manner in which the King was recieved and with the grandeur of the scene that they expressed repeatedly their satisfaction at having come.

I mentioned to you in a former letter the embassy of foreigners who went with an address to the national assembly.—Their reception encouraged the few Americans who were here, and some days ago Paul Jones put himself at the head of them and went with an address. They were well recieved. The answer of the President M. de Bonnai, was very much applauded. These gentlemen wished me to go with them and deliver the address, but it would have been so manifestly improper, that I declined it without hesitation.

It is true that the Queen of Portugal has appointed M. Friere her chargé des affaires at London, Minister Resident in America. I should have supposed this appointment would not have been made without some previous overture which insured a reciprocity, and yet a late letter from you does not allow me to doubt on this subject.—[I mentioned in a former letter the different places where I supposed Congress would keep representatives, and my desire to be employed at one or the other of them in the case of some other person being sent here. I would not repeat it now if I were sure that letter would arrive safe. I give the same excuse for the tedious repetitions respecting myself which you will find in all my late letters. Not knowing which will arrive safe, I mention nearly the same things in all—viz. my desire to remain in France for some time to come, or to be employed in some other court, my reasons for it, and for not wishing to return to America at present, my mortification at finding the probability of some other being preferred to me for the place heightened by the opinion which prevails here and which must necessarily change to a supposition that nothing but my incapacity could occasion it as you are the head of the foreign department and must necessarily direct all the operations made in it.][1]—I inclose a letter for the President which the Abbe Sieyes sent me yesterday. He was President of the assembly when it was ordered to be written.—Nothing has transpired since my last relative to the Negociation at Madrid. It is no longer doubted that the letter from Bilbao was premature. If my letters partake of a confusion inseparable from my present uncertain and anxious state of mind I hope you will excuse it in, Your friend & servant,

W. Short

RC (DLC); at head of text: "*Private*"; part of text deleted in manner indicated in note to Short to TJ, 11 July 1790 and also not deleted in PrC (DLC: Short Papers); endorsed as received 2 Nov. 1790 and so recorded in SJL. The enclosed communication from the Abbé Sièyés is discussed in TJ to Washington, 9 Dec. 1790.

The ADDRESS which Short declined to participate in is printed in *Gazette of the United States*, 6 Oct. 1790; it was signed by Joel Barlow, John Paul Jones, Samuel Blackden, James Swan,

George Washington Greene, and others. Short probably enclosed among the papers a copy of *Journal de Paris* (DLC: TJ Papers, 56, 9605) containing an account of the address and the response of the Abbé Sièyés, who noted that America "a conquis sa liberté par des flots de sang; la France doit la sienne aux progrès de la raison."

[1] Matter enclosed in brackets (supplied) comprises the part of text obliterated as indicated above.

To Martha Jefferson Randolph

MY DEAR PATSY   New York July 17. 1790.

I recieved two days ago yours of July 2. with Mr. Randolph's of July 3. Mine of the 11th. to Mr. Randolph will have informed

you that I expect to set out from hence for Monticello about the
1st. of September. As this depends on the adjournment of Congress
and they begin to be impatient, it is more probable I may set out
sooner than later. However my letters will keep you better informed
as the time approaches.—Colo. Randolph's marriage was to be
expected. All his amusements depending on society, he cannot live
alone. The settlement spoken of may be liable to objections in
point of prudence and justice. However I hope it will not be the
cause of any diminution of affection between him and Mr. Randolph
and yourself. That cannot remedy the evil, and may make it a great
deal worse. Besides your interests which might be injured by a
misunderstanding be assured that your happiness would be infinitely
affected. It would be a cankerworm corroding eternally on your
minds. Therefore, my dear child, redouble your assiduities to keep
the affections of Colo. Randolph and his lady (if he is to have one)
in proportion as the difficulties increase. He is an excellent good
man, to whose temper nothing can be objected but too much facility,
too much milk. Avail yourself of this softness then to obtain his
attachment. If the lady has any thing difficult in her dispositions,
avoid what is rough, and attach her good qualities to you. Consider what are otherwise as a bad stop in your harpsichord. Do not
touch on it, but make yourself happy with the good ones. Every
human being, my dear, must thus be viewed according to what
it is good for, for none of us, no not one, is perfect; and were we
to love none who had imperfections this world would be a desert
for our love. All we can do is to make the best of our friends: love
and cherish what is good in them, and keep out of the way of what
is bad: but no more think of rejecting them for it than of throwing
away a piece of music for a flat passage or two. Your situation
will require peculiar attentions and respects to both parties. Let no
proof be too much for either your patience or acquiescence. Be you,
my dear, the link of love, union, and peace for the whole family.
The world will give you the more credit for it in proportion to the
difficulty of the task. And your own happiness will be the greater
as you percieve that you promote that of others. Former acquaintance, and equality of age, will render it the easier for you to cultivate and gain the love of the lady. The mother too becomes a very
necessary object of attentions.—This marriage renders it doubtful
with me whether it will be better to direct our overtures to Colo.
R. or Mr. H. for a farm for Mr. Randolph. Mr. H. has a good tract
of land on the other side Edgehill, and it may not be unadviseable

to begin by buying out a dangerous neighbor. I wish Mr. Randolph could have him sounded to see if he will sell, and at what price; but sounded thro' such a channel as would excite no suspicion that it comes from Mr. Randolph or myself. Colo. Monroe would be a good and unsuspected hand, as he once thought of buying the same lands. Adieu my dear child. Present my warm attachment to Mr. Randolph. Your's affectionately,   Th: JEFFERSON

RC (NNP). PrC (MHi). Martha's letter of 2 July 1790 and MR. RANDOLPH'S OF JULY 3 have not been found but are recorded in SJL as received 15 July 1790, the former being written from "Presqu'isle."

COLO. RANDOLPH'S MARRIAGE:

Martha's father-in-law had recently married Gabriella Harvie, daughter of John Harvie (Robert Isham Randolph, *The Randolphs of Virginia*, p. 51). See TJ to Harvie, 25 July 1790; also Malone, *Jefferson*, II, 320.

Plans and Estimates for the Diplomatic Establishment

I. PLANS PRESENTED TO WASHINGTON, 26 MARCH 1790
II. PLANS PRESENTED TO THE CONFERENCE COMMITTEE, 21 JUNE 1790
III. OBSERVATIONS ON THE DIPLOMATIC ESTABLISHMENT AS PROVIDED FOR BY CONGRESS, 17 JULY 1790
IV. ESTIMATES OF FUNDS REQUIRED FOR THE DIPLOMATIC ESTABLISHMENT, 1790-1791

EDITORIAL NOTE

Soon after the passage of the Act providing the means of intercourse with foreign nations, a writer in the *New-York Journal* declared that the appropriation of $40,000 would cause "ambassadors . . . to be maintained at splendid courts, by a nation which has recently compounded with its creditors, and postponed payment, because she felt herself barren in *ways* and *means*." He asked rhetorically: "Has America ever realized any substantial advantage from foreign ministers? . . . This [foreign] department has been maintained with borrowed monies, and with great expence, and the character of America has not been exalted by most of our representatives. Spain has sent us an *Escargado de Negocios*—Great Britain has insulted us—France has flattered us with very respectable commissions, and we endeavored to return the compliment. We did not send them a *Count* or *Marquis*, but we sent them an *elegant philosopher*, and a *civilized Poet*. This account current of civilities is balanced. . . . It is a folly for a young republican country, removed by the kindness of nature, from the quarrels of Europe, to get entangled in the intrigues of European courts."[1] This spirit of economy, of republican simplicity, of antipathy to courts and courtiers, and of a pervading prejudice in favor of insularity in American policy was reflected through the country generally and in Congress particularly. "I consider the money as worse than thrown away," declared Senator Maclay, "for I know not a single thing that we have for a minister to do at a single court in Europe. Indeed, the less we have to do with them the better. Our business is to pay them what we owe, and the less political connection the better with any European power. [The bill] was well spoken against. I voted against every part of it."[2] Maclay has been called, with little justification, the original Jeffersonian, but on this issue as on others he could scarcely have taken a more remote position from that of Jefferson, who had no exalted opinion either of courts or of the generality of diplomats but who grasped as few Americans of the time did the importance of maintaining an adequate foreign establishment on a liberal allowance and who intuitively understood both the art and the importance of diplomacy.[3]

The issue had been joined even before Jefferson arrived in New York, and the reports from France revealing republican attitudes of economy toward diplomatic and consular establishments did nothing to weaken the convictions of those who felt as Maclay did. The new secretary of state at once displayed his sensitiveness to the prevailing mood by submitting to Washington alternative plans at their second extended interview.[4] His policy called for higher salaries, more generous allowances, and provisions for an outfit and for a return at regular intervals. Economies would be effected by choosing lower grades of diplomatic officers and by restricting their number rigorously to those nations with which the United States was likely to have important concerns. The issue involved not merely attitudes of economy and insularity: it also was concerned with the constitutional question of the right of Congress to determine places to which emissaries should be sent and to fix the rank to be assigned.[5]

A bill to provide compensation for diplomatic officers was debated,

---

[1] *New-York Journal*, 17 Sep. 1789. The *Journal* was even more critical of the proliferation of offices in the treasury department. "The objects of America should be," it declared in one of a series of articles opposing Hamilton's funding measures, "to cultivate national economy, humility, and honesty" and questioned whether his object might be "under the head of current service, or *Exegencies*, a political increase of salaries, and multiplication of offices, to give a ministerial strength to party, and political energy to a confederation which *must destroy the states or be destroyed*" (same, 2 July 1790). The concluding phrase was turned about by Hamilton himself a few months later when Virginia remonstrated against the assumption: "This is the first symptom of a spirit which must either be killed, or will kill the constitution of the United States" (Hamilton to Jay, 13 Nov. 1790; William Jay, *John Jay*, ii, 202).

[2] Maclay, *Journal*, ed. Maclay, p. 304.

[3] See, for example, Vol. 13: 269-70, for TJ's opinion of courts.

[4] Document i, below; see also TJ's opinion under 24 Apr. 1790, and notes there of his early consultations with Washington.

[5] Washington, *Diaries*, ed. Fitzpatrick, iv, 107, 109-10, 115, 122, 128, 129, 130; for notes to TJ's opinion on the constitutional question, see under 24 Apr. 1790.

amended, and passed through two readings soon after Washington's general recommendations had been made.[6] It was scheduled for the third reading on 28 Jan. 1790 but when the engrossed bill was read, Sherman observed that $40,000 was appropriated by it "to uses with the propriety of which no gentlemen seemed to be well acquainted." He thought that the house could not be warranted "in passing a bill disposing of so large a sum of money without further information," and therefore moved that it be tabled.[7] A further inducement to this action lay in the fact that Madison at this time was actively pressing Jefferson to accept the office of secretary of state and his arrival in New York was momentarily expected. The engrossed bill was taken up on 24 Mch. 1790, the day after Jefferson had had his first formal conversation with Washington on the question of the diplomatic establishment. It was committed to Sedgwick, Huntington, and Lee—the committee with which Jefferson presumably discussed the alternative plans that he laid before the president on the 26th.[8] A substitute bill was reported on 31 Mch., but not debated until late April, when it was amended, passed, and sent to the senate. It was read the second time on the busy first Monday of May. "Full one half of our time," wrote Senator Maclay, "was taken up in two speeches on the subject of etiquette and expense attending and necessary to constitute the very essence of an ambassador. The lowest farthing should be three thousand pounds sterling, besides a year's salary at setting out. Much of what he [Adams] said bore the air of the traveler; in fact, I did not believe him, and, of course, voted in the face of all his information." The bill was sent to committee and, much to his surprise, Maclay was designated as a member. The others were Strong, Ellsworth, Carroll, and Few. At this point Washington took such an unusual interest in the committee that it is difficult to believe the secretary of state was not involved in the manoeuver. On the Friday following the commitment, he recorded in his diary: "As the House of Representatives had reduced the Sum, in a Bill to provide for the expences of characters in the diplomatic line, below what would enable the Executive to employ the number which the exigencies of Government might make necessary, I thought it proper to intimate to a member or two of the Senate the places that were in contemplation to send persons to in this line—viz:—to France and England (when the latter manifested a disposition to treat us with more respect than she had done upon a former occasion) Ministers Plenipotentiary—and to Spain, Portugal and Holland Chargé des Affaires, and having an opportunity, mentioned the matter unofficially both to Mr. Carroll and Mr. Izard."[9] Three days later Washington fell gravely ill, but when the committee met late in May Carroll could scarcely have forgotten what the president had dared to "intimate."

[6] JHR, I, 142-3, 144, 146-8; this was House bill No. 35 for which House bill No. 52 was later substituted.

[7] *Annals*, I, 1130.

[8] Washington, *Diaries*, ed. Fitzpatrick, IV, 109-10; see Document I, below.

[9] JHR, I, 182, 186, 202, 205; *Annals*, II, 1599, 1602; JS, 65; Maclay, *Journal*, ed. Maclay, p. 254; Washington, *Diaries*, ed. Fitzpatrick, IV, 128, under 7 May 1790.

John   Tuskatche Mico or Birdtail

Creek Indian Chiefs whom Jefferson met at the Treaty of 1790.
(See p. xxix-xxx.)

Indian figure presented to Jefferson.
(See p. xxx.)

Market Street, Philadelphia, looking east toward offices of Department of State and Residence of Secretary of State. (See p. xxx.)

The offices of the Department of State in Philadelphia, 1790.
(See p. xxx-xxxi.)

Jefferson's chart of national diplomatic establishments.
(See p. xxxi.)

The most intransigent opponent of a diplomatic establishment who sat on that committee has left a memorable account of Jefferson's first appearance before members of the senate.[10] Maclay was obviously captivated as he heard the secretary argue that it was "better to appoint a *chargé* with a handsome salary than a minister plenipotentiary with a small one," as the senator translated the expression used by Jefferson. He was in fact so much absorbed that he erred in thinking that the committee had, at the conclusion of the interview, struck out the provision allocating any specific sum to a foreign emissary, agreeing instead to a total appropriation of $30,000. But it may have been what he called "the main business" before the senate—the question of the permanent seat of government—as well as Jefferson's scattering "information wherever he went, and some even brilliant sentiments" that diverted Maclay. At any rate, the amendment proposed by the committee allowed $9,000 to a minister plenipotentiary "for all his personal services and expenses," $3,000 to a chargé d'affaires for the same, and $1,350 to any of their secretaries, with allowance of one quarter of a year's salary if recalled or given leave to return.[11] The senate readily accepted this but the house rejected it by a vote of 38 to 18.[12] Both bodies stood firm. A conference was asked by the senate and King, Izard, and Read were appointed managers to meet with Gerry, White, and Williamson from the house. There the matter stood until 21 June when Jefferson appeared before the conference committee and presented the alternatives shown in Document II of the present series.[13] This compromise was acceptable to the committee as perhaps the best that could be obtained, for in return for the limitation placed upon ministers' and chargés' salaries at $9,000 and $4,500 respectively—the latter was the minimum that Jefferson stipulated—the total sum of the appropriation was raised from $30,000 to $40,000.[14] This was accepted by both houses.[15]

But not without opposition. In the house the committee of conference was charged with having exceeded its powers in agreeing to an alteration of the sum of $30,000 which both bodies had already voted. It was argued that more than one minister was unnecessary and that a chargé d'affaires in London would suffice, an argument that seemed to gain strength from the fact that it appeared to be the same as that advanced by the secretary of state. The committee, in defending its course, said that it had not relied on its own judgment entirely, but had consulted "the Secretary of Foreign Affairs. His opinion was, that in the present situation of this country with respect to foreign nations, two Ministers and two Chargés des Affaires were necessary; a Minister at the Court of Versailles is generally conceded to be requisite. The peculiar situation of this country with respect to the posts, the Northern

---

10 Maclay, *Journal*, ed. Maclay, p. 272; for a quotation of Maclay's account of TJ's appearance as taken from the original manuscript, containing one significant variation from the published version, see notes to TJ's opinion on the constitutional question, 24 Apr. 1790; see also, TJ to Short, 27 May 1790, note.

11 JS, 66, 70, 82, 84; JHR, I, 224.

12 JHR, I, 224-5.   13 JS, 88, 89, 92; JHR, I, 227, 231.

14 JS, 120, 124, 137; JHR, I, 249, 250, 251, 252, 253.

15 JS, 143; JHR, I, 254; *Statutes at Large*, I, 128-9.

and Eastern frontiers, and the state of our commerce in respect to Great Britain, can scarcely leave a doubt of the necessity and importance of sending a minister to that country. This being the state of affairs, a less sum than that proposed, it is demonstrably evident, will not be found adequate."[16] The qualifications that Jefferson had made and the intimations that Washington had given to Izard and Carroll coincided in general with this position. But it is clear that the object the administration had in view was primarily to augment the total appropriation, not to guarantee the appointment of more than one minister at that particular moment. The house acquiesced. In the long interval between the designation of a conference committee and the rendering of its report, Maclay, preoccupied with the residence question, had all but forgotten about the intercourse bill, as it was called. Now, he found, "the thing was neither dead nor sleeping. It was only dressing and friends-making. . . . I concluded they had secured friends enough to support it before they committed it to the House. This turned out to be the case."[17]

The legislative history of the bill reveals Jefferson's touch at every point, hidden though the maneuvers were. The constitutional question of the right to designate rank and places had been settled for the time being, though it would arise again.[18] The actual appropriation had been increased by a third, with the president's right to stipulate salaries being only partially limited and with the limitation on the salary of chargés d'affaires being increased by half. The latter point is significant as reflecting the general tendency of Jefferson's argument before the senate and conference committees. His method now, in persuading the president on the manner of allocating the whole sum, was different but equally effective: a glance at the figures was enough to show that the plan the president had intimated to Carroll and Izard was scarcely feasible. In consequence, Jefferson's outline of the probable demands on the appropriation, as set forth in Document IV, represents approximately what he had recommended to the president at their first discussion.

In meeting this issue of economy and insularity, Jefferson employed characteristic methods. He went through the archives of the office of foreign affairs to find what practices had prevailed under the Articles of Confederation.[19] He consulted such experienced men as Adams, Jay, and Barclay. And he compiled information in tabular form to show

[16] *Annals*, II, 1709; *Gazette of the United States*, 26 June 1790.

[17] Maclay, *Journal*, ed. Maclay, p. 304.

[18] See TJ's opinion on the constitutional question under 24 Apr. 1790; for the revival of the issue at a later date, see TJ's opinion under 4 Jan. 1792.

[19] See Document III and enclosures. It is obvious that TJ selected his examples in order to point to them as precedents for liberality of treatment (see, for instance, the allowance to Dana for postage and even for the depreciation value of his carriage; Document III, enclosure 3, viii). He could have cited examples of extravagance, since he had among his papers some notes that he had taken in Paris of Silas Deane's claimed "public" expenses (see TJ to Jay, 3 Aug. 1788, and notes). But he chose to confine the selected extracts to those exhibiting reasonable claims for allowances made by persons whose probity had not been drawn into question. (TJ did not have access to his papers at this time, but the Deane volumes from which the extracts were taken were available in the Department of State.)

what foreign emissaries, in what rank and number, could be found at the various capitals of Europe. This remarkable document, based on a variety of sources that included even the implausible Lucy Ludwell Paradise, made two points crystal clear. The first was that, in rank, in numbers of diplomats, and in nations represented, the capital of France was beyond question the principal nexus of world diplomacy. The second, equally emphatic, was that even the diplomatic establishments supported by such minor powers as Sardinia and the Sicilies dwarfed that now projected for the vast empire of the new world.[20]

Washington, on receiving the enrolled act on 30 June 1790, carefully noted in his diary all of the provisions it contained.[21] He was receptive to Jefferson's arguments drawn from the records of the previous Congress tending to show that officers of the diplomatic establishment should be given handsome salaries and "should live in such a stile and manner . . . as they may find suitable and necessary to support the dignity of their public character." Indeed, with respect to the importance of enabling public officers to support requisite form and etiquette out of public funds, Washington was naturally inclined to go far beyond Jefferson. But neither past experience nor present actuality could persuade the president to allow one item that Jefferson and others had regarded as being among the obvious public expenses of a diplomat. In his view, the item of stationery was a personal, not a public charge.[22] This was not niggardliness but a scruple that others shared. And both the president and the secretary of state understood well that obtaining

20 The following summation of the chart illustrated in this volume appears on its verso (MS in TJ's hand, DLC: TJ Papers, 232: 41620; see notes to illustration and to Document III):

A State of the Diplomatic establishments of the principal courts	I. Ambassadors	II. Envoys	III.			
			Residents	Min. Plenipo.	Min.	Chargés
Rome	12					
France	12	2	4	17	1	3
Spain	6	6	..	5	..	2
Venice	5	..	4			
Emperor	4	9	2	9	2	2
England	3	11	3	3	1	
Holland	2	8	3	2		
Russia	1	12	1	3	3	2
Portugal	2	6	3			
Sardinia	2	5	1	4	1	1
Sicilies	2	4	1	4		
Sweden	1	8	..	..	2	1
Denmark		10	3	..	1	
Prussia		9	5	2	4	2
America				1	..	1

21 Washington, *Diaries*, ed. Fitzpatrick, IV, 130-1.

22 TJ to Short, 6 June 1790. In a comment on Short's account (DLC: TJ Papers, 56: 9536-9) listing sundries purchased for public use, TJ excluded an item under 17 Mch. 1790 for copying paper as being contrary to "the late rule by the President which does not allow stationary."

what, under the circumstances, was a fairly liberal appropriation for the diplomatic establishment was not the vital question. The real problem was put in Jefferson's ciphered message to Short on 26 July 1790: "We are extremely puzzled to find characters fit for the offices which need them."

I. Plans presented to Washington

[26 March 1790]

	Dollars
Establishment for	
A Minister Plenipotentiary. His salary	11,250
his Secretary	1,350
postage, couriers &c.	400
Outfit, suppose it to happen once in 7. years will be equal to an annual sum of	1,607[1]
	14,607
A Chargé des affaires. His salary	4,500
his Secretary	1,350
postage, couriers &c.	400
Outfit, as above	643[2]
	6,893
The Agent in Holland. His salary is	1,300
postage, couriers &c.	400
	1,700

1st. Plan

	Dollars
1. Versailles. Minister plenipotentiary	14,607
London. Chargé des affaires	6,893
Madrid. do.	6,893
Lisbon. Do.	6,893
Amsterdam. Agent.	1,700
	36,986

2d. Plan.

Versailles. Minister Plenipotentiary	14,607
London. Do.	14,607
Madrid. Chargé des affaires	6,893
Lisbon, do.	6,893
Amsterdam. Agent	1,700
	44,700

3d. Plan.

Versailles. Minister Plenipotentiary	14,607
London. do.	14,607
Madrid. Chargé des affaires	6,893
Lisbon, do.	6,893
Hague. do	6,893
	49,893

MS (DNA: RG 59, MLR); entirely in TJ's hand, undated; endorsed by Washington: "Diplomatic Establishmt." Dft (DLC); with variations noted below; at foot of text: "communicated Mar. 26. 1790."; endorsed by TJ: "Diplomatic establmt." Tr (DNA: RG 59, SDC).

[1] At this point Dft has an entry not in MS, reading: "Return. On same principle adds annually 402 D."

[2] At this point Dft has an entry not in MS, reading: "Return. Will add annually 161."

II. Plan presented to the Conference Committee

[21 June 1790]

Estimate of the expences of the diplomatic missions proposed for the U.S.

	Dollars
[A Min]ister Plenipotentiary. His salary	11,250
His Outfit, suppose it to happen once in 7. years, will equal annual sum of	1,607
His Return, suppose it to happen once in 7. years, will equal annual sum of	402
His Secretary	1350
Postage, Couriers &c. about	400
	15,009

A Chargé des affaires. His salary	4500
His Outfit, suppose it once in 7. years	643
His Return. do.	161
His Secretary	1350
Postage, Couriers &c. about	400
	7054

Estimate, on a lower scale

	Dollars
[A Mi]nister Plenipotentiary. His salary	9000
His Outfit, suppose it once in 7. years will equal annual sum of	1285
His Return, do.	321
His Secretary	1350
Postage, Couriers &c. about	400
	12356

A Chargé des affaires. His salary cannot be proposed lower than 4500. Dollars, &c. as above.

PrC (DLC: TJ Papers, 55: 9467); entirely in TJ's hand; at foot of text: "Communicated to Commee. of Conference June 21. 1790."

III. Observations on the Diplomatic Establishment as provided for by Congress

[17 July 1790]

The bill on the intercourse with foreign nations restrains the President from allowing to Ministers plenipotentiary or to Chargés more than 9000. and 4500. Dollars for their 'personal services and other expences.' This definition of the objects for which the allowance is provided, appearing vague, the Secretary of state thought it his duty to confer with the gentlemen heretofore employed as ministers in Europe, to obtain from them, in aid of his own information, an enumeration of the expences incident to these offices, and their opinion which of them would be included within the fixed salary, and which would be entitled to be charged separately. He therefore asked a conference with the Vicepresident, who was acquainted with the residences of London and the Hague, and the Chief justice who was acquainted with that of Madrid, which took place yesterday.

The Vice-president, Chief justice, and Secretary of state concurred in opinion that the salaries named by the act are much below those of the same grade at the courts of Europe, and less than the public good requires they should be. Consequently that the expences not included within the definition of the law, should be allowed as an additional charge.

1. Couriers, gazettes, translating necessary papers, printing necessary papers, aids to poor Americans. All three agreed that these ought to be allowed as additional charges not included within the meaning of the phrase 'his personal services and other expences.'

2. Postage. Stationary. Court fees. One of the gentlemen being of opinion that the phrase 'personal services and other expences' was meant to comprehend all the *ordinary expences* of the office, considered this second class of expences as *ordinary*, and therefore included in the fixed salary. The 1st. class beforementioned he had viewed as *extraordinary*. The other two gentlemen were of opinion this 2d. class was also out of the definition, and might be allowed in addition to the salary. One of them particularly considered the phrase as meaning 'personal services and personal expences,' that is, expences for his personal accomodation, comfort and maintenance. This 2d. class of expences is not within that description.

3. Ceremonies; such as diplomatic and public dinners, galas, and illuminations. One gentleman only was of opinion these might be allowed.

The expences of the 1st. class may probably amount to about 50. dollars a year. Those of the 2d. to about four or five hundred dollars. Those of the 3d. are so different at different courts, and so indefinite in all of them, that no general estimate can be proposed.

The Secretary of state thought it his duty to lay this information before the President, supposing it might be satisfactory to himself, as well as to the diplomatic gentlemen, to leave nothing uncertain as to their allowances; and because too a previous determination is in some degree necessary to the forming an estimate, which may not exceed the whole sum appropriated. Several papers accompany this, containing former opinions on this subject.

The Secretary of state has also consulted, on the subject of the Marocco consulships, with Mr. Barclay, who furnished him with the note of which a copy accompanies this. Considering all circumstances,[1] Mr. Barclay is of opinion we had better have only one Consul there, and that he should be the one now residing at Marocco, because, as Secretary to the emperor,[2] he sees him every day, and possesses his ear. He is of opinion 600. Dollars a year might suffice for him,[3] and that it should be proposed to him, not as a salary, but as a sum in gross intended to cover his expences, and to save the trouble of keeping accounts. That this Consul should be authorised to appoint agents in the Seaports, who would be sufficiently paid by the consignments of vessels. He thinks the Consul at Marocco should most conveniently recieve his allowance through the channel of our Chargé at Madrid, with whom also this Consulate had better be made dependant[4] for instructions, information, and correspondence, because of the daily intercourse between Marocco and Cadiz.

The Secretary of state, on a view of Mr. Barclay's note, very much doubts the sufficiency of the sum of 600. Dollars: he supposes a little money there may save a great deal; but he is unable to propose any specific augmentation till a view of the whole diplomatic establishment and it's expences may furnish better grounds for it.

MS (DNA: RG 59, MLR); entirely in TJ's hand; endorsed by Washington: "Respecting Diplomatic and the Allowances made by Congress." PrC (DLC: TJ Papers, 56: 9621-2, 9624); at foot of text there is the following (not in MS): "Th: Jefferson July 17. 1790." FC (DNA: RG 59, SDC); at head of text: "Observations &ca. respecting Diplomatic matters, and the Allowances made by Congress"; in clerk's hand, including date and signature. N (DLC: TJ Papers, 232: 41538); entirely in TJ's hand; endorsed: "Marocco. Mr. Barclay's information." This memorandum, which TJ must have set down after conferring with Barclay, contains interesting variations from the expressions employed in the above observations sent to Washington (see notes below). Enclosures: (1) The copy of Barclay's NOTE, undated, reads: "Most of the foreign Consuls live at Tangier, the Dutch Consul at Mogadore, and the French at Rabat. They are all furnished at the expence of their several Countries with the means of making the necessary presents, with the expences of Couriers, travelling expences, particularly to and from Morocco.—They charge for authenticating papers, some

of them for Consulage on the vessels belonging to their nations; the English Consul in particular charges twelve Spanish dollars for each. Exclusive of which they have the following Salaries.—

English	£800 Sterling per annum
France	19000 Livres per annum, with an addition of 1000 livres made in favor of Mr. De Roché the present Consul General.
Spanish	4000 ⎱ Spanish dollars
Danish	4000 ⎰
Swedish	3000 ⎱
Dutch	3,400 ⎰ Spanish dollars
Venetian	2,800 ⎰ Who is the American Agent at Tangier

Francisco Chiappe
  at Morocco
Josephus Chiappe
  at Mogadore   ⎱ American Agents"
Gérolamo Chiappe
  at Tangier

(Tr in DLC: TJ Papers, 233: 42194; in Taylor's hand. MS in DNA: RG 59, PCC No. 91; in Barclay's hand, endorsed by TJ: "Mr. Barclay's note of the foreign Consuls in Marocco"). (2) Chart in TJ's hand showing number and rank of diplomatic officers maintained by different countries at the principal European courts (DLC: TJ Papers, 232: 41620; entirely in TJ's hand in tabular form [see illustration in this volume]; PrC in same; another tabular MS, in TJ's hand, is in DNA: RG 59, MLR; and another, in clerk's hand, is in DNA: RG 59, SDC). (3) "Extracts from the Secret Journals of Congress respecting allowances made to their Diplomatic characters, abroad," containing copies of the following: (i) resolution of 28 Sep. 1776 "that the Commissioners should live in such a stile and manner at the Court of France, as they may find suitable and necessary to support the dignity of their public character," keeping account of their expenses, which would be reimbursed, and that, in addition, "a handsome allowance be made to each of them as a compensation for their time, trouble, risk and services," with the secretary of the embassy being allowed a salary of £1,000 sterling; (ii) resolution of 7 May 1778 repeating the substance of the foregoing for the commissioners appointed for the courts of Spain, Tuscany, Vienna, and Berlin; (iii) resolution of 6 Aug. 1779 allowing 11,428 livres, calculated at £500 sterling per annum, as compensation for each of the commissioners, to be computed from the time of their leaving their places of abode to three months after their notice of recall; (iv) resolution of 4 Oct. 1779 allowing ministers plenipotentiary at the rate of £2,500 sterling per annum, and each secretary at the rate of £1,000 sterling per annum, in full for both services and expenses; (v) resolution on report of committee of 10 May 1783, consisting of Williamson, Carroll, and Osgood on letters of Franklin and Adams concerning allowances, that payment of couriers and postage should be charged to the United States exclusive of salaries; (vi) resolution of 7 May 1784 that after 1 Aug. 1784 the salary of a minister at a foreign court should not exceed $9,000 per annum; (vii) resolution of 11 May 1784 that after 1 Aug. 1784 the secretary of a commission or an embassy should not exceed $3,000 per annum; (viii) resolution of 22 July 1785 that Francis Dana be allowed "the sum of four hundred three Dollars and fifty one nineteeths, on account of the charges of Postage accrued whilst he was in a public character in Europe," and, in addition, "three hundred eleven dollars and twenty three ninetieths on account of travelling expenses . . . and a loss sustain'd by him on the sale of a Carriage intended for his reception at the Court of Petersburgh," plus the "necessary expence for a private secretary," all to be exclusive of salary; (ix) resolution of 27 Dec. 1782 approving purchase John Adams had made of a house at The Hague for the use of the United States; (x) extract of letter from Arthur Lee to the secret committee, 2 Apr. 1778, stating that his account of expenses had been kept as minutely as possible and that, including two journeys, they had not exceeded the sum allotted, "tho' the being acknowledged will necessarily augment the expence"; (xi) extract of letter from Lee to the committee, 1 June 1778, stating that he agrees with Adams "that it would be better for the public that the appointment of your public ministers were fixed, instead of being left at large and their expences indefinite," and adding: "From experience I find the expence of living in that character cannot well be less than three thousand pounds sterling a Year, which I believe too is as little as is allowed to any public Minister above the rank of a Consul. If left at liberty I believe most persons will exceed this sum"; (xii) extract of letter from John Adams to John Jay, 13 May 1785, reporting on his conversation with the British ambassador concerning the presentation of himself and family to the king and queen of England, and adding: "I hope, Sir, you will not think this an immaterial or a trifling conversation, when you consider that the single circumstance of presenting a Family to Court will make a difference of several hundred pounds sterling in my inevitable annual expences. This is not the first serious Lecture that I have had upon the subjects of Etiquette, and even dress. I have formerly related to you in conversation another much more grave, which I had five years ago from the Count de Vergennes. I believe I have also reported to you similar exhortations made to me even by the best Patriots in Holland. There is a certain appearance in proportion to rank, which all the Courts of Europe make a serious point of exacting from every body who is presented to them.—I need not say to you, Sir, because you know it perfectly, that American Ministers have never yet been able to make this appearance at any Court. They are now less able to do it than ever. I lament this necessity of consuming the Labour of my fellow Citizens upon such objects as much as any man living: but I am sure that the consequences of debasing your Ministers so much below their rank, will one day have consequences of much more importance to the Husbandman, artisan, and even Labourer." At this point the following note is appended: "Note. Mr. Adams at this period received 9,000 Dollars per annum"; (xiii) extract from Jay's answer to the foregoing, 3 Aug. 1785, stating that the expenses of presentation at court would doubtless be considerable and that he had long felt Adams' salary was not equal to what it should be, adding: "Custom and fashion often exact a Tribute which however just and virtuous to refuse, is often very expedient to pay. In short, your salary is more than what a private Gentleman may with care live decently upon, but is less than is necessary to enable you to live as other Ministers usually and generally do. Whether Congress will make any alterations in this respect is very uncertain. There are men in all the States who make a merit of saving money in small matters without sufficiently attending to the consequences of it"; (xiv) extract of a report by Robert R. Livingston to Congress, 29 Apr. 1783, on a peace establishment for the department of foreign affairs, reading: "The Ministers of the United States at foreign Courts should in my opinion be of the second and third Orders, that is Ministers Plenipotentiary and Ministers. Ministers Plenipotentiary derive some advantage from their station in conversing with the great; they are more readily admitted to audiences, and obtain easier access at Court. For which reason as well as on acount of the compliment to the Prince to whom we are so greatly indebted, I would maintain a Minister Plenipotentiary at the Court of Versailles, where even after the War we shall have very important matters to settle, and where our Commerce and our Debts will leave us many points to discuss. I would pursue the same measure with Spain—her Trade—the vicinity of her Territories and the intimate connexion between the branches of the House of Bourbon, render an

influence at the Court of Madrid important to us. The pride and ceremony of the Nation induces me to believe that a Minister Plenipotentiary will best obtain it. At London, Lisbon and the Hague, I conceive the interests of the United States may be as well attended to by a Minister of the third order, as by one of higher rank.—The salaries of the Ministers must depend upon their characters and the places at which they reside. A *Minister Plenipotentiary* in France or Spain ought, I should conceive, with proper œconomy to be supported for about Ten thousand Dollars. A *Minister* in England, Portugal and Holland for about seven thousand Dollars, inclusive of house hire and all contingent expences, except the Postage of Letters and the purchase of public prints, which I would give them no inducement to œconomize in"; and concluding (xv) with the following note: "Dr. Franklin in a Letter dated Philadelphia 29th November 1788 and directed to the President of Congress mentions that he has settled his accounts with Mr. Barclay but had not finally closed them, because he had some equitable demands for extra services respecting which he wished the opinion of Congress, Mr. Barclay not conceiving himself empowered to allow them. He refers to and encloses in this letter, one he wrote to Mr. Barclay dated Passy 25 June 1785 wherein he claims and continues to charge for his salary under an Act of Congress of 5th October 1779. £2500 sterlg per annum; and says that the subsequent Act which reduces the salary of a Minister Plenipotentiary to £2000 can only relate to such plenipotentiaries as should be afterwards appointed, as he conceives that Congress after promising a Minister £2,500 a year and thereby encouraging him to live in a certain stile for their honor, which salary only can support, could not think it just to diminish it one fifth, and leave him under the difficulty of reducing his expences proportionably, a thing scarcely practicable." (DNA: RG 59, SDC.)

1 N reads: "considering the smallness of our fund."

2 N reads: ". . . at Marocco, viz [Francisco] Chiappe, who is one of the Emperor's Secretaries and sees him every day."

3 N reads: ". . . and give to the

Consul 600 Doll. *to answer expences of couriers &c.* and ever more if necessary, and to let him know that nothing can be allowed to the agents."

⁴ N reads: "He thinks it will be better to make that Consulate dependant altogether on the Chargé at Madrid, and let him correspond with him altogether; to send a new Consular commission to Mr. Carmichael for [Francisco] Chiappe."

IV. Estimates of Funds Required for the Diplomatic Establishment, 1790-1791

[19 July 1790]

Estimate of the expences of a Minister Plenipotentiary.

	Dollars
Minister Plenipotentiary. His salary	9000.
His Outfit. Suppose it to happen once in 7. years, will average	1285.
His Return at a Quarter's salary, will average	321.
Extras. viz. Gazettes, translating, printing, aids to poor American sailors, couriers and postage about	350.
His Secretary	1350.
	———
	12,306.

Estimate for a Chargé des affaires.

Chargé des affaires. His salary	4500
His Outfit, once in 7. years, equal to an annual sum of	643
His Return at a Quarter's salary, do.	161
Extras as above	350
	———
	5654.

The Agent at the Hague. His Salary	1300.
Extras about	100
	———
	1400.

Estimate of the annual expences of the Establishment proposed.

	Dollars
France. A Minister Plenipotentiary	12,306
London. Do.	12,306
Madrid. A Chargé des affaires	5,654
Lisbon. Do.	5,654
Hague. An Agent	1,400
Marocco. A Consul	1800
Presents to Foreign ministers on taking leave, @ 1000. Doll. each, more or less, according to their[1] favour and time. There will be five of them. If exchanged once in 7. years, it will be annually	715
	39,835.

Estimate of the probable calls on our Foreign fund from July 1. 1790. when the Act for foreign intercourse passed, to July 1. 1791.

	Dollars	
France. A Minister Plenipotentiary. His Outfit.	9000.	
His salary, suppose it to commence Aug. 1.	8250	
Extras	320	
Secretary	1237.5	18,807.5
Chargé. Suppose him to remain till Nov. 1.		
Salary	1,500.	
Extras	117.	
His return, a quarter's salary	1,125	2,742
Madrid. A Chargé. His Salary	4,500	
Extras	350	4,850
Lisbon. A Chargé (or Resident) his Outfit	4,500	
His Salary. Suppose it to commence Jan. 1. 1791.	2,250	
Extras	175.	6,925
London. An Agent. Suppose to commence Oct. 1. @ 1350. D. Salary	1,012.5	
Extras (@ 100. Doll. a year)	75	1,087.5

Hague. An Agent		1,400.
Marocco. Consul		1,800
Presents to Foreign ministers. The Dye about	500.	
2. Medals and chains	2000	2,500
		40,112

MS (DNA: RG 59, MLR); entirely in TJ's hand; endorsed by Washington: "Diplomatic Establishm. and Estimates." PrC (DLC); after PrC was executed, TJ wrote following at bottom of page, not on MS: "given in to the President July 19. 1790." Tr (DNA: RG 59, SDC); also dated 19 July 1790.

It is to be noted that the projected figures for the chargé d'affaires in France contemplated his return by 1 Nov. 1790, a clear indication that TJ supposed Washington had decided not to appoint William Short minister (see TJ to Short, 26 July 1790). It is also possible that TJ may have deliberately included the full cost of an outfit for a minister and those for the chargé's salary and return (which would not have been required at all in the latter case or wholly in the former if Short had been named minister) in order to suggest to the president's mind that a saving on these items might be applied to the cost of supporting a minister in London, thus appealing to Washington's views in order to advance the nomination of Short. But this is not a probable motive.

[1] TJ first wrote: ". . . according to their grade and favour" and then altered the passage to read as above.

From James Monroe

DEAR SIR   Albemarle July 18. 1790.

My last from Richmond in answer to yours of the 20th. of June has no doubt been received. The more I have reflected on the subject, the better satisfied I am of the impolicy of assuming the state debts. The diminishing the necessity for State taxation will undoubtedly leave the national government more at liberty to exercise its powers and encrease the subjects on which it will act, for that purpose, and if that were absolutely a necessary power of the government, and no objections applied to the transfer itself of the publick creditors from one government to the other, without their consent, (for such a modification as leaves them not even a plausible alternative, amounts to the same thing, and such I understand the report to be) or to the probable inefficiency of the national government comparatively with those of the States in raising the necessary funds, I should perhaps have no objections to it at present. Even in our time we may hope to see the whole debt extinguish'd or nearly so, and we must be the favor'd people, if no occasion should hereafter arise, that would make it necessary for the general government to tax highly, and raise considerable revenues. Such exigency can never apply hereafter to those of the States, so that merely for the sake of preserving an equality at present, I should think it useless to balance the debt, between them. But as I believe this (upon speculation only) a defect in the government, and presume thro that medium, the prepondrance of one over the other, will be settled,[1] I would avoid throwing any thing occasionally into that scale from which I apprehended most danger. On the other hand as the government now rests on its own means, for the discharge of its engagements, I would always use its powers for the purpose, nor would I endanger the publick credit rather than exercise a power, which was of questionable propriety, or in some instances thought so. Thus things would have their regular course, proper experiments would be made and we should ultimately be landed where we should be. The weight of all the State creditors thrown into the national scale at present, might also perhaps produce some disorder in the system, as it would occasion a fortuitous but severe pressure from that quarter, affecting them from the heart to the extremities, before either their legislators by moderate experiments, had acquir'd sufficient knowledge for the purpose, or the people given sufficient proof of what they could, and what they would bear. Will not this from necessity as well as policy, compel them to glean whatever they can from trade, pressing that resource upon trial likewise, beyond what perhaps for the sake of revenue, it can bear, and introducing a system of œconomy in other respects very oppressive on some parts of the U. States: For in the present State of arts and industry in America, the moment that medium is pass'd, that forms the basis of a wise commercial policy for the whole, diffusing its beneficial effects to every part, will it degenerate into a tyrannous sacrifice of the interests, of the minority to that of the majority; and that precise medium which will be most productive in point of revenue and beneficial in other respects, can only be discover'd by gradual operation and gentle experiments, which the assumption, for the reasons above will entirely prevent.—As to the residence I will only hazard one Idea. We find that for its removal to Phila. the representatives of that State rely on those of this, and the other southern States or some of them. They do not expect that the Eastern States will vote to remove it further from them—place it in Philadelphia and how doth this principle apply? Will our and their members harmonize so well afterwards, will they unite in forwarding it to Georgetown? Or will it not rather immediately bring about an harmony of sentiment and cooperation elsewhere? And shall we not be left dependant on a resolution of Congress which holds its tenure upon the pleasure of 8. States, who (whatever their true interests may be) have always shewn they consider'd it as consisting in keeping the seat of government as near home as they could. As soon as they get fix'd in Phila. (and the shorter the term allotted for their residence there the more active will this principle be) the representatives of that State will look with a jealous eye toward their brethren of the South. Any attempts to forward the erection of buildings at Georgetown will at first be received coolly and afterwards with disgust. Common interest in this as in other respects will unite them, and we shall soon find a well form'd plan, regularly pursued, that shall be best calculated to promote them. We have often found that an union on some great question, which was consider'd as primary or ruling in the view of parties, gave a tone to their proceedings on many others; how much more reasonable then is it to expect it, when there are so many predisposing causes to promote it? I should therefore wish to see the funds appropriated and commissioners appointed to carry on the work, plac'd as completely without the reach of Congress as possible afterwards, before we acceded to any thing upon this subject only; much less would I give a consideration for any thing less.—I hinted in my last I would mention to you a subject of importance to myself in cypher, but as you expected to return to France when you left it tis possible you omitted to bring it with you. As tis a matter which does not press immediately, and which perhaps you may conjecture, and tis possible we may meet before I come to any decision on it unless I have a private opportunity, I shall decline mentioning it untill one of those events takes place. We are well and hope you are completely restor'd. I am with the greatest respect & esteem your affectionate friend & servant, JAS. MONROE

RC (DLC); endorsed as received 7 Aug. 1790 and so recorded in SJL, being the same day that TJ received Monroe's letter of 26 July 1790.

1 At this point Monroe wrote, and then deleted, "sometime or other."

From J. P. P. Derieux

MONSIEUR   Charlotteville ce 20 Juillet 1790.

Nous avons appris avec beaucoup de satisfaction que vous etiés heureusement arrivé à New-york, et nous voyons encore avec un plaisir plus sensible s'approcher le tems où nous devons vous revoir et vous offrir de nouveaux et foibles temoignages de notre reconnaissance.

Je vous apprendrai avec doulleur que je n'ay point encore reçu de lettres de ma Tante Bellanger, ny même de Mr. Mazzei, et que je crains beaucoup d'avoir perdu dans l'esprit de l'un et de l'autre, sans à ma Connoissance y avoir donné lieu; vous me rendriés le plus grand service, Monsieur, de decouvrir si mes inquiétudes sont fondées, et si elles le sont, vous seul pourriés remettre les choses dans leur premier etat. L'evenement a desja assés prouvé jusqu'a quel point je puis esperer des bontés que vous voudrés bien avoir pour moi et ma famille, et que sans le secours de ces mêmes bontés, que je sollicite, je ne puis ny ne dois beaucoup esperer. Voullés vous bien me faire la Grace de leur faire passer les deux Lettres cy joint.

Depuis votre depart j'ai beaucoup reflechi aux moyens de me replacer promptement en Campagne pour m'occuper entierement des occupations rurales. Le Commerce n'offre point de ressources dans cette ville, et l'agriculture y a des inconveniens locales, qui s'opposent à sa progression. Cette decouverte, faitte plutot, m'auroit sauvé 3 ans d'epreuves desagreables, mais n'y ayant trouvé que de l'encouragement, auprès même des personnes les mieux instruittes du Local, je crus bien faire de l'entreprendre; mais l'experience du contraire a eclairé mes Erreurs, et je suis dans le plus grand Empressement de quitter la Ville, pour reprendre la routte heureuse que vous aviés bien voulu me tracer dans le principe. J'ai été en Consequence voir plusieurs plantations qui sont à Vendre, mais elles sont pour la pluspart, ou des terres usées, ou des terres incultes, dont on demande au dela de ce que je puis donner, et où il faudroit beaucoup de tems et de depenses pour batir: de maniere que je ne me suis encore determiné pour aucune.

Je vous avouerai, Monsieur, que, soit mon attachement pour Collé, soit le desir que Mde. de Rieux me temoigne d'acquerir cet endroit, qu'elle a de tous tems regardé comme devoir lui appartenir, je m'arrete toujours avec plaisir à l'idée d'y faire encore notre demeure; et si cette inclination naturelle ne m'aveugle pas sur les ressources de cette petite plantation, je me persuade que je pourrois y trouver le necessaire pour moi et ma famille. Je sais que la terre a eté très affoiblie par ses productions reppetées en Corn, mais on me dit qu'avec de profonds Labours et des recoltes en petittes graines, il seroit aisé de la rendre productive, et je crois qu'avec des prairies artificielles et beaucoup de pommes de terre, propres à l'Engrais des Bestiaux, on remplaceroit aisement la corn que l'habitude, plutot que la necessité, fait regarder ici comme une récolte indispensable. Nous nous proposons, ma femme et moi, d'y aller avec nos enfants passer huit ou quinze jours, pour nous delasser de l'ennui de la Ville, dont il n'est pas possible d'etre plus fatigués.

Si vous avés reçu reponse de Mr. Mazzei, et que vous ayés pu en obtenir des termes raisonnables, je ferai tout le possible pour empecher que Collé ne passe dans des mains Etrangeres. Je ne verrois pas d'ailleurs sans beaucoup de deplaisir s'échapper cette occasion de devenir votre voisin. Vous pouvés certainement, plus que personne, persuader à Mr. Mazzei que la degradation de ses Batiments et l'inferiorité de sa terre réduisent le tout à une valleur très mediocre.

Je suis actuellement en Negotiation avec le frere du Col. Samuel Lewis pour lui rendre sa maison avant l'expiration des cinq ans. Il m'a fait proposer par Col. Bell il y a quelque tems de me remettre en argent les 300. pound qui me sont dus, et après avoir recu ma reponse conforme à ses desirs, il n'a plus offert que son billet pour le tout. Je lui ay repondu que cela ne pouvoit pas me convenir et, pour le determiner, je lui ay ajoutté que s'il ne reprenoit pas sa maison, j'allois la sous louer pour les deux ans qui me restent encore à jouir. J'attends sa reponse tous les jours, et je crois qu'elle me sera favorable, ayant appris depuis peu qu'il venoit de recevoir 15 ou 16. cent pound en argent comptant, et qu'il avoit le plus grand desir de degager cet objet de mes mains. Mais il paroit qu'en homme rusé il a voulu tenter s'il pourroit me faire prendre son billet. C'est un homme de beaucoup de fortune et de credit dans la comtée de Botetourt, et dans tout autre cas que le mien, je ne crois pas qu'il y auroit le moindre danger à prendre son Billet. Mais j'ai besoin de cette somme pour m'aider à acheter Collé et des negres. Je ne ferai rien au surplus sans avoir eu l'honneur de vous consulter la dessus et savoir si, ne pouvant absolument recevoir cet argent, je pourrois remplir ces deux objets, en negotiant son Billet qu'il m'offre avec interets.

En outre de la Lettre pour Mr. Short, dans laquelle je vous prie de voulloir bien inclure celles de ma tante Bellanger et Mr. Mazzei, je prends la liberté de vous en adresser plusieurs autres pour France et la Martinique. Je vous demande pardon de cet embarras et vous supplie d'excuser mon importunité.

Mde. de Rieux vous prie d'agreer l'assurance de son respect, et j'ay l'honneur d'etre dans les sentiments de la plus parfaitte reconnoissance et du profond respect, Monsieur Votre très humble et très obeisst. Serviteur   P. De Rieux

P.S. J'ai l'honneur de vous observer, Monsieur, que si Mr. Mazzei ne trouvoit pas suffisantes les offres que vous avés recu pour Collé et qu'il preferat ne pas le vendre quant à présent, que je serois très satisfait que vous voulliés bien m'y laisser retourner pour quelques années. Cela ne pourroit etre, dans la suitte, que d'un grand avantage pour la Vente de cette plantation, qui a absolument besoin de nouvelles finses et cela me donneroit le tems de me mieux pourvoir par la suitte, et de faire batir à mon aise, dans le cas où j'acheterois des terres en friche. Je vais faire tout le possible d'ici a votre retour, pour tacher de me debarasser de cette maison de La ville, et pouvoir vers La fin du mois prochain, commencer a Ensemencer toutte La terre de collé, si je puis avoir L'honneur de recevoir pour ce tems, votre reponse a cet Egard.

Dans mes Lettres a ma tante et Mr. Mazzei Je ne fais pas mention de mon desir de quitter La Ville, je crois qu'il vaut mieux attendre que je sois fixé et mieux Etably ailleurs.

RC (MHi); endorsed as received 21 Aug. 1790 and so recorded in SJL. Enclosures not further identified.

From William Temple Franklin

Dear Sir   Philadelphia, 20th. July 1790.

I received duly your Favor of the 16th. Inst. Since my Return here, I have not been inattentive to fulfil your Wishes relative to a House; but have hitherto met with so few suitable, and on which I could depend, that I have been loath to write to you, till I could do it with more certainty.

Mrs. Buddens Houses, which I thought would suit you, and of which you seem to have the same Opinion, I now think would not. I find they are situated much higher up Chesnut Street than I informed you they were, which will render them very difficult of access in Winter, as our Pavement in that Street only extends to Seventh Street, and those Houses are between 9th. and 10th.—There are so few Houses in that Part, that there is little probability of the Pavement being continued further for several Years. Besides which, on Visiting those Houses, I found that Mrs. Budden lived in the only one finish'd, and the others in no forwardness, and on Enquiry, little Expectation was given me of their being carried on with any degree of Spirit, Mrs. Budden being Absent and her Fortune much deranged. Some say they must be soon sold to pay Part of her late Husbands Debts. From these Circumstances I gave up all thoughts of them, and visited others that I thought might suit. Among these, those that pleased me the most are two new houses of Mr. Leipers, adjoining each other, built entirely on the same Plan and situated in Market Street between 8th. and 9th. Streets. The whole of the Building is 50 Feet front, each house being 25. Ft. There are a number of Workmen employ'd about them, and there is no doubt of their being compleatly finish'd by the 1st. of Octr. I immediately applied to Mr. Leiper for the Refusal of them, but he had already promised One to Mr. John Vaughan, who has I believe taken it for his Father. This he (Mr. L.) regretted, as he would much rather have you for a Tenant; and told me that if I could persuade Mr. V. to give up the House he would immediately open Doors in the Rooms so as to convert the two Houses into One, and do any thing else that might be agreable to you.—The Houses and the Landlord pleased me so well, that I immediately made Application to Mr. Vaughan on the subject, and he has promised me to write to the Person for whom he has engaged the House (not saying it was for his Father) to know if it would be equally agreable to him to exchange for another House nearly of the same size and exactly opposite to it. Of this I have some Hopes, having been very urgent with Mr. Vaughan, as they appear to me to be the only ones at present here that would exactly suit, according to your Idea of living on One Floor and having your Offices under the same Roof.— But that you may better judge, I shall endeavor to describe them. They are situated on the South side of Market Street, and both Foot and Street Pavement extend to them. They are well built and are to be finish'd in the best Manner. Each House is 25 Feet front and 44 Feet deep, besides which the Part containing the Stairs is 18 by 11. And the Kitchen 18 Feet in length on the Yard, with two stories of Chambers over it. The Drawing Rooms are 23. Ft. 9. by 20. in the Clear, the Back Chambers 20. by 17. The Parlours below are rather small, owing to the Entry being wide, and an arch'd Passage through the two Houses to the Yards. But as you would use these as Offices it would not be of much consequence. The Front Parlours are 20 Ft. 9 In. by 14. Ft. 3. and the

Back Parlours 19 Feet 19 In. by 14 Ft. 3. Up two Pair of Stairs the Chambers are the same Size as on the 1st. Floor, excepting that a Small Dressing Room and Closet is taken off each front Room. The Garrets are good and have fire Places. The Rent of each House is 150£ which is only 6 pr. Cent for the Building and Lot. Stables are to be erected on a back Street, for which an additional Rent will be expected. Handsome and convenient as these houses are I do not think them dear. On the first Floor, by means of a Door of communication you would have four good Rooms.— The two largest for your Dining and Drawing Rooms and the others for your Bed Chamber and Study. As they all communicate they would make a handsome suite, and constitute what the french call *un Appartement complet*. As to the situation I think it a good one, so high up Market Street as not to be incommoded by Waggons, and your Chamber and Study being back from the Street you would not be disturbed by Noise. It is likewise not more than 3 Squares from the House intended for the President, and the State House. I should not write thus temptingly of them but that I have great hopes of Mr. Vaughan's relinquishing the One he has taken. The other I am to have the Refusal of at any Rate. For fear however of this failing I have made application for Mr. Gurneys House in Chesnut Street next Door to Mrs. Allen's. This is a large House 3 Rooms on a floor but two only communicating. It Rents at present with Stabling &c. for near 300£ a Year, but there would be no place for your Offices.—The present Tenant and Landlord being both absent, I have not been able to get a positive Answer. I have also applied to Mrs. Keppele for a large House of hers, situated at the N:E: Corner of Arch and 4th. Street. This a Roomy House and might be sufficient for yourself and one of your Officers. It will not be rented under 300£. I am however promised the Refusal. The Lady would not at present fix the Rent, but said she would let me know by the middle of August. The Houses I have mentioned are I think the only ones that would suit you of those that are to be had. And I have no doubt of obtaining one or the other of them. But Leipers I think by far the most convenient as well as the cheapest: as the Offices would be accommodated, which would be a considerable deduction from your Rent.—Mr. Leiper who built these Houses, and is a man of considerable Property, has likewise agreed (in case you are willing) to build a House on any Plan you may please to give him, not exceeding 50 Feet front, on a Lot he has on Market Street between 10th. and 11th Streets, provided you will agree to take the same when finish'd, till the end of the Ten Years allotted by Congress for their temporary Residence here, and pay him for Rent the Interest of his Money laid out in the Building and the Value of the Lot. This according to the present Rate of Building would not be a dear Rent.

I have not heard of Mr. Randolph's Arrival. When I do I will wait on him, and mention your Wish of being in the same Neighbourhood with him; and when you have fix'd, will endeavor to accommodate him accordingly.

I beg you will excuse this long scrawl, and let me know your Opinion of the Houses I have mention'd, as also whether you would wish to have one built for you on the Terms proposed. It might be got ready in about Twelve Months. I am Dear Sir, with affectionate Esteem, Your most obedt. & most humble Servt.,

W. T. FRANKLIN

RC (DNA: RG 59, MLR); with marginal note in TJ's hand opposite final paragraph reading: "Lengthen living room. Outrigger room over kitchen. No front benches. Stables wanted" (see TJ to Franklin, 25 July 1790); endorsed as received 21 July and so recorded in SJL.

From Mary Jefferson

DEAR PAPA   Eppington july 20, [1790]

I hope you will excuse my not writing to you before tho I have none for myself I am very sorry to hear that you have been sick but flatter myself that it is over. My aunt skipwith has been very sick but she is better now. We have been to see her two or three times. You tell me in your last letter that you will see me in september but I have received a letter from my Brother that says you will not be here before February. As his is later than yours I am afraid you have changed your mind. The books that you have promised me are Anacharses and gibbons roman empire. If you are coming in september I hope you will not forget your promise of bying new jacks for the pianeforte that is at monticello. Adieu my dear Papa. I am your affectionate Daughter   MARY JEFFERSON

My Uncle and Aunt desire to be affectionately remembered to you.

M.J.

RC (ViU); slightly mutilated; wholly lacking in punctuation, a deficiency remedied editorially for the sake of clarity; endorsed by TJ as received 6 Sep. 1790 and so recorded in SJL, where the date is given as 2 July.

From Lucy Ludwell Paradise

I have the pleasure of acquainting your Excellency that the Queen of Portugal has appointed Monsr. le Chevr. de Freire to be her Minister to America. This Gentleman was to have gone to another Court, but Monsr. le Chevr. de Pinto, knowing that Monsr. de Freire had been imployed here to negotiate the Treaty between Portugal, and America, and also, as he was personally acquainted with your Excellency, and Our Vice President Mr. Adams, and understood perfectly the English Language, the Queen altered her first intention, and appointed him immediately as her Minister to our States. You will find him worthy of every attention you will be pleased to shew him, as a private Gentleman, and also as a Minister. He is possesed of every Virtue which constitutes a truly great and good Man. It will make him happy to be upon the strictest friendship with you. He has been Three times Chargé des affair's here. He is greatly beloved and respected by all his acquaintance. He is extremely sorry to leave this Country. I have told him, I hope he will find America and the Americans in every respect as agreeable as the people of this Country. I have taken the liberty to tell him, I am certain you and Mr. Adams will Make it a point to contrive to Make him pass his time in the Most agreeable Manner. He would be happy to know what things he Must bring, or if it would be better for him to buy them in America. Being Unacquainted with the business, I told him, I would take the liberty to trouble you. It is as followes, whether he can find a House ready furnished, and if not furnished, would you advise him to buy his furniture here or in America. There being numberless things necessary for a Minister which I am a total Stranger to you will add greatly to the many obligations you have already confered upon Me to send Me a particular account of every thing I have desired. I have heard from so many persons that My dearest Friend Miss Jefferson has changed her Name, that, I think, Mr. Paradise and Myself may join in congratulating you on the event, which we sincerely pray may make you the happiest of Fathers. We have heard that her Sister lives with her at your Seat in Virginia. We must trouble you to present our Congratulations to Mr. and Mrs. Randolph and the now Miss Jefferson, and assure them, that we often, and often, talk of them, and think of the happy Days, we passed with them. On Sunday July the 3d, arrived in this City Mrs. Barlow the Wife of Mr. Barlow. I was in hopes she would have brought us Letters from Our Friends at New York, but great was our Uneasiness when she said she had none. Mrs. Blagden is come from France to Conduct her to her Husband. My Daughter in her last Letter acquaints me she had Answered your Excellencies Letter, and was affraid, as she had not heard again from you, You had Not received her Answer. I did not know Your Excellency had ever written to her. This puts Me under another obligation, and for which I beg you will accept My thanks. Dr. Bancroft is still the same, good, and kind friend. Mr. P. is perfectly sober, and is in perfect health and should be happy to be employed by his Country to which he now belongs as a Citizen.

All Europe is in a great Bustle, France seems in My humble opinion to be the Most wise in every respect. My wish is that they would stop, and go no further, as things over done is generally spoilt. We beg you will present our respectful Compliments to our President his Lady and family and our Compliments to our Vice President and his Lady and Family and to all our Friends both Ladies and Gentlemen. Mr. Paradise and Myself join in Affectionate and Grateful Compliments and a Thousand Thanks to your Excellency for all your favours. Dear Sir I have the Honour to be your ever Affect. Humble. Servant   LUCY PARADISE

I shall be greatly obliged to you Sir, if you will be so good as to send the inclosed Letter to my Cousin.

P.S. I am told Lord Hawksbury is to be the Minister for the foreign department in the room of the Duke of Leeds who it is said will resign.

RC (DLC); endorsed as received 22 Nov. 1790 and so recorded in SJL. Enclosure not further identified.

To William Fitzhugh

DEAR SIR   New York July 21. 1790.

Your favor of the 11th. came to hand three or four days ago. As my servant Bob went from here to place himself at Fredericksburgh, I took for granted he would fall in your way, and give you an account of Tarquin. Some time after his arrival here he was taken with a lameness which continued perhaps three or four weeks, not severe, but so as to render him unfit to be used. By leaving him at rest, it went off; and I have since avoided using him but merely for little rides about town. As this is my principal use for him, I hope he will answer my purpose. I am much attached to him for his size, form and properties, so that I beg you to consider yourself as under no responsibility for him, in which light I have ever considered you. The remittance of his price has been delayed longer than I expected. On my arrival here I proposed to draw a bill of exchange, for a considerable sum, on the bankers of the U.S. at Amsterdam, but exchange was then far below par, and I found an idea that the loss would be mine, which I did not think right. As exchange was rising fast, I was advised to wait and thus avoid dispute. It was expected that at the sailing of the last packet it would be at par; but it was not. I am assured it will be so at the sailing of the next, which will be about the 8th. of August. Whether it is or not, I shall draw, and then remit you the £75. say 250 dollars in any way I can devise or you advise. Or if you please to draw on me for that sum, payable[1] the [7]th. of Aug. your draught shall be honored, and this would be the most agreeable to me, as the channel of remittance might, in my unskilful hands, occasion a delay, useless to me, and inconvenient to you.

The question of war and peace between Spain and England is still unsettled as far as we know. Congress will adjourn early next month, and the President go to Mount Vernon soon after. I hope to visit Virginia about the beginning of September. In that month and October I presume the removal of the offices to Philadelphia will take place. With my best respects to Mrs. Fitzhugh I am Dr. Sir Your most obedt. & most humble servt,   TH: JEFFERSON

PrC (ViU); containing first page only, the second page being in DLC: TJ Papers, 57:9765 (see note 1).

TJ had received TARQUIN, a large, elegant roan of distinguished blood lines, at Alexandria on 11 Mch. 1790. Upon such an animal he would have made an impressive entrance at the seat of government, but the heavy snow forced him to take the regular stagecoach (TJ to Fitzhugh, 11 Mch. 1790). Isaac, a Monticello slave whose reminiscences are remarkably revealing though sometimes inaccurate, said that "Mr. Jefferson never had nothing to do with horse-racing or cock-fighting: bought two race-horses once, but not in their racing day: bought em arter done runnin. One was Brimmer, a pretty horse with two white feet. . . . Tother

was Tarkill: in his race-day they called him the Roane colt: only race-horse of a roane Isaac ever see: old master used him for a ridin-horse" (Rayford W. Logan, ed., *Memoirs of a Monticello slave*, Charlottesville, 1951, p. 33). TJ identified Tarquin's sire as Eclipse and his dam as a roan mare "of the blood of Monkey, Othello, and Dabster" (Account Book, 11 Mch. 1790). Monkey was one of the first English-bred horses to be established in America and was distinguished for two things: his is the only known portrait of a horse imported into America before the Revolution and, as a pioneer who found few blooded mares in Virginia, he bred up the native stock, "imparting something magical to his filly foals which made of them the foundation stock for successful quarter racers which it was the privilege of Janus ultimately to galvanize" ([Fairfax Harrison], *The Roanoke Stud 1795-1833*, privately printed, Richmond, 1930, p. 113-7). Monkey, if not imported by Nathaniel Harrison of Brandon, certainly stood in the Brandon stud, as did Othello, who was described by Harrison himself as being "as high bred a horse as ever came to America" (*Virginia Gazette*, 11 Apr. 1777). Dabster, another import from the English turf, was in the Carter and Byrd studs from 1743 to 1761. Tarquin's dam was a roan mare owned by Peyton Randolph (Betts, *Farm Book*, p. 96). On the side of his sire, his lines may have been even more distinguished. TJ's description in the Account Book states that the gelding was 9 or 10 years old and that he excelled "in 2. mile heats 140. ℔." Betts, *Farm Book*, p. 95-6, points out that he could not have been quite so old if his sire was the Eclipse owned by R. B. Hall, for that courser had been on the English turf in 1781-1783 and had been imported into Maryland in 1784. But there were two stallions of this name in Virginia, either of which could have sired Tarquin. One was Harris' Eclipse, foaled in 1771, "a beautiful bay 15 hands 3 inches high," owned by John Harris (1749-1800) of Powhatan. The other was Burwell's Eclipse, foaled 1774, bred by Lewis Burwell (1738-1779) of Gloucester, and exported to Georgia at an indeterminate date; he was also a bay fifteen hands high. Both horses were the get of Old Fearnought, who was "entitled to the palm in preference to any stallion that had preceded him in giving the Virginia turf stock a standing equal to that of any running stock in the world" ([Fairfax Harrison], "The Equine F. F. Vs," VMHB, XXXV [1927]. 359-60, quoting "An Advocate for the Turf [George W. Jeffreys]," whose *Annals of the Turf*, originally published in the *Petersburg Intelligencer* in 1826, was the first systematic study of the bred horse in colonial Virginia). Fearnought was also called "the Godolphin Arabian of America," the summit of praise, and his get were noted for size, stamina, and distance running. It seems very probable that Tarquin's sire was Harris' Eclipse, for in Oct. 1790 TJ bought Brimmer from Carter Braxton and that horse was a grandson of Harris' Eclipse.

William Fitzhugh of Chatham, a noted horseman (and not to be confused with William Fitzhugh of Marmion who was a neighbor and kinsman of Nathaniel Harrison of Brandon), had written TJ on 11 July 1790 that he was very anxious to know the fate of Tarquin, having "never heard a Tittle respecting him" since TJ's letter acknowledging delivery, and added: "I must beg leave to request of you, when disengaged from more weighty Concerns, to inform me whether he has answer'd your Purpose. It is possible his lameness may have returned, and that he has not been equal to the Business, for which you intended him. If it shou'd be so, I am still willing that you shou'd dispose of him, on my Account, for any thing you may think him worth; but if on the contrary he has proved a good Horse, and you can, with the most perfect Conveniency to yourself, contrive me the seventy five Pounds, by some safe Conveyance, you will do me a singular Favour.—The Loss of my Tobacco and Corn last year, has thrown me so much in Arrears, that even a tolerable Crop of Wheat will not relieve me" (RC in MHi; endorsed as received 17 July 1790 and so recorded in SJL). On 7 Aug. 1790 Fitzhugh replied to the above letter, saying that he had that day drawn for $250 in favor of John Proudfit of Fredericksburg, adding: "I am much pleased to hear you are satisfy'd with the Horse. His figure is elegant, and I am in Hopes with gentle usage, he will recover his Lameness, and be equal to what you require of him. When you return to Virginia, if you can make it convenient, I shall be happy in seeing you at Chatham" (RC in MHi; endorsed as received 15 Aug. 1790 and so recorded in SJL). TJ thought that Tarquin had only one fault: he stumbled in going down hill. In the Albemarle region, this was enough to cause him to dispose of the animal, and in 1793 he gave him to Thomas Mann Randolph, Jr. It is worth noting that, in 1784 when TJ went northward to depart for France, he rode another grandson of Old Fearnought, Assaragoa, and sold the animal in Boston (Betts, *Farm Book*, p. 94-5).

[1] Text of PrC (ViU) ends at this point.

To David Howell

DEAR SIR   New York July 21. 1790.

I have duly recieved your favour of the 6th. and attend to your recommendation of Mr. Carter for promulgating the laws of the U.S. The act for that purpose directed me to have them published in three states at least. I have in fact ordered them in five states, which is as far as I think it right to extend the implication of the law as yet. Should it be thought expedient still to add to the list I will pay due respect to what you say of Mr. Carter. So also should any future and other cause arise of employing a printer in that state. I have the honor to be with great respect & esteem Dear Sir Your most obedt. humble servt.,   TH: JEFFERSON

PrC (DLC).

The Consular Establishment

I. MEMORANDA ON CANDIDATES AND PLACES FOR CONSULAR APPOINTMENTS, CA. 1 JUNE 1790
II. LIST OF CONSULAR VACANCIES, 21 JULY 1790

EDITORIAL NOTE

At the time that Jefferson arrived in New York, only one consular appointment had been made by Washington, that of Samuel Shaw for the port of Canton.[1] On his initial consultation with the president in regard to diplomatic and consular offices, he brought forth the letter of 14 Nov. 1788 that he had written to Jay at the time of the signing of the Consular Convention. In that letter Jefferson had not only indicated the places in France to which consuls and agents might be sent, together with the names of persons that he and others recommended, but he had called for the enactment into law of what he described as "the rule of 1784" so far as this applied to the office of consul. That rule was developed by a committee of which Jefferson was a member and was adopted by Congress on 16 March 1784. The resolution affirmed "That it is inconsistent with the interest of the United States to appoint any person not a citizen thereof, to the office of Minister, chargé des affaires, Consul, vice-consul, or to any other civil department in a foreign country."[2] The modification that Jefferson had sug-

[1] Washington sent Shaw's name to the senate on 9 Feb. 1790 and the appointment was confirmed on the 10th; JEP, I, 37, 39, 40. Shaw had been elected consul in China in 1786 (JCC, XXX, 28-9).

[2] JCC, XXVI, 144. A copy of this was transmitted to Franklin, Adams, and Jay. Washington was probably not familiar with the resolution when he recommended the appointment of the son of Sir Edward Newenham to a vice-consulship (see below).

gested in 1788 recognized both the advantages and disadvantages in the appointment of natives to consular posts and was a realistic attempt to embrace the former and minimize the latter. By his plan the office of consul would be confined to natives, but as it could happen that bankrupts fleeing creditors, "or young, ephemeral adventurers in commerce without substance or conduct" would be the only Americans available in some foreign ports, the office of vice-consul could be held by foreigners, their duties to be suspended when the consul was in port.

This recommendation may have appeared less realistic on 16 Apr. 1790 when Jefferson had another long conference with Washington "on the proper places and characters for Consuls or Vice Consuls."[3] And in the next three weeks, faced with the need of creating a consular establishment that would be co-extensive at least with the salient features of America's far-flung commerce, that would recognize the commercial claims of the northern states and not disappoint the expectations of those in the south, and that would avoid men who "might disgrace the consular office, without protecting our commerce," Jefferson saw the inevitability of modifying the view he had expressed in France. Even for the very restricted diplomatic establishment that was being created, he had said that the administration was "extremely puzzled to find characters fit for the offices which need them."[4] And for the much larger consular system, aggravated by the claims of individuals with powerful backing and by the certain risk of incurring censure in the bestowal of patronage—always a painful function for Jefferson—the problem was greatly magnified. The feeling of many Americans that such offices should bear salaries did nothing to lessen the difficulty of finding and appointing proper personnel.[5] Here, too, the constitutional question was raised and Washington discussed with both Jefferson and Madison "the propriety of consulting the Senate on the places to which it would be necessary to send persons in the Diplomatic line, and Consuls." And the designation of consuls for the French West Indies raised a question from La Forest concerning the construction of the Consular Convention of 1788.[6] But these issues, like the proposed modification of the Rule of 1784, were more easily disposed of than the perplexing question of naming suitable candidates, of having them confirmed by the senate, and of inducing them to accept once appointed.

It is possible that Washington consulted Madison about proper candidates for consular offices as well as about the constitutional problem, for the original of what is here presented as Document i is to be found in the Madison Papers. Jefferson obviously prepared it for the president, but it is equally possible that Washington asked Jefferson to show it to Madison and discuss the matter of appointments with him. Certainly both Washington and Jefferson engaged in the search. In late April the president noted in his diary that he had "Fixed with the Secretary of State on places and characters for the Consulate—but as some of the latter were unknown to both of us he was directed to make enquiry

[3] Washington, *Diaries*, ed. Fitzpatrick, iv, 107, 115.
[4] TJ to Short, 26 July 1790.   [5] See below, note 25.
[6] TJ to Short, 26 July 1790.

respecting them."[7] Just before his own illness, and while Jefferson was incapacitated himself, Washington again noted that he had "Endeavoured through various channels to ascertain what places required, and the characters fittest for Consuls at them." Late in May Jefferson was able to take up the problem again, just as he received damaging allegations about the mal-practices of a vice-consul in Canton.[8] Even so knowledgeable and interested a person as Robert Morris found himself unable to nominate more than a few suitable candidates, being uncertain of some and naming two that he later felt constrained to withdraw, though they were men of good family and character.[9] Jefferson's memoranda and notes, during this period, with names entered and deleted and with arrangements by states represented among the candidates being considered, reflect the difficulty of the search.[10] Early in June, still uncertain of the acceptance of the office by some of those named, Jefferson presented to Washington a list of thirteen names.

On 4 June 1790, having added a fourteenth name that Jefferson had supplied on Robert Morris' recommendation, Washington submitted the list of nominations to the senate. Those named as consul were: Richard Harrison of Maryland for Cadiz; Edward Church of Massachusetts[11] for Bilbao; John Marsden Pintard of New York for Madeira; James Maury of Virginia for Liverpool; William Knox of New York for Dublin; Joseph Fenwick[12] of Maryland for Bordeaux; Burrill Carnes of Massachusetts for Nantes; Nathaniel Barrett of Massachusetts for Rouen; Sylvanus Bourne of Massachusetts for Hispaniola; and Fulwar Skipwith of Virginia for Martinique. Those named as vice-consul were: Thomas Auldjo of England for Cowes; Etienne Cathalan of France for Marseilles; La Motte of France for Le Havre and John Parish of Hamburg for Hamburg.[13] On the 7th all of those nominated for the office of consul were confirmed save Edward Church. Action on those nominated as vice-consul was postponed. On the 17th a resolution was offered in the senate to the effect "that it may be expedient to advise and consent to the appointment of foreigners to the offices of Consuls or Vice-Consuls for the United States." An effort was made to amend this so that such appointments "should be confined to citizens of the United States, except in cases of urgent necessity, but the amendment failed and the resolution was adopted as introduced. There is no evi-

[7] Washington, *Diaries*, ed. Fitzpatrick, IV, 122, 128.

[8] Sarly to TJ, 22 Dec. 1789.

[9] Morris to TJ, 1 May 1790; see Document I, note, where the letter is summarized.

[10] These memoranda are summarized in note to Document I.

[11] TJ listed Church as being from Massachusetts, Washington so presented him to the senate, and the senate so confirmed him (see summary of TJ's list, Nos. 4 and 5, note to Document I; JEP, I, 47, 51). But the *Gazette of the United States* for 19 June 1790 listed him as "Edward Church, of Georgia, formerly of Massachusetts."

[12] TJ listed him as James Fenwick and the senate so confirmed the appointment, but on 23 June 1790 Washington sent the correct name to the senate and the record was set straight; JEP, I, 52.

[13] JEP, I, 47-9.

dence that Jefferson's earlier suggestion about modifying the Rule of
1784 and enacting it into law was brought forward at this time, but
the confining of nominations of foreigners to the office of vice-consul
shows that some remnant of the proposal remained in his mind. Until
"near two o'clock," Maclay wrote, "we were engaged on the subject of
consuls and vice-consuls. The grand question, was whether foreigners
were eligible to those offices. It was admitted that they were, and a
number accordingly appointed."[14] Church, Auldjo, Cathalan, and Parish
were confirmed on this day, but La Motte was not confirmed until
22 June. On 2 Aug. 1790 Washington sent to the senate the names
of Joshua Johnson of Maryland to be consul at London; Francisco
Sarmento of Spain to be vice-consul at Tenerife; John Street of Portugal
to be vice-consul at Fayal; and Ebenezer Brush of New York to be consul
at Surinam. All were promptly confirmed save Sarmento, who was
rejected, a rather surprising action in view of the fact that Sarmento
was married to a Philadelphian, was recommended by Thomas Fitz-
Simons as being a man of character and substance, and was evidently
supported by Robert Morris.[15] Thus, of the two original groups of
nominations to office in the consular establishment, six of the eighteen
were foreigners, three—excluding Church—were from Massachusetts,
three from Virginia, three from New York, and two from Maryland.
"I find the President and Secretary of State are impressed," wrote John
Adams, "with an apprehension of censure, for appointing too many
[consuls] from one state."[16] The geographical distribution of the nominees confirms the judgment, but there were other considerations as well.
In 1788 Jefferson had strongly recommended John Bondfield as consul
at Bordeaux, considering him as "unexceptionable in every point of
view."[17] When the son of George Mason saw Jefferson in Paris, soliciting the post for his partner, Joseph Fenwick, Jefferson declined to make
any change in the recommendation. His notes as described in the note to
Document I in the present series show that he continued to hold Bondfield in mind for the office. But not for long: George Mason, a bitter
foe of the Constitution whose good will toward the federal government
was worth cultivating, wrote Jefferson in March recommending Fenwick
and offering criticism of Bondfield. A line was struck through the
latter's name and on 13 June 1790 Jefferson wrote that Fenwick had
been appointed "according to your desire."[18] It is scarcely to be credited
that this was done by the secretary of state without informing the
president of the circumstances in the case.

Other recommendations perhaps no less weighty with Jefferson or the
president were not accepted. The speaker of the house reported during
the early days of Jefferson's illness that he had been requested by "some
Gentlemen in Philada. to mention Mr. Collins . . . as a Gentleman well

14 Maclay, *Journal*, ed. Maclay, p. 297.
15 JEP, I, 51-2, 53-4, 54-5, 56; see Document I.
16 John Adams to John Codman, Jr., 10 Oct. 1790 (MHi: Adams Papers).
17 TJ to Jay, 14 Nov. 1788.
18 Mason to TJ, 16 Mch. 1790; TJ to Mason, 13 June 1790.

qualified to act as a Consul for the United States in Ireland."[19] Daniel Denton Rogers recommended one Bromfield, saying that he also had the support of John Adams and was "an American Gentleman now settled in London . . . regularly bred to Business, and in the prosecution of it in America, Holland, France, and in London has had greater Opportunity for acquiring a Knowledge of the Commerce of this Country than perhaps any other man." Rogers added to this high praise the statement that Bromfield had "ever been the decided Advocate for the Liberty of his Country" and was known to the secretary of war.[20] Robert Morris, after talking with Jefferson in March, gave C. F. Baudin of St. Martin's, Île de Ré, reason to believe that he would be appointed to the consulship he had solicited of Jefferson in Paris.[21] And among the applications and recommendations that Remsen listed for Jefferson as being recorded in the departmental records, Jefferson found one that seemed to be supported by influence no less weighty than that of Benjamin Franklin and the president himself. This concerned an application by Sir Edward Newenham for the appointment of his son as consul at Marseilles. But that matter had been disposed of by Washington in 1787 by appealing to the Rule of 1784 as a justifiable principle to which, for the sake of consistency, he could ask no exception.[22]

On 17 June 1790 Senator Maclay, having listened to discussions in the senate on the eligibility of foreigners for the offices of consul and vice-consul, was informed by the speaker that a bill had been introduced in the house for granting salaries to such officers. "Thus it is," he declared, "that we are led on, little by little, to increase the civil list; to increase the mass of public debt, and, of course, the taxes of the public. This, however, is all of a piece with former management from the offices."[23] Maclay's sentiment was characteristic, being similar to the attitude of economy if not of penury he had displayed toward the diplomatic establishment, but his information was faulty. The pressure for salaries came not from the administration but from those seeking office.[24] And the proposal in the house, made by Gerry, was not for the adoption of a bill but for the appointment of a committee "to consider and report whether any, and what, fees, perquisites, or other emoluments, shall be annexed to the office of Consul and Vice-Consul." A

[19] J. P. G. Muhlenberg to TJ, 5 May 1790 (RC in DLC: Applications for Office under Washington); Collins was described as a native of Ireland.

[20] Rogers to TJ, dated Broad street, New York, 25 June 1790 (RC in same; endorsed by TJ as received 26 June 1790 and so recorded in SJL).

[21] Baudin to TJ, 11 July 1790 (RC in same; endorsed by TJ as received 11 Jan. 1791 and so recorded in SJL); see Vol. 12: 70, 155, 432-3.

[22] For Washington's correspondence on this request, which obviously gave him some embarrassment, see Washington, *Writings*, ed. Fitzpatrick, XXIX, 50, 156, 175, 204-6, 346. Washington's letter of 20 Apr. 1787 conveying the information to Newenham (same, XXIX, 204-6) is also printed under the erroneous date 20 Apr. 1797 (same, XXXV, 437-8) from a typescript furnished Fitzpatrick by the Mount Vernon Ladies Association. For Remsen's list of applications and recommendations, see Document I, notes.

[23] Maclay, *Journal*, ed. Maclay, p. 297.

[24] See, for example, the letters of Sylvanus Bourne and Richard Hanson Harrison in this volume.

bill was brought in providing for fees, permitting American citizens who were consuls or vice-consuls to own vessels in their own names or in partnership with other American citizens, and was passed on 21 July 1790. James Madison introduced an amendment to this bill authorizing the president "to appoint one or more Consuls on the coast of Barbary, at a salary of nine thousand dollars per annum."[25] But the senate failed to act on this bill during the session.

One part of his recommendations of 1788 Jefferson definitely had not given up. He had then urged the use of such an establishment in gathering intelligence, though one of the very reasons for which Congress had rejected the Consular Convention of 1784 was the fear that it might introduce such a system into the United States for the benefit of a foreign power and to its own disadvantage. In preparing his memoranda for Washington, Jefferson now favored the establishment of a consulship at Angra in the Azores because this was the harbor at which ships from Brazil touched "and where intelligence of that country may be had." His preference in this instance, over opposing recommendations by Morris and others, is a measure of his continuing interest in Brazilian affairs.[26] The appointment of Joshua Johnson as consul at London was inspired largely, if not primarily, by the desire to obtain intelligence.[27]

[25] JHR, I, 243, 255, 256, 274, 275; *Annals*, II, 1698, 1714, 1715-6, 1742. It is to be noted that the amount proposed by Madison as a salary for a consul on the Barbary coast was precisely the amount to which a minister plenipotentiary's salary was limited by the act passed three weeks earlier. Two plausible explanations occur for this action: first, that it was a deliberate move to embarrass the bill, or, second, that it was an effort to ease the burden on the diplomatic establishment, since TJ's estimate of probable calls on that fund had included an item of $1,800 for a consul in Morocco, and the adoption of this amendment would have rendered this provision unnecessary.—The proviso permitting American citizens who were consuls to own trading vessels may have been introduced in part because of Samuel Shaw, who at this time held commission as consul at Canton and was on the high seas as supercargo of the *Massachusetts*, a vessel of which Shaw & Randall were principal owners (Shaw to Daniel Parker, 15 Mch. 1790; Shaw to Randall, 12 Mch. 1790; MHi: Knox Papers; Lear to Shaw, 13 Feb. 1790, enclosing commission; DNA: RG 59, MLR). See also TJ to Boudinot, 29 June 1790.

[26] See, for example, TJ to Jay, 4 May 1787.

[27] See TJ to Johnson, 7 Aug. 1790.

I. Memoranda on Candidates and Places for Consular Appointments

[ca. 1 June 1790]

Gottenburgh.

This is a considerable deposit of our rice for the consumption of the Northern countries of Europe: being very free in it's commerce, it is a good deal frequented by our vessels; and might be worthy of a consulship were a good native citizen to desire it, or

Sweden.
Hamburgh.

an Englishman, as the English have great privileges there. John Parish named by Mr. Morris.[1]

Holland.   *Amsterdam.* Mr. Greenleaf is married and settled there. Mr. Cassinove speaks of him as a discreet young man. If we should have a Chargé des affaires there, it would be less important who should be the Consul. But if we have no Chargé there, I imagine it would be important to appoint such a person Consul as might be rendered useful in the very great money transactions we shall have there; and who might keep an eye over our bankers there, which will be found necessary.

Spain.   *Cadiz.* Richard Harrison already nominated. Welsh asks the appointment. I believe he is a native of Britain. With respect to these a general observation must be made. In those countries disposed to be friendly to us, and not so to Great Britain, the governments would be jealous of seeing a Briton employed as American Consul, because they could so easily cover British bottoms under the American flag. In France, where we have considerable privileges denied to the English, the government has been much perplexed and defrauded by British ships under false American colours. And these suspicions have produced embarrasments to vessels really ours. Tho' I do not know that we have any privileges in Spain which the English have not, yet that government is not friendly to the British, and therefore the appointment of a native of Britain to be American Consul might draw an unfavorable shade over the appointment. In countries where British commerce is favored, it might be advantageous sometimes to appoint an Englishman our Consul, in order to partake of the favor of his nation.

Bilboa. Edward Church of Massachusetts already named.

The Canaries.   *Teneriffe.* Thomas Thompson of Virginia already named. Sarmento asks it. He is said by Mr. Fitzsimmons to be a Spaniard, married to a Miss Craig of Philadelphia, settled at Teneriffe, to have a good deal of the American business and to be of excellent character.

Qu. if it be sufficiently important to have any appointment here, unless it were a good native?

Portugal.   *Lisbon.* John Marsden Pintard, of New York, will probably prefer this to Madeira. He is not at present in New York.

Madeira Is. Azores.   *Madeira.* Wm. Hill Wells is proposed, if Mr. Pintard does not accept. He is the nephew of Henry Hill of Philadelphia. Mr. Morris sais he is a very clever fellow. He is 22. years old.

I. CANDIDATES AND APPOINTMENTS

Angra, in the island of Tercera, is the metropolis of the Azores. It is said to be the only station for ships in all the seven islands, and is the residence of the English, French and Dutch consuls. It is the port at which the Brazil ships refresh, and where intelligence of that country may be had.

Fayal. Messrs. Morris and Fitzsimmons recommend John Street of Fayal to be Consul. They say he is a native of England, but has resided in Fayal so long that he is considered as a Portuguese: that he is 30. years old and of very good character.

St. Michaels. Thomas Hickling of Boston, asks the consulship of the Azores or Western islands. He sets forth that he has resided several years at St. Michael's, is well versed in the Portuguese language and in their laws and customs respecting trade: that on the acknolegement of our independence, he, being the only American residing in those islands, was appointed by the Chief judge Consul for the protection of our commerce to the Western islands in which he has acted since 1783. Mr. Yates of New York sais that Hickling is a respectable man of property, and that he has long corresponded with him.

Qu. if this appointment might not as well be left in it's present state till some good native can be found who will settle at Angra which is central to all the islands? It's connection with Brazil gives it advantage over any other position in these islands.

London.

Liverpool. James Maury of Virginia already named. Is not this port sufficient for the Western coast?

Cowes in the Isle of Wight. This is a port at which many of our vessels touch, and where patronage against the Custom house officers will certainly be useful. Thomas Auldjo, a native of Britain, of the house of Strachan, Mackenzie & co. is recommended by Mr. Morris. I know him personally, and think him a good man. The Custom house officers seem devoted to him. He is the only merchant of any note there, and has the care of almost all the Carolina rice deposited there. This port would suffice for all the Southern coast of England.

Great Britain.

Dublin. William Knox, of Massachusetts, decidedly prefers this consulship to all others. He will decide within two or three days whether he will accept it.   Randall, who was nominated, declines accepting. Mr. Morris recommends a Mr. Wilson of Dublin.[1]

Ireland.

Newry.[2] Wm. Eugene Imlay of Jersey already nominated.

France.   *Marseilles.* Stephen Cathalan, a Frenchman.
Bordeaux. Joseph Fenwick, of Maryland.
Nantes. Burrell Carnes, of Massachusetts.
Havre. La Motte, a Frenchman.   } already nominated.
Rouen. Nathaniel Barrett of Massachusets.
Lorient.

Isle of Rhé. Very unimportant in my opinion. Perhaps it would be as well to let the Consul for Nantes (to which place I believe it is nearer than Bordeaux) appoint T. Baudin his Agent there. Baudin desires it for the sake of the honor, and sais he has done several good offices for our vessels there. He is a Frenchman.

French Islands.   *Hispaniola.* The ports are the Cape, Port au Prince and aux Cayes. Sylvanus Bourne already named.

Guadaloupe.   *Point à petre.*

Martinique.   *Port royal.* Fulwar Skipwith of Virginia already named.

St. Lucie.   *Carenage.*
Tobago.   *Scarboro.*   } These two islands lying nearer to Martinique than to any other Consulship, and seeming too inconsiderable for separate Consulships, may as well perhaps be agencies under the Consul of Martinique. And indeed, considering how many Consuls are destined for France and it's dependancies, it may be doubted whether it would not be better to make Guadaloupe also an Agency of Martinique (to which it is so near) till a very good native shall offer for it?

Isle of France.

China.   *Canton.* Samuel Shaw of Massachusetts already named. Thomas Randall Vice-Consul. There is a complaint against him for malpractice; recieved from Jacob Sarly.[3]

MS (DLC: Madison Papers); entirely in TJ's hand; undated, but written after 27 May, when TJ received the complaint from Sarly about Randall that is mentioned in the final paragraph, and before 4 June 1790, when Washington submitted the first list of nominations to the senate. PrC (DLC: TJ Papers, 55: 9343-6); containing variations not in MS (see notes 2 and 3).

Several documents preceded or followed the above in the period when Washington and TJ were discussing consular appointments late in April. All are undated, but they reveal that geographical as well as political considerations were involved in the search for suitable nominees. These may be described as follows:

(1) Memorandum in TJ's hand, mutilated, DLC: TJ Papers, 233: 41617, reading:
"Newry Wm. Eugene Imlay Jersey
Isle of Bourbon
Lorient (Franklin / Murray) Vail N. York
Mediterranean. Nice. Sasserno.
  Piemontese
  Civita Vecchia (D. Carrol)
W.I. Braxton
Lisbon.Bristol. London.}
  John   Cowper   of | recommended
  Portsmouth   } by Josiah
St. Domingo. Bristol. | Parker"
Wm. Stokes. Virga. }

The recommendation for an appointment made by Daniel Carroll refers to a letter from John Carroll to Daniel Carroll, 14 Feb. 1790 (RC in DLC: Applications for Office under Washington; endorsed by TJ: "Consulate for Civita vecchia. Mr. Carrol's Letter asking it for Alexander Sloane"). This was really an endorsement of part of a letter from "Mr. Thorpe" reading as follows: "Mr. Alexander Sloane, a Scotch Gentleman, has been settled in business, during several years, at Civita Vecchia, where he has born an uniform character of honesty and industry, and obtains very considerable credit. He sollicits the appointment of Consul for the United States in that port. He asks no salary, and expects none to be annexed to the office; but only desires the advantage of holding that rank, and taking those eventual emoluments, which are customary, when there shall be need for his assistance."

(2) Memorandum in TJ's hand, DLC: TJ Papers, 233: 41618, with James Greenleaf designated for Amsterdam; Paul R. Randall of New York and Richard Codman of Massachusetts for Cadiz (the latter having "Mr. Dalton" beside his name as a sponsor); "T[homas] Thompson Virginia" and "Sarmento Portugee" for the Canaries; "(D.Carroll) Portugee" for Oporto; "Street (R. Morris) Portugee" for the Azores; and "Donald.A" and "Bromfield" for London, together with a recommendation by "(Mr. Morris)" that is not discernible because of the mutilation in MS.

(3) Memorandum in TJ's hand, DLC: TJ Papers, 233: 41619, listing on its recto the names of ports and opposite to these the names of those being considered for nomination. The ports correspond with those listed in Document I above, except that the Azores and Cowes are omitted. The names designated for these ports correspond with those above except that Moylan was assigned to Lisbon, Pintard to Madeira, Randall to Dublin, and, for Bordeaux, Marseilles, and Martinique, respectively, the names of Bondfield, Larreguy, and Benjamin Thompson are deleted and those of Fenwick, Cathalan, and Skipwith are substituted for them. On verso TJ listed the appointments by states, as follows:

"Massachusetts

√Sylvanus Bourne
   Hispaniola
√Nathaniel Barrett
   Rouen
√Burrel Carnes
   Nantes
√   Church
   Bilboa
⟨James Greenleaf
   Amsterdam⟩
√William Knox
   Dublin
√Samuel Shaw
   Canton

Rhode Island

⟨Dunn⟩
   Hispaniola

New York

√John Marsden Pintard
   Madeira
⟨Paul R. Randall⟩
   Dublin

New Jersey

⟨Stephen Moylan⟩
   Lisbon
⟨Benjamin Thompson⟩
   France or Fr. islds.
⟨enquire character of
   R. Morris⟩
√Wm. Eugene Imlay
   Newry
   Q. of Mr. Bland Lee
   of Virga. and member of N. Jersey. Patterson.

Maryland

⟨Richard Harrison⟩
   Cadiz
√Joseph Fenwick
   Bordeaux

Virginia

√James Maury
   Liverpool
√Thomas Thompson
   Teneriffe
√Fulwar Skipwith
   Martinique

Foreigner.

⟨John Larreguy⟩
   Stephen Cathalan
   Marseilles
   La Motte
   Havre
   Auldjo
   Cowes
   Parish
   Hamburgh."

The foregoing tabulation was clearly employed from late April until after Document I was drawn up, as the deletions and additions show, thus indicating that TJ kept a geographical distribution of the appointments clearly in mind during the whole period.

(4) PrC of list of proposed nominees, DLC: TJ Papers, 55: 9340, in TJ's hand. This is the list of those whom TJ describes in Document I as being "already named" or already nominated, except that the nominees for Teneriffe, Bilbao, and, of course, Canton are not included. The names of "Stephen Moylan of New Jersey" for Lisbon and "Paul R. Randall of New York" for Dublin have lines drawn through them, indicating that the list was drawn up about 1 May 1790, since Washington wrote to Moylan a day after that asking if he would accept the appointment "as it is not proposed to give salaries the rewith" (Washington, *Diaries*, ed. Fitzpatrick, IV, 126).

(5) PrC of list of proposed nominees, with one exception, in DLC: TJ Papers, 55: 9347-9, in TJ's hand. This list is cast in the form in which Washington presented the nominations to the senate, the first of which reads: "Cadiz. Richard Hanson Harrison of Maryland, Consul of the United state of America for the port of Cadiz in the kingdom of Spain and for such parts of the said kingdom as shall be nearer to the said port than to the residence of any other consul or vice-consul of the U.S. in the said kingdom." There were thirteen nominations in this list; the fourteenth was that of John Parish for the port of Hamburgh that was evidently added to the (missing) manuscript before Washington transmitted it to the senate on 4 June 1790. See Editorial Note above.

(6) MS in Remsen's hand listing applications and recommendations for consular appointments as follows: "*Andrew Christian Tilebein*, to be Consul for the District or Kingdom of Catalonia in Spain. He resides at Barcelona and is recommended by the Marquis d'Yranda.

John Marsden Pintard to be Consul for Lisbon and Madeira.

Sir Edward Newenham of Ireland, appointment of Consul for his Son at Marseilles, recommended by Dr. Franklin and Genl. Washington.

Robert Montgomery, to be Consul at Alicant in Spain.

Richard Harrison, to be Consul at Cadiz

John Bondfield, to be Vice Consul at Bordeaux, recommended by Dr. Franklin and Mr. Barclay.

Nathaniel Cutting to be Consul at Havre de Grace.

Paul Randall, offering himself as a Candidate for a foreign Appointment.

Mr. Thomas Barclay was recommended as Consul General for G. Britain by Mr. John Adams. [*In TJ's hand, in pencil*:] Broadway, 2 doors below Crown str. Mrs. Barclay's.

Mr. Uriah Forrest, to be Consul General for Do." (MS in DLC: TJ Papers, 69: 11904; at head of text: "Applications for Foreign Appointments").

On Washington's correspondence with Sir Edward Newenham concerning a consulship for his son, see Editorial Note.

(7) A letter from Robert Morris, 1 May 1790, expressing regret that he had not met TJ "Yesterday at either of the reciprocal calls on each other," and adding: "When Mr. Morris came to reflect on the Persons to whom the Consular Appointments might be desirable, He could recollect but few, and even of these He has set down two Americans that He is not sure of, Mr. Geo. Harrison and Mr. Edwd. Hall. They are Young Gentlemen of good Character and if desired Mr. M. would consult them on the subject" (RC in DNA: RG 59, MLR; on verso TJ wrote and then deleted the names of Wilson, Baudin, Parish, Sarmento, and Haller, substituting for them the names of Wilson, Welsh, Baudin, Auldjo, and Parish). The names that Morris set down are listed as follows:
"For Consuls
Dublin .... Mr. Philip Wilson
Cadiz .... Mr.   Welsh of the House of Dominick Terry & Co.
Lisbon .... Mr. Stephen Moylan
St. Martins Isle of Rhé .... Fr. Baudin
Marseilles .... Estienne Cathalan
Bourdeaux .... Mr.   Mason of Virga.
      Mr. Geo. Harrison of Philada.
      Edwd Hall of Maryland
Cowes Isle of Wight .... Mr   a Nephew of Strachan Mackenzie & Co.
Hamburg—Denmark .... Mr. John Parish."

(8) In DNA: RG 59, MLR, there is a copy of the foregoing in the hand of Thomas FitzSimons that contains the following additions and variations: for Cadiz the name of "Mr. Harrison"

was added to that of Welsh; for Bordeaux the name of "J. Verney" [Jacob Vernes] was added to that of Mason; the names of Harrison and Hall were designated for Le Havre, and opposite these TJ wrote in the margin: "withdrawn by Mr. Morris"; for Tenerife, FitzSimons wrote: "Mr. Sarmento, a Spaniard, married Miss Craig of P[hiladelphia] settled at Teneriff. He has acquired a great p[art] of the American business and has applied for this appointment"; and for Marseilles he added the name of "Mr. Haller, nephew to the Banker Haller of Paris" to that of Cathalan.

MR. CASSINOVE: Théophile Cazenove, of Amsterdam, who had recently arrived in New York as a representative of Dutch mercantile and banking houses, bearing letters of introduction to Washington and others. Washington treated the matter with punctilio. When Van Berckel, the Dutch minister, informed the president that Cazenove had arrived with letters which he wished to deliver in person and requested to know when it would be agreeable for him to do so, Washington recorded in his diary: "It was thought, before this should be done, it might be proper to know whether they were of a public nature, and whether he was acting in a public character. If so, then let them come to me through the Secretary of State—if not, then for him to send them, that the purport might be known before he was introduced, which might be at the next Levee, when he might be received and treated agreeably to the consequence he might appear to derive from the testimonials of the letters. It being conceived that etiquette of this sort is essential with all foreigners to give a respect to the Chief Magistrate, and the dignity of the Government, which would be lessened if every person who could procure a letter of introduction should be presented otherwise than at Levee hours in a formal manner" (Washington, *Diaries*, ed. Fitzpatrick, IV, 105-6). This was only two days before Washington held his first interview with Jefferson, but the letters of introduction were evidently not handled through the secretary of state since they must have concerned private rather than public affairs.

On the COMPLAINT AGAINST Randall received from Sarly, see Sarly to TJ, 22 Dec. 1789. WILLIAM KNOX was the brother of Henry Knox. The recommendation by FITZSIMMONS may have been in a (missing) letter of 31 July recorded in SJL as received same day.

1 This sentence interlined by TJ before PrC was executed.

2 In PrC TJ deleted "Newry" and substituted "Limerick," a change made after PrC was executed.

3 At this point PrC has an additional sentence not in MS and therefore added after the former was executed: "Hamburgh. John Parish, merchant of Hamburgh vice-consul for Hamburgh."

II. List of Consular Vacancies

Consulates still vacant, Candidates, of what country,
and by whom recommend[ed.]

Port.	Candidates	Of what Country	by whom recommended.
Gottenburg.			
Amsterdam.	James Greenleaf.	Massachusets.	
Cadiz.	Paul R. Randall.	New York	
	Richard Codman.	Massachusets.	Mr. Dalton
Canaries. viz.	Thomas Thompson	Virginia.	T. Pleasants
Teneriffe.	named.		
Ferro	Sarmento	Portugal	
Canary &c.			
Lisbon.	Paul R. Randall	New York.	
	Thomas Thompson.	Virginia.	
	. . . .	Portugal.	D. Carrol.
Azores. viz.	Street	Portugal.	R. Morris
Tercera.			
Fayal.			
St. Michael &c.			
London	. . . Bromfeild	Massachusets.	Vice-president. Mr. Dalton
	Walter Stone.	Maryland	R. Morris
	Alexr. Donald	Scotland.	His own letter.
Newry	Wm. Eugene Imlay	Jersey.	
Isle of Bourbon			
Lorient.	Vail	N. York.	Franklins & Murray merchts. N.[Y.]
Civita Vecchia	. . . .	Scotland.	D. Carrol
Nice	Sasserno	Piedmont.	
[a]ny place	Braxton	Virginia.	A. Donald

Th: Jefferson
July 21. 1790.

PrC (DLC: TJ Papers, 56: 9633).

From William Short

Dear Sir   Paris July the 22d. 1790.

Since my last the federal deputies from the provinces have been
leaving Paris daily to return to their respective homes. The most
perfect harmony continued to the last, which was contrary to the
fears or hopes of every party.

The assembly are at present employed in discussing their judiciary system, and the organisation of their army. There is little
hope however that they will adopt the best plan. Their attention
is so often diverted from constitutional objects by those which are
incidental. The different parties are so opposed and so violent, that

there is nothing like cool and continued discussion.—Their decrees for some time past have shewn this spirit, and it becomes so evident that the assembly is too numerous and too heated to form moderate and wise deliberations, that all parties out of the house begin to express a wish for their separation. It had been hoped that they would have fixed before the departure of the federal deputies the term at which the next legislature should be convoked. This having not been done it is feared now they will prolong their session until public clamour shall announce to them the necessity of finishing it. This could not fail to produce a bad effect and therefore all the friends of the revolution wish them to confine themselves strictly to the formation of the constitution and finish it in time to anticipate such an event.

The negotiations in the North hold out the prospect of a peace in that quarter. Those between England and Spain are carried on in a manner which presents little official information to public view. It is certain that this court takes a very inactive part in the negotiation, and that circumstance leads to a variety of conjectures concerning the result. One of them is that Spain displeased with the principles which prevail at present in France, and taking it for granted that a compliance with the family compact cannot be counted on, will go into the English balance by a political alliance, in order to avert the present storm which would seem to threaten her American possessions: and that she will make a commercial treaty with England which shall extend to her European dominions only, and by that means have her exclusive commerce on the coast of America guaranteed by the power from whose interference she had the most to fear. By this arrangement England will have divided the house of Bourbon, and will have obtained what she has long desired, a commercial treaty with Spain. This will leave her also more perfectly at liberty to support the King of Sweden by sending a fleet into the Baltic if it becomes necessary.

These I give you as conjectures. *They lead to others which regard us and which I have heard mentioned here in conversation. They are that England and Spain being allied, and France considered as a non entity at present, they may be disposed to join in finishing their unsettled business with the U.S.—the navigation of the Mississipi, the British forts and debts, and under these pretexts carry their pretensions as much further as circumstances and their force may enable them.—I mention these as mere conjectures for which I know no foundation except the present peculiar situation of Eu-*

rope, and the well known malevolent disposition of the King of England and the present exultation of the nation which will necessarily be encreased if they succeed with Spain. Still I cannot help communicating them to you as I have heard them.[1]

I am sorry not to have a more sure and speedy conveyance for this letter. It will be sent to Havre to wait there for the sailing of some vessel. I inclose you the Leyden gazettes, and the memorial on the Algerine business mentioned in a former letter.—Your furniture is not yet all ready. I have hurried the Packers and Petit as much as possible. They have lost no time that could have been avoided, and will certainly be in a condition to despatch every thing for Havre in a very few days. I am with sentiments of the most perfect attachment, Dear Sir, Your most obedient Servant,

W. SHORT

PrC (DLC: Short Papers); at head of text: "*No. 37*"; partly in code, accompanied by text *en clair* of coded passage, in Short's hand on separate page; lacks complimentary close which has been supplied from Tr (DNA: RG 59, DD), having coded passage decoded interlineally. Recorded in SJL as received 2 Nov. 1790. On the enclosed memorial, see 28 Dec. 1790.

[1] The passage in italics is written in code and has been supplied from Short's text *en clair*. Code No. 10 was employed.

To George Washington

Thursday July 22. 1790.

Th: Jefferson has the honor to inclose to the President the extracts he desired from his letter of May 4. 1787.

He finds by a note, which he does not know however where he got, that the city of Mexico is about 200. miles from the sea.

RC (DNA: RG 59, MLR); addressed: "The President of the United States"; endorsed by Washington: "22d. July. 1790 State of the Portuguese in So. America." Not recorded in SJL. FC (DNA: RG 59, SDC). The text enclosed (printed below) is a summary rather than an extract from TJ to Jay, 4 May 1787, plus information derived from conversations with José da Maia.

ENCLOSURE

Jefferson's Notes on Brazil and Mexico

BRAZIL contains as many inhabitants as Portugal, that is to say about two millions. These are of the following descriptions.

1. Portuguese. They are very few, and are married and identified with the Brazilians, having lost sight of their native country.
2. Native Whites. They form the body of the nation.

3. Black and mulatto slaves. As numerous as the Whites, and will take their side.

4. Indians, civilized and savage. The former have no energy. The latter would not meddle.

20,000 regular troops; originally they were Portuguese, but as these have died off they have been replaced by natives, who now form the greatest mass and may be counted on by their country.

Rio Janeiro, the metropolis, contains 50,000 inhabitants. It is considered as the strongest port in the world after Gibraltar.

The king's fifth of the mines yeilds annually 6½ million of dollars. Diamonds and other precious stones yeild him about half as much. The remaining produce of the mines is 26. millions.

MEXICO. It's inhabitants are of the following descriptions.

1. Spaniards, possessing most of the offices. Very few in number.

2. Native Whites, forming the body of the nation, and much disposed to revolt.

3. Slaves, mulatto and black. Will side with their masters, and of important weight, being equal to them in numbers.

4. Indians, conquered and free. The former of no consequence. The latter brave and formidable, but so distant as not to be likely to intermeddle.

The city of Mexico contains 300,000 inhabitants.

MS (DNA: RG 59, MLR); in TJ's hand. FC (DNA: RG 59, SDC).

From Madame de Corny

23 juillet

Je vous ai ecrit en octobre, vous me repondez le 2 avril, et je recois votre lettre le 20 juillet. Autant vaudroit dater des champs elisées que de New york. Ah, je l'avois bien dit que je ne vous reverrois jamais; mes adieux ont devances les votres, et lorsque je fus chez vous apres le depart, ma tristesse extreme fut un pressentiment bien juste. Enfin soyez heureux, comme vous lentendez, a votre maniere, bien loin de moi, separé meme de vos filles. Il est donc bien vrai que je ne vous reverrai jamais. Je nay dautre affaire que celle daimer et de regretter mes amis; ainsi, mon souvenir vous est assuré, mais le vôtre, ah, quil est douteux.—Je vais vous predire votre sort, vous vous remarirez, oui, c'est sur, Votre femme sera heureuse et vous aussi, je lespere bien; mais qui me retracera a votre souvenir? Allons, encore un sacrifice a la necessité.

Votre fille est donc mariée, et son gout s'est raporter avec le votre. Les bons peres doivent etre ainsi recompensé par leurs enfans. Et cette chere Pauly qui parle de moi, pourquoi navez vous pas eu assez de confiance pour me la laisser? Mais non, il eut ete trop difficile de vous la rendre. Faitte mille amitie a ces deux chere filles. Je parie que laînée a deja sa jolie taille gâté.—Mr. Short crain de quitter paris. Lhistoire de notre revolution est interessante a suivre, quoique tout les gens sensés trouvent que depuis longtems nous avons passé le but. Lordre judiciaire et le militaire ne sont pas encor organisé; la municipalite de paris n'est encor que provisoire. Et pourtant lon a fait beaucoup de choses: en destruction il ny a plus rien a inventer. Loperation sur le clerge est un bien pour le siecle a venir mais le present est dur a suporter. Mr. Neker est perdu aux yeux de la multitude. Le 12 juillet de cette année, juste le bout de l'an ou Msrs. les duc dorleans et Neker ont ete portes comme idole du peuple, ce même peuple les insulte et les place dans la boue. Quelle versatilité dans lopinion et que pour longtems encor les bonnes gens aimeront a vivre ignoré et loin de la Capitale.—Nous avons fait choix dune abbaye fort simple, fort isolée, pour lachetter, mais jay des concurrens et je crains de ne pas lobtenir.—Nous fessons tout ce que nous pouvons pour subsister et croire aux assignats, le numeraire disparoit largent sachette un prix fou.—Ah pourquoi un si grand espace nous separe til? Jaimerois a chercher près de vous un repos après lequel je soupire. Mr. de Corny aime votre pays, il forme bien des voeux.—Mais il faudroit realiser sa fortune, ma jolie maison est a vendre mais on ne veut pas lachetter. Je ne puis concevoir qui arrette Mde. De brean [Brehan]. Je voudrois être a sa place, je vous lassure.—Mr. de Corny a bien souffert pour sa santé, il ma donné des inquiétudes très vives. Le malheur la vieillesse se peignoient sur son visage. Je le trouve mieux. On na pas encor remboursé sa charge et on ne luy en paye pas même les interets. Degoutez bien toute vos dames de venir en France et assurez les que leur imagination peut seul embellir paris quil ne faut plus venir chercher.

Mr. de Corny est penetre destime pour vous, il vous regrette, et pour luy, et pour moi. Donnez moi vos commissions, donnez en a Mr. de Corny. Lon disoit lautre jour que l'assemblée nationale ne vouloit plus dambassadeurs. Les Cours etrangeres suivroient ce même exemple. Alors chacun naura plus quun agent corresponde[nt]. Si ce roman a lieu, songez a Mr. de Corny. Il aime a soccuper et je le crois plus malheureux de navoir rien a faire que dêtre presque ruiné.

Mr. Short me donne quelquefois de vos nouvelles. Je voudrois qu'il fut possible de ne pas le remplacer. Il me semble qu'il méritte dêtre bien traité. Mais, sil en est autrement, ne madressez pas celuy qui vous succedera. Je crois quil me feroit de la peine de le voir.

Mr. de la fayette justifie bien ladoption quon en a fait en amerique. Cest une prudence, une tranquilité, une perseverance qui le font adorer. Je crois quil ne peut y avoir que les mechans qui [luy] refusent justice. Adieu mon cher Monsieur croyez a mes sentiments pour vous, ils sont inalterables.

Mr. Church est membre du parlement Angelique se porte très bien. Kitty ne mécrit plus. Mais l'essentiel, cest que sa mère soit contente delle et elle l'est.

RC (DLC); unsigned; endorsed as received 20 Nov. 1790 and so recorded in SJL. A separate slip accompanying RC contains the following in TJ's hand: "Me de Corny aux boulevards presque vis-a-vis les bains Chinois Numero 5." Madame de Corny's letter to TJ was that of 25 Nov., not OCTOBRE, 1789.

From Tench Coxe

SIR   Maiden lane. July 23d. 1790

Mr. Matthew Carey of Philadelphia wishes for the honor of conversing with you on the republication of the several treaties of the United States. Tho he cannot expect to insert them in his Museum by your *Authority*, he justly conceives it of great importance that they be strictly true copies. I proposed to have done myself the honor of waiting upon you with him to ask for him the favor of such aid to his object as it might be within your convenience and pleasure to afford; but have been prevented by an application for some papers for the use of the Legislature. I beg leave to say that Mr. Carey's work has received the Sanction of several of the first names in the public and literary line in the united States, and that the republication of the Treaties in the Museum will place them in near two thousand hands in the several States. I have the honor to be, with the most respectful Consideration, Sir Your obedient Servant,   TENCH COXE

RC (DLC); endorsed as received 23 July 1790 and so recorded in SJL.

As a result of this first meeting with Mathew Carey, the *American Museum* or, *Universal Magazine* carried the texts of the definitive treaty of peace of 1783, the treaty of amity and commerce with Prussia of 1785, the consular convention with France of 1788, the treaty with the Creek Indians of 1790, and the Indian treaties negotiated at Hopewell in 1785 and 1786 (Aug. and Oct. issues, 1790, VIII, Appendix 2, p. 18-21, 21-7, 27-31, 50-4, 54-5, 56-7). Only the treaty with Prussia and that with the Creeks were attested by TJ.

To Roger Alden

DEAR SIR   New York July 25. 1790.

I receive this moment your favor of to-day. Tho' I shall ever be pleased with every event which may promote your interests, yet I cannot be without regret altogether that one of the consequences of the advantageous propositions you embrace is that they deprive me of the continuance of your assistance. I have been too short a time in the office to know as yet it's duties myself. It was on the special recommendation of the President of the United states that I appointed you to the direction of it. His judgment in the characters of men is too well known to me to leave a hesitation in my mind to give you a preference over the numerous applications made to me for the same office. And during the four months you have assisted me in it, I have had every reason of gratitude to the President for having so well directed my choice. I thank you for your kind expressions of esteem for me. I assure you they are reciprocal, and that I shall sincerely rejoice in every circumstance which shall give you success and happiness. I am with very sincere esteem & attachment Dr. Sir Your most obedt. and most humble servt.,

TH: JEFFERSON

PrC (DLC).

This letter was in response to Alden's of the same date stating that he was disposed to accept some flattering proposals because his estate was "small, and that little not increased from any compensations . . . received from the public," and that, with TJ's permission, he would resign his post and leave New York the next day. He enclosed some "honorable testimonials" and asked TJ to contribute his own "if . . . favorable impressions or the opinion of others" provided the basis for such (RC in DNA: RG 59, MLR; recorded in SJL as received the same day).

To Nathaniel Anderson

[DE]AR SIR   New York July 25. 1790.

I have duly recieved your two favors of July 12. and 14. I have a good deal of confidence that Harvie's lands may be saved to Sam. Carr notwithstanding the suit. It is very interesting to him that every possible delay be used, because it will give more time to be receiving profits and paying off, and because he may come of age in the mean time and make valid engagements for money to save the lands if that be necessary. Not having Mr. D. Carr's will here I do not know whether Mr. O. Carr and myself are joint guardians, or myself solely. If the latter, say nothing about it; let them run out their tether against Mr. O. Carr, and when he shall have answered that he is no guardian, they will have to amend their bill, and make me defendant. I shall be much obliged to you if you can inform me, what was the original amount of the debts? How much has been paid off? How much can be annually paid off? I have reason to believe the widow has committed waste on the lands by working more hands than she ought to have done on it. If so, she forfeits the lands wasted and treble damages. I forbore to enquire minutely into this and to bring an action as long as she abstained from law: but I will now enquire into it and act accordingly. I shall be in Virginia in September. It is still doubtful whether there will be war between Spain and England. Appearances are in favor of it. If there is, France will probably engage in it. I am with great esteem Dr. Sir your friend & servt., TH: JEFFERSON

PrC (MHi). Anderson's TWO FAVORS OF JULY 12. AND 14. have not been found, but are recorded in SJL as received, respectively, on 20 and 23 July 1790.

From Madame Plumard de Bellanger

ce 25 juillet 1790

MONSIEUR ET RESPECTABLE AMI (AGRÉES CE TITRE)

J'ay étté bien charmée de recevoir de vous une lettre. Impatiente d'apprendre de vos nouvelles, j'en croyois le moment passé. Je croyois qu'un si long trajet de Mer et des objets si agréables pour vous à retrouver avoient effacé quelques sentimens flatteurs pour moi, s'ils avoient jamais existé. Mon Cousin m'ayant écrit au mois de decembre m'apprit les détails de votre arrivée, de laquelle Monsr. Short ne m'avoit dit que votre débarquement en bonne santé. Cette lettre m'apprit aussi les attentions pleines de bonté que vous eûtes pour lui et sa femme. Aucun détail du premier diner qu'il put avoir l'honneur d'aller faire chés vous ne lui avoit échapé. Le soin que vous prîtes de lui cacher le refroidissement que je devois ressentir de son omission longue à m'écrire le touchoit beaucoup, il m'a touché également. Vous presumiés, Monsieur, que mon amitié pour lui se retrouveroit la même lorsque j'apprendrois qu'il n'y avoit pas de sa faute. J'ay jugé par les expressions de sa lettre qu'elle n'avoit pas du être la seule qu'il m'eut écritte, mais je n'en ai pas recu d'autre. Vous ne voulés pas que nous nous haissions, et qui y a-t-il de plus propre à me le rendre interessant que tout le bien que vous avés la bonté de m'en dire. Un éloge de votre part a bien plus de valeur que ceux qu'on entend faire ordinairement. Les marques d'estime dont vous l'honnorés, Monsieur, sont bien propres à lui donner de la considération parmi ses voisins, ses bons voisins qui sont si honnêtes que de me savoir gré d'avoir fait du bien à mon cousin. Cela prouve leur amour pour la bienfaisance. Dans la lettre que vous m'avés fait l'honneur de m'ecrire, il m'a paru que vous croyiés que j'ay mis à fond perdu la pareille somme que je lui ai donnée: je ne l'ai pas fait et je ne puis guère, quelque envie que j'aye de lui procurer de l'aisance, penser à le faire, à cause de l'incertitude de touttes les fortunes en France. Je crois que les finances d'Amérique vont prendre une stabilité qui sera l'effet de la bonne constitution que tous les Etats Unis ont adoptée maintenant. Je verrois avec confiance mon Cousin y mettre des sommes, elles lui seroient d'un plus grand rapport qu'ici, mais je n'ai pas même pu encore retirer mon bien de la main des héritiers de feu mon masi. J'ai avec cela un autre Cousin qui est son frere qui n'a pas moins besoin des mêmes secours. Ces deux frères s'aiment et le vôtre croit sans sujet que son frère de la Martinique va venir le joindre.

J'ay appris avec beaucoup de joye le mariage de Mademoiselle Jefferson; recevés en, je vous prie, Monsieur, mon Compliment sincère. Permettés aussi qu'en lui faisant pareillement compliment je lui souhaitte tout le bonheur dont on peut jouir dans ce lien quand on se convient bien. Mon Cousin, à qui vous avés fait l'honneur d'être de la Noce, m'en a fait part.

Il y avoit un peu de tems lorsque j'ay recu votre lettre, Monsieur, que [je] savois votre acception de la place où votre mérite vous a appelé. Ce qui est un bien pour votre Païs est une perte pour celui ci, et particulierement pour ceux qui avoient l'avantage d'être en connoissance et en societté avec vous. Il n'y a personne qui le sente plus que moi. Je devois vous revoir et vous m'ecrivés une lettre d'adieux. Ah, quelle triste chose que ce mot! Quoy vous avés la bonté de priser tant les témoignages de consideration et d'attache-ment que je vous ay donnés pour me dire que vous en ressouviendrés toutte votre vie, ne pourrés vous plus me donner de vos nouvelles si chères? Ce sera la preuve que vous me tiendrés la parole de ne point m'oublier. Vous me souhaités une longue vie; il ne faut pas faire ce souhait aux personnes malheureuses. Pour vous, dont la conservation est véritablement précieuse, avés vous assés soin de votre santé? Ce cruel mal de tête vous est donc revenu et vous a causé une maladie grave. Croyés plus à la Medecine. Vous avés, dit-on, de bons medecins. N'omettés rien de ce qu'il faut pour prevenir le mal.

Vous êtes, je crois, assés informé de tous les événemens de notre révolution pour que je pense à vous en instruire. Je vous dirai seulement que je vois avec satisfaction notre constitution se consolider. La grande conféderation qui vient de se faire a présenté aux yeux un grand spectacle et à la raison de grands sujets de joye et de securitté pour l'avenir. La lecture que je viens de faire des observations sur la vente des biens Nationaux par Mr. Le Couteux et sur la dette publique me rassurent aussi beaucoup sur la prétendue banqueroutte. Il n'y a que les ennemis de la revolution, qui malheureusement sont en grand nombre, qui cherchent les moyens de la faire faire en l'annonçant.

On va faire ici en Public l'eloge funeraire de Monsr. Franclin. Puissent les grands hommes qui comme lui ont eu part à l'heureuse révolution d'Amérique faire longtems notre admiration et ne nous mettent en deuil qu'après un tems bien eloigné.

Je vous prie de recevoir les assurances des sentimens pleins d'un tendre attachement ainsi que d'une considération distinguée avec lesquels j'ay l'honneur d'etre, Monsieur Votre tres humble et tres obeissante servante PLUMARD BELLANGER

RC (MHi); endorsed by TJ as received 20 Nov. 1790 and so recorded in SJL. See TJ to Madame de Bellanger, 4 Apr. 1790.

On the same day, Madame de Bellanger wrote Derieux: "I consider you very fortunate, my dear cousin, to have won the friendship of such a man as Mr. Jefferson. He collected all the pleasant things your neighbors had said to him about you to tell me in his letter. I see that he has continued all the time that he has been near you to show you the same friendship. He invited you to the wedding of Mademoiselle, his daughter, and perhaps she herself has been to your house. It is in this country a mark of great esteem" (*Correspondence of . . . Comte de Rieux*, ed. Elizabeth Lancaster, privately printed, Richmond, Va., 1913).

To Elizabeth Wayles Eppes

DEAR MADAM   New York July 25. 1790.

Your favor of June the 4th. with Mr. Eppes' of May 30. came to my hands only the 8th of July. Consequently they must have been all the month of June getting from Eppington to Richmond, from which last place they would be but 8. or 9. days coming. I mention this as an apology for being so late in acknowleging their reciept. Patsy has written me on the subject of a maid also, but adds that it will be time enough when we meet at Monticello. She will certainly never want any thing I can add to her convenience. I am in hopes, while in Virginia, to bring about arrangements which may fix her in Albemarle: and that this will be one inducement the more for you to continue to visit that country sometimes. Can you not do it in September, and make us all happy? The season will be mild, and will the better admit of your roughing it, for which you must come prepared. I am sure Maria will vote for the excursion, and will do all she can to lessen your sufferings while at Monticello. I have always thanks to return you on her account: she will live longer to feel what she owes you than I shall. I wish to consult you about her, and this can be best done at Monticello. In hopes of meeting you there then, I conclude with assurances of the warm attachment & respect of dear Madam Your affectionate friend & humble servt.,   TH: JEFFERSON

PrC (MHi). Mrs. Eppes' FAVOR OF JUNE THE 4TH. has not been found, but is recorded in SJL as received 8 July 1790. The letter from PATSY . . . ON THE SUBJECT OF A MAID was probably that of 2 July 1790 (received on the 15th), which is also missing.

To Francis Eppes

DEAR SIR   New York July 25. 1790.

I have duly recieved your favor of May 30. inclosing Mr. Ross's accounts &c. I observe that almost the whole of the balance he makes, results from turning money into tobacco at 20/ and then turning it back again into money at 36/. If there was ever any agreement between Mr. Ross and me to pay him any part of the account in tobacco, it must be paid him in tobacco. But neither justice nor generosity can call for referring any thing to any other scale than that of hard money. Paper-money was a cheat. Tobacco was the counter-cheat. Every one is justifiable in rejecting both except so far as his contracts bind him. I shall carry these papers to Virginia, and there settle the matter.—War or no war, between England and Spain is still a doubtful question. If there be war, France will probably take part in it. This we cannot help, and therefore we must console ourselves with the good price for wheat which it will bring us.—The assumption of the state debts will, I believe, be agreed to; somewhat on the plan mentioned to you in my last. They assume particularly for the state of Virginia the exact quota she will be liable to of the whole sum assumed. But the same justice is not done to the other states. More is given to some, who owed more, and less to others who owed and asked less. It is a measure of necessity. I hope to set out about the beginning of Sep. for Monticello. I am in hopes the season will invite Mrs. Eppes and yourself to make an excursion there, which will make me very happy. It is a society which will ever be dear to me. Adieu, my dear Sir. Your's very affectionately,

TH: JEFFERSON

PrC (DLC). For the attempted settlement of the account of David Ross, see TJ to Ross, 25 Oct. 1790.

To William Temple Franklin

DEAR SIR   New York July 25. 1790.

On a review of the houses you are so kind as to propose to me, I have no hesitation to prefer one of Mr. Lieper's. The part of the town, the price, and the landlord determine me to this: and the latter article is not a small consideration, as you tell me you like the landlord. On my part I can say with truth I never had a pin to cavil with a landlord in my life on quitting a house. I take care of it myself, and exact rigorous care from my servants. While the price of a single tenement encourages me to take one, it is such as will prevent me from taking both. There has never been paid more than 80.£ for an office for my department, and therefore I must endeavor to get one of that price. Confining myself to a single one of these houses, I shall be obliged to appropriate to myself the room over the kitchen, which must therefore be well finished, and at the end of that, externally, to have built another across the whole lot, such as you saw to the house I live in here. This additional room to be supported on pillars below, and no room above it. The breadth should be 14. feet, and as, Mr. Lieper is proprietor of the adjoining lot perhaps he can let it's length extend into that as far as the breadth of the other kitchen extends. It will be no inconvenience to the neighboring tenant, for I conceive those houses to be somewhat as here represented. Suppose A. the one I am to have, and I should prefer it, because it's out-building will front West. Then the additional room will be supported on the pillars 1. 2. 3. and might go on to 5. without incommoding the neighboring tenant. As it is intended for a book room, length becomes important,

[267]

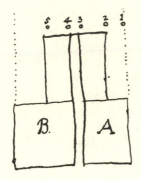

and [we] cannot give it length by running it lengthwise of the tenement instead of across it, for then it would front West. There will be no occasion to derange Mr. Vaughan's views on one of these houses; and indeed if it is intended for his father, I shall be glad of such a neighbor. I wish it may be practicable to divide the two lower rooms otherwise than as you mention. You state them as 20 f. 9 I. and 19 f. 9 I. I should like much better an antichamber in front, of [14.] feet length, and a dining room, back, of [26.] feet long. The breadth 14 f. 3 I. will do for a dining room. But as well as I recollect, the Philadelphians do not place their chimnies at the ends of the rooms as the New Yorkers do, which admits of moving the partition back or forward as one pleases; but I believe in Philadelphia the chimney is in the partition between the two rooms, and hinders their relative dimensions from being varied. If so, we must submit to it. I shall want stables for 5. horses, and a carriage room for 3. carriages.—No seats at the street door to collect lounging servants.—I expect of course a reasonable addition to the rent for the additional book-room. To take a house, built on my own plan, for 10. years, would be wedding myself to the seat of government longer than I would chuse. Were the adjoining lot, on the other side, Mr. Lieper's, perhaps we could agree for a cheap house which might do for the offices, taking however the second floor to myself and also the ground, and adding them to my own rent, so as to leave the residue not more than £80. to the public.—I beg your pardon, my dear Sir, for troubling you with all these details. But I do not mean you should perplex yourself with them, but only hand them on to Mr. Lieper. Should there be a possibility of going to Philadelphia before Congress rises, I will do it. If not, I shall be there about the last of [August] on my way to Virginia, and then can settle all small arrangements about the house. I am with great esteem Dr. Sir Your most obedt. humble servt.,

Th: Jefferson

P.S. On further turning in my mind the idea of a building on the adjacent lot, I find it might accomplish my views perfectly with a very unexpensive building. Two rooms on a floor and two stories high, with doors of communication with the present building, would suffice. In that case I should assign the four rooms of the ground floor for the offices and occupy all the rest of the two tenements myself. The present division of the two rooms below would not need to be altered: but the additional book-room would be differently placed. If the adjoining lot be vacant and belong to Mr. Lieper, I could wish for such a disposition of it. If it belongs to any body else, perhaps they would improve it in this way. The addition of a kitchen, when I should leave it, would render it fit for any other tenant. Could this be effected, I would try hard to come to Philadelphia, and see to the arrangement of it.

PrC (MHi); without indication of addressee, but is a response to Franklin to TJ, 20 July 1790 and is so recorded in sjl; badly faded.

To George Gilmer

DEAR DOCTOR   New York July 25. 1790.

I wrote you last on the 27th. of June. Since that we have had great appearance of an explosion between Spain and England Circumstances still indicate war. The strongest fact against it is that a British Ambassador is actually gone to Madrid. If there be war, France will probably embark in it. I do not think it can disturb her revolution. That is so far advanced as to be out of danger. Be these things as they may, there will be war enough to ensure us great prices for wheat for years to come, and if we are wise we shall become wealthy.—Mc.gillivray and about 30. Creek chiefs are here. We are in hopes this visit will ensure the continuance of peace with them.—The assumption in a proportionate form is likely to pass. The sum to be assumed is 21. millions. Of this 3½ millions are allotted to Virginia, being the exact sum it is supposed she will have to contribute of the whole assumption, and sufficient also to cover the whole of her remaining domestic debt. Being therefore to recieve exactly what she is to pay, she will neither lose nor gain by the measure. The principal objection now is that all the debts, general, and state, will be to be raised by tax on imports, which will thus be overburthened: whereas had the states been left to pay these debts themselves, they could have done it by tax on land and other property, which would thus have lightened the burthen on commerce. However, the measure was so vehemently called for by the state creditors in some parts of the Union, that it seems to be one of those cases where some sacrifice of opinion is necessary for the sake of peace.—Congress will probably rise between the 6th. and 13th. of August. The President will soon after that go to Mount-Vernon: and I will take advantage of the interregnum to see my neighbors in Albemarle and to meet my family there. I suppose it will be the 1st. of Septemb. before I can set out from this place, and shall take that occasion of having my affairs removed hence to Philadelphia. Present me affectionately to Mrs. Gilmer & all my friends. Adieu Dr. Doctor. Your sincere friend & humble servt.,   TH: JEFFERSON

PrC (DLC).

To John Harvie, Jr.

DEAR SIR   New York July 25. 1790.

I received yesterday your favor of July 12. by Mr. Austin and am glad of the occasion it's acknolegement furnishes me of resuming a correspondence which distance and business have long interrupted, but which has never wanted the urgency of motives of sincere friendship on my part. Mr. Austin shall certainly recieve every aid I can give him. That which he asks from Congress I suppose very doubtful. No body can say where such a precedent would carry them. A contract to supply government with the lead it may want I should think him entitled to on principles of sound policy.

It is still uncertain whether there will be war between Spain and England. If there is, France will probably embark in it. Her revolution is so far advanced that it cannot be disturbed by a war. Perhaps it may improve their constitution by adapting it to that circumstance. As yet appearances indicate war, tho there is a leading fact against it, that of a British Ambassador having actually gone to Madrid. Be this as it will, there will be war enough to give us high prices for wheat for years to come; and this single commodity will make us a great and happy nation.—The assumption will I believe pass in the form in which you see it in the publick papers. That is to say a fixed sum will be assumed and divided among the states. The partition is governed by a combination of their census and their circumstances. The greatest proportions by far are given to Massachusets and S. Carolina because they were indebted in a still higher proportion. That Virginia might lose no benefit from the paiments she has made of her domestic debt, they assume for her exactly what it is supposed she will have to furnish of the whole sum assumed. It is imagined too this sum will cover the whole of her remaining domestic debt. To other states which owed and asked less, less is apportioned. With respect to Virginia, the measure is thus divested of it's injustice. It remains liable however to others founded in policy. I have no doubt that the states should be left to do whatever acts they can do as well as the general government; and that they could have availed themselves of resources for this paiment which are cut off from the general government by the prejudices existing against direct taxation in their hands. They must push therefore the tax on imports as far as it will bear, and this is not a proper object to bear all the taxes of a state. However, the impossibility that certain states could ever pay the debts they had contracted, the acknolegement that nine tenths of these debts were contracted for the general defence as much as those contracted by Congress directly, the clamours of the creditors within those states, and the possibility that these might defeat the funding any part of the public debt, if theirs also were not assumed, were motives not to be neglected. I saw the first proposition for this assumption with as much aversion as any man. But the developement of circumstances have convinced me that if it is obdurately rejected, something much worse will happen. Considering it therefore as one of the cases in which mutual sacrifice and accomodation is necessary, I shall see it pass with acquiescence. It is to be observed that the sums to be assumed, are to be on account only. McGillivray and his chiefs are here. We hope good from this visit. Congress I think will adjourn between the 6th. and 13th. of August. The President will very soon after set out for Virginia. I shall avail myself of this interregnum to visit Virginia.

Be so good as to present my best respects to Mrs. Harvie & to be assured yourself of the sincere esteem of Dear Sir Your affectionate friend & humble servt.,   TH: JEFFERSON

PrC (DLC).
The special emphasis given to the expression of friendship here voiced should perhaps be interpreted in the light of the circumstances set forth in TJ's letter to Mrs. Randolph, 17 July 1790 (see note).

To Mary Jefferson

New York July 25. 1790.

No letter from you yet, my dear Maria. You now owe me four, and I insist on you writing me one every week till you shall have paid the debt. I write to you every three weeks, and I think you have quite as little to do as I have, so that I may expect letter for letter. The account stands at present as follows.

Maria Jefferson Dr.		to Th: Jefferson Cr.	
April 11. To letter of this date	1	April 25. By letter of this date	1
May 2. To do. of this date	1		
23. To do. of this date	1	May 23. By do. of this date	1
June 13. To do. of this date	1		
July 4. To do. of this date	1	Balance due T. J.	4
25. To do. of this date	1		—
	—		6
	6		

I am in hopes of seeing you at Monticello early in September, and that your aunt and uncle will find it convenient to come and rough it with us awhile, and to partake of the pudding you are to make for us by way of shewing your skill. However good, be assured it will be a great additional gratification to see that you are improved in Spanish, in writing, in needle work, in good humor, and kind and generous dispositions; and that you grow daily more and more worthy the love of, dear Maria, Your's affectionately,

Th: Jefferson

Tr (MHi).

From Le Veillard

Monsieur   Passy Les Paris 25 Juillet 1790

Je n'ai reçu Votre lettre du 5 avril dernier que le 22 du présent et il y avoit deja longtemps que nous savions la mort de mon amy, de Votre illustre compatriote. La France lui a rendu des honneurs dont le récit doit indubitablement faire mourir de désespoir certaines personnes de Boston.

Peu de temps apres votre départ, Monsieur, on m'a remis, d'après son ordre, 150 pages in folio des mémoires de sa vie jusqu'en 1757. Cette partie n'est peut être pas celle qui plaira le plus à ceux qui ne peuvent être émus que par des évènements qui tiennent immédiatement à la destinée des empires, mais ils auront le plus grand intérest pour ceux qui aiment a voir ce qui les prépare et comment la force d'un grand genie surmonte les circonstances et le mene dans tous ses rapports a la plus haute élévation. Je vous assure, Monsieur, que j'ay singulierement regretté que vous ne fussiez pas en France lorsque j'ay reçu cet intéressant ouvrage. Quoyque monsieur Franklin me recommandat de ne le confier qu'a monsieur de La Rochefoucauld, je l'aurois communiqué sans scrupule, et avec la certitude de n'être pas desaprouvé par l'auteur, à l'homme le plus capable de les apprécier et pour qui je connoissois ses sentimens.

Je savois aussi depuis quelque temps Monsieur que probablement je ne vous reverrois plus, et j'en ai ressenti beaucoup de peine. Malgré la constante uniformité de nos opinions et l'accueil que vous vouliez bien me faire, votre différente maniere d'exister et la crainte que j'ay par dessus toute chose d'être importune ne m'ont pas permis de profiter souvent du bonheur de vous connoitre. Permettez qu'aujourdhuy que je n'ai pas a craindre en vous montrant mes sentimens pour vous, que le desir que vous avez d'obliger ne vous engage a quelque sacrifice en ma faveur, je vous déclare avec la plus grande sincérité que je ne connois personne avec qui j'aimasse mieux passer ma vie, que je vous demande permission de vous le rappeler de temps en temps, et que je vous prie de me faire quelque fois savoir que vous ne m'avez point oublié.

Je vois souvent monsieur Short dans la maison de La Rochefoucauld ou il est parfaitement reçu a cause de luy et a cause de Vous. Nous desirons tous de le garder, cependant je crois que Mr. W.T. Franklin pourroit souhaiter une mission en Europe. Il a le projet d'y venir pour l'édition complette des oeuvres de son ayeul, et sans doute il a des droits pour demander, mais je ne puis solliciter pour luy que dans le cas ou ses prétentions ne contrarieroient pas vos projets.

Notre état est toujours critique. L'assemblée nationale, au milieu des séances les plus tumultueuses, les plus bruyantes et quelquefois même les plus scandaleuses produit une multitude de décrets très sages, mais les finances que les grandes économies déjà statuées peuvent retablir ne sont pas encore reglées, nous n'avons point de force publique pour y parvenir, et faire cesser les desordres et les moyens de surmonter ces difficultés ne sont pas aisés a trouver. Toutes nos ressources de sureté sont réunies sur la seule tête qui s'est déjà si bien montrée chez vous pour pareille cause. Si nous la perdions, personne ne s'entendroit plus et quoyque les intentions de la tres grande pluralité soient uniformes, je ne vois pas par qui ni comment on viendroit a bout de les remplir.

Me. Le Veillard est bien sensible a votre souvenir, elle vous présente ses complimens, et mes enfans y joignent leurs respects.

Voulez vous bien agréer les assurances du respectueux et inviolable attachement avec lequel je suis, Monsieur, Votre tres humble et tres obeissant serviteur,   LE VEILLARD

RC (MoSHi); endorsed as received 22 Nov. 1790 and so recorded in SJL.
For TJ's earlier correspondence with Le Veillard concerning Franklin's MEM-OIRES, see TJ to Le Veillard, 9 May 1786 and enclosures.

To Thomas Mann Randolph, Jr.

DEAR SIR   New York July 25. 1790.

This being my week of writing to Maria, I should not have troubled you but to inclose the copy of a letter I write this day to Colo. Randolph. You see that I have taken great liberties in hazarding ideas on which you ought to have been previously consulted: however I do it in such a way as to leave them open for your correction, and when we meet at Monticello, the arrangements may be finally put into such a shape as may suit all. Congress will probably rise between the 6th. and 13th. of August, and I may set out for Virginia about a fortnight after their adjournment. A quotaed assumption, which will leave Virginia to pay exactly what she will recieve, will probably be agreed to. No certainty yet of war between Spain and England. Present my best love to Martha and be assured of the esteem of Dear Sir Your's sincerely & affectionately,
                                              TH: JEFFERSON

RC (DLC). PrC (CSmH). TJ made two press copies of the following letter, and evidently enclosed one of them in this.

To Thomas Mann Randolph

DEAR SIR   New York July 25. 1790.

It is not till now that I begin to relinquish the hope you had given me of visiting New York this summer. Besides the pleasure on which I had counted, of seeing you here, I had proposed to see whether we could not arrange together a matter which our children have at heart. I find it is the strong wish of both to settle in Albemarle. They both consider Varina as too unhealthy, a consideration too important, nor to overbear every other. Besides I have always believed it better to be settled on a small farm, just sufficient to furnish the table, and to leave one's principal plantations free to pursue the single object of cropping without interruption. You expressed a disposition to sell to Colo. Harvie a part of your Edgehill lands, 600. acres I believe, at 30/ the acre. It is of less consequence to him, than to your son, to be the purchaser. Suppose then you let your son have this, or even a smaller quantity on the same terms proposed by Colo. Harvie. It will suffice as a farm to furnish his table with every necessary and himself with occupation and amusement. I should propose to him in that case to make use of the house at Monticello, which would relieve him from the necessity of building and furnishing a house for some years, and enable him to abandon the profits of Varina to the paying you for the farm in Albemarle; and perhaps he could not effect this sooner than by leaving that in your hands awhile. To these means of making the paiment to you, I will add any assistance in my power, which shall be arranged between us on my return to Virginia this autumn; and my wishes to arrange this settlement for him are so strong as to engage me to every thing necessary to render it agreeable and convenient to you.—In the short conversation I had with you the morning I left Richmond you mentioned that you meant to have your daughters portions raised by the sale of the Edgehill lands, and that to add these to what you had given, and destined to give him, would be injustice to your other children. I will never, on any consideration, wish an injustice to them, even in his favor. But if it be possible to save for him so valuable and convenient a tract of land, he paying the daughters portions, I think it desireable for all parties. And this I think can be arranged among us on my return, without deranging any view you have as to those lands. I think that Mr. Randolph, occupying the house and appendages at Monticello, furnishing his table &c. from the farm I have proposed he should purchase from you immediately, and his other expences from his plantation at Poplar Forest, would be so much at his ease, that he could appropriate all the profits of Varina to the accomplishment of our wishes respecting Edgehill. Think of this, my dear Sir, and write me a line on the subject. If it leaves Richmond before the 12th. of August it will surely find me here. I do not know but that I may set out to Virginia the latter part of that month, but pretty certainly by the beginning of September. I wish it may be possible for you to come and spend a few days with us at Monticello. It will compleat a circle which will fill up the measure of my happiness.—We are still uncertain here whether the war between Spain and England will take place. It seems rather probable. France will certainly take part in it. This will ensure great prices for wheat many years. I believe the assumption will take place in the form in which you now see it in the public papers. It has been so shaped, principally to quiet Massachusets and S. Carolina the two states most in need of it, and Virginia the most opposed to it on account of the great progress she has made in paying her debt. The sum assumed for her will pay all her remaining debt, and it is exactly the quota she will have to contribute of the whole sum assumed. So that she will neither gain nor lose. Present my best esteem to your family and believe me to be with the most sincere attachment, my Dear Sir Your affectionate friend & humble servt.,

TH: JEFFERSON

PrC (MHi). Another PrC (DLC); badly faded (see note to preceding letter).

From Benjamin S. Barton

SIR   Philadelphia, July. 26th: 1790.

I take the liberty of enclosing to you a paper of *Proposals* for a work which I have been engaged in writing, for some considerable time, and which is now nearly ready for publication. I am confident your *name*, Sir, as a subscriber, will add not a little to the consequence and success of my undertaking, and as you have long distinguished yourself as a friend of literature, I have ventured to request *it*.

You will observe, Sir, from the title of the work, that the subjects which it involves are both curious and important:—how far it may be worthy of the public attention, time must determine; as it embraces, however, a variety of new and striking facts, I flatter myself, it may be of service.

Unknown, as I am, to you, I cannot but apologize for the liberty of this letter: but, my apology I have already hinted at; the importance of your name to an undertaking of this nature, in the New:World. I have the honour to be, with the greatest respect, Sir, your very humble Servt.,   B. S. BARTON

RC (MHi); endorsed as received 28 July 1790 and so recorded in SJL.

From James Monroe

DEAR SIR   Charlottesville July 26. 1790.

A few days past your favor of June 11. was presented me by your relation Mr. G. Jefferson expressive of your friendly and benevolent wishes toward that young gentleman. Colo. Lewis is on a visit to Bedford, so that whatever depends on him will remain in suspense, untill his return, which will be in a few days. In the interim he will remain with me, and indeed untill he shall be comfortably establish'd in the neighbourhood. Be assur'd I shall be happy to render him every possible service in my power, being gratified with an opportunity of shewing my regard to whomever you may wish to possess it, especially so near a connection of your own.

Tis reported here that the subject of residence has received a final decision, which has terminated in favor of the head waters of the Potowk. as the permanent, and Phila. as the temporary seat. The precise modification has not reach'd us: if they have not plac'd it too high up the country in the 1st. instance, suffer'd it to remain too long in Phila. in the next, and left the erection of the buildings in some measure dependent on subsequent votes of Congress, I shall heartily approve of it. If they have plac'd the latter business under the direction of the Executive it will most probably succeed. If this interesting subject has been clos'd in the manner represented to us, and shall be *bona fide* executed, I shall consider it as a liberal and magnanimous trait in the operations of the government which will do those who discharge its functions the highest credit. And altho' I did not expect upon this subject, from their former conduct on it, such a decision, yet as nature has pass'd no inhibiting law to the contrary, I shall conclude it is the case. I am sincerely your affectionate friend & servant,   JAS. MONROE

RC (DLC); endorsed as received 7 Aug. 1790 (the day TJ also received Monroe's letter of 18 July 1790), and so recorded in SJL.

To William Short

DEAR SIR   New York July 26. 1790.

My publick letters to you have been of the 28th. of March, the 6th. and 30th. of April. Yours, which remain to be acknowledged, are of Mar. 9. 17. 29. Apr. 4. 12. 23. and May 1. being from

No. 21. to 28. inclusive except No. 23. which had come to hand before.[1] I will state to you the dates of all your letters received by me with the times they have been recieved, and length of their passage.

date		received		length of passage
Jan.	12	April	5	83 days
	23		17	84.
	23	May.	27	124.
Feb.	10		27	106.
Mar.	3	May	5	63
	4		5	62
	9	June	10	93
	17		10	85
	25	May	25	61.
	29	June	15	78.
Apr.	4		17	74.
	12		17	66
	23	July	12	80
May.	1		20	81.

You will percieve that they average eleven weeks and a half, that the quickest are of 9. weeks and the longest are of near 18. weeks coming. Our information thro' the English papers is of about 5. or 6. weeks, and we generally remain as long afterwards in anxious suspence till the receipt of your letters may enable us to decide what articles of those papers have been true. As these come principally by the English packet, I will take the liberty of asking you to write always by that packet, giving a full detail of such events as may be communicated thro that channel. And indeed most may. If your letters leave Paris 9. or 10. days before the sailing of the packet we shall be able to decide, on the moment, on the facts true or false, with which she comes charged. For communications of a secret nature you will avail yourself of other conveyances, and you will be enabled to judge which are best by the preceding statement. News from Europe is very interesting at this moment, when it is so doubtful whether a war will take place between our two neighbors.

Congress have passed an act for establishing the seat of government on the Potowmac[2] from the year 1800. and in the mean time to remove to Philadelphia. It is to that place therefore that your future letters had better be addressed. They have still before them the bill for funding the public debts. That has been hitherto

delayed by a question whether the debts contracted by the particular states for general purposes should at once be assumed by
the general government. A developement of circumstances and more
mature consideration seem to have produced some change of opinion
on the subject. When it was first proposed a majority was against
it. There is reason to believe by the complexion of some later votes,
that the majority will now be for assuming these debts to a fixed
amount. 21. millions of dollars are proposed. As soon as this point
is settled, the funding bill will pass, and Congress will adjourn.
That adjournment will probably be between the 6th. and 13th. of
August: they expect it sooner. I shall then be enabled to inform
you ultimately on the subject of the French debt, the negociations
for the paiment of which will be referred to the Executive and
will not be retarded by them an unnecessary moment. [A bill is
past authorising the President to raise the salary of the Chargé
des affaires to 4500. dollars, from the 1st. day of July last. I
am authorised by him to inform you that yours will accordingly
be at that rate, and that you will be allowed for gazettes, translating
or printing papers where that shall be necessary, postage, couriers,
and necessary aids to poor American *sailors*, in addition to the
salary, and no charge of any other description except where you
may be directed to incur it expressly. I have thought it would be
most agreeable to you to give you precise information, that you
may be in no doubt in what manner to state your accounts. Be
pleased to settle your account down to the 1st. of July last, and
state the balance then due which will be to be paid out of the
former fund.]³ From that day downwards a new account must be
opened, because a new fund is appropriated to it from that time.
The expences for the medals directed in my letter of April 30.
must enter into the new account. As I presume the dye will be
finished by the time you recieve this, I am to desire you will have
a medal of gold struck for the Marquis de la Luzerne, and have
put to it a chain of 365 links, each link containing gold of the
value of two dollars and a half, or 13. livres 10. sous. The links
to be of plain wire, so that their workmanship may cost as it were
nothing. The whole will make a present of a little more than 1000
dollars, including the medal and chain. As soon as done, be pleased
to forward them by a safe hand to the Marquis de la Luzerne in
the name of the President of the United states, informing him that
it is the one spoken of in my letter to him of April 30. 1790. Say
nothing to any body of the value of the present, because that will

not always be the same in all cases. Be so good as to have a second medal of gold struck in the same dye and to send this second, together with the dyes, to Philadelphia by the first safe person who shall be passing. No chain to be sent with this.

We are impatient to learn the progress and prospect of the Algerine business. Do not let it languish a moment, nor leave us a moment uninformed of any thing relative to it. It is in truth a tender business, and more felt as such in this than in any other country.—The suppression of the farms of tobacco, and the free importation of our salted provisions will merit all your attention. They are both of them objects of first-rate importance to us.

The following appointments of Consuls have taken place.
Joseph Fenwick, Consul for Bordeaux.
Burrell Carnes do. for Nantes.
Nathan'l. Barrett do. for Rouen.
Steph. Cathalan the youngr. Vice-Consul for Marseilles.
Monsr. de la Motte. do. for Havre.
Sylvanus Bourne. Consul for Hispaniola.
Fulwar Skipwith do. for Martinique.
James Maury do. for Liverpool.
Thomas Auldjo. Vice-Consul for Cowes.
William Knox. Consul for Dublin.
John Parish. Vice Consul for Hamburgh.
Edward Church. Consul for. Bilboa.
John Marsden Pintard. Consul for [Made]ira.

Their jurisdictions in general extend to all places within the same allegiance which are nearer to them than to the residence of any other Consul or Vice-Consul. As yet only their commissions have been made out. General instructions await the passage of a bill now depending. Mr. La forest at this place remarked our appointment of Consuls in the French islands. In the first project of a Convention proposed on the part of France, the expressions reached expressly to the kingdom of France only. I objected to this in writing as being narrower than the 29th. article of the treaty of amity, which was the basis of the Consular convention and which had granted the appointment of consuls and viceconsuls in their respective 'states and ports' generally and without restriction. On this the word 'France' was struck out and the 'dominions of the M.C.K.' inserted every where. See the 5th. 9th. 12th. 13th. and 15th. articles particularly, of the copy of the draughts of 1784. and 1788. as I had them printed side by side. The object of this alteration was the appointment of Consuls in the freeports allowed us in the French West-Indies, where our commerce has greater need of protection than anywhere. I mention these things that you may be prepared, should any thing be said to you on the subject. I am persuaded the appointment will contribute eminently to the preservation of harmony between us. These consuls will be able to prevent the misunderstandings which arise frequently now between the officers there and our traders, and which are doubtless much exaggerated and misrepresented to us by the latter.

I duly recieved the copy you were so kind as to send me of the Bishop of Autun's proposition on the subject of weights and measures. It happened to arrive in the moment I was about giving in to Congress a report on the same subject which they had referred to me. In consequence of the Bishop of Autun's proposition I made an alteration in my report substituting 45.° instead of 38.° which I had at first proposed as the standard latitude. I[4] send you a copy of my report for the Bishop, and another for M. Condorcet, Secretary of the Academy of sciences. By taking the second pendulum or rod of the same latitude for the basis of our measures, it will at least furnish a common measure to which both our systems will refer, provided our experiments on the pendulum or rod of 45.° should yield exactly the same result with theirs.

The newspapers as usual will accompany the present which is to go by Mr. Barrett. I have the honor to be with great esteem and attachment Dear Sir Your most obedient & most humble servt.,

TH: JEFFERSON

RC (DLC: Short Papers); endorsed by Short (three times) as received 24 Sep. 1790. FC (DNA: RG 59, PCC No. 121). For note on printed text of enclosed copies of report on weights and measures, see under 4 July 1790.

The SECOND MEDAL OF GOLD was intended for De Moustier, but in asking that it be sent to Philadelphia TJ was fully aware that the French minister would not return to America: the request was obviously a device to conceal the true circumstances of De Moustier's recall. The medal, however, was not finished in time and so was presented by Short in France (see TJ to De Moustier, 2 Mch. 1791; TJ to Short, 8 Mch. 1791; Short to TJ, 8 Feb. 1792).

1 TJ first wrote: ". . . except No. 23. between those of Mar. 17 and 29 which had not yet come to hand," and then altered the passage to read as above. No. 23 was that of 25 Mch., received 25 May 1790.

2 TJ first wrote "at Georgetown" (FC reads thus) and then altered it to read as above.

3 The paragraph in brackets (supplied) was repeated in the letter from TJ to Carmichael, 6 Aug. 1790.

4 At this point in RC TJ placed an asterisk and at the bottom of page wrote: "sent by Mr. Barrett."

To William Short

DEAR SIR   New York July 26. 1790.

My publick letter of this date will convey to you public information and there is little of a private nature which the newspapers will not give you. Your last letter to me was of Mar. 25. and was acknoleged in mine of May 27. Since that I have written you three short letters of June 6. July 1. and 8. to apprize you of the removal of government from hence to Philadelphia on the bare possibility they might get in time to change the destination of Petit and my furniture to Philadelphia instead of this place. Be so good as to make my acknoledgements to the club des quatre vingts dix for the honor of their choice of me as a member. Other destinations will prevent the President, Dr. Franklin and myself from the honour of meeting them in person, so you must make the compliments of us all.

A minister will be sent to Paris, but to this moment I do not know who it will be. A conversation with the President today convinces me he has not made up his mind; that he is even undecided whether he will name one immediately, or put it off to December. As the Senate will sit but a few days longer, my next will inevitably inform you whether you will be relieved this fall or the next spring. Make up your mind to come and enter sturdily on the public stage. I now know the characters on it, and assure you candidly you may be any thing you please at home or abroad as soon as you shall make yourself known and possess yourself of American affairs. We are extremely puzzled to find characters fit for the offices which need them.[1] The President pays a visit to Mount Vernon soon. I shall to Monticello. Adieu. Yours affectionately.

RC (ViW); at head of text: "Private"; unsigned; partly in code, with interlinear decoding in Short's hand; endorsed as received 23 Oct. 1790. PrC (DLC); accompanied by the text *en clair* on a separate sheet for the coded passage.

TJ erred in referring to the QUATRE VINGTS DIX club (see Short to TJ, 28 Jan. 1790): the "Société de 89" was founded by Lafayette to provide his followers with "un centre de concert et d'action . . . où les députés et les nouvellistes frayaient avec les grands seigneurs et les banquiers. Il [Lafayette] ne dédaigneit pas les hommes à gages: quand les démocrates s'emancipèrent, il publia des feuilles de combat et une claque remplit les tribunes de l'Assemblée" (Georges Lefebvre, Raymond Guyot, and Philippe Sagnac, *La Revolution Française*, Vol. XIII of *Peuples et civilisations*, Paris, 1930, p. 42; see also Catalogue of the Lafayette exhibition, Archives Nationales, Paris, 1957, p. 69, article signed Marcel Reinhard). In commenting to Washington on the probability of a counter revolution by the aristocrats, Lafayette remarked: "I am rather more concerned with a division that rages in the popular party. The Clubs of the Jacobines, and *89* it is called, have divided the friends of liberty who accuse each other, Jacobines being taxed with a disorderly extravagance, and *89* with a tincture of ministerialism and ambition. I am endeavouring to bring about a reconciliation" (Lafayette to Washington, 23 Aug. 1790, *Letters of Lafayette to Washington, 1777-1799*, ed. Louis Gottschalk, privately printed, N.Y., 1944, p. 349-50).

1 All of the preceding part of this paragraph is written in code; the passage is supplied from TJ's text *en clair* and has been verified by the Editors, employing a partially reconstructed key for Code No. 10.

From George Washington

United States July 26th 1790

The President of the United States transmits to the Secretary of State, to report thereon, a memorial of Monsr. de le tombe, Consul of France, to the Legislature of Massachusetts, respecting certain parts of the Consular Convention agreed upon by and between his most Christian Majesty and the President of the United States, together with a Resolution of that Legislature upon said memorial; and a letter from Governor Hancock to the President enclosing said Memorial and Resolution.—And

A Representation, addressed to the President and Senate of the United States, from many Merchants and Inhabitants of the Commonwealth of Massachusetts, of the inconveniencies resulting to Americans who settle in the French West India Islands, from the Droit d'aubaine prevailing against them there;—and praying an interference on the part of the United States with the Court of France on this subject. Four other papers attesting the facts stated in the Representation accompany it.

RC (DLC); in a clerk's hand. Not recorded in SJL. Enclosures: (1) John Hancock to Washington, 20 July 1790, referring to him the following documents (RC in DLC: TJ Papers, 56: 9629; address cover, postmarked "BOSTON. JULY 20" and endorsed by TJ "Consular convention. Explanatory law," is in same, 236: 42387). (2) Memorial of Philippe de Létombe, French consul at Boston, to the Massachusetts legislature, 7 June 1790, enclosing a text of the Consular Convention of 1788 and stating that Article IX empowering him to arrest deserters from French vessels and send them back is in conformity with two laws passed by the legislature at his request 6 Mch. 1782 and 2 Mch. 1787, but that the stipulation setting them at liberty and holding them immune from further arrest if not returned within three months has "an inconvenience . . . particular to the climate and temperature of this State where no French Vessell hardly ever comes in from the month of November till the month of March or April" because of storms; that, as a French naval fleet had entered Boston every year since 1787 in August or September and remained until October or November, this Article produced another "difficulty of a greater magnitude for this State especially," one that would be exacerbated in time of war owing to the increased numbers of squadrons or vessels entering and to the impossibility of sending their deserters back, which might "operate as an insurmountable bar to their coming here in future" and thereby be prejudicial to the interests of France and to the trade, agriculture, and industry of Massachusetts; that, in consequence, he requests that a law be passed to the effect that "the Deserters from any French Vessel whatsoever shall after having been duly claimed by the Consul or his Vice Consul before one of the Justices of the peace be committed to Jail, at the expence of the said Consul and sent back to France or the French Islands . . . by the first opportunity"; that Article XII, empowering the Consul to decide all differences and suits between French subjects, especially those pertaining to wages and terms of engagement of crews of French vessels, presents another local difficulty by failing to provide for the execution of such judgments in Massachusetts and he therefore requests the legislature to order "That the Consul of France or his Vice Consul shall have within this Commonwealth the coercive authority necessary to compel a compliance with his own Decrees, that is, by applying to any Sheriff, Constable, or other executive officer of this Commonwealth"; that he considers this request "to be right and just—right because the Convention cannot have granted him an illusory power; Just because the authority of determining gives necessarily the authority of causing the judgment to be put in execution"; that he "believes, in this case, that the Convention being expressed in general terms, has left implicitly to every State of the Union the right to prescribe the mode of executing the said Convention, that mode being particular to each State relative to their laws and customs and to their individual interests"; that he "has taken, on those difficulties, the advice of eminent persons in this State, and he will add to that authority, that the Convention being a reciprocal contract between the two nations, friends and allies, no inconveniences can result from the extension of any of these clauses, but on the contrary, that the extension cannot but corroborate the good understanding and the common interests of the two contracting nations especially this local extension or rather that confirmation of the federal will being pronounced by a State itself Sovereign and independent"; and that he therefore "humbly hopes that such laws will be enacted as your Honors wisdom shall concieve to be proper on the occasion" (Tr in DLC: TJ Papers, 55: 9357-9, in French and English in parallel columns, attested by John Avery, Jr.). (3) Resolution of the senate and house of representatives of Massachusetts, 24 June 1790, requesting the governor to transmit the memorial of Létombe to the president of the United States that he might "take such order thereon as the importance of the subject justly deserves" (Tr in DLC: TJ Papers, 55: 9490, signed by Samuel Phillips, president of the senate, and David Cobb, speaker of the house of representatives; attested by John Avery, Jr.).

To Nathaniel Barrett

SIR   New York July 27. 1790.

I have duly recieved your favor of the 18th. I thank you for the information you give me relative to the present state of our whale fishery, and shall be glad to recieve the further information of Mr. Jones. I do not apprehend any danger of our privileges as to whale oil in France being put on a worse footing than they now are, unless it be caused by some act of our own legislature, of which I am not without fear. I shall be obliged to you, while in France, to watch particularly the state of the fisheries of France and England, and to procure for me if possible, and forward to me annually, as exact a statement as you can get of every year's equipments, expressing the number of seamen employed, the number and tonnage of the vessels in each fishery.

I trouble you with two packages for Mr. Short, the smallest being the most important. The larger contains newspapers, and also some letters covering Consular commissions. If you do not go directly to Paris yourself, I believe they may be trusted by the post of that country. Wishing you a safe and pleasant voyage I am with great esteem Dear Sir Your most obedt. humble servt.,

TH: JEFFERSON

P.S. General instructions to the Consuls await the passage of a bill now depending on that subject.

PrC (DLC). Enclosures: The public and private letters to Short of 26 July 1790, with the package containing newspapers and letters to consuls.

A letter from Barrett to TJ of 3 Aug. 1790 is recorded in SJL as received on the 9th, but it has not been found. On 11 Aug. 1790 TJ acknowledged this letter and added: "I . . . now inclose you further letters for Mr. Short. The smaller one is so important that I wish it to go thro' no hand but your own, or one you can as fully rely on.—In case of your absence at any time, from Rouen, it would be proper to leave an Agent.—An indisposition obliges me to add nothing more than wishes for a good passage & assurances of . . . esteem" (PrC in DLC). The further letters to Short enclosed in this were the private and public letters of 9 and 10 Aug. 1790 respectively, of which the latter was the one deemed by TJ to be of such importance. With these TJ also sent his letter of 11 Aug. 1790 to Thomas Auldjo of Cowes, reading: "This letter will be delivered you by Mr. Nathaniel Barrett, consul of the U.S. for Rouen. As he will land at Cowes and cross the channel from thence, I take the liberty of introducing him to your acquaintance, and the rather as, from the neighborhood of your positions, you may sometimes perhaps have occasion to correspond. I take for granted you will have received a letter from me covering a commission in which the President wished you might find it convenient to act for the U.S. at your port" (PrC in DLC).

To Ferdinand Grand, Jr.

DEAR SIR   New York July 27. 1790.

I did not arrive at this place till the last of March, and an illness which came on me soon after put it long out of my power to attend to any business. I have at length obtained information on the subject of the loan office certificates which you desired me to enquire after. This is contained in the inclosed papers, and being stated by a person more familiar with the subject than I am, I shall not undertake any additional explanations. I have written to Mr. Smith, loan-officer of Pennsylvania, to know whether Mr. Holker has received any of the interest on the new certificates, and tho I have not yet his answer, it is probable I may be able to get it to you as early as the present letter, which goes by Mr. Barrett, appointed Consul for Rouen. If I can be of further use to you in this business I shall be so with pleasure, as far as the duties of a laborious office will permit, and a general resolution to have nothing to do with the reciept or paiment of money not my own, or the opening an account. Be so good as to present me affectionately to Mr. and Mrs. Grand the mother and daughter, and to accept yourself assurances of the esteem & attachment with which I have the honor to be Dr. Sir Your most obedt. & most humble servt.,   TH: JEFFERSON

PrC (DLC); at foot of text and in SJL entry the recipient is identified as "Mr. Grand junr." See Grand to TJ, 7 Sep. 1789; TJ to Smith, 27 July 1790.

From Madame d'Enville

LaRocheguyon ce 27 juillet 1790.

Si j'étois amériquain, Monsieur, et dans votre gouvernement je n'aurois pas hésité a vous y donner une place, mais françoise a deux mille lieuës de votre pays je n'ai pu apprendre sans une peine sensible que je vous avois dit un éternel adieu. Je ne perdrai jamais le Souvenir de tout le bien que Vous procuriez a mon âme lorsque j'avois le bonheur de Vous voir Versailles pendant les premiers orages de notre nouvelle constitution. Nous parlons souvent de vous avec M. Schordt; nous desirons vivement de le conserver ici. Un jeune homme formé sous vos yeux ne peut être qu'infiniment intéressant; nous l'aimons tous beaucoup; laissez-le nous pour notre consolation. Il joint a la gayeté de la jeunesse la Solidité d'un âge beaucoup plus avancé.

Je crois comme vous, Monsieur, que tout citoyen qui vous ressemble doit adopter sans hésister toutes les fonctions que l'autorité publique veut lui assigner, mais je crois aussi que si les hommes très ordinaires ou d'une mauvaise valeur savoient s'aprécier ils n'ambitionneroient point des places ou les vertus et les lumières sont de première nécessité. Croyez vous que le perfectionnement de la nature humaine puisse monter a cette élévation? Quel beau Spectacle ce seroit pour lors, qu'une assemblée nationale! Je souhaiterois que tous les membres qui la composent pratiquassent aussi bien que vous votre excellente morale. Nous n'aurions pas eu les momens de crise que nous avons éprouvés; la belle conduite de M. de la Fayette nous en a beaucoup sauvé. Ce jour peut-être un peu précoce de la fédération s'est passé avec un ordre et une tranquillité qui a déconcerté tous les pamphlets et tous les propos qui annonçoient les plus grands troubles. Lorsque notre constitution sera entièrement perfectionnée et la Subordination rétablie je crois que la terre n'aura jamais eu, malgré les horreurs que nous avons éprouvées, une révolution terminée a moins de frais, mais ce tems n'est pas arrivé; on ne peut encore prévoir le terme de l'assemblée, nous allons cependant entrer dans le quinzième mois.

Vos prédictions, quoique bien plus favorables que celles de Jérémie, ne sont pas encore entièrement vérifiées quoiqu'elles Soutiennent mes espérances par mon extrême confiance en vous.

Non; Dieu n'a point fait l'homme dans sa colère, cette passion nous appartient et nous la lui prêtons. Si nous suivions constament notre raison nous serions toujours bons, mais les passions de douze cens personnes l'obscurcisse quelquefois. Je fais les mêmes Souhaits que Vous en faveur de toute l'Europe et je me flâte que Vous aurez le bonheur d'apprendre que Votre exemple lui a rendu la liberté. Je ne Vous parle point en détail des nouvelles de l'assemblée, M. Short vous en instruit mieux que je ne pourrois faire. Je me contente de Vous assurer, Monsieur, que je desire passionnément de mériter l'opinion que Vous voulez bien avoir de moi, aucun Suffrage ne me paroît aussi flâteur; c'est avec ces Sentimens que je vous prie d'être persuadé, Monsieur, de la profonde estime et de la Vénération avec lesquelles j'ai l'honneur d'être Votre très humble et très obéissante servante,   LAROCHEFOUCAULD D'ENVILLE

RC (DLC); endorsed as received 20 Nov. 1790 and so recorded in SJL.

To Thomas Smith

Sir   New York July 27. 1790.

On the 5th. of May 1789. Mr. Holker recieved from you new loan-office certificates to the amount of 43,646 dollars specie value for 405,100 dollars paper value which had been burnt in his house. These certificates are issued in his name; but the property of them is in himself jointly with Messrs. Le Coulteulx & co. and Ferdinand Grand. The latter has desired me to enquire whether Mr. Holker has recieved any and what sum of interest on these certificates. Your information on this subject will oblige me, as I am about writing to Mr. Grand on the subject. I am happy to have this occasion of renewing an antient acquaintance with you, and of assuring you of the esteem with which I have the honor to be Sir Your most obedt. humble servt.,   TH: JEFFERSON

PrC (DLC).
Smith replied to the above on 29 July 1790; his letter, recorded in SJL as received two days later, has not been found.

Opinion on McGillivray's Monopoly of Commerce with Creek Indians

July 29. 1790.

Colo. Mc.Gillivray, with a company of British merchants, having hitherto enjoyed a monopoly of the commerce of the Creek nation, with a right of importing their goods, duty-free, and considering these privileges as the principal sources of his power over that nation, is unwilling to enter into treaty with us, unless they can be continued to him. And the question is how this may be done consistently with our laws, and so as to avoid just complaints from those of our citizens who would wish to participate of the trade?

Our citizens, at this time, are not permitted to trade in that nation. The nation has a right to give us their peace, and to withhold their commerce, to place it under what monopolies or regulations they please. If they insist that only Colo. Mc.Gillivray and his company shall be permitted to trade among them, we have no right to say the contrary. We shall even gain some advantage in substituting citizens of the U.S. instead of British subjects, as associates of Colo. McGillivray, and excluding both British and Spaniards from tha[t] country.

Suppose then it be expressly stipulated by treaty, that no person be permitted to trade in the Creek country, without a licence from the President, that but a fixed number shall be permitted to trade there at all,[1] and that the[2] goods, imported for and sent to the Creek nation, shall be duty free. It may further be either expressed that the persons licensed shall be approved by the leader or leaders of the nation, or without this, it may be understood between the President and Mc.Gillivray that the stipulated number of licenses shall be sent to him blank, to fill up. A treaty made by the President with the concurrence of two thirds of the Senate, is a law of the land, and a law of superior order, because it not only repeals past laws, but cannot itself be repealed by future ones.[3] The treaty then will legally controul the duty-act, and the act for licensing traders, in this particular instance.—When a citizen applies for a license who is not of Mc.Gillivray's partnership, he will be told that but a given number could be licensed by the treaty, and that the number is full.—It seems that in this way no law will be violated, and no just cause of complaint will be given: on the contrary the treaty will have bettered our situation, tho' not in the full degree which might have been wished. TH: JEFFERSON

MS (DNA: RG 59, MLR); entirely in TJ's hand; addressed "The President of the United States"; endorsed by Washington: "29th. July Respecting the Treaty negotiating with the Creek Indns." PrC (DLC); with supplementary note not in RC or FC (see note 3 below). FC (DNA: RG 59, SDC).

Coming from a foe of monopoly and from one solicitous for the rights of states even when the national authority was unequivocal (see TJ's opinion on the Yazoo grants, 3 May 1790), this remarkable opinion places TJ's broad construction of the treaty power squarely in line with a long series of decisions beginning with Marshall in *Ware* v. *Hylton* (3 Dallas 199 [1796]). Indeed, not until *Missouri* v. *Holland* (252 U.S. 416 [1920]) was the position here assumed by TJ given its fullest validation, for the object was not only to legitimatize a monopoly but to accomplish this by treaty when it could not be done by statute. Marshall himself did not fail to note this opinion when, under other circumstances, TJ came to hold a more restricted view of the treaty power (Marshall, *Washington*, V, ch. ix; Gibbs, *Administrations of Washington and John Adams*, I, 308; TJ's memorandum of cabinet discussion, 21 Nov. 1793; TJ to Madison, 27 Mch. 1796; TJ to Madison, 31 May 1798). Federalists seized upon Marshall's reference to the above opinion and there is no doubt that their barbs penetrated. One of these, over the pseudonym *B* in the *National Intelligencer* of 24 Feb. 1816, caused TJ to draft a rebuttal signed *A* and to assume the further disguise of one who had been a member of Congress in 1790 and also at the time Jay's Treaty was under discussion. In this defense he argued that Marshall had quoted "two or three little lines only" of the above opinion and added: "if we could see the whole opinion, it might probably appear that it's foundation was the peculiar circumstances of the Creek nation. We may say too, on this opinion, as on that of a judge whose positions beyond the limits of the case before him are considered as obiter sayings, never to be relied on as authority" (MS dated 13 Mch. 1816, DLC, entirely in TJ's hand). (TJ's article, signed *A*, was published in the *National Intelligencer*, 18 Mch. 1816.)

But the above opinion became the basis of authority immediately. On 4 Aug. 1790 Washington sent a message to the Senate pointing out that the treaty with the Creeks caused "much embarrassment" owing to the fact that the trade of that nation was "almost exclusively in the hands of a company of british Merchants, who by agreement make their importation of Goods from England into the Spanish ports." Washington then revealed the extent of the dilemma and the solution offered by TJ: "As the trade of the Indians is a main mean of their political arrangement, it is therefore obvious that the United States cannot possess any security for the performance of treaties with the Creeks, while their trade is liable to be interrupted or withheld at the caprice of two foreign powers. Hence it becomes an object of real importance to form new channels for the Commerce of the Creeks through the United States. But this operation will require time, as the present arrangements can not be suddenly broken without the greatest violation of faith and morals.—It therefore appears to be important to form a secret Article of a treaty similar to the one which accompanies this message." The accompanying draft of such an article provided that the commerce necessary for the Creeks should be carried on through "the Ports and by the Citizens of the United States," if arrangements could be made before 1 Aug. 1792. In the meantime the contracting parties agreed to permitting existing arrangements to continue, except that, in case of war or prohibitions by Spain, any interruption could be countered by appointment of particular persons to carry on trade through the United States to the Creeks to the extent of $60,000 annually free of all duties (Washington to the Senate, 4 Aug. 1790, *Writings*, ed. Fitzpatrick, XXXI, 74-5).

McGillivray, an extraordinarily astute forest diplomatist engaged in playing off the United States against Spain in the middle of the war crisis, had Washington impaled on a cruel dilemma. In 1789 he had scorned Washington's overtures—the "Talleyrand of Alabama" had no such estimate of David Humphreys talent as a negotiator as Washington had (McGillivray to Panton, 8 Oct. 1789, Lawrence Kinnaird, ed., *Spain in the Mississippi Valley*, III, 283). In the spring of 1790 Washington sent Marinus Willett to invite McGillivray to negotiate at New York a treaty "as strong as the hills and as lasting as the rivers." Arriving at a moment when war between England and Spain seemed inevitable, McGillivray pressed every advantage, seeing himself as the equal of Washington: "A Treaty concluded at N. York ratified with the signature of Washington and McGillivray," he wrote to his associate in the trading combine of Panton, Leslie and Company, "would be the bond of Long peace and revered by Americans to a very distant period" (McGillivray to Panton, 8 May 1790, in John W. Caughey, *McGillivray of the Creeks*, p. 41-2, 259-62). In view of the war crisis, the delicate problem of the Yazoo grants, and the close watch Spain and England were both keeping on the negotiations through George Beckwith and Carlos Howard, this secret article caused the greatest difficulty of all, threatening to disrupt the negotiation until the last moment. TJ's opinion was not merely aimed at reducing the threat of an additional enemy on the Spanish border but also in sustaining national authority in the Yazoo question. On the eve of the treaty McGillivray himself wrote to the Spanish agent: "Another stipulation was directed toward taking our trade from its present source. After much debate it was decided to defer the consideration of this point until the end of two years; and it seemed to me the best way to escape this article, the most difficult point to adjust. It occupied us several days, because the Georgians and other interested persons insisted that the cessions made to them should be confirmed on the part of our nation" (McGillivray to Howard, 11 Aug. 1790, same, p. 273-6).

The Secretary of War was designated as sole commissioner to negotiate the treaty (Tr of commission, signed by Washington and TJ, dated 7 Aug. 1790, DNA: RG 59, MLR). But the principal contributor to the most vexed point in the negotiations was the Secretary of State. Washington did not reveal to the Senate the fact that McGillivray was a partner to the monopoly. Maclay, the Residence Act passed, had departed for home and so his comments on a secret article and his views of a suspected monopoly were never to be recorded. The Senate immediately gave its advice and consent to the secret article (JEP, I, 55-6). TJ had not advised that the solution be made secret, but this was doubtless an inevitable part of the dilemma. His own dilemma was summed up in the accurate description of the above opinion in an entry in SJPL which Marshall and *B* who criticised it in the *National Intelligencer* would have been interested in seeing: "[July] 29. Opinion Th: J. on treaty with Creeks giving monopoly of trade. Paramountship of treaty over laws." But the treaty that was to outlast the hills and rivers did not in fact outlive the term of the secret article. On promise of an increase of his pension almost three times that given by the United States, McGillivray on 9 July 1792 negotiated a treaty with the Spanish governor that repudiated the one negotiated at New York.

1 In MS at this point TJ first wrote and then deleted: "that they shall be in partnership with M'Gillivray."

2 TJ first wrote "their," then altered the word to read as above.

3 In PrC TJ inserted a cross at this point, keyed to a passage written at the bottom of the page, probably much later: "unless with the consent or default of the other contracting party. It may well be doubted too, and perhaps denied that the treaty power can controul a law. The question here proposed was then of the 1st. impression. Subsequent investigations have proved that the contrary position is the more general truth."

From Thomas Upshaw

Essex, Virginia, 27 July 1790. Some time ago he ventured to write John Page of his desire to be "usefull to society, and my Country" and to request a letter of introduction to the president. He reminded Page of the peculiar confidence the governor of Virginia had in him during late war and he hopes TJ will remember the order in council of 1 Oct. 1779 which was signed by him and containing "high incommiums as to steadiness and confidence." He is desirous of filling "a moderate post, if there should be any such" and thinks his service of four or five years as an officer and his reluctant yielding to the entreaties of Governor Henry and several members of the council to leave his command to undertake other trusts justify "flattering expectations." He solicits TJ's interest and interposition with the president: "I am very desirous to prove to the world, and to a few enemies in particular that I still retain a zeal for the public weal of my native Country.—Perhaps some vacancies may be to fill up in conducting afairs respecting the New Seat of Government."

RC (DLC: Applications for Office under Washington); endorsed by TJ as received 7 Aug. 1790 and so recorded in SJL.

From Montmorin

A Paris le 31. Juillet 1790.

J'ai reçu, Monsieur, la lettre par laquelle vous me faites l'honneur de m'informer que votre mission en France étoit cessée par votre nomination à la place de Secrétaire d'Etat des Etats Unis.[1] Je ne puis, Monsieur, que vous Temoigner le regrèt sincere que j'éprouverois en cette occasion, si je ne Trouvois pas un véritable motif de satisfaction pour moi dans la nouvelle marque de confiance qui vous est donnée et qui justifie de plus en plus l'opinion qui vous est duë et que vous avez laissée de vous dans ce pays ci.

J'ai l'honneur d'être avec un très sincere attachement, Monsieur, votre très humble et très obéissant Serviteur, MONTMORIN

RC (DLC); in clerk's hand, signed by Montmorin; endorsed as received 12 Jan. 1791 and so recorded in SJL. Dft (Arch. Aff. Etr., Corr. Pol., E.-U., XXXV; photostats in DLC); one variation noted below. Tr in English (DNA: RG 59, MLR); endorsed in part: "sent to the President Jany. 14th. 1791."

Another Tr in English (DNA: RG 59, SDC).

1 Dft originally read: ". . . nomination à une place de l'administration intérieure des Etats Unis" and was then altered to read as above.

To William Blount

SIR   New York August 1st. 1790

Your favour of July the 7th has been duly received. On information from Doctr. Williamson that you are not possessed of the acts establishing the western Governments, I have now the honor to enclose to you 1. The Ordinance of the ancient Congress for the Government of the Territory North West of the Ohio. 2. An act of the present Congress for the Government of the same. 3. Their Act for the Government of the Territory South of the Ohio.

It is expected Congress will rise this week. As soon as their Acts are printed a complete copy of them shall be sent to you. I presume they must be directed to you at your new residence, from whence we shall be happy to receive as full and frequent communications as shall be convenient to you.

It is not yet known whether a war has taken place between Spain and Great Britain. Colonel McGillivray and the Creek Chiefs are now here, and we hope that friendly arrangements will take place.— I have the honor to be with great esteem and respect &c.

FC (DNA: RG 59, PCC No. 120); at foot of text: "(signed) Thomas Jefferson." Enclosures: (1) Ordinance of 13 July 1787. (2) Act of 7 Aug. 1789 for the government of the Northwest Territory. (3) Act of 26 May 1790 for the government of the Southwest Territory. Enclosures are printed in Carter, *Terr. Papers*, II, 39-50, 203; IV, 18-19. The terms of the Act for the government of the Southwest Territory were identical with those for the government of the Northwest Territory, with one exception—acceptance of the ten conditions stated in the North Carolina deed of cession, one of which was that the territory should be formed into a state or states conformably to the Ordinance of 1787 provided that no regulations made by Congress should "tend to emancipate slaves" (texts of the North Carolina Act of cession of

22 Dec. 1789, of the deed of cession of 25 Feb. 1790, and of the Act of acceptance of 2 Apr. 1790 are printed in Carter, *Terr. Papers*, IV, 3-8, 9-17; TJ transmitted two authenticated copies of the Act of acceptance to the governor of North Carolina on 6 Apr. 1790, together with a copy of the Act of 2 Apr. 1790 to prevent the exportation of goods not duly inspected according to the laws of the states [circular: FC in DNA: RG 59, PCC No. 120; RC to governor of Pennsylvania, NN; to governor of Maryland, MdAA; to governor of North Carolina, NcR]).

Blount's letter of 7 July 1790 acknowledged receipt of his commission as governor of the Southwest Territory and asked TJ to inform the President that he had a "very perfect Sense of the Honor" and that he accepted the office "with a firm Determination to perform the duties of it to the best of Abilities" (RC in DNA: RG 59, SWTP; endorsed by TJ as received 23 July 1790 and so recorded in SJL; at foot of text in pencil in TJ's hand: "Letters for Govr. Blount must be put in mail for Washington in N. Carolina. Send him the act for government N. W. of the Ohio"). For TJ's summary of information concerning candidates for office in the Southwest Territory as derived from letters of members of Congress from North Carolina (Hugh Williamson, Timothy Bloodworth, John B. Ashe) and no doubt from conversations with his friends John Brown of Kentucky and Benjamin Hawkins of North Carolina, see under 7 June 1790 (texts of Williamson to Washington, 28 May 1790; Bloodworth to Washington, 5 June 1790; Ashe to Washington, 5 June 1790, which were utilized by TJ are in Carter, *Terr. Papers*, IV, 19-23). The commissions to Blount as governor, to Daniel Smith as secretary, and to David Campbell as judge, are all dated 8 June 1790; TJ's letters of transmittal of these commissions, together with that covering the commission of John McNairy as judge of the Southwest Territory, are all dated 15 June 1790 (FCs in DNA: RG 59, PCC No. 120; texts in Carter, *Terr. Papers*, IV, 24-6, 29-30).

From William Temple Franklin

DEAR SIR   Philada. 1. August 1790

I was not in Town when your Letter of the 25th. July arrived: but according to the Directions I had left, it was opened and shew'd to Mr. Leiper; who has, I find, in consequence thereof, and in order to accommodate you as much as possible, sent his Master Carpenter to New-York to receive your Directions relative to the Augmentation you wish to the house. This I have much approved of, as it will save a great deal of writing, and prevent any misunderstandings.—I did not, I believe, mention to you, that there are not at present any Stables or Coach house erected, but Mr. Leiper intends building such either at the End of the house Lot, or on a Lot not far distant. These however, as well as the new Room, will increase the Rent somewhat. The lot adjoining your House, does not as you suppose belong to Mr. Leiper, but in consequence of your Wish to have your Offices near you, he has endeavor'd to purchase it; but has not effected it, the Owner being, as he thinks, too exorbitant in his Demand. There is a House on it that might suit for the Offices, and perhaps it may be possible to rent it.

Adieu, my Dear Sir; I beg you would not think you give me any Trouble, when you afford me an Opportunity of being either useful or agreable to you, being very sincerely, and with great Regard, Your affectionate and very humble Sevt.

W. T. FRANKLIN

RC (DLC); endorsed as received 3 Aug. 1790 and so recorded in SJL. On this same day TJ recorded the receipt of a letter from Thomas Leiper of 29 July 1790; this letter has not been found, but it probably was a letter of introduction for Leiper's MASTER CARPENTER, Thomas Carstairs, who evidently brought along with him drawings of the plans of Leiper's house (see TJ to Leiper, 4 Aug. 1790).

From Robert R. Livingston

SIR   ClerMont 1st. Augt. 1790

Having flattered myself that I had fallen upon a new meathod of diminishing the friction in heavy machines, I take the liberty to communicate it to you, and to beg that you would do me the favour to inform me if I have deceived myself, or made a useful discovery?

Let the end of the spindle pass thro, and be strongly fixed to a peice of light wood whose solid contents should be two square feet and whose length should be twice its breadth. Let the point of the spindle be fixed in a vessel large enough to receive it with its cylinder, leaving a space of ⅛ of an inch at the side and ¼ of an inch at the bottom, between itself and the cylinder. Fill this space with quicksilver a cubick foot of which weighs 947. If then the pressure on the spindle should be 2000 ℔. the weight on the point of it will be reduced to 106, the rest being supported by the bouyancy of the wood. The little friction that may exist between the mercury and the sides of the vessel will be more than compensated by reducing the point of the spindle, which in this case will not bear ⅒ part of the weight necessary if no quicksilver was used. You will easily see sir, that this principle (if not erronious) may be applied to every species of fixed machines, and that in many cases water may be made to answer the purpose of quicksilver.— I have the honor to be Sir with respect & esteem your Most Ob. Hum. Servt.,   R. R. LIVINGSTON

RC (DLC); endorsed by TJ as received 5 Aug. 1790, but recorded in SJL under 4 Aug.

To David Rittenhouse

Dear Sir   New York. August 1. 1790.

I do myself the honour of inclosing you a printed copy of the
report on measures &c. You asked in your letter whether the papers
I had sent you were to be kept or returned. They are now useless
and therefore may be done what you please with. They were only
copies of what I had retained.

Congress will rise this week, and I hope to be able within a
fortnight after them to leave this place for Virginia, passing a
few days in Philadelphia on my way, where I shall have the pleasure
of seeing you, and of consulting you privately as to what you could
do, were the French and English to propose to us to concur with
them in their operation.—I am with great esteem Dear Sir Your
sincere friend & humble servt.,   Th: Jefferson

PrC (DLC). For note on printed text of enclosure, see under 4 July 1790. In
SJL under 28 July TJ records receipt of a letter dated 26 July 1790 from Rittenhouse; it has not been found.

From Joseph Fenwick

Portland, [*Maine*], *2 Aug. 1790.* Arrived yesterday and will embark
in two or three weeks on vessel now loading for Bordeaux. The law,
when adopted, "respecting the particular duty and purquisates of Consuls, and the general instructions" from the Secretary's office may be
sent by way of "*George Town on Potomack*" if no opportunity offers
from New York.—"When in Boston I was credibly informed that the
American company establishd in France under . . . a Mr. —— Roach
[William Rotch] at Dunkirk for the purpose of carrying on the Whale
Fishery and instructing the French in that branch was endeavoring to
obtain an interdiction of the american oil into France and from Roach's
advice to his friends he was sanguine in his expectation of succeeding.
Now from the manner in which that Company carry's on the business, it
is obvious (at least to me) that the expected advantages cannot result
from it to the french nation. If they go on to give that company the exclusive right of supplying oil, it will tend to enhanse the price not only
to the loss of that nation, but to the great injury of the commerce of
these States. All the Company vessels in the business are built, fitted,
and manned from America except 3 or 4 supernumery french Men or
Boys aboard of each and they very frequently return here before they
land oil in France. The profits of the business will centre in this Country
as all the friends and connexions of the Company live here and they
themselves mean no doubt ultimately to return. In this point of view it
will prove injurious to this Country only as a monopoly.—These are the

thoughts that have occured to me on that business which I take the liberty to submit to your Excellency and ask if you do not think it advisable some endeavors should be made to counteract the design of that Company . . . [*In postscript*:] While I was in New Port R. Island early in July there arrived there a Brigg from whaleing. She had fitted out as the Capt. told me from Nantuckett had made successfull cruise and was then on her way to France where she expected to receve the bounty given by the Government to Mr. Roach's company being one of their vessels. At R. Island she entered and paid Tonnage as an American."

RC (DNA: RG 59, CD); endorsed as received 11 Aug. 1790 and so recorded in SJL.

From John Harvie, Jr.

DR SIR   Richmond August the 3rd. 1790

Your very Acceptable Letter of July 25th. is this moment handed to me, when I am about setting out to join my wife and Daughters who are on a Visit to her father. The prospect of a renewed Correspondance with you is so flattering to me, that I must do myself the pleasure of thus Acknowledgeing that it will at all times Contribute greatly to my Satisfaction.—I am pleased to find that Mr. Austin's Manufactory meets with your Countenance, as I think it certainly Merits some Encouragement from Government.—The Assumption under any Modification will I fear be Considered as a Bitter pill in this State, the publick Voice being against it, Arguments of Accomodation will have but little Avail, and the Circumstance of the persevereing States withholding their Concurrence to funding the Acknowledged part of the Continental Debt, unless this favorite Scheme makes a part of the System Carry with it a Legislative temper that forebodes jealousy which some other Untoward proposition may kindle into a dissension dangerous to the Union. If the Measure is Adopted the friends to the Government must soften it to the people as far as truth and Reason will justify.

It gives me pleasure to hear that you propose during the Recess of Congress to Visit Virginia. I hope Richmond will enjoy some part of your time where all your friends in this City will be happy to see you, and none more so than him who had the Honour of your patronage in the Early part of his Life, and who at all times since has felt with Gratitude the Advantages it was of to him, with these Sensations give me leave to Subscribe myself Dr Sir Yr Most Oblidged & Obt. Svt.,   JNO. HARVIE

RC (DLC); endorsed as received 12 Aug. 1790 and so recorded in SJL.

From Petit

Monsieur je prans laliberte de vous Ecrire pour vous dire que mes parans Sesont oposé pour que jail vous rejoindre. Outre Cela Cest que les gages que vous me proposé Sont trop mediocre pour alle Siloiens. Je fais, tout henballe, tout pour le mieux. Je crois que vous de vé recevoir le tout Bien condisionné. Vous dite Si il iaduvin dele faire maittre henboutele. Voila omoiens troiy ans quil ne vous est poiens venu duvin henpieces. Il sitrouve 600 Boutele devin tont que Konyacque que grave et pagnerais et frontignon et autre vin des pagne. Il ia dons toutes les Caisses des Carte de tout les noms des vin. Monsieur jai pris laliberte de garde un lit de plume qui est mavais. Si il avait de Ete duduvais Comme les deux autre je vous lorais henvoie pour mesouvenir devous. Cest pour quoies que jepris laliberte dele garde. Cependant si vous le trouve movais je vous ontreindre Conte si vous le juge apropos. Il imanque Bien des petite choses. Il se trouve voute petite Cuiliere a caffait de perdu. Du tons que ses de maisaile etoit a lhotele jeme on a perduune et les autre Cetoit Salais qui les maitoit dons lentichambre pondont que jenetoit pas la et les personne qui venais les prenais. Comme les serviete mamesele mon a Bocoup perdu el onvoiais des paquet de Cotés et dautre et on ne ronvoais poient les cerviete. Ain si monsieur tout Ce quil iadesur je ne garde rien autre choses que le lit de plume. Les pagnole ma de mande delui lesse un matela et une Couvertur et un mauvaises paire de drap. Je lui elesse. Comme letout est tres movais jepansé que vous le troverais Bien. Il onreste hen caure 3 ala maison pour Couche henri et le coche qui est portie. Monsieur Shorte a change la croix et a mis henriy henplacer a tondu que la croix etoit volleur. Il mont prie bien des choses. Pour moies je Conte mon retourne dons mon paiié. Comme jai un paux de Bien je conte alle le faire valoir.

Monsieur Shorte madit que vous avie ete uncomode ce qui mafait Bocoup de painne, ainsi qua tout le monde qui restoit. A, nous oubliront jamais la perte que nous avons fait quande lon nous a dit avous ne revenie plus. Nous nou sommis tous a nous regarde et nous maittre a pleure dela paine que Sa nous faisait daprandre que nous perdion le Roiy des maittre et que jamais nous trouveron vottre pariele. Cest Ce qui me fait dessider a mon retourne dons mon paiié.

Ainsi monsieur je finie hen vous faisant mon dernie adieux et prie le tout puisant pour la conservassion de vos jour. Je sui a

vecque tout le plus grant respect Monsieur, vottres humble et tres
obeissant serviteur   PETIT

Jesoite bien le Bonjour a jemme ain si qua salais.

Si josais je vous prirais dassure de mes respais a monsieur et
madame adame.

RC (MoSHi); addressed: "Monsieure de Jefferson Minitre des affaire hetrangere ⟨aux a neucres⟩ Philada"; postmarked: "FREE" and "N YORK july 16"; endorsed by TJ as received 19 July 1791 and so recorded in SJL. Petit's punctuation is even more puzzling than his phonetic spelling, and much of it has been supplied for the sake of clarity.

To Thomas Mann Randolph, Jr.

DEAR SIR   New York Aug. 3. 1790.

In my letter of the last week I believe I did not acknoledge the
reciept of yours of July 3. With respect to Mr. Thompson he had
been named to the Consulship of the Canaries: but as these offices
have no direct emoluments, depending for indemnification on the
consignments and other business they may produce, he has declined
accepting any. Your application needed no apology. I know the
impossibility of your avoiding those sollicitations, and therefore
scarcely consider your wishes as coupled with your nomination. On
my part, the applications are so numerous, and the line of duty
so cogent to recommend the best subject to the President, that I
am sure you will always wish the person you name to be postponed
to a better. So that all that is necessary in this case is to understand
one another. Where two candidates are otherwise perfectly equal,
I should be justifiable in giving a preference to the one who has
asked your sollicitation. On the other hand you will understand,
if he has been postponed that it has been in favor of a competitor
with some better qualification. I will ask of you to give always the
true and naked character of the person as far as you can come at it.

The English packet arrived yesterday morning. Peace and war
still undecided, tho the nation eager for the latter. The parliament
was dissolved. This and some other circumstances rather point to
a war. Matters in France were going on well.

I inclose you two copies of a report of mine on Measures, weights
and coins. As it is a mathematical subject, and I can have few or
no occasions of rendering myself a member of any value to the
Society at Edinburgh of which you were so kind as to have me

named, I will beg the favor of you to forward one of the copies in my name to the society, if there be no impropriety in it.

I have never sent you my description of my mould-board because it will be difficult to make it from a description. I have had a small model made, which I will forward to you if any person should be going before myself. Otherwise I will bring it. Congress will rise this week. I shall set out for Virginia within a fortnight after they rise. But as I must stay a while in Philadelphia to see about a house, I suppose I shall not leave that place till the 1st. of Sep. nor be at Monticello till the 10th. or 15th. of that month. I shall hope to meet yourself and the girls then or as soon after as you can conveniently be there. Present my best love to my dear Martha, and to Maria if you are together, and be assured of the sincere esteem & attachment of Dear Sir Your's affectionately,

TH: JEFFERSON

RC (DLC). PrC (DLC); first page only. PrC (ViU); second page only. Randolph's letter of JULY 3 is recorded in SJL as received 15 July 1790 but it has not been found.

From Nathaniel Cutting

SIR   St. Marc, Island of St. Domingue 4th. August, 1790.

Since I did myself the honor of writing you from hence under the 6th Ultimo, a series of Political Events has presented in this Colony which I presume you will deem worthy your notice; therefore without any further apology I shall take the liberty of transmitting you a slight sketch of them. Conscious that I am but a shallow Politician, I shall not presume to make Conjectures nor Comments; but only briefly narrate the principal occurrences as they presented themselves to my observation. Please to know then that on the 10th. July an Express from the Cape brought advice to the General Assembly sitting at this place, that the Assembly of the Northern District (whose Powers are totally superseded by the appointment of a Colonial General Assembly) had taken upon itself to issue an order for the suppression of the Municipalitie lately established at Cape François. The members of that Municipalitie refused to acknowledge the authority of said Provincial Assembly, protested against its proceedings, and then dispatch'd a Courier to the General Assembly with advice of these transactions.—The General Assembly had lately past a Decree that on the 14th. July,

which is the Anniversary of the Capture of the Bastile, Te Deum
should be chanted and other public demonstrations of Joy exhibited
throughout the Colony in commemoration of that happy Event
which destroy'd one of the principal props of Despotism in France:
—and moreover that the Citizens should at the same time take the
oath of allegiance to the Nation, the Colony, the Law and the King.
Ordering also that the same Ceremonies should be observed throughout the Colony on the anniversary of that day ever after. This
Decree was transmitted to the Governor General, M. Le Comte de
Peinier, for Sanction and Promulgation, he publicly refused both;
alledging that the Assembly arrogated to itself powers which had
not yet been conceded to it by the National Assembly and the King
of France.—The Decree however was published by authority of
the Assembly, agreably to the Basis of a Constitution which has
been form'd by it for this Colony and which has been dispatch'd
to France for the Royal sanction.

In conformity to this Decree, at this place the 14th. of July was
usher'd in by the ringing of Bells and the discharge of Artillery.—
The appointed Ceremonies were observed by and in Presence of
the Assembly. At Evening the Town was illuminated.

On the 18th. July the Citizens of St. Marc convened at the
Church for the purpose of chusing a Mayor and other Municipal
Officers agreably to the Decree of the General Assembly; which
Decree the People seem determin'd to carry into execution though
the Governor General still persists in refusing his assent to it. The
variance between that Personage and the General Assembly daily
increased; The firmest and most Sagacious Patriots have long
entertain'd the opinion that the General and his Partizans *here*,
under the auspices of M. de la Luzerne and the Aristocratic Party
in *Europe*, would endeavour to retain this Colony in the shackles
of Despotism, and by means of its importance in the scale of
national Commerce, together with the immense wealth and influence
of its Proprietors, endeavour to effect a Counter-Revolution in
France. Numerous occurrences confirm'd this suspicion. It was observ'd that those anti-Revolutionists had their Emissaries dispersed
in every quarter, who industriously instigated and fomented dissentions among the Colonists. A convincing and at the same time
an alarming Proof of their too great success was the defection of
a great majority of the Inhabitants of the Cape, which was notified
at St. Marc on the 20th. July.

Cape François was divided into twelve Districts or Wards; at a general meeting of the Inhabitants about that time, nine Wards out of the twelve voted for an abolition of the municipalitie which had been so lately established under the auspices of the General Assembly!

The Governor General and his Party, in justification of their opposition to the General Assembly and of their indefatigable attempts to invalidate all its measures, how-well-so-ever they may be calculated for the public good, hold out the specious pretext that it has not critically conform'd to certain Arrets of the National assembly of France dated the 8th. and 28th. of March ultimo, but assumes to itself certain Legislative Powers wherewith it is not legally invested.

The Truth is that previous to the arrival of those two Decrees abovemention'd, the Assembly General of this Colony had form'd the Basis of a Constitution for it, which was forwarded to France for approbation, as I have before observ'd. This Basis differ'd in some particulars from the Plan of Legislation and Government proposed by the National Assembly, but agreed so well with it in the main, that the Colonial, alias, General Assembly, has not scrupled to Legislate agreably to a mode which they have the strongest presumption will be approv'd and confirm'd by the Supreme authority of the nation. It seems to be the opinion of most judicious persons with whom I have conversed on the subject, that the discretionary powers wherewith the General is invested, would fully authorize his temporarily sanctioning any Laws fram'd by the Colonial Assembly for the purpose of promoting the peace, well-being, and good government of the Colony; but he is surrounded by evil Counsellors who warp his judgement and have apparently wrought an irreconcileable difference between him and that Representative Body where he ought to preside. In fine, the animosity of the contending Parties has arisen to such a heighth as to threaten this flourishing Colony with all the horrors of a Civil War.

On the 20th. July a Decree past the General Assembly for admitting American Vessels into all the Ports of this Colony without exception, from the date of the Decree till the first of next march; but I do not learn that it takes off any of the restrictions wherewith the exportation of the produce of this Colony in foreign Bottoms, was previously saddled; so that I concieve it cannot be advantageous to any Class of men except the French Planters.

I am told the Governor refuses his assent to this Decree likewise and threatens that he will station arm'd Cruizers with orders to make seizure of every American Vessel that may presume to visit any Port in the Colony except those previously declared free-Ports.

On the 23d. July it was reported here that the Inhabitants of Leogane had appointed their municipal Officers, agreeably to the direction of the Assembly General, and immediately took possession of the Military Magazine in that Town. The Inhabitants were then forbidden to obey any requisition of the King's Commandant at that place, but to hold themselves accountable for their Conduct to the Municipality and to the General Assembly. On the 24th. July information was given to the General Assembly that M. Le Comte de Peinier had issued private orders to the Commandant at this place to embark the Powder that was in the Magazine that night and with it the Corps under his Command, and to repair with them to Port-au-Prince as soon as possible. The Assembly was much alarm'd; but the *Mayor* quieted all apprehensions by declaring that he and the Citizens would be responsible for the safety of the powder. On the 26th. July, two Commissaries from Colonel Mauduit, Commander of the Regiment of Port-au-Prince, arriv'd here to renew the Oath of allegiance of the soldiers belonging to the detachment station'd here. The usual Oath has been "to be faithful to the Nation, the Law and the King." Colonel Mauduit, doubtless with permission of the General, has added to it on the present occasion a clause purporting that they "will not obey any requisition of the Colonial General Assembly or of the municipalities by them establish'd." The Troops station'd in this *Colony* are paid by *it*; the General Assembly therefore on the 28th. took upon itself to declare them freed from their engagements to Government, and by a Public Decree invited them to form a new Patriotic Corps under the auspices of said Assembly;—promissing additional pay to those who would thus renew their engagements;—those who did not chuse to continue soldiers, should be permitted to pursue any useful occupation in the Colony, and those who preferr'd returning to Europe, should be furnish a passage at the public Expence.— A considerable number of the detachment station'd at this place, refused the new oath tender'd them by their Officers, and threw themselves on the protection of the General Assembly. On the 29th. a soldier who refused to take the new Oath, and was leaving his Barracks in consequence of the late Decree, was arrested by a subaltern Officer, put in Irons and closely confin'd. The instant this outrage against the predominant feelings of the Citizens was reported abroad, several of them flew to arms and were for rescuing the Soldier instantaneously. A *Seance Extraordinaire* of the General Assembly was immediately held on the occasion. Many of the members were so irritated by the insult offer'd their Body by the Officer daring to impede the opperation of its Decree, that the powers of speech would scarcely enable them to give vent to their resentment. After much useless vociferation, M. Archevesque Thibaud was permitted to make an uninterrupted harrangue, wherein he observ'd that it was not probable a subaltern Officer would dare take such a step without the order of his superiour:— and then in a very animated manner advised the assembly to command the immediate attendance of the Commandant. This was done instantly through the medium of the Committee of St. Marc who transact the Public business of the Town till the municipal Officers are all elected and established.

M. Le Chevalier de la Grémonville, the Commandant, return'd for answer that "he did not hold himself accountable for anything that respected the discharge of his Duty as a Military Officer, to any but the General who station'd him here," or to that effect. When this was read by the President of the Assembly, the Croud of Auditors who were in the Gallery, as usual, cried aloud that they would go and bring the Commandant to the Assembly by Force. One of the members of the Assembly who is a Relation of the Commandant, begg'd permission of that Body to visit him, declaring that he would engage to bring him immediately before the House. After some altercation leave was given, and in a few minutes he return'd with the Commandant, who had put off his Uniform and was drest in a plain Frock. When the President began to interrogate him rather austerely on the Business of that afternoon, M. de la Grémonville, to the astonishment of all present, replied that he did not then present himself before that Assembly in quality of *Commandant*, but merely as a simple *Citizen*, in which Character he begg'd he might ever thereafter have the honor to be consider'd, for from that moment he relinquish'd his Commission, renounced the principles of those who were inimical to the Colony, and hoped that his future conduct would entitle him to the esteem and confidence of his Fellow Citizens, with whom he wished to live on the most amicable terms. He then declared that he had not given any order for arresting the Soldier in question.—This regeneration of the Commandant caused the most unbounded bursts of applause to reverberate from side to side of that sacred Edefice which has of late become a Theatre where Patriotic Enthusiasm displays its facinating energy.

In course of that Evening it was decreed that the Committee of the Town should take charge of the Arsenal and the Powder Magazine, and be accountable for the military stores therein contain'd to none but the General Assembly.

The next morning, M. Le Chevalier de la Grémonville, conformably to his public professions, resign'd his Commission into the hands of the President of the General Assembly. In course of the day the soldiers all left their Barracks; some were enroll'd anew as Patriotic Troops, others proceeded to Port-au-Prince.

On the 30th. a ship came into the Road from Port-au-Prince, bound to France. The General Assembly had information that a Packet of Letters from M. Le Comte de Peinier, were very privately convey'd aboard that Ship, where they were then secreted. The Committee of the Town sent a deputation aboard and found the packet conceal'd in a Bed. It was addrest to M. de la Luzerne. The Letters were publicly read, whereby the secret advisers of the Governor General were discover'd, as well as some of their intentions. One part of the Plan of opperations was to send a Frigate round to this Road with Troops aboard to join those station'd here, and then disperse the General Assembly by force of arms.

On Saturday the 31st. July, advice was receiv'd that a Skirmish had taken place at Port-au-Prince between the Patriotic Citizens and a detachment of Troops under command of Colonel Mauduit, wherein five Citizens were kill'd, about twenty were wounded, and near forty taken Prisoners. The Citizens of St. Marc as well as the General Assembly were much alarm'd at the expectation that a Frigate was coming into this Road with hostile intentions. Order was taken to put the Batteries in order with all possible dispatch. The Company of Voluntiers and Chasseurs paraded under arms, and made a very respectable appearance. Advice had been receiv'd by particular members of the General Assembly, though not in an official way, that there was a defection among the Officers and Crew of the Leopard, laying at Port-au-Prince, the only ship of the Line station'd in this Colony. The *Maitre d'Equipage*, with the other warrant officers and Crew had declared themselves in favour of the General Assembly, and had actually obliged the Commander, M. de la Gallissonnière, with several of his Lieutenants, to quit the ship.

After much debate on all these interesting points, it was determin'd to pass a formal Decree declaring M. Le Comte de Peinier and

Colonel Mauduit guilty of high Treason. The Assembly order'd a Proclamation to be printed and dispersed throughout the Colony offering a reward of Eight thousand Dollars for the apprehending and delivering into Custody of the General Assembly either of the Persons thus attainted. It was also decreed by the General Assembly to send a deputation aboard the Leopard to thank that Ship's Company for their Patriotic declarations, &c.

On the Afternoon of the same day a *seance Extraordinaire* of the General Assembly was held on account of the arrival of a Packet of intercepted Letters, from M. de la Luzerne to M. de Peinier.— They were publicly read, were dated in June, and tallied exceedingly well with the wishes and even with the public regulations which had been proposed by the General Assembly. This was a cause of much rejoicing, not only to the members of the Assembly but to the numerous Citizens who crouded the Galleries on this occasion.—On Sunday morning 1st. August, The General Assembly held another *seance extraordinaire*. One of the Patriotic Patroles on the Road leading from Port-au-Prince to this place, in course of the preceding night had arrested a Person in the garb of a Sailor, who on examination proved to be one of the Marechaussé. A Packet of Letters was found in his possession addrest to a merchant in this Place. By the suspicious manner in which this Packet was convey'd and the doubtful Character of the Person to whom it was addrest, People expected that some new Treason would be discover'd by it, but that did not prove to be the case. The Letters were publicly read:—one was from the Lieutenant Colonel of the Port-au-Prince Regiment, addrest to a Military officer now confin'd here, giving an account of the late skirmish, and lamenting that the Citizens had the advantage of ground so that Colonel Mauduit's Field-pieces could not do the execution which he wish'd, because they could not be sufficiently elevated! Another Letter was from the Commandant of a Corps of degenerate Citizens who falsely style themselves *Patriotic Volunteers* at the same that they have link'd themselves with a band of *Petty Despots and Assassins*. This Letter is addrest to the Commandant of the Voluntiers at St. Marc, and asserts the cause of the late melancholly catastrophe at Port-au-Prince to be as follows; viz. The Committee of that Town had in various instances attempted to counter-act Royal authority:—and had even carried its audacity so far as by a liberal distribution of money and fair Promises to seduce some of the officers and Crew of his Majesty's ship the Leopard, and had influenced them to refuse obedience to their

Captain who was likewise Commander in chief of the marine on this station. And even had prevail'd on them openly to profess themselves abettors of the said Committee and of the Colonial General Assembly. That for these reasons the Governor General had determined on the measure of arresting the members of said Committee. The Execution of this order, which was agreed to in Council, was committed to Colonel Mauduit, with a detachment of Troops and Voluntiers, on the night of the 29th. July, and brought on the skirmish wherein several Persons lost their lives, &c. The Writer then exhorts the Voluntiers of St. Marc to join the Corps under his command in its intention of assisting the Governor to disperse the General Assembly. A Proclamation of the Governor issued immediately after the Massacre at Port au Prince accompanied these Letters. I herewith inclose a Copy of it.

The appearance of a large Ship in the offing early this morning, very much alarmed the General Assembly and the Inhabitants of St. Marc. Everyone was flying to arms, supposing it might be the Frigate which it was known M. de Peinier had it in contemplation to send round here with Troops. The arms in the Public arsenal were distributed. The Records and other Papers of the General Assembly were dispatch'd to a place of safety in the Country. Notice was sent to the neighbouring Parishes and their aid requested. Everything breathed war and confusion.—The General Assembly directed the Committee of the Town to send a Flag of Truce aboard the suspected Ship, which was done about nine o'Clock. The Members of the Assembly became so alarm'd that they determin'd on quitting the Town. They all arm'd themselves, some with Fusils, some with Pistols, some with Swords or Cutlasses, and some particulars with all those weapons. About ten o'Clock they commenced their retreat toward the River Artibenite, attended by a few Patriotic Soldiers and four Brass Field-Pieces under the direction of M. Le Marquis de Cadusch, whom the Commons of St. Marc had appointed Captain General pro. temp.

As the ship approach the Town she was known to be the Leopard and of course all apprehension of danger subsided. The General Assembly return'd to Town, and at 4 P. M. held a *Seance Extraordinaire* to receive several officers of the Leopard, who had left that ship in the offing and were just then landed. They were usher'd into the centre of the assembly amidst the acclamations of a surrounding multitude, and were there cordially saluted by reitterated clapping of hands and other demonstrations of joy. What a Contrast did this Evening Scene form to that of the morning! The Public thanks were render'd by the President to the Officers for their *Patriotism*. The Inferior Officers and Crew have appointed *M. Le Baron de Sancto Domingo*, Commander of the Leopard. He is a native of this Colony, educated in France and has Rank in the French Marine as Commander of a Frigate. Two second Lieutenants are the only other Commission'd officers that remain with the Ship. The said Lieutenants with many inferior officers were of the deputation that day sent to offer the Ship and the services of her Company to the General Assembly and likewise to claim its protection and support. When the *applaudissements* of the audience subsided, the Assembly Decreed that a medal should be struck and presented to each of the Officers of the Leopard in testimony of the high sense that Body entertain of their Patriotism and attachment to the principles of Consitutional Freedom. It was also decreed that an addition should be made to the name of the Ship, and that in future she should be call'd *Le Sauveur des Français!*

The same night two Gentlemen arriv'd Express from the Cape with advice that by order of the Governor General a Detachment of 7 or 800 men were to embark at that place on monday morning, to come round under convoy of a Frigate, and land at Gonaive, about 14 leagues westward of St. Marc. There they were to wait for orders from Port-au-Prince, and when the Forces at *that place* were prepared, both those Bodies were to approach St. Marc by Land in order to effect a dissolution of the General Assembly.

The fortunate Event of the Leopard's being at the disposal of the Assembly places it in perfect security as to the personal freedom of its members; some of them have proposed to embark altogether, proceed first to America in order to procure Stores and Provisions and from thence directly for France.

The Leopard came to anchor in the Road of St. Marc on the 2d. Current. Many Inhabitants of the neighbouring Parishes came into Town on Sunday Evening and on monday the 2d. Current, to marshall themselves under the orders of the assembly. The Mails that came from Port-au-Prince that day ⅌ Courier, were open'd in presence of the General Assembly, all Letters to and from suspected Persons were stopp'd; many of them were publicly read. Different Packets contain'd great numbers of Proclamations issued by the Governor General on the 1st. Current, stigmatizing the General Assembly as a Band of Traitors, and peremptorily commanding its immediate dissolution.

Most of the late Transactions of the Governor and his Party confirm some of the most sagacious Patriots in the opinion that the Aristocratic Party in Europe yet fondly cherish the hope of effecting a Counter Revolution in France through the medium of St. Domingue. Colonel Mauduit is known to be one of those who fled from France in the Suite of the Comte d'Artois, and accompanied that Prince to Italy. No doubt he was selected as a man of proper Talents to promote the nefarious views of Despotism in despair:— However, from the present aspect of affairs here, it is generally thought that he has now taken an irretrievable Step toward defeating the execrable purposes of his imperious Coadjutors.

On the other hand, these sticklers for Arbitrary sway accuse the General Assembly of aiming at Independance, notwithstanding all its professions and transactions hitherto have been perfectly consonant to the *spirit*, though perhaps they may have differ'd a little from the *Letter* of that mode of Legislation and Government which the King and National Assembly of France have voluntarily prescribed for this Colony.

The Question whether the General Assembly shall remain at St. Marc or embark on board the Leopard and transport itself to Aux Cayes or some other safe place where it may be sure of a cordial reception and spirited support, has been several times agitated; but the debates thereon have been desultory and indecisive. A Majority of the Inhabitants of St. Marc and its Environs have earnestly besought the assembly to remain where it is, engageing at the same time to defend it to the last extremity. It might perhaps be more conveniently succoured and supported at aux Cayes; but from the apparent dispositions of the Inhabitants in the Western and even in the Northern District, there is no doubt that it will triumph over all its opponents. A considerable number of Patriotic Voluntiers came into Town this day from Plaisance; We are told that the Inhabitants of Gonaive, Port-Margot and Olimbé are in motion for the same service; in fine it is not improbable that in a few days several thousand determin'd Freemen will be collected under the Banners of the General Assembly. The most timid members of that Body begin to be assured, and now only say that *rather than cause an effusion of Human Blood* they will voluntarily retreat to some other part of the Colony where the Governor will not have the temerity to follow them. Other members again have proposed that while the spirits of People are high and their resentment strong against Mauduit and his Banditti, they be led against

Port au Prince, at the same time that the Leopard be sent round to Blockade that Place by Sea, and by one *Coup de main* put an end to the Contest.

The Commons of St. Marc, &c. have reappointed the Marquis de Cadusch as General and Commander in Chief of the Patriotic Troops assembled and assembling at this place.

The archives of the General Assembly were this morning convey'd aboard the Leopard, under charge of certain Commissioners specially appointed to guard them.

When I began this narrative, I did not think I should have intruded so far on your time and patience; but I could not well omit any part of the detail without breaking that chain of occurrences which only could give you a competent idea of the present distracted State of this Colony. In addition to their domestic troubles the Colonists are apprehensive of being involv'd in a War with the English, as by the latest accounts from France we are taught to believe that great naval armaments are yet kept up on both sides the British Channel.

I expect to take my departure for Havre de Grace on Sunday next, on board the Ship Hero, Captne. du Jardin.—Permit me here to repeat the observation that if I can render you any service in that Country, you have but to command me. I have the honor to be, most respectfully, Sir, Your most obedt. & very huml. Servt.,

Nat. Cutting

Augt. 6th. From advices this day received, it is beyond a doubt the Forces from the Cape are or will be this day at Gonaive. Reinforcements continually coming into St. Marc, but badly provided with arms and amunition.—no other material occurrence since the 4th. Current.

RC (DNA: RG 59, MLR); addressed: "The Honble Thomas Jefferson Esquire, Secretary of State, New-York"; endorsed as received 6 Sep. 1790 (the day TJ received Cutting's letter of 6 July 1790), but not recorded in SJL.

To Thomas Leiper

Sir   New York Aug. 4. 1790.

On considering the plan of your house, I find it will make considerable odds to me that in the room over the kitchen, the door be placed in a corner of the room; I presume it must be in the left hand corner as you enter, or the Northeast corner of the room.

Perhaps it may be better to leave this door in it's present state, whatever that be, and also the cornice &c. in that end of the room (the North end) till I come to Philadelphia, which will be within two or three weeks. It will be essential for me that the house, stables &c. be in readiness by the 1st. of October. I explained to Mr. Carstairs the manner in which I wished to have the additional room made. I am Sir Your most obedt. humble servt.,

TH: JEFERSON

PrC (MHi); faded and mutilated, some words being verified from Tr (MHi). MR. CARSTAIRS was Leiper's master carpenter (see Franklin to TJ, 1 Aug. 1790).

From Warner Lewis

Warner Hall, Virginia, 4 Aug. 1790. A rumor prevails in Virginia that Congress intends "immediately to fit out a certain [nu]mber of Cutters . . . to be employed in preventing as far as it is possible the practice of smuggling. Cap't Francis Bright, who commanded an armed vessel, some years ago, in the little navy of this State, and who through the whole course of my acquaintance with him in that capacity, conducted himself in the most proper manner, is anxious to obtain an appointment to one of the Cutters. As, from being a member of the Virginia navy-board, I had repeated opportunities of inspecting the conduct of Cap't Bright, and as I can affirm that it was in every instance unexceptionable, he thinks that a declaration of this sort made by me to some gentleman at New York, who will take the trouble of mentioning it to the President, may be a means of procuring him the command he solicits. I take the liberty of asking your assistance for him. . . . I really think him a man of merit." He will always be gratified to hear from TJ, "for I most truly assure you that neither distance nor time can ever lessen the affection that I have always had, and still retain, for you."

RC (DLC: Applications for Office under Washington). Not recorded in SJL.

On 4 Sep. 1790 Bright wrote to Lewis (same) saying that he would sail for New York on the return of the packet that brought John Page, that he was not certain TJ would be there when he arrived, that he hoped Lewis would give him an open letter instead of the one he had previously written which Bright therein returned, and that he expected to make use of it with the secretary of the treasury, who would "superintend the appointment" and to whom he would apply if TJ happened not to be in New York. The above letter is presumably the one that Bright returned and Lewis may have sent it back to Bright instead of writing another.

From William Short

DEAR SIR   Paris August the 4th. 1790

Some time ago the Count de Mercy made an application to M. de
Montmorin for a passage of some troops on the territory of France,
on their march to the low countries. On its being known in that
quarter that the passage was promised, the *directoire du département* sent an express to the national assembly to take their orders
on it, previous to the arrival of the troops. This circumstance had
excited a considerable degree of fermentation in the province. The
inhabitants had neglected their harvests and fled to arms.—The
communication of this intelligence created much uneasiness in the
assembly and alarm in the capital. Libels were immediately circulated asserting the treachery of the ministry and exciting the
people to a massacre of them and a number of others suspected by
the libellists of being in a plot to effect a counter-revolution by
introducing foreign armies into the Kingdom. In the midst of this
disorder the assembly went into a full deliberation on the present
situation of France relative to foreign powers. Six commissaries
were immediately named to go to the offices of war and foreign
affairs and enquire there into the nature of the orders given for
the passage of foreign troops, and into such information as has
been lately received respecting the political situation of neighbouring powers.—From the report of the committee of six it appeared
that the ministry had not considered the passage of the troops
contrary to the decree of the assembly respecting the introduction
of foreign troops into France.—Some of the members were for
violent measures being taken against the ministry, but the assembly only decreed that the orders given should be considered as
void, and that they would deliberate on the passage of the troops
as soon as they were officially informed of their numbers, destination &c.—The report of the committee respecting neighbouring
powers shewed that England continued her military preparations,
that she had encreased her regular troops and was embarking a
considerable number of them, that the militia was assembled, that
four Dutch ships of the line had joined and that six others were
expected, that they do not think the fleet intended for the Baltic,
first because the Ships are too large to pass the sound, and secondly
because the season is too far advanced, that the negotiations between
England and Spain continue, and that it appears impossible that
the dispute between them should be the motive of such extensive

preparations, having cost already to England 36. millions of livres. The report respecting Spain shewed that her military preparations were such as could give no uneasiness to France—Respecting Prussia that her alliance with England was certain and her influence in Holland immense—That the German Princes who have possessions in Alsace were endeavouring to excite an insurrection there—that the troops of the Germanic body were assembling either to march to Liege or other places more alarming for France—that the Bishop of Spire, and the Cardinal de Rohan (who has left the assembly and gone beyond the Rhine) were endeavouring by their envoys at the Diet of the Empire to stir up that body—that the King of Sardinia had few troops on this side of the Alps.

A decree was passed, among other things, for desiring the King would give orders for distributing arms to the citizens wherever the defence of the Kingdom may render such a precaution necessary.— The Cardinal de Rohan is recalled to take his seat and render an account of his conduct to the assembly.

During these discussions Mirabeau proposed to the Assembly to pass a decree for confiscating the property of the Prince de Condé, unless he disavowed a manifest which had been sent to several municipalities with the plan of a counter-revolution and which was attributed to him. This was grounded on the suspicions of M. de Montmorin respecting the Prince de Condé, communicated by him to the President of the committee des recherches. The assembly however did not think proper to adopt Mirabeau's proposition. The day before yesterday M. de Montmorin sent a letter to the assembly informing them that the continued military preparations of England rendered it necessary to increase the armaments in the French ports, and at the same time desiring the decision of the assembly on the letter of the Spanish Ambassador requiring the fulfilling the conditions of the *pacte de famille*. The letter of the Ambassador was dated the 16th. of June. M. de Montmorin had postponed communicating it till now because he had hopes that the result of the negotiations would render it unnecessary. In this letter the Ambassador says among other things "Sa M. C. me charge d'ajouter encore que l'état actuel de cette affaire imprevue exige une determination très prompte, et que les mesures que la Cour de France prendra pour venir à son secours soient si actives, si claires et si positives, qu'elles évitent jusqu'au moindre sujet de méfiance; autrement *S. M. T. C. ne devra pas être surprise que l'Espagne cherche d'autres amis et d'autres alliés parmi toutes les autres puissances de l'Europe, sans en excepter aucune, sur qui elle puisse compter toujours en cas de besoin.*" These communications were referred to a diplomatic committee lately named for the purpose of examining treaties and conferring with the Minister of foreign affairs.—It is impossible to say what would have been the decision of the assembly; for although some of the more enlightened members saw clearly that the letter of the Ambassador of Spain denoted an alliance with England, and were deeply affected by it, yet the majority seemed determined not to extend their attention beyond the confines of the Kingdom. A letter sent to the Assembly yesterday by M. de Montmorin prevented their taking up this subject: He informed them that an express passing through Paris on his way to London had brought a copy of a declaration between Spain and England signed the 24th. of July, and that there was reason to believe this would stop the military preparations making in England.—By the declaration it is said that His Ca. M. is disposed to give satisfaction for the injury complained of by his B. M. to restore the vessels and indemnify the parties: "bien entendu que la présente declaration ne pourra rien préjuger sur les établissemens que les Sujets de S. M. B. pourroient prétendre former dans la dite Baie de Nootka." By the counter declaration the British Ambassador accepts this satisfaction on behalf and by order of his master, "bien entendu qu'il n'en resultera ni exclusion, ni prejudice à tout établissement que ses sujets voudroient faire dans la dite Baie de Nootka."—Thus you see Sir that the matter of right is still left open to discussion. It seems to me highly probable that it will all end in a political alliance and commercial treaty between the two powers.—What changes this political phaenomenon may produce it is impossible to say, but it cannot fail to have a preponderating influence on the present state of the world. We shall know in a few days whether England discontinues her armaments, and from thence be able to form an accurate idea of their real object. Many think that they are too considerable to be destined against Spain alone—they suppose still that England has designs in the Baltic. In that case the present situation of the King of Sweden will render it necessary that no time should be lost and of course we shall soon know what opinion to form on that subject. His fleet has lately been forced to escape from the Russian with the loss of ten Ships of the line. It is true however that fortune favored him some days after (the 9th. of July) the two flottillas met and he gained a complete victory over the Prince Nassau. But his fleet will not again be able to put to sea until he receives foreign aid to augment their number.

Since[1] *my last the rumors of the designs of England against us have become so public and common that it is impossible not to pay attention to them.—The report the most credited is that one of the Princes of England is to be declared Stadtholder in the United States.* I cannot find from whence these *reports* arise, nor do I suppose they *have any real foundation.—*Still they lead *one*[2] *to believe that the English cabinet* may cherish *hostile projects—*perhaps make use of her *present armed situation* in order to demand an *immediate payment of debts*[3] *or endeavour* to make some arrangement respecting *the forts by which they may keep them or*[4] *in fine* take some step to try to destroy the *rising credit of our finances. Yet their armament, being large ships of war, is not what they would make use of against us. The troops they have put on board as mentioned by Montmorin, I believe are only those substituted to marines.—*I am sorry not to be able to *give you more certain information. At present* I have thought it *proper* to *inform you of what is said and repeated here every day.—*The communication between this place and New-York is such as disables me from giving you so regular and so early intelligence as I would wish to do.[5] But I hope this letter will find an immediate conveyance from Havre.

The merchants of Havre have made complaints to Mr. Necker and the Minister of Marine concerning the heavy tonnage to which they are subjected in the United States, and particularly the repeated duties to which they are subjected in going from one part of the United States to another. The present situation of affairs here does not admit of their paying attention to these complaints, and I hope the present arrangements making by Congress will render them unnecessary, as I do not doubt every facility will be given to the commercial intercourse between the two nations. Any example of this kind set by us will certainly be followed here, as soon as they can find time to attend to their commercial regulations.—In the conversations I have had with the committee of commerce they have frequently expressed a desire that the two countries should form a treaty on the footing of the most perfect reciprocity with respect to this subject, and such as might increase the articles of exchange. I shall send by the diligence a bundle of newspapers which will arrive at Havre nearly as soon as this letter, and probably go by the same vessel. I am with sentiments of the most perfect attachment my dear Sir, your friend & servant,   W. SHORT

FC (DNA: RG 59, DD); at head of text: "No. 38. W. Short to Secty of State"; partly in code, with interlinear decoding. PrC (DLC: Short Papers); accompanied by text *en clair* for coded passages on a separate page. Recorded in sJL as received 20 Nov. 1790.

1 This and subsequent words in italics are in code and have been decoded by the Editors, employing a partially reconstructed key for Code No. 10; the interlinear decoding varies from this decoding in some particulars, one of which is noted.

2 This was decoded as "us"; but both the text *en clair* and the code symbol call for the above reading.

3 In text *en clair* the preceding three words are interlined in substitution for "compliance with the treaty," deleted.

4 In text *en clair* the following is deleted: "settle the disputed boundary."

5 This sentence appears in text *en clair* but was not encoded.

From William Short

DEAR SIR   Paris August the 4th. 1790

Your furniture is at length all packed up, and the last articles are this moment gone to Neuilly to meet the vessel which is to take them in there. They are all plumbed so as not to be opened any where. They will be recieved at Havre by M. de la Motte, who promises to take charge of them. Your directions with respect to the mode of packing the several articles were not strictly followed. The Packer gave good reasons for deviating in some instances, particularly with respect to the chairs, and on the whole I thought it more prudent to let him pursue his known and accustomed way, than to endeavour to make him follow new instructions. I hope you will recieve all these packages safe. They will be accompanied by a list not only explaining their contents, but the manner of unpacking them. Every article you had here is sent agreeably to your directions, except such things as were of the more common kind. They consist in your Secretaire (which is not yet sold because Petit has not been able to get a third of its value), the cases in which your books were placed, two or three tables, five dumb waiters, three white flagbottomed chairs and seven of a coarser kind. Petit lays claim to a part of the bookcases, i.e. all except the two which stood in your cabinet. He says when Mr. Adams left Paris he gave him all such things and is sure your intention if here would be the same. As the articles are trifling I have supposed it proper to comply. I have desired him to sell the other articles as soon as possible for whatever he can get, and particularly the Secretaire. Your servants were discharged and paid the two months agreeably to your directions at the time of recieving your letter. They had none of them places. Petit and Henri were employed till now, the latter in the place of Nomeny, to assist in the packing. After the elopement of Nomeny Henri applied to be put on the same footing as to wages. It was done because the augmentation was small, because you were then expected to return in a very short time, and because Petit and myself thought that being debarassed of Nomeni, you would employ Henri in his place, and because he said his wages were not sufficient for his subsistence independent of your table. I yeilded the more easily to this and paid him the wages of Nomeny, because your servants now cost you less although he was paid more.—The coachman, in applying for his two months gratification, was supported by Petit who said at the time of your departure, you were in arrears to him for clothes and that you promised on your return to indemnify him. Besides he has always considered himself as at your service, and regards himself at present as without place, knowing that he will be discharged as soon as I can find a tolerable price for your horses. I found also on enquiry that even should your servants be placed custom entitled them to a gratification, but as yet they are all without places. Petit talks of returning to his family, in order to become a farmer. He has no hopes of a place except from your successor.—The hatter has presented an account for a hat made for Miss Jefferson a few days before your departure. I objected for some time to paying it, because you had told me there was nothing of that sort to be paid, but as the servants recollected his coming here two days after your departure with the same demand, and as he was ready to affirm the truth of it, I thought it better to pay so trifling a sum than to dispute, particularly as I was persuaded it was just. These are the only sums I have paid without an express warranty from you.

The memoire of the Emballeur amounts to upwards of six thousand livres. I have given it M. Gautier who promises to have it examined that I may know whether it is reasonable. It seems to us both a very large sum.—All your commissions have been executed, except that of the clock. The workman after promising faithfully it should be finished for the 15th. of July, had not at that term even begun it. I am at a loss whether to have it made at present, as I know not whether you would wish to have it sent alone. I will thank you to give me further instructions respecting it as soon as possible. The workman I believe is going on with it, but I shall be perfectly master to take it or not, agreably to our conditions, and shall be a good deal guided by the manner in which it is executed. Petit has paid for all the articles purchased, and has the memoires and reciepts in his hands. I am going to give him an order on M. Grand for their amount, as soon as we have examined and added them together. I shall then forward them to you. These sums together with my account against you consisting in the wages of your servants which I have paid monthly, and the boxes made by Upton agreably to your orders, which I have paid also, the forrage of your saddle horse until he was sold and two or three trifling articles, make the sum of your debts here. I shall send you the details of my account in my next, and shall draw on the bankers in Holland for its amount. Your house rent forms an article a part and has not yet been paid. I mentioned to you in my former letters the interpretation put on the lease, by which you are obliged to keep the house three years to count from the last renewal of the lease. I have as yet not been able to learn any thing from your Landlord who is in Switzerland, but his brother who is his attorney here claims the compliance with the lease. He has written to his brother long ago on the subject and has not yet communicated to me his answer. Several people have talked of hiring the house and Mr. Grand is now trying to dispose of it in that way, in order to diminish your loss. House rent however has much fallen so that you will inevitably lose something. Besides Langeac is endeavouring to sell it, and in that case you will lose nothing. At worst I imagine he will be satisfied with a small sacrifice in ready money, and it is Mr. Grand's advice to make this. I hope however to hear from you soon on this subject, that I may know what you wish to be done.

I forgot to mention that there is another of your commissions which is not executed—that respecting the gun locks. The smith after making me hope for some time that I should recieve them sent me word some days ago that he could not make them until he had had a private conversation with me. I sent to him to call on me; but he has not yet come. The person who was here on his behalf seemed not to concieve the possibility of the locks being lost, and to apprehend an improper use would be made of them by those who had taken them either in France or America. I will make a point however of seeing the Smith soon, and of removing such difficulties as he may have. Some of them I believe arise also from the inquisitorial eye with which the districts and municipality regard the manufacture of arms at this moment. I inclose you a number of letters sent me by your friends here. You will observe that from Mde. D'Enville has only a wafer. It is because she complies with the decree in not making use of her arms. I add to them such letters as came here to your address after your departure, and which from inadvertence were not forwarded as soon as I knew of your being fixed at N. York.—I say nothing to you about myself in this letter because I have already said perhaps too much, and because I suppose my fate will be decided before its arrival. Adieu my dear Sir believe me unalterably your friend & servant, W: SHORT

RC (DLC); at head of text: "Private"; endorsed as received 20 Nov. 1790 and so recorded in SJL. PrC (DLC: Short Papers).

To W. & J. Willink, N. & J. Van Staphorst, & N. Hubbard

GENTLEMEN   New York Aug. 4. 1790.

This serves to advise you that, on the 31st. of July, I drew on you in favor of Messieurs Leroy and Bayard of this place, for four thousand and thirty six florins courant of Holland paiable at 60. days sight, which be pleased to honor and charge to the account of the United States of America, as for arrears of Salary due to me as their late minister plenipotentiary in France and payable out of their monies in your hands. That the place from which I drew might excite no doubts in your mind, I procured previously a letter of approbation from the Secretary of the Treasury to you which you will recieve herewith, and in which the sum could not be exactly fixed at the time of it's date. I have the honor to be Gentlemen Your most obedt. humble servt.,   TH: JEFFERSON

PrC (DLC); at foot of text: "Messieurs Willem & Jan Willink, Nicholas & Jacob Van Staphorst Amsterdam." Enclosure not found. Under this date TJ wrote the following in his Account Book: "signed bills of exchange on Messrs. Willinks & V. Staphorst for 4036. florins courant paiable at 60. days sight to Leroy & Bayard for arrears of salary, with the approbation of Colo. Hamilton who wrote them accordingly. The bills were dated July 31. to make them agree with his letter. Note these were sold @ 3/1 the gelder (the par is 3/2) so they come to £622-4-5 N.Y. currency which I leave in the hands of Leroy & Bayard. It is equal to £350. sterl." See TJ to Hamilton, 9 July 1790.

To William Carmichael

SIR   New York August 6th. 1790.

I have had the honor of writing to you on the 10th. of April and 31st. of May. In order that a review of the channels you have adopted for the conveyance of your letters may enable you to judge which of them are best, and whether better may be found, I send you the dates of those of the last seven years, and the time of their reception.

They are as follows.

date of letter	receipt	date of letter	receipt
1784. October 12	1785. Februy 10.	1787. July 3.	1788. Feby 4.
1785. July 25.	Octr. 27.	August 19.	Jany. 21st.
Decr. 9.	1786. April 4.	1788. April 29.	July 5.
1786. July 15.	Novr. 7.	Novr. 5.	1789 May 12.
Augt. 14	Ditto	8.	Ditto.
Septr. 2.	Ditto	28.	Ditto.
10	1787 Feby. 3.	Decr. 2.	Ditto.
		1789. May 6.	Septr. 2.

You will perceive that they come slowly, and also that they are more rare than we could wish, the last being now fifteen months old, and indeed being the only one of the years 1789. and 1790. I make no doubt but that some miscarriages have shortened the list, and I know that it is difficult to find conveyances from Madrid. Cadiz and Lisbon I suppose to be the ports within your reach from which vessels come most frequently; at the former we shall have a Consul named probably in the course of the present year, and as to the latter you can make arrangements with Col. Humphreys, so as to give us the hope of hearing from you more frequently, say once a month.

Congress have passed an Act for establishing the seat of Government on the Potomac from the year 1800, and in the mean time to remove to Philadelphia; it is to that place therefore that your future letters had better be addressed. They have also passed bills for funding our debts foreign and domestic.[1] . . . from that day downwards a new account must be opened, because a new fund is appropriated to it from that time; which will still however be in the hands of our Bankers at Amsterdam, on whom your draughts will therefore continue to be made.

As you may sometimes have occasion for foreign correspondents on matters interesting to the United States, I have the honor to inform you of the following appointments of Consuls for them in the following ports.[2]. . .

Fayal. John Street. Vice-Consul.

Surinam. Ebenezar Brush. Consul.

Their jurisdictions in general are made to extend to all places within the same allegiance, which are nearer to them than to the residence of any other Consul or Vice-Consul of the United States.

We learn through the channel of the public papers that the Emperor of Morrocco, our friend, is dead. It is much wished that we could know as soon as possible, whether Francesco Chiappe holds any place near the present Emperor, as he did with the former.

As the introduction of uniformity in weights and measures is in contemplation in some parts of Europe, I send you two copies of what is proposed here on that subject, the one for yourself, the other for Monsr. de Campomanes. You will receive herewith a cypher for our future correspondence, and the public papers. I shall endeavour to furnish in future for the use of your Office, copies of the federal laws, as conveyances shall occur. I have the honor to be with great esteem &c.   THOMAS JEFFERSON

FC (DNA: RG 59, PCC No. 121); recorded in SJL as "public." On the enclosed cypher, see TJ to Remsen, 9 Aug. 1790, note.

¹ The passage omitted here is that enclosed in brackets in TJ to Short, 26 July 1790 (see note 3).

² The names of the consuls and their jurisdictions are omitted here because, except for the two names given above, they are identical with those stated in TJ to Short, 26 July 1790.

From James B. Pleasants

SIR   August 6th. 1790.

I have this moment received information that induces me to believe that some mistake has arisen on the subject on which I wrote you some time since the application of steam by means of a perpetual Cylinder. The name I mentioned is not Evans, the name is Cruce. If Evins has imposed himself by the name of Cruse the Imposition appears to me to be so gross as not to admit of a doubt of detection.—If there is any mistake in the business I have no doubt of its being rectified.—I am with the highest sentiments of respect,

JAMES B. PLEASANTS

RC (DNA: RG 59, MLR); endorsed as received 12 Aug. 1790 and recorded in SJL on that date though the place of origin (Baltimore) is not there mentioned. Pleasants' former letter is that of 5 May 1790.

To George Washington

Friday Aug. 6. 1790.

Th: Jefferson has the honor to inform the President that in a conversation with Mr. Hawkins yesterday evening, it came out that he had seen Mcgillivray's letter to Govr. Houston, and Houston's answer: he thinks they were dated the latter end of 1784. but is sure they were some time in the year preceding the treaty of Galphinton to which he was sent. He recites the substance and purport of Mcgillivray's letter, but does not recollect that of Houston's. Previous to the treaty of Galphinton, some of the Indians disavowed to him that of Augusta, and declared the lands ceded were of those which belonged to the whole nation, and not to the lower creeks in particular. I am not certain whether he did not say this conversation was in 1784. But I am sure he repeated it as precedent to the treaty of Galphinton.

RC (DNA: RG 59, MLR); addressed: "The President of the United States." FC (DNA: RG 59, SDC). Not recorded in SJL.

To James Brown

SIR   New York Aug. 8. 1790.

As I shall shortly set out for Virginia, and shall have occasion there for some necessaries, I take the liberty of stating them herein, and of asking the favor of you to send them to me by the first conveyance after the reciept of this. Any waggon going to Charlottesville may deliver them at Colo. Nichs. Lewis's, unless my own were to be passing, which might carry them directly to Monticello. I have noted a quarter cask of wine. I would prefer good Lisbon; next to that Sherry, next to that Calcavallo; but still a good quality of the latter would be preferable to an indifferent quality of the former. If none of these, then claret. Whatever kind you can procure me, be so good as to have it bottled before sent.

The papers which I received from Mr. Donald, I inclosed to the Secretary of the Treasury, desiring he would return them to me if the prosecution was to go on. He has not returned them. I shall be able before I leave this, to know what is intended: and will let you know it. I am with great esteem Sir Your most obedt. humble servt.,   TH: JEFFERSON

Coffee 20. ℔
double refined sugar 2. loaves
single do. 2. loaves
brown sugar. 30 ℔.
rice 50. ℔.

raisins 10. ℔.
almonds 10. ℔.
pepper. black. 1. ℔.

cinnamon mace cloves ginger nutmegs allspice	1. oz. of each.

capers. 3. bottles
mustard. 3. bottles
candles. a box, small. spermaceti if to be had.
1. cheese.
French brandy 10. gallons. if none, then good rum.
common rum 5. gallons.
wine. a quarter cask, bottled.
cod-fish. 15. or 20. ℔.

If the wine you send me be either Lisbon, Sherry, or Calcavallo, then I would be glad of 3. or 4. doz. in addition, of any sound weak wine, either red or white, which would be good for mixing with water, the kinds specified not being proper for that.

P.S. I send from hence 2½ doz. Windsor chairs, which I have desired to be delivered to you, and will beg the favor of you to forward them as quick as you can to Mr. Lewis's or to Monticello.

RC. (Mr. Ike Hayman, Rutherford, N.J., 1950). PrC (MHi).

Brown acknowledged the above on 16 Aug. 1790, saying that he had "some Sherry Wine of first quality . . . imported by Mr. Donald 18 months ago direct from Cadiz" and that he would "have a Qr. Cask Bottled Off"; he also repeated his expression of gratitude to TJ for his good offices in the disagreeable affair with Heth (RC in MHi; endorsed as received 24 Aug. 1790 and so recorded in SJL). On 30 Aug. 1790 John Brown wrote for his brother that he was sending the above order by Philemon Richards, including 12 dozen bottles of sherry, 3½ dozen bottles of port, "56 ℔. Tallow Candles (no Spermaceti to be got)," 4 loaves "S[ingle] Refin'd Sugar (No Dble. R[efined] to be got)," and other articles as specified except "No Cheese nor fish to be got" (RC in MHi; endorsed by TJ as received [at Monticello] 19 Sep. 1790 and so recorded in SJL).

From Diodati

Paris le 8 Aoust 1790

Vous m'avez prévenu mon cher Monsieur et j'allois Vous écrire ayant appris que Vous Vous étiez décidé a accepter le poste qui

Vous étoit proposé et que Vous restiez en Amérique, pour Vous en faire mon compliment, sil peut contribuer Votre bonheur mais pour Vous temoigner aussi, tous mes regrets mes profonds et sincères Regrets, de ce que je ne vous verrai plus dans ce pays, de ce que je ne pourrai plus Vous témoigner toute mon estime, toute la vraye amitié que je Vous ay Vouée, qui me portoit à vous avec une entière confiance, puisqu'il m'avoit paru que Vous m'accordiez aussi des Sentiments analogues aux miens. C'est un des malheurs de la Vie que de perdre la société et les Relations habituelles qui conviennent a toutes sortes d'égards. On en trouve si peu en général, et vous aurez trouvé comme moi, que le Corps diplomatique en présente très peu.

Je ne suis nullement surpris que le Congres ayt cherché à s'appuyer de Votre Travaill et de Vos lumières en Vous confiant le département des affaires Etrangères. Je souhaitte seulement que le Travaill qu'il nécessite ne fatigue point Votre Santé et que les affaires tournent a Votre Satisfaction. On a voulu dire icy qu'il y avoit plusieurs de Vos provinces qui regrettoient la domination Anglaise, mais j'ay peine a le croire, puisqu'il ne dépend que d'elles, d'être tres heureuses et libres. La France a recouvré sa liberté, mais elle est devenüe Licence, qui se manifeste de toutes les façons et par beaucoup de réformes, tellement que l'exces, la continuité et l'Umpunité pourroient bientôt conduire des Tetes françoises légères et accoutumées au joug, d'y rentrer librement. On peut tout croire et tout craindre, de l'état actuel des choses qui est une véritable anarchie, dans laquelle il est impossible qu'elles restent, et il faut nécessairement qu'il survienne quelque Evènement, dont personne ne sçauroit dire et prévoir la Nature et la Tournure. Je n'entrerai pas dans de plus grands détaills sur tout ce qui se passe, présumant que M. Short est éxact à Vous en donner. Je l'ay prié de Venir quelques fois chez moi, ce dont il a la complaisance, et de me donner de Vos Nouvelles, que je rechercherai toujours avec le plus grand empressement.

Je suis de Retour de Genève seulement depuis 3 mois, y ayant passé pres dune année, et puis à peine étois-je arrivé que Mad. Diodati a été obligée d'y retourner pour aller rendre des soins à une Tante mourante qui l'a élevée, qui la demandoit, de façon que je suis seul. Je lui ay fait part de Votre obligeant souvenir, mon cher Monsieur, et que nous Vous perdions décidément. Elle même témoigne ses Regrets pour elle et pour moi, puisqu'elle partage bien ma façon de penser. Tronchin m'a prié de Vous exprimer aussi les siens et je m'en acquitte avec plaisir.

Il me sera bien douce d'apprendre de vos Nouvelles, mon cher Monsieur, et il me le seroit encore plus de pouvoir Vous étre de quelque Utilité icy. Certainement Vous pouvez compter sur moi. Certainement vous pourrez toujours compter sur l'amitié sincère que je Vous ay vouée, comme sur tous les sentiments pleins d'estime et de Considération avec lesquels j'ay l'honneur d'étre, mon cher Monsieur, Votre tres Humble & tres Obéissant Serviteur,

LE CTE DIODATI

RC (DLC); endorsed as received 20 Nov. 1790 and so recorded in SJL.

To Nicholas Lewis

DEAR SIR   New York Aug. 8. 1790.

Congress have resolved to rise the day after tomorrow and if nothing unforeseen happens, I think I may be at Monticello from the 1st. to the 8th. or 10th. of September, where I hope to remain a month. I have this day written to Mr. Brown of Richmond to send up some necessaries for which I shall have occasion during my stay. We must once more trouble our neighbors on the score of beds. If the bedding of my daughters is still at Monticello, 3. beds and bolsters in addition to theirs will do. There will be no need of either sheets or blankets. It is the last time we shall have occasion to trespass in this way, as I have ordered from Europe a sufficient supply of what is necessary in this line for Monticello, which I had hoped would be arrived before this. How-[ever] it is not, and cannot now come in time.—You will be so good as to direct a sufficient stock of fattened meats. It will be the season for good woodland beef, which is the best possible.—I have received my bacon and venison hams here in good condition, for which I must thank Mrs. Lewis in particular: adding due acknolegements to Colo. Bell. I inclose a letter from France for Monsr. Derieux.

No certainty yet whether England and Spain will be engaged in the war. Enough are engaged however to ensure a good price for wheat for years to come. It is at a dollar here. As I shall see you within a week or fortnight after you recieve this, I shall only add affectionate respects to Mrs. Lewis, and assurances of the esteem &

attachment with which I am Dear Sir your sincere friend & servt.,

TH: JEFFERSON

PrC (MHi). Enclosure not found.

The letter from Mrs. Lewis about the BACON AND VENISON hams is printed above (Vol. 1: 40-1) under the erroneous date of 14 [April?] 1770. The figures in the date are deceptive, but the correct reading is obviously that supposed by TJ in an entry in SJL for 12 May 1790, which reads: "Lewis Mary, Albem. 14 (April [1790] I suppose)." COLO. BELL was probably Thomas Bell (d. 1800), an Albemarle neighbor (VMHB, XXI [1912], 8-9). The

term WOODLAND BEEF is not recorded in DAE, but, given the date and the context, the meaning is clear: i.e., beef cattle fattened in woodland ranges as distinguished from stall-fed beef. In the earlier phases of colonial agriculture woods were burned annually in the spring to promote the growth of grass for cattle (DAE, *Wood*, I, b.). TJ's lease of Shadwell to Craven Peyton on 1 Oct. 1799 provided that "his stock shall have free range on all the uninclosed woodlands . . . on the same side of the river" (Betts, *Farm Book*, 167-8).

To Robert R. Livingston

DEAR SIR   New York Aug. 8. 1790.

I duly recieved your favor of the 1st. inst. and have withheld acknoleging it in hopes of finding time to consider it thoroughly. But this hope advancing before me, like my shadow, I must hasard thereon the ideas which occur extempore. I think it ingenious, well worth trying, and that probably it will lessen the friction. One consideration occurs to me. Suppose it the case of the tub mill, with it's pivot armed with wood as you propose and turning in a vessel of mercury, instead of running on a pivot and ink as usual. A cylinder of wood 2. feet long and containing 2. cubical feet, must be of $13\frac{1}{2}$ inches diameter. The pivot then will be a compound one, the central part of iron running on the iron bottom, surrounded by an annulus area of wood of 144 square inches—the area of a section of the iron part. This annulus area resting on a surface of mercury, and turning on it, is really a part of the pivot, and, tho, the body on which it turns being fluid, the friction will be small, yet considering that it will act from $6\frac{3}{4}$ inches from the center of motion, down to (suppose) $\frac{1}{2}$ inch, it's effect may become sensible. I join with you in thinking the friction on the curve surface of the cylinder will be small, and on the whole think it worth an experiment, and will be glad to know it's issue if you try it.

Finding that you amuse yourself mathematically, I inclose you a report of that nature made to Congress on the subject of measures and weights.—Be so good as to present me respectful-

[ly] to Mrs. Livingston and to be assured of the esteem & attachment with which I have the honour to be Dear Sir your most obedt. & most humble servt.,   Th: Jefferson

PrC (DLC). Enclosure: *Report of the Secretary of State, on the subject of establishing a uniformity in the weights,* *measures and coins of the United States* (New York, Childs & Swaine, [1790]).

From Josiah Parker

New York, 8 Aug. 1790. John Cowper, Jr., of Portsmouth requested him "to name him as a candidate for a Consulship at . . . London, Bristol, Lisbon, or Bilboa." After obtaining "a more than common Education," Cowper was sent to Liverpool to be educated in the mercantile line, where he served in house of Crosbie & Greenwood for five years. He then returned to Virginia to conduct "the Mercantile concerns of his Father Mr. Wills Cowper of Portsmouth" until the spring of 1789 when he went to Bordeaux "long enough to acquire a tolerable knowledge of the French language" and their mode of business. He would prefer Bordeaux, but does not offer himself for that as a consul is already appointed there. He "is a young Gentleman of address and abilities and supports a very good Character." Mr. William Stokes of Virginia also desires to be made consul "at a port in St. Domingo or at Bristol"; he has been unfortunate in business but "conducted himself in such a manner as to support an unblemishd Character. Both these Gentlemen are attached to their Country and the present Government of it."—TJ "will please to name those Gentlemen to the President."

RC (DLC: Applications for Office under Washington); at foot of text: "Secretary of the States"; endorsed by TJ as received 7 Aug. 1790 and so recorded in SJL (since there were several other entries on this date, not in alphabetical order, the error in date was probably that of Parker). To the endorsement TJ added "for Lisbon," but neither Cowper nor Stokes is mentioned among the recommended candidates in the list of vacancies submitted to the President on 23 Feb. 1791. Parker's use of the imperative in the final sentence may reflect his view of prerogative as a member of the Virginia delegation in the House of Representatives. There is no evidence that TJ responded to the above letter and the silence on these two candidates may be due to a feeling in the administration that Virginia and Maryland already had a full share of the appointments, particularly those for such key ports as London, Liverpool, Bordeaux, and Martinique (see documents on the Consular Establishment under 21 July 1790 and notes there).

To Martha Jefferson Randolph

New York Aug. 8. 1790.

Congress being certainly to rise the day after tomorrow, I can now, my dear Patsy, be more certain of the time at which I can be at Monticello, and which I think will be from the 8th. to the 15th. of September: more likely to be sooner than later. I shall leave this about a fortnight hence, but must stay some days to have arrangements taken for my future residence in Philadelphia. I hope to be able to pass a month at least with you at Monticello. I am in hopes Mr. Randolph will take dear Poll in his pocket. Tell him I have sent him the model of the mould-board by Mr. David Randolph who left this place yesterday. I must trouble you to give notice to Martin to be at Monticello by the 1st. of September that he may have things prepared. If you know any thing of Bob, I should be glad of the same notice to him, tho' I suppose him to be in the neighborhood of Fredericksbg. and in that case I will have him notified thro' Mr. Fitzhugh. I have written to Mr. Brown for some necessaries to be sent to Monticello, and to send on some chairs which will go hence to the care of Mr. D. Randolph at the Hundred, to be forwarded to Mr. Brown at Richmond. If Mr. Randolph can give a little attention to the forwarding these articles we shall be the more comfortable. Present me to him and Maria affectionately, and continue to love me as I do you, my dear. Most sincerely,   TH: JEFFERSON

RC (NNP). PrC (ViU); partial text owing to folds in paper when being put through copying press, accompanied by early Tr of PrC showing result of an attempt to reconstruct text.

From Nathaniel Cutting

SIR   St. Marc, Isle of St. Domingue 9th. Augt. 1790.

After what I took the liberty to write you from hence under the 4th. Current, with a hasty Postscript of the 6th., I presume it will be agreable to you to know that a temporary suspension of all altercation between the General Assembly of this Colony and M. Le Comte de Peinier has taken place by mean of as unexpected and I think as extraordinary an occurrence as is recorded in the History of mankind. It is no other than that the General Assembly, with its archives, has embark'd aboard the *Leopard*, surnam'd *Le Sauveur des Français*, and has actually sail'd for France!

In my Letter abovemention'd I acquainted you that this Step had been proposed by several members of the assembly so early as the 1st. Current; but the voices of the Commons of St. Marc and many other Parishes, were then against it. However, when it was found that M. de Vincent had actually arriv'd at Gonaive at the Head of eight hundred men or upwards, including Cavalry and Artillery, with the intention of cooperating with the Governor General to disperse the Assembly;—When certain intelligence arriv'd that a Reinforcement of one thousand men were ready to come to his assistance in case of necessity, and that Le Comte de Peinier could muster at least one thousand men on the opposite side St. Marc;—When it was known that Comte de Peinier had sent a Corvette to the Commandant at Martinique requesting him to send down all his Majesty's Forces that could possibly be spared —the Assembly wisely consider'd that though its friends might eagerly press to defend it, and might far out-number their opponents, yet they were but badly appointed, neither had they military stores or Provisions to sustain any considerable contest:—But another consideration weigh'd more with the General Assembly than every thing else; viz. That whichever Party might prove victorious in the deathful Conflict, the invaluable Blood of many worthy Citizens must stain the Soil. To avoid bringing things to this extremity, which would be the inevitable consequence of its continuing embodied at St. Marc;—at the same time to avoid exposing its members to personal insult and danger by *dispersing*, and being unwilling *thereby* to gratify the arbitrary views and implacable enmity of a sett of imperious aristocrattes;—likewise to prove the rectitude of its intentions;—being conscious that its transactions would bear the strictest investigation, and confident of meeting the approbation of that Supreme authority which must judge between it and its adversaries in the last resort,—The General Assembly on the Evening of the 6th. Current came to the Resolution of departing immediately for France in the Leopard.— This Resolution was no sooner past by a large majority than a great number of the members sent their Baggage aboard. The President, Vice President and above thirty members slept aboard that night, being apprehensive that some treachery would be practiced against them if they remain'd at their usual Lodgings. The next day a *Seance* was held at the usual place;—About 4 P.M., The Vice President in the Chair, The Assembly took Public leave of the municipalitie of St. Marc, and directly after was escorted down to the Water-side by the different Patriotic Corps under arms, Drums beating and Colours display'd. It was really a solemn and an affecting sight! This step of the assembly ought to convince its most inveterate Enemies of the rectitude of its intentions. It eagerly seeks to make a *personal appeal* to that supreme authority which only has a right to take cognizance of, and to controul its transactions. Among the Members of their Assembly there are some men of first-rate abilities, and of Capital Fortunes, some also who have resided twenty to thirty years in this Colony, and who thought never to have quitted it. What an immense sacrifice they make in departing thus at a moment's warning, in forsaking ease and affluence to brave the inconveniences and dangers attending a passage across the Boisterous Ocean, merely from the patriotic motive of securing to the Inhabitants of this Colony and their Posterity the blessings of a liberal constitution, calculated to promote the happiness of all who dwell beneath its salutary influence! Whatever may be the consequence of this manly though excentric manoeuvre, each Individual of the Assembly who is gone to present himself before his Sovereign will enjoy the supreme satisfaction of reflecting that by thus "patiently persevereing in the ways of well-doing," that is to say, by obeying the dictates of Eternal Reason, he insures to himself "honor, Glory and Immortality"!

A very small number of members of the General Assembly remain behind, and are dispersing to their respective Parishes.

On Sunday Evening about 8 o'Clock the Leopard weigh'd and stood to Sea. Those Inhabitants of different Parishes who voluntarily came hither to support the Assembly have quietly retired to their different places of abode, and the Town of St. Marc is now as tranquil as if the voice of Politics or War had never been heard within its Boundaries.

These extraordinary occurrences have unexpectedly detain'd me here till the present moment. The Captain with whom I take passage for Havre has just given me notice that he will take his departure to morrow.—I have the honor to be, with the greatest Respect, Sir, Your most obedt. & very huml. Servt.,

NAT. CUTTING

RC (DNA: RG 59, MLR); addressed; endorsed as received 22 Nov. 1790 and so recorded in SJL.

To Henry Remsen

Monday morn. [9 Aug. 1790]

Th: Jefferson being to go to the President's at 8. aclock, and perhaps for the day, would be glad to see Mr. Remsen at least a quarter before 8. and that he will bring with him whatever printed cyphers he has of the kind furnished by Th: J. in order to compare them with two he has received from Mr. Adams.

RC (George A. Ball, Muncie, Indiana, 1945); undated; addressed: "Mr. Remsen" and written on fragment of memorandum from Remsen to TJ containing information about costs of removal of the offices to Philadelphia: "a waggon will take One ton at 12/ per 100 is £12.0.0. Four days journey is £3.0.0. per day each waggon" (see note below). Neither Remsen's note nor the above is recorded in SJL. The date is assigned on the basis of TJ's letter to the President of 8 Aug. 1790 (Document V in group of documents on the war crisis) in which he alludes to the letter to Carmichael of 6 Aug. 1790 and mentions the fact that cyphers needed to be prepared. Having transmitted the important budget of documents to Washington on Sunday, TJ—according to this conjectural reconstruction of the chronology—expected to go over these with him on Monday morning "at 8 aclock, and perhaps for the day." The memorandum to Remsen must, then, have been written quite early. No other episode at this time involving cyphers required such urgency.

The cypher key transmitted to Carmichael in the letter of 6 Aug. 1790 was to replace that sent by TJ to him on 1 Feb. 1788. TJ had every reason to believe that the Spanish ministry had access to that cypher (Code No. 11); W. C. Ford, *The United States and Spain in 1790* (Brooklyn, N.Y., 1890), p. 18, states "that before Carmichael's letters could leave Spain, or Jefferson's be delivered to him, the Spanish court had read them and were perfectly cognizant of what they contained. Even the cypher used between

these two was known to it."

In DLC: TJ Papers, 66: 11553 there is the remainder of the document noted above in which Remsen gathered information about freight costs to Philadelphia. The remnant reads: "Freight of articles to Philadelphia by water.

7d. per square foot.
2/. per barrel
from 6d. to 1/6 per chair, according to quality of chair.
2/8 per bed, tied up in a small compass in a blanket.

A vessel capable of containing 500 barrels can be freighted for £35, and the passage of servants in her will not be charged; but they must find themselves. This vessel will contain

Mr. Jefferson's furniture.
The effects belonging to the Offices that are to be removed by water
The effects of the persons in the Office.

And such other Effects as may offer. The expence of transporting articles to Philadelphia, by water to Amboy, by land from Amboy to Bordentown, and by water from Bordentown to Philadela. 4/9 per hundred weight, and 7/ for a passenger. The expence of transporting effects to Philadelphia by land, from Powles hook, the ferriage from N York to Powles-hook exclusive, 10/ per hundred weight for a single Ton, and 8/4 for seven Tons, to be carried in covered waggons."

It is obvious from the date of the foregoing that TJ initiated an inquiry into the costs of moving the departmental offices as soon as the residence Act had been passed.

To William Short

[New York] Aug. 9. 1790.

Congress rises tomorrow. Your successor will not be appointed till they meet in December. Consequently he cannot go till the next spring.

RC (DLC: Short Papers); entirely in code, except for date, having interlinear decoding in Short's hand; at head of text (also in code): "private." PrC

(DLC); accompanied by text *en clair* in TJ's hand. Decoding verified by Editors, employing partially reconstructed key to Code No. 10. Entry in SJL shows that both this and the letter to Short of 10 Aug. 1790 were conveyed "by Barrett."

From Edmund Randolph

SIR   New York August 10th. 1790.

I have examined the papers which you did me the honor of submitting to me yesterday, on the subject of the Georgia confiscations. But in the present mutilation of the necessary documents, it is impossible for me to form a satisfactory opinion. The act of May 1782 is not among the enclosures of Sir John Temple, but is the groundwork of the proceeding complained of. The last act appears in part only, nor does the Governor's reasoning supply any of these defects.

I trust therefore, that you will see the propriety of my declining to enter into the question at this moment at least. Perhaps at any time the proper answer will be, that the executive of the United States ought to leave the whole business to the judiciary. On this however I do not now presume to decide. I have the honor to be &c.   EDMUND RANDOLPH

FC (DNA: RG 59, PCC No. 120); at head of text: "From the Attorney General for the United States"; at foot of text: "(signed)." Not recorded in SJL. See TJ to Temple, 11 Aug. 1790.

Randolph's allusion to "enclosures" suggests that Temple transmitted the papers by letter, but such a letter has not been found and is not recorded in SJL. The LAST ACT of the legislature of Georgia was that of 10 Feb. 1787: for reference to that and other documents evidently alluded to in Temple's representation, see Enclosure I, TJ to Temple, 11 Aug. 1790.

From Elizabeth Wavles Eppes

DEAR SIR   Eppington August 11. 1790.

With pleasure would we embrace your kind invitation to Monticellow if it was possible, but Mr. Eppes will at that time be so engag'd in manufacturing, it will be impossible to leave home tho' flatter our selves we shall be favour'd with your company at Eppington. Your compliment with regard to dear Polly, I assure you would be no small inducement (tho' I am assured your own judgment is quite sufficient) for I have every thing much at heart that can tend in the smalest degree to her happiness. She has lost a month in consequence of my attending on my poor Sister Skipwith who has been very near bidding us a final adieu with a nervous fever but, thank God she is now doing very well.—I have the highest sense of your attentions to both the dear girls and am well assur'd they have only to communicate their wants, and you will supply them. Your plan of fixing dear Patsy in Albemarle were you to be there your self I should wish to take place, as I would not deprive you of the happiness you must have in such a daughters being near you, but as I suppose that will not be the case, must confess from selfish views I can not be pleased with it as I flatter my self we shall now see her frequently, tho' she has set out but badly. We have been favour'd with her company only once. We had the pleasure to hear she was well last week. I am sorry to hear you have been so much afflicted with the head ache and sincerely hope the pure air of Monticellow will put an end to it. Yours with sincere friendship,   E EPPES

RC (MHi); addressed: "Mr. Jefferson New-York"; endorsed as received 28 Aug. 1790 and so recorded in SJL. The above was probably enclosed in one from Francis Eppes to TJ of the same date (also recorded in SJL as received with it), but that letter has not been found. Eppes' letter also may have covered three undated letters from Mary Jefferson as well, for these, too, are recorded in SJL as received 28 Aug. 1790. Only one of Mary's letters has been identified (see under 11 Aug. 1790).

From Benjamin Huger

Lisbon, 11 Aug. 1790. Forwarding enclosed letter gives him pleasing opportunity "of returning you the most sincere thanks for the kind reception my last from Geneva met with. Your favor in answer, and the letters which accompanyed it, reached me not till my arrival at Florence late in September, nor could any thing, but the supposition of your haveing embarked for America before that period, have prevented me from testifying to you immediately my sense of your good nature, and affability. . . . The recommendations you were so obligeing as to furnish me with, were of great utility to me."

RC (MHi); endorsed as received 4 Oct. 1790 and so recorded in SJL. Enclosure: Kinloch to TJ, 26 Apr. 1789.

From Mary Jefferson

DEAR PAPA   [ca. 11 Aug. 1790]

I have just received your last favour july 25 and am determined to write to you every day till I have discharged my debt. When we were in Cumberland we went to Church and heard some singing Masters that sung verywell. They are to come here to learn my cousins to sing and as I know you have no objections to my learn- ing any thing I am to be a scholar and hope to give you the pleasure of hearing an anthem. We had pease the 14 of may and straw- berries the 17 of the same month tho not in that abundance we are accustomed to in consequence of a frost this spring. As for the martins swallows and whippoorwills I was so taken up with my chickens that I never attended to them and therefore cannot tell you when they came tho I was so unfortunate as to lose half of them for my cousin Bolling and myself have raised but 13 between us. Adieu my Dear Papa believe me to be your affectionate daughter,

MARY JEFFERSON

RC (ViU); endorsed by TJ as re- ceived 28 Aug. 1790 and so recorded in SJL, along with two other undated letters (see Mrs. Eppes to TJ, 11 Aug. 1790, note).

To Sir John Temple

New York, August 11th. 1790

Mr. Jefferson presents his compliments to Sir John Temple: he has paid due attention to the enclosed papers which he returns in the first moment in his power. The validity of the laws in ques- tion being purely a judiciary question, will, by our Constitution, be to be decided on by the Federal Court, before whom the parties in- terested will of course take care to bring it. He is happy to believe that the characters of the individuals who compose that Court are such as to leave no doubt in the mind of any party that right will be done.

FC (DNA: RG 59, PCC No. 120). Enclosures: Printed below.

TJ here more explicitly assumes for the federal courts the right of judicial review of state legislation than did Ran- dolph, to whom he had submitted the papers relating to the action of Georgia on British debts (Randolph to TJ, 10 Aug. 1790). In this he was merely re- flecting the natural and prevalent as- sumption. Even Phineas Bond, British consul at Philadelphia and commissary for commercial affairs in North Amer- ica, had expressed this view some months earlier: ". . . whatever rules and regulations may have been heretofore adopted by the courts of the several states, the definitive treaty is acknowl- edged to be the law of the land. . . . If therefore any British subject meets with injustice in the recovery of debts from the subjects of these states, or of the lawful interest due on the same, he may have justice done him by applying to the federal courts now established agreeably to the constitution." A few weeks later Bond added: "The estab- lishment of judiciary courts under the New Constitution promises some relief in the controul of local laws which press hard upon the interests of the British creditors and in correcting a system of delay which had been highly oppressive" (Bond to Leeds, 23 Sep. and 11 Nov. 1789, PRO: FO 4/7). The "system of delay" reflected in the enclosures to this letter showed what a long and tortuous road there was to the decision in Ware v. Hylton, but the implications of Article IV of the Treaty and of Article VI of the Constitution were clear. To the obstacles presented by inherent difficulties of the issue and by such legislation as that of Georgia was added the action of the federal government in ratifying the Treaty of 1794. It is ironic that John Jay, whose brilliant report of 1786 called upon the states to recognize the Treaty of Peace as "binding and obligatory on them," should have negotiated that which removed the issue of British debts from the American judiciary where it belonged and where in 1790 it seemed certain to remain—an irony heightened by the fact that the negotiator was also head of the federal judiciary (see Vol. 14: 79-80; S. F. Bemis, *Jay's Treaty* [New Haven, 1962], p. 434-9; for a good account of the litigation over debts in Virginia, see Isaac S. Harrell, *Loyalism in Virginia*, p. 153-78; Monroe to TJ, 1 May 1792; for an account of the issue that places it in the context of imperial problems in the years between 1748 and 1764, see Lawrence H. Gipson, "Virginia Planter Debts before the American Revolution," VMHB, LXIX [July, 1961], 259-79). It was not until TJ became President that the Convention of 8 Jan. 1802 annulling Article VI of the Treaty of 1794 and confirming Article IV of the Treaty of Peace restored the matter to its proper status as "purely a judiciary question" so far as the future operation of Article IV was concerned (TJ to Senate, 29 Mch. 1802).

The action of Georgia was protested by British merchants trading in that state as contravening the Treaty of Peace and as being "still more oppressive and unjust" than the numerous violations they had reported theretofore. On 11 Mch. 1790 the auditor of Georgia had summoned all persons indebted to British merchants to render an account of such indebtedness as confiscated under the act of 4 May 1782 and as further enforced by that of 10 Feb. 1787.

The merchants therefore asked for protection in those rights under the Treaty they felt themselves "so fully and clearly entitled to, and . . . so manifestly guaranteed them" (John North and others to Leeds, 13 July 1790, PRO: FO 4/8). This and other appeals, particularly those protesting the South Carolina instalment act of 1788, led to Temple's presentation of the Georgia situation to TJ. The Secretary of State had himself drafted the Virginia act of sequestration of 1779 (Vol. 2: 279-84). But he stood at the opposite pole from those who sought to interpose the authority of a state against the binding obligations of the Treaty. Some months before Jay made his report of 1786 TJ embodied its substance in a letter to Monroe. He suggested that "Congress . . . recommend a mode of executing that article respecting the debts, and send it to each state to be passed into law. Whether England gives up the posts or not, these debts must be paid, or our character stained with infamy among all nations and to all times. As to the satisfaction for the slaves carried off, it is a bagatelle which if not made good before the last instalment becomes due, may be secured out of that" (TJ to Monroe, 10 May 1786). Long before the complicated issue of the debts came before him as Secretary of State, TJ had determined to settle his own debts privately under principles of "exact justice . . . without needing any obligation but that of morality," and he had in fact done so (TJ to Jones, 1 June 1789 and documents on his debt to Farell & Jones, Vol. 15: 642-77). Though shared by many in Virginia, this position evidently was not that of the majority in the state (see instructions to Caroline delegates in the House of Delegates affirming "the impolicy, injustice, and oppression, of paying British debts"; *Pennsylvania Journal*, 8 Nov. 1783).

Immediately on the adjournment of Congress and the day following this reply to Temple, TJ initiated the inquiry into state legislation on debts and other matters considered to be infractions of the Treaty of Peace, thus laying the foundation for his powerful reply to Hammond two years later (TJ to Harison, 12 Aug. 1790; TJ to Hammond, 29 May 1792).

I

Report of the Governor of Georgia on Confiscation Acts

In Council 15th. July 1789.

The Governor, who by the order of Council of the 12th. June last, was requested to draw up and report a state of facts from the several papers which were then read to wit, the Auditors letter, the report of the Committee of Council, the Act of banishment and confiscation, the definitive Treaty of peace between the United States and Great Britain, the Acts of Assembly of the 13th. February 1786, and of the 10th. February 1787, together with the resolutions of Congress of the 21st. March 1787, and their letter to the States founded thereon of the 13th. April following—States and Reports.

That in order to give a clear view of the business it is necessary to recur to original principles and to incidental facts.

He therefore says, that the District of Country lying on the Atlantic Ocean, from New Hampshire to Georgia inclusive, prior to the 4th. day of July 1776, formed several Provinces of the Crown of Great Britain. That several of the Acts of the Legislature of the Kingdom having been considered as oppressive and inovative of the Constitutional and the Charter rights of the Provinces, the authority of them was disputed, and their operations opposed.

Open and avowed hostilities ensued.

In this state of warfare and uncertainty the several Provinces sent Deputies to Philadelphia and formed a general Congress, which after the adoption and pursuit of various measures to restore peace and obtain justice, the common safety and future welfare compelled them, on the said 4th. day of July 1776, to declare the said Provinces to be Independent States; and Articles of Union were afterwards formed and agreed to, by which they were leagued by a general confederation with the powers of war and peace.

Treaties of commerce and alliance were also made and entered into with foreign powers; and by them the Independence of the States was explicitly recognized, and finally acceded to by Great Britain.

From the 4th. day of July 1776, therefore, the Acts and proceedings of the several States are those of sovereign and independent powers, and binding in their relation with the Union and with other nations, and within this description is the act of confiscation of this State.

The object then of this inquiry is, whether certain debts mentioned in the Auditors letter, were bonafide confiscated before the definitive Treaty of peace, and if so, whether the same was not done away by the said Treaty. The documents will speak for themselves.

By the 1st. clause of the act of confiscation, the property of every kind of many of the Merchants who resided in this State at the commencement of the war and who are therein named, is expressly confiscated and their persons banished, and by the 4th. and fifth clauses, the monies and the Estates, real and personal, belonging to the british Subjects, whose persons were not in the power of the State, were sequestered, confiscated, and appropriated to the use of the State. In virtue of which many of the Estates of british Subjects, as well of the merchants named, which were discovered, have been already sold, both before and since the definitive Treaty; and it may be ascribed to the difficulty of the coming at the knowledge and evidence of the debts, that the same, together with the act of 1786 and 1787 for that purpose, have not been carried into more full effect. But should the merchants who fled this State during the war, with their books, or those whose debts are confiscated, generally return, or come and put them in suit, it is presumed the attorney General would understand the extent and line of his duty from the several acts themselves, and the instructions under which he acts.

The definitive Treaty of peace between the United States and Great Britain goes something further than other Treaties; by not only expressly acknowledging the Independence and Sovereignty of the States, and relinquishing all right, and pretensions to right, in form, but by recognizing the acts of confiscation and guarantying the navigation of the Missisippi.

It is dated the 3d. day of September 1783, the act of confiscation the 4th. day of May 1782; the former being posterior and the latter recognized by it, the act on this foundation, and without question on any other, is in force, and it is not this or that part that is so, but the whole.

It has already been acted upon to considerable extent: and so far as the actual appropriations have gone, Great Britain has made adequate compensation.

The 4th. article of the Treaty respects such mercantile transactions as are not affected by confiscation prior to the Treaty, which is the case in this State. This article and the two succeeding ones, may be explained by a resolution of Congress, entered upon the Secret Journal, and transmitted to the Ministers Plenipotentiary for their government and anterior to the Treaty. It is known to the writer and had reference to the acts of confiscation. It asserted the Sovereignty and right of the States to make laws which they could not controul, and restricted the Commissioners, with respect to them, in the entering into any Treaty, as the confiscations could not be conceded by the Commissioners, the 5th. and 6th. clauses were agreed to as the alternative.

These have been fully carried into effect by the act of Congress of the 14th. January 1784, and by the resolutions and letters herein before mentioned: But however much the body recommending was respected, it was altogether optional with the Sovereignty of the States, how far they would yield in that regard; and so it was universally considered on both sides the atlantic, nor did any of the States give up their acts or cease carrying them into effect. That there shall be no more confiscations made, was understood on all sides to be a confirmation of the past, and a provision against future acts of the kind; nor has any since taken place in either of the States.

The letter of Congress to the States breathes a spirit of peace and benevolence, with a desire of forgetting the animosities of the war, in the contemplation and pursuit of national prosperity. In their place, and urged by their Embassador, it was good policy to repeat and go thus far, but this opinion could not affect the right. The State in opposition of the right, had her alternative. Our liberty and independence are the price of our blood; The confiscation—of our excessive losses by the ravages of the war, and the monstrous alienations of the usurpation.

Note. The principles and facts upon which this case is stated, arose and existed within the periods of independence and the establishment and operation of the federal Constitution, which has no retrospect.

FC (DNA: RG 59, PCC No. 120); at head of text: "Georgia"; at foot of text: "Extract from the minutes. J. Merewether Sy. E.C." Tr (PRO: FO 4/7).

II

Order in Council Respecting Suits Concerning Confiscation

Georgia. Richmond County.
Present the honorable Henry Osborn and
George Walton Esquires.

Chambers, Augusta May 11th. 1790.

The attorney and Solicitor general moved for a rule to make his Excellency the Governor, for the time being, plaintiff in behalf of the State, in all cases where the State has claims for property founded on the Act of banishment and confiscation, passed the 4th. day of May 1782, and comprehending as well Lands and Tenements, negroes, Stock, Furniture, monies, debts which are due at the time of passing the said Act to british subjects or merchants, and of any nature and kind whatsoever, within the intent and meaning of said Act. Whereupon it is ordered, that a rule be granted for constituting parties for the establishment of Justice with respect to the premises, and that upon application of the attorney or Solicitor general, upon all occasions, and within the several Counties within this State, the respective Clerks do receive a copy of this order, as a sufficient warrant of attorney for the Governor for the time being to appear as a party, and entered of record as such by either of the said Executive law officers, as fully and effectually as any other person, party, or suitor might or could do, by the 7th. rule of the superior Courts.

FC (DNA: RG 59, PCC No. 120).

To Richard Harison and other
District Attorneys

SIR   New York August 12th. 1790

It is desirable that Government should be informed what proceedings have taken place in the several States since the Treaty
with Great Britain, which may be considered by that Nation as
infractions of the Treaty, and consequently that we should be
furnished with copies of all acts, orders, proclamations, and decisions, legislative, executive, or judiciary, which may have affected
the debts or other property, or the persons, of british subjects or
american refugees. The proceedings subsequent to the Treaty will
sometimes call for those also which took place during the war. No
person is more able than yourself, Sir, to furnish us with a list of
the proceedings of this kind which have taken place within your
State, nor is there any one on whom we may with more propriety
rely for it, as well as to take the trouble of furnishing us with
exact copies of them. Should you be so kind as to state any facts
or circumstances which may enter into the justification or explanation of any of these proceedings, they will be thankfully received;
and it is wished the whole may come to hand between this and the
last of October.

While I am troubling you with this Commission, I am obliged
to add a second, which, being undertaken at this time, will abridge
the labour of the first. It is found indispensable that we be possessed
here of a complete collection of all the printed Laws and Ordinances, ancient and modern of every State of the union. I must ask
the favour of you, Sir, to have such a collection made for us, so
far as relates to your State. The volumes of this collection which,
being more modern, may be more readily found, I will ask the
favour of you to send immediately by whatever conveyance you
think safest and best; those more rarely to be had, you will be
so good as to forward from time to time, as you can get them.
For your reimbursement, be pleased to draw on me, only expressing in your draught that it is for 'the laws of your State purchased
and forwarded for the United States.' Or if it should be more convenient to you, I will at any time send you an order from the
Treasury for your reimbursement on the Collector most convenient
to you. This shall be as you please.

Your zeal for the general service needs not to be excited by information that it is with the special approbation of the President of the United States that I address you on this occasion.—I have the honor to be with great regard Sir Your most obedient & Most humble Servt.,

TH: JEFFERSON

RC (Miss Elizabeth Harison, New York, 1950); at head of text: "(Circular)"; at foot of text: "Richard Harrison esquire"; in hand of George Taylor, signed by TJ. Recorded in SJL as to "Attorneys of districts. Circular." This text is accompanied by the following memorandum in the hand of Henry Remsen, Jr.: "Note. There are already in the Office two Vols. of the Laws of New-York, Containing those passed from the first to the twelfth session inclusive, and published by Hugh Gaine under the superintendence of Samuel Jones and Richard Varick; those therefore are only wanted which will be requisite to complete this Set." FC (DNA: RG 59, PCC No. 120); at head of text: "To the Attornies for the several Districts of the United States, Maine and Kentucky excepted." Recipients' copies of the circular addressed to William Channing, attorney for the Massachusetts district, and to George Read, Jr., attorney for the Delaware district, were sold in 1957 at the Forest G. Sweet Sale, Parke-Bernet Galleries, Inc., Catalogue No. 1756. The above text is actually a signed press copy, indicative of the system TJ had long employed to make the copying press serve as a duplicating machine.

TJ's initiation of this inquiry concerning possible infractions of the Treaty of Peace was anticipated by similar action of the British ministry more than a year earlier. On 24 Feb. 1789 the Committee of Merchants Trading to North America protested against the 1788 instalment law of South Carolina as being a "violent infraction of the Treaty of Peace" and also as "contrary to the Federal Constitution." They asked protection of government and called attention to the fact that on former representations of infractions of the Treaty Congress had recommended in "the most pressing and honorable manner a repeal of the laws" (Memorial to Carmarthen, 24 Feb. 1789; Carmarthen to Bond, 4 Mch. 1789, PRO: FO 4/7; on Jay's report and Congress' appeal to the states, see Vol. 14: 79). On 18 June 1789 the Lords of the Committee for Trade directed Leeds to instruct consuls and other agents in America to report on duties imposed on tonnage by Congress or the states; on discrimination in port or tonnage duties; on the increase or diminution of grain, rice, tobacco, and other production and the natural, commercial, or political causes thereof; on the state of manufactures and bounties, premiums, or other encouragement for their increase; on the number of ships and their tonnage belonging to citizens of each state; on the number of ships and their tonnage that belonged to European nationals and entered American ports after 1783; on the number of indentured servants or redemptioners brought into the states from British dominions; on the emigrants from the states to other regions under American jurisdiction, whether for the purpose of establishing colonies or new governments or in order to settle in British-American colonies; on the increase or diminution of population; and on the proceedings of those who had gone from the states to settle on "the banks of the Great Lakes, the Ohio, the Missouri, and the Mississippi, with a view to establish themselves in those parts, to provide subsistence, to form governments, or to carry on any branch of commerce." The fourth article of this comprehensive inquiry directed the consular and other agents to report on "what Laws have been made, and are now in force and what Rules or Regulations have been adopted by the Courts of Justice in the Countries belonging to the said United States, for obstructing the Recovery of debts owed by the subjects of the United States to British subjects or to the subjects of other Foreign Countries, or to deprive them of lawful Interest . . . or to oblige them to receive in payment depreciated Paper Currency or other Effects not equal in value to Sterling Money" (Lords of the Committee for Trade to Leeds, 18 June 1789; Leeds to Bond and other consuls, 30 June 1789, PRO: FO 4/7). The most comprehensive reports in response to this inquiry came from Bond ("Letters of Phineas Bond," *Ann. Rept. Am. Hist. Assn. for 1896*, I, 513-659; same for 1897, p. 454-568; many of Bond's important enclosures are only listed and should be consulted in PRO: FO 4). British merchants calculated the total debt at £4,764,364 11s as of 1 Jan. 1790, a figure that included a rough estimate of £2,000,000 in interest for the fourteen years after 1775. A year later the total was set at £4,930,656 13s 1d, including interest at "two million and upwards." Of this total £2,-305,408 19s 2d was of Virginia origin. Under the circumstances it is not surprising that, as George Hammond later conceded, the amounts were grossly exaggerated (PRO: FO 4/8, filed under the date given; the latter figure was presented 5 Feb. 1791 and the subtotals are to be found in S. F. Bemis, *Jay's Treaty*, p. 140). The merchants were more accurate and more useful to the ministry in compiling a record of legislative and judicial proceedings tending to impede recovery of debts. The resultant pamphlet, *Abstract of*

the laws of the American states, now in force, relative to debts due to Loyalists, subjects of Great Britain, was printed in London in 1789 and enclosed in a memorial of Jan. 1790 (John Hamilton, Cumberland Wilson, and Robert Gilmore to Evan Nepean, Jan. 1790, PRO: FO 4/8).

ALL THE PRINTED LAWS: The resolution proposed by Vining on 23 July 1789 calling for the establishment of a home department required the secretary to procure copies of the printed laws of the several states (*Annals*, I, 692). The supplemental act creating the Department of State failed to make such a provision and the oversight was remedied by a joint resolution adopted immediately thereafter: "That it shall be the duty of the Secretary of State to procure from time to time such of the statutes of the several states as may not be in his office" (18 Sep. 1789; JHR, I, 114, 119, 120).

To Henry Knox

DEAR SIR   Thursday eveng. [12 Aug. 1790]

May I invite the three Chargés des affaires to attend the ceremony? May they be permitted to bring respectable strangers of their nation with or without limitation of numbers? Do ladies go? If they do, Mrs. Otto must be named in the invitation to Mr. Otto. I will beg the favor of your answer to these queries and govern myself accordingly. Only be so good as have reserved for them a seat in a respectable position. Yours affectionately & respectfully,

TH: JEFFERSON

RC (MHi: Knox Papers); addressed: "The Secretary at War"; endorsed: "A Note from Mr. Jefferson." Not recorded in SJL.

The above was in response to one from Knox written the same evening: "The President of the US proposes to ratify the treaty with the Creeks in the representatives chamber tomorrow at 12 oClock" (Dft in MHi: Knox Papers; not recorded in SJL). Knox' answer to TJ's inquiry reads: "I imagine that the ... charges des affaires might be permitted to bring any number of their nation without limitation. Respectable seats shall certainly be assigned the princapals. The ladies by all means.—

The president proposes to have it informally notified to the Senators and representatives in Town and who may find it convenient to attend.—Will you suffer me to call upon you at ½ past seven in the morning to decide upon the particular arrangements?" (Dft in MHi: Knox Papers; not recorded in SJL). THE THREE CHARGÉS: Louis Guillaume Otto, who served as French chargé from the time De Moustier left until the arrival of Ternant in the summer of 1791; José Ignacio de Viar, secretary of Spanish legation, acting as chargé; and Franco Petrus van Berckel, minister resident for the United Netherlands.

The CEREMONY was the formal occasion on 13 Aug. 1790 in Federal Hall when "the President, in behalf of the people of the United States, and the Kings, Chiefs, and Warriors of the Creek Nations" solemnly ratified the treaty." Among the witnesses to the instrument were TJ's young friends Thomas Lee Shippen and John Rutledge, Jr. ([N.Y.] *Daily Advertiser,* 14 Aug. 1790). A fortnight earlier when the Indians were received by the Society of St. Tammany with speeches, songs, and toasts, TJ was also present, smoked the calumet of peace, and joined in the "*shake-hands* . . . obtained from all the head men, in the Creek fashion by the whole society passing their line *in* Indian file" (same, 4 Aug. 1790).

To Juan Nepomuceno de Quesada

SIR   New York August 12th. 1790

I am charged by the President of the United States of America to acknowledge the receipt of your Excellency's polite and friendly letter of the 17th. of July, to congratulate you on your accession to the Government of Florida, and your safe arrival there, and to thank you for your offers of friendly service to the United States. I am authorized to assure your Excellency that on the part of the United States there is a strong sense of the advantages of being on terms of the strictest friendship with their neighbours, and a disposition to cultivate that friendship by all the attentions and good offices in their power. Having the honor to be charged with the department of foreign affairs in our Government, I may perhaps have occasion sometimes to solicit the permission of your Excellency to make such communications as may tend to preserve and promote a good understanding between our two Countries; and shall count among it's other advantages the personal one of repeating to you assurances of the sentiments of respect and esteem with which I have the honor to be &c.,   THOMAS JEFFERSON

FC (DNA: RG 59, PCC No. 120). Not recorded in SJL.

Quesada's letter to Washington, dated at St. Augustine, 17 July 1790, announced that he had commanded that town and province since the 7th and expressed the hope that some circumstance might enable him to be useful both to Washington and to some of the states (RC in same, MLR, together with translation in English by Isaac Pinto; FC in same, PCC No. 120). As an example of the sort of COMMUNICATIONS TJ knew he would probably be obliged to make, see TJ to Carmichael, 11 Apr., 31 May, and 29 Aug. 1790. Indeed, Quesada raised the question of slaves in his reply of 28 Aug. 1790 to the present letter, the expressions in which he said gave him "indecible gusto, quando confirman la reputacion de Luces, y virtud que esa Republica naciente establece": he declared that he had received royal instructions not to permit for any reason whatever the introduction and liberation in that province of slaves from the United States, and that he took advantage of the first opportunity to pass on this gratifying recognition of the interests of both nations (RC in DNA: RG 59, MLR; endorsed by TJ as received 25 Oct. 1790 and so recorded in SJL). See TJ to Quesada, 10 Mch. 1791. But the question of fugitive slaves was not confined to Spanish-American relations: Alexander McGillivray, with

whom the government had just concluded a treaty, had helped to build up
his ascendency among the Creeks by
receiving a great number of slaves fleeing from Georgia plantations and by
incorporating them among his followers (De Moustier to Montmorin, 5 June
1788; Arch. Aff. Etr., Paris, Corr. Pol.,
E.-U., xxx).

To William Short

DEAR SIR   New York Aug. 12. 1790.

Being just now informed that a vessel sails this afternoon for a
port of Normandy, and knowing that the President wished to have
some Champagne, and that this is the season to write for it, I have
been to him, and he desires 40. dozen bottles. The execution of this
commission I must put upon you, begging the favor of you to procure it of the growth of M. Dorsay's vineyard at Aÿ opposite to
Epernay in Champagne, and of the best year he has, for present
drinking. His homme d'Affaires when I was there was a M. Louis,
and if the same be in place it will perhaps best to write to him,
and it may give him the idea of a more standing customer if he
knows that the application comes through the person who bought
the remains of his wine of 1783. in April 1788. being in company
with a M. Cousin. It is to be *Non-mousseux.* M. Dorsay himself
lives in Paris. We have not time to procure a bill to inclose you
herein, but I will take care to forward one immediately by some
other conveyance. I am anxious this wine should not move from
Champagne till the heats are over, and that it should arrive at
Philadelphia before the spring comes on. It will of course be in
bottles. Adieu Dear Sir Your's affectionately,

TH: JEFFERSON

P.S. call for the best possible, and they may be sure of a continuance of such an annual demand as long as it comes of the best.

RC (ViW); endorsed as received 24
Sep. 1790; recorded in SJL as "private."
PrC (DLC). In DLC: TJ Papers, 57:
9707 there is a memorandum in TJ's
hand, endorsed "Washington Presidt,"
reading:

Sauterne	30.	doz.	1/	432
Segur	20.	doz.	3#	720
Frontignan	10.	doz.	1/	144

Champagne 40. doz. 3.#10s. 1680."
At the bottom of this memorandum
are TJ's calculations of costs of the
wines named, with shillings transposed
into livres, so that all of the totals are
in the latter currency. On TJ's visit to
Epernay and the purchase of the last
of M. Dorsay's WINE OF 1783, see Vol.
13: 29-32.

Documents Relating
to Departmental Personnel
and Services

EDITORIAL NOTE

Following passage of the Residence Act various departmental details obtruded upon the attention Jefferson was giving to Indian affairs, fiscal and commercial policy, British aims in the northwest, the Mississippi Question, and the secret mission to Spain. Few in government could have found personnel vacancies and office routines less congenial than he, for clerical chores had been one of the oppressive factors that caused him to hesitate so long before accepting office. But he faced these duties with the same love of system that he brought to large affairs. In this respect no one in the administration equalled him, not even Washington. Unimportant in themselves, these details gain significance as being another reflection of a style of administration that became apparent at once on Jefferson's assuming office, a style manifest in everything from the purchase of supplies to the shaping of policy. It was indeed impossible for Jefferson to regard a mastery of detail as being irrelevant to or divorced from the forming of policy. These were integral and both were to be brought under the rule of common sense and system. Nature and experience, not theory, had prepared him for such a conception of administration.

The problems of foreign relations faced by the Secretary of State, to be sure, were essentially the same as those confronted by the Secretary for Foreign Affairs. There was also a far greater element of continuity in bureaus, personnel, and administrative procedures than is generally supposed.[1] Despite this and despite Jefferson's assertion

[1] Edmund C. Burnett, *The Continental Congress*, p. 726, points out that most of the executive departments of the old Congress were carried over intact into the new government. Leonard D. White, *The Federalists*, p. 1, places almost exclusive

that he had not disturbed Jay's arrangements in the office,[2] it is not surprising that he brought a new approach to the old issues and a different system of management, for in personal attributes and in concept of policy he differed markedly from his predecessor.[3] Change was also in part a natural consequence of the new distribution of governmental powers brought about by what many Americans of the day thought of as "the revolution of 1789," though the influence of this factor has been much overestimated. The impact of the more violent upheaval in France the same year also had its effect. But these obvious influences on attitudes and methods of administration have thrown into obscurity, indeed almost into oblivion, a factor of central importance: that is, that the decisive event of 1776, by the very act of repudiating a hierarchically-ordered society, elevated both the citizen and the official to a new plane of moral responsibility. Since this was the dominant influence in Jefferson's life, it could scarcely have been other than a decisive force governing his view of responsibility as a public administrator. It is necessary to emphasize this most subtle but no less potent of the factors bringing about a new concept of public service because it has been neglected, is difficult to assess, and at the time was not perceived by everyone or embraced with conviction by all who were sensitive to its pervading implications.

Jefferson, who grasped the dimensions of the moral proposition more clearly than any other public figure of the time both in its risks and in its implied duties, cannot be gauged as a public administrator without taking into account the intensity of conviction with which he accepted the idea that the public interest, thenceforth, was the paramount responsibility both of the private citizen and of the public official. In Jefferson's view the latter indeed had a special obligation to be utterly disinterested in the management of public affairs, and he was at pains to make this manifest by managing his personal affairs so as to avoid the danger of a conflict with his public responsibility. This was the essence of the matter. In the new order of things the incumbent at every level of public office from that of clerk to that of chief magistrate was obliged in all matters to give precedence to the public interest over every other consideration. Washington at the head of the administration was an embodiment of this concept. Jefferson, in the details of office management, in the handling of personnel, in the emerging interdepartmental jealousies, and in the determination of

emphasis on the new beginnings. These appraisals on the first and last pages of two indispensable works of original scholarship symbolize what has been lost by the fact that one ends where the other begins. In the point of view set forth in the above note and elsewhere (e.g., Vol. 16: vii-ix), discontinuity is accorded much less emphasis and TJ's stature as an administrator given far more elevation than in the pioneering work of White. See also, James, Hart, *The American Presidency in Action, 1789: a Study in Constitutional History* (New York, 1948), and L. K. Caldwell, *The Administrative Theories of Hamilton and Jefferson* (Chicago, 1944).

[2] TJ to Barton, 12 Aug. 1790 (Document II); TJ to Pinto, 28 Aug. 1790 (Document VI).

[3] Julian P. Boyd, "Two Diplomats between Revolutions John Jay and Thomas Jefferson," VMHB, LXVI (Apr. 1958), 131-46.

policy, not only embraced the concept as a matter of personal principle, but made it an integral part of the profound "contest over principles of administration" that took place from the very beginning between the Jeffersonian and Hamiltonian points of view. This was in fact a central element in the contest and the opposing concept of administration makes that of Jefferson stand out the more clearly because of the stark contrast. The idea of gaining support for government by multiplying the ligaments of private interest was at the other pole from that which animated him. The bonds of strength that he sought to encourage were those grounded in moral sanctions, expressed most succinctly in the view that every citizen has a portion "in whatever is public."[4] The contrasting concepts were matched by contrasting conduct. It is therefore not at all surprising, though generally overlooked, that a disinterested administration of public affairs met with public response and commendation in the culminating contest of 1800.

Jefferson was prepared by experience as master of the many facets of plantation economy to fill the role of a man of business—to use the phrase in the sense, now obsolete, in which it was employed in his day to designate a man of public affairs.[5] This was a unique schooling in management and in such notable examples as Washington and Jefferson the plantation system produced distinctive qualities of leadership and administrative capacity. Neither law, merchandising, nor commerce could equal that system in the range and depth of experience that it afforded as a training ground for managers. A knowledge of all these was in some degree necessary for the planter, to say nothing of other skills not demanded of the merchant or shipper. Supervision of slaves required in the nature of things an unremitting attention to the planning and execution of all aspects of operations. Plantation labor might include artisans capable of performing such varied tasks as ironmongery, carpentry, masonry, distilling, and even fairly sophisticated cabinetwork, but slaves constituted no such body of knowledgeable clerks and tradesmen as the merchants of Boston and Philadelphia could command. Stewards and overseers required an equally close supervision. Few could be depended upon in such a system and it is doubtful if any planter could have delegated to his steward the full degree of authority that the merchant or shipowner was obliged to confer upon the master of a vessel or the supercargo. This need for close supervision obliged the planter to attend to all of the details of providing for the housing, sustenance, and health of both a laboring force and a large community of families; of planning the year-round sequence of planting, cultivation, harvest, and marketing; and, at the same time, of keeping in view the ultimate ends, both political and economic, which sustained the system. At one end of the broad spectrum of his duty as a planter Washington could spend many hours counting and weighing seed, not as a matter of idle speculation but as a necessary and useful task, and at the other he was obliged as a burgess to deliberate upon the effects of imperial and local legislation on the plantation econ-

4 TJ to Correâ, 26 Apr. 1816.
5 OED, *business*, 22 (a).

omy. In his extraordinary effort to breed mules for carriage and farm uses Washington was prompted by one of the elementary concerns of an administrator: that of obtaining a more efficient, cheap, and dependable source of power than that afforded by horses and oxen. Jefferson, in making endless estimates of the time required for a particular task by a given number and kind of slaves—for example, the quantity of nails that a boy might reasonably be expected to produce in a day—was also a manager engaged in calculating efficiency and in adapting the labor force of different sexes and varying degrees of maturity and strength to appropriate tasks. The absence or scarcity of a circulating medium also schooled the planter in the nature and uses of credit. This is reflected in Jefferson's continuing concern for supporting the national faith and credit, culminating in the remarkable and all but unknown letters on public finance written in his years of retirement.

Given such a schooling, it was thus scarcely an accident that Jefferson rather than a Nantucket whaleman or a merchant produced the most thorough study of the whale fishery in 18th-century America. Nor is it surprising that the most systematic approach to the problem of uniformity in weights and measures, a study also concerned with minute details of merchandising and with broad aspects of national policy, should have been produced by a planter and not by a merchant or financier from the commercial centers of the north. The plantation system had many and grave defects, most particularly —as Jefferson saw in deep anxiety—those deriving from slavery. For men lacking in will or stamina its manifold invitations to indolence, lethargy, and abdication of responsibility produced in his countrymen those qualities that Jefferson described so acutely.[6] But the plantation school of administrative experience was nevertheless an excellent preparation for office. Washington and Jefferson were the two most conspicuous examples of those who mastered its hard lessons. Both loved system and method, but Washington was an innovator only in the pursuit of husbandry whereas Jefferson's disposition to experiment, to test by exact knowledge, and to adopt useful and promising reforms extended to all areas of human endeavor. This was a disposition common neither to the plantation nor to the commercial community. Robert Morris saw no need to establish a uniform standard of weights and measures and, while he was glad to accommodate Jefferson in 1784 by ordering from London one of James Watt's new copying machines, he ordered none for his own counting house: everyone knew what a bushel was from New Hampshire to Georgia and clerks could continue the satisfactory if inefficient routine of copying letters into letter-books. But Jefferson had been in office as Secretary of State less than a month when he introduced into government practice a method of multiplying copies that would one day be routine in almost all public offices and mercantile establishments. The essential difference between him and such exemplary products of the plantation and commercial worlds as Washington and Morris is that, being ardent in looking for means

6 TJ to Chastellux, 2 Sep. 1785.

of improvement, he was able so often and in so many variant ways to anticipate what another age would adopt.

William Wirt thought that the law and the tutelage of George Wythe imparted to Jefferson "that unrivalled neatness, system, and method in business, which, through all his future life, and in every office that he filled, gave him, in effect, the hundred hands of Briareous."[7] These were important influences, but the plantation system must take rank with them. Transcending all of these, of course, was the spirit of scientific inquiry that Jefferson had absorbed in part from William Small but mostly from the age. Public administration was not exempt from that pervading influence insofar as it fell under his hand.

7 William Wirt, *A Discourse on the Lives and Characters of Thomas Jefferson and John Adams* (Washington, 1826), p. 27-8.

I. Thomas Jefferson to William Barton

SIR   New York Aug. 12. 1790.

I have been duly honored with your's of the 7th. instant, and in order to answer it must enter into a detail of facts.

In the formation of the higher departments there were some endeavors in Congress to establish a separate minister for the domestic business. This was disapproved by a considerable majority of Congress, and they therefore united that with the foreign business under the department of the Secretary of state.—When I arrived here I found Mr. Alden at the head of the home-office, and Mr. Remsen at that of the foreign office. Neither could descend to a secondary appointment, and yet they were each so well acquainted with their respective departments and the papers in them, that it was extremely desireable to keep both. On this ground of their peculiar familiarity with the papers and proceedings of their respective offices, which made them necessary to me as indexes, I asked permission to appoint two chief clerks. The legislature recieved the proposition with some jealousy, lest it might be intended to bring forward again the plan of two departments and tho the bill past, it was after considerable delay, and being quite satisfied I had no other view than to be enabled to keep the two gentlemen so peculiarly familiar with the papers under their care. One of them chusing afterwards to engage in another line, I could do nothing less, in return to the complaisance of the legislature, than declare that as the ground on which alone they were induced to allow the second office, was now removed, I considered the office as at an end, and that the arrangements should return to the order desired by the legislature: this declaration has been given to some applications already made for this office.

I should have had real pleasure, Sir, in serving you on this occasion, but the preceding detail of facts will serve to shew you that the appointment cannot be renewed. The testimony I have recieved would be quite sufficient to convince me that I could not fill the office better than by naming you, were it considered as now existing. I beg you to recieve, with the faithful expression of my regret, assurances of the regard with which I have the honor to be Sir Your most obedient & most humble servt.,

TH: JEFFERSON

PrC (DLC).

The attempt to establish a separate office FOR THE DOMESTIC BUSINESS was linked to the resignation of the faithful secretary of the Continental Congress from 1774 to 1789, Charles Thomson. After the bill for establishing a Department of Foreign Affairs had passed the House but before it was approved on 27 July 1789, Vining of Delaware moved a resolution calling for the establishment of a department to be headed by "the Secretary of the United States for the Home Department," whose duty it would be "to correspond with the several States, and to see to the execution of the laws of the Union; to keep the great seal, and affix the same to all public papers, when it is necessary; to keep the lesser seal, and to affix it to commissions, &c.; to make out commissions, and enregister the same; to keep authentic copies of all public acts, &c.; and transmit the same to the several States; to procure the acts of the several States, and report on the same when contrary to the laws of the United States; to take into his custody the archives of the late Congress; to report to the President plans for the protection and improvement of manufactures, agriculture, and commerce; to obtain a geographical account of the several States, their rivers, towns, roads, &c.; to report what post roads shall be established; to receive and record the census; to receive reports respecting the Western territory; to receive the models and specimens presented by inventors and authors; to en-ter all books for which patents are granted; to issue patents, &c.; and, in general, to do and attend to all such matters and things as he may be directed to do by the President" (*Annals*, I, 692). These sweeping administrative and executive powers were such as no department had been specifically directed to perform. But Charles Thomson, sole remaining symbol of government under the Articles of Confederation, still served as custodian of its records and seals. When the new government came into existence, he was offered the post of secretary of the Senate. This he declined, countering with the proposition that he be made "Secretary of the Senate and of the United States or Congress," with custody of the great seal and records, and that his office be made repository of "the acts, laws, and archives of Congress" (Thomson to Robert Morris, 7 Apr. 1789, quoted in L. R. Harley, *Charles Thomson*, p. 128-9). Unquestionably, Thomson hoped the extensive powers contemplated in Vining's resolution would be only an enlargement of his existing custodial function. The terms of this remarkable and unrealistic motion, reflecting as it does an intimate knowledge of all phases of the operations of government such as Thomson alone possessed, suggest that it was drafted with his assistance if not inspired by him.

Much as he deserved office on the score of integrity, fidelity, and competence, Thomson's refusal of the Secretaryship of the Senate and Vining's attempt to stake out too broad a range of powers for an office framed to fit his constituent's peculiar talents combined to bring about an emphatic defeat of the resolution. During the debate Thomson visited Maclay, who saw clearly the injustice of the treatment accorded him, but thought it "certainly bad policy for him to refuse the offer of his friends. The political door is harder to be opened than any other if once it is thrown in a man's face" (Maclay, *Journal*, ed. Maclay, p. 106). Immediately on defeat of the motion, Thomson sent his resignation to the President and Washington expressed his regret at losing the services of "so old, so faithful, and so able a public officer." He directed him at the same time to "deliver the Books, Records and Papers of the late Congress, the Great Seal of the Federal Union, and the Seal of the Admiralty, to Mr. Roger Alden, the late Deputy Secretary of Congress" (Washington to Thomson, 24 July 1789; *Writings*, ed. Fitzpatrick, XXX, 358-9). Washington's letter touched Thomson, evoking a response that was almost effusive but still could not conceal an ambition to serve in the new administration (quoted in L. R. Harley, *Charles Thomson*, p. 131-2). It could not have been comforting to a man held in honor by Washington, Jefferson, Franklin, Adams, and others that, only a week after his resignation and on the heels of the Act creating the Department of Foreign Affairs, there was introduced a bill enlarging the function of that department so as to accommodate the functions and records which, as Washington felicitously expressed it in his letter to Thomson, bore a "Name so honorably connected with the verification of such a multitude of astonishing facts." The functions of offices pertaining to finance, war, and foreign affairs had had uninterrupted continuity from the old to the new government. But Thomson's effort to have his office elevated to the status of an executive department only served to call attention to an omission and to produce the exact reverse of what he desired. With the defeat of Vining's motion the functions that he had performed so long and so faithfully in "minuting the birth-records of a nation" (DAB) were annexed to the amplified and re-named Department of State. On Thomson's resignation the last vestige of the old government disappeared.

Thus when TJ came into office his deputies stemmed from two separate bureaus, but the Act creating the Department of State had failed to amend that part of the Act of 27 July 1789 which allowed only one chief clerk. Both Washington and Jay urged upon TJ the respective claims of Roger Alden, who had been assistant to Thomson, and Henry Remsen, Jr., who since 1784 had served under the Secretary for Foreign Affairs (Washington to TJ, 13 Oct. 1789; Jay to TJ, 12 Dec. 1789; TJ to Jay, 14 Feb. 1790). There were other aspirants. Charles Storer appealed to John Adams to intercede in his behalf with TJ for "the office of his first Secretary." Adams ended the hope quickly: "Mr. Remsen has been many years in the office of foreign affairs and has qualifications and merits which preclude all competition. Mr. Alden is another in a similar predicament, so that there is not a possibility of your success in your first thought" (Storer to Adams, 23 Feb. 1790; Adams to Storer, 26 Mch. 1790, both in MHi: AM). Another problem was Alden's compensation. No funds had been provided for the discharge of duties assigned to him by Washington on Thomson's resignation. On 29 Jan. 1790, therefore, Alden petitioned the House of Representatives for compensation for himself, for a clerk he had employed, and for the expenses of the office incident to the custody of "the records and papers of the late Congress, the great seal of the Federal Union, and the seal of the admiralty, which were delivered to him on the twenty-fourth of July last, by Charles Thomson . . . pursuant to the order of the President of the United States." This was allowed by Congress at the rate of $1,000 per annum for Alden and $500 for his clerk, the former being authorized to receive the salary only "until the Secretary of State shall enter on the duties of his office" (JHR, I, 149, 152, 153). Hence when TJ assumed office, he found two chief clerks in fact and an appropriation for only one. Moreover, one of these had been allowed a compensation for the preceding eight months greater than that provided by law for the single one he was authorized to designate as chief clerk. He accordingly made the request for authority to appoint TWO CHIEF CLERKS soon after taking office. On 4 Apr. 1790

Roger Sherman of Connecticut introduced a resolution authorizing the Secretary of State to employ an additional clerk at a salary of $800, the amount fixed by the Act of 11 Sep. 1789 for the salary of the chief clerk. The resolution was referred to Vining, Sherman, and Lee, who reported a bill on 13 Apr. but it did not become law until 4 June 1790. Shortly thereafter TJ submitted an estimate of expenses providing salaries of $800 each for one clerk in the Home Office and another in the Foreign Office (JHR, I, 188, 193, 194, 205, 227, 233, 234; Annals, II, 1571, 1602; Vol. 16; 512-13). In this the compensation for both was provided for from 1 Apr. 1790. Alden, of course, was obliged to accept a reduction in salary. The salaries of clerks in the public offices, as Adams had assured Storer and as TJ frequently asserted, were "a bare subsistence." Such able clerks as Alden and Remsen were often men of family and this fact combined with the low salaries accounts in general for their leaving government service.

Alden's resignation of 25 July 1790 prompted the letter from Barton OF THE 7TH. INSTANT, but this was not the first time he had sought TJ's patronage. On 20 Apr. 1790 David Rittenhouse wrote TJ from Philadelphia: "Having been informed that the office of Deputy Secretary to the Treasury is Vacant, and that application has been made to the Secretary in favour of my Nephew William Barton, and thinking it may probably fall in your way to befriend him, I cannot forbear giving my testimony to his Character. He has had a liberal Education and has studied the Law. His abilities are certainly more than equal to the Office, as he has given some Specimens sufficient to convince us that he might be a very agreeable writer. His principles and morals are unexceptionable and his Conduct in every respect such as must endear him to his friends and acquaintances. Your goodness will excuse the liberty I take" (RC in DLC; endorsed as received 24 Apr. 1790 and so recorded in SJL). Barton called on TJ with this letter and TJ applied to the Secretary of the Treasury, who responded: "Mr. Hamilton presents his respectful compliments to Mr. Jefferson and returns him the letter from Mr. Writtenhouse on the subject of Mr. Barton. As Mr. Bartons merit is well ascertained, if Mr. H——

can be of service to him in any other way he will take pleasure in being so" (RC in DLC, 29 May [1790], not recorded in SJL). Tench Coxe received the assignment and TJ surmised that "the successor had been decided on" even before the vacancy became known (TJ to Rittenhouse, 15 June 1790).

On learning of Alden's resignation, Barton wrote TJ on 7 Aug. 1790: "Situated as I am, with a pretty numerous family, and having a small as well as precarious income, I concluded to offer myself a Candidate for that Vacancy. . . . If, Sir, you should be disposed to favor my Views, on the present occasion, I beg leave to announce the Names of Mr. Secretary Hamilton and Mr. Tench Coxe, Mr. Speaker and most of the delegates from Pennsylvania, Mr. Page, Mr. Madison and Mr. Boudinot, besides Mr. Rittenhouse . . . all of whom, I trust, would bear satisfactory testimony to the respectability of my Education, Connections and general Deportment. Were it proper, I might refer to the President, to whom I have been amply recommended" (RC in DLC: Washington Papers; endorsed by TJ as received 10 Aug. 1790 and so recorded in SJL). Barton eventually became principal clerk in Coxe's office as commissioner of revenue (Account number 4564, 30 Sep. 1793, DNA: RG 217, MTA; see Barton to Hamilton, 9 Aug. 1790, Syrett, Hamilton, VI, 553).

When the consular establishment was before the Senate, Maclay, without noting that salaries were not involved, declared: "we are led on, little by little, to increase the civil list" (Maclay, Journal, ed. Maclay, p. 297). There was indeed a steady augmentation of the civil list in the departments of War and Treasury. This was necessarily so with respect to the latter, with the large numbers of clerks required in the offices of the secretary, the comptroller, the auditor, and the register, to say nothing of what TJ described in 1792 as "the hundred clerks of his [Hamilton's] department, the thousand excisemen, customhouse officers, loan officers &c. &c. &c. appointed by him, or at his nod, and spread over the Union" (TJ to Washington, 9 Sep. 1792). But in declaring one OFFICE AS AT AN END, TJ provided the single example of a voluntary retrenchment undertaken out of respect for what he considered to be the original intent of Congress. In keeping his departmental force for three more years at a level below that set at the beginning of his incumbency, TJ seemed to be endeavoring to provide in this fact also a contrast with the principles of administration that gave tone to Hamilton's department.

II. John Meyer to Thomas Jefferson

SIR   New York August 12th. 1790

It appears probable that it will not be convenient to the persons, who have heretofore been employed in your department as Interpreters, to proceed to Philadelphia, when the removal of the Offices shall take place, and that of Course there will be a vacancy.

If this be the case Sir, and it should correspond with your Arrangements, to make an Appointment for that purpose, I would with great deference beg leave to offer my Service as translator of the French, German and Low dutch Languages.

I have not procured an introduction Sir, but I take the Liberty of referring You to Mr. Hamilton, in whose Office I hold an employment, who, I have reason to believe, will give a Satisfactory Testimony, respecting my character, and who may also be able to give an opinion with regard to my Abilities in that Line.—I am Sir, with the greatest respect, Your most obedient hble Servt,

J. MEYER

RC (DLC: Applications for Office under Washington); endorsed by TJ as received 13 Aug. 1790 and so recorded in SJL.

It would be easy to exaggerate the significance of this document and equally so to dismiss it as just another appeal for employment. But the facts and the circumstances seem to point to far more important reasons prompting the application. Meyer was an employee in the Treasury. He was applying for a position of minor importance in another city. As his later record showed, he did enjoy the confidence of the Secretary of the Treasury and moved steadily upward in rank. He gave the name of his superior as a reference, an act of which custom required he should have first informed Hamilton. He clearly intended to remove to Philadelphia when the government did, otherwise the application and the reason given for it would be meaningless. Yet the compensation of an interpreter—half that of an ordinary clerk—was inadequate as a means of support or as a reason for transferring from one department to another, thus allowing the inference that Meyer intended to remain in the Treasury while engaged in translating for the Department of State. In view of this, the question whether this was an effort on the part of the Secretary of the Treasury to infiltrate the office of the Secretary of State cannot be avoided.

On the matter of interdepartmental relations, TJ early formed a policy of non-interference in the affairs of other departments (TJ to Washington, 9 Sep. 1792). There is no evidence that he departed from this general rule. The case of Tench Coxe in 1791 is generally cited as a move initiated by TJ to counter Hamilton's growing influence and to place a confidant in the Treasury (White, *The Federalists*, p. 224-25). But the facts do not sustain this interpretation: it is more correct to say that Hamilton himself prompted Coxe's application (see Coxe to TJ, 17 Apr. 1791; TJ to Washington, 17 Apr. 1791, notes). The Secretary of the Treasury, on the other hand, had no scruple against interfering in the conduct of affairs belonging to the Department of State. This is amply demonstrated not only in his relations with Beckwith during the war crisis of 1790 and in his confidential conversations with David Humphreys, but in a general pattern of conduct which even Hamilton's most sympathetic biographers acknowledge (e.g., Frederick S. Oliver, *Alexander Hamilton*, p. 213-14, cited by White, *The Federalists*, p. 224, in connection with his own statement to this effect: "Hamilton recognized no limits to the extension of his official activity and influence. The War Department fell into his orbit; and foreign policy had such an essential connection with his fiscal and domestic plans that he threw himself into diplomatic negotiations with the same attention he gave to financial operations"). Such an exercise of interference was by no means confined to overt moves. It would, in fact, have been quite characteristic of Hamilton to have endeavored to place a trusted subordinate in a position that would have given him as ready access to the communications of the French minister as he already had with respect to those of the British secret agent Beckwith. That he did so in respect to Meyer's application must remain conjectural, but the facts in the case do not in any sense contradict the possibility.

Since 1786 German translations under Jay and TJ had been made by the distinguished professor of German and geography at Columbia, John Daniel Gros. Dutch documents were translated by Remsen, Spanish and Italian by Isaac Pinto. On 11 Sep. 1790 Gros was paid £5 for four years of translations. During his similar period of service in the Office of Foreign Affairs, Pinto earned only £8 12s. 4d., though he received £20 15s. 9d. for translations in the first six months of TJ's tenure (Cashbook, Office of Foreign Affairs and Department of State, 1785-1795, DNA: RG 59, General and Departmental Accounts, under various dates from 15 Mch. 1787 to 15 Sep. 1790). Meyer aimed not at these minor compensations but at the position of "clerk for foreign languages" for which there was a fixed salary of $250. He also must have known already that its incumbent was not planning to move with the government to Philadelphia.

The incumbent of this clerkship was John Pintard (1759-1844), book collector, friend of Jeremy Belknap and Ebenezer Hazard, founder of the New-York Historical Society, proposer in 1789 of "an American Antiquarian Society," promoter in 1790 of a museum of natural and historical materials, and, in his own words, possessor of an increasing "passion for American history." Few men of the day displayed a keener interest in young men of intellectual promise than did the Secretary of State, as his correspondence with Short, Shippen, Rutledge, and many others demonstrates. But Pintard evoked no such response. TJ accorded him none of the sympathetic interest in matters of history that he gave so generously to Hazard, Wirt, Girardin, and others. So far as the record reveals, no such congenial or friendly relations existed between TJ and Pintard as prevailed between him and Remsen (see note, Document VI). So far as known, TJ wrote only a single letter to Pintard during his lifetime—a brief acknowledgement of his election to membership in the New-York Historical Society (TJ to Pintard, 9 Jan. 1814). Pintard had informed TJ of that election, but the only other letter he is known to have written the man under whom he had served for five months and of whom he was about to take leave is the following: "In behalf of the Trustees of the American Museum, belonging to the St. Tammanys Society in this city, I take the liberty to request, in case there should appear any supernumerary papers, Gazettes, &c. in your Department, not worth the trouble and expence of removal to Philadelphia, that you would be pleased to deposit them in the Museum where they will be carefully preserved and tend to form a collection which will always be open to the curious. —The object of this institution is to collect and preserve whatever relates to our Country in art or nature, as well as every material which may serve to perpetuate the Memorial of national events and history. A small fund is appropriated to support this design which is yet in its infancy, but we rely chiefly on what may be obtained by donations.

The plan is a patriotic one and if prosecuted may prove a public benefit by affording a safe deposit for many fugitive tracts which serving the purpose of a day, are generally afterwards consigned to oblivion tho' ever so important in themselves, useful to illustrate the manners of the times.—I am induced to intrude this letter, the more as I am well aware that you are much disposed to promote any measure that may be advantageous to our common country. Without further apology I have the honor to be therefore Your obed. hum. Servt." (Pintard to TJ, New York, 26 Aug. 1790, RC in DNA: RG 59, MLR; endorsed by Remsen as received the same day and so recorded in sjl. FC in DNA: RG 59, PCC No. 120. PrC in DLC).

Pintard chose one of the busiest days of the Secretary of State in 1790 to address his only known leave-taking in the form of a request for government property. There was no answer. As if to emphasize the fact, TJ caused the letter to be transcribed for the official files, an unusual procedure, and retained a copy of this for his own records.

A merchant belonging to an old mercantile family in a city in which that interest adhered generally to the Hamiltonian position, Pintard was a leading Sachem in the Society of St. Tammany and he declared that the principles of the society were his: "it is a political institution founded on a strong republican basis, whose democratical principles will serve in some measure to correct the aristocracy of our city" (MHS, *Colls.*, 6th ser., IV, 469-70). This was a prophetic utterance, but it would be a misreading of the evidence to assume that Pintard and the Secretary of State regarded either "supernumerary papers" or republican views in the same manner. The clerk for foreign languages, for all of his zeal in promoting civic institutions, seemed closer to his neighbor the Secretary of the Treasury than to his superior in the Department of State. In 1791 he became involved in and ruined by the "pyramid of magic paper" of Hamilton's former assistant secretary, William Duer. He is said to have been so ardent in republican principles that he changed the names of such streets as King, Queen, Duke, Princess, and Crown to "good republican names" (Joseph A. Scoville, *Old Merchants of New York*, II [New York, 1864], 217, 223, 224, 242, 256). But his republicanism seems an instrument of promotion rather than a conviction. Nothing is clearer on the basis of the record than that TJ was on far greater terms of cordiality and esteem with Henry Remsen, son of a Loyalist merchant, than he was with this zealous advocate of "democratical principles."

There is no evidence that TJ replied to Meyer's application and the position of clerk for foreign languages was allowed to remain vacant until it was given to Philip Freneau. According to TJ's later statement, he had been "applied to on behalf of Freneau" when the government was still in New York and had given the answer that there was no vacancy (TJ to Washington, 9 Sep. 1792; Brant, *Madison*, III, 334-5). Meyer in 1790 was a clerk in Hamilton's own office in the Treasury and evidently was paid at the rate he was receiving early in 1791—$400 per year. On 1 Apr. 1791 his compensation was raised to $500. Two months later he was paid at the rate of $600, being one of two clerks in the office to receive that sum. By 1792 he was listed as one of Hamilton's two principal clerks and was receiving $800 per year, thus having had his salary doubled in less than two years (DNA: RG 217, M235/1, 2, 3, and 7: accounts number 1196, 1135, 1371, 1613, 1859, and 3010). He was a man of family and was one of those who came under the Act of 1791 allowing reasonable and necessary expenses incurred by clerks on the removal of the offices to Philadelphia. On 31 Mch. 1791 he received $95.70 for the expense of removing himself and family (DNA: RG 217, M235/1, account number 1115; Meyer was the first of nineteen clerks on the list and one receiving the highest compensation; George Taylor, Jr. in the Department of State received $47; Remsen's account was settled separately—account No. 3953, same, M235/10). In view of this record there can be little doubt that Meyer was fully justified in feeling that the Secretary of the Treasury would GIVE A SATISFACTORY TESTIMONY in support of his application. The question is whether Hamilton or his subordinate was the more disappointed at TJ's failure to fill the vacancy.

III. James Wilson to Thomas Jefferson

DEAR SIR   Philada. 13th Augt. 1790

I am just now informed that the Place of Clerk for recording the Laws of the United States and keeping the Papers of the former Congress is vacant and in your Gift. If the Information is true; permit me to recommend to you for this Office, a Friend of mine William Nichols Esquire Clerk of the Court of Quarter Sessions and of the Orphans Court in the County of Philadelphia. I can recommend him with Confidence; and you will lay me under a particular Obligation by appointing him. I have the Honour to be, Sir, with much Esteem, dear Sir Your most obedient and very humble Servant   JAMES WILSON

RC (DLC: Applications for Office under Washington); endorsed by TJ as received at the office on "Aug. 17. by Th: J. Aug. 21," when he returned from Rhode Island; recorded in SJL under the latter date.

There is no evidence that TJ replied to this letter. It is, indeed, remarkable and perhaps significant that there exists only one letter from him to Wilson —that of 17 Apr. 1793 concerning some ingeniously designed bookshelves. Both men were lawyers, both were learned in the study of government, and both had taken similar and advanced positions in 1774 on the nature of the British imperial constitution.

But Wilson's identification with the leading principles of the Revolution was somewhat scholastic, tinged with opportunism, and marred by a self-seeking ambition. The two men had little in common: one who argued that a Bill of Rights was unnecessary and who in addition gave evidence that this argument was tempered "for the Audience to whom it was addressed" could scarcely win the admiration of one who believed that "a bill of rights is what the people are entitled to against every government on earth, general or particular" (TJ to Madison, 20 Dec. 1787).

IV. Richard Bland Lee to Thomas Jefferson

DEAR SIR   Alexandria Aug. 19. 1790

You may recollect that I mentioned Mr. Daniel Brent to you as a young gentleman of merit who would be happy to be employed in some of the public offices as a clerk. If any vacancy should happen in your department in consequence of the removal to Philadelphia, your patronage of this gentleman would be useful to him, and I flatter myself without injury to you or the Public.

The assumption will probably endanger my election:—I shall be a willing victim, if the government should be established and prosper.—With very great esteem & respect I am your obt: huml. servt,   RICHARD BLAND LEE

RC (DLC: Applications for Office under Washington); docketed by clerk; endorsed by TJ as received 28 Aug. 1790 and so recorded in SJL.

Brent became a clerk in the Treasury Department. Lee was not defeated, but served in the House of Representatives until 1795. He was one of the two members of the Virginia delegation, Alexander White being the other, who voted for the ASSUMPTION as a result of the conference arranged by TJ.

Lee was a strong Federalist and had evidently been committed to vote against assumption. Of his action in doing so Richard Henry Lee later wrote: "It was generally supposed that the Assumption part of our Bill would be rejected by the H.R. but Messrs. R. B. Lee and White from our Country with Gale and Dan'l Carroll from Maryland, changing sides, the Assumption was agreed to" (*Letters of Richard Henry Lee*, ed. J. C. Ballagh, II, 535).

V. Thomas Jefferson to Isaac Pinto

SIR   New York August 28th. 1790

I have made it very much my rule to preserve the arrangements which Mr. Jay had established in the office for foreign affairs. In your case indeed I was led on the representations I received through or from Mr. Remsen to raise the allowance for translating which had been given by Mr. Jay: in this I went as far as I thought an impartial judge ought to go, deciding between the public and an individual. No new cause occurring to produce any change of opinion, I doubt not you will yourself approve of my not going beyond what I believe to be right. I am Sir &c.

FC (DNA: RG 59, PCC No. 120).

In a letter to Jay of 13 Nov. 1789, Pinto referred to his appointment as Spanish interpreter in the Office of Foreign Affairs and added: "When I received that Appointment, altho' no Salary was arranged, I took it for granted that the employ would have been of considerable advantage to me; you will be apprised of the little benefit I have derived therefrom when I acquaint you that the whole amount for my Service is no more than £8. 12. 4 in the very near Three Years. . . . I therefore concieve it no impropriety in me to hope or even expect some further Compensation. I am persuaded you will think what I have received not an Object for an appointment from your Office. I rest the matter Sir on your own Equity and Feelings to fix the Compensation, in Confidence that it will be agreeable to my wishes" (RC in DNA: RG 59, MLR; Tr in same, PCC No. 120). Pinto enclosed a copy of this letter in one to TJ of 16 Aug. 1790, stating: "Mr. Jay . . . seem'd to think my Expectations of more Advantage from my Appointment were well founded and a Subject of relief; yet as he was then Circumstanced, cou'd not take it upon himself making me the Compensation I wish'd for, and recommended an application to you for that purpose" (RC in DNA: RG 59, MLR; endorsed by TJ as received by the office on 17 Aug. and by him on 21 Aug. 1790, and so recorded in SJL).

VI. Salary Account of the Department of State

[1 Apr. 1791]

Account of Salary due to the Secretary of State, his Chief and other Clerks, and the Office-keeper and Messenger, and of Rent of the House lately occupied by the Office in New York, and of the one now occupied by the Office in Philadelphia.

Names	Station	Commencement	Ending	Salary ⅌. Anm:	Quarter's Salary	
Thomas Jefferson	Secy of State	1st Jany: 1791	31st Mar: 1791	3,500	875	
Henry Remsen Junr.	Chief Clerck	ditto	ditto	800	200	
George Taylor Junr.	Clerk	ditto	ditto	500	125	
Jacob Blackwell	ditto	ditto	ditto	500	125	
William Lambert	ditto	ditto	ditto	500	125	
Sampson Crosby	Office-keeper, &c.	ditto	ditto	200	50	
Office Rent in New York		ditto	ditto	200	50	Cents
ditto in Philadelphia		ditto	ditto	186.66 2/3	46	66 2/3
				Dollars	1,596	66 2/3

MS (DNA: RG 217, MTA); in Remsen's hand, with notations by others showing settlement with Auditor and examination by Comptroller on 1 Apr. 1791, and registry the next day by Register of the Treasury under account No. 1128.

This document is the earliest statement of account showing departmental personnel and salaries during TJ's tenure that has been found. It may be taken as the standard for estimating the size and status of the staff from 1790 through 1793. In his estimated departmental needs of 17 June 1790, TJ listed two clerks at $800, three additional clerks at $500, and one messenger at $200. When Alden resigned at the end of July, 1790, the clerical staff remained as in the above statement. Other statements of account for salary lists are to be found in DNA: RG 217, MTA. These are incomplete but suffice to show the small and stable force that prevailed throughout TJ's incumbency. These are as follows: (1) Account number 1372 for the quarter ending 30 June 1791, showing the same personnel as above and totalling $1,563.42 (office rent included in this and following figures). (2) Account number 1609 for the quarter ending 30 Sep. 1791, showing the same personnel as above and totalling $1,546.67. (3) Account number 3011 for the quarter ending 30 Sep. 1792, totalling $1,621.67 and showing that George Taylor, Jr. had succeeded Remsen as chief clerk, that George Pfeiffer had been added as the third clerk, and that Philip Freneau had become "clerk for foreign languages" at $250 per annum. (4) Account number 4229 for the quarter ending 30 June 1793, totalling $1,465.11 and with the same personnel as in preceding statement. (5) Account number 4572 for the quarter ending 30 Sep. 1793, totalling $1,575 and showing that Benjamin Bankson had succeeded William Lambert during the quarter. (6) Account number 4757 for the quarter ending 31 Dec. 1793, totalling $1,512.50 and with the same personnel as in preceding statement.

The last was TJ's final report of his salary list, but Edmund Randolph submitted for the next quarter a statement showing that between 19 Nov. and 31 Dec. 1793 eleven extra clerks were employed in the office of the Secretary of State preparing documents for Congress. This was in the last few weeks of TJ's incumbency when the report on commerce, the report on relations with the Barbary powers, and the copying of the extensive correspondence with the British and French ministers needed to be completed in addition to the normal work of the department. Other periods in these four years had brought intensive spells of work for the staff and especially for the Secretary of State, as was true in the summer of 1790. But this was the only period when the sustained pressure of performance against a time limit was such that it was necessary for the clerical staff to be expanded. No comparable spate of activity in any other period or in any other department during Washington's two administrations can be said to equal this final burst coming at the end of a disillusioning and frustrating experience in office. In all the eleven clerks put in a total of 291⅓ days plus 100½ days in extra time in the last six weeks of 1793. Bernard Webb spent thirty-three hours copying correspondence with the British and French ministers. James Young wrote from nine in the morning to ten each night between the 28th of Nov. and the 7th of Dec., including Sundays. Richard Johnson put in 50½ days between 29 Nov. and 31 Dec. plus 17½ days extra. Edward Robinson, in a period only four days longer, worked 100 days exactly, an incredible performance of more than two regular clerk's days (six hours constituted a day) for each calendar day of the period, Sundays and holidays included. George Taylor, Jr. certified that all of this was done "by desire of Mr. Jefferson, late Secretary of State . . . and that the duty was performed by each under the usual oath of office faithfully to execute the trust reposed" (Account number 5245, DNA: RG 217, MTA, 2 Apr. 1794).

Expressed in other terms, the departmental salaries for 1790 were at the rate of $6,800 per year, in 1791 at $6,000, in 1792 at $6,500, and in 1793 at $6,000. Actual expenditures for salaries from 4 Mch. 1789 to 31 Dec. 1791 (the figure is not broken down by years) were $10,855.37, for 1792 were $6,502, and for 1793 were $6,078.45 (DNA: RG 39, Register of Civil List Accounts, 1789-1808). This becomes all the more impressive by contrast with what preceded and followed. During the last year of government under the Articles of Confederation—surely a quiescent period for the Office of Foreign Affairs and the Office of Secretary to Congress—these two bureaus had salary lists of $5,600 and $4,700 respectively, or a total of $10,300, almost the equal of that required in the two years 1792 and 1793 when the functions of these offices were combined under the Department of State (DLC: Force Collection, Treasury Accounts, 1784-1790, p. 257, 262). During the first year after TJ left office there were added to the four clerks held over from his administration—Taylor as chief clerk at $1,000, and Blackwell, Pfeiffer, and Bankson—four other clerks. Thus while the number of persons regularly employed and the amount of salaries were actually less at the end of 1793 than they had been in 1790, both increased sharply in 1794, the total number of the clerical staff being raised to eight and the salary account to $8,250 (Accounts number 5258, 5968, and 6289 for the quarters ending 31 Mch., 30 Sep., and 31 Dec. 1794, DNA: RG 217, MTA; this was in addition to the sums for extra clerks at the end of 1793 and also to the $250 paid Blackwell and Bankson for extra services in "Recording American Ministers Letters &c. out of office hours by direction of the Secretary of State" from 1 Feb. to 30 Sep. 1794 [same]). There is no evidence to suggest that the work of the department in 1794 had undergone a commensurate increase. Indeed, it is quite doubtful whether any single year of the decade equalled in complexity and extent the burdens that fell upon the departmental staff in the critical year 1793 when TJ, until the last few weeks in office as he faced an extraordinary series of tasks to be discharged before departing, managed with a smaller staff than he had had four years earlier. Even in 1792 TJ described the work of a clerk in the department—indeed, that of the chief clerk—as being "one continued scene of drudgery in copying papers and close attendance from morning till night" (TJ to Barton, 1 Apr. 1792). But both the size of the staff and the total of salaries continued to mount during the decade. By 1800 the civil list of the Department of State called for an appropriation of $24,911.99, more than four times the total expenditure in the last year TJ was in office (DNA: RG 39, Register of Civil List Accounts, 1789-1808).

The staff during the years 1790-1793 included the following: ROGER ALDEN: In office at beginning of TJ's tenure, and resigned as of 25 July 1790. HENRY REMSEN, JR. In office at beginning of TJ's tenure, resigned as of 1 Apr. 1792 (TJ to Taylor, 1 Apr. 1792; TJ to Remsen, 14 Apr. 1792). GEORGE TAYLOR, JR.: In office at the beginning of TJ's tenure, having served as clerk in the Office of Foreign Affairs since 1785; became chief clerk on 1 Apr. 1792 and served throughout TJ's term (Taylor to TJ, 17 Mch. 1792). JACOB BLACKWELL: In office at the beginning of TJ's tenure and at its close (TJ to Blackwell, 1 Apr. 1792). JOHN PINTARD: Clerk for foreign languages in office at the beginning of TJ's tenure, resigned 26 Aug. 1790 (see notes, Document II; see also TJ to Washington, 9 Sep. 1792; TJ to Speaker of the House, 2 Jan. 1793). WILLIAM LAMBERT: Employed as clerk late in 1790, resigned in 1793 (Lambert to TJ, 8 June 1793). SAMPSON CROSBY: Served as messenger throughout TJ's term of office, also occasionally furnished firewood (see Document VII). PHILIP FRENEAU: Appointed "clerk for foreign languages" in Aug. 1791, though his salary only began 1 Oct. 1791 (see Document X, also TJ to Washington, 9 Sep. 1792). GEORGE PFEIFFER: Appointed clerk Apr. 1792 and served remainder of TJ's tenure of office (Pfeiffer to TJ, 2 Apr. 1792). BENJAMIN BANKSON: Employed for a few days in Sep. 1790 as "additional clerk" (Document VII); appointed in 1793 to vacancy created by resignation of Lambert in June 1793. ISAAC PINTO: Temporary translator of Spanish documents in 1790 (see Document V). One James P. Puglia apparently served as an occasional interpreter in 1792-1793 (Puglia to TJ, 21 June 1808). John Carey began as a clerk on 25 Jan. 1793 but was only temporarily employed (Account number 3834, DNA: RG 217, MTA).

As Secretary of State TJ was obviously a rigorous taskmaster who administered an office characterized as much by its discipline and systematic methods as by the tone of republicanism that he gave to it. It is equally evident that he stood on terms of agreeable, friendly, and mutually respectful relations with his subordinates. His leave-taking letters to Alden and Remsen are expressed in terms of genuine respect and even affection. With the latter he maintained a life-long friendship: the close of a moving letter that he wrote Remsen in the last months of his life reads: "I retain for you a sincere and affectionate friendship and respect" (TJ to Remsen, 25 Mch. 1826). No hint of scandal or charge of betrayal of secrets was ever levelled at the clerks of the Department of State during TJ's tenure of office and none was ever discharged for such reasons as was the case in the Department of the Treasury (see Appendix, Vol. 18). No open hostility ever developed between the Secretary of State and a subordinate as there did between the Secretary of the Treasury and Andrew G. Fraunces. It is true that Taylor and Blackwell, after many years of service to the government, were summarily dismissed in 1798 for allegedly accepting passport gratuities (White, *The Federalists*, p. 286-7). But even in doing so the Secretary of State, Timothy Pickering, declared that Taylor and Blackwell "sustained fair characters, had been long in the office, would have been recommended for their fidelity to any employment, were careful, steady, industrious, and the chief clerk, from his long and accurate acquaintance with the books, papers, and business of the office was eminently useful" (Pickering to the Rev. John Clarke, 26 Jan. 1798, same, p. 287). But the discharge of two such men cannot be dissociated from the fact that Pickering himself had been publicly accused of the misconduct and that he attributed this to the work of the "Jacobinic scoundrels" (*Aurora*, 24 Jan. 1798). Further, the side of the case that is known is that of the accusing official.

This episode, imperfectly known as it is, does indeed tell "a good deal of the temper of the times" about the conduct of government employees (White, *The Federalists*, p. 286). But this leaves much left unsaid. The fact that clerks of acknowledged rectitude at the end of the decade should have come to consider the taking of gratuities for public service as a matter of accepted conduct requires that some note be taken of an important distinction. This is that two opposing philosophies of administration—two opposite ways of looking at government and its ends—inevitably produced differing concepts of ethical conduct in office at every level. Under an administrative theory aimed at gaining support for government by appealing to ligaments of interest—of considering that "every man ought to be supposed . . . to have no other end, in all his actions, but private interests"— it was quite natural that underpaid clerks should have imitated the modes of conduct they observed in their superior officers. Incidents such as those involving the arrearages of pay for Revolutionary soldiers and the purchase of Baron Glaubeck's claim, to say nothing of the revelation of state secrets such as those discussed in the group of documents pertaining to the war crisis, could not help but affect the general tone of the offices. A theory that, by contrast, called at every point for sub-.

ordinating private interest to that of the public and for avoiding all conflict between the two could not help but produce a contrary effect at all levels. This distinction stands confirmed by the record. During his incumbency as Secretary of State, TJ presided over a staff that, so far as the evidence reveals, was above suspicion of improper conduct. This cannot be said of the clerks in the offices of the Secretary of the Treasury. In his own department in the turbulent climate of the early 1790's TJ set the standard in every aspect of departmental affairs by his profound loyalty to principles of equality, justice, and disinterested conduct. His own view of man and society diffused its humane influence over the small, close-knit group of subordinates. Their response reflected the same steady, industrious, reliable, and smooth-functioning performance that characterized the administration in his presidential years. A philosophy of administration could not do everything, but it could elevate.

VII. Contingent Expenses of the Department of State, 1790-1793

1790		New York Currency		
Jany. 14.	By cash paid Archibald McLean for two sets of the daily Gazette from 1st. May 1789 to 1st. inst. at 48/. per annum	£	3. 4. 0.	
	By cash paid Thomas Allen for sealing wax, paper, binding of books and other articles of Stationary for the office		9. 7. 6.	
21.	By cash repaid Wm. Constable, the postage on a packet of letters he had received from Mr. Jefferson, for Mr. Jay		0. 18. 4.	
23.	By cash paid Jacob Marseilles for three cords nut wood, inspection and carting		6. 4. 3.	
	Sawing and piling the said three cords		15. 0.	
Feby. 2d.	By cash paid Francis Turner for 350 best quills		2. 7. 6.	

[1790]

Apl. 14. By cash paid Francis Turner for 300 best quills	2. 5. 0.
15. By cash paid Abrm. Okie for sundries for the office, including tea water for 4 months, candles, sweeping of chimneys, charge attending the yard, &c.	2. 5. 9.
19. By cash John Fenno for four sets of the Gazette of the United States from 15 Oct. 1789 to 14 Aprl. 1790 at 24/. each per annum	2. 8. 0.
21. By cash paid Monsr. le Prince for a copying press and apparatus to copy letters	20. 0. 0.
Carting the said press to the office	6. 6.
[26. By cash paid William Vanwart for one load nut wood, carting, &c.	0. 12. 4.
May 3d. By cash paid Isaac Pinto for translating and copying a number of papers concerning Don Blas Gonzales, and translating other Spanish papers	20. 12. 9.
5th. By cash paid William Morton for the morning post, from 5th. May 1789 to 5th. May 1790	1. 12. 0.
6th. By cash paid Abm. Okie, for one load nut wood, carting, &c.	0. 13. 4.
14th. By cash paid Childs & Swaine for two sets of the daily advertiser from 1st. May to 1st. August 1789, £1. 4. 0. One set of the advertiser from 1st. August 1789, to 1st. May 1790, £1.16. 0., and two printed reports of the Secretary of the Treasury respecting public credit, 10/.	3. 10. 0
By cash paid Archibald McLean for two sets of the daily Gazette from 1st. January to 1st. May 1790, at 48/. each per annum.	1. 12. 0.
15th. By cash paid John Fenno for printing five quires of sea letters for vessels, and finding paper	1. 10. 0.
29th. By cash paid Samuel Loudon, for sundries since July last, viz: 26 skins of parchment at 4/6 £5.17.0. one dozen and one papers ink powder 10/. and binding a set of the Journals of Congress at 4/. per Vol.: £2.12.0.	9. 3. 6.

[1790]

July 1st.	By cash repaid Mr. Alden for sundries for the office, among which was the seal for the Secretary's office that cost £2.3.4.	2. 13. 10.
30	By cash paid John Fenno for printing fifty blank commissions or warrants for the officers of the customs, and finding paper	0. 14. 0
Sepr. 1st	By cash paid the freight and primage of a box of books sent by Mr. Dumas to the department of State, and for a permit and the cartage	0. 17. 0.
	By cash paid George Faber for his services as additional messenger to the department of State from April 20th. to this day, at the rate of 100 dollrs. per annum	14. 13. 2.
2.	By cash paid Benjamin Bankson for his services as an additional clerk in the department of State, from the 25th. to the 29th. of August, at the rate of 500 dollars per annum	2. 13. 8.
11th.	By cash paid Revd. Dr. Gros for translating a number of German papers at different periods, since his appointment of German interpreter in September 1786	5. 0. 0.
15th.	By cash paid Henry Remsen for translating sundry dutch papers since April 1st. 1789	3. 4. 10
	By cash paid Isaac Pinto for translating sundry spanish papers since May last	0. 3. 0
Octr. 1st.	By cash paid Abrm. Okie for sundries for the office, [including tea water for six months, candles, marking pot and brush, expence attending the yard, &c.][1]	2. 18. 0
	By cash paid the cartage of that part of the effects of the office that was to go to Philadelphia *by water* from the office to the vessel, being 21 loads	2. 7. 0.
2d.	By cash paid George Faber for hasps to secure the chests, and nail them on, and for his labor in assisting to pack up	2. 8. 7.
5th	By cash paid, for carting the effects in the city Hall that were to go by land, to the office in Broadway, the corpora-	

[1790]	tion having required the delivery of the rooms, being nine loads	0. 14. 0.
8th	By cash paid Thomas Allen, for a five quire blank book, sealing wax, paper and binding of french newspapers for the *foreign* office, and for paper, ink powder, sealing wax and quills, furnished Col: Smith, in exchange for six reams of thin quarto paper, and two and an half dozen of ink powder for the *copying press*	28. 5. 6.
	By cash paid Berry and Rogers for a variety of Stationary and blank books for the *home* office, since February 19th. 1790.	28. 18. 3.
9th	By cash paid Andrew Wright for making a number of rough boxes to case the cases, and casing them, &c.	13. 19. 0.
13th	By cash paid Thomas Thomson for the freight of the effects of the office to Philadelphia, *by water*	23. 9. 4.
	By cash paid the cartage of the said effects from the wharf to the office in Market Street £1.8.0. and a labourer in assisting to unpack and carry them in 8/	1. 16. 0.
14th	By cash paid Thomas Allen for two sticks sealing wax	0. 2. 0.
15th	By cash paid the cartage of that part of the effects of the office that were to go to Philadelphia *by land*, from the office to the Brunswick boat, being 8 loads	0. 14. 0.
17th	By cash paid John Fenno for four sets of the Gazette of the United States from April 15th. to October 15th. 1790. at 3 dols. each per annum	2. 8. 0.
Nov. 1st	By cash paid Archibald McLean for the daily gazette from May 1st. 1790 at 48/. per annum	1. 4. 0.
	By cash paid Childs and Swaine for the the daily advertizer from May 1st. 1790 at 48/. per annum and some wrapping.	1. 6. 0.
5th	By cash paid William Morton for the Morning post from May 5th. 1790 at at 32 per annum	0. 16. 0.
10th	By cash paid the cartage of the effects of the office, that came *by land*, from the wharf to the office in market street	0. 8. 0.

[1790]

20th	By cash paid Augustine Davis for the Richmond paper for two years, ending the 4th. of Octr. last	2. 0. 0.	
26th	By cash paid George Taylor for 3 1/2 cords of hickory wood, cartage, sawing and piling £7.19.11. and for sundries for the office 7/1	8. 7. 0.	
Dec. 18	By cash remitted the attorney for the district of New Jersey the amount of his expenditure for a set of the laws of that State 30 1/3 dollars	12. 2. 8.	

1791

Jany.

3rd   By cash paid Andrew Brown for publishing in the federal Gazette printed *at Philadelphia*, the acts passed at the 2d. session of the Congress of the United States 88 1/2 dollars   35. 8. 0.

4th   By cash paid John Aitken for four dozen pieces of Mahogany[2] to be used in filing papers   1. 5. 7.

14th   By cash paid William Lambert for ink powder and sundry ingredients for making ink, an inkstand, and for firewood, while he wrote at his lodgings   2. 0. 0.

16th   By cash paid George Taylor for sundries for the office   0. 4. 1.

18th   By cash paid Augustine Davis for publishing in the *Virginia* Gazette, the acts passed at the 2d. session of the Congress of the United States, 88 1/2 dollars   35. 8. 0.

22d   By cash paid Benjamin Russell for publishing in the Columbian centinel printed at *Boston* the said acts, 88 1/2 ds.   35. 8. 0.

25th   By cash paid John Fenno for publishing in the Gazette of the United States, printed at *New York* the said acts, 88-1/2 ds.   35. 8. 0.

Feby.   1st   By cash paid Jacob Blackwell for 6 and 5/8 cords of hiccory wood, and the cartage and sawing of the same £16.0.5. Sweeping of chimneys 3/. and 3℔. of candles 3/3   16. 6. 8.

21st   By cash remitted the attorney for the district of Virginia the amount of his expenditure for certain laws of that State, respecting british subjects, &c. 38 1/2 dollars   15. 8. 0.

[1791]   By sundry disbursements, vizt: laborers in New York, 4/. putting a door lock at the office there, 1/6. Two of Gaine's almanacks for the year 1791 for Messrs. Short and Carmichael, 2/.   0.   7.   6.][3]

Dollars

[March 1st   By balance due on the account last settled and transferred to this   47.58

By cash paid the cartage of a chest containing printed laws of the United States to the Amboy boat 12 1/2 cents (the transportation of it to Philadelphia remains unpaid) and the cartage from the boat to the office in Market street 25 cents   .37 1/2

Apl.   2d   By cash remitted the attorney for the district of Georgia, the amount of his expenditures for certain laws of that State   17.14

3d   By cash remitted the attorney for the district of Maryland the amount of his expenditures for certain laws of that State   25.25

10th   By cash paid Andrew Brown for publishing in the federal Gazette printed at Philadelphia the acts passed at the 3d. session of the Congress of the United States   37.87

May   7th   By cash remitted the Attorney for the district of Connecticut, the amount of his expenditures for certain laws of that State   15.25

13th   By cash remitted Joshua Johnson, American Consul at London, the amount of his expenditures for British newspapers and pamphlets   15.11 1/4

20th   By cash paid Henry and John Ingle for sundries for the office, vizt: putting on and repairing door locks, and repairing and putting up venetian blinds, and for two sets of new venetian blinds, at £2.0.0. each and carpenter's work   18.93 1/3

24th   By cash paid Bart: Carter for Norman's map of the United States, and chart of the West Indies   2.50

June   23   By cash remitted the attorney for the district of Massachusetts the amount of

[1791]   his expenditures for certain laws of
that State   5.84

28   By cash paid Childs & Swaine for pub-
lishing in the daily advertised printed at
New York, the acts passed at the 3d.
Session of the Congress of the U.S.   37.87

By cash paid Childs and Swaine for
printing 100. proclamations respecting
permanent seat of Government, 3 ds.
$^{50}/_{100}$—fifty proclamations respecting
James O'Fallon, 2 ds.; seventy heads to
blank parchment commissions 2 ds.
$^{50}/_{100}$ twenty two quires of blank commissions for officers of the customs and
revenue, 20 $^{25}/_{100}$ and for nine copies of
acts passed 1st Session, and two of 2d.
Session, 13 dollars.   41.25

By cash paid Augustine Davis, for publishing in the Virginia Gazette, the acts
passed at the 3d. Session of the Congress of the United States   37.87

July 1st By cash paid Michael Roberts for the
following articles of Stationary, viz:
writing and wrapping paper, £14.10.0;
1 ream copying paper, 30/. 2 doz. copying ink, 45/; 1 wetting and one drying
book, 9/; 4 half and 4 quire sheets
oiled paper, 21/6; 3 pen knives, 15/.
one dozen ink powder 8/4; 20 skins of
parchment, 60/; 3 ℔. sealing wax, 42/-
6; 1 ℔. wafers, 15/; 400 crown wafers
for great seal, 20/; 500 quills, 75/; 6
black lead pencils, 5/; 1 ℔. black
sand, 1/3; 3 pr. of snuffers, 14/; 1 doz-
en red tape, 12/; 1 double piece silk
taste 7/6; 2 fountain inkstands, 10/6;
Glasses for inkstands, 2/6; 2 1/2 doz-
en scuttle bone, 2/9; 2 pounce boxes,
3/9; a tinder box and apparatus, 2/6;
Chambaud's french dictionary, 2 vols.
quarto, 75/.   107.74

July 20th By cash paid Sampson Crosby for 2
cords hickory wood, carting and sawing, 69/6; expence of procuring salt
water, and making experiments thereon,
40/1; 13 ℔. candles, 11/11; water
pitchers and tumblers, 6/8; sweeping
chimnies, 3/10; dowlas for covering a

[1791]	book, and the copying press, 13/1; transportation of Maryland laws to the office, 5/5; cleaning the office, 6/; and for sundries, 6/1.	21.81½
25	By cash paid John Fenno for 30 reports on the fisheries, 7 ds. ⁵⁰⁄₁₀₀; four sets of the Gazette of the U.S. from Oct. 27th. 1790, to April 27th. 1791, 8 dols., and for printing 150 blank commissions or warrants for officers of the customs, 3 dols.	18.50
	By cash paid the postage and penny postage on sundry letters directed to the chief clerk on public business	1.50
Augt. 6	By cash paid Ann Timothy for publishing in the South Carolina State Gazette, the acts passed at the 3d. Session of the Congress of the U.S.	37.87½
	By cash paid Alexander Hale for 500 wafers for great seal	3.33⅓
	By cash paid Benjamin Russell for publishing in the Columbian centinel, printed at Boston, the acts passed at the 3d. Session of the Congress of the U.S.	37.87
11th	By cash remitted the Attorney for the district of Rhode Island the amount of his expenditures for certain laws of that State	45.
	By cash paid John Bringhurst for 1 hammer, 3/9; 1 pull back lock, 4/; a screw driver, 1/3; a pair of bellowses 6/; 6 flat steel candlesticks, 18/; 1 sweeping, 2 hearth and 1 desk brush, 83/; a large door lock with two keys, 20/; a smaller door lock, 3/6; and a case lock, 2/6;	8.97
12th	By cash paid Archibald McLean for 50 papers of the daily Gazette to complete that file of papers	1.57
15th	By cash paid Thomas Greenleaf for 13 papers to complete a file of newspapers	0.54
Oct. 19th	By cash paid Henry and Joseph Ingle for a small writing desk	5.
25th	By cash paid for thirteen cords of hiccory wood, measuring, carting, sawing and piling	78.43

[1791]

29th   By cash paid for the Delaware Gazette, commencing October 1st. 1790 and ending October 1st, 1791   2.

Novr. 12   By cash paid Sampson Crosby for cleaning the office and for sand, 6/6; 3 lb. candles, 2/9; ingredients for ink, 4/11; dowlas and thread for book covers, 4/; carting the journals of the old Congress to Mr. Beckley's office, 15/6; and for sundries, including chimnies swept, 4/1   5.4

18th   By cash paid John Fenno for five sets of the Gazette of the U.S. from April 27. to October 26. 1791, 7ds. $^{50}/_{100}$, and for advertising for information respecting L. Raus, 1 dollr.   8.50

26   By cash paid Benjamin Franklin Bache for publishing a proclamation respecting James O'Fallon, 1d. $^{50}/_{100}$; for 14 papers to complete the file of the General advertiser, $^{60}/_{100}$; for a set of said advertiser from October 1st. 1790 to Septemr. 30. 1791, 5 $^{50}/_{100}$ dollars; for 6 quires of blank bills of exchange, 9 $^{50}/_{100}$ dol; and for advertising for information Claud Causin, 1 dollr.   16.10

28th   By cash paid the Attorney for the district of Delaware the amount of his expenditures for certain laws of that State   14.

By cash paid Mathew Carey for 4 sets of the constitutions of the different States, 18/9; and for 12 sets of the examinations of Lord Sheffield's observations, 56/3.   10.][4]

Decr. 13th   By cash paid Monsr. Hallet for two drafts of the federal town, made out by the direction of the President of the U.S. for the Senate and House of Representatives, 100 ds.; and the joiner for fixing mahogany rollers to said drafts, 2 dols.   102.

By cash paid Mr. Dallas for making an index to the acts passed at the 1st 2nd. and 3d. Sessions of the 1st. Congress   200.

[1791]
28th By cash paid for the Pittsburgh Gazette commencing October 19, 1790 and
[1792] ending October 19, 1791[5] 2.
Jany. No. 1. By Cash remitted Christopher Gore for set of copies in the case between Stephen Hooper and T. Pagan 19.50
Feb. 10 2. By Cash paid Henry Remsen postage of a public letter from Colo. Humphreys to him 1.31
20 3. —— George Faber for attending the Office of the Secy. of State, during the illness of the stated Doorkeeper from 14th. Jany. to 16 Feb. 1792 inclusive, and for Cash he paid for a lock 6/3 and cleaning the office, 7/. 18.
Mar. 1 4. —— Andrew Brown, subscription for Fed. Gaz. from Octr. 1790 to 1. Jany. 1792 5.62
5. Andrew Brown for 6 vol. laws of US at 1.75 10.50
10 6. Benj. Russell for Mass. Centinel, 1. Oct. 90 to 1. Oct. 91. 2.24
13 7. Michael Roberts for Quills, 13D. 35 cts. black lead pencils, 1.73; parchment, 19.99; Bank post paper, 1.34; Ink powder, 2.21; Carlton's map, 2.50; Fools cap paper, 5.34; 6 qrs. thin cartridge paper, 1.50; 2 R. best thick Extra 4to. post paper, 9.D.; 1 ℔. black sand, 13cts; 3 ℔. sealing wax, 4D.4cts; 1 Glass for an Ink Stand, 7 Cents 63.16 [i.e., 61.20]
8. Sampson Crosby, for the Office, viz: 6 news carries new Years Gift, 11d. each. Candles, Wood, &c. 12.12
14 9. George Breining, for repairing the screw press for the Seals 2.
15 10. Augustine Davis, Virga. Gaz. 4 Oct. 90 to 4. Oct. 91. 2 sets 5.
17 11. Sampson Crosby, 1 Cord wood, £2.5.4. paste boards 4/; inkstand, 5d. 6.63
19 12. B. Bohlen, 2,000 dutch quills (best) 31.33
20 13. Hugh Gaine, 6 Pocket Almanacs .50
26 14. John Dodds for transporting two packages of public papers from New Castle to Phila. .27

[1792]

	31	15. Executors of Govr. Livingston, deceased, for 2 vols. of N.Jersey laws, @ 1 Guinea each, 9.33 transportation from Trenton, 1.	10.33
Apr.	1	16. Henry Remsen, 1 Ream copying press paper	4.67
		17. Henry Remsen, postage of letters 27cts repaid Brs. Coster & Co. of N. York for postage of letters sent to go by their vessel to Amsterdam 25	.52
	24	18. Thomas Dobson, 1 Ream of paper	2.67
	27	19. Muir & Hyde. 12 blank books, binding returns of enumeration 1 Vol. of laws of US., 2 Vols. daily advertiser, 2 Vols. Gazettes, 2 Vols. morning post, 1 Vol. N.York packet, 1 Vol. Gaz. US., 1 Vol. N.York Journal and 1 Set Rymers Fœdera, viz: 10 Vols. fol. Calf, lettered being from May 10, 1791 to March 29, 1792	104.27
May	10	20. John Melcher, New Hamp. Gaz. 1. Oct.90 to Apl. 92, 2.25; sealing up @ 25 Cts. per annum,.37	2.62
	12	21. John Dunlap one daily advertiser, 1 Jany. to 31 Decr. 91, £3.; binding do. £1.2.6. inserting proclamation respecting seat of Govt., 16/10	13.24
	19	22. Peter Stewart, 1 vol. No.Caro. laws	6.
		23. Vincent M. Pelosi, Marine list 1791	4.67
June	1	24. Andrew Brown for publishing laws 1 Ses. 2d. Cong.	64.50
	4	25. John Fenno, Gazette US., 6 mos. ending 25 Apr. 1792 (5 setts)	7.50
	28	26. Ann Timothy on account of printing laws 1st Ses. 2d. Congress	60.

			D. Cts.
July	18	27. Childs & Swaine, 15 blank patents on parchment	1.75
		8 quires demy blank commissions including paper	8.
		3 Vol. Octav. laws at 1.75	5.25
		14 do.	24.50
		2 do. 1st. sess. folio	2.
		1 do. 2d. ses.	2.
		1 do. 3d. do.	.50
		8 reports on lands	4.

[1792]   3 Journals House of Rep. 1

Sess.   4.50

5 do.   10.

5 do.   3 do. 7.50

1 vol. laws   1.75

12 copies report on Isaac's Me-

morial   2.

6 reports Secy. of Treasury

on Manufactures   2.25

3 do.   on public debt .50

1 vol. folio laws   3.50

135 copies ratification of amend-

ments to Constitution 30.

paper for the above 3.12

33 copies octav. laws 57.75

laws of Western Territory 45.

2½ Reams paper for do. 9.

Stitching the same 4.37

30 blank patents on parchment 2.

Sewing in blue boards 182

copies Acts 1st Ses. 2d.

Congr.   25.48

15 copies acts 1 Ses. 2d. Cong. 6.50

Subscription for the daily

advertiser from 1 Nov. 90

to 1 May 1792, 18 mos.

@ 6 D.   9.

Publishing therein laws 1

Ses. 2d. Congr. 64.50 333.72

Sep. 6 28. Sampson Crosby, 12 Cords Wood,

sawing, &c.   69.11

29. do. for 1 cord wood, carting, &c.,

2 Tumblers, sweeping the chimneys

cleaning the office, being from Apl. to

30 Sep. 1792   18.61

Octr. 6 30. John Fenno, 60 numbers Gaz. US. 1.50

7 31. John Sitgreaves, acts of No. Caro.

as to but property 6.

Iredell, laws No.Caro. 6.50

Davis', do. 5.50 Moselys', do. 4. 9.50 22.

31 32. Philip Freneau, 7 Sets Nat.Gaz.

1 Nov. [91] to 31 Oct. 92 21.

Nov. 8 33. Goddard & Angel, Maryland Jour-

nal, 10 Sep. 90. 10 Sep. 92 5.33

16 34. Augustine Davis, for publ. laws

1st. Sess. 2d. Cong.   64.50

[1792]

	20	35. Brynberg & Andrews, their paper from 1. Oct. 91 to 1. Oct. 92		2.
	27	Remitted to B. F. Timothy the balance due to the late Mrs. Ann Timothy for pub. laws 1st. Sess. 2. Cong.		4.
Dec.	4	36. John Parker, 6 mos. sub. for courier de l'Amerique, due this day		1.50
	14	37. Benjamin Russel, pub. laws 1st. Sess. 2d. Cong.		64.50
	22	38. John Fenno, 6 sets paper ending 26 Oct. inst.	9.	
		Binding 3d. Vol. of his paper	1.	10.
	28	39. George Breining for a fender for an open stove, fitting another fender, mending a latch, &c.		3.42
	31	40. Michael Roberts	D. Cts.	

8 Qrs. best F. cap	1.80
1 Ream do.	5.
2 doz. Tape	3.20
1 Qr. F. cap	27
7 black pencils	93
1 Penknife	67
3 Qrs. paper	80
1 R. extra Qto. paper	4.50
1/2 ℔. Scuttle bone	50
1 Penknife	67
1 Ream paper	2.67
1 Wetting book	60
1 Drying book	60
1 Qr. Sup. Atlass paper	2.67
1 R. paper	4.50
1/2 R. Cartridge paper	2.
1/2 Doz. inkpowder	.55
1 R. F. cap paper	5.
2 R. 4to. paper	9.
8 do. do.	36.
1 Glass inkstand	67
12 Skins parchment	8.
1 Doz. pencils	1.34
1 lb. sealing wax	2.
1 Doz. inkpowder	1.11

being from 14 March to 31 Decr. 1792 incl.   95.50   [i.e., 95.05]

1793
Jany.   1   41. Sampson Crosby, 2 Rittenhouse Stoves, for carting them to the office, and putting them up, 4 ℔. Candles, sweeping the Chimneys, &c., &c.   31.71

[1793]

Feb.	12	42. John Scull, pittsburg Gaz. 1 Year ending 19 Oct. 92	2.
		Cash paid for postage of a public Letter from Messrs. Markland and McIver, printers Charleston to Geo. Taylor Jr.	.20][6]
[Feb.		1. By cash paid Anthony Haswell, Vermont Gaz. 1st. Aug. 91 1 Feb. 1793	2.50
Mar.	2	2. Andrew Brown, Fed. Gaz. 1 Jany. 1792 to 1. Jany. 1793	5.
		3. Benjamin F. Bache, Genl. Advertiser, 15 months from 1st. Oct. 1792, and 76 newspapers	10.87
	24	4. Francis Trumble, 6 windsor Chairs	6.
	30	5. Samuel Benge, rehanging 3 pulley venitian Blinds with new tape, line, &c. 4 Green curtains for office windows with cords, fixing two setts of blinds in 3rd. Story and hanging 2 Setts of blinds	5.77
April	1	6. John Carey, for index to laws of 2d. Congress	200.
	4	7. Benjamin Russel, publishing in the *Centinel* acts of 2d. Session of 2d. Congress and 2 proclamations, one of 15 Sep. the other of 12 Dec. 1792	45.75
		8. A. Hale, 500 large and 100 small wafers	3.60
	6	9. David Seckel, one Quarter's office rent due 1 Apl.	46.67
	10	10. George Breining, 11 Keys for chest and other locks, fitting 8 old keys and Ketches on chests and closets	4.53
		11. Andrew Brown, publishing laws 2.Ses. 2d. Congr. and 2 Proclamations	45.75

			D	Cts.
	11	12. Sampson Crosby		
		5 ℔. Candles		.60
		Oswald's bill for newspapers from 7 Jany. 92 to 7 Jany. 1793		2.67
		Sweeping Chimneys		2.13
		Wm. Owens for carpenters work		5.17
		Laborers for moving effects of the office		8.
		Carting 6 loads wood		1.
		1 pair of andirons shovel and Tongs		4.50
		Cohoan & McKey for putting up stoves, &c.		2.20

[1793]		Wm. Owens, carpenter work	9.02	
		Woman for cleaning office	80	
		1 Oz. Gum arabic	12	36.21
	12	13. Henry Ingle, repairing writing	[£]S d	
		table	8 4	
		small packing box	4	
		mahogany Table	2 15	8.98
	22	14. John Dunlap, Am. daily advertiser,		
		1 Jan. to 31 Dec. 92	8 Dol.	
		Binding do.	3	11.
	25	15. B. Bohlen, 1,000 quills		13.33
	27	16. Robert Harpur—exemplification		
		of 5 indian deeds		12.50
	30	17. Childs and Swain, publishing		
		laws, 2d. Sess. 2d. Cong.	43.50	
		two proclamations	2.25	45.75
May	8	18. Thomas Greenleaf, N.York Journal for 1792, closing with the year		3.
	10	19. George Breining, 2 new Keys for the office, mending andirons, &c. &c.		2.
	11	20. John Fenno, 6 sets of Gaz. US. 6 mos. ending 27 Apl.		9.
	27	21. J. & N. Johnson Georgia Gaz. 7 Oct.90 to 7 Oct.92		9.32
June	5	22. By cash paid Augustine Davis Virga. publishing Acts 2d. Sess. 2d.Congr. and 2 Proclamations		45.75
	20	23. Markland & McIver, So.Caro. do.		45.75
	28	24. Child and Swaine, for printing, viz:		

21 sheets laws 2.Sess. 2d. Cong.		210.
9 do. including index Octavo		90.
30 copies acts for the States		15.
7 Reams foolscap paper at	3D	21.
5 do. medium	4	20.
1 ½ do. demy	8	12.
14 copies acts first cong.	2.	28.
20 do. 2 Cong.	3/8	
		7.50
2 Reports on weights and measures		1.
30 proclamations on parchment		12.
25 extracts law concerning intercourse with indians, on parchment		14.

[1793]		100 letters patent on parch-		
		ment	8.	
		250 Safe conducts	6.	
		250 Consular bonds	8.50	
		6 quires blank Commissions	8.50	461.50
July	3	25. John Dunwoody 1 Quarters		
		rent due 1 Inst.		66.67
	5	26. Michael Roberts, Stationery		
		from 10 Jany. to 21 June 93. viz:		
		6 wedgwood inkstands	2.	
		1 Penknife	.50	
		1 Ream foolscap paper	4.67	
		1 large ind. rubber	.50	
		1 Ream foolscap paper	2.67	
		1 Pr Scissors	.33	
		1 Pr. dividers	.25	
		1 Ream demy paper	10.67	
		1 vial red ink	.25	
		2 ink Glasses	.13	
		2 ℔. sealing wax	4.	
		1 ℔. sup. wax	2.67	
		1 pint black sand	.25	
		1 piece blue taste	.50	
		2 skins parchment	6.67	
		3/4 ℔. scuttle bone	.75	
		1 pounce box	.25	
		1 pr. folders	.67	
		16 Skins large parchment	10.67	
		24 do. small	13.34	
		1 piece red taste	.50	
		3 Doz. large parchment	24.	
		1 leaf Gold foil	.25	
		2 Qr. cartridge paper	.80	
		1 Ream 4to. copying paper	4.67	
		3 Sheets foil from J. Anthony	.60	
		1 Doz. pencils	1.33	
		1 Qr. thick folio	.50	
		50 Skins parchment	30.	
		1 Ream folio paper	9.	
		2 paper folders	.50	
		1-3Qr. book 1/2 bound	1.20	
		1 Ream thick paper	9.	
		1 Doz. inkpowder	1.11	
		1 small wedgwood inkstand	.25	
		4 Reams 4to. copying paper	18.67	164.37
Octr.	3	27. John Dunwoody, 1 Qrs. rent due		
		1. inst.		66.67
	18	28. A. Hale, 3,000 large wafers		20. 1

Nov. 23	29. James Beaumont, whitewashing the office completely, and putting up stove		7.74
Decr. 6	30. T. Jefferson, for expenses at Germantown		16.94
14	31. Abel Thomas, for 5 cords wood		38.75
	32. James Ph. Puglia for translating letter of 30. Nov. 93 from Messrs. Viar and Jaudenes and 3 inclosures		6.12
19	33. A. Hodge, North Caro. Journal, 1 Year No. 1 a No. 52		2.50
28	34. G. Taylor Jr., translating correspondence of Mr. Genet with the Secy. of State		40.
29	35. John Fenno, 3 sets Gaz. US. 4 3/4 months at 3D.		5.94
31	36 Sampson Crosby from 4 Apl. to 31 Dec. inclu. viz:		
	to Poyntell for Hutchins map	£ 1. 2. 6	
	porterage for 2 boxes	2. 3	
	postage of Books called the *"bee"* from Boston	3.11	
	Hales bill for large wafers	2.10.	
	1 Mallet for cutting papers for Great Seal	2. 9	
	Viser & Jones' bill for carpenter work	3.15.	
	2 Tumblers	1. 2	
	Hales' bill for wafers for Gt. Seal	5. .	
	1 pair Hinges for case in the office	1. 3	
	Wookerer's bill for tool to cut papers for Gt. Seal	1.10.	
	2 tin cases for dispatches to M. Morris	10. 6	
	Pelosis bill for marine list 1 Year ending Jany. 93.	1.15.	
	washing and cleaning the office	4. 9	
	for conveying a letter with Commission to Colo. Moylan	7. 6	
	Hales' bill for wafers	12. 6	
	5 Gallons vinegar for sprinkling the office	9. 4 1/2	

[1793]

1 ℔. Juniper berries for smoking in the office	9	
penny post carrying letters during yellow fever	8. 3	
Horse hire, conveying letters from the office to seat of the Secy. of State	1.17. 6	
Washing the office	7. 6	
5 Cords wood, sawing, &c.	12.17	
Horse hire to Germantown with letters for Secretary of State	16. 3	
6 ℔. Candles	5.	
13 ℔. do.	17. 4	
altering position of the office stove	11. 3	
repairing door locks	4. 2	1/2
masoning up a fire place	7. 6	
3/4 cord wood	1.14.10	
Carting, &c	7.11	
2 1/2 cords wood and sawing &c.	7. 8. 2	1/2
1 Cord wood and Sawing, &c.	2.18. 4	
2 1/2 Yds. dowlas for sand bags	2. 7	
4 news carriers, their new year's Gift	3. 9	
Carpet, 3 1/4 by 3 1/2 Yds: 11 1/4 Yds at 5/3	2.19.	
24 Sheets tin, at 11d.	1.2.	
Sawing and piling 5 Cords wood	1. 5.	
2 ℔. candles	3.	

£55. 6. 6 1/2   147.53][7]

Extracts from MS Cashbook for the Office of Foreign Affairs and the Department of State, 1785-1795 (DNA: RG 59, General and Departmental Accounts); in various clerks' hands, though chiefly that of Remsen, and containing records of disbursements of contingency funds from 19 Jan. 1785 when John Jay was Secretary for Foreign Affairs to 5 Feb. 1795 when Edmund Randolph was Secretary of State; the above extracts omit the debit side of the account covering warrants on the treasurer and fees (see notes below for summary of these) and include only the disbursements during TJ's incumbency. This very informative volume, for which no counterpart exists for the Department of State during the years 1795-1798 (or until the beginning of the Daybooks for Miscellaneous and Contingent Expences in 1798), contains in its last fifteen pages the names of several hundred persons—mostly French émigrés returning to Port au Prince and Cap François, with a few American citizens—to whom passports were issued between 25 June 1799 and 30 Oct. 1801, with dates of issue, destination, remarks giving reasons for request of passports, and the names of persons recommending them (among these were Benjamin Rush, James McHenry, Francis Kinloch, William Bingham, and Joseph Hopkinson). See *Preliminary Inventories, Number 157, General Records of the Department of State* (The National Archives, 1963), p. 62.

The actual statements corresponding to the above account of disbursements of contingency funds are to be found in the "Miscellaneous Treasury Accounts" of the General Accounting Office (DNA: RG 217). These, being submitted with vouchers, are less detailed than the Cashbook entries in respect to names and itemized records of expenditure (the actual vouchers are not to be found in RG 217, MTA). The difference between the entries in the Cashbook and those in the corresponding statements have not been indicated except where the latter contain information not to be found in the former (see textual notes below). The statements can be most conveniently located under the number assigned when registered in the office of the Register of the Treasury, in RG 217. See *List of National Archives Microfilm Publications 1961* (National Archives, 1961), p. 26, where the publication for series RG 217 is designated as M 235. In the following list of statements of account paralleling entries in the Cashbook, the designation M 235/3: No. 1267 indicates that statement number 1267 is to be found on reel three of publication M 235. References in textual notes below are made to these statements as numbered in the following sequence:

(1) MS "State of the Account of Thomas Jefferson Esq. for Contingent expences" (DNA: M 235/1, No. 1267), covering the period 26 Apr. 1790-2 Feb. 1791, in Remsen's hand, dated 1 Mch. 1791; with notations in other hands showing settlement was made with the Auditor on 3 May 1791 and indicating that during the period covered four treasury warrants totalling $1,404 had been issued; examined by the Comptroller 5 May 1791 and registered 7 May 1791.

(2) MS statement "The Department of State in account with the U.S. for contingencies &c." (DNA: M 235/3, lacking that part showing settlement and registry hence lacking a number but following No. 1930), covering the period 1 Mch. 1791-28 Nov. 1791, the entries for 13 and 28 Dec. 1791 being lost with the covering sheet; in Remsen's hand.

(3) MS "State of the Account of Thomas Jefferson Esqr" (DNA: M 235/10, No. 3777), covering the period 1 Jan. 1792-12 Feb. 1793, in hand of George Taylor, Jr. dated 9 Mch. 1793; with notations in other hands showing settlement with Auditor 14 Mch. 1793, examination by Comptroller 31 Dec. 1793, and registry on the same date. The statement shows on its debit side that three treasury warrants totalling $1,241.16 had been issued during the period covered; that on 9 Aug. 1792 a remittance of $102 had been received from the Commissioners of the City of Washington for advance made by the Department on 13 Dec. 1791, and that as of 6 Mch. 1793 the Department had received in fees for authenticated copies of documents a total of $10.24½.

(4) MS "Contingent Account of The Department of State" (DNA: M 235/17, No. 5606), covering the period 1 Feb. 1793-15 Apr. 1794, in the hand of George Taylor, Jr., dated 16 Apr. 1794; with notations in other hands showing settlement with Auditor 17 June 1794, examination by Comptroller on 19 June 1794 and registry the same day; the debit side of the statement showed that two treasury warrants had been issued during the period covered totalling $1,851.67 and that $2.81 in fees for authenticating documents had been received. In this statement only the names of persons receiving payment were recorded.

(5) MS "State of the Account of Thomas Jefferson Esqr. for Contingent expences" (DNA: M 235/17, No. 5609); being a final settlement of account with TJ for contingencies and transference to the debit of Edmund Randolph of the balance on hand as shown on statement No. 3777 plus treasury warrants as indicated there; with notations showing the account was audited 17 June 1794, examined by the Comptroller 19 June 1794, and registered the same date; accompanied by a certificate of registry dated 14 June 1794 and signed by George Morton for Joseph Nourse.

From this list of expenditures for services and supplies for the Department of State in the years 1790-1793 it is easy to reconstruct in imagination the general appearance of the departmental offices. The simple building of three storeys on the northwest corner of Market and Eighth streets had Venetian blinds, green curtains, bare floors. Clerks worked at plain tables and sat in Windsor chairs made by Francis Trumble—a chair TJ liked so much he bought many for Monticello from the famous maker. Filing cases, maps, newspapers, a few books, vast amounts of quills, paper, and all the paraphernalia of clerical work—fountain ink wells, red taste (or tape), small mahogany boards for bundling papers, parchment skins for commissions, blotting sand—were much in evidence. The copying press for duplicating texts and the screw press for affixing the great seal stood as symbols of the department. Open fireplaces and stoves furnished heat in winter. Tea was served members of the staff. Tumblers occasionally appeared to sweep the chimneys. Newspaper boys appeared at New Year's to deliver their verses and to claim their gratuities. During the Yellow Fever epidemic the floors were sprinkled with vinegar, the walls were whitewashed, and juniper berries were burned as precaution or as incense.

There was a "Secretary's room" in this modest home of the Department of State, but it is very doubtful whether TJ used it for any official purposes except perhaps the signing of documents or the performance of other routine tasks. He naturally preferred seclusion for correspondence, study, drafting state papers, and conference. His most important duties as Secretary of State were undoubtedly performed at his residences at 57 Maiden Lane in New York and at 274 Market street in Philadelphia. The latter was diagonally across the street from the offices of the department, being the fourth house west from Eighth on the south side. This house, like that in New York, had been altered to accommodate his idea of an efficient arrangement for privacy, study, and entertainment. It contained an ample dining with an ante-room, a library adjacent to TJ's bedroom, and a special garden structure with sky light but no fenestration, designed as "a place to retire and write in . . . unseen and un-

disturbed" even by servants (TJ to Leiper, 16 Dec. 1792). In these quarters, when the alterations were finally completed, TJ installed fifteen cases of books that had been acquired in Paris and were arranged in specially constructed bookshelves (TJ to James Wilson, 17 Apr. 1793). This in effect was the library of the Department of State and its presence provides the basis for rejecting the role generally accorded the first Secretary of State as founder of the departmental library. That honor belongs rather to C. W. F. Dumas, who presented Rymer's *Foedera* and to Edmund Randolph, who soon after coming into office sold to the Department of State his own copies of Burlamaqui, Postlethwayt, Bynkershoek, and others (DNA: RG 59, MS Cashbook, 1785-1795). TJ possessed these and other works concerning diplomacy and the law of nations and so had no need to concern himself with the establishment of a departmental collection to the same degree that he busied himself in gathering statutes of the states and newspapers.

TJ's Philadelphia residence in its elegant appointments stood in strong contrast to the simplicity of the departmental offices. When his furnishings finally arrived from Paris, those who gathered at the home of the Secretary of State found themselves in surroundings of Parisian taste—crimson and blue damask curtains, chiffoniers, paintings, busts, "gilded chairs with gay damask covering, beds with upholstery of blue silk, commodes and tables with decorations or ormolu," and, of course, the imposing column with its flattering description that had been presented by Madame de Tessé (Marie Kimball, "Thomas Jefferson's French Furniture," *Antiques*, XV [Feb. 1920], 128; Dumbauld, *Jefferson, American Tourist*, p. 160-3; TJ to Madame de Tessé, 27 Aug. 1789). In this atmosphere of gentility the Secretary of State received visits from foreign ministers, discussed public matters with Madison and others, and conducted the real business of the department, even to the extent of keeping in his custody there, for purposes of security, the communications from American ministers abroad. His very surroundings seemed a reflection of his policy of multiplying the bonds of friendship and commerce with France.

1 The words in brackets (supplied) are not in statement No. 1267 (see MS 1 above) and the total there is £2 0s. 0d. but under date of 25 Sep. 1790 there is an entry in statement not in Cashbook: "paid Maule & Bullock for a trunk to hold laws 0-18-0," an amount included in the entry above under 1 Oct. 1790.

2 MS reads "hany"; statement No. 1267 (see MS 1 above) reads "Mahogany."

3 Matter enclosed in brackets (supplied) embraces that part of Cashbook entries covered by statement No. 1267 (see MS 1 above).

4 Matter enclosed in brackets (supplied) embraces that part of Cashbook entries covered by statement lacking number but filed after No. 1930 (see MS 2 above).

5 At this point Remsen placed the following note at foot of page addressed to George Taylor, Jr.: "N.B. This account immediately precedes that which was opened before I left the office, and which I delivered to you, with the balance of cash in my hands. It would have been entered with former ones, but the book was not large enough to admit of it. It was my intention, to have copied all these accounts, beginning with the first opened under Mr. Jay, into a 3 or 4 quire book of foolscap paper, as I thought it very necessary to have in the office a full account of it expences, especially as so many items entered into it, which were unforeseen, and which magnified it so considerably"; signed by Remsen and undated but evidently written late in 1791 or early in 1792. This was the last entry in Remsen's hand in Cashbook.

6 Matter enclosed in brackets (supplied) embraces that part of Cashbook entries covered by statement No. 3777 (see MS 3 above).

7 Matter enclosed in brackets (supplied) embraces that part of Cashbook entries covered by statement No. 5606 (see MS 4 above).

VIII. Memoranda from Henry Remsen, Jr.

[ca.30 Aug. 1790]

All the Letters received for Mr. Jefferson after his departure, and Fenno's paper[1] are to be forwarded to him by post AT MONTE CELLO in Virginia, until the last[2] of Septr., after which time, those that are received are to be kept for him 'till he returns.

Mr. Jefferson will please to give H. R. junr. any directions he may chuse to leave with him, respecting the removal of his furniture to Philadelphia, the payment of the transportation of it there &c.

About the 20th. of September we shall begin to pack up the effects belonging to the Offices, and in the mean time bring up and examine the records. On the 1st. of October the next quarter's salary will be due, and as soon after as it is paid, the effects and persons will remove. One will be at Philadelphia to receive them, and one travel with them. The papers to be removed by land; the printed journals, books, newspapers, models and furniture by water. H. R. junr. takes the liberty to observe, that it will be very acceptable for those belonging to the Office to receive their salary before they leave N. York, and as the other Offices will not probably remove until the middle, or latter end of Octr., no inconvenience can arise from the Office of State being kept here until the beginning of it.

If Mr. Jefferson on his arrival at Philadelphia, will have time to look at the house contemplated for an Office, and write to H. R. junr. where it is, and to whom he must apply for possession, it will be very serviceable, or if that house is not fit, and Mr. Jefferson cannot remain long enough at Philadelphia to procure another, to write to H. R. Junr. directing him what to do, whether to go to Philadelphia previous to the removal to procure one, and what it's situation and size and rent must be. It is to be observed that the house should have at least two large rooms, one for the foreign and the other for the domestic papers, besides other rooms for the models, Journals, and Newspapers. The Cases as at present would fill a large house, but they may be reduced in number when the Papers are better arranged, at least those of the domestic kind. But when they are arranged they will occupy much space. Mr. Jefferson will be able to judge of the size of the house wanted, by the cases containing the foreign papers, which are comprized in as small a compass as possible. The cases to contain the domestic papers must be, I should judge, rather more numerous.

The balance of the money granted for contigencies, will be absorbed by the accounts now against both Offices for contingencies, and the demands of the German translator (who has never yet been paid for his services) and Spanish and Dutch translators. The two last have but a small sum due to them.

Will it not be best to apply for a further grant of money, sufficient to pay the additional messenger (whose wages are not provided for by the last appropriation act), to remove to Philadelphia, and lay up wood for the next winter. The account can be settled the moment the Treasury Department is established there. And if Mr. Jefferson applies for a sum, and goes before a warrant issues, a Note from him to the Treasurer requesting payment of it, will be necessary to procure it's receipt. To obtain the proportion of the warrant for the salary due on the 1st. of October, a similar Note will be necessary. Mr. Jefferson's own salary can remain with the Treasury or not, at his election. The proportion of the warrant wanted will be, vizt.

	Dolls.	Cents
The whole account amounts to	1504.	16
Mr. Jefferson's qrs. salary	875.	
	629.	16

629.16 for the Chief and other Clerks, Interpreter and door-keeper.

To obtain the payment of the warrant now to be issued for arrears of salary and House rent, in case Mr. Jefferson sets out before it is issued, a similar Note will be necessary.

The collection of laws for the Executives &c. to go by post, will need a frank to exempt them from postage, and if Mr. Jefferson speaks to the Secretary of the Treasury or Secretary at War, they will undoubtedly frank the packages.

Mr. Lambert (at Mr. Beckley's Office) will continue the Record of the Laws when he comes back from Virginia, if Mr. Jefferson desires it, and his business under Mr. Beckley will admit of it.

Mr. Bankson who is now in Mr. Otis's Office, was formerly in Mr. Thomson's, and was appointed Register of the Court of appeals just before the Judges of that Court went out of Office. A part of the papers of that Office he now has. He kept them in Mr. Thomson's Office in one of the cases, until he entered Mr. Otis's, when he removed them to his lodgings. He wishes to know what he must do with them, and says that a chest is wanted to put them in. I have told him he must speak to the Chief Justice, Mr. Jay; but he thinks that they ought, at least for the present, be deposited in the Office of State. I suppose he wishes not to incur the expence of removing them, lest he may not get reimbursement.

I have purchased two sets of the fœderalist in boards for Mr. Short, 2 Vols. in each set, the price for both is 2 dollars.

The proprietor of the Stage will furnish covered waggons to go to Philadelphia, and take what may be sent by land, at 10/ per hundred for a single ton, and 8/4 if there are several tons. H. R. junr. will enquire the price of freight by water.

MS (DLC); in Remsen's hand, with two insertions by TJ; at head of text: "Memorandums"; undated but certainly written before 30 Aug. 1790 (see TJ to Hamilton, 30 Aug. 1790).

[1] Preceding three words interlined in TJ's hand.
[2] This word interlined in TJ's hand in substitution for "25th," deleted.

IX. Further Memoranda from Henry Remsen, Jr.

[ca. 1792]

If the Secretary of State should think it necessary, when the recording of his Letters while abroad and other foreign Letters will allow of it, that a Set of the Journals of Congress respecting foreign Affairs should be copied for the foreign Office from the Set which is now in the Home Office, the one to be copied may contain, besides the Matter in the other, all the foreign Treaties, and Letters received by Congress from the Sovereigns of Europe and written by them to those Sovereigns, which will render it very complete and save the Necessity of opening several Books to be denominated differently. A continuation of this Journal will commence with the first act of a foreign Nature that took place under the Administration of the new Government, and contain all Matters of a foreign Nature, such as Ratifications of Treaties &c. on the part of the President, Letters written by him to and received by him from the Sovereigns of Europe, Commissions to our Ministers, Chargé des Affaires and Consuls which are not entered agreeably to the present System of the Office in other Books. And this Continuation may be immediately begun.

Papers to be entered in the foreign Journal, or Journal of foreign Affairs, being a Continuation of that in the Home Office, Viz.

Recorded in the Office of the Secretary of the Senate

The President's Message to the Senate, delivered by Mr. Jay June 11th. 1789, on the Subject of the Consular-Convention.

idem

The President's Message to the Senate, delivered by Mr. Jay 16th. June 1789, informing them he had given Mr. Jefferson Leave of Absence, and nominating Mr. Short Chargé des Affaires.

idem

The act of the Senate consenting to, and advising the Appointment of Mr. Short, passed June 18. 1789.

Report Book 4 Vol.

Mr. Jays report of 25 July 1789, made in pursuance of an Order of the Senate of 22 July directing him to report, whether the Faith of the U. S. is engaged to ratify the Consular Convention in its present Sense and Form.

public Acts

The Act to establish the Department of foreign Affairs, passed July 27. 1789.

Office of Secy. of Senate.

The Resolve of the Senate of 29 July 1789 consenting to, and advising the President to ratify the Consular Convention.

IX. FURTHER MEMORANDA

The Ratification of the said Convention on the part of the President, which will take in the Convention in full, both original and translation, and the Powers to the respective Plenipotentiaries to form it.

Register of Treaties

The Commission to Andrew Ellicott to survey the Boundary between the U. S. and the States of New York and Massachusetts, and to make some astronomical Observations within the Government of Canada, dated September 4. 1789.

Record of Commissions in home Office

The 1. 3. 4. and 5. Sections of the Act passed 15 September 1789 altering the Name of the Office.

public Acts

Letter from his most Christian Majesty to Congress announcing the Death of the Dauphin, dated 7 June 1789.—The President's Message to both Houses communicating it, delivered by Mr. Jay the 29 September—and the President's Letter of Condolence to his most Christian Majesty of 9 October 1789.

In a book to be opened for the purpose

The Commission of the Secretary of State—dated (I believe) 13th. Oct. 1789.

Home Office

Mr. Jay's Note to the President of 28 Novemr. communicating an account of the Negociations, Treaty and Affairs with Morocco, and the President's answer of 1st. Decemr. approving of the Draft of a Letter to the Emperor, to be signed by him.

Journal of fo: Office, and book to be opened for the purpose

The President's Letter to the Emperor of Morocco of 1st. Decem. 1789.

idem

Mr. Shaw's Commission to be Consul for Canton—Feby. 10. 1790.

Book of fo: Commissions

The President's Message to the Senate of 15 February 1790 relating to the Eastern Boundary of the U. S.—the Act of the Senate in consequence and subsequent Proceedings

Senate's Office

The President's Letter to his most Christian Majesty of 6 April 1790 recalling Mr. Jefferson.

Book to be opened for the purpose

The President's Proclamation requiring an Observance of the Consular Convention, April 9. 1790.

Register of Treaties

Book of for:
Commissions

Commissions to Mr. Short and Mr. Carmichael, dated 20 April 1790.

idem

Consular Commissions—dated 7. 17. and 22 June 1790.

Qu: Will it be necessary to have recorded the messages from the President to the Senate nominating for Consulships and other foreign Offices, and the Acts of the Senate consenting to, and advising the appointment of the persons nominated, or rejecting them, as the Case may be?

Instead of continuing the Journal of foreign Affairs on the aforegoing Plan, the Consular Convention as ratified and the Proclamation requiring it's Observance, together with all Treaties, Conventions &c. which may in future be formed, can be recorded in the Register of Treaties in the *home* Office, which contains all the Treaties, Conventions (the Consular one excepted) and Contracts that have been made; and that Register can be removed to the *foreign* Office for that purpose.

The Letters received by Congress from the King of France and other Powers, and written by them to him and them; and those received by the President from those Powers, and written by him to them, may be recorded in a Book to be opened for their reception only.

The Commissions to our Ministers, Chargé des Affaires and Consuls may be entered in a Book by themselves, to commence with those granted under the present Administration, or to go back to the first Commissions granted, as there is no Record of them other than the Secret Journals of Congress.

NB. other acts have arisen since the date of the last. There are printed forms of Sea letters or passports, which only need filling up when applied for. See record thereof.

The form of a passport granted to individuals going to travel. See rough journal of the foreign office.

Patent
business

The board of arts meet the last Saturday in each month and **Mr.** Crosby is to notify the members thereof the preceding day. When they meet all applications received since the former meeting to be read, and to lie a month under consideration. The Board does not even decide on them then, unless they are accompanied with specifications, drafts, or models properly prepared. No models to be delivered to the persons depositing them, after the patents are issued, without the orders of the Secy. of State: And no patents already made out or which may be made out, to be delivered unless the claimants produce models, drafts and specifications. The specifications to be executed according to the usual form. If by an Attorney see specification enclosed in patent No. 6[1] but if by the claimant him self, see specification enclosed in patent No. 21. Should you be in doubt as to the want of explicitness in the specifications drafts or models, Mr. Jefferson will remove it on application. When a patent is granted label the model, as I have done, or the models, as sometimes two models of the same thing are deposited.

Such of the *Foreign letters* as are not filed away in the cases, are for the present put on my desk in the two pigeon holes at the right hand side. The *Consular returns* are at the bottom of said desk right hand side: and so are the *Letters from the Attornies of districts*, which are tied together. The *drafts of foreign proceedings*, such as ratifications, exequaturs on foreign consular commissions, letters to European powers, are filed in said desk left hand pigeon hole. The letters from our Ministers and Chargé des affaires now in commission Mr. Jefferson keeps. All the foreign letters received before Mr. Jefferson came into Office, are filed away as the others were in the time of Mr. Jay. For any particular letter see book relating to files in the desk already alluded to.

Papers to be furnished to our Ministers and Chargé des affaires.

Each of them to receive one copy of the laws in octavo, one copy of the Journals of the Senate, one copy of the Journals of the House of Representatives, one of Freneau's papers, and one of Fenno's papers, with such pamphlets as Mr. Jefferson may specially direct.— Mr. Short to receive, in addition to these one Richmond paper, there being two received. See my several memorandums.

We take *one* piece currently which is to be divided equally among them.

One set of Fenno's paper to be preserved and half bound for the use of the Office; and *two* sets of Freneau's.

Mr. Jefferson has a number of letters, which when he has done with, he'll return to the Office to be re-filed. They are principally foreign Letters.

Petitions for patents are to be endorsed according to the present mode, the day of their receipt, and noted in the minute book, in which petitions are filed together in the desk up stairs in one of the pigeon holes. In the said desk are filed in another pigeon hole, the petitions decided on; and also the drafts of patents issued, which drafts the law for promoting useful arts directs to be recorded. Some of the specifications are in said desk, and others in the closet.

Journals of old Congress. There are ten Sets complete in the chest in the third story; and twenty sets in the garret which want the 4th. Vol. to make them so. Mr. Dunlap can supply them, and I have spoken to him to do it. I should think when he furnishes the Vols., that as many Vols. of the Laws of the United States should be added to them as there are sets, making in the whole 30. sets. None of these are to be delivered out without the express order of Mr. Jefferson.

Detail of the business in the Department of State

Home-Office. In this office is a journal wherein is to be noted its transactions; also the receipt of Laws from the President, and at the end of every Session a receipt mentioning their titles is to be made out and given to his Secretary. Note also in it all papers received from the President to be filed: and the receipt of books, maps &c., filed by authors under the act for the encouragement of learning.

The distribution of the laws as mentioned in the aforegoing Journal to be continued. See that Journal.

Newspapers are to be filed, and at the end of the year half bound.
Laws of the several States. —— Do. —— Do.

☞ A little attention will be necessary in separating the foreign from the domestic letters, as they are sent to the Office of Mr. Jefferson to be filed. My rule in making the separation was by reading them. The *domestic* letters to be filed in the Office down stairs, the foreign Letters in the Office upstairs.

☞ whenever leisure will allow, the foreign letters and papers should be filed anew, as some of the boxes are too full to admit of more being put in them. There is a new c[ase?] and 12 new paper boxes to go in it provided for the papers. When you go thro' this business, take all the foreign letters out of the iron chest, and file them away with other papers, agreeable to the present mode which is the best for preserving them, and for enabling a person to find them.

Foreign Office. The letters from our Ministers, Chargé des affaires, and Consuls will be sent to the Office to be filed from time to time by Mr. Jefferson; who will direct which shall be recorded. Observe the present mode of filing them. His foreign letters will be recorded in the foreign letter book, and his domestic letters in the domestic letter book, as before, and at the close of every year. Material papers enclosed and referred to in letters he writes, to follow the letter in the record.[2]

MS (DNA: DNA: RG 59, Reports of Bureau Officers); undated and entirely in Remsen's hand except for passage noted below and the following endorsement in Taylor's hand: "Mr. Remsen's Memo. of the disposition of the papers in the Dept. of State." On the 4th page Taylor also noted: "Some ideas of Mr. Remsen relative Business of the office."

There can be little doubt that this memorandum was drawn up early in 1792 and certainly before 1 Apr. 1792 when Remsen resigned as chief clerk. Its object obviously was to familiarize his successor, George Taylor, Jr., with his own methods of filing, recording, and carrying out office business. But it reveals TJ's hand in the concern for bound sets of Journals, in the provision for sending one copy of the *Virginia Gazette* to Short, and especially in the fact that files of letters from American "Ministers and Chargé des affaires . . . in commission" were kept in the custody of TJ himself. This last was in keeping with his practice in Paris where only TJ had access to his files—a practice in marked contrast to the laxness of Franklin in this respect. Even after his return to America these files continued to be kept under lock and key and were accessible only to himself (TJ to Washington, 17 Oct. 1792). The Secretary of State had full confidence in his clerks —with reason—but close attention to security in all matters of public business was a deeply ingrained habit with him. MODELS as well as documents were involved in the problem of security. George Beckwith reported in a missing letter to Lord Dorchester of 27 July 1790 the arrival of "a model of Arkwright's cotton mill" in America and soon thereafter reported that "A com-

plete model of Arkwright's cotton machine is lodged in the office of the Secretary of State" (Brymner, *Report, 1890*, p. 148; Beckwith to Grenville, 10 Aug. 1791, PRO: FO 4/12, f. 164-8). How the secret agent learned of this is not known though his confidant, Alexander Hamilton, was well aware of the presence of the model by virtue of his responsibility as a member of the BOARD OF ARTS. A year later when Hamilton went to New Jersey to unfold his plan for the Society for Useful Manufactures, Beckwith reported upon it with much concern as a matter that promised "ultimate effect upon the interests of The Empire" in the United States. He also informed Grenville that at the meeting "Models of different machines were produced and amongst others a model of Arkwright's cotton mill"—the same one that he had told Dorchester about the preceding year (same). How and under what circumstances the model was taken from the custody of the Department of State and made available for the promotion of Hamilton's famous enterprise is not known. But in view of TJ's strong feeling about security and of Hamilton's known habit of informing the agent of official secrets, it is at least a plausible inference that Beckwith learned of the model from his principal source of information in the government.

[1] The figure might be interpreted as 61, but the above seems more likely.

[2] At end of the text there appears the following note in pencil by an unidentified clerk, perhaps written around 1799 when numerous passes were being issued (see note, Document VII): "file the affidavits of citizenship for passes with Am. letters."

From Edmund Randolph

E. R. to Mr. Jefferson   Friday [13 Aug. 1790]

The inclosed letter is from Charlton. If you approve it, let the sum be settled in what I owe you for the Encyclopedia; and I will send a receipt.

Will the president be obliged to publish a proclamation in consequence of the Indian treaty? He desired me to inquire into this matter from you, as he wishes me to draw it, if to be issued.

I am glad to hear, that you have shaken off your late indisposition.

RC (DLC); endorsed as received 13 Aug. 1790; undated and not recorded in SJL, though enclosure is there entered on this date. Enclosure: Jane Charlton to TJ, 26 June 1790, reading: "Your generosity and politeness towards me on a former address has encouraged me to take the liberty of reminding you of having Honourably resettled an account of Mrs. Jeffersons, paid in 1777 and by your own statement left a balance in my favour with £12-9-5 with interest till paid. Your letter with the Statement has been shewn to Mr. Eppes but he declined settling it. Mr. Randolph does me the favour of presenting this to you and whenever it is Convenient for you to discharge it, will be acknowledged Confering a singular favour on Sir your obliged Hble Servt. J. Charlton" (RC in DLC; endorsed as received 13 Aug. 1790 and so recorded in SJL). Mrs. Charlton's "former address" and TJ's letter in reply have not been found. The original settlement with Edward Charlton is recorded in TJ's Account Book for 20 May 1777; TJ's calculation of interest on the balance for thirteen and a half years, making the total £20 18s., is stated in his hand at the foot of Jane Charlton's letter, where a receipt is signed by Randolph for the balance after debiting Randolph for the Encyclopédie; and the settlement is recorded in Account Book 25 Nov. 1790 with the statement that it is "the principal and interest of a balance to Charlton to make up the depreciation of an antient paper payment."

Washington wrote Randolph on 12 Aug. 1790 that he would not withhold concurrence in his wish to go to Philadelphia the following Monday but that, "as it may be necessary for me in pursuance of the law to regulate trade and commerce with the Indian tribes to issue a Proclamation . . . it might be best for you to see the Secretary of State or the Secy of War, or both . . . before your departure" (DNA: RG 59, MLR; Washington, *Writings*, ed. Fitzpatrick, XXXI, 90).

The proclamation alluded to was not that pertaining to the treaty itself. Tobias Lear drafted the form for proclaiming the treaty with the Creeks, dated 14 Aug. 1790 (Washington, *Writings*, ed. Fitzpatrick, XXXI, 92). The full text of the treaty (except, of course, the secret article) as confirmed and ratified by Washington, as attested by TJ, and as signed by all of the Indian chiefs and witnesses, was published in the (N.Y.) *Daily Advertiser* and in the *Gazette of the United States* of 14 Aug. 1790, the latter having also an article on the Creek nation (as TJ noted on a slip in DLC: TJ Papers, 59: 10012). But the proclamation which Washington asked the Attorney General to draw in consultation with TJ and Knox presented a much more delicate problem. The Act of 22 July 1790 established regulations for carrying on trade and intercourse with the Indians for a period of two years, but the treaty with the Creeks as published, unlike the comparable Hopewell treaties of 1785 and 1786, contained no article concerning trade since that was the sole object of the secret provision. Washington therefore wished Randolph, TJ, and Knox to consider whether a proclamation was obligatory in consequence of the Indian treaty. The result was not brought forth for another two weeks.

An early draft of the proclamation, signed by Washington, attested by TJ, and dated 26 Aug. 1790, has been incorrectly attributed to TJ as being in his handwriting (Washington, *Writings*, ed. Fitzpatrick, XXXI, 99). It is in fact in the handwriting of Randolph (MHi: Knox Papers, LIII, 50). This draft shows that the original intention was to publish the Act of 22 July 1790 and the Hopewell treaties of 3 Jan. 1786 and 10 Jan. 1786 with the Choctaw and Chickasaw nations, for it contains no allusion to the treaty with the Cherokee nation at Hopewell on 28 Nov. 1785. All three of these treaties were virtually identical. They defined the boundaries, forbade settlement in Indian territory by other than Indians, provided for the mutual return of prisoners and for the restoration of slaves and other property taken by Indians, prohibited punishment by retaliation as unjust, required trial of robbery, murder, and other capital crimes under laws of the United States, and retained for the nation "sole and exclusive right of regulating the trade with the Indians." The final text of the proclamation of 26 Aug. 1790 as published in the *Federal Gazette and Philadelphia Daily Advertiser*, 15 Sep. 1790, with texts of the Cherokee, Choctaw, and Chickasaw treaties in that and the next two issues, reads as follows (caption, signatures, and sigillary paragraph omitted): "Whereas it hath, at this time, become peculiarly necessary to warn the citizens of the United States against a violation of the Treaties made at Hopewell, on the Keowee, on the twenty-eighth day of November, one thousand seven hundred and eighty-five; and on the third and tenth days of January, one thousand seven hundred and eighty-six between the United States and the Cherokee, Choctaw, and Chickasaw nations of Indians; and to enforce an act entitled, 'an act to regulate trade and intercourse with the Indian tribes;' copies of which treaties and act are hereunto annexed: I have therefore thought fit to require, and I do by these presents require all officers of the United States, as well civil as military, and all other citizens and inhabitants thereof, to govern themselves according to the treaties and act aforesaid: as they will answer the contrary at their peril" (texts of the treaties themselves are conveniently found in JCC, XXX, 187-95, and in *Indian Affairs: Laws and Treaties*, ed. Charles J. Kappler, II, 8-16).

It was indeed "peculiarly necessary" that such a proclamation of warning be issued, but not for the reasons given. The secret article of the Creek treaty required enforcement but could not be published. The solution to this delicate problem was quite as ingenious as TJ's proposal that the monopolistic trade guarantee to McGillivray, on which the entire negotiation depended, be legitimatized by treaty when this could not be done by law (see opinion, 29 July 1790). It is therefore natural to suppose it was the Secretary of State who suggested the possibility of rendering the secret article enforceable by a proclamation which, reaffirming old treaties negotiated under the Articles of Confederation, made no allusion whatever to the treaty of which that article was a hidden part. TJ had long been familiar with those treaties and with the fact that all three vested exclusive control of Indian trade in the United States, thus supplying the deficiency which—on its public surface—the Creek treaty exhibited (see Hawkins to TJ, 14 June 1786).

To Francis Hopkinson

DEAR SIR   New York. Aug. 14. 1790.

I wrote you a good while ago ·on the subject of the quilling of the harpsichord and you were so kind as to answer me with an account and model of your cork tongue, instead of quill. My object was a pettifogging one: but I pursue it. I have at home a well toned Spinette; the jacks of which have strayed away, in a good degree, since it was in use. It is the only instrument there at present, and as I am to meet my daughters there early in Septemb. I wish to fix it up for all our amusements. Foreseeing this, I brought with me from home one of the jacks thinking that, by that as a model, a workman would make me a set (for a Spinette) and tongue them in your method. Business has kept this out of my mind till perhaps it is too late. I shall leave this place about the 30th. inst. and shall stay two or three days in Philadelphia on my way home. It would make a whole family and it's friends gay and happy, if any workman would be so friendly as to complete me a set of jacks in that time according to the model now inclosed. This is a case in which I must be troublesome to you, because I am sure you must know the best workman, and have interest with him. Will you then be so good as to get him to undertake this job, and thus add another to the numerous obligations under which you have laid Dear Sir Your sincere friend & servt.,

Th: Jefferson

PrC (DLC).

To Thomas Mann Randolph, Jr.

Dear Sir   New York Aug. 14. 1790.

I am setting out on a trip to Rhode-island with the President tomorrow, by water. We shall be absent about 5. or 6. days, and of course his departure hence to the Southward will be that much later than he intended, and my departure, which must be after his, a little delayed. Still I hope to reach Monticello by the 15th. of September, or from that to the 20th. We have just concluded a treaty with the Creeks, which is important, as drawing a line between them and Georgia, and enabling the government to do, as it will do, justice against either party offending. Congress separated the day before yesterday, having in the latter part of their session reacquired the harmony which had always distinguished their proceedings, till the two disagreeable subjects of the assumption and residence were introduced. These really threatened, at one time, a separation of the legislature *sine die*. They saw the necessity of suspending almost all business for some time; and, when they resumed it, of some mutual sacrifices of opinion. It is not foreseen that any thing so generative of dissension can arise again, and therefore the friends of the government hope that, this difficulty once surmounted in the states, every thing will work well. I am principally afraid that commerce will be overloaded by the assumption, believing it would be better that property should be duly taxed. Present me affectionately to my dear daughters and believe me to be sincerely yours,   TH: JEFFERSON

RC (DLC).

From Benjamin Rush

DEAR SIR   Philadelphia 15t August. 1790

The bearer of this letter Mr. Andrew Brown has applied to me as One among many witnesses of his zeal in promoting the Adoption of the fœderal constitution by means of his paper, and has requested me to add my testimony, of his faithful and meritorious services, to that of his Other friends. His sacrifices to his principles, and to the best interests of our Country have been great. The Acknowledgement and reward of them by government therefore cannot fail of having an useful influence upon public spirit. Mr. Brown will make known to you the nature of the favors which he goes to New York to solicit. I beg leave to refer you to him, and am Dr Sir with the warmest sentiments of respect your most Obedient humble Servant,   BENJN RUSH

P.S. I beg your Acceptance of a copy of a small tribute to One of my old friends, and what is much more, One of the friends of Mankind.

RC (DLC); endorsed by TJ as received 26 Aug. 1790 and so recorded in SJL. Enclosure: Rush's *An eulogium in honor of the late Dr. William Cullen, professor of the practice of physic in the University of Edinburgh; delivered before the College of Physicians of Philadelphia*, Philadelphia, 1790; Sowerby, No. 523.

Among the OTHER FRIENDS who wrote TJ in behalf of Andrew Brown, publisher of the *Federal Gazette and Philadelphia Daily Advertiser*, was William Bingham, who said he "could not resist the solicitations of Mr. Brown, to furnish him with a Letter . . . expressive of the Circumstances on which he founds his Pretensions to your Patronage of his Views." He added that

Brown had served as an officer in the war with "considerable merit" and that as a printer he was "very industrious and correct, and has Supported a daily Paper with considerable Reputation" (RC in DNA: RG 59, PDL; endorsed by TJ as received 26 Aug. 1790 and so recorded in SJL). Brown was given patronage by TJ and later, on presenting TJ with a bound set of the *Federal Gazette* for the year ending 1 Apr. 1791, he wrote: "To you, Sir, this Gazette owes much of its present reputation; and its proprietor will ever retain a grateful remembrance of your patronage" (Brown to TJ, 6 Dec. 1791; RC in MHi, endorsed by TJ as received 6 Dec. 1791 and so recorded in SJL). Alexander Hamilton wrote to Edward Carrington on 26 May 1792 that this patronage had led Brown's paper to take an increasingly hostile attitude toward him (cited in Malone, *Jefferson*, II, 425 n.). See TJ's report on Brown's memorial, 5 Feb. 1791.

From William Short

DEAR SIR   Paris Aug. 15. 1790

I recieved your letter of July the 1st. some days ago, and in time to comply with its instructions. Two days before, I had understood that there was such a probability of Congress removing to Philadelphia that I had desired M. de la Motte to send your furniture to that place. I have this moment recieved a letter from Rouen which informs me that your effects had arrived there in safety and had been despatched to Havre, or were to set off yesterday. At the same time I recieved a letter from Havre which informs me there is a vessel there bound for Philadelphia, and that your goods if they arrive in time shall be shipped on her board. It is further said I shall have time to write by the return of the post which I am now hastening to do, in hopes of this letter going by the same vessel. I shall send you the usual newspapers also to which I refer you for public news.

Mr. Gautier has returned me the memoire of the emballeur. The person by whom he had it examined thinks the articles are charged too high. The emballeur spoke a language to Mr. Gautier which shewed he was determined not to diminish his charge. It is the advice of Mr. Gautier to have the memoire reglè (which I suppose will be done) if the emballeur persists in his full claim. He is to call on me to-morrow when it will be decided. I inclose you a copy of my account (amounting to 5063.^{tt} 6s) of monies paid for you, the medal boxes are included because as you had ordered them before your departure and paid I believe for some which were then finished, it seems more simple that the account should go to Congress through your hands. As I shall have occasion for the money I shall draw on the bankers for it, to be charged to you. Petit's memoires for articles which he has purchased for you amount to 3393.^{tt} 14s. I have not yet given him an order for the amount, because I am waiting until the emballeur's memoire is settled that I may pay them both at the same time and by one bill of exchange on Amsterdam. I will then send you the details of these memoires.

Langeac's brother and attorney here, keeps aloof. I have endeavoured in vain for some time past to have an interview with him. I know not whether to attribute this to his dissipated mode of life, or to a desire to know whether your successor will rent the house, or in fine to endeavour to sell it, before he shall come to a definitive explanation with respect to the lease.

A day or two after the date of my last letter (the 4th. inst.), the carriage house was forced open and robbed. A plated cabriolet harness, the cushions of my carriage and cabriolet and some other articles were taken off. The robbers passed through the garden, the treillage being broken down so as to be not even the appearance of an obstacle. I apprehended they would return some other night and perhaps carry off the horses, as there was nothing to oppose such an attempt. I determined therefore not to risk it, but to move into Paris and lodge at the Hotel D'Orleans, Rue des petits Augustins, until I should learn something of my future destiny. I therefore had the horses put in the petites affiches, determining to keep only my cabriolet in Paris. Several people came to see them and to my great astonishment and mortification the highest price offered was twenty guineas. I could not determine to let them go at that price, as twenty five had been formerly offered and refused by me, because I was sure your successor would be glad to give more for them. I felt now how dangerous it was to act with too much latitude in a case which regards others, and confess I am sorry to have refused the twenty-five guineas, although I then thought and still think them worth much more. They have been taken the best care of and are in perfect order. I cannot omit at present that when I refused the twenty-five guineas, I was induced to do it exclusively from a regard to your interest, and without consulting any convenience of mine. The proof of it is that I had then the intention of making several trips into the country (which I have since realised and shall realise) during which time the horses and coachman were a dead useless expence. I have been twice to La Rocheguyon and post both times and I shall do the same to Mareil. I mention these particularities because the late experiment has made me fear I have miscalculated for your interest in having refused the twenty-five guineas, unless your successor of which I cannot however doubt, should be disposed to take them at that or an higher price. As to myself I know that I should be glad to do it, and I judge of others from myself. On the whole I had determined rather than to sell for twenty guineas at present to give up my plan of going to lodge in Paris, and to submit to the anxiety which the apprehension of another visit from the robbers submitted me to in remaining here. Luckily the Duke de Pienne, having more horses than stable-room has asked leave to put some of them in the vacant stable. I have granted it because he keeps a guard with them who sleeps in the stable together with a bull dog; so that I am in hopes we shall be secure from robbers on that side in future.

I have heard by letters recieved in Paris that Congress had determined to adjourn on the 16th. of July.—I have a letter from London also which mentions that the sum of 40 thousand dollars had been voted for the foreign establishment, on your representing that Congress could not keep less than two ministers and two chargès des affaires in Europe. I am sorry your letter of the 1st. of July did not give some intimation on these subjects. In the present want of information however from America I am glad to catch it any where. From the two letters I infer that the appointments were made previous to the 16th. of July or very shortly after. I suppose the second minister will be at Madrid and the two chargé des affaires at the Hague and Lisbon, and yet I should imagine that the Queen of Portugal having sent a minister to America an equal grade would be expected from thence. I form a thousand conjectures and am wearied to death with them having no kind of data to go on except such intelligence as I pick up here and there. The present situation appears to me now the most disagreeable possible, on account of its uncertainty, and still when matters come to be ascertained I shall find that situation perhaps still more so. On the whole the time present is filled with anxiety and pain for me, and I fear that which is to come.—The reserve of your late letters shews I have every thing to fear. I do violence to myself in not enlarging on this subject, but I feel that I have already said too much on it in my former letters in the abandon of my heart. To any other than [yourself I should certainly have been silent. To you I should have said much more if I had been sure of my letters arriving in time, or much less if I had been sure of their arriving too late. All that I said partook of that uncertainty, doubt, and perplexity in which my mind was at the time of writing. I hope and believe you will excuse it, as it is the continuation of the habit to which I have been so long accustomed with you, of disclosing without reserve to you whatever relates to myself. Under any other circumstances or to any other person, my letters would have made an impression different from what I intended.][1]

I inclose you at present a list of your articles according to the

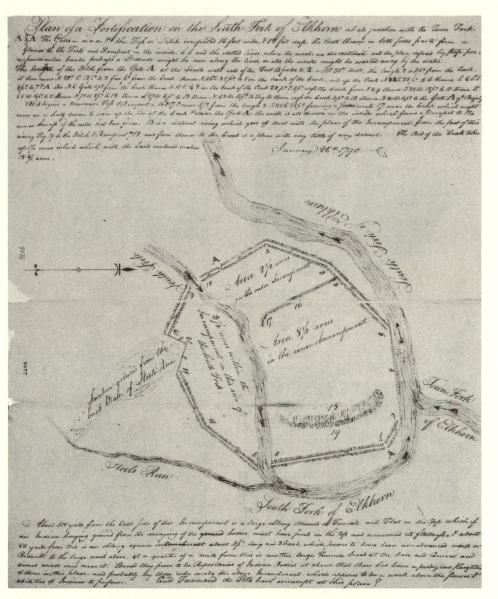

"Plan of a Fortification on the South Fork of Elkhorn"
(See p. xxxi-xxxii.)

William Loughton Smith

Arthur St. Clair

Medal awarded Henry Lee

Robert Morris

different packages as numbered by the Packer. It is copied from his memoire. He promised me also to give a paper containing instructions of the manner of unpacking each case, but as yet it has been impossible to get it from him. He has promised it definitively for to-day: should it arrive before my letter is finished it shall be inclosed.[2]

The conferences of Reicheinbach have ended in preliminary articles between the Kings of Hungary and Prussia. The former to give up all that has been taken from the Turks during the late war. The latter to use his mediation with the Porte for extending the Austrian territories to the Unner.—You will see the particulars in the newspapers sent.—Nothing as yet done with respect to Russia, but she will probably be forced to an immediate peace with a cession of her conquests. Some even suppose that her renunciation to the Crimea will be insisted on.

[The reports which circulated here some time ago and which I mentioned in the cypher of my last letters have subsided in a great measure. I have taken some pains to find from whence they came. But I have not been able to learn that there was the least foundation in reality for them.][3]—You will see in the Moniteur an article taken from an English newspaper, relative to a demand supposed to be made to Congress by the British ministry, and the answer. It is believed here because it has been printed in England. Many have enquired of me respecting the truth of it. I have always answered that I had no knowlege of any such demand.

The committee of commerce have got the tariff of duties to which French Ships and merchandize are subjected in the United States. They are now having it translated. They wish to open as free a communication as possible between the two countries and I don't doubt will be easily induced to do whatever they may suppose will contribute to it. I have had several conversations with the rapporteur of the committee. He is a man of information and well disposed. He has promised to communicate to me his report as soon as it is completed. I should hope from his desire to encrease the commerce between the two countries that he will be brought to see the propriety of counteracting the tendency of American produce to go [to] England, by proper encouragements here, or at least by removing every obstacle.

The committee of imposition is divided into two parties so opposed that it is impossible to say with certainty what will be the result as to tobacco. One party headed by Dupont is for continuing the farm of that article. The other led by Roederer, a member from Alsace is for abolishing all duties whatsoever on it, and thus throwing away a revenue of thirty two millions, which it is now said to have produced in former years. It is an article of cultivation in Alsace, and as the barriers are now to be removed to the frontiers, it will be necessary either to render this article free, or to subject its cultivation to such an inquisition as that province, he says, will not submit to. The question will necessarily come on now, as both parties of the committee say, in eight or ten days.

The horizon becomes more and more obscure every day. For a long time the government has been disorganised and without force —consequently a diminution of taxes and an increase of expence. Notwithstanding all the suppressions made by the assembly and which have reduced thousands from the highest to the lowest, to real want, it is evident public expences and losses increase. Every municipality considering itself sovereign puts an army on foot at every alarm of a plot or counter-revolution. This army being composed of gentlemen volunteers cost much more than any other. The reports of foreign invasion either from Spain, Savoy, or Germany, and which are circulated with design, have kept on foot for some time past, all the gardes nationales of the frontiers.—In the mean time several regiments of regular troops have imprisoned their officers under pretence of their being aristocrats, or having embezzled the funds of the regiment. In this situation they plunder the treasury of the army in their garrison, force their officers to sign bonds for large sums, which they transfer, and spend the whole in debauch in the taverns. The whole garrison of Metz has disbanded, consisting of near ten thousand men. The Intendant and the son of M. de Bouillé who commands these, were siezed and narrowly escaped with their lives. No body knows how or where this insubordination will end. It is evident that the enemies of the revolution triumph in it. The popular party which has been divided into two factions for some time past, begin to fear that their work has been ill done. They are endeavouring now to unite as the only means of saving public affairs. There are however such personal animosities among them that I fear it will be difficult to keep them together.

It has been impossible as yet to get the Marquis de la fayette to set for his picture. He always says he will do it, but never keeps his word and indeed he has not time—not even one moment to spare. Still if it is possible it shall be done.—Adieu my dear Sir and accept assurances of the sentiments of attachment & affection with which I am your friend & servant,

W: SHORT

RC (DLC); at head of text: "Private"; endorsed as received 20 Nov. 1790 and so recorded in SJL). Mrs. (DLC: Short Papers). Tr of Extract (DNA: RG 59, DD); see note 3, below.

1 The matter in brackets (supplied) is heavily crossed in RC by TJ through the use of small diagonal lines striking through each letter. Since Short's handwriting was minuscule and almost illegible even to TJ, this effectively blocked out the self-revealing passages.

2 This paragraph in RC has seven diagonal marks drawn through it which in no way obscure the text. At this point there appears in an unidentified hand the following caption: "Extract of a letter from Paris dated Aug. 15th. 1790," indicating possible publication though none has been found.

3 That part of the text in brackets (supplied) consists of the whole of the Tr of Extract.

From Benjamin Franklin Bache

HONOURED SIR   Philada Aug. 20. 1790

When the removal of Congress to this City was determined, I understood that Messrs. Childs & Swaine intended setting up a press here. I have since heard that they have no thoughts of moving. Perhaps you may have not yet fixed upon a person to print the laws here; in this case permit me to offer myself. I am just setting out in the printing business with an extensive assortment of materials and would endeavour to merit your approbation should you think proper to employ Dear Sir, Your most obedt & most hble Servant,   BENJN: FRANKLIN BACHE

RC (DNA: RG 59, PDL); endorsed as received 21 Aug. 1790, and so recorded in SJL.

From Robert Montgomery

Alicante, 21 Aug. 1790. He has corresponded constantly with Mr. Carmichael and given him all the useful information possible about "Our Commercial and political affairs on this coast of the Mediteranean," and did not trouble TJ since his letter of 15 Oct. 1787. Duty and inclination prompt him to congratulate TJ and the country on his appointment. "The Algerians continue to cruise on this coast, but the vessels they employ . . . are so small as not to be able to keep the sea above three months during the Summer, and none of them would be equal fires to one of ours mounting ten or twelve guns. Indeed, for the most part they are but boats with two or four guns and a number of Men, their large Vessels being at present in the Turkish service and entirely out of the way of Our trade. Their success in cruising on this coast for some years past has been so very little as not to pay one quarter part of the expence of their Armaments. We have now about Sixteen prisoners at Algiers who from their own accounts are the least uncomfortable of any in that situation.—The Portuguese Squadron are pretty constant cruising within the Streights mouth. Their primary object seems to be that of preventing the enemy corsairs getting into the Atlantic. The Spanish Armaments continue notwithstanding they have ceded their claim of Nootka sound and given up the two Vessels taken there. The remaining demand of Britain I believe is a commercial treaty in which they could not succeed in a friendly negociation proposed through Mr. Eden." As appointment of consuls is now in TJ's hands, he reminds him that such is needed on this coast perhaps more than in any other part of Europe. He trusts that his long services will recommend him to first consideration. As "you did me the honour to mention in your Letter of the tenth of September, that a letter addressed to Mr. Jay on that subject would suffice, but your being now in the office he then exercised, I beg leave to address this to your self." [*In postscript*:] "It had been reported some time since that Muly Azid the Young Emperor of Morroco, was Poisond: but without foundation and he is now said to be before Ceuta with a very large Armey.—Last post from Madrid brings advice that a very considerable part of that city was on fire and burning when the post came away. The Damage will be to individuals only."

RC (DNA: RG 59, CD); at head of text: "Second"; endorsed by TJ as received 22 Nov. 1790 and so recorded in SJL. The copy that Montgomery presumably designated as "First" is recorded in SJL as received 22 Jan. 1791, but it has not been found.

The above was forwarded from Boston by John Montgomery to TJ, 2 Nov. 1790, who said that he had just established himself in business there "in conjunction with my Brother Robt of Alicante" (RC in DNA: RG 59, MLR, endorsed as received 22 Nov. 1790 and so recorded in SJL).

To Nathaniel Colley

DEAR CAPTAIN   New York Aug. 22. 1790.

For fear that your uncertainty what was become of me should have prevented your executing the memorandum I gave you for the tables, I have copied it again on the next leaf. If you have already purchased them, and sent them to France, I shall get them with my furniture from thence: or if you have brought them with you, I will beg you to ship them to Philadelphia for me. But if you have not got them at all, I will still beg the favor of you to get them according to the note now sent. In any of these cases, either draw on me for what I may be in your debt, and it shall be paid at sight; or let me know to whom and where to pay it and it shall be punctually done.—Drop me a line of information for the present, if you please, and send it by post to Richmond, noting on the letter 'to be forwarded to Monticello,' where I shall be within three weeks.

My daughters were well when I last heard from them. The elder is married to Mr. Randolph the younger of Tuckahoe.

I saw your arrival at Norfolk announced in the Philadelphia papers, and on the strength of that write to you. I hope you have had a pleasant passage, & am Dear Captain your most obedt. humble servt.,   TH: JEFFERSON

PrC (MHi); accompanied by "Du-plicate of Note given on board the Cler-mont Nov. 16. 1789" (printed above under that date).

To Pierre Delivet

SIR   New York, August 22. 1790.

In answer to your several letters complaining of an illegal imprisonment of your person, I have to observe to you that the constitution of the United States having lodged the Executive and Judiciary powers in different bodies, and the Judiciary alone having the power to imprison or to enlarge the person, the Executive cannot interfere nor give any order in your behalf. Such an order would be disregarded as a mere nullity. To the judiciary alone then you can apply, and if your imprisonment is contrary to law, there is no doubt they will release you.

If I have been long in answering you, it was from a knowledge I could do nothing for your relief; from a presumption that your sentence has been according to law, because pronounced by your Consular Court, pronounced by the Federal Court, and not complained of by your Minister here, the natural Patron of the King's subjects: and from a multiplicity of business, which does not leave me time for correspondencies, as useless to the individuals they may concern as to the Public.—I am Sir, your very humble servant,

                 TH: JEFFERSON

FC (DNA: RG 59, SDC). Not recorded in SJL.

The first of Delivet's SEVERAL LETTERS was dated "a la Prison de Baltimore Le 9: May 1790" and described its author as "Pierre Delivet, Sous Lieutenant des Vaisseaux du Roy, Capitaine Commandant et Gerant par permis de Sa Majesté tres Chretienne un Batiment du Commerce du Havre en Normandie."

Delivet stated that he arrived in Baltimore in April 1786 on "une petite Expedition" for a company of merchants of Le Havre, Rouen, and Paris; that one of the Paris associates, because of "Difficultés de Compte," entered suit in the consular court of Baltimore, where sentence was pronounced 22 Oct. 1789; that he learned of this 18 Feb. 1790 and appealed the next day to the parlement of Rennes in Brittany, but that one of the judges, prior to the trial, had been given full powers by his former associate and two others were prejudiced; that the judges had invoked the laws of Maryland although forbidden to do so by French law and the Consular Convention; that on 24 Mch. 1790 a writ of ejectment was served on him and on the same day another writ compelled him to appear before the federal court at Annapolis, whereupon he was arrested, being kept in a "Lugubre Prison" until the 6th of May when he was taken to the Annapolis prison; that the next day his cause came on for trial, whereupon he presented to the court a copy of the gazette of 20 Apr. 1790 containing the text of Art. XVI of the Consular Convention and showed them, in addition to his letters of appeal to the parlement of Rennes, Arts. IV and V, but "n'ont eu auquun Egard"; that on the 8th the court remanded him to the prison at Baltimore, where he now is; and that he therefore appeals to TJ to give orders to whomever it may concern to nullify the writ of ejectment and the writ pending in the federal court as being contrary to the Consular Convention (RC in DNA: RG 59, MLR; recorded in SJL as received 14 May 1790; another letter from Delivet of 21 July 1790 is in RG 59, MLR; it is recorded in SJL as received on the 27th). On 16 Aug. 1790 Delivet wrote again, this time in English, saying that he had hoped TJ's honor and humanity would prompt him to answer but that he found "I am Mistake of Both . . . and I find that I perish in Geal. My health, My Liberty Captive, My Reputation Loss, and the ruin of my Interest for the sake of the Bad Conduct of Some Judges that have Refuse to Read, or to observe and Perform the Article XII of the Convention, where all my Cause is Explain and interpret in full. . . . What the federal Court have to interfere there-

in our Article forbid them to take any Cognisance" (RC in DNA: RG 59, MLR; endorsed by TJ as received 21 Aug. 1790 and so recorded in SJL). On the evening of 21 Aug. 1790 Washington and TJ returned from the presidential jaunt to Rhode Island (Dumbauld, *Jefferson*, p. 156-8). The next morning, Sunday, TJ wrote the above letter and soon thereafter received one from Tobias Lear enclosing another from Delivet "which the president found on his arrival last evening" (Dft in DNA: RG 59, MLR; FC in same, SDC; not recorded in SJL). TJ at once replied to Washington, saying he had not answered Delivet's letter of "some time ago" because of "some expectation that, if [the imprisonment] were unjust, Mr. Otto would complain of it"; he enclosed a press copy of the above letter and added: "If the President would wish any other or further answer to be given, Th: J. will be ready to do it; he cannot suggest any thing additional unless the President would chuse that he should recommend to the Attorney of the District to attend to the case of Delivel" (FC in DNA: RG 59, MLR; dated "Sunday August 22nd. 1790"; not recorded in SJL). Evidently Washington suggested that TJ write to the federal district attorney, for on 23 Aug. 1790 he stated the facts about "Peter Delivel" to Richard Potts of Baltimore and added: "The circumstances however which he mentions himself excite a presumption that his imprisonment is regular; nevertheless, as it may be otherwise, and he, as a stranger, may not know how to obtain relief, I take the liberty of requesting you to make such enquiry into his case as may satisfy yourself; and if you find the case to be such as is relievable in law, that you be so good as to put him into the way of obtaining it" (FC in DNA: RG 59, PCC No. 120).

To J. P. P. Derieux

DEAR SIR   New York Aug. 22. 1790.

I recieved yesterday your favor of July 20. and as I expect to be in Albemarle between the 12th. and 20th. of September I should have deferred answering it till I might have the pleasure of doing it verbally, were it not that your purpose of making preparations for a crop at Colle requires a speedier answer as to that particular. You know I told you that I should not consider myself as having any authority to meddle with that place but in the event of selling it: that in the mean time it would certainly remain as Mr. Mazzei had placed it, under your care. Consequently you have a perfect right to occupy it yourself if you please. With respect to the sale, I have informed Mr. Mazzei of the price you offered, and those offered by others, which were much higher than yours. Should he authorize me to sell it for whatever it will bring, I should think it my duty to get the most possible for it, indulging as far as I could, without prejudice to him, my inclination to give you a preference over every other bidder on equal terms.—Your letters shall be duly forwarded. As to all other particulars I refer them till I have the pleasure of seeing you, & am with respects to Madame de Rieux, Dear Sir Your most obedt. humble servt.,

TH: JEFFERSON

PrC (MHi).

From Le Mesurier & Cie.

SIR   Havre the 22d. Augt. 1790.

We have been advised from Rouën, that your effects from Paris are reembark'd on board Two Traders for this port so that we may expect them in a few days—provided they are not detained by contrary winds or any accident. You will receive the packages we are directed to send to Philadelphia by the Henrietta Captn: Weeks; as to those for Virginia, they must wait an opportunity, none offering for the present.

By Mr. Shorts' Letters accompanying the present, he will undoubtedly inform you of the plan presented to the National Assembly, by the Committee of Taxes, an article of which will abolish the Farm and make Tobacco a free article of Trade, with liberty to manufacture and cultivate it, without restraint.

We shall be able by our next to announce the Decree, there being no doubt (in our mind) but the Assembly will adopt the Committee's plan which seems a very popular one on the whole. We have the honor to be very respectfully Sir Yr. most obedient humble servants,   PAR LE MESURIER & COMP.

RC (DNA: RG 59, MLR); endorsed as received 20 Nov. 1790 and so recorded in SJL. Dupl (DLC); enclosed in Le Mesurier & Cie. to TJ, 27 Aug. 1790, and received 22 Nov. 1790.

Short had already advised Delamotte to send TJ's goods to Philadelphia and received the altered instructions confirming this decision after the effects were en route by water carriage to Rouen: there was also the usual doubt about available vessels and even about the number of parcels involved (TJ to Le Mesurier & Cie., 13, 16, and 18 Aug. 1790; DLC: Short Papers). On this day the Le Havre firm acknowledged Short's letters and said that Le Blanc of Rouen had announced the forwarding of TJ's goods to Le Havre and had drawn on them for payment of his costs, which they had refused but would pay if Short authorized it. Short directed payment on the 24th and at the same time gave the merchants a detailed analysis of the new regulations proposed in the report on TOBACCO, not then public (Le Mesurier & Cie. to Short, 14, 22 Aug. 1790; Short to Le Mesurier & Cie., 24 Aug. 1790; DLC: Short Papers).

To Martha Jefferson Randolph

MY DEAR DAUGHTER   New York Aug. 22. 1790.

The last letter I recieved from you was of the 2d. July. In mine of the 14th. inst. to Mr. Randolph I informed him I should set out the next day to Rhode island with the President. I did so, and returned yesterday, after a very pleasant sail of two days going and two days returning thro the Sound. We visited Newport and Providence, where the President was received with great cordiality. He expects to leave this place the 30th. My letter of about that date will inform Mr. Randolph of the day I shall set out from hence, which will probably be about the 1st. of Sep. and allowing for my necessary detention at Philadelphia, I shall in that case be at Monticello between the 14th. and 20th. of September, where I shall hope the pleasure of passing a month with you. I am afraid you will suffer inconvenience from the detention of your harness; but without it I could not have used my carriage till I recieve my own harness from France which I hardly expect now till September.—I think you understood Lady Caroline Tufton was about to be married. But in a London paper put into my hands by Mr. Rutledge I saw her attendance at court mentioned and under the name you knew her by.—We have no news yet whether the war between England and Spain has commenced. Kiss dear Poll for me, and remember me to Mr. Randolph. Adieu my dear. Your's affectionately,   TH: JEFFERSON

RC (NNP). PrC (MHi).
On the same day TJ wrote a letter to Thomas Mann Randolph, Jr.: "In my letter of to-day as well as in that of last week I forgot to ask the favor of you to look out for a fine red bay horse to match the best of mine, young, broke to the carriage, of good properties (for

it is in this point I dislike one of mine) rather larger than smaller, and to know his price. I am not decided to buy one, tho I believe I shall, and therefore would only wish to know where I may get one while I am in Virginia, without engaging absolutely, till I come. One of mine turns out fine in form and properties, the other indifferent in both. —I write this in hopes the post is not yet gone off, and supposing you will have time to make enquiry for me before your departure for Monticello" (RC in DLC: addressed: "Thomas Mann Randolph junr. esquire at Richmond"; postmarked: "New-York august 23"). TJ's "letter of to-day" was that of this date to Martha. On the search for a bay horse, see TJ to Fitzhugh, 24 Aug. 1790.

From Philip Schuyler

Sir   Albany August 22d. 1790.

Being on the point of embarking for this place, when I was honored with your note, of the 14th: inst:, and much engaged, I neglected to send you all the memorandums, I had made when perusing your report.

The novelty of the Subject, the ingenuity Evinced in its discussion, the pleasure it afforded, added to a sence of duty, induced me to examine the principles, and make the calculations. The former appeared to me demonstratively Just, the latter thro error of the press, or mistake in Notation, I found somewhat incorrect, but in so trifling a degree that I should neither have noticed or mentioned them to you If I had not been perswaded that perfection is your aim, as far as it is attainable, in whatever you offer to the public.

The length of a Pendulum, which shall vibrate Seconds in the latitude of 45 degrees, and the Rod thence deduced, as a Standard of measure, being 58.72368 inches, English, this Rod divided into five equal parts to be called feet, each foot will then be 11.744736 Inches English, which Cubed, will produce 1620.05506862 (the Cubic inches English, in the Standard foot,) now as 1000. ounces averdupoise, of pure rain water, will Exactly fill a Cubic foot English, or 1728 Cubic inches English, and as the Standard foot contains, only 1620.05506862 Cubic Inches English, it is evident, that if the water, which will exactly fill this Cube, be divided into 1000 Equal parts, Each of the parts, will be less in bulk, and consequently less in weight, than the former, in the ratio of 1728. to 1620.05506862, therefore, we shall have as 1728 (the Cubic inches English in a Cubic foot English) to 1620.05506862 (The Cubic Inches English in the New Standard Cubic foot) so is 437.5 (The grains Troy in an ounce averdupoise) to 410.17019243 the grains Troy, in the new or Standard Ounce, 11/12ths of which, is the pure Silver in the Unit, or dollar, that is 375.989343 Grains Troy, and hence the Expression of the Unit, or dollar, when the Avoirdupoise ounce shall consist of only 18 penny weights, or 432 Grains Troy, will be found by the following proportion, as 437.5, to 432. so 375.989343, to 371.2626277 the Expression of the pure Silver in the Unit.

If my Calculation be founded, then the report will require the following amendments.

page	37.	Line	9th:	dele	376.02985	Substitute	375.989343
			18th:	ditto	371.30261	ditto	371.2626277
page	41.	line	6th.	ditto	1620.23	ditto	1620.05506862
do.	42.	last line		ditto	376.02985	ditto	375.989343
do.	43.	line 2d.		ditto	.38985	ditto	.349343

And lest the English foot, Inch &c. Should be taken for the Standard foot, Inch &c. Perhaps the following amendments might also be proper.

Page 40. line 2d: Page 41. last line before "foot" insert *Standard*

do. 40. 20th. between "100" and "feet" insert *Standard*

do. 41. line 5th: and 15th. page 42. line 5th and 6th. and page 43 line 5th. before "Cubic" insert *Standard*

do. 41. line 6th: before "Bushel" insert *Standard*

do. 42. do. 3d: 6th: and 18th: and Page 43 line 5th. dele "an" Substitute *a Standard*

do. 42 7th. dele "the" Substitute *this*

Your observation, page 40. that, "It may be better generally to retain the name of the nearest present measure," has led me to enquire, if it was not possible to find Standards for measures, weights, and Coins, which while unchangeable in their nature, should be of such determined length, Capacity, and Weight, as that the New or Standard *Unit* in each may not only retain the name, but as often as may be, coincide in length, Capacity and Weight, with those now in use within the united States, and that where they do not so coincide, the proportional numbers, for converting the expression of the one, into that of the other, may be composed altogether of pure Integral numbers, or pure terminated decimals; probably this may be affected, in a great degree, by means of your

Standard Rod of 58.72368 Inches English, for if it be increased, by some Equal part of its own length, it will still be an invariable, unchangeable *Standard*.

Let us then increase the Rod, by one forty sixth part of its own length, and it will become 60.0002817 Inches English, and as the fraction above 60. is so extremely small, that it may safely be rejected, in all the computations which are the subject of your report, let us state the length of the *Standard*, at 60 Inches English, let it be divided into five Equal parts, let each part be called a Standard foot, which will be the same, as an English foot, let the Standard foot be divided into 10 Standard Inches, each standard inch will then be Equal to 1.2 Inches English, and then we may have the following Series as in your report,

A point.
10 points a Line
10. Lines an Inch
10. Inches a Standard foot
10. Feet, a Decad
10. Decads, a Rood
10. Roods, a Furlong
10. Furlongs, a Mile

Then the Standard Mile will consist of 1. Mile 3. Quarter 1. furlong 32 Yards and $\frac{44}{100}$ English, and the former will be to the latter as 10000. to 5280.

Superficial Measure.

Superficial Measures have been Estimated, and so may continue to be, in Squares of the measure of length (**A**) Except in the Case of Lands, which have been Estimated by Squares called Roods and Acres.

Let the chain be of 100 links, each link of 6 Inches and 6 lines Standard, then the chain will be 66. Standard feet, but 66 Standard feet are the same as 66 English feet, hence the Standard chain, will be the same as Gunters chain. Each link 6.6. Standard Inches, is equal to 7.92 English Inches, which is the length of a link in Gunters chain, hence the area of a Survey, whether made by the Standard, or Gunters chain, may be computed in the manner now in use, and the Areas will coincide, and be expressed, as now, in Acres, Roods &c.

Measure of Capacity.

Let the measure of Capacity, be the Standard Cubic foot, to be called a Standard Bushel. It will contain 1000. Standard Cubic Inches, be very nearly 1/5. less than the Winchester Bushel, of 8 Gallons Corn measure English, and 1 1/4 Standard Bushel will be only, 8 Cubic Standard Inches more, than the Winchester bushel, and then we may have the following Series as in your report.

A Metre, the least measure which will be of a Cubic Standard Inch

10. Metres, a Demi-pint.

10. Demi-pints a Pottle.

10. Pottles, a Standard Bushel (**B.**)

10. Bushels, a Standard Quarter (**C.**)

10. Quarters, a Last or double Ton

The measures for use being four Sided, and the Sides and bottoms rectangular, the Standard bushel will be a Standard Cubic foot.

The Pottle 5 Standard Inches square, and four deep.

The Demi-pint 2 Standard Inches square, and 2 1/2 deep, hence any person, with a Standard foot Rule, divided into Standard Inches, may readily determine if his measures of capacity be true or otherwise.

Weights

Let the weight of a Standard Cubic Inch of rain water, or the thousandth part, of a Standard Cubic foot, be called a Standard ounce, then this ounce will be precisely of the same weight, as the avoirdupoise ounce, now in use, and then we may have the following Series as in the report.

A Mite, the least Nominal weight

10. Mites, a minim or demi-grain

10. Minims, a Carat

10. Carats, a double Scruple

10. double Scruples, an Ounce (**D**)

10. Ounces, a pound (**E**)

10. Pounds a Stone. (**F**)

10. Stone a Kental (**G**)

10. Kentals a hogshead (**H**)

Coins

Let the money Unit be a dollar, and let its weight be Equal to a Standard Cubic Inch of rain water, that is equal to an avoirdupoise Ounce, or 437.5 grains troy. Now the pure Silver in a dollar, was by the Act of the late congress of the 8th. of August 1786. to be 375.64 Grains Troy, and 34.15 grains Troy of alloy, making together 409.79. Grains Troy. If then the standard dollar be of 437.5 Grains, there must be more Alloy, and as this encrease of Alloy is of some value, there must consequently be an equivalent value of the Silver less, in the Standard dollar, than in the dollar of 1786; Supposing the Alloy to be worth about 11. Cents ℔r. pound Avoirdupoise, the Encrease of Alloy will be equal to very nearly 8.64 grains, or $\frac{64}{100}$ th of a grain Troy of Silver, equal in value to 1 7/10 mill, and this deducted from 375.64 grains troy the weight of the Silver in the dollar of 1786; there will remain the weight of the Silver in the Standard dollar Equal to 375. Grains Troy, the difference between this, and 437.5 Grains, is the Alloy, for the Standard dollar, and is 62.5 grains Troy, or 1/7 part of the whole, hence the Standard Dollar will consist of 6 parts pure Silver, and one part Alloy, and now we may have the following Series.

A Mite, the least Weight Equal to 0.04375. Grains Troy
10. Mites, a Minim, or demi-grain, or 0.4375   ditto
10. Minims, a Carat, or   4.375   ditto
10. Carats, a double Scruple, or   43.75.   ditto
10. double Scruples, an Ounce, or   437.5   ditto **(I)**
10. Ounces, a Pound or   4375.   ditto

(A)   If the Sides of a Superficies be given, in entire Standard feet, the Area will be the same, and Expressed in like manner, as if the Sides had been given in English feet.

If the sides of a Superficies be given in Standard feet and Inches, Lines, and Points, the feet in the product, will be indifferently Either Standard, or English feet, and the decimal parts of the product, will consist of Standard Inches, lines, and points, which may be converted into English Inches, Quarters &c., by the usual mode of Converting decimal, to Vulgar Fractions.

If the Sides of a Superficies be given in Standard Inches, Lines, and points, the product will be Standard, and will be to the English as 100. to 144.

(B)   The Standard Bushell will be to the Winchester bushell as 17280. to 21504.

[407]

(C) The Standard quarter will be only 64 Cubic Standard Inches, or 64 Metres, more than the English quarter, of 8 Winchester bushels, the Standard Quarter is, to the English Quarter, as 17280. to 21504.

(D) The Standard Ounce, is of Equal weight with the averdupoise ounce, and also of a Standard Cubic Inch of rain water, and also of a Metre of rain water.

(E) The Standard Pound is equal to 5/8th. of an Averdupoise Pound, also Equal to a Standard demi-pint of rain water. The Standard pound, is to the averdupoise pound, as 10. to 16.

(F) The Standard Stone, is Equal to 6 1/4 pounds averdupoise, also Equal to a Standard pottle of rain water.

(G) The Standard Kental is Equal to 62.5 Pounds Averdupoise, also equal to a Standard or english Cubic foot of rain water, and Equal to a Standard bushel of rain water.

(H) The Standard Hogshead is Equal to 625. Pounds Averdupoise, also equal to 10. Cubic Standard feet, also Equal to 10. Standard Bushels of rain water in weight.

(I) The Standard ounce, is equal to the Averdupoise ounce, also equal to a Cubic Inch of water, also equal to a Metre of rain water.

(K) From this coincidence, between Weights, and Measures of Capacity, it is Evident that Either, might be applied as a Substitute for the other.

Thus if I wanted to weigh, a Kental of Wool, and have no Standard weights, but have a standard bushel, place the empty bushel in one scale, counterpoise it by something in the other, then fill the bushel with water and Counterpoise the whole by Wool on the other Scale,—and so of the others.

No Standard, other than that which is derived from yours, has hitherto occurred to me, that will combine an equal number of advantages; should I discover any, I will with great pleasure communicate it. If what I have detailed on the Subject can be improved to any public advantage you are perfectly at liberty to make what use of it you may think proper. I have the Honor to be Sir With much respect Your Obedient Servt., PH: SCHUYLER

RC (DLC); in a clerk's hand, signed by Schuyler; endorsed by TJ as received 28 Aug. 1790 and so recorded in SJL. What appears to be a rough draft, dated 19 Aug. 1790 at Albany and entirely in Schuyler's hand, is in NA: John Williams Papers, being accompanied by the enclosed Table. But this evidently was a fair copy that Schuyler intended to send but did not. So far as the text goes, it agrees in substance with the above, save for the concluding paragraph which Schuyler marked for deletion. This deleted paragraph reads: "It is probable that better standards may be obtained [than] this. Should we totally neglect any coincidence between the new and the Old measures, this appeared to me an eligible one under the present prejudices arising from long habits. If any public use can be made of what I have said on the subject you are perfectly at liberty to apply It as you please." The draft of the substitute paragraph, together with various calculations and drafts of the enclosed Tables, undated and all in Schuyler's hand, are in DLC: Hamilton Papers, f. 1249, 1471-5, perhaps being furnished to the Secretary of the Treasury at the time he was preparing the Report on the Establishment of a Mint and was obliged to consider the value of the money unit as established by the resolution of Congress of 8 Aug. 1786 (see Syrett, *Hamilton*, VII, p. 467; Tench Coxe to Hamilton, 31 Dec. 1790, same, VII, 396). These calculations and memoranda vary in detail from the above.

In MHi there is an undated memorandum from Schuyler to TJ, obviously written soon after he received TJ's (missing and unrecorded) note OF THE 14TH: INST:, reading: "Mr. Schuylers Compliments. He is this moment going to embark for Albany, and has not time to make a fair copy of his Calculation, therefore begs Mr. Jefferson to excuse him for sending the rough copy of the Calculation he has made. He will perceive that the difference is very trifling" (not recorded in SJL and not endorsed by TJ, but evidently received just before TJ departed on 15 Aug. 1790 for Rhode Island or just after he returned on the 21st.; on that journey TJ recorded in SJL that he wrote Alexander Hamilton "on the Packet" and the letter may have referred to this calculation, but it has not been found). The enclosed calculation showed that, as in the above, Schuyler found the "expression of the [money] unit in new grains will be 371.26262" grains, whereas "the Secretary of State makes It 371.30261."

ENCLOSURE

Table to compare Standard with English long, square, and cubic Measure and with English measure of Capacity.

Standard denomination of Measures in length	The Expression when the Unit is a Standard foot	Equivalent expression in English Inches in length	Equivalent Expression in English square Inches when the Standard is Squared	Equivalent Expression in English Cubic Inches when the Standard is Cubed
The point	.001	.012	.000144	.000001728
Line	.01	.12	.0144	.001728
Inch	.1	1.2	1.44	1.728
Foot	1.	12.	144.	1728.
Decad	10.	120.	14400.	1728000.
Rood	100.	1200.	1440000.	1728000000.
Furlong	1000.	12000.	144000000.	1728000000000.
Mile	10000.	120000.	14400000000.	1728000000000000.

Standard denomination of measures of Capacities	The expression when the Unit is a Standard Bushel	Equivalent Expression in English Cubic inch: when the Standard is Cubed
The Mitre	.001	1.728
demi-pint	.01	17.28
Pottle	.1	172.8
Bushel	1.	1728.
Quarter	10.	17280.
Last	100.	172800.

Table to compare Standard with English Weight and coin

Standard denomination of Weights	The Expression when the Unit is a Standard Pound	Equivalent Expression in Avoirdupoise Pounds	Equivalent Expression in Troy Grains	
The Mite	.00001	.00000625	.04375	
Minim	.0001	.0000625	.4375	
Carat	.001	.000625	4.375	
double Scruple	.01	.00625	43.75	
Ounce	.1	.0625	437.5	
Pound	1.	.625	4375.	
Stone	10.	6.25	43750.	
Kental	100.	62.5	437500.	
Hogshead	1000.	625.	4375000.	
Standard denomination of Coin	The Expression when the Unit is a Standard Dollar	Equivalent Expression in Avoirdupoise Ounces	Equivalent Expression in Troy Grains	
			Silver	Alloy
The Mill	.001	.001	.375	.0625
Cent	.01	.01	3.75	.625
Dime	.1	.1	37.5	6.25
Dollar	1.	1.	375.	62.5
Eagle	10.	10.	3750.	625.

MS (DLC: TJ Papers, 57: 9731); in a clerk's hand, the first table being on recto and the second on verso. Dft (NA); in Schuyler's hand, both tables being on recto. Another Dft (DLC: Hamilton Papers).

From William Short

Dear Sir   Paris Aug. 22. 1790

This letter is begun merely to introduce to you Monsieur de Tevernal an officer of artillery, and M. des Rochers, his friend, who are going to settle on the Siota. They intend to land at Philadelphia and the Marquis de la fayette desires me to recommend them to your civilities. He gives them a letter to the President. I am persuaded I need say nothing further to insure them such marks of attention from you as may be in your power.—This leaves me also more time to inform you of the present state of your affairs here, before they call to take the letter.

Since my last of the 15th. inst. I have sent to Havre a particular invoice of the effects contained in each of the packages. I mentioned to you their departure from Rouen for Havre. As yet I have no account of their arrival there but I expect it daily. The memoire of the emballeur has been reglé. It was reduced only 180.^{tt} He has been paid the amount 6443.^{tt} Petit has been also paid. The two sums together with a second memoire which I paid to Goldsmith amount to ten thousand and sixty livres 3.s. 6.d. I have drawn for their amount on Willinck & Van Staphorst in favor of Mr. Grand and directed them to charge it to their account with you. I gave them notice also that I should shortly draw on them for my account current with you. I wait until I shall have paid the draught of Le Mesurier of Havre, which I expect daily, for their disbursements on account of the transportation and other charges relative to your effects. There are some articles here also still to be sold. After that the account will be settled and I will send you the details of it. I enclosed you in my last a copy of the advances made on your account by me at different times, and I hope in my next to state the whole.

Langeac has surprized me lately in the most agreeable manner possible. His brother and attorney here called on me to inform me that your Landlord was sensible there could be no doubt that the expression of the lease was such as authorized him to insist on its continuance for three years from the last renewal. He says further that you understood it so, but that there was a verbal agreement between you by which you were authorized to give the congé when you pleased, and that he was ready to accept it from the end of the term which expired the 15th. of July. He is in treaty for the sale of his house and has hopes of effecting it very soon.

When I desired Mr. Grand to charge the house rent to Congress so that it might not enter into your account, he objected that he had at present no account open with Congress. It was true that he had 66000^{tt} livres of theirs in his hands. But as that had been appropriated to a particular purpose and subject only to your order or mine it could not be considered as a public fund. I have authorized him therefore to appropriate a part of it to the payment of the house-rent, and this I have done as well because there is no probability of its being employed in the manner you expected, as because of the danger of its depreciating here.—The same consideration makes me wish that it could be applied to the payment of the interest on the foreign officer's debt. There would be always time enough to draw on Amsterdam in the case of its being wanted for the Algerine business and I suppose there is no danger that such a sum in future could not be commanded there at any time at a moment's warning. This renders the appropriation in Mr. Grand's hands unnecessary.

Mr. Grand shewed me some days ago his correspondence with Drost on the subject of your letter. He authorizes Mr. Grand to make you propositions as he may judge proper, and says he will abide by them. He gives his opinion at the same time. It is that his expences should be paid, and that he should recieve in addition a thousand pound sterling ℞ Ann.—He thinks it will be proper and necessary that he should pass some time in Paris in order to have executed such parts of the machine as can be better done here than in 'America.' Mr. Grand is to write to you on the subject and I expect his letter in order to be sent with this.

I have received a letter from Mr. de Crevecoeur at Caen, which tells me that he shall send by the first opportunity your reveille watch intrusted to his care. As soon as I get it I shall put it into the workmans hands.

I saw the Gun-smith a few days ago. The difficulty that he has in furnishing the six locks, is that his machine is not mounted at present, and that he cannot mount it for so small an object. However he hopes to be able to collect by some means or other that number in ten or fifteen days when he will send them to me, and they shall be forwarded to you by the first opportunity.

Charpentier has recieved your sketch of the copying press. He understood it perfectly and promised it should be finished by the end of the month.

I have always forgotten to mention to you why De Lorme was not employed to pack the clocks and other articles you desired. Petit thought the packer employed would be displeased with it and might perhaps be less attentive to the other objects and more disposed to augment his charges. Besides he knew him to have been employed for a long time in packing the most difficult articles and to stand in reputation second to none except De Lorme. As yours were to go by water and were not of the most difficult kind I yielded to his observations. I hope no ill will result from it. I yielded the more readily because he assured me it would be difficult to get a good packer who would agree to undertake only such things as were not thought fit to be trusted to another. It was at least probable that such a sacrifice of *amour propre*, would have induced an augmentation of charge.

I recieved a letter from Parker yesterday which informs me that Rumsey has been delayed beyond all expectation, that his engine is now perfect, but that he has found that his boiler is too small. He is making another which will be completed next week.

He adds that "his present boiler had enabled him to make 200 strokes with his engine on the vessel and that the effect of moving her forward was *fully proved*."

I send by the bearer your silver medal of P. Jones which you desired should be made for you. I omitted sending it with your furniture. It has been a long time since I have had the pleasure of hearing from you. Your last was of the 27th. of May, for I don't count that of the 1st. of July. I cannot attribute your reserve (at a time when you know in what a state of anxiety I must be) to any other circumstance than your desire to put off as long as possible the communication of bad news. It is impossible that you should not have known long ago what was intended in this business. —I fear much that every thing will have been decided before you recieved my letters in answer to yours mentioning your acceptance of the place with Congress. I repent now most sincerely having not known this before you left Paris. I feel now that I could have put matters in a train which would have been agreeable to me and presented the subject to you in a light in which you perhaps have not seen it.—For I still think that I can be more useful here than any other who has not a knowledge of the country. Adieu my dear Sir. Yr. friend.   W: SHORT

RC (DLC); at head of text: "*Private*"; endorsed as received 23 Nov. 1790 and so recorded in SJL. PrC (PHi); consisting of first page only.

The LETTER FROM MR. DE CREVECOEUR, which was dated 12 Aug. 1790, stated: "in opening my Trunk I have found a box containing a reveille matin Watch, which Mr. Jefferson Intrusted to my care and desired I shou'd deliver to you: hope my forgetfullness has not caused any uneasiness: 'tis safe and you shall receive it as soon as I can find a safe opportunity." What Short did not tell TJ was that Crèvecoeur asked a question about the matter uppermost in Short's mind: "Are there any hints or news of a diplomatick successor? Mr. Maddison might be the man and then we shou'd keep his and Mr. Jefferson's friend here, Mr. William Short" (RC in DLC: Short Papers, signed "St. John" because, as Crèvecoeur explained in a postscript, "Their Seignorie name being done away with, with pleasure I return to the simple American one by which I have been known in the Country upwards of Twenty years").

From William Short

DEAR SIR   Paris Aug. 22. 1790

The committee of impositions have not yet made their report to the assembly although they have announced the outlines. Their plan at present after violent debates between the two parties mentioned in my letter of the 15th. inst., is the result of mutual sacrifices. It is considered as defective by both who say that nothing but mere necessity can justify it. It is to admit of the cultivation of tobacco in France (I allude to what relates to that article particularly), and to form an exclusive company for the purchase of it from foreigners. They are sensible that this measure keeps the door shut as to the commercial intercourse which the free reception of that article from the United States would have established, but they say it is combined with other more important operations. It is useless to add all the stupid reasoning I have heard on the subject. You will be convinced of the impossibility of avoiding this decision in the committee, when you are told that they were put in full possession of the subject as well by your memorial, presented to Count Vergennes as by whatever occurred to me relative thereto—and that the Marquis de la fayette has taken the same active part in the measure to which you know him accustomed in similar cases. The only hope now left is that the assembly will modify the report of the committee as to the exclusive company. Some merchants who are here intend to make observations and remonstrances on the subject. They will probably be aided by their partners and correspondents in the ports. The result will be known very shortly, as I believe the report is to be made tomorrow, and I shall lose no time in informing you of it.

The Minister of the Marine announced yesterday to the assembly that the Algerines exacted reparation for the violence offered to some of their vessels on the coasts of France some time ago, which I then mentioned to you. His memorial on the subject was not read, so that the particulars are not known. The result however will probably be the paying damages, and making other pecuniary sacrifices in reparation.

You will be surprized to learn that this memorial of the minister on so pressing a subject gave way to a discussion which lasted the whole day, on the punishment to be inflicted on one of their members for having printed a speech which the assembly had refused to hear in the tribune, and having added that he considered himself honored by the censure of the assembly. It was moved to put him in the prison of the Abbaye for eight days. There was no doubt of its passing when one of the members of the *coté droit* M. Faucigny, rose and running towards the middle of the arena, cried "*puisq*u'il y a guerre ouverte il faut tomber à coups de sabre sur ces gaillards-là."—The President de Frondeville, the author of the printed speech, seeing the effect this was about to produce, flew to the tribune and in the most distressing tone declared he acknowleged his fault, that he felt himself guilty from the moment he had seen the dangerous effect about to be produced, begged that the wrath of the house might fall on him alone, and that he was ready to go to prison or submit to any other punishment that might be inflicted. The assembly were induced to change the original motion into a resolve "qu'il se rendroit aux arrêts et les tiendroit dans sa maison pendant huit jours." They determined at the same time to excuse M. de Faucigny who made every acknowlegement and declared that he had been for a moment out of his senses. This tyrannical measure in the assembly has produced little impression on the minds of the public, but it is evident on that principle that the majority of the assembly have an absolute power over the liberty of the minority. It is to be observed also that when the rules of the house were formerly adopted, there was a proposition for the members being imprisoned in particular cases by the order of the house, and that it was then rejected on the principle of its being too severe, and of the assembly not having a right to deprive his constituents of the presence of their member in the house.

The naval preparations are still going on in England, and such profound secrecy is observed as to their object that no person seems possessed of any thing more than conjectures respecting them. The most probable seem to be that the negotiations with Spain not being finally determined, Mr. Pitt thinks the best mode of insuring and expediting them, is to shew a formidable warlike countenance. It has been said here within these two days that Spain had lately shewn an obstinacy which had not been expected. As she is forced into this negotiation against her will it is not surprizing that ill humour from time to time should make her recalcitrate for a moment, but after reflexion will probably induce her to subscribe to such conditions as may be insisted on. It is probable also that Mr. Pitt wishes to be in an armed state at the negotiations which will take place, as it is supposed between Russia, Sweden and the Turk. He will no doubt attempt to secure to England commercial advantages in the Baltic and the Levant.

I send you the usual newspapers to this date, and hope you will continue persuaded of the sentiments of respect & attachment with which I have the honor to be Dear Sir, your most obedient humble servant,   W. SHORT

PrC (DLC: Short Papers); at head of text: "*No.39*"; noted in SJL as received 23 Nov. 1790. Tr (DNA: RG 59, DD).

To Sylvanus Bourne

Sir   New York August 23d. 1790.

Your favor of the 15th. instant has been duly received and laid before the President.

You will permit me to recall to your memory that when I proposed to you the Consulship of Hispaniola, I informed you that neither salary nor perquisites were annexed to the office, nor probably would be: that it was in contemplation of the Legislature to consider the subject, but that the result was too uncertain to be counted on. On this ground you took a day or two to make up your mind, and finally accepted. The ground has not changed at all, it is now exactly what it was then. The bill which was brought into Congress, has not been passed, and to delay your departure till it does pass, may be a delay without end. The probabilities of a general war taking place, the revolution now actually going on in Hispaniola, and the expediency that the representations, now asked from them by the mother Country, should be pointed to our common good, render it peculiarly interesting to the United States that the Consul of that Island should be in his place, and will, I am sure, justify in your judgment the wish of Government that you should repair thither with due dispatch. I have the honor to be, Sir &c.,

THOMAS JEFFERSON

FC (DNA: RG 59, PCC No. 121).

On Bourne's insistent plea concerning SALARY, see note to Bourne to TJ, 24 Mch. 1790. In a letter to TJ of 8 July 1790 Bourne returned to the attack, saying that he had learned from the press that Congress had "rejected the plan of granting Consuls some small douceur from Vessells" and asked: "Will Congress consent to give a certain sum in the first instance . . . whereby we may be assisted in making our establishments?" Bourne added that he had been surprized to learn that the French government in the West Indies had "lately put in practice the droit d'Aubine in one or two instances Contrary to the Convention lately published" and that a memorial to Congress on this subject was "in contemplation" among Boston merchants. He also said that L'Étombe, the French consul, was "about to request of Government that some provision should be made directing in what manner the decrees of

Consuls shall be put in force by the Executive Power where they reside" (RC in DLC: Applications for Office under Washington; endorsed by TJ as received 14 July 1790; on 5 Aug. 1790 Bourne again wrote TJ, but only to let him know that instructions would reach him in Boston and that he would not return to New York before departing; RC in same; endorsed by TJ as received 11 Aug. 1790 and so recorded in SJL). On the 15th Bourne wrote the letter that provoked the above peremptory reply: "as I am told by Mr. Thatcher that the Senate have assigned [the Consular Bill] over to the next session, I have to request permission from you to delay my departure for Hispaniola till this Bill is finished, of the probability of which you must be acquainted. I feel an anxiety to know on what grounds and principles I can support my oficial situation with a pride of having my public Conduct guaranteed by some legal sanction, and though the idea of a direct consulage seems to be exploded Government I think will have the manliness to allow some kind of pay for business to be done and will not require in return for an empty title the sacrifice of the time and services of Individuals whose peculiar situation will illy allow either.—Pardon, my respected Sir, the warmth of my feelings which do not arise from any disappointment relating to pecuniary emolument but of an ingeneous wish to support with a proper dignity a Commission from under the Seal of the United States of America" (RC in DLC: Applications for Office under Washington; endorsed by TJ as received 21 Aug. 1790 and so recorded in SJL).

To Sylvanus Bourne

SIR   New York Aug. 24. 1790.

I have the honor to inclose you a letter addressed to me from the Secretary of the Treasury, accompanying papers in the case of Capt. Brown, who having sold the sloop Polly at Port-au-Prince, her register was detained. You will see by the letter of the Secretary of the Treasury the inconveniencies to which this practice leads in this country, and as the detention of the register, when a vessel is sold, seems to be attended with no advantage to the Government where it is sold, we have reason to hope that the friendship always manifested towards us by the Sovereign and subjects of France will induce those in power in the island of Hispaniola to listen with attention to the temperate and friendly representations you will make to them against this practice, and to accomodate their and our convenience by such a relaxation as they shall find practicable. I am with great esteem Sir Your most obedient & most humble servant,   TH: JEFFERSON

RC (NjP). FC (DNA: RG 59, PCC No. 121); accompanied by list of enclosures. Enclosures: Hamilton to TJ, 20 Apr. 1790, and its various enclosures.

To William Fitzhugh

DEAR SIR   New York Aug. 24. 1790.

Your bill for 250 dollars for the horse was yesterday presented by Messrs Ludlow & Gould and paid on sight.

The President leaves this the 30th. I shall set out within a day or two after him, but am incertain whether I shall strike off from Alexandria by Newgate, or go by the way of Fredericksburgh. If the latter, I shall surely have the pleasure to call and ask you how you do. Mr. Madison and I travel together.

Not knowing whether my servant Bob is in your neighborhood,

I must ask the favor of you, if he be there, to direct him to be at Monticello by the 10th. or 12th. of September.

I believe I shall have occasion while in Virginia for a carriage horse, blood bay, of 4f. 10 or 4f. 11 I. high, finely formed, young, broke to the carriage, and of good dispositions. Should you know of such an one, I will thank you to drop me a line to remain at the post office of Alexandria, till called for. I gave £30. for the horse to which I want a better match, the one I mean to dismiss as being vicious. I would not chuse any engagement to be made till I am further decided in my mind. Pardon me, my dear Sir, for asking information of you in a line wherein you can have it and I cannot; & believe me to be with sincere esteem Your friend & servant,

Th: Jefferson

PrC (MHi).

See note to TJ to Fitzhugh, 21 July 1790, and to TJ to Martha Jefferson Randolph, 22 Aug. 1790. Fitzhugh replied to the present letter on 5 Sep. 1790, saying that BOB had been with George Carter of Williamsburg for some time and that he had written to Charles Carter of Albemarle, asking him to pass on TJ's request; he added that he would continue to look for a horse for TJ but feared it would be a difficult matter to find such a one as described, though he was on the point of going "in a few Days to the County of Culpepper, where . . . there are some likely geldings" (RC in MHi; recorded in SJL as received 14 Sep. 1790). TJ returned by way of FREDERICKSBURGH, stopping at Mt. Vernon en route; later in the autumn he returned northward the same way, but probably missed Fitzhugh both times. On 10 Oct. 1790 Fitzhugh wrote again from Chatham: "Soon after I received your Tickett, I waited on Mr. Vernon to know the Price of his Horse, and found it to be two hundred Pounds, which is more I presume, than you would wish to give, even for a Stud: of this I should have inform'd you long since if an Opportunity had offer'd. I have not yet met with a gelding that I think woud suit you. Whenever I do, you shall hear from me" (RC in MHi; recorded in SJL as received 25 Oct. 1790, at Monticello; TJ's "Tickett" has not been found and is not recorded in SJL). TJ acknowledged this four days later: "Mr. Vernon's horse is beyond my price four or five times over. I purchased one on my arrival at home which died within three days. I have since that purchased another, so that I am no longer in pressing want. Still if you were to see a horse of capital figure and of the other descriptions I have troubled you with of from 30£ to 50£ I would thank you to write me. I set out for Philadelphia the 8th of next month. Should I take the route of Fredericksburg I will endeavor to have the pleasure of seeing you" (PrC in MHi). TJ arrived at Monticello from New York on 19 Sep. 1790; there is no record of the purchase of a horse that died three days afterward, but on 4 Oct. 1790 he recorded in his Account Book the purchase at Richmond of a "horse of Carter Braxton 5. years old last spring got by Brimmer, who was got by Eclipse." According to the slave Isaac, this horse (also named Brimmer) was a racer: it is thus interesting that the two horses of the turf that TJ is said to have owned were both acquired in 1790 and both were in the blood lines of the noted Eclipse. TJ paid for him by note "for 116⅔ Doll. paiable at Phila. Dec. 31. or at Richmd. Jan. 15." He sold the animal early in 1793 (see TJ to Samuel Clarkson, 2 Feb. 1793). On 16 Nov. 1790 Fitzhugh acknowledged TJ's letter of 29 Oct., promised to continue the search for a horse, and then offered another opportunity: "It is possible that you may be in want on a young Gentleman of Character and Abilities in your Office. If you shou'd be, I take the Liberty of recommending to you, the Gentleman who will deliver you this Letter, Mr. Mortimer. He is a young Man of a most amiable Character, has been genteelly educated, and will I am persuaded, acquit himself with Honour in any Department that may be assign'd him. He received the latter part of his Education in the House of an eminent Merchant in Philadelphia, by whom he is warmly recommended. He writes a pretty Hand, is Master of Figures, and I am inform'd has some Knowledge of the French Language" (RC in MHi; recorded in SJL as received 14 December 1790).

To John Hancock

SIR   New York August 24th. 1790

The Representatives of the United States have been pleased to refer to me the representation from the General Court of Massachusetts on the subject of the Whale and Cod fisheries which had been transmitted by your Excellency, with an instruction to examine the matter thereof and report my opinion thereupon to the next Session of Congress. To prepare such a report as may convey to them the information necessary to lead to an adequate remedy, it is indispensible that I obtain a statement of the fisheries, comprehending such a period before and since the war as may shew the extent to which they were and are carried on: with such a statement under their view, Congress may be able, by comparing the circumstances which existed when the fisheries flourished, with those which exist at this moment of their decline, to discover the cause of that decline, and provide either a remedy for it, or something which may countervail it's effect. This information can be obtained no where but in the State over which your Excellency presides, and under no other auspices so likely to produce it. May I, therefore take the liberty of soliciting your Excellency to charge with the collecting and furnishing me this information, some person or persons who may be competent to the object. Taking a point of commencement at a proper interval before the year of greatest prosperity, these should be stated in a table year by year under different columns as follows.

1. The number of vessels fitted out each year for the cod-fishery.
2. Their Tonnage.
3. The number of seamen employed.
4. The quantity of fish taken. 1. of superior quality. 2. of inferior.
5. The quantity of each kind exported. 1. to Europe, and to what countries there. 2. to other and what parts of America.
6. The average prices at the markets. 1. of Europe. 2. of America

With respect to the Whale fishery, after the three first articles, the following should be substituted;

4. Whether to the Northern or Southern fishery.

5. The quantity of oil taken 1. of the Spermaceti whale. 2. of the other kinds.

6. To what market each kind was sent.

7. The average prices of each.

As the ports from which the equipments were made could not be stated in the same table conveniently, they might form a separate one. It would be very material that I should receive this information by the 1st. of November, as I might be able to bestow a more undisturbed attention to the subject before than after the meeting of Congress, and it would be better to present it to them at the beginning than towards the close of a Session.

The peculiar degree of interest with which this subject must affect the State of Massachusetts, the impossibility of obtaining necessary information from any other quarter, and the slender means I should have of acquiring it from thence, without the aid of your Excellency, will I hope be a sufficient apology for the trouble I take the liberty of giving you; and I am happy in every occasion of repeating assurances of the respect and attachment with which I have the honor to be &c.,   THOMAS JEFFERSON

FC (DNA: RG 59, PCC No. 120); at head of text: "To the Governor of Massachusetts."

To Sylvanus Bourne

SIR   New York August 25th. 1790.

I enclose you herein sundry papers containing a representation from Messrs. Updike & Earle of Providence, who complain that their Sloop Nancy was seized in the Island of Hispaniola, and though without foundation as her acquittal proved, yet they were subjected to the payment of very heavy expenses. It is to be observed that in no Country does Government pay the costs of a defendant in any prosecution, and that often though the party be acquitted, there may have been colourable cause for the prosecution. However this may have been in the present case, should the parties think proper to endeavour by their own agent to obtain a reimbursement from the Government or from individuals of Hispaniola, I take the liberty of recommending their cause to your patronage so far as evidence and law shall be in their favor. If they address the Government, you will support their demands on the ground of right and amity. If they institute process against individuals, counterpoise by the patronage and weight of your public character, any weight of character which may be opposed to their obtaining of justice. I am Sir &c.,   THOMAS JEFFERSON

FC (DNA: RG 59, PCC No. 121); followed by listing of the three enclosures, as follows: (1) John Updike and William Earle to Theodore Foster, 25 June 1790, concerning seizure of *Nancy* by French officers. (2) Protest of John Russell, master, before notary public, Providence, 19 June 1790. (3) Account of costs and damages sustained by owners of *Nancy* as a result of the seizure.

On this same day TJ wrote Messrs. Updike & Earle saying that he had received the papers in the case of the *Nancy* and had laid them before the President, adding: "It is concluded that the only proper way in which Government can interfere, will be through the Agency of Mr. Bourne, now at Boston, who is going out as our Consul to Hispaniola. . . . I enclose you a copy of my letter to him, and recommend to you to concert with him before his departure, the steps it may be expedient for you to take" (FC in DNA: RG 59, PCC No. 120).

From Stephen Sayre

Le Havre, 25 Aug. 1790. Finding the *Henrietta* going out with TJ's articles, he recalls himself to TJ as bringing letter from Massachusetts and Virginia delegates in 1785 "recommending your appointing me to the place, which *I found so honorably fill'd by Mr. Lamb.*" Requests "some employment in Europe if I may be thought worthy of it."

RC (DLC: Applications for Office under Washington); endorsed by TJ as received 22 Nov. 1790 and so recorded in SJL.

To William Short

DEAR SIR   New York Aug. 25. 1790.

The President will leave this on the 30th. for Mount Vernon and will return to Philadelphia towards the latter part of November. I go hence a day or two after him, for Monticello, and shall return to Philadelphia about the last of October. The other offices will be removed to Philadelphia between the middle of October and of November. I very much wish my letters, written for this purpose, may have reached you in time to change the destination of my furniture to Philadelphia directly.

I must beg the favor of you to get Houdon to have made of a light cheap silk, couleur d'ardoise, the actual costume he formed for the President's statue. It consisted of a gilet, and cloak which fell behind the back so as to shew the form of the body clear of it. Let it be made of the size of the life.—This is not meant to bring in[to] doubt the original order to make the statue in the real costume, to wi[t,] the military uniform. I must ask the favor of you to pay for it and charge it to me. I must also beg the favor of you to place for me in the hands of Mr. Grand 574^{tt}. the balance of money remitted me by Mr. Drayton of the S. Carolina agricultural society, to be subject in Grand's hands to the draughts of M. Cathalan of Marseilles or to your or my orders. Mr. Mazzei borrowed of me (I think in 1787) 1200^{tt}. From this is to be deducted £8-14-6 3/4 Virga. currency=157^{tt}-2s. which I am to recieve on his account from J. Blair; also the price of a portrait of Castruccio Castracani he was to get for me from Florence. This would reduce the debt to something less than 1000^{tt}. Besides this there was a bond of mine to him, in the hands of Bowden for £146-4-6 paper money=£18-5-7 silver, Virga. currency=329^{tt}. with interest from Nov. 4. 1778. The bond was dated Jan. 29. 1779. I wrote to him to know whether this bond had never been settled between us? If not, whether I was to take credit for it against the 1200^{tt}. or to pay it to Bowden? He can tell you this. If it is not already settled, and I am to take credit for it, it will reduce his debt to me to about 500^{tt}. I wish you could intimate to him (but not as if it came from me) that the expences of sending on my baggage and other calls on my account will exceed the sums which you can command for me, and that therefore it would be convenient if he would pay you the balance whether of 1000^{tt}. or 500^{tt}. or thereabouts as he shall settle it. If he talks of my collecting money here for this balance, the answer is that, if there be any thing to collect, it would oblige me to enter into the settlement of his affairs, which my occupations render impossible. Pardon my troubling you with this business. It is to answer the double purpose of settling with him, and furnishing you with money for my affairs.

Congress separated about a fortnight ago. Your successor will not be named till the session of December.

This goes by the French packet which will sail a few days after my departure. Mr. Remsen will try to find a passenger by whom to send the two copies of the Federalist you desired, so as to avoid postage. The newspapers will give you the news, small and great. I probably shall not write to you again till my return to Philadelphia, unless it be merely to cover a bill of exchange for the President's wine as soon as I recieve it from him. Adieu my dear Sir Your affectionate friend, TH: JEFFERSON

RC (ViW); at head of text: "(private)"; endorsed as received 22 Oct. 1790. PrC (DLC).

Circular to American Consuls

SIR   New York August 26th. 1790

I expected 'ere this to have been able to send you an Act of Congress, prescribing some special Duties and Regulations for the Exercise of the Consular Offices of the United States; but Congress not having been able to mature the Act sufficiently, it lies over to their next Session. In the mean while I beg Leave to draw your Attention to some Matters of Information which it is interesting to receive.

I must beg the Favor of you to communicate to me every six Months, a Report of the Vessels of the United States which enter at the Ports of your District, specifying the Name and Burthen of each Vessel, of what Description she is (to wit, Ship, Snow, Brig &c.), the Names of the Master and Owners, and Number of Seamen, the Port of the United States from which she cleared, Places touched at, her Cargo outward and inward, and the Owners thereof, the Port to which she is bound, and Times of Arrival and Departure; the whole arranged in a Table under different Columns, and the Reports closing on the last Days of June and December.

We wish you to use your Endeavours that no Vessel enter as an American in the Ports of your District which shall not be truly such, and that none be sold under that Name which are not really of the United States.

That you give to me from time to time Information of all military Preparations, and other Indications of War which may take place in your Ports; and when a War shall appear imminent, that you notify thereof the Merchants and Vessels of the United States within your District, that they may be duly on their guard: and in general that you communicate to me such political and commercial Intelligence, as you may think interesting to the United States.

The Consuls and Vice-Consuls of the United States are free to wear the uniform of their navy, if they chuse to do so. This is a deep blue coat with red facings, lining and cuffs, the cuffs slashed and a standing collar; a red waistcoat (laced or not at the election of the wearer) and blue Breeches; yellow buttons with a foul anchor, and black cockades and small swords.

Be pleased to observe that the Vice-Consul of one district is not at all subordinate to the Consul of another. They are equally independent of each other.

The ground of distinction between these two officers is this. Our Government thinks that whatever there may be either of honor or profit resulting from the Consular office, native Citizens are first entitled, where such of proper character will undertake the duties; but where none such offer, a Vice-Consul is appointed of any other Nation. Should a proper native come forward at any future time, he will be named Consul, but this nomination will not revoke the Commission of the Vice-Consul: it will only suspend his functions during the continuance of the Consul within the limits of his jurisdiction, and on his departure therefrom, it is meant that the Vice-Consular authority shall revive of course without the necessity of a re-appointment.[1]

It is understood that Consuls and Vice-Consuls have authority of course to appoint their own Agents in the several ports of their district, and that it is with themselves alone these Agents are to correspond.

It will be best not to fatigue the Government in which you reside, or those in authority under it, with applications in unimportant cases. Husband their good dispositions for occasions of some moment, and let all representations to them be couched in the most temperate and friendly terms, never indulging in any case whatever a single expression which may irritate. I have the honor to be &c.   THOMAS JEFFERSON

FC (DNA: RG 59, PCC No. 121); this text does not contain the paragraph indicated in note 1 below, which is here inserted from the text addressed to vice-consuls; at head of text: "To the Consuls of the United States"; at foot of text there is a list of the consuls to whom this circular was addressed: Joseph Fenwick at Bordeaux; Burrill Carnes at Nantes; Nathaniel Barrett at Rouen; Sylvanus Bourne at Hispaniola; Fulwar Skipwith at Martinique; James Maury at Liverpool; William Knox at Dublin; Edward Church at Bilbao; John Marsden Pintard at Madeira; Joshua Johnson at London; and Ebenezer Brush at Surinam. RC (DNA: RG

59, CD); in hand of Henry Remsen, Jr., with TJ's signature cut away; endorsed in part by its recipient, Joshua Johnson: "Receivd October Answ'd 2 Novemr. [1790] ℔ the Two Brothers Capt. Sely." FC (DNA: RG 59, PCC No. 121); at head of text: "To the Vice-Consuls of the United States"; at foot of text: "To Monsr. De la Motte Vice-Consul at Havre. The Sieur Etienne Cathalan the younger Marseilles. Thomas Auldjo Esquire. Cowes. John Parish. Hamburgh. John Street. Fayal." Not recorded in SJL. Printed text of this circular is in DLC: Silvanus Bourne Papers, being incorporated, along with a text of TJ's circular to the consuls

[424]

of 31 May 1792, in Edmund Randolph's circular of 31 Dec. 1794 referring to the "rule of office" established by TJ in this general communication.

1 This paragraph appears only in the text of the circular that was addressed to vice-consuls.

Jefferson's Opinion on Fiscal Policy

On consideration of the letter of our bankers of Jan. 25. 1790. the Secretary of the Treasury's answer to it, and the draught of powers and instructions to him, I am of opinion, as I always have been, that the purchase of our debt to France by private speculators would have been an operation extremely injurious to our credit; and that the consequence foreseen by our bankers, that the purchasers would have been obliged, in order to make good their paiments, to deluge the market of Amsterdam with American paper of all sorts and to sell it at any price, was a probable one, and the more so as we know that the particular individuals who were engaged in that speculation, possess no means of their own adequate to the paiment they would have had to make. While we must not doubt that these motives, together with a proper regard for the credit of the U.S. had real and full weight with our bankers, towards inducing them to counterwork these private speculations, yet to ascribe their industry in this business wholly to these motives, might lead to a too great and dangerous confidence in them. It was obviously their interest to defeat all such speculations because they tended to take out of their hands, or at least to divide with them, the profits of the great operation of transferring the French debt to Amsterdam, an object of first rate magnitude to them and on the undivided enjoiment of which they might count, if the private speculators could be baffled. It has been a contest of dexterity and cunning, in which our champions have obtained the victory. The manoeuvre of opening a loan of three millions of florins has on the whole been useful[1] to the U.S. and, tho unauthorized, I think should be confirmed. The measure proposed by the Secretary of the Treasury, of sending a superintendant of their future operations, will effectually prevent their doing the like again, and the funding laws leave no danger that such an expedient might at any future time be useful to us.

The report of the Secretary of the treasury, and the draught of instructions present this plan to view. 1. To borrow, on the best terms we can, not exceeding those limited by the law, such a sum as may answer all demands for principal or interest of the foreign debt, due, or to become due before the end of 1791. (This I think he supposed will be about 3 1/2 millions of dollars.) 2. To consider two of the three millions of florins already borrowed by our bankers as, so far, an execution of this operation; consequently that there will remain but about 2 1/2 million of dollars to be borrowed on the old terms. 3. To borrow no more as yet, towards completing the transfer of the French debt to Amsterdam, unless we can do it on more advantageous terms. 4. To consider the 3d. million of florins already borrowed by our bankers, as, so far, an execution of the powers given the President to borrow 2. millions of dollars, by the act of the 12th. of August. The whole of this appears to me to be wise. If the 3d. million be employed in buying up our *foreign paper* on the exchange of Amsterdam, by creating a demand for that species of paper, it will excite a cupidity in the monied men to obtain more of it by new loans, and consequently enable us to borrow more and on lower terms. The savings of interest too of the sum so to be bought, may be applied in buying up more principal, and thereby keep this salutary operation going.

I would only take the liberty of suggesting the insertion of some such clause as the following into the instruction. 'The agent to be employed shall never open a loan for more than one million of dollars at a time, nor open a new loan till the preceding one has been filled, and expressly approved by the President of the U.S.' A new man, alighting on the exchange of Amsterdam, with powers to borrow 12. millions of dollars, will be immediately beset with bankers and brokers, who will pour into his ear, from the most unsuspected quarters, such informations and suspicions as may lead him exactly into their snares. So wonderfully dexterous are they in wrapping up and complicating their propositions, they will make it evident, even to a clear-headed man (not in the habit of this business) that two and two make five. The agent therefore should be guarded, even against himself, by putting it out of his power to extend the effect of any erroneous calculation beyond one million of dollars. Were he able, under a delusive calculation, to commit such a sum as 12. millions of dollars, what would be said of the government? Our bankers told me themselves that they would not chuse, in the conduct of this great loan, to open for more than two or three millions of florins at a time, and certainly never for more than five. By contracting for only one million of dollars at a time, the agent will have frequent occasions of trying to better

Robert Morris moves the Seat of Government to Philadelphia. (See p. xxxiv-xxxvi.)

I. "View of C-o-n-ss on the road to Philadelphia."

II. "Cong-ss Embark'd on board the Ship Constitution of
America bound to Conogocheque by way of Philadelphia."

The Residence Bargain Satirized.

the terms. I dare say that this caution, tho not expressed in the instructions, is intended by the Secretary of the Treasury to be carried into their execution. But perhaps it will be desirable for the President that his sense of it also should be expressed in writing.

TH: JEFFERSON

Aug. 26. 1790.

MS (DNA: RG 59, MLR); entirely in TJ's hand; endorsed by Lear: "The Secretary of State respecting the Loan made by the Agents of the U.S. in Holland." PrC (DLC). FC (DNA: RG 59, SDC). Entry in SJPL reads: "Opn. Th: J. on borrowing money in Holland."

It is clear that this report was drafted on the same day that Washington asked for TJ's opinion about the ratification and acceptance of the loan of 3,000,000 florins that had been opened on 1 Feb. 1790 by W. & J. Willink', N. & J. Van Staphorst, & N. Hubbard in a desperate maneuver by that firm to forestall efforts of speculators to purchase the American debt to France. For the Holland bankers' lengthy explanation of their reasons for that unauthorized action in their letter of 25 Jan. 1790 to the Secretary of the Treasury and Hamilton's brief and necessarily noncommittal response of 7 May 1790, both of which TJ had before him while drafting the above opinion, were only transmitted by Hamilton to Washington in his letter of 26 Aug. 1790 recommending that the President give his sanction to the loan and that authority for this be subsumed under both Acts of Congress of 4 and 12 Aug. 1790, the former authorizing a loan of $12,000,000 and the latter a loan of $2,000,000 (U.S. Statutes at Large, I, 138-44, 186-7; texts of the letters are in Syrett, Hamilton, VI, 210-18, 409-10, 568-70). Washington's POWERS AND INSTRUCTIONS to Hamilton exist in two copies and bear the date 28 Aug. 1790, being therefore presumably later versions than those read by TJ. The former authorized Hamilton under the two Acts to borrow a sum not to exceed $14,000,000 and the latter directed him to limit the loans to the amount needed for principal and interest due on the foreign debt to the end of 1791, unless this could be done for the residue of the debt on terms more advantageous than those existing. The instructions also included the following: "Except where otherwise specially directed by me you shall employ in the negotiation of any Loan or Loans which may be made in any foreign country   "—a blank later filled by the name of William Short (Tr in DLC: Washington Papers; Short's copy has his name in the text, DLC: Short Papers; texts of Washington's letter of authorization and his letter of instructions are in Syrett, Hamilton, VI, 578-80). Some months earlier when Necker, angered by the Amsterdam bankers' move, had pointedly solicited the application of the whole 3,000,000 florins to the debt of the United States to France, Short himself had written Hamilton: "I suppose it useless to repeat here the advantage which might be derived from Congress having some representative in Europe authorized to control their finances at Amsterdam" (Short to Hamilton, 4 Apr. 1790, Syrett, Hamilton, VI, 350; see also, Short to TJ, 7 July 1790). About the same time Gouverneur Morris, acting on TJ's suggestion, appraised the standing of the American banking agents in Holland, concluded that it would not be prudent or right to place fiscal affairs in other hands, and added: "but I am fully convinced of the Propriety of your Idea that the person who may be sent to manage our Affairs there should have full Power to dismiss them if needful" (Morris to TJ, 10 Apr. 1790). TJ took care immediately to place these observations before the President (TJ to Washington, 15 June 1790). Knowing and respecting Morris' ability as a financier, he may have done so in the hope that Morris would be given such a responsibility—a strategy that would have had the double advantage of placing that charge in capable hands and possibly of lessening the claim Morris had to be named minister to Paris in consequence of his agency in England (see documents on the war crisis, Editorial Note).

By this time Washington, Hamilton,

and TJ were all aware of the state of Morris' negotiations in London and the Secretary of the Treasury was far less confident of Morris as an agent than he had been when he recommended him the previous year. Some difficulty over the choice of a fiscal agent must have caused a delay, for the instructions were submitted on the 26th but the blank was not filled with Short's name until the 31st, the day after Washington left New York. On that day Hamilton informed the Secretary of State that the President had expressed to him "a preference of Mr. Shorts being employed, if he could be spared the requisite time from France, without injury to the affairs depending there." He stated to TJ that it would be necessary for Short to proceed at once to Amsterdam and remain there perhaps three months, with occasional journeys thereafter. TJ was of opinion that "Mr. Short might be spared from France without injury to the public service," a judgment which Hamilton accepted as conclusive and, as he reported to Washington, "it only remained for me to fulfil your intention and I accordingly requested him to make proper communication on his part to Mr. Short, and have since transmitted instructions to that Gentleman in conformity to the general tenor of those which I received from you" (Hamilton to Washington, 3 Sep. 1790, Syrett, *Hamilton*, VII, 22-3). Washington approved both the appointment and the instructions (Washington to Hamilton, 18 Sep. 1790, same, VII, 59). Both letters are ambiguous in phraseology and leave room for doubt as to whether Hamilton or Washington proposed Short, though Hamilton's use of the word "preference" suggests that Short's name was not the only one considered. Short was dismayed at the "sudden and unexpected change which took place between the 25th. and 31st. of August" and it may be presumed that TJ, though doing what he could to advance Short's wishes, was quite convinced that it was to his best interest to return to America (Short to TJ, 25 Oct. 1790; TJ to Short, 24 Jan. 1791).

It is very clear, however, that the limitation on amounts of the new loans that TJ suggested and the extensive powers of the fiscal agent that he recommended were adopted. The authorization given by Hamilton to the Amsterdam bankers concerning the loan already opened recited the purpose of the two Acts giving the President power to borrow $14,000,000 in the United States or abroad, declared that the execution of this power had been committed to the Secretary of the Treasury, and concluded: "after due consideration I have concluded to accept and ratify it." This limited the loan to 3,000,000 florins and the covering letter announced the determination to apply half of the sum to the debt to France on instructions from Short. The letter to Short explained these arrangements and directed him to consult "the Secretary of State for instructions with regard to the timing of the intended payment" (Hamilton to the bankers, 28 Aug. 1790, with enclosed powers; Hamilton to Short, 29 Aug. 1790, Syrett, *Hamilton*, VI, 580-6; TJ to Short, 31 Aug. 1790). The choice of Short to negotiate the new loans had not at this time been settled. Three days later, after Washington had named Short as his preference, Hamilton gave the latter full instructions, stating as a primary and principal object of his attention the acquisition of exact knowledge of the state of the money market in Holland, of "the principal houses and brokers concerned in the negotiations of foreign loans; their characters, comparative solidity and influence with the money lenders; the terms upon which their agency is afforded to their employers," and so on, this information to be partly for the use of the Treasury and partly to enable Short to determine whether to continue the former fiscal agents or, if continued, to induce them to meliorate their terms. Hamilton admonished Short to use circumspection, for the agents had risked themselves and their fortunes on American affairs "when the doing it was not without serious hazard." As far as known, he declared, "they deserve well of us. My object is, in entering upon a new stage of our affairs, to have the ground over which we have passed well examined, that we may better judge whether to continue or alter our course." The commission authorized Short to borrow a sum not exceeding $14,000,000 "on behalf of the United States in any part of Europe." The covering letter stipulated that no loan should be opened for more than a million dollars and that no new loan should be undertaken until the previous one had been reported to the President and had received his sanction (Hamilton to Short, 1 Sep. 1790, enclosing commission, Syrett, *Hamilton*, VII, 6-15). These limitations were in accord with a separate instruction from Washington to Hamilton on 26 Aug. 1790, written after he had received TJ's above opinion recommending them. Thus, as is evident from this chronology, Hamilton transmitted his draft of powers and instructions for himself from the President, Washington submitted this draft to the Secretary of State, TJ drew up the above opinion, and Washington gave his sanction to Hamilton's draft, subject to the additional stipulations suggested by TJ—all on the same day, 26 Aug. 1790, a fact which incidentally adds significance to the unusual delay in giving the commission to Short. The separate instruction was transmitted by Tobias Lear to Hamilton and was made necessary, he explained, "for reasons which he [the President] will assign to you" (Lear to Hamilton, 26 Aug. 1790, same, VI, 566; it is this letter which proves that Hamilton had prepared and submitted to Washington the draft of his own powers and instructions).

But it is extremely doubtful that Washington ever informed Hamilton of the fact that TJ was in effect author of the additional instruction, whatever reasons he may have assigned for making it. This assumption is based upon Washington's administrative method and upon events of 1793 involving this opinion. In his Report on Foreign Loans of 13 Feb. 1793, Hamilton attached a copy of Washington's powers and instructions of 28 Aug. 1790 (Syrett, *Hamilton*, VI, 578, 580, notes). Soon afterward he asked for TJ's opinion as to the object to which the loan of 3,000,000 florins had been intended. TJ told Madison that Hamilton had asked for a statement "perhaps to shew it to some friends whom he wished to satisfy as to the original destination of the 3. mill. of florins, and that he meant to revive this subject" (TJ to Madison, 31 Mch. 1793). The reply to Hamilton that he drafted is the famous letter of 27 Mch. 1793 which exists in two states but has only been published in one, with no indication of the important differences in the texts. This has helped confuse attempts to prove TJ's hypocrisy and use of deception (Schachner, *Hamilton*, p. 314) and also attempts at defense (Malone, *Jefferson*, III, 527-8), both of which have missed the central point through failure to note the significant variations between the two drafts of TJ's letter to Hamilton.

In the first draft (rather, a fair copy) of the letter of 27 Mch. 1793, TJ said that he could answer Hamilton's request with more certainty because he happened "to possess a paper" whereon he had "committed to writing some thoughts on the subject at the time, that is to say, on the 26th. of Aug. 1790" (PrC in DLC, with this phrase at head of text in TJ's hand: "not sent"). TJ then took the intended recipient's copy of this text, made extensive alterations in it, and sent it to Madison as the "rough draught" of a letter that he supposed would not answer Hamilton's purpose (MS in DLC: Madison Papers; PrC from the [missing] RC or fair transcript in DLC; this is the text that is printed in previous editions: L & B, IX, 57-9; Ford, VI, 208-9). In this revised text which he dispatched to Hamilton, TJ made a number of alterations and two of these are significant: (1) the "paper" of 26 Aug. 1790 that enabled him to reply with a degree of certainty became "an official paper" and (2) a paragraph was added at the close not in the previous text: "I have thus, Sir, stated to you the view I had of this subject in 1790. and I have done it because you desired it. I did not take it up then as a Volunteer, nor should now have taken the trouble of recurring to it, but at your request, as it is one in which I am not particularly concerned, which I never had either the time or inclination to investigate, and on which my opinion is of no importance." The depreciatory comment at the end obscures the emphatic meaning of the change in the text. The official paper of 26 Aug. 1790 written not as "a Volunteer" could mean only one thing: TJ was informing Hamilton of a fact he surmised the President had never informed him, otherwise he would have known what TJ's opinion in 1790 had been. He was telling him, in brief, that the President had asked for his opinion of Hamilton's draft of instructions and that he gave this to him, as the letter itself stated, two days before Washington issued the powers and instructions to the Secretary of the Treasury on 28 Aug. 1790. As that letter also shows, what TJ had before him as he drafted it so carefully was not a "memorandum" made at the time (Malone, *Jefferson*, III, 527). It was, in fact, the above official opinion, the order and the phraseology of which TJ copied with precision in the letter that Hamilton could not use for his purpose.

For the significant fact, which TJ made quite clear in the 1793 letter, lies in TJ's inference drawn from Washington's final instructions of 1790 to Hamilton, dated but not written two days after the President had received both Hamilton's draft and the above opinion: "I observed that he had therein neither confirmed *your* sentiment of employing a part of the money *here*, nor *mine* of doing it *there*, in purchases of the public debt; but had directed the application of the whole to the *foreign debt*: and I inferred that he had done this of design, and on full and just deliberation, well knowing he would have time enough to weigh the merits of the two opinions, before the million of dollars would be exhausted here, or the loans for the foreign debt over-run their legal measure there. But in this inference I might be mistaken. I cannot be however in the fact that these instructions give a sanction to neither opinion"

(TJ to Hamilton, 27 Mch. 1793, PrC of final text). What TJ was really telling Hamilton was that documentary proof supporting his own and the President's view existed in the form of the above official opinion. Further, as he knew to be the case from having had before him Hamilton's own draft of his powers and instructions when that official opinion was drawn up, he was informing him that he was aware Hamilton could not produce equally valid evidence to substantiate his position. He seemed indeed to be offering the Secretary of the Treasury a challenge to ask the President for such a statement as Hamilton had asked of him, knowing full well that this could no more be done than that Hamilton could find satisfaction in his own response.

On TJ's views concerning the desirability of transferring the American debt from France to Amsterdam, see Vol. 14: 190-209 and the sources cited in Editorial Note; see also W. & J. Willink, N. & J. Van Staphorst, & N. Hubbard to TJ, 24 Sep. 1789.

¹ This word interlined in substitution for "advantageous," deleted.

To Henry Knox

DEAR SIR   New York Aug. 26. 1790.

On the hasty view which the shortness of time permits me to take of the treaty of Hopewell, the act of cession of N. Carolina and the act of acceptance by Congress, I hazard the following sentiments.

Were the treaty of Hopewell, and the act of acceptance of Congress to stand in any point in direct opposition to each other, I should consider the act of acceptance as void in that point: because the treaty is a law made by two parties, and not revocable by one of them either acting alone or in conjunction with a third party. If we consider the acceptance as a legislative act of Congress, it is the act of one party only; if we consider it as a treaty between Congress and N. Carolina, it is but a subsequent treaty with another power, and cannot make void a preceding one, with a different power.

But I see no such opposition between these two instruments. The Cherokees were entitled to the sole occupation of the lands within the limits guaranteed to them. The state of N. Carolina, according to the jus gentium established for America by universal usage, had only a right of preemption of these lands against all other nations. It could convey then to it's citizens only this right of preemption, and the right of occupation could not be united to it till obtained by the U.S. from the Cherokees. The act of cession of N. Carolina only preserves the rights of it's citizens, in the same state as they would have been, *had that act never been passed.* It does not make imperfect titles, perfect; but only prevents their being made worse. Congress, by their act, accept on these conditions. The claimants of N.C. then and also the Cherokees are exactly where they would have been, had neither the act of cession, nor that of acceptance been ever made; that is, the latter possess the right of occupation, and the former the right of preemption.

Tho' these deductions seem clear enough, yet the question would be a disagreeable one between the general government, a particular government, and individuals, and it would seem very desireable to draw all the claims of preemption within a certain limit, by commuting for those out of it, and then to purchase of the Cherokees the right of occupation. I have the honor to be, my dear Sir Your's respectfully & affectionately,   TH: JEFFERSON

RC (MHi: Henry Knox Papers); at foot of text: "The Secretary at war"; endorsed: "Augt. 26. 1790 Mr. Jeffer- son—The treaty of Hopewell." PrC (DLC).

To William Short

DEAR SIR   New York August 26th. 1790

My last Letters to you have been of the 26th. of July and 10th. instant. Yours of May 16th. No. 31. is come to Hand.

I enclose you sundry Papers by which you will perceive that the expression in the 11th. article of our treaty of amity and commerce with France, Vizt. that 'the Subjects of the United States shall not be reputed Aubaines *in France*, and consequently shall be exempted from the droit d'Aubaine, or other similar duty, under what name soever,' has been construed so rigourously to the letter, as to consider us as Aubaines in the *colonies* of France. Our intercourse with those colonies is so great that frequent and important losses will accrue to individuals if this construction be continued. The death of the master or supercargo of a vessel, rendered a more common event by the unhealthiness of the climate, throws all the property which was either his, or under his care, into contest. I presume that the enlightened assembly now engaged in reforming the remains of feudal abuse among them, will not leave so inhospitable an one as the droit d'Aubaine existing in France or any of it's dominions. If this may be hoped, it will be better that you should not trouble the minister with any application for it's abolition in the colonies as to us. This would be erecting into a special favor to us the extinction of a general abuse, which will I presume extinguish of itself. Only be so good as to see that in abolishing this odious law in France, it's abolition in the colonies also be not omitted by mere oversight; but if, contrary to expectations, this fragment of barbarism be suffered to remain, then it will become necessary that you bring forward the enclosed case, and press a liberal and just exposition of our treaty so as to relieve our citizens from this species of risk and ruin hereafter. Supposing the matter to rest on the 11th. article only, it is inconceivable that he who with respect to his personal goods is as a native citizen in the mother country, should be deemed a foreigner in it's colonies. Accordingly you will perceive by the opinions of Doctor Franklin and Dr. Lee two of our ministers who negotiated and signed the treaty, that they considered that rights stipulated for us *in France*, were meant to exist in all the *dominions of France*.

Considering this question under the 2d. article of the Treaty also, we are exempted from the droit d'Aubaine in all the dominions of France. For by that article 'no particular favor is to be granted to any other nation, which shall not immediately become common to the other Party.' Now by the 44th. article of the treaty between France and England, which was subsequent to ours it is stipulated 'que dans tout ce qui concerne — *les successions des biens mobiliers* — les sujets des deux hautes parties contractantes auront *dans les etats respectifs* les memes privileges, libertés et droits, que la nation la plus favorisée.' This gave to the English the general abolition of the droit d'Aubaine enjoyed by the Hollanders under the 1st. article of their treaty with France of July 23. 1773. which is in these words. 'Les sujets des E.G. des P.U. des pays-bas ne seront point assujettis au droit d'Aubaine dans les Etats de S.M.T.C.' This favor then being granted to the English subsequent to our treaty, we become entitled to it of course by the article in question. — I have it not in my power at this moment to turn to the treaty between France and Russia, which was also posterior to ours. If by that the Russians are exempted from the droit d'Aubaine '*dans les Etats* de S.M.T.C..' it is a ground the more for our claiming the exemption. To these you will be pleased to add such other considerations of reason, friendship, hospitality, and reciprocity as will readily occur to yourself.

About two or three weeks ago a Mr. Campbell called on me, and introduced himself by observing that his situation was an awkard one, that he was come from Denmark with an assurance of being employed here in a public character, that he was actually in service though un-announced. He repeated conversations which had passed between Count Bernstoff and him, and asked me when a minister would be appointed to that court, or a character sent to negotiate a treaty of commerce: he had not the scrip of a pen to authenticate himself, however informally. I told him our government had not yet had time to settle a plan of foreign arrangements, that with respect to Denmark particularly, I might safely express to him those sentiments of friendship which our government entertained for that country, and assurances that the king's subjects would always meet with favor and protection here; and in general I said to him those things which being true, might be said to any body. You can perhaps learn something of him from the Baron de Blome. If he be an unauthorized man, it would be well it should be known here, as the respect which our citizens might entertain, and the credit they might give to any person supposed to be honoured by the king's appointment, might lead them into embarrassment.[1]

You know the situation of the new loan of three millions of florins going on at Amsterdam. About one half of this is destined for an immediate payment to France; but advantage may be gained by judiciously timing the payment. The french colonies will doubtless claim in their new constitution a right to receive the necessaries of life from whoever will deliver them cheapest; to wit, grain, flour, live stock, salted fish and other salted provisions. It would be well that you should confer with their deputies guardedly, and urge them to this demand if they need urging. The justice of the National Assembly will probably dispose them to grant it, and the clamours of the Bordeaux merchants may be silenced by the clamours and arms of the Colonies. It may co-operate with the influence of the colonies if favorable dispositions towards us can be excited in the moment of discussing this point; it will therefore be left to you to say when the payment shall be made, in confidence that you will so time it as to forward this great object:

and when you make this payment you may encrease it's effect, by adding assurances to the minister that measures are taken which will enable us to pay up within a very short time all arrears of principal and interest now due; and further that congress has fully authorized our government to go on and pay even the balance not yet due, which we mean to do if that money can be borrowed on reasonable terms, and that favorable arrangements of commerce between us and their colonies might dispose us to effect that payment with less regard to terms. You will of course find excuses for not paying the money which is ready and put under your orders, till you see that the moment is arrived when the emotions it may excite may give a decisive cast to the demands of the colonies.[2]

The newspapers as usual will accompany the present. I have the honor to be with great esteem and attachment Dear Sir Your most obedient & most humble Servt.,   TH: JEFFERSON

Dft (Lloyd W. Smith, Madison, N.J., 1946); in TJ's hand except for text *en clair* of the paragraph in code (see note 2, below), which is in the hands of Remsen and Taylor and is accompanied by a sheet containing the code symbols in Taylor's hand, the last addressed by TJ: "Mr. Remsen" and endorsed by Remsen: "*Cyphers* in the Letter to Mr. Short August 26. 1790." RC (NjP); in Remsen's hand, signed by TJ, with interlinear decoding in Short's hand; endorsed by Short as received 22 Oct. 1790. FC (DNA: RG 59, PCC No. 121). Enclosures: (1) Memorial signed by Stephen Gorham and fifty-two other merchants of Boston to the President and Senate setting forth their alarm "at the appearance of a disposition in some of the [French] Islands to infringe and misconstrue an important article [in the treaty of amity and commerce], which in its future operation must impede, if not totally annihilate, the amicable and advantageous commerce which ought to subsist" between them and the United States. The memorialists stated that Article XI was intended to apply to the French dominions; that "upon the faith of this rational presumption strengthened by Legislative sanction" on the part of Massachusetts, many persons in that state had "ventured their capitals in the French Islands . . . formed commercial establishments and . . . embarked in a more extensive and flourishing commerce than actually subsists

between America and Old France"; and that "under the pretence that the [eleventh] Article must be literally restricted to the Kingdom of France, the most minute and trifling articles of . . . property [of those Americans who have died in the colonies] have been seized by the officers of Government and appropriated to the public use." The following two paragraphs in the memorial were not included in the copy enclosed in the above letter to Short, as indicated by marginal note in FC: "That should this construction be suffered to prevail the Americans residing in the Colonies will be compelled to withdraw their persons and effects, or contract new ties of allegiance with the King of France inconsistent with their duty and affection for their native Country, to which under the present administration they have every cause to feel new and increasing attachments.—It is however with peculiar satisfaction that your Memorialists can now prefer their petition to a supreme and competent authority which possesses energy to enforce it's remonstrances, and a disposition to extend its ample protection to it's affectionate and dutiful constituents." (2) Affidavit of James Perkins, Jr., 22 Apr. 1790, stating that he was merchant of Boston who for about seven years had resided chiefly at Cap François; that he had "particularly and with anxious concern noticed the conduct of the Government in that Island, in respect to the property and effects of

Americans dying there; that on the deaths of "Mr. James Dennie, formerly of Boston . . . a Mr. George Richardson . . . [and] Mr. Silas Cook Brenton late of Newport," their most minute effects had been seized and converted to public use; and that, on Perkins' protest and calling Article XI to the attention of the judge and attorney general, they replied that the article did not apply to the islands. (3) Letter from Sartine, the Minister, 1 Jan. 1777, to the councils at Port au Prince and Cap François, stating that it was erroneous to conclude that "en vertu des traités conclus avec diverses puissances le droit d'aubaine est aboli aux Colonies comme il est en Europe." (4) Letter from Sartine, 25 July 1779, to the council of Cap François concerning differences of opinion over the subject and declaring: "C'est un principe certain que les traités pour l'abolition du droit d'aubaine n'ont aucune application aux Colonies." (5) Letter from James Perkins, Jr., to Benjamin Franklin, Boston, 7 Jan. 1790, calling attention to Article XI and asking "whether this *local* application was the design of the contracting parties." (6) Benjamin Franklin to Perkins, Philadelphia, 19 Jan. 1790, reading in part: "I was indeed one of the Commissioners on the part of the United States for making that treaty, but the Commissioners have no right now to explain the treaty. Its explanation is to be sought for in its own words, or in case it cannot be clearly found there, then by an application to the contracting powers.—I certainly conceived that when the *Droit d'aubaine* was relinquished in favor of the citizens of the United States, the relinquishing clause was meant to extend to all the dominions of his most Christian Majesty, and I am of opinion that this would not be denied if an explanation were requested of the Court of France: and it ought to be done if any difficulties arise on this subject in the French Islands, which their Courts do not determine in our favor. But before our Congress is petitioned to make such request, I imagine it may be proper to have the case tried, in some of the French Islands, and the petition made in consequence of a determination against us." (7) Samuel A. Otis to Arthur Lee, 13 Jan. 1790, asking his opinion on the subject in behalf "of a friend in the West Indies." (8) Arthur Lee to Samuel A. Otis, 21 Jan. 1790, reading in part: "The words of the treaty furnish no answer to his [Perkins'] question direct and decisive. I do not remember any discussion on the subject. It was taken for granted that as the object of the treaty was to encourage commercial intercourse . . . and the abolition of this right was one means of encouraging it, it's being abolished in France would necessarily abolish it in her Colonies who derived it from her.—I am much inclined to believe that the Court of France will give this interpretation to that article." FC's of all of the foregoing are to be found in DNA: RG 59, PCC No. 121. The deletion of the two paragraphs in the first enclosure was as obviously TJ's doing as the suggested approach to the French court on the abolition of THIS FRAGMENT OF BARBARISM and the timing of payment on the French debt was characteristic of his method in diplomacy.

[1] TJ wrote "embarrasment" and one of his clerks, George Taylor, inserted a caret and added an additonal s.

[2] This paragraph is in code and Short's interlinear decoding has been verified by the Editor with partially reconstructed key to Code No. 10.

From Le Mesurier & Cie.

Le Havre, 27 Aug. 1790. Enclose duplicate of theirs of 23rd by the ship *Citoyen.* TJ's effects arrived on 25th from Rouen. "To save time, as the Ship Henrietta was kept in waiting and to prevent the Furniture's being tumbled, we obtained a permit from the Custom House to Ship the Cases on board Capt. Weeks without landing, and were proceeding in that manner Yesterday morning, when a great number of people assembled and by force Obliged us to land the greatest part of the Effects. We applied to our Municipality who endeavoured by agreement to dissuade the Populace from insisting on having the Cases opened, but their endeavours being fruitless, we requested a Piquet from the National Guards to keep order and proceeded to the examination in the face of the multitude. You have a note hereunder of the Cases that were examined, and we hope that the Busts have received no damage tho' we are sensible they are not repacked in so compleat a manner as when the Case left Paris. However we were ourselves present at the opening and handling of the contents of every Package, resolved as we were that no shadow of doubt should remain on the minds of the most ignorant of the regularity and fairness of every declaration. By the time we came to the opening of the eight Package the Ringleaders of the Tumult had sneaked off and we were enabled to close the business. This day we have embarked the whole, and inclosed you have the Bill of Lading of the 78 Packages shipt for Philadelphia on board the Henrietta, Captn. Weeks, the remaining Eight Packages shall be sent by the first Vessel for Virginia. We shall send our Account Charges to Mr. Short and draw on him for the amount.—We understand the populace had been excited against the passengers on board the Citoyen and foolishly imagined your Effects belonged to them and must of course contain a great deal of specie. Considering no mischief has ensued, we are not sorry the examination has taken place, for otherwise no power on earth could have dissuaded the people from their prevention, whilst now the most violent are both ashamed and convinced."—The British fleet "of 31 Sail of the Line sailed last week from Torbay, and it is said the Spanish Fleet remains at sea." [In postscript:] "Packages Opened. No. 7, 8, 14, 32, 57, 77, 82." The two carriages, shipped from Rouen on second lighter, not yet arrived, must be sent to Virginia with six other packages, or by Philadelphia ship if one offers earlier. Invoice enclosed.

RC (DLC). Recorded in SJL as received 22 Nov. 1790. Dupl (DLC). Not recorded in SJL. Enclosures: (1) Le Mesurier & Cie. to TJ, 22 (not 23 as stated above) Sep. 1790. (2) The preliminary list or invoice of the 86 parcels. Short's letters of 4 and 15 Aug. were addressed to TJ under a double cover, with the preliminary invoice under the first. Short instructed Le Mesurier & Cie. to open it, copy off the items for Virginia, and then forward the original with the letters to TJ (Short to Le Mesurier & Cie., 16 Aug. 1790, and their reply, 13 Sep. 1790; DLC: Short Papers).

Le Mesurier & Cie. also described the actions of the mob to Short and gave the firm's assurance that "nothing has been pilferr'd or . . . damaged in any shape." They added that parcels Nos. 77 and 78 containing "the Marble Pedestals . . . were compleatly unpack'd, being suspected from their weight to contain money. The three Busts No 32 have likewise been unpack'd. The other packages opened were Books and wearing apparel. On the whole no mischief has been done and Mr. Jefferson's character has appeared in its proper light in the eyes of an inflam'd and ignorant Multitude, whose passions had been excited against the Passengers on board the Citoyen which sailed a few days ago and who foolishly imagined these Effects belonged to the same persons." They also stated that the workmen employed to open and repack the cases had caused "a few extra charges" but they said these would prove trifling (Le Mesurier & Cie. to Short, 27 [i.e. 29] Aug. 1790; DLC: Short Papers). The variations between the firm's letters to Short and those to TJ arouse conjecture. If, as stated to Short, the mob thought the parcels belonged to the passengers on the *Citoyen*, it is difficult to see how TJ's character could have been brought into question. The disappearance of the ringleaders, the fact that the cost of unpacking and repacking fell upon the innocent party, the random selection of parcels with the heaviest being brought ashore presumably before the mob could have had its suspicions fixed on them because of weight, and above all the failure of the consignee to oppose the examination of parcels on the ground that they were being shipped under diplomatic passport—these and other facts all point to the probability that Le Mesurier's explanation to TJ was the true one: that is, that the examination resulted in allaying suspicions. They also suggest that the affair may have been preconceived by those having access to a complete invoice of goods, and so prearranged in order to divert well-grounded public suspicion from the secretive exportation of gold and objects of wealth by émigrés. Diplomatic passports were neither inviolate nor above suspicion, of course: John Adams related how his friend "Count Sarsfield, one of the most learned and sensible French Noblemen" he had ever known, once asked him in London to permit him to import mirrors under his diplomatic privileges. Adams replied that he had never done such a thing in any country and could not do it then. Sarsfield said that he had expected such an answer, and added: "Il ne vaut pas, un sous d'etre votre Ami" (Adams to Dr. Walsh, 10 Oct. 1790; FC in MHi: AM).

From William Short

DEAR SIR   Paris August 27th. 1790

The diplomatic committee made their report the day before yesterday on the subject of the Family-compact. It was extensive and eloquent of which you will easily be persuaded when you know that Mirabeau was the author. Still there did not appear a perfect accord between the principles laid down in the report and the decree proposed by the committee in consequence of them. It was said that there was 'l'espérance presque certaine que la paix ne sera pas troublée' — 'que le territoire de l'Amérique en question n'appartient ni à l'Angleterre ni à l'Espagne' — and still they propose that the assembly should vote an augmentation of their ships in commission to thirty. As England does not claim the territory it would seem as if the committee meant to decide that Spain was in the wrong.

The committee did not confine the result of their report to what regarded the family-compact alone. They proposed that the assembly should decree that all treaties heretofore made with other nations should be considered as binding until they should be changed 'd'après le travail qui sera fait à cet egard, et les instructions que le Roi sera prié de donner à ses agens auprès des differentes puissances de l'Europe' and that in the mean time these powers should be informed that a regard for peace being the basis of the constitution of France, the nation cannot acknowlege any other stipulations made in the treaties except such as are merely defensive and commercial.

The report was after some deliberation adjourned to yesterday for further discussion. It was debated the whole day, and ended in adopting all the propositions relative to Spain, and omitting the two articles mentioned relative to treaties in general, as not being the proper moment for taking them up. The number of vessels is increased as you will see by the decree which I inclose you from thirty to forty-five ships of the line.

It is to be remarked that this decree was adopted almost unanimously and warmly supported by many of the *enragés* as they are called who have for some time past been the loudest in their cries against supporting Spain, and in pretending that the quarrel with England was merely to draw France into war in hopes of turning their attention from the object which at present occupies them, and which is so formidable to all the courts of Europe, the establishment of a free constitution.

The continued activity of the British armaments notwithstanding the signature of the declarations at Madrid, and the profound secrecy with which the British cabinet have enveloped their designs, are the causes of this sudden change in the minds of the popular party here. I should have feared that Spain had already taken arrangements with England, either commercial or political, which would render the measure adopted yesterday by the assembly inadequate to the preservation of the family-compact. But the pleasure which manifested itself on the countenance of the Spanish Ambassador on being informed of the decree, makes me hope that the negotiations were less advanced than had been suspected. This hope is strengthened also by the report mentioned in my last, by the unremitting activity which both nations have observed in their naval preparations, and by the circumstance of both their fleets being now at sea. The English fleet consists of thirty one ships of the line commanded by Admiral Howe. It is generally supposed it will return after a short cruise and that it will not go further than the bay of Biscay.

Within these few days accounts have been received of several regiments in the different garrisons which had disbanded, having returned to their quarters, shewn marks of repentance, and declared their determination to observe the most exact discipline in future. This is an agreeable symptom for the present, but little hope can be founded on a discipline that depends on the mere will of the soldiery. And it is certain that there is no where a sufficient degree of force placed in the present government for inforcing discipline in the army, or the preservation of order in the nation.

The continuance of peace between the Kings of Hungary and Prussia is preserved by the result of the negotiations of Reichein-bach, which you will have seen in the papers I forwarded you on the 22d. Since then we have had no demonstrations of the designs of the Prussian cabinet relative to Russia. The Empress, however, as cannot be doubted, will be forced to a peace, and if we may judge from the known dispositions of her present antagonists, it will be on humiliating and disadvantageous terms. A Congress is to meet at the Hague, for completing the preliminaries signed at Reicheinbach relative to the low countries. Count de Mercy goes there on behalf of the King of Hungary. One would suppose that the Belgick Congress would give up all hopes of resisting the award of such powerful arbitrators. Still their publications breathe nothing but resistance and war and they lose no opportunity of attacking the Austrian troops when they meet with them.

Since my last I have had a conversation with one of the members of the committee of impositions, who is charged with that part of the report which regards tobacco. I expected it would have been proposed to the assembly before this time. The day had been fixed, but as yet it has been delayed. The final result, and that to which the committee adheres with obstinacy is to allow the cultivation of tobacco in France without any kind of restraint. Its sale and manufacture also, (I speak of that made in France) is to be entirely free.

As to foreign tobacco it is to be subjected to a regie—viz. the nation is to be the sole purchaser and manufacturer of it. In their words the nation is to keep "la seule boutique du tabac étranger." They calculate that the increase of this cultivation in France will diminish considerably its importation. They suppose that the nation will pay three millions for the first purchase of this article, and that they will sell it after being manufactured in such a manner as to have fourteen millions clear. They intend to take on the account of the nation the machines for the manufacture of this article which at present belong to the farmers general, and they hope by the superiority of their manufacture to find a certain sale for what they purchase. They agree, however, that there are no data which warrant their calculation of fourteen millions. They present it to the assembly as the means of obtaining their assent to the scheme of abolishing the present prohibition to the culture of tobacco in France.

They are all sensible of the defects of this plan, but they say that its connexion with other subjects rendered any other result impossible. For instance, the province of Alsace being a frontier, and not too well disposed to the revolution, it was absolutely necessary not to render them absolutely hostile, and particularly as they are the neighbours to those German Princes whose intrigues in foreign Cabinets against the present revolution are known and feared here. Alsace has hitherto enjoyed the privilege of cultivating tobacco, and relative to that article was considered as a foreign country. There were barriers kept up between that Province and France to prevent the introduction of that article. At present those internal barriers are every where to be demolished. Alsace will therefore be a part of France under every consideration. It is impossible under the pretext of rendering its inhabitants free to deprive them of a privilege which they enjoyed under the reign of despotism, (the cultivation of tobacco) and to which they are attached in proportion to the rigour with which it was prohibited in France.—Besides it is observed that every freeman has a right (which no legislature is authorized to violate) of cultivating on his own soil whatever he may judge proper.

These are the considerations which lead to abolishing the farm of tobacco as to France: And as this is sacrificing a revenue of thirty two millions, the committee think themselves bound to adopt that plan which holds out the greatest prospect of gain on foreign tobacco. They are fully convinced that that is by a national regie, and consequently absolutely decided to propose it to the assembly.

There will be the same conflict in the assembly that there was in the committee—viz. one party will think that no consideration can warrant the loss of a revenue of thirty two millions at the present moment and will be therefore for preserving the farm of tobacco in its present situation.—A few will be sufficiently enlightened to see that the advantages to be derived to their manufactures and agriculture, and the revenue which would result from admitting the article of tobacco as a means of commerce with the United States, and receiving the duty in the ports, are much more than sufficient to overbalance the plan of the regie which proposes a certain exclusion of the American commerce so far as it concerns tobacco, and offers only an uncertain revenue, or at least one not more certain than that proposed under the idea of the article being of free commerce. A third party and I fear the more numerous one will be for adopting the plan of the committee. Almost all the plans of the committees are adopted without discussion, arising from the lassitude of the assembly and their fear of only retarding without bettering the system, if they reject such plans as have undergone a long and laborious examination by their committees.

It seems to me unavoidable that this plan, if adopted, will place the article of tobacco on a worse footing than it has ever been. The regie will necessarily keep the imported tobacco at so high a price as to encourage its cultivation. That made in Alsace is of an inferior quality and consequently could not enter into competition with ours for the use of the rich, but I am well assured, and by persons not suspect, that many parts of the southern provinces produce this article of a quality much superior to ours. Mr. Alexander, whom you know, and who is here at present told me that he had known tobacco made at Clairac to sell as high as a guinea the pound. Under these considerations the quantity of our tobacco consumed must exceedingly diminish and besides as the nation is to keep the regie, and has determined to adopt this scheme merely to recover as great a part as possible of the thirty two millions without any regard to commercial advantages, they will necessarily exempt themselves from those conditions to which the farmers general were subjected in their modes of purchase and make use of every means of getting the most tobacco possible for the three millions they propose laying out in the first purchase.

I have gone into this long detail Sir, on the change to which this article will probably be subjected, because I know it will be very unexpected in America. I am persuaded your knowlege of this business will enable you to see clearly that nothing which could have been done by a foreign minister here could have avoided it: and that as to yourself you will have no doubt that every thing which could be done has been done. But as it is probably expected in America that the present revolution should remove the shackles of commerce, and consequently increase that with the United States, I fear an unacquaintance with all the subjects with which this business is connected may induce some to suppose that it might have been avoided by proper exertions, and of course attribute it to a want of zeal or exertion in me. I hope therefore if this should be the case that you will do me the justice to represent this matter in its true light. I need not repeat here what I have mentioned to you before that your memorial was put into the hands of the committee, that I have fortified it by a variety of considerations which the present circumstances suggest and that the Marquis de la fayette has exerted his customary zeal in this business.

I think a short time will open their eyes on this business, and that when they have experienced the error they will be disposed to correct it.

I beg you to accept assurances of the sentiments with which I am, dear Sir, Your friend & servant,   W. SHORT

FC (DNA: RG 59, DD). PrC (DLC: Short Papers); at head of text: "No. 40." Recorded in SJL as received 15 Dec. 1790.

From Ezra Stiles

SIR   Yale College Augt. 27th. 1790.

Be pleased to accept my Thanks for the printed Copy of the Report of the Secretary of State upon the Subject of a national Uniformity of Weights, Measures and Coins, which you did me the Honor to send me last Post. I had before read it as published in the Papers; and was so extremely pleased with it as a philosophic Production that I immediately communicated it to the higher Classes of the Students, [advising?] them to pay Attention to it, as what would probably [meet wi]th general Reception thro' the United States: and [particul]arly led them to see the Certainty and Sufficient Immutability of the *Pendulum* Standard, especially the second Rod, on 45th Deg. of Latitude; and of the *cubic Foot of Rain Water* in Cellar Temperature as the National Standard of Weights.

Some years ago you was pleased to ask me my Authority for asserting that the Roman Imperial Debt was over in the Times of the Caesars 300 Mill. Sterg. I hoped to have been able to refer to classic originals: and taking time to search for this, has occasioned my delay. In truth I had it from second hand. In a Minute which I extracted in 1763 from one of the Folio Volumes of the General Genealogical History or rather Biography, I find that "when Vespasian came to the Empire, he told the Senate that he found the Public Debt . . . Sesterces, computed to be about three hundred Millions Sterling. Adrians Remission to the People, which rendered him so popular as by S.C. to be Voted Pater Patriae, was about Twenty two Millions 500 Thousand Golden Crowns." A similar

Account is to be found in Eckards Roman History, but without referring to classic Authority. We have not the General Genealogical Dictionary in New Haven, nor have I read it since I lived at Newport, when I found it in the public Redwood Library. But according to my Recollection the original Roman Historian is not referred to in that Author. However, I do not doubt but it may be found. I had very much finished my reading of the Greek and Roman and other Antient History in Course 30 years ago. After finishing this Course we look into [de]tached parts of History pro re natâ and as referred to by second[ary and] subsequent Authors. For above 27 years past I have [not searched?] formally for and had thot I could easily advert to the Passage, [and have?] also searched for other Historical accounts of the Times, and Manner of extinguishing that national Debt of 300 Mill. but thro' incessant Interruptions and want of Time for a thoro' Search, I have hitherto failed. Some one will find it, and will wonder that it should be overlookt. We too must content ourselves with perusing the modern inaccurate and injudicious Retailers of ancient History neglecting the original Historians, whether in the original Languages or their Translations. I have repeatedly told some of my senior Pupils in their Course of reading antient History especially the roman, to look out for this historical Fact, but they read only the modern Writers or Compilers of antient History, and I have failed here also. It must be some ingenious young Classical Scholar so good a linguist and of so classical a Taste, as to read the Roman Historians in the Original. It is such an one only who can be charged with this Examination. We have good Classical Scholars, but none that have gone to the fountains for their Antient History. I have heretofore gone over the greater part of the Latin and Greek Historians, in their Originals, and had I leisure even in Old Age, would read them through again, for I am very sick of your Gibbons's, Robertsons, Rollin the best of them. They are at best but Manuductions and should be read with a Constant Recourse to the Original Authors as to principal Characters, and Descriptions of great public Events. Purius et Forte bibuntur Aquae. I expect your Sagacity and indefatigable Attention and thoro' Researches will ascertain this matter. And should you find it, I shall be obliged by the Communication.

I am rejoyced that the United States are honored with your Counsels and Abilities in the high Department of the Secretary of State. This I say without Adulation, who am a Spectator only and a most cordial Friend to the Liberties and Glory of the American Republic, tho' without the least Efficiency or Influence in its Councils. There are four Characters which I cannot flatter; their Merit is above it. Such are those of a Franklin, an Adams, an Ellsworth, a Jefferson and a Washington. I glory in them all; I rejoice that my Country is happy in their useful Labors. And for yourself I can only wish, that when that best of Men, the present President, shall be translated to the World of Light, a Jefferson may succede him in the Presidency of the United States. Forgive me this Effusion of the Sentiments of sincere Respect and Estimation, and permit me the honor of Subscribing myself, Dear Sir, Your most affectionate, Obliged, & Hble Servt,

EZRA STILES

RC (CtY); mutilated, and some words conjecturally supplied; endorsed by TJ as received 31 Aug. 1790 and so recorded in SJL.

From George Washington

DEAR SIR   Friday Morning 27th. July [i.e. Aug.] 1790

Enclosed is the report (I mentioned to you on our Passage to Rhode-Island) of the Officer who was directed to explore the Navigation of Big Beaver &c.—When you have read, and taken such extracts from it as you may be inclined to do, please to return the papers to me, as they will have a place with some other Papers I mean to take with me to Virginia.

The short and rough Extracts also enclosed, were taken at the time of reading another report of the Ouabash River Navigation. Yrs. &c.,   G W——N

RC (DLC); misdated and corrected by TJ both on the letter and in SJL entry; addressed: "Mr. Jefferson"; endorsed as received 27 Aug. 1790 and so recorded in SJL.

For six years TJ and Washington had corresponded about the great object of tapping the "source of wealth and power . . . from the Western country" by way of the Potomac and Ohio rivers to Lake Erie (TJ to Washington, 15 Mch. 1784; Washington to TJ, 1 Jan. 1788; see also Madison to TJ, 9 Jan. 1785). Now the threat of war between Spain and England, the increasing impatience of the western inhabitants at the closure of the Missis-

sippi, the growing danger that disaffected persons in that region would look to England or to Spain for the securing of their vital interests, the decision to locate the permanent residence of government on the Potomac, the restiveness of the Indians in the Northwest, and the rumors of military preparations in Detroit for a possible descent on Spanish territory—all of these public and some private interests brought the subject again to the fore. The journey to Rhode Island offered perhaps the first opportunity the two men had had in some years to discuss the results of Washington's various efforts to procure information about navigation to Lake

Erie (see Washington to Richard Butler, 26 Nov. 1786 and 10 Jan. 1788; to William Irvine, 10 Jan. and 31 Oct. 1788, *Writings*, ed. Fitzpatrick, *Writings*, XXIX, 89, 369-71; XXX, 123; Freeman, *Washington*, VI, 23-6). Immediately on their return Washington's first business was connected with such information, but with military not commercial objectives—that of planning the expedition against the Indians (see note, TJ's second opinion, 29 Aug. 1790, Document XI in group of documents on the war crisis).

Washington and TJ had also long been interested in the approach to Lake Erie by way of the Big Beaver creek; the latter looked forward to the improvement of the navigation of the Potomac and the Ohio and to the junction of the Big Beaver and the Cuyahoga by canal as likely to "spread the feild of our commerce . . . Westwardly . . . beyond any thing ever yet done by man" (TJ to Madison, 8 Dec. 1784; TJ to Washington, 6 Apr. 1784). In DLC: TJ Papers, 56: 9541, attached to Rittenhouse to TJ, 2 July 1790, there is a leaf of notes in Rittenhouse's hand giving the boundaries of Pennsylvania, with particular distances and locations of intersections of the western boundary with Little Beaver creek and with the branches of Big Beaver. But it is unlikely that TJ received this document in 1790, for it seems to belong to the period 1786-1787 when he was engaged in revising the map for *Notes on Virginia* and was urgently requesting information about the western boundary (see TJ to Page, 4 May 1786; TJ to Hopkinson, 14 Aug. 1786; see also Rittenhouse to TJ, 28 Sep. 1785 and 8 Nov. 1788).

E N C L O S U R E   I

Jonathan Heart to Josiah Harmer

SIR

The big Beaver empties into the Ohio 29 miles below Fort Pitt, is 150 yards wide at the mouth, gradually decreasing in width to the crossings at the Mahooning Town, which is about 85 miles by water from its mouth; at this crossing it is 100 yards wide. From the mouth of Beaver to the Block House at the foot of the Falls 3 1/2 miles good water. Up the first Falls 1 1/2 mile; to foot of second or upper Falls 1/2 mile gentle current up the second Falls one mile much more rapid and rocky than the first—along the first Falls high Hills adjoin the River on west side—the banks on the East side a gentle slope from the water edge rising back to a white oak flatt—level flatts on both sides along the gentle current between the lower and upper Falls—high and impassable Hills adjoin the River on East side, level flatt on west side along the upper Falls—a good road may be made from the Block House along the East side, crossing to the west side at the gentle current, thence along the west side to the head of the upper Falls, and indeed the Country is good for roads in general to the crossings of Beaver above Kaskaskias, and thence to the crossings 11 miles above the Pennsylvania Line; from the head of the Falls the waters are gentle for 6 miles thence more rapid and many Islands; for 10 miles high Hills adjoining the River on both sides—thence very good water to the crossing 11 miles above the Pennsylvania Line—the banks generally stoney not subject to being washed away—bed of the River stone and gravel—in no place less than four feet of water except at the Crossing above Kaskaskias where there was only 3 1/2 feet—it is however to be observed the River was 3 1/2 feet higher than when Ens. McDowel reconnoitred it—the information of a Mr. Wilson who may be depended on assures that when there is water sufficient to come to the crossing 11 miles above the Pennsylvania Line as above mentioned, there is also sufficient to go up to the Mahooning Town which is 30 miles by water tho' only 15 1/2 by Land south 80 west—from Mahooning Town at the crossing of Cayahoga to the standing stone 24 miles N. 77 west—the Country very level no Hills, generally white oak flatt some low wet Lands, but not swampy—one bad stream which the present path crosses three times, but by going a little round, the path will be much better and twice crossing avoided. The Cayahoga at the standing Stone is 50 yards wide rapid and difficult crossing, 1 1/2 mile below, the River is only 25 feet wide, high solid banks and a Bridge easily made across. The Cayahoga from the standing Stone is very rapid for 2 1/2 miles, thence gentle 5 miles, thence a continual descent by stages of 10 to 20 feet perpendicular Falls, for 4 miles, thence rapid to the crossings at the old Cayahoga Town which is three miles more. From the Standing Stone by land to Cayahoga Town 11½ miles S. 60 west and very good Lands for roads except a few spots of low swamp. The River at Cayahoga Town is 50 yards wide and 6 feet depth at the crossings which from information is 3 feet higher than in common summer seasons. The old Cayahoga Town stood on the south side of the River on an Eminence beautifully situated at the bend of the River, where it turns quick to the N.W. which is the general course of it; from this place to the Lake is about 45 miles by land and double that distance by water; the common current at this time the rate of 5 miles an hour. At 11 miles from the Town commences what is called the upper rapids, and continue 4 miles at the rate of 8 miles an hour— at one place are rocky difficult and dangerous. At the foot of those rapids met two loaded canoes which the Indians said they could push up to the head of the rapids by sunset which was about three hours. The Indian who piloted me down said the rapids were much more difficult at this stage of the water than when either higher or lower—22 miles still lower down are the lower rapids which continue also about 4 miles, are neither so rapid or difficult as the upper. From thence to the Moravian Town is 20 miles. From Cayahoga Town to this place which is called the head of navigation, depth of water from 6 to 10 feet and 70 yards wide. From this place to the mouth which is 20 miles, depth of water from 10 to 15 feet and widens to 200 yards and becomes a little more gentle before it reaches the Lake. At the very entrance into the Lake, not more than 100 yards wide and scarcely water at this time for a Canoe to pass into the Lake, which is always the case during and immediately after a north west wind, though at other times large vessels can come in. The Cayahoga is exceeding rapid and crooked, continually meandring from one side to the other of an extensive bottom; the banks low, rich and loose soil subject to washing; great quantities of Trees and drift wood in the bends, which in places, nearly obstructs the passage, and added to the rapidity makes the navigation dangerous. The bed of the River is generally a gravel and sand, very few rocks either in the River or along shore. The Indians who live along the River and particularly a Chippewa Chief, says when the Delawares lived at Cayahoga Town, he has often been up the River with Canoes for the French Traders, that they could push a Canoe from the mouth to the Town in 4 days, that he had often done it, and that except very dry seasons there was water sufficient for large Canoes to go up loaded. The lands at the mouth of Cayahoga on west side, low bottom for great distance, on East side high flatt, no heighth in commanding distance. From the mouth of Cayahoga to Presq' isle is near 100 miles. At 35 miles distance is a large River called Cheauga, rises between the waters of Beaver and Cayahoga is as large as the Cayahoga, much better entrance into it and did not appear so rapid. The Indians who live on the River say it is not rapid and that it is but a little way from the salt Springs to where the river is canoeable. One of the Delawares who was with me says he went up with a large canoe three days when the Corn was in blossom. There are other considerable Streams which empty into the Lake but none of them are likely to afford a water communication except this. The information of different Indians say that from Cayahoga Town across south to the head waters of the Muskingum is only 6 miles, that canoes can go down from that to the mouth. A Mr. Wilson who is well acquainted along the Lake and whose information may be depended on, says there is a path from the Salt Springs in a direct course to the mouth of Cayahoga, which path is along high ridges except one swamp which is not very bad; that the distance is about 50 miles—that the path from the standing Stone to the Moravian Town is only 25 miles and through lands capable of making good roads, though in places low and wet.

With respect to the communication between the Lake and the waters of French Creek, Presq' isle is an excellent harbour, and the only good one between Niagara and Detroit on the south shore of the Lake—from Presq' isle to Le Beuf is 15 miles through high heavy timbered Country and very wet at some seasons, but is by no means a Swamp, as has been by some represented—from thence to the mouth of French Creek is 40 miles by land and 65 by water, a crooked Stream, rapid as well as shallow in some places, but no where dangerous or very difficult; high Hills come into the river and at some places rocky shores. When there is water in the Allegany to come to the mouth of French Creek, with very little difficulty the same Boat may be carried to Le Beuf. A Mr. Hulings who has been long acquainted with these waters, says he has been at Le Beuf with a boat of 3 1/2 Ton burthen while that Post was in possession of the British. In September 1787 the Commissioners who run the Northern Line of Pennsylvania went up French Creek with very large Canoes, and during my residence at Fort Franklin, Canoes often went up; the information of all agree that from the mouth 3 miles up is much the most difficult in the whole distance to Le Beuf, and this by no means impracticable.

With respect to Chattaucq Lake, the Allegany waters continue to the mouth of the Connewago branch much the same as below, as to depth and rapidity, from the mouth of French Creek to Connewago is 80 miles, thence up the Connewago for 10 miles the waters are shallow and rapid, not Canoeable during summer season—from thence to the upper end of Chattaucq Lake is about 60 miles good water—from thence by Land is only 9 miles and good lands for a road, indeed there has formerly been a good waggon road, but it [is] agreed by all that there is no harbour even for Boats, and much less for vessels, being high and rocky banks along the Lake for great distance. The waters of the Allegany below the mouth of French Creek are too well known to need any observations being made on them.

Have thus according to the best of my abilities reported such remarks and observations on the different waters and Portages &c. as the lateness of the season would admit of my making.—I have the honor to be with due respect Sir Your most obedent & Humble Servt.

(signed JONA. HEART
Captn. 1st. U. S. Regt.

Tr (DLC); undated, but early 1788; in hand of Jacob Blackwell; endorsed by TJ.

The above report was evidently enclosed in an undated letter from Captain Jonathan Heart to General Josiah Harmar giving an account of his exploration of the navigability of the Big Beaver between 8 Nov. and 30 Dec.

1787 (Tr in DLC: TJ Papers, 80: 13917-8; in hand of Henry Remsen, Jr.). Washington asked TJ to return the above and the "rough Extracts" (Enclosure II, following) in order that he might take them to Virginia, in consequence of which TJ found it necessary to have one clerk transcribe the report, give its covering letter to his chief clerk, and himself copy the second enclosure.

ENCLOSURE II

Report on Navigability of Rivers in Northwest Territory

Major Hamtramick's report

	leagues
From Post Vincennes to the mouth of the Wabash is called	60
From do. to Tomhoute (no rapids and a good navigation)	40.
From Tomhoute (or Terrehoute) to Vermillion river on the North side. (the navigation as good as before)	20.
To the Weeha (the navigation is still better)	20.
To the river and town Ibossicanoes on the N. side. (the navigation is excellent	6.
To la Vache qui pisse (where there is a flat rapid of about 10. acres and sometimes not more than 1. foot water)	2.
To la Coulle (the channel is on the left going up, and sometimes not more than 8. inches water for 15. acres in length.)	4.
To Petit Roche (here is a strong rapid of 8. acres but plenty of water and directly above the Rapid is a flat of ½ a league and sometimes not 6. I. water)	6.
To mouth of Eel river N. side (a good navigation)	2.
To the Great Rapid 15. acres in length, and in some places not above 8 I. water. Above the Rapid is a flat of ½ a league with 6. I. water)	1.

To Calumet river S. side (where is a Rapid of 10. acres, but good water)	4.	
To an island (passage on the left) and above it of 1. acre and about 6. I. water)	1	
To Rapid St. Cyre (which is ½ a league but good water)	3.	
To river Mussissinone S. side. (here is a rapid of 12. acres long sometimes not more than 1. foot water)	2.	
To the Hospital (through very low country and very little water.—At the Hospital there is 1. league that is uncommonly low, insomuch that Periaguas are obliged to lighten to ascend it. This place is remarkeable by a rock on the N. side.)	7	
To river Salaminia (here is an island. the passage is on the S. side where is a rapid of 3. acres with good water)	3.	
To the Bended maple (where the navigation terminates)	1	122.
To Little river N. side (here you take this little river to go to the Miami and quit the Wabash on the S. side)	4	
To the portage of the Miami	12	
To the Miami village on the river St. Joseph	3½	
To the Rapid of the Wolf. (here sometimes you are obliged to unload and the intermediate navigation is full of small rapids but with plenty of water)	3.	
To la roche debout (good water)	3.	
To lake Erie	6	
To the mouth of the river Detroit	12	
To the Fort (plenty of water)	6	219[1]

Tr (DLC: TJ Papers, 80: 13906); in TJ's hand; undated, but submitted by Major John Francis Hamtramck about 1788-1789.

[1] The figure should be 231½ leagues, according to TJ's copy of Hamtramck's figures.

From Ferdinand Grand

MONSIEUR   Paris 28 Aoust 1790

Il faut donc que je me Contente de votre Buste au lieu de L'original que je regreterai toujours par une suitte des Sentiments que vous m'avés Inspiré. Ma position me met dans le Cas de relations avec des persones d'un si grand Merite que je ne me fais point à leur perte. Vous Monsieur, Mr. Franklin et Mr. Jay, me le faites trop eprouver pour que je ne renonçe pas à me Lier avec vos Ministres futurs; j'en excepte Mr. Schort si Comme je le desire vous nous le laissés.

Ceci doit vous prouver une grande Verité, C'est que vous avés

Laissé icy en Moy une persone qui vous est devouée et qui ambitione que vous lui fournissiés les moyens de Vous en Convaincre.

A la reception de votre premiere lettre, j'en fis passer l'extrait à Mr. Droz à Londres. C'est un honete Garçon qui n'entend et ne Conoit que son Etat, de sorte que, tant pour abreger une Correspondance Lente, que pour vous procurer plus promptement la Reponse que vous attendés, je me suis determiné à amalgamer ses Idées avec les mienes pour en former le projet de Convention que Voicy. Je le fais d'autant plus Volontiers qu'il men a prié [en] s'en rapportant à moy entierement, ainsy que je lai fait voir à Mr. Schort en lui Communiquant Les Lettres.

Quoyque Mr. Droz ne soit point embarrassé de lui, jai Lieu de Croire quil Ambitione plus détablir un Hotel des Monoyes de sa façon, que de travailler sur un qui auroit les deffauts de L'ancienne Methode quil est si difficille de deraciner Comme il l'a éprouvé icy.

Je ne doute donc pas que si d'une maniere ou d'autre vous lui proposés un sort honete, il ne le preffere aux offres qui lui sont faites de plusieurs endroits et notamment de L'Espagne.

Depuis votre Depart Monsieur nous avons fait des pas de Geant, en marchant comme des tortues, parce qu'à Mesure que nous avançons les difficultés des hidres qui nous devoroyent s'élevent et se multiplient d'une maniere effrayante quelques fois, de sorte que nous somes travaillés par touts les bouts et de touts les Cotés du Royaume.

Si nous n'avons plus de Livrée, il nous reste encorre des Vestiges de Titres.

Il est Singulier que nous souffrions [. . .] beaucoup de la privation des richesses factices pendant que les réelles abondent, car nous avons une riche recolte et infiniment peu d'argent. Si vous ne brillés pas par là, non plus, Vous en etes bien Amplement dédomagés par une Excellente Constitution pour la formation de laquelle vous aviés des Vertus, et nous navons que des Vices qu'il faut détruire avant de pouvoir Espérer la fin de nos Maux.

Houdon ne quitte plus le Marbre de Mr. Wasington et jusques icy il reussit parfaitement. Il est rare de ne pas trouver de mauvaises Veines dans un si gros bloc.

Vous tenés aujourdhuy Monsieur une des raines de votre Gouvernement. Elle ne pouvoit etre en meilleures mains. J'espere quelle ne vous fatiguera pas autant que la notre icy, surtout à present.

Toutte ma famille se reunit à moy pour vous offrir L'expression de nos Sentiments. Je vous prie de les agréer et de me Croire plus que persone Monsieur Votre très humble & tres obeiss Servit

GRAND

RC (DLC); endorsed by TJ as received 23 Nov. 1790 and so recorded in SJL. The enclosed PROJET DE CONVENTION was forwarded by TJ to Hamilton on 24 Nov. 1790 and has not been found. For earlier correspondence concerning Droz, see TJ to Jay, 9 Jan. and 1 Feb. 1787, and TJ's report on coinage, 14 Apr. 1790.

From Alexander Hamilton

New York, 28 Aug. 1790. Requests two copies of "An Act making provision for the debt of the United States" and of "An Act making provision for the reduction of the public debt," together with two copies of his commission as secretary of the treasury, all "certified and exemplified under the Great Seal." A vessel is expected to sail for Amsterdam in the evening by which he wishes to send some of the copies and so he will "be obliged by their being ready as soon as possible."

RC (DNA: RG 59, MLR); in Hamilton's hand, signature missing. Not recorded in SJL.

Tench Coxe had written TJ on 24 Aug. 1790 requesting two copies each of these same two acts "for transmission to Europe"; Hamilton's request was evidently a repetition caused by the need for haste (RC in DNA: RG 59, MLR; not recorded in SJL). On 30 Aug. 1790 Hamilton requested "two more authenticated copies of his Commission as Secretary of the Treasury . . . and three Copies of his Commission or power for making the Loan," adding: "Mr. Hamilton will probably stand in need of those instruments before he will have an opportunity of seeing Mr. Jefferson (RC in same; endorsed by Remsen as received same day; not recorded in SJL). One of the attested copies of the act for the reduction of the public debt was sent to William Short (DLC: Short Papers; the attestation is in Remsen's hand, signed by TJ with seal of office attached, is dated 28 Aug. 1790, and has a printed text of the act annexed).

George Washington to John Hancock

SIR New York, August 28, 1790.[1]

Your favor of July 20th. came safely to hand, together with the Memorial of Monsieur de Latombe of the 7th. of June, and the Resolve of the Legislature of Massachusetts of the 24th. of the same month. On considering the nature of the difficulties which have occurred in the execution of the Consular Convention, they appeared to be such as could not be removed but by a legislative Act. When these papers were received the session of Congress was already drawn so near to a close, that it was not thought expedient to propose to them the taking up at that time a Subject which was new, and might be found difficult.[2] It will remain there-fore for consideration at their next meeting in December.[3]—With due consideration I have the honor etc.

FC (DLC: Washington Papers). PrC (DLC); in TJ's hand, with varia-tions as indicated in notes below. See notes, Washington to TJ, 26 July 1790. Entry in SJPL reads: "[Aug. 2] draught of letter from G. W. to Govr. Hancock on French Consular Conven-tion," an entry proving that TJ was more characteristically prompt in pro-viding the draft than the date of its dispatch would seem to indicate. The delay was doubtless calculated so that the letter would be dispatched after the end of the session.

[1] Dateline does not appear in TJ's draft.
[2] At this point in PrC the following is deleted (obviously by TJ rather than by Washington, since the dele-tion was made before PrC was exe-cuted): "Monsieur Laforest, the Con-sul of France here, was spoken to on the subject, and concurred in the opinion."
[3] At this point wrote, and then de-leted, the words "when they"; text of PrC ends here.

Fixing the Seat of Government on the Potomac

EDITORIAL NOTE

Washington, Madison, and Jefferson—as well as Richard Bland Lee, Alexander White, Daniel Carroll, John Page, and other members of the Virginia and Maryland delegations—headed homeward at the end of the second session in full awareness of the fact that mere enactment of the Residence Act was by no means a guarantee that the permanent seat of government would ever come to the Potomac. They could scarcely have felt otherwise. The newspapers were filled with derisive comments about the way in which the Virginians had been trapped by Robert Morris and the Pennsylvania delegation. To these were added equally derisory remarks about the Potomac. Freneau's exchange be-tween the New York and Philadelphia housemaids seemed to sum up the general feeling to the northward:[1]

[1] (N.Y.) *Daily Advertiser*, 15 July 1790; Griswold, *Republican Court*, p. 235.

My master would rather saw timber, or dig
Than see them removing to Conogocheague—
Where the houses and kitchens are yet to be framed
The trees to be felled, and the streets to be named.

During the acrimonious debates in the House, Vining of Delaware declared it would take twenty years to determine the question of permanency. A newspaper wag thought the only kind of permanence would be a peripatetic government, as under the Articles of Confederation, and suggested that Pierre L'Enfant design a mobile capitol on wheels.[2] Long before the bargain had been sealed, a more serious correspondent warned the Southerners: "get Congress to Philadelphia, and farewell for ever to the Patowmac."[3] A writer in the Stockbridge *Western Star* called the bargain a "Virginia delusion" and made this prediction: "The probability that Congress will ever remove from Philadelphia, after it shall have been so long the seat of government . . . has been treated in that ludicrous point of view in which it must appear to every unprejudiced mind."[4] No one had made the point with a sharper sense of ridicule than Jefferson's friend Elbridge Gerry, who declared in the House debates:[5]

> . . . if the residence of Congress was to be fixed at Baltimore, there would be some prospect of our establishing a permanent residence. But what prospect does the bill afford of permanency, by placing it at Connogocheque? Enquiries will be made, where in the name of common sense is Connogocheque, and I do not believe that one person in a thousand in the United States knows that there is such a place

2 Vining's remarks occurred in the debates of 9 June, *Gazette of the United States*, 12 June 1790; in a satirical report of speeches by two members of the House that appeared in the *New-York Journal* of 15 June 1790, one commented on the whispers "that there had been a bargain between our assumptionists and our non-assumptionists, and that the unexpected majority in this house [on the residence bill] is the effect of juggling"—a comment made on the day that Robert Morris told Maclay of Jefferson's suggestion for a temporary residence. Typical of the satirical pieces was that concerning "Miss Assumption" who had been delivered of twins, *Philadelphia* and *Potowmacus*, the former destined to long life and prosperity, while the latter "was very feeble, and scarcely breathed in the birth, and lived but a few moments after the ceremony of baptism, which was hurried with precipitancy, by those who had any connection with this prude and prostitute. The friends to the girl rejoice in his death, because it would have cost an expensive sum to have preserved his feeble constitution, and to have given him a decent settlement in the world. The transient existence of this fortuitous and illegal offspring, stands recorded in the parish books, and this concise history is to be inscribed on his monument, which is to be fixed in some *church window*, in the ancient dominion.—[*encircled in mourning border:*] 'To the memory of *Potowmacus*, who was the twin of *Philadelphia*—He was the child of *Miss Assumption*, a deluded female—He was born in New-York, in the year 1790, on the 10th of July, and died on the same day: if he had lived, the wilderness of the ancient dominion would have blossomed like the rose, and our sweet scented tobacco would have perfumed the mountains of *Alleghany*'" (*New-York Journal*, 31 Aug. 1790).

2 *New-York Journal*, 15 June 1790.

3 *New-York Journal*, 3 June 1790.   4 *New-York Journal*, 3 Aug. 1790.

5 Debates of 6 July, in (N.Y.) *Daily Advertiser*, 10 July 1790.

on earth. If the second class of American nobility, the Society of St. Tammany . . . had passed a vote to celebrate their festival in their wigwam at Connogocheque, I should have thought that there was some propriety, some stile in the measure; but for the grave council of the United States, to pass a bill that the seat of government should be removed to that place, is a measure too ridiculous to be credited. Few will suppose that Congress are serious. It will be generally viewed, as has been stated, [as] a mere political manoeuvre. You might as well induce a belief that you are in earnest by inserting Missisippi, Detroit, or Winnipipiocket Pond, as Connogocheque. . . . Can it be conceived that after ten years residence, Congress will remove from the city of Philadelphia?

But the wielders of ridicule and the practical politicians erred in two respects. The mistake of lesser importance was that the Potomac was not the wilderness they conceived it to be. It was instead a pleasant land of farms, meadows, and woodland watered by a noble river, inhabited by families that had cultivated the soil there for three or four generations, boasting commercial towns in Alexandria and Georgetown whose vessels were quite as closely in touch with Bordeaux and Liverpool as were those of New York and Philadelphia. The second and more important mistake was that they underestimated the political resourcefulness of the Virginia leaders of that day. No one was more acutely sensitive to the possibility that the bargain might become unsealed than those who had made it. Washington, Jefferson, and Madison—though the President had nothing but an eloquently silent part in the legislative transactions—were all thorough realists, experienced in politics and long united in the wish of fixing the national capital on the Potomac. The declaration on the statutes was only an opportunity, as they well realized, and they had ten years in which to translate it into reality. Even so, from the moment they left New York there was a sense of urgency in everything they did touching the seat of government. Washington kept an attentive eye upon all details, but at this stage the guiding hand in the strategy of planning what one day would become the political capital of the world was that of Jefferson, with Madison assisting.

Confused dating of the first relevant documents Jefferson drafted after the Residence Act had become law is in part responsible for minimizing both his sense of urgency and the role that he played. The program that he drew up even before leaving New York, perhaps at the request of the President and in consultation with Madison, has always been considered to be the product of his reflections after he had returned to Philadelphia almost three months later.[6] It was actually a precis of the provisions of the Act and of ideas for the President to bear in mind on his way to Mount Vernon. Jefferson knew that the gentlemen of Georgetown and Alexandria, as well as the principal landowners in the neighborhood, would be prompted by self-interest to indulge in local competitions for the seat of government comparable to those that had taken place in Congress. This called for the closest secrecy about the exact

6 See Document I.

location and it is clear that for several months no one could say with certainty where this would be. Yet in the second document produced in his planning—now datable two and a half months earlier than the accepted date—the desired and ultimate location was fixed in Jefferson's mind, as no doubt it was also in the President's.[7]

It is natural that these earliest documents should have been taken to reflect the deep interest in architecture and the concern for a well-planned capital exhibited by one who had employed the Roman temple at Nîmes as the model for the Virginia capitol. But it is equally significant to note that Jefferson's agenda of suggestions stretched the law to the limit. The Act fixing the permanent seat of government did not stipulate that a capital city be laid out. It did not even direct that a district of ten miles square be claimed for the federal government. Like the Constitution, it merely set this as the maximum limit. The government under the Residence Act could have functioned quite as easily within the limits of Georgetown as Jefferson and Washington feared it might continue to do permanently in Philadelphia.[8] It is now certain, however, that as Jefferson rode southward the basic assumptions concerning the capital had become clearly established in his mind: the opportunity would never occur again if this fair one were to be lost; it would be "dangerous" as well as illusory to rely upon Congress or the legislatures of Virginia and Maryland for means to improve the opportunity; there would be a new city laid out and planned so as to be worthy of the rising empire; the district for the seat of government would be of the maximum size permitted by the Virginia and Maryland resolutions and allowed by the law; and to attain the great object it would be necessary to press forward immediately and vigorously and to appeal to the self-interest of the landowners in the vicinity. In the effort to seize the opportunity that might never come again, Jefferson's basic strategy was to keep the decisions in the hands of the executive and away from those of the legislative bodies as much as possible. This was not only permitted by the law but aided by its vague phraseology as to the amount of land to be acquired for governmental purposes, and Jefferson took full advantage of these openings. The means, in brief, were those normally called Hamiltonian. But what Jefferson did in holding out inducements to the local landowners, just as he had recently done in holding out inducements to Spain to open the Mississippi, was thoroughly characteristic. So was his conception from the beginning of a spacious capital city and so, too, was the strategy he devised to make an asset of competing local interests.

It is now evident from the reordering of the chronology of the documents that the opening discussions with Daniel Carroll, Benjamin Stoddert, and William Deakins, Jr. by which this strategy was set in motion took place at Georgetown on the 13th of September. This significant event in the history of the capital found its most graphic chronicler in

[7] See Document II.
[8] A memorial signed by Peter Robert and other inhabitants of Georgetown urging that the capital be located there was, in fact, presented to Congress on 28 June 1790 (Columbia Historical Society, *Records*, XI, 211).

the person of young Thomas Lee Shippen, just returned from Europe where two years earlier he had drawn the most memorable portrait of Jefferson at the Court of Versailles.[9] Washington himself had stopped at Georgetown two days earlier, ostensibly to hold a conference on affairs of the Potomac Company and no doubt to plan the tour of inspection that he made later. But the actual opening of negotiations he left to Jefferson, whose report of the conversations was drafted on the 14th when he was at Alexandria. Jefferson was in haste to reach Monticello and doubtless intended the document as an aide-mémoire to be handed to Washington as he stopped at Mount Vernon on the 15th. In it he declared that the landowners would doubtless come forward soon with proposals.[10] Two weeks later the Georgetown *Times and Patowmack Packet* announced that local inhabitants would offer to the President 400 acres of land for the seat of government.[11] The signed proposals were ready to be given to Washington when he arrived in Georgetown in mid-October.

On Saturday the 16th of October the President spent a day in company with the leading citizens of the town, viewing the adjacent countryside as Jefferson had done a month earlier, then departed early Sunday morning for the Great Falls and Conogocheague, over seventy miles upriver. The local newspaper, in an obvious attempt to penetrate the secret, reported that this trip of inspection around Georgetown was made "in order to fix upon a proper situation, for the GRAND COLUMBIAN FEDERAL CITY" and then added: "We are informed, that since the arrival of the President in our parts, bets respecting the Seat of Government run high in favor of George-Town; by the return of the President [from Conogocheague], we hope to have it in our power to lay a circumstantial account of this important matter before the Public."[12] Washington's interest in the progress of the Potomac Company's works was genuine and profound, but he could not have been unaware of the value of such a journey as a feint to cloak his purpose. He was authorized by the Residence Act to locate the capital anywhere on the Potomac in an eighty-mile stretch between the Eastern branch and the Conogocheague and his journey served to stimulate rumors that the choice might actually fall upon a spot far above tidewater.[13] But it is obvious that the proposals Jefferson had in mind in making the suggestions to Carroll, Stoddert, and Deakins were quite different from those advanced by Robert Peter and others. The latter were not intended as free dona-

[9] See Documents III and IV, with enclosures to the latter. See also, Vol. 12: 502-4n.

[10] Document IV.

[11] Cited by Louis Dow Scisco, "A Site for the 'Federal City': The Original Proprietors and their Negotiations with Washington," Columbia Historical Society, *Records, 1957-1959*, p. 128, under date of 29 Sep. 1790.

[12] *The Maryland Journal and Baltimore Advertiser*, 26 Oct. 1790, under a Georgetown date-line of 20 Oct. 1790, printed in Allen C. Clark, "Origin of the Federal City," Columbia Historical Society, *Records*, XXXV-XXXVI (1935), 26-7.

[13] William Force, "History of the Selection of the Permanent Seat of Government for the United States," in *Special Report of the Commissioner of Education on the Condition and Improvement of Public Schools in the District of Columbia* (Washington, 1871), p. 187 (41st. Cong., 2d sess., Ex. Doc. No. 315).

tions, the acreage was far less than Jefferson desired for the capital, and the tracts lay in the immediate environs of Georgetown, not in the location bordering on the Eastern branch of the Potomac that Jefferson already envisioned as the site of the capital.

On the day after Washington set out for the Conogocheague the Georgetown landowners engaged a surveyor to map the various tracts owned by each proprietor "within the lines laid down"—lines apparently indicated by the President.[14] Speculation continued as to the exact location. By mid-November it was rumored that Washington had ordered three sites on different parts of the Potomac to be surveyed, but the *Times and Patowmac Packet* admitted that nothing certain was known.[15] At the end of the month Samuel Davidson, a Georgetown merchant, wrote a friend that not a doubt remained but that "the Grand Federal City will soon rear its august head in the vicinity of this town," that the President had fixed the place but had not made it known with certainty, that his address to Congress in December would reveal the secret, that the location would be between Rock Creek and the Eastern branch, and that "on the height of Peter's Slashes plantation will stand the Stadt House."[16] But not until the message to Congress and the public proclamation late in January was all doubt removed. Washington's presumed indication of the inclusive lines near Georgetown and his authorization of the surveys in the vicinity of the abandoned townsite of Hamburg helped cover the secret.[17]

It is a measure of Jefferson's deep concern that, after leaving Mount Vernon on the 16th of September, he decided to make an appeal to the local interest of the state in addition to the reliance he placed on the self-interest of the landowners. With Madison's help he sought to influence several members of the General Assembly to induce that body to appropriate funds for building ten private dwellings a year for ten years in the district to be fixed upon as the seat of government.[18] He no doubt urged this upon the delegates from Albemarle as he certainly did upon Zachariah Johnston, who had been a member of the Virginia Convention of 1788 and had represented his county in the House of Delegates since 1778.[19]

[14] William Deakins, Jr. to Washington, 3 Nov. 1790, quoted in Allen C. Clark, "Origin of the Federal City," Columbia Historical Society, *Records*, XXXV-XXXVI (1935), 27.
[15] *The Maryland Journal and Baltimore Advertiser*, 16 Nov. 1790, under a Georgetown date-line of 10 Nov. 1790, printed in same, p. 27.
[16] Quoted in Louis Dow Scisco, "A Site for the 'Federal City': The Original Proprietors and their Negotiations with Washington," Columbia Historical Society, *Records, 1957-1959*, p. 130; Davidson's letter, to an unidentified person, is dated 28 Nov. 1790.
[17] Same, p. 130; Allen C. Clark, "Origin of the Federal City," Columbia Historical Society, *Records*, XXXV-XXXVI (1935), 28.
[18] See Document V. That this plan was an afterthought is proved both by the reordered chronology of the documents and by the fact that TJ did not report it to Washington until later (see TJ to Washington, 27 Oct. 1790).
[19] Zachariah Johnston (1742-1800), son of an immigrant from the North of

This attempt was characteristic but hopeless. The General Assembly was in no mood for taking such a gamble as Jefferson had urged upon it once before.[20] Estimated revenues for the coming year amounted to £246,232, while expenditures were figured at only £179,386. Yet the members were determined not only to reduce taxes but even to limit the collection of those imposed. Their own great capitol looked imposing from a distance, but it was far from finished. The lead covering for the roof authorized at a cost of £2,873 was still incomplete and not secure against the weather, the committee rooms and offices were not plastered, and pay for the workmen was in arrears. One of the chief reasons for this arrearage was that funds in the hands of the commissioners for sales of public property were unproductive because collections could not be made of the estate of Archibald Cary for lots and buildings long since sold.[21] With this unhappy experience staring them in the face and calling for deficiency appropriations to forward the work on the capitol, legislators were not likely to embark upon other real estate ventures depending so much upon political decisions of the future.

Ireland who was one of the first settlers in the Valley of Virginia, was an ardent republican, a man of some substance, a believer in emancipation, and a supporter of the Statute for Religious Freedom. At the session of the General Assembly in 1789 Johnston, on an urgent appeal from George Mason, obtained the passage of an Act authorizing the removal of the courthouse from Alexandria to a place nearer the center of Fairfax county (JHD, Oct. 1789, 1828 edn., p. 132; Hening, XIII, 79; *Tyler's Quarterly*, V [1924], 189-90). Mason himself had drawn the petition and had obtained more than 550 signatures to it. The next year, only three weeks after TJ solicited Johnston's aid in behalf of the Federal City, Mason wrote Johnston: The benevolent Intention of the Assembly has . . . been frustrated, by Justices of the Twon-Faction; who have presumed to dispense with a Positive Law, and are now using all the arts of Misrepresentation and Falsehood, to obtain a Repeal of it. This has laid us under the necessity of applying to the Legislature to enforce their own Authority, by such Amendments to the former Act, as will compel the due Execution" (Mason to Johnston, 3 Nov. 1790, quoted in John G. Paxton, "Zachariah Johnston," *Tyler's Quarterly*, V [1924], 185-92). This feud of long standing between Mason and the "Alexandria Faction," whom he accused of controlling the county court, of corrupting and perverting the administration of justice, and of "continually gaining Strength by the Power of appointing Militia Officers, Commissioners of the Tax and other money-jobs," illuminates TJ's report to Washington concerning Mason's opinions of Alexandria and Georgetown—opinions, incidentally, that Washington could scarcely have obtained otherwise in view of the rift that had developed between Mason and himself since the Federal Convention of 1787 (same; see Document IV in the present group; see also, Vol. 16: 143n). On Johnston's minor role in the Virginia Convention of 1788, see A. J. Beveridge, *John Marshall*, I, 474.

20 See Vol. 6: 362, 367-8.

21 JHD, Oct. 1790, 1828 edn., p. 122-3, 148, 151, 156, 167. At this session the General Assembly passed an Act authorizing various alterations in the Virginia capitol and the purchase of "a fit and sufficient bell," as well as stoves for the House of Delegates and the Senate chambers; Hening, XIII, 201. It also authorized payment of $120,000 to be advanced for the public buildings to be erected at the seat of government as provided in the resolution of 10 Dec. 1789, these payments to be made in three equal instalments annually and the warrants to be "payable . . . to the order of the President of the United States"; Hening, XIII, 43-4, 125. The fact that payments were specifically directed to be made to Washington suggests that TJ or Madison may have prompted this in accord with the general plan to keep all of the affairs of the Federal City in the hands of the President as much as possible.

Further, even if this had not been so, the mood of the session was one of angry resentment against the assumption Act, which the members in a solemn remonstrance demanded to be repealed as impolitic, unjust, and unconstitutional. Jefferson no doubt told Zachariah Johnston as he had told others how essential it had been to acquiesce in assumption for the sake of union, perhaps also how the measure had been combined with the question of the seat of government. Johnston voted against the protest. In the initial stages of the acrimonious debate a milder form of remonstrance was approved in committee of the whole by the House of Delegates and a more vigorous amendment was voted down by a vote of 88 to 47. But the longer the contest waged the more emphatic became the language of the House of Delegates, ending at last with the ominous declaration that the consent of the state legislatures should be obtained before the assumption Act could "assume a constitutional form."[22] Suspicion was also directed at the Senate of the United States for the adoption of such a measure, and early in the session the House of Delegates unanimously resolved that the Virginia Senators should do their utmost to make it possible for citizens to have free admission to the debates in that chamber and that the legislatures of the various states should be invited to frame similar instructions.[23]

Just as Jefferson arrived back in Philadelphia for the opening of the third session of Congress, Andrew Brown's *Federal Gazette* printed an early version of the Virginia resolutions and made this comment:[24]

The resolution of the Virginia Assembly respecting the Assumption of the State Debts . . . exhibits a very curious phenomenon in the history of the United States. The majority who voted in favor of the resolution, it seems, fell asleep in September 1787, (just before the rising of the Federal Convention) and did not awake till a few weeks ago; during which time the Federal Government was adopted and established throughout all the States. Their vote therefore must be ascribed to *ignorance* of what passed during their long sleep. The *Resolution* is calculated only for those years of anarchy, which preceded the general ratification of the present HAPPY NATIONAL GOVERNMENT. It is now nugatory and ridiculous. . . .

Thus, as Jefferson set out with such a sense of urgency to rivet the seat of government to the Potomac, he heard the reverberations of *Junius Americanus'* words questioning the constitutionality of one part of the bargain over the residence and assumption measures. Now, in a

22 The resolutions were adopted in committee of the whole on 3 and 5 Nov. 1790 and the final remonstrance was passed by the House of Delegates on 17 Nov. 1790; JHD, Oct. 1790, 1828 edn., p. 35, 44, 80-1, 141, 150.

23 Same, p. 81.

24 *Federal Gazette*, 20 Nov. 1790. In this and other comment at the time the resolutions agreed to in committee of the whole in the House of Delegates were mistakenly regarded as resolutions of the Virginia General Assembly. In the *Federal Gazette* of 23 Nov. 1790, under a Richmond date-line of 17 Nov., there appeared the text of the amendment that had been defeated in the committee of the whole on 3 Nov. 1790.

far more menacing roll of thunder, he heard the other part so branded by his fellow Virginians—the "first symptom of a spirit which must either be killed or will kill the constitution of the United States."[25] But this was a spirit that refused to die and continued to threaten. Fortunately, Jefferson was not required to respond to this menacing challenge as he had been obliged to answer *Junius Americanus*, but he was well aware that the bargain which gave the government so precarious a seat on the Potomac had borne bitter fruit.

[25] Hamilton to Jay, 13 Nov. 1790, enclosing copies of the resolutions as adopted in committee of the whole in the House of Delegates on 3 and 5 Nov. 1790, Syrett, *Hamilton*, VII, 149-50.

I. Jefferson's Draft of Agenda for the Seat of Government

[29 Aug. 1790]

Proceedings to be had under the Residence act.

A territory not exceeding 10. miles square (or, I presume, 100 square miles in any form) to be located by metes and bounds.

3. commissioners to be appointed.

I suppose them not entitled to any salary. [If they live near the place they may, in some instances, be influenced by self interest, and partialities: but they will push the work with zeal. If they are from a distance, and Northwardly, they will be more impartial, but may affect delays.]

The Commissioners to purchase or accept 'such quantity of land on the E. side of the river as the President shall deem *proper for the U.S.*' viz. for the federal Capitol, the offices, the President's house and gardens, the town house, Market house, publick walks, hospital. For the President's house, offices and gardens, I should think 2. squares should be consolidated. For the Capitol and offices one square. For the Market one square. For the Public walks 9. squares consolidated.

The expression 'such quantity of land as the President shall deem *proper for the U.S.*' is vague. It may therefore be extended to the acceptance or purchase of land enough for the town: and I have no doubt it is the wish, and perhaps expectation. In that case it will be to be laid out in lots and streets. I should propose these to be at right angles as in Philadelphia, and that no street be narrower than 100. feet, with foot-ways of 15. feet. Where a street is long and level, it might be 120.

feet wide. I should prefer squares of at least 200. yards every way, which will be of about 8. acres each.

The Commissioners should have some taste in Architecture, because they may have to decide between different plans.

They will however be subject to the President's direction in every point.

When the President shall have made up his mind as to the spot for the town, would there be any impropriety in his saying to the neighboring landholders, 'I will fix the town here if you will join and purchase and give the lands.' They may well afford it from the increase of value it will give to their own circumjacent lands.

The lots to be sold out in breadths of 50. feet: their depths to extend to the diagonal of the square.

I doubt much whether the obligation to build the houses at a given distance from the street, contributes to it's beauty. It produces a disgusting monotony. All persons make this complaint against Philadelphia. The contrary practice varies the appearance, and is much more convenient to the inhabitants.

In Paris it is forbidden to build a house beyond a given height, and it is admitted to be a good restriction. It keeps down the price of ground, keeps the houses low and convenient, and the streets light and airy. Fires are much more manageable where houses are low. This however is an object of legislation.

MS (DLC: DCP); entirely in TJ's hand; undated but in SJPL the following entry, which can relate only to this document, appears under date of 29 Aug. 1790: "Note of Th:J. on agenda in the 10. miles square." Ford, v, 252, and Padover, *National Capital*, p. 30, both assign the date of 29 Nov. 1790 and the latter incorporates this text with that of the report made to Washington after consultation with Carroll and others, as if both were integral. But the above was obviously prepared for Washington's use prior to his departure for Virginia and the report was made to him subsequently.

II. Jefferson's Report to Washington on Meeting Held at Georgetown

[14 Sep. 1790]

In conversations with Mr. Carrol, Mr. Stoddard and Mr. Dickens they were properly impressed with the idea that if the present occasion of securing the Federal seat on the Patowmack should be lost, it could never more be regained, that it would be dangerous to rely on any aids from Congress, or the assemblies of Virginia or Maryland, and that therefore measures should be adopted to carry the residence bill into execution without recourse to those bodies: and that the requisites were 1st. land enough to place the public buildings on; and 2dly. money enough to build them, and to erect moreover about 20. good dwelling houses for such persons belonging to the government as must have houses to themselves, about as many good lodging houses, and half a dozen taverns.

To obtain this sum, this expedient was suggested to them. To procure a declaration from the proprietors of those spots of land most likely to be fixed on for the town, that if the President's location of the town should comprehend their lands, they would give them up for the use of the U.S. on condition they should receive the double of their value, estimated as they would have been had there been no thought of bringing the federal seat into their neighborhood. It was supposed that 1500 acres would be required in the whole, to wit, about 300. acres for public buildings, walks &c. and 1200 acres to be divided into quarter acre lots, which, due allowance being made for streets, would make about 2000 lots. The vacant lots in George town now sell at £200. Those of Alexandria at £600. Suppose those of the new town should bring only £100 clear. This would produce 200,000£. a sum adequate[1] to the objects before mentioned. It was further supposed that the assembly of Maryland would interpose to force the consent of infant or obstinate proprietors for a reasonable compensation.

It was also suggested as a more certain means of ensuring the object, that each proprietor within the whole ten miles square, should cede one half his lands to the public, to be sold to raise money. Perhaps this would be pushing them too far for the reputation of the new government they were to come under, and farther than is necessary when we consider the sum which may be raised by the sale of lots, the donation of 120,000 Dollars by Virginia, and the possible donation of an equal sum by Maryland. At least it might shew a commendable moderation not to push this proposition till experiment should prove the other resources inadequate.— Great zeal appeared in the gentlemen beforementioned, and they seemed to approve the proposition for the 1500. acres. That for a moiety of all the lands within the 10. miles square was hazarded only to Mr. Carrol. They will probably proceed immediately to make the best arrangements practicable, and to come forward with them to the President.

Queries. 1. Would it not be well, if a position below the little falls should be decided on, to begin the 10. miles just above the commencement of the canal; and accept from Maryland, for the present, only from thence down to the Eastern branch, supposed about 7. miles; and to accept from Virginia 10. miles beginning at the lower end of Alexandria, and running up as far as it will extend, which probably will be as far up as the commencement on the Maryland side. This being accepted, and professedly (as to Maryland) in *part* only of their cession, when Congress shall meet they may pass an amendatory bill authorising the President to compleat his acceptance from Maryland by crossing the Eastern branch and compleating the 10. miles in that direction, which will bring the lower boundary on the Maryland side very nearly opposite to that on the Virginia side.—It is understood that the breadth of the territory accepted will be of 5. miles only on each side.

2. In locating the town, will it not be best to give it double the extent on the eastern branch of what it has on the river? The former will be for persons in commerce, the latter for those connected with the government.

3. Will it not be best to lay out the long streets parallel with the creek, and the other crossing them at right angles, so as to leave no oblique angled lots but the single row which shall be on the river? Thus

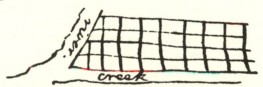

MS (DCP); entirely in TJ's hand; undated.

Padover, *National Capital*, p. 30-6, assigns this document the date of 29 Nov. 1790 and prints it with TJ's draft of agenda of 29 Aug. 1790 as if the two were a single document. The report was certainly written after TJ left Georgetown on the 14th and before he arrived at Mount Vernon on the 15th, for the conversations here discussed and the EXPEDIENT SUGGESTED are mentioned in TJ to Washington, 17 Sep. 1790 (Document IV).

TJ was correct in supposing that Maryland might interpose to force the

CONSENT OF INFANT OR OBSTINATE PROPRIETORS. On 28 Nov. 1790 the Maryland legislature passed such an act, limiting the amount to be obtained by a jury called by the sheriff to value the land at 130 acres—the exact amount of land held by various absentee owners in the old Hamburgh site (Scisco, "A Site for the 'Federal City': The Original Proprietors and their Negotiations with Washington," Columbia Historical Society, *Records, 1957-1959*, p. 130.

¹ This word interlined in substitution for "sufficient," deleted.

III. Thomas Lee Shippen to William Shippen

My dear Sir   Alexandria Sep. 15. 1790

I arrived here late at night the day before yesterday and yesterday I was so engrossed by the Lees who abound here that I could not find time to write to you. My journey was a delightful one from Chester town to George town whether spoken of for the excellence of the Society, my fare, the weather or the roads. For I overtook as I told you I expected I should, my two valuable friends Messrs. Jefferson and Madison. At Rock Hall 12 miles from Chester town we waited all that day for want of a vessel to take us over, and I never knew two men more agreable than they were. We talked and dined, and strolled, and rowed ourselves in boats, and feasted upon delicious crabs. A six hours passage over the bay for us, and one of eighteen for my poor Baptist. I had made him go with my horses and carriage in a different boat from that we went in, as there was not room for all and wonderful to tell, although at one time they had got before us on the passage, we arrived 12 hours before them at Annapolis. There I saw my dear friend Shaaff and found him the same thing I had ever known him. He was overjoyed to see me and we were constantly together. I introduced him to my fellow travellers and he became our Ciceroni. We passed 3 hours on the top of the State House steeple from which place you descry the finest prospect in the world, if extent, variety Wood and Water in all their happiest forms can make one so. My good friend Shaaff was not displeased at my comparing him to the Diable Boiteux whose office he seemed to fill in opening the roofs of the houses and telling us the history of each family who lived in them. Mann's Inn at Anna[poli]s is certainly to be placed among the most excellent in the world. I never saw so fine a turtle or so well dressed a dish as he gave us the second day for dinner. Every thing was of a piece —Old Madeira £80 a pipe to season it. He has made two additions to his house both very handsome one of them magnificent—But enough of Annapolis. After the turtle feast we proceeded as far as Queen Anne's a dirty village 13 miles from Annapolis. Here a most perfect contrast to Mann's—Musquitos, gnats, flees and bugs contended with each other for preference, and we had nothing decent to eat or drink. You may imagine how much we slept from the company we were in—breakfasted next morning at Bladensbgh.

with an old black woman who keeps the best house in the town and calls herself Mrs. Margaret Adams. She diverted us with an account of the resentment which discovered itself towards her because the President and his family had preferred her house to lodge at as he passed through Bladensburgh. After trying every other expedient to distress her, they pulled down her temple of Cloacina and there was the demolished building when we arrived, a monument at the same time of the envy of her fellow citizens and her own triumph. Dined at Georgetown—were waited upon after dinner by Col. Forrest, Mr. Dan Carrol, Colo. Dickins, Mr. Stodart &c. &c. who reside in the town. They proposed our setting off in the early morning of the next day to view [the falls?] and fine prospects which the vicinity of G. [affords?]. We acceded to their proposal, breakfasted in the [morning?] at a beautiful seat of Mr. Notley Young who among other gracious things told me he had gone to school with you 30 or 40 years ago. We traversed the whole country were joined by the different gentlemen who lived upon the confines and had at last a cavalcade of thirteen: dined at Forrest's and after dinner went in a boat to the falls 4 miles above the town —romantic scene. At 1/4 past 7 at night I left my companions who accompanied me in the boat to this side of the Potowmac—they returned to George town—I came on to Alexandria. Eight miles I travelled in the night a new road, but arrived without any adverse accident at a little after 8 at my uncle's house on the bank. My horses perform wonders—my carriage is delightful. Yesterday I passed at Ludwell's seat a mile from Alexandria, with my uncle Mr. Fendall—Flora—Ludwell and Molly of Chantilly. The place is called Shuter's Hill and is infinitely handsomer than the one in England of that name. The house is handsome and spacious. Today they dine with us—Tomorrow I pass at Mt. Vernon and on the day after hope to set off on my tour. My uncle accompanies me throughout the whole of it. Had I room I would tell you our plan but I will write again soon and tell you all. My love to all my friends my dear Mama & yourself in particular your own,

T L Shippen

I find my poor friend Harrison here sick.

RC (DLC: Shippen Papers); addressed: "Doctor William Shippen Junior Fourth Street Philadelphia."

For Shippen's memorable description of TJ at the Court of Versailles, see Vol. 12: 502-504n. It is pleasant to speculate that the hours spent on the steeple at Annapolis may have resulted from Shippen's asking whether TJ on his several stops at Annapolis had ever himself taken the advice he urged upon Shippen, Short, and Rutledge in 1788: "Go to the top of a steeple to have a view of the town and it's environs." More likely it was there that TJ had learned how important an elevated view of the countryside was. Shippen should have remembered, and no doubt did, TJ's other remark that obviously came from experience: "The steeple of the Cathedral [at Strasbourg] . . . I believe is the highest in the world, and the handsomest. Go to the very top of it; but let it be the last operation of the day, as you will need a long rest after it" (Advice to young Americans, 1788, Vol. 13, 267-8; note also the famous description of the view at Harper's Ferry in *Notes on Virginia*).

Shippen had no less than nine living uncles among the LEES WHO ABOUND in Virginia (Hendrick, *Lees of Virginia*, chart at p. 438). COL. FORREST, MR. DAN. CARROL, COLO. DICKENS, MR. STODART: Uriah Forrest, Daniel Carroll, William Deakins, Jr., and Benjamin Stoddert, all of whom later figured prominently in affairs of the District of Columbia, public and private. Carroll was the key person in this group.

IV. Thomas Jefferson to George Washington

SIR   Fredericksburg Sep. 17. 1790.

In the course of the visit we made the day we left Mount Vernon, we drew our host into conversation on the subject of the federal seat. He came into it with a shyness not usual in him. Whether this proceeded from his delicacy as having property adjoining Georgetown, or from what other motive I cannot say. He quitted the subject always as soon as he could. He said enough however to shew his decided preference of George-town. He mentioned shortly, in it's favor, these circumstances. 1. It's being at the junction of the upper and lower navigation where the commodities must be transferred into other vessels: (and here he was confident that no vessel could be contrived which could pass the upper shoals and live in the wide waters below his island.) 2. The depth of water which would admit any vessels that could come to Alexandria. 3. The narrowness of the river and consequent safeness of the harbour. 4. It's being clear of ice as early at least as the canal and river above would be clear. 5. It's neighborhood to the Eastern branch, whither any vessels might conveniently withdraw which should be detained through the winter. 6. It's defensibility, as derived from the high and commanding hills around it. 7. It's actual possession of the commerce, and the start it already has.

He spoke of Georgetown always in comparison with Alexandria. When led to mention the Eastern branch he spoke of it as an admirable position, superior in all respects to Alexandria.

I have committed to writing a Memorandum for Mr. Carroll of the kind of conveyance I suggested to him, and which I had not the opportunity then to put on paper. I inclose it open for your perusal, and take the liberty of asking you to put a wafer into it, when you are done with it, and forward it to Mr. Carroll. I have the honor to be with the greatest respect and attachment, Sir, Your most obedient & most humble servt., TH. JEFFERSON

RC (DLC: District of Columbia Papers); addressed: "The President of the United States at Mount-Vernon"; endorsed in Washington's hand: "From Thos. Jefferson Esq. and Mr. Madison 17th. Sepr. 1790." Not recorded in SJL. Enclosures printed below.

OUR HOST: George Mason of Gunston Hall.

E N C L O S U R E   I

Thomas Jefferson to Daniel Carroll

[Fredericksburg, 17 Sep. 1790]

T.J. has the honor to present his Compliments to Mr. C——— and to send him a memorandum of the substance of the conveyance he suggested to him as best calculated to remove the difficulties which were the subject of conversation between them. He had not the residence act under his eye at the time of writing the memorandum, not being able to get a copy of it: which must account for its deviations from that act, if any should be found. As far as his memory serves him he has adhered to the letter of the Act.

Tr (DLC: District of Columbia Papers); in Washington's hand. Not recorded in SJL.

It is evident from the terms of the draft conveyance that this involved the proposition suggested to Carroll, Stoddert, and Deakins, and applied to *possible* locations of the site of government, not to that applicable to the whole district of ten miles square suggested to Carroll alone (see Document II). The DIFFICULTIES were obviously, first, to secure the cooperation of local landowners without revealing to any of them what the ultimate site would be; second, to minimize competitions between the Georgetown and other locations; and third to contrive the conveyances of land and gifts of money so as to make it unnecessary to obtain further authority from Congress.

E N C L O S U R E   II

Sketches for the Conveyance of the Lands whereon the Federal Seat is to be fixed.

The Conveyance to be executed, according to the forms of the laws of Maryland, by the Proprietors of the land designated by the President for the federal seat.

The preamble to recite the substance of that part of the residence act which authorises the President to receive grants of *lands* and *money* for the use of the United States and to declare that the object of the conveyance is to furnish both *land* and *money* for their use.

The body of the Deed to convey the lands designated for the Seat (suppose 1500 acres) to A and B and their heirs in trust for the following purposes.

1. To reconvey to the Commissioners their heirs and successors to be named by the President, such portions of the said lands, as the Presi-

[467]

dent shall designate for the scite of the public buildings, public walks streets &c. to remain for the use of the U.S.

2. To reconvey the residue in such lots, to such persons, and in such conditions as the Commissioners shall direct, for the purpose of raising money, and the money when received to be granted to the President for the use of the U.S. according to the residence act.

The effect of this last clause will be such that the President (without any further legislative authority from Congress) may proceed to lay out the town immediately into: 1. public lots: 2. public walks or gardens: 3. private lots for sale: 4. streets.—The 1. 2. and 4th. articles to be reconveyed to the Commissioners, and the 3d. to private purchasers as above proposed.

It is understood that this conveyance will have been preceeded by Articles of Agreement signed by all the Proprietors of the lands in and about those several spots which have such obvious advantages as render it presumeable to every one that some one of them will attract the President's notice and choice.

Tr (DLC: District of Columbia Papers); entirely in Washington's hand; at head of text: "From T. J. Esqr. to CC. Esqr"; caption in text is same as that given above. Not recorded in SJL. Washington's endorsement, if intended to indicate that the letter was addressed to Charles Carroll of Carrollton, is clearly erroneous.

V. Thomas Jefferson to Zachariah Johnston

DEAR SIR   Monticello Octob. 7. 1790.

As the assembly will soon meet, I presume you will be passing down to it a few days before. I shall be at home at that time, and will always be glad to see you here when I am here: but particularly I wish it at this time, as it is highly interesting to our country that it should take up a particular matter now in it's power, and which never will be so again. This subject can only be opened in private conference. Knowing the weight you have justly acquired with our public councils, and your zeal to promote the public interest I have taken the liberty of asking to see you on your way down. My house will be a convenient stage for you the first day, and if you can have time to tarry a day with me it will be very desireable to me, and I trust not unfruitful to our state in general and our particular part of it. I am with great esteem Dear Sir your most obedt. humble servt.,

TH: JEFFERSON

PrC (DLC). RC (Miss Anne Johnstone, Lexington, Va., 1945).

VI. Proposals by Georgetown Landowners

[13 Oct. 1790]

The object of the subscribers to the paper annexed is to accommodate—they will cheerfully consent to any other arrangement, that may be thought reasonable, should their Lands, or any part of them be selected for the Federal City.

They are induced to make the offer of their Lands under the Idea, that if the Federal City should be erected on navigation, no place in the small distance from the mouth of the Eastern Branch, to the highest Tide Water, offers so many advantages—and that to none there can be so few solid objections as to George Town and its immediate vicinity.

In point of healthiness of situation, goodness of water and air, considerations of so much weight, there are but few spots in the United States, which can boast any advantages over the one now in contemplation:—and, it is conceived, that the hilliness of the Country, far from being an objection, will be thought a desireable circumstance, as it will at once contribute to the beauty, health and security of a City intended for the seat of Empire.—For a place merely commercial, where men willingly sacrifice health to gain, a continued flatt, might perhaps be preferred—but even in this view, the Friends to an entire flatt might be gratified from the Lands now offered—the whole of which includes a sufficient variety to please.

For at least nine months in the year, the Harbour of George Town is as secure as any in the United States, and is sufficient to contain several hundred ships, and it is a fact easily to be proved, that any vessel which can pass the mud some distance above Maryland Point, can come to George Town, and load at the Wharves.— It is not a good winter harbour in its present state, and probably cannot be made so for many ships, without considerable expense; the subscribers cannot think it very material as undoubtedly, the lower part of Mason's Island can be made a place of security for any number of ships that might winter here—and even if this was not the case, the Eastern Branch would afford the utmost safety and would be found no inconvenient place for the merchants in the Federal City, to lay up their Ships; for when Ships must be Idle, it is of little consequences whether they remain under the owners Eye, or at the distance of four or five miles.—Whenever they could sail from the Eastern Branch they could load at George Town—

the only difference is this, that they might sometimes be loaded in the Eastern Branch and ready to sail as soon as the Ice disappeared; whereas at George Town, they would only begin to load, when they could sail from the Branch, which might be attended with a delay of 6 or 7 Days—not more; and this could not probably happen to more than one vessel in every hundred.—Alexandria, in this particular, stands and must remain unrivalled, there, opportunities are generally afforded of dispatching ships every 12 or 15 days during the Winter, from partial openings of the Ice— an advantage, which experience evinces, cannot be enjoyed by any place above Alexandria. But even this advantage will be thought less important, when it is considered that large commercial towns on the Patowmack must derive their chief support from the Produce brought down the River—and that Ships can always remain at George Town, at least as long as the River above can be navigated; and consequently long enough to take off all the produce brought down by Water.—In one particular, and that a very important one, George Town must always retain great advantages over any places below it—there is seldom any swell at George Town—never one quarter of a mile above it, the vessels therefore, which bring the produce down the River, can empty at George Town, which from their construction and the swell in the River, it is thought they can never do, much below.

Should it be necessary to raise money for the public buildings by the sale of lotts, the place now offered would probably afford greater advantages than any other which could be selected under the Act of Congress; for the seat of government, being fixed in the neighbourhood of a Town already in possession of no very inconsiderable, and increasing Trade, the lotts that might be laid off adjacent to the Town, would immediately command a ready and an extensive sale, and would produce money in the beginning, and when it would be most wanted—Whereas, should any spot at a distance from Town, be chosen, it would likely be many years before the lotts would sell, or be improved—Doubts would arise, whether after all, the Seat of government would be on Patowmack;—and if no such doubts were to exist, commercial men would long hesitate about setting down and erecting expensive buildings, on a spot, between two Towns, each of them possessing superior natural advantages to any place between; and one of them certainly better calculated to remove the objections entertained by some parts of the Union, against Patowmack on the score of health.

VI. PROPOSALS BY PROPERTY OWNERS

The subscribers cannot but be of opinion (and where their observations are just, they will not have less weight for coming from Men Interested) that the speediest means of extending the Town all over the Country between George Town and the Eastern Branch, would be, to erect the Federal buildings adjacent to George Town—in such an event, no doubts could be entertained of the rapid improvement of the City and Country around it—no buildings would be omitted in consequence of apprehensions that the seat of government might not after all be on Patowmack, for all Men would be satisfied, that if disappointed in this favorite object, their improvements would still afford them ample compensation for their expences, from being in a large Commercial Town.[1]

We, the subscribers, do hereby agree and oblige ourselves our heirs, Executors, and administrators, to sell and make over by sufficient Deeds, in any manner which shall be directed by General Washington, or any person acting under him, and on such terms as he shall determine to be reasonable and Just; any of the Lands which we possess in the vicinity of George Town, for the uses of the Federal City, provided the same shall be erected in the said vicinity.

Witness our hands this thirteenth day of October, 1790.

ROBERT PETER for One hundred Acres shoud
   so much of mine be thought necessary.

THO. BEALL of Geo.	J M LINGAN
BENJ. STODDERT	GEORGE BEALL
URIAH FORREST	ANTHONY HOLMEAD
WILL DEAKINS, JUNR	
JOHN THRELKELD	

  any Land on the north
  side of my meadow

MS (DNA: RG 42, Records of the Commissioners for the District of Columbia, "Deed Book"); in hand of Benjamin Stoddert except for signatures and consisting of five pages, the fifth page of which (once wafered to the statement at point indicated in note 1 below but now disjunct) comprises THE PAPER ANNEXED, on the verso of which is this endorsement: "13th October 1790. Agreement of Sundry persons to relinquish their Lands for Federal City."

[1] The statement of proposals ends at this point (see preceding note).

To William Carmichael

New York August 29th. 1790.

You will receive by the present conveyance my letters of the 2d. and 6th. instant.

In my letter of April 11th. I enclosed to you a duplicate of Mr. Jay's of September 9th. 1788 complaining of the practice of the Spanish Governments bordering on Georgia, of receiving and withholding the fugitive slaves of that State, and urging redress. My letter of May 31st. covered a triplicate of Mr. Jay's, with some new evidence of a continuation of the practice and desired your pointed attention to that object. I now enclose two letters from the Commanding Officer of the United States on St. Mary's River, giving information of a recent instance of the same violation of good neighbourhood, and shewing you that it cannot be continued peaceably. Be so good as to press for immediate orders to their Governor to discontinue this practice, and to convey an answer speedily to me.

Being to leave this place within 3 or 4 days for Virginia, from whence I shall return to Philadelphia after about a month's stay at my own house, you will probably receive no other letter from me dated earlier than the latter end of October. With the present, the newspapers to this date will be handed you. I have the honor to be &c.

FC (DNA: RG 59, PCC No. 121). Not recorded in SJL. Enclosures: (1) Captain Henry Burbeck to Henry Knox, St. Mary's, 31 July 1790, saying that a few days since a "Mr. Jones in a vessel" on St. Mary's river with three negroes, his principal property, anchored off Cumberland Island opposite the Spanish galley and during the night two of his negroes stole his boat and went to the island "where they were free men." Burbeck added: "Mr. Jones was obliged to borrow a boat to go in pursuit of his Negroes, and found them at the Spanish Garrison as good christians as himself. He . . . was obliged to return without his boat and insulted by his negroes; the Captain told him that the negroes would want the boat to go to Augustine. The man was almost raving mad, and came to me for advice. I told him that he had better go immediately to Augustine as the new Governor had arrived, and it was expected had some orders respect- ing run away negroes. . . . There are but few inhabitants in this part of Georgia that have not had negroes, who have obtained their freedom by crossing the St. Mary's to Florida, and the people have been impatiently waiting for the arrival of the new Governor, expecting that he would have orders not to harbour them: but in case he countenances it and grants them protection, you may rely on the inhabitants making reprisals; for they will no longer consent to losing their property without any redress" (same). (2) Burbeck to Knox, 2 Aug. 1790, saying that Jones had gone to St. Augustine, had waited on the governor informing him of his business, and had been asked by the governor "how he presumed to come there without permission and . . . if he did not know that runaway negroes coming from the United States to Florida were all free men." Burbeck added: "He answered that he was sensible that it had been the case, but it was expected that his Excellency would have orders to give them up. The Governor told him, that he had nothing further to say to him. He then asked him for a passport to return. The Governor told him that he came without permission and that he should return in the same way.—Mr. Jones saw his negroes acting as servants in the Governors House" (same).

To Alexander Donald

DEAR SIR   New York Aug. 29. 1790.

Your favor of July 2. is now before me. The consulates of the W. Indies had been already filled. Mr. Braxton's name however shall be kept on the list of candidates, and all shall be done for him which can be justly done, that is to say, between equal competitors your recommendation shall turn the scale in his favor as far as shall depend on me. The suggestion for your other friend was also too late. Mr. Joshua Johnson had been already decided on by the President. I will continue my attentions to Mr. B's affair. The papers have not been returned to me, which is of good augury.—The President sets out tomorrow for Virginia. I shall do the same the next day. He will return to Philadelphia in November, I in October. In the mean time it is expected the flames of war will be kindled between our two neighbors. Since it is so decreed by fate, we have only to pray their souldiers may eat a great deal. Our crops of wheat are good in quantity and quality, and those of corn very promising. So far also this (I hope our last) crop of tobacco looks well. Little will be done in that way the next year, and less and less every year after. Adieu my dear Sir. Your affectionate friend & servt.,   TH: JEFFERSON

PrC (DLC).

To Thomas Mann Randolph, Jr.

DEAR SIR   New York Aug. 29. 1790.

The President sets out tomorrow. I shall follow two or three days after, so that allowing for stoppages on the road I shall be at Monticello about the 18th. of Sep. unless I should go by the way of Mt. Vernon which will add a delay of two or three days. I hope I shall have the happiness of meeting yourself and my daughters there. Tho' I count on remaining there a month, yet it will be subject to my being called away every moment, and at a moment's warning. The dissolution of parliament, and speech of the British king on that occasion, with many smaller indications render war almost a certain event. It is tolerably certain that France will join in it. We may rely with great safety on a high price for wheat for several years, and may in my opinion prepare our crops accordingly. Tobacco will be less affected in it's price by the circumstance of war. Kiss my dear daughters for me and be assured of the sincere esteem of Dear Sir Your's affectionately

TH: JEFFERSON

P.S. Wheat of this year's harvest in Maryland sells at a dollar and a third a bushel.

RC (DLC); addressed: "Thomas Mann Randolph junr. esq. Richmond"; franked; postmarked: "NEW-YORK * august 29."

To Alexander Hamilton

DEAR SIR   New York Aug. 30. 1790.

During my absence from the seat of government, which will be for about two months, the removal of my office, and other circumstances will call for advances of money which I am absolutely unable to calculate before hand. The following heads may give some idea what they will be.

		Dollars
Sep. 30. for a quarter's salaries		1504.16
Arrearage account	about	325.
debts due here	about	25.[1]
expences of removal		

Thus unable to fix a precise sum, and having perfect confidence in the discretion of Mr. Remsen, I must beg the favor of you to have his draughts for the above purposes answered at the treasury, on account, and I hereby render myself responsible for the due application of the money, of which an account shall be rendered, on my return.

The collection of the acts of the last sessions are to be sent to the members of Congress by post, and ought to be franked; but I shall not be present to perform that duty. If you would be so good as to frank the packets, I shall be much obliged to you. I know of no other official papers to be dispatched in my absence. Yet if any such should occur, I would venture to ask your extending the same favor to them also, on Mr. Remsen's explaining to you the nature of the occasion. I have the honor to be with the most perfect esteem & respect Dear Sir Your most obedt. humble servt.,

TH: JEFFERSON

PrC (DLC).

The ACTS sent to members of Congress were evidently not accompanied by a covering letter signed by the Secretary of State, but on this same day TJ sent to each of the governors of the states "a collection of the Acts passed by the Congress of the United States at their second session, to which are annexed all the Treaties which have been already made and promulged under the authority of the United States" (FC in DNA: RG 59, PCC No. 120; RCs in hand of Benjamin Bankson, signed by TJ, and addressed to governors of North Carolina, Rhode Island, and Virginia, are in NN, RPA, and Vi respectively).

1 MS torn; there may be three digits.

To La Forest

SIR   New York August 30th 1790.

I asked the favour of the Secretary of the Treasury to consider the 4th. Article of the Consular Convention and to let me know whether he should conclude that Consuls not exercising Commerce, were exempt from paying duties on things imported for their own use. I furnished him no explanation whatever of what had passed on the subject at the time of forming the Convention, because I thought it should be decided on the words of the Convention as they are offered to all the world, *and that it would only* be where these are equivocal that explanations might be adduced from other circumstances. He considered the naked words of the article, and delivered me as his opinion, that according to these, the first paragraph "The Consul and Vice Consuls &c.—as the natives are" subjected all their property in whatever form and under whatever circumstances it existed, to the same duties and taxes to which the property of other individuals is liable, and exempts them only from *taxes on their persons*, as Poll taxes, head rates for the poor, for Town charges &c. and that the 2d. paragraph "Those of the said Consuls &c.—or other Merchants" subjected such of them as exercised commerce even to the same *personal taxes* as other Merchants are: that the 2d. paragraph is an abridgement of the first, not an enlargement of it; and that the exemption of those not Merchants which seemed *implied* in the words of the 2d. paragraph could not be admitted against the contrary meaning directly and unequivocally expressed in the first.

Such, Sir, was his opinion, and it is exactly conformable to what the Negociators had in view in forming this Article. I have turned to the papers which passed on that occasion, and I find that the first paragraph was proposed in the first project given in by myself, by which the distinction between taxes on their property, and taxes on their persons is clearly announced and was agreed to: but as our Merchants exercising Commerce in France would have enjoyed a much greater benefit from the personal exemption than those of France do here, M. de Rayneval, in his first counter project, inserted the second paragraph, to which I agreed. So that the object was in the first paragraph to put Consuls, not being merchants, on the same footing with Citizens, not being Merchants, and the second to put Consuls, merchants, on the same footing with Citizens, merchants.

This, Sir, we suppose to be the sense of the Convention, which is become a part of the law of the Land, and the Law you know in this Country is not under the controul of the Executive, either in it's meaning or course. We must reserve, therefore, for more favourable occasions our dispositions to render the situations of the Consuls of his Majesty as easy as possible, by indulgences depending more on us, and of proving the sentiments of esteem and attachment to yourself personally, with which I have the honor to be, Sir, &c.

FC (DNA: RG 59, PCC No. 120). The PAPERS WHICH PASSED ON THAT OCCASION may be found in Vol. 14: 66-177.

To John Bondfield

DEAR SIR New York Aug. 31. 1790.

You will have understood perhaps that in the appointment of Consuls which has taken place, another than yourself has been named for Bordeaux. I feel it a duty to explain this matter to you lest it should give you an uneasiness as to the cause. No nomination occasioned more difficulty, nor hung longer suspended. But the Senate refused in every instance, where there was a *native*[1] *citizen* in any port, to consent to the nomination of any other. While this explains the reason of your not having been appointed, I trust it will also excuse those with whom the appointment rested. With respect to myself particularly, I beg you to be assured that I shall be happy in every occasion of being useful to you, and of proving to you the sentiments of esteem & attachment with which I have the honour to be Dear Sir Your most obedt. & most humble servt, TH: JEFFERSON

PrC (DLC).

¹ Both words are underscored and the first is doublescored.

From Arthur Fenner

SIR State of Rhode Island. Providence Augt. 31 1790

Having been informed that it was in contemplation to procure the Laws of the United States to be printed, in one of the News-papers in each of the States, I therefore take the liberty to recom-mend the Paper published by Mr. Bennet Wheeler entitled *The United States Chronicle political commercial and Historical* as suitable to be employed for the purpose, should such a measure be Adopted.

This paper has been published to general satisfaction nearly six Years and I believe has a more extensive Circulation in this State than any other paper published in it. The Publication of the Laws therefore in this paper would cause a Knowledge of them to be more generally diffused and would give perhaps as much or more satisfaction than if published in any other Paper in this State. I have the Honour to be Sir with the Highest sentiments of Esteem & Regard your most Obedient & humble Servt,

ARTHUR FENNER Govr.

RC (DNA: RG 59, PDL). Recorded in SJL as received 26 Sep. 1790.

On 26 Aug. 1790 Bennett Wheeler wrote TJ that he had received infor-mation that the laws of the United States "are published in the News-papers of *some* of the States by your Order at the Expence of Government, and that it was in Contemplation to have it done in *each* State"; he there-upon offered "the United States Chron-icle for that Purpose, upon the same Terms as are allowed to others. Our Paper has the most extensive Circula-tion of any in the State, and no Atten-tion of mine shall be wanting to have the Work well done" (same; also en-dorsed and recorded in SJL as received 26 Sep. 1790). Jabez Bowen wrote TJ also, 3 Sep. 1790, saying that Wheeler's paper had as large a circu-lation and was "as Correctly Printed as any one in the State"; he hoped Wheeler would be given the business "if 'tis not pre-engaged" (same; en-dorsed by TJ as received 26 Sep. 1790 and so recorded in SJL).

To William Short

DEAR SIR New York Aug. 31. 1790.

Since writing my letter of the 26th. it has been decided to commit to your care the transaction of very important money matters at Amsterdam. It is thought necessary that you should go there immediately, and remain there about three months to possess yourself of the ground. The Secretary of the Treasury will detail to you the particulars requisite there.

With respect to our affairs at Paris, we trust, in your absence, to the friendship of the Marquis de la Fayette for such things as are important enough to merit his attention. Two of the subjects lately given you in charge are of this description. As to all others, do them by letter or otherwise as you can. It will be necessary for you doubtless, sometimes to ask the attention of the Marquis, by letter; and where you think the moment requires essentially your presence, it is understood you will come to Paris express, returning again to Amsterdam as quickly as circumstances will admit. The facilities of travelling in Europe admit of this. Should you think it necessary, you may appoint a Secretary during your absence to remain at Paris, and communicate with you, allowing him a salary of four thousand livres a year. If you think this not necessary, you of course will not make the appointment. I am with sincere and great esteem Dear Sir your most obedient humble servt.,   TH: JEFFERSON

RC (ViW); endorsed by Short as received 28 Oct. 1790 and marked "duplicate" by him. Dupl (DLC: Short Papers); at foot of text in TJ's hand: "Duplicate"; endorsed by Short as received 22 Oct. 1790. Surprisingly, since both texts show evidence of haste in drafting and both are in TJ's hand, he did not employ a press copy but transcribed the text again for the duplicate. FC (DNA: RG 59, PCC No. 121).

From George Wythe

G.W. TO T.J.   Williamsburgh, 31 of Aug. 1790.

The report which you, my much respected sir, sent to me, had been seen and read over and over again by me three weeks ago. Thanks are due for it, and it is deposited among my treasures.

RC (DLC); endorsed by TJ as received 14 Sep. 1790 and so recorded in SJL.

From Stephen Cathalan, Jr.

SIR   Marseilles the 1st. Sepber 1790

As I had hoped, that your Excy. would have returned in France and not knowing Positively your usual residence in America, I have perhaps too much postponed of Paying you my Respects.

In congratulating your Excy. on the Eminent Post of Secretary of State in Foreing Affairs, which your Country has Confered on you, in Reward of the important Services you have rendered to America, I Sincerely regret that Such Circumstances deprives me, perhaps for ever of Seeing you Again, even to have frequent opportunities of Cultivating the Friendship you honour'd me when we were not so distant; be however well Persuaded, that, I will be always ready to your Commands in whatever I may be usefull to you and to United States of America; and beg you to furnish me opportunities, directly, or by the channel of Mr. W. Short or any other Person Appointed in the Ministry of united States in France.

You may be too well advised by your Friends at Paris of the actual revolution in France, that I may give you any news on that account; you have forseen Long time ago a good Part of what happens; I am too Far of the Stage to Judge if all together Cooly considered, our nation collectively will become more happy, have they not been too Far. Time and Experience will resolve the Problem.

Meantime it will not be an Easy Matter to Submit to the Laws So much Common People, who have mistaken Licence for Genuine Liberty, when their too exalted Spirit, is intirely Corrupted; now tho' they have Sworn at the Federation of the 14th. Last July, to Lett the free Circulation of wheats amongst the different provinces of this kingdom and to protect it, they will not allow any enportation Even from a Municipality to an other, and have threaten the exporters of hanging them.

The appearances of the Last Crop were very Promising, but at the harvest it is not proved So in the Southern Provinces of France, and prices which had fallen in the Beggining of July Suddenly fell £44.ᵗ to 30.ᵗ⅌ charge have Since Rised progressively and are now at £40.ᵗ If we had not been So abbundantly provided Last winter and Spring by the Kingdoms of Naples and Sicily, the Southern Part of France would have experienced the horrors of the most dreadful Famin; we Can't enport the Same Supplies now from those Part, their crops being but Indifferent, and as prices will go on the rise as we will advance in the Season, you may with Safety encourage Americans Merchants to Send this way wheat and flour, any quantity will meet ready and advantageous Sales at £38. to 40.ᵗ⅌ charge the wheat and 40.ᵗ to 42ᵗ⅌ Bu. the Superfine Flour.

We have yet about 800 hhd. Tobacco unsold, the prices are from £30.ᵗ to 33.ᵗ℔ ql. Marc Wheights; it appears by the repport of the commitée of Finances, that this article will be no more a Farm, and the Cultivation in our own Lands allowed, but it will require time before a quantity may be reapped, and I find that American Tobacco will become to a Lower price and of a Better quality; and delivered of the Farmer's, it will become a Large Branch of Trade between our two Nations, as soon as it will be decretted and sanctionned.

I have a Large Parcel on hand of American Beef and Pork, that article being landed here, on account of the Gabelle, could be exported only to our west Indies, without Paying a duty of 3.ᵗ ℔ ql. Marc Brut, but as well for others forting Places, or the Consumption of our vessels or this of this and neighbouring Places, this duty ought to be Paid, I received orders in the Last Month, (as I could not Sale Such parcel on account of that duty,) to Send it to Cadix, but that duty being asked to me, I have made a Petition to the National assembly and Ministry, Subscribed by other Merchants and our Board of Trade, and hope very Soon that the duty will be taken off.

Till now Mr. Barclay has paid to me nothing of the Large Sum he owes me, and proposes me 25℔ ct. only on the Capital, the 7 years of Interest Lost for me, other wise he Says, he will declare him self a Bankrupt, I will consent to an abbattment to finish with him, but not to such Bad Conditions, better have been offered to Messrs. P. & W. French & Nephew, Bordeaux, who have acted rigorously with him, when, I rely'd on his word of honor, that he would pay me in full. I writte by this Same opportunity to Messrs. Willing Morris & Swanwick my attorneys, to Settle with him in receiving in ready money 25℔ ct. and others 25℔ ct. in a Short time under a Good Quaranty; I beg you to Speak to Mr. Barclay in my Favor, and if he will prevent the Bankrupt, what I ask is very reasonable; I am in a great need of that money Since the heavy losses I have Suffered in the American Trade.

By the report of M. Mirabeau we will Sustain our pact of Late of Family but now national Pact, with Spain, and 30 Mens Warr will be put into Commission to prevent England to be intirely despots at Sea.

I am intirely at your Service and to that of United States of America, and to any of your Friends who will Command me; all my Family present you their Respects and I am very respectfully Sir of your Excellency the most obedt. humb. Servt.,

STEPHEN CATHALAN Junr.

RC (DNA: RG 59, CD); addressed and docketed beneath address by J. Swanwick as having been forwarded by him on 20 Dec. 1790; endorsed by TJ as received 20 Dec. 1790 and so recorded in SJL.

From Alexander Donald

MY DEAR SIR   London 1st. Septemr. 1790

I arrived here a few days ago after a very pleasant passage of five weeks and three days.

Before I left America, I had intended to ask the favour of you to give me a letter of introduction to one of the Farmers General of France; but I was so much hurried that it escaped my memory. It is reported here, that the Tobacco Trade in France is to be put upon nearly the same footing that it is on in this Country, indeed I believe it is so ordered by the National Assembly. This I recollect you mentioned to me when I had the pleasure of seeing you in Virginia, but notwithstanding of that, it is probable that some of the Farmers may still incline to do business in the Tobacco line, and I am willing either to contract to furnish any given quantity, or to purchase in Virginia upon Commission. I would go over to Paris if I had been fortunate enough to have brought with me a letter from you.

I hope you have used your good offices with Mr. Hamilton so effectually as to prevent Mr. Brown any further Trouble about the Bowman's business. The Papers which I forwarded to New York before I left Virga. would satisfie every unprejudiced person that there were no grounds for Heth's Conduct, nay he himself told Mr. Harrison after seeing the Papers that he was satisfied. I always thought, and ever shall, that the whole proceeded from envy or malice in Mr. Heth.

The appearance of war is stronger now than it was three days ago. The National Assembly of France have ordered 32 ships of the Line to be put into Commission, which will make the Spaniards more forward when they find they are to be so powerfully supported by France. I hope America will not be involved in it. I sincerely wish for war, and on her account only, as she will, by observing a strict neutrality, become the carrier for all the Belligerent Powers, and will find a very proffitable market for all her superfluous grain and Lumber in their West India Islands, and I am really sorry to find that some such market appears to be necessary, For from all the information I have been able to procure since I came here, the demand from Europe will not be great, for in general every Country has made sufficient to supply its own consumption, and I have not heard of any that apprehends a scarcity.

There was only a small part of your Crop of Tobacco brought to Richmond when I left it, but I suppose it would get down soon afterwards. You will find that the money will be very punctually paid, which I hope will induce you to give Mr. Brown the refusal of your Crops in future. I took the liberty of mentioning to you and of writing to Colo. Lewis, that it would be much your Interest to import your coarse goods, if you do not manufacture enough for to cloath your People; Or if there is any thing that this Country affords, which you may want for yourself at New York, I trust I have no occasion to tell you that I will be most happy in Executing any of your commands. I am with much respect & esteem My Dear Sir Your mo. obt. Sert.,   ADONALD

RC (DLC); endorsed as received 20 Nov. 1790 and so recorded in SJL.

From Lucy Ludwell Paradise

DEAR SIR   London Sept. the 1st. 1790

I have done Myself the honour of writing to your Excellency by Mr. Broom. The purpot of that Letter was to acquaint you that the Queen of Portugal had appointed Chevr. de Freire to be her Minister to our States. He was to have gone to a Court in Europe. But Monsr. le Chevr. de Pinto knowing Mr. Freire knew more of Amerca then, perhaps, any of his Countrymen, and also, as he had the honour of knowing you, and Mr. Adams personally, the Queen altered her first intentions, and appointed him Minister to America. I have assured Mr. Freire he will be more pleased with America, and the Americans then he at present supposes. I have taken the liberty to tell him, I make no doubt he will be pleased with the attentions he will meet with from your Ecellencies. I hope you have received all the Money you had the goodness to lend Mr. Paradise during his stay at Paris. I should be obliged to your Excellency to let me know. The beginging of November we shall quit our house in London, as it is too dear a place for Us to live in. I believe we shall go to Bath to Lodge and Board for a few Months. Therefore I shall esteem Myself honoured if you would be please to write to Me and direct your Letter for Us to Mr. Anderson our Merchant and put them under cover to him and desire him to be particular to deliver your Letter safe to Us. Dr. Bancroft is the Same good and true friend. Indeed, I do not know what I should do, if I had not him to assist Me. I wish greatly to return home, but, I fear, I may wish long enough for until all the Debts are paid here I must stay. I have told Mr. P I wish to go and see America once More before I get too old and that I would return to him again. Indeed, I think it necessary. The longest time I wish to stay is one year. Will you My dear Sir have the goodness to give Me your Advice upon the Subject? Mr. P is perfectly Sober, and well, only a little nervious owing to the heat of the Summer. He is at present in the Country for a few Days. You and your Amiable family enjoy the Blessing of health and happiness, I hope to the highest degree. I beg you to present Mr. Paradise and my affectionate Compliments to your amable family and respectful Compliments to all our Noble Friends &c &c &c &c. I remain with every sense of Gratitude Your ever Oliged, and Humble Servant and Friend,

LUCY PARADISE

RC (DLC); endorsed as received 7 Dec. 1790 and so recorded in SJL.

From William Vernon

SIR   Newport Rhode Island 1st. Septemr. 1790

Agreeable to your Advice I have wrote to the Honble. William Short Charge des Affaires at the Court of France, and also to the Consul Joseph Fenwick Esqr. at Bourdeaux, respecting the most probable methods to be taken in Order to get my Son Mr. Wm. Vernon Home; and if no other will succeed to take effectual Measures to compel him to return Home.

I have, with your Permission, made Use of your Name to those Gentlemen; and do, Sir, earnestly entreat your Influence to accomplish what I have been assiduously pursuing these Eight Years to no Purpose.

You will perceive my Anxiety to save a Son from total Ruin and Destruction has led me to resolve upon Methods that must be very humiliating and disgraceful to him if no other should prevail. Indeed this was what Doctr. Franklin advised me to, upon his Return to Philadelphia; and wrote me that he wou'd furnish me with Letters that shou'd effectually answer the Purpose; and I regret that I did not, at that Moment, close with his Advice and kind Offer.

The above mention'd Letters are inclosed, *unseal'd*, for your Perusal, which, if conformable to your Sentiments, I pray you will strengthen by a Line. If not, please to erase such parts as you dislike and close them.

I shou'd fail in Words to express my Obligations to you, Sir, for this unmerited Favor; but I make no Doubt that the Satisfaction of restoring a Subject to the United States, and a Son to a Parent, will give you more Pleasure than Ten Thousand Compliments, but my Thanks are unfeigned, and the Favor will never be forgot, by Your most obliged & most humble Servant,

WM. VERNON

P.S. I shou'd be glad to know if you receive these Letters timely for the Packet.

RC (DLC); endorsed as received 31 Aug. 1790 and so recorded in SJL without any notation concerning the inconsistency between the date of the letter and the date of its receipt.

From Richard Harison

SIR   New York Sept. 3d. 1790

I have been honored by your Letter of the 12th. [ins]tant and in consequence have made Enquiries for a Set of the Laws of this State, excluding those published by Messrs. Varick and Jones. With some difficulty I have found such a Set consisting 1st. of a Volume compiled by Peter Van Schaack under the Directions of the Legislature, comprehending all the Acts that were in force in 1773. inclusive. 2ndly. of the Acts passed in 1774 and 1775. 3rdly. of a Volume containing the Acts from the first Meeting of the Legislature after the Revolution to 1784 inclusive. 4th. of the Acts from 1784 to 1789 inclusive.

These are not all of them bound up in regular Order. The Acts of 1774 and 1775 having been very scarce, were bound with other Acts by Gentlemen of the Profession, as they could be procured. The Edition of Laws already in the Office of State, contains all those public Acts which were in [force] in March 1789, with perhaps one or two Exceptions. Consequently *they* exhibit the Legislation of New York in its State at that Time, the other Volumes which I have mentioned, shew its Progress. I have directed these Books to be reserved until I am honored with your further Commands upon the subject.

Previous to Mr. Van Schaack's Edition of our Laws, there had been several mentioned in his preface. Some of these may perhaps be met with, if it should be thought of any Importance.

I have not supposed it necessary to obtain the Laws of this State passed in July 1789, and in the present Year. They may be had by sending to Messrs. Child & Loudon, Printers to the State at those Periods.

Be assured, Sir, that your other Commands will be executed with that Attention which their Importance appears to demand, and that I shall be ready to exert myself with the utmost Zeal, upon every occasion where the general service may render it necessary. With the highest Respect, I have the Honor, to be, Sir, Your most obedt. and most humble Servt:,   RICH: HARISON

RC (DNA: RG 59, MLR); endorsed by TJ as received 26 Sep. 1790 and so recorded in SJL.

From Madame de Houdetot

au chateau du Marais ce 3 September 1790

I received Sir the letter which you did me the honor of writing to me by Monsieur de Crevecœur. If the kind sentiments it contained gave me sincere pleasure how afflicting is it to me to think, I can no longer enjoy them near you. You left us in a storm of troubles. I believe before your departure you knew of the horrid outrages of the sixth of October. This storm so far from producing a calm, leaves us the fear that we shall be for a long time the victims of the errors of our Legislators, and of the ill intentions of some of them; at least we dare not hope, or even expect a speedy calm, and that permanent happiness the result alone of a good administration. Two circumstances absolutely necessary to form a solid basis for the edifice of a new constitution seem to me wanting, namely, a national representation by proprietors, and a proper balance of powers. The means of insurrection that have been adopted, and the abuse still made of it, have thrown the whole Kingdom into a state of general fermentation. The terrible method they have employed they themselves are no longer the masters of. Already it has gained part of the army, and may perhaps be the means of perverting the whole. The steps taken to restablish the finances, which are ever readily abused, appear rather to have diminished, than increased the public credit. The effects of anarchy are experienced in every part of the kingdom, nor is it to be wonderd at, since it has as yet been found impossible to establish order and no power exists to enforce it. I fear that to arrive at the wished for point of amendment, we must pass through a labrynth of difficulty, and disorder, and that the only good that can be expected, must spring from the excess of evil. The executive power has no longer any authority, even in the maintenance of salutary laws. The characteristic diffirence between your revolution, and ours, is that having nothing to destroy, you had nothing to injure, and labouring for a people, few in number, uncorrupted, and extended over a large tract of country, you have avoided all the inconveniences of a situation, contrary in every respect. Every step in your revolution was perhaps the effect of virtue, while ours are often faults, and sometimes crimes. Excuse this melancholy account; It is the effect of a well placed confidence that your reasoning, and enlightend understanding, which have always led me to hope an happier issue, will diminish the impression, which those events have left upon my mind. You Sir have perhaps been a witness of the last moments of that great man, who will be for ever the object of the admiration of succeeding ages, and who was to me also that of my peculiar esteem and attachment. I could say in the words of Nestor that I have seen such men, as posterity never can. Your country has produced more than one, and those whom it still boasts, must be considerd amongst the richest gifts of nature. Adieu Sir preserve for me a place in your remembrance, of which I feel the full value, and indulge me sometimes with the proofs of it.   LALIVE DHOUDETOT

RC (DLC); addressed: "A Monsieur Monsieur Jefferson"; endorsed by TJ as received 11 Jan. 1791 and so recorded in SJL.

From N. & J. Van Staphorst & Hubbard

SIR   Amsterdam 3rd. September 1790.

It was with sincere pleasure we learned from Mr. Short, and from our Connexions in America, Your Safe return to your native Country, and your acceptance of the high Office of Secretary of State, to which you were appointed during your absence; Confident that your Exercise of it will tend to the honor and Credit of the United States, and We Sincerely hope also to your own Satisfaction and Happiness.

We are informed by our attornies in South Carolina, that Some difficulty will probably be started against crediting us for the amount of the 150 Bonds passed by Commodore A. Gillon to Bearer in his quality of Agent for that State, owing to the legislature having most imprudently issued a special Indent for the same object, to Persons pretending to be Owners thereof. In order to convince the state of the true Nature and evident Justice of our Claim, and thereby to avoid having recourse to extremities that are ever disagreeable to us, we have added our Friend Mr. Theophe. Cazenove to our former Attornies, with full authorisation to represent us in the Business, in consequence of which He will proceed if necessary to So. Carolina. But this we hope will not become requisite as we flatter ourselves the Representation He and our other agents will make to the State, will procure us all we ask, Justice. Should he request you Sir, not to deliver up to the state the Bonds We deposited with you, until the state shall have consented to give us credit on the Treasury Books for their amount, You will greatly oblige us, by granting his Suit, and if upon the Communication of the whole of this business, that we beg of him to make you, You would take the trouble to write to the State your Opinion upon the Subject, we shall esteem it an additional favor to the many you have already conferred on us, for which we retain the most lively Gratitude: As you might perhaps thereby induce the state not to Compromise further its Credit in an affair so very clear.—Having found on examination of our Books a Charge of Holld. Cy ƒ100 against you, We have discovered it to arrise from an Error in your letter to us of 3d. May 1789, on reference to which you will see, that the addition of our disbursments therein contained was made by you ƒ237.60 whereas it ought to be Holld. Cy ƒ337.6. We inclose you Copy of said letter for your Government in case you should not have your Papers at hand; The difference ƒ100 you may remit us an order for or pay on our account to our Friends Messrs. Le Roy & Bayard of New-york, whichever you prefer.

Should we be so happy as to be able to render you any useful or agreeable offices, we desire you to dispose freely of us. With greatest Esteem and Respect we are Sir! Your most obt. hble. servts.,   N. & J. Van STAPHORST & HUBBARD

RC (DLC); endorsed by TJ as received 11 Dec. 1790, but recorded in SJL under 10 Dec. 1790.

From Nathaniel Colley

DEAR SIR   Norfolk Septre. 5th. 1790

I have just Received your favour of the 22nd. Augst. Enjoining a Duplicate of your Small Memorandum. I Did not Get the Tables made when in London last As Mr. Cutting informed me you did not Return to France again and I thought they might attend with trouble trasporting them there and back. I am exceedingly happy I Received your Letter in time as I this Day Sail for London again and Mr. Brown and Col. Eppes of Richmond whom I called on to know where to Direct the tables to when I Returned informed me you would not now want them they Supposed which would have prevented my Getting them. But you may Depend on my Bringing them when I return and will Send them to Philadelphia Imeadeatly. Mr. Cutting was Exceedingly Kind and rendered me a great deal of Service when in London at the time of my peoples being imprest, as he undertook to Draw of petitions for us and hand them in himself, through which means we obtaind an order for Our American Seaman. I am happy to hear yourself and Daughters are all well. So having no more at present I conclude with Assuring you I am Dr. Sir your most Obdt. Hbl. St.,   NATHL. COLLEY

RC (MHi); endorsed by TJ as received 26 Sep. 1790 and so recorded in SJL.

From William Short

DEAR SIR   Paris Sep. the 5th. 1790

Since my last in which I mentioned that the national assembly had voted an augmentation of their armament to forty-five ships of the line, nothing has transpired in England to shew what effect it produced in the British cabinet. We know only that on the exchange war is considered as inevitable in consequence of it. I should suppose however that Mr. Pitt would not take any decisive measure on account of the vote of the assembly, but would wait to see whether that vote can be carried into effect, for he must certainly know that there is a great difference between the vote and its execution in a disorganised government. Should France not be able to arm under the present circumstances, it is leaving matters in the very posture which Mr. Pitt must desire, and of course I should imagine he would not risk the uniting the several parties here by an hostile attack, under the hope of the advantages to be gained from commencing the war against them unprepared.

Whatever be the designs of the British cabinet, it is certain that their naval preparations are carried on with unremitting ardour. I still suppose that their original design was to frighten Spain into a commercial treaty, and if possible into a political alliance, that the expense of the first preparations having not effected that purpose, it has been judged proper to add a second stake in hopes of recovering the first loss, and that finally if it were possible for France to fit out her fleet and shew a firm and decided countenance, the game would be abandoned, and that arrangements as to Nootka sound would be proposed and accepted as the only object of the negociation.

These preparations in England have embarassed our commerce and harrassed our seamen there beyond measure. A merchant of Boston who was with me yesterday assured me there had been more than three hundred American sailors impressed into the British service, that the expence and difficulty of rescuing them from their captivity was such as to deter many of the owners from attempting it and particularly as so many obstacles are thrown in their way as to render their applications for the most part useless. I imagine you will have recieved particular accounts of this business from Mr. Cutting who has exerted himself in it with much zeal and activity.

I mentioned to you in my last the apparent repentence of several regiments who had mutinied. Since then the Regiment du Roi in garrison at Nancy has relapsed and been the occasion of vigorous measures being taken which fortunately met with success. An inspector was sent by the King to Nancy to settle the accounts of the revolted regiments, as the want of that settlement was the pretext of their disorder. This inspector being ill treated by a Swiss regiment in garrison there and in revolt he drew his sword, wounded several and made his escape to Luneville. In this extremity M. de Bouillé was ordered by the King to take such troops as he thought proper, and such a number of gardes nationales as he could procure and march against the garrison of Nancy. On arriving near Nancy he harangued his army, read to them the decree of the assembly, and finding they were willing to support him determined to act with vigour. Deputations were sent to him from the three regiments who composed the garrison desiring to capitulate. He refused their demand and ordered them to retire out of the town to receive his orders. A part of the two French regiments obeyed. The Swiss and some soldiers of the Regiment du Roi refused and defended the entrance of the town. As soon as the column of M. de Bouillé's army approached the gate they were fired on by the guard posted there. An engagement immediately ensued. The gate was forced and the garrison made prisoners after a combat of several hours in which three or four hundred were killed. Two commissaries are sent to enquire into the causes of this revolt which is attributed to a variety of circumstances. Some say it is owing to the severities exercised by the officers, who are all aristocrats, against the soldiers on account of their patriotism. This as you may suppose is the most popular reason and that which is most readily adopted. Others think that a faction in the assembly whose power depends only on disorder, have excited these revolts in the several garrisons to strengthen their party. The most natural cause however seems to be, the example which the garrison of Nancy had already seen of several regiments having imprisoned their officers and pillaged their military chests with impunity.

The intelligence of this engagement at Nancy and its success made a very different impression here, in and out of the assembly. The assembly voted their thanks to the municipalities and gardes nationales who had taken a part in this business, and approved the conduct of M. de Bouillé and the regular troops. The mob of Paris on the contrary assembled. Money is said to have been distributed amongst them. Several feuilles volantes were circulated to animate them against M. de Bouillé, who it was said had begun the counter-revolution by massacring the most patriotic regiments and the peaceable citizens of Nancy. It was said also that a majority of the assembly were bribed by the government and had abandoned the cause of the people, and that the people should avenge

themselves on them and on M. de la fayette who had supported
M. de Bouillé. The mob insisted also on the ministers being
turned off, and many on their being hanged. Motions were also
made for going to bring the King from St. Cloud where he then
was. No attempt was made to disperse the mob, but strong guards
were placed before the houses of the ministers to prevent their
entering them. M. Necker, who is no longer a favorite with the
people retired to his country-house in alarm, and the Minister of war
also thought it prudent to pass the night out of his house. A heavy
rain which came on dispersed the mob, and since then the assemblies of the people in the Thuilleries and Palais-Royal have not
been more numerous than usual.

Many journalists continue to spread inflammatory writings
against the assembly, ministry and M. de la fayette, on account
of the affair of Nancy. Nothing is more common now than to hear
motions made in the Palais-Royal for hanging the latter as having
deserted their cause. There is some reason to fear also that the
gardes nationales of Paris are not unanimous in approving those
who acted under M. de Bouillé. This shews that M. de la fayette
has less influence on them than had been hoped. Still however
there is no doubt that a great majority place implicit confidence and
are much attached to him.

Mr. Necker as you know has been long intending to go to the
waters on account of his health. This late mob and the pressing
solicitations of Madame Necker have determined him to realize
his intention. He has written a letter to the assembly notifying
it. This is considered as the resignation of his office; on the
receipt of his letter, and its being read, the order of the day
was called for and no further notice was taken of it. What is still
more extraordinary, it has had no effect whatever on the stocks.
The other ministers seem to be determined to try to keep their
places. It is as yet uncertain whether they will succeed. The best
and only security they have for them is that no member of the
assembly can accept a place in the ministry.

The last public ministerial act performed by M. Necker was
to send a memorial to the assembly against a plan which is now
before them for emitting two milliards of paper money for paying
off what is called the *dette exigible*. You will receive this memorial
with the plan for the emission and the debates on the subject in
the newspapers and journals which I sent yesterday to M. de la
Motte to be forwarded to you. The statement of the committee

of finance which brings on this subject divides the whole national debt into three heads: 1. *la dette constituée* viz. rentes viageres and perpetuelles, where the Nation is only answerable for the interest annually, and can never be called on for the principal; 2. *la dette exigible* consisting of arrears due, and the price of venal offices suppressed, &c. 3. the debt which will become due hereafter at fixed terms. It is proposed to pay off the dette exigible by the sale of ecclesiastical and Royal lands. One plan for effecting the sale is to give certificates to the creditors of the exigible debt bearing an interest until the sale, and to recieve them in the purchase of the lands. Another is to pay off these creditors by a paper money, which shall also be redeemed by the sale of the same lands. The difference between these two plans as you will see, consists principally in this, that in one instance the public creditor recieves a certificate bearing interest until the lands are sold; in the other he recieves a paper money, with which he can pay his own private debts. Mirabeau who has hitherto been the avowed enemy of paper-money both in his writings and speeches is now the most vigorous supporter of this paper-money scheme. Its advocates insist on its being not paper-money, because there is a pledge for its immediate redemption. They are answered several ways, but irresistibly by those who tell them that the value of the pledge is not known, and that it may be and probably will be far inferior to the emission. The apprehension of this paper money has rendered specie more scarce than ever. The commercial towns and some of the provinces will certainly remonstrate against it, and as the assembly has determined that the question shall not be decided before the 10th. of this month, the disposition of the assembly will perhaps change. Hitherto it has appeared in favor of the paper money.

Among the papers which I sent you yesterday is one called L'Ami du peuple. It is published and circulated here daily. I have sent it to you to give some idea of the liberty of the press of this country. There are several others of the same kind. Some feeble attempts were made to prevent these papers being cried in the streets, but in vain, and lately the national assembly directed the Procureur du Roi au Chatelet to prosecute the author of one called *c'en est fait de nous*, in which he tells the people that the only remedy to their present evils is to seize and kill the queen, imprison the dauphin, and hang seven or eight hundred members of the assembly with Mirabeau at their head.

The report of the committee of impositions has not yet been laid before the assembly although several days have been fixed for it. They adhere to their plan relative to tobacco. It will probably pass, as well because it is the shortest way of getting rid of the business, as because the merchants only among the members of the assembly will oppose it.

We remain still ignorant here of the proceedings of Congress. The only intelligence that I have had for a long time has been through letters recieved here by the Americans at Paris and in London. It is on this authority alone that I have answered the variety of enquiries made me ministerially and otherwise. Your two last letters which have come to my hands were of July 1. and 8. You will soon see I hope that they produced the effect you desired. I beg you to be persuaded of the sentiments of real attachment with which I am, dear Sir your friend & servant,

W. SHORT

PrC (DLC: Short Papers); at head of text: "No. 41." Tr (DNA: RG 59, DD). Recorded in SJL as received 15 Dec. 1790.

To Joseph Fenwick

DEAR SIR   Philadelphia Sep. 6. 1790.

According to your permission I trouble you with a commission to recieve and forward to me some wines for the President and myself. They are written for in the inclosed letters to the respective owners of the vineyards, and are as follows.

M. la comte de Lur-Saluce	30. doz. Sauterne for the President
	10. doz. do. for myself
M. de Mirosmenil	20. doz. vin de Segur for the President
Madame de Rozan	10. doz. vin de Rozan for myself.
Monsieur Lambert at Frontignan	10. doz. Frontignan for the President
	5. doz. do. for myself

To these I must beg you to add 10. dozen for me of a good white vin ordinaire, or indeed something better, that is to say of such a quality as will do to mix with water, and also be drinkable alone. Such I suppose may be obtained at Bordeaux for ten sous the bottle. I would wish you to buy it of the person who makes it, and give me his name and address, that, if it suits me, I may always

[493]

be sure of the same quality. This letter will go under cover to Mr. Short, who will furnish you with the means of paiment. Be so good as to have the wines delivered immediately and forward them by the first safe vessel bound from Bordeaux to Philadelphia. I have directed those for the President to be packed separately and marked G.W. and mine T.I. You will recieve them ready packed. Those from Frontignan cannot probably be forwarded so soon as the others. You need only send the letter to Dr. Lambert at Frontignan, with a note of your address, and he will forward them to Bordeaux and draw on you for the amount of the wine and expences. I am with great esteem Dear Sir your most obedt. humble servt.,   TH: JEFFERSON

PrC (DLC). Enclosures: (1) TJ to Madame de Rausan, 6 Sep. 1790, reading in part: "Quoique je n'ai pas l'honneur, Madame, de vous etre personellement connu, j'ai eu l'avantage, dans un tour que j'ai fait pendant ma sejour à Paris, de sçavoir, en visitant le canton des bons vins de Bordeaux, que ceux nommés *de Rozan*, de votre cru, sont d'excellente qualité"; he asked that she send ten dozen bottles "du meilleur pour la service actuelle," bottled and packed at the vineyard, and added: "Je vous demanderai encore la grace, Madame, de m'en annoncer l'expedition, et de me dire comment je devrai m'adresser de tems en tems pour des envois du meme genre." (2) TJ to Miromenil, 6 Sep. 1790, reading in part: "Quoique je n'ai pas l'honneur Monsieur de vous etre personnellement connu, j'ai eu l'avantage . . . en visitant le canton des meilleurs vins de Bordeaux d'avoir vu votre vigne qui donne les vins nommés *de Segur*, et de sçavoir que c'est un des meilleures crues de ce canton. J'en ai fait cette eloge à notre President le General Washington, et il me charge consequemment de vous prier d'avoir la bonté de lui en fournir une vingtaine de douzaines de bouteilles de votre meilleur pour la service actuelle," to be bottled, packed, and marked G.W. at the vineyard; he said that it was more than probable that he would renew the order each year and added: "Ayez seulement la complaisance de m'en annoncer l'expedition, et de m'assurer que les vins sont veritablement de votre cru." (3) TJ to Lambert, 6 Sep. 1790, reading in part: "Quoique bien eloigné de vous

actuellement, Monsieur, je suis encore à portée de recevoir de vos excellens vins. Ayez la bonté donc de m'en expedier dix douzaines de bouteilles pour notre President le General Washington, et cinq douzaines pour moi, du blanc et du rouge, mais du dernier en bonne proportion," the shipments to be separately packed and marked as indicated above; he stated that Fenwick would receive the shipment, paying all costs, and added: "J'aimerais [moi-] meme que les cinque douzaines pour moi soient mises en bouteilles de demi pinte si vous en avez, qui feroient alors dix douzaines de demi pinte." (4) TJ to Lur-Saluces, 6 Sep. 1790, reading in part: "Le vin blanc de Sauterne, de votre cru, que vous avez eu la bonté de m'envoyer à Paris au commencement de l'année 1788. a eté si bien approuvé des Americains qui y en ont gouté, que je ne doute pas que mes compatriotes generalement ne le trouvent aussi conforme à leur gout. Actuellement que je me suis etabli ici, j'ai persuadé à notre President, le General Washington, d'en essayer un echantillon. Il vous en demande trente douzaines, Monsieur, et moi, je vous en demande dix douzaines pour moi-meme," to be bottled, packed separately, and marked as indicated above "afin d'arranger les malheurs qui peuvent arriver en voyage"; he asked that the shipment be made to Fenwick, who would pay all costs, and to inform him when sent. Press copies of all of the foregoing enclosures, dated "à Philadelphie ce 6me. 7bre. 1790," are in DLC.

From Henry Remsen, Jr.

The intelligence which I had the honor to communicate to you in my last Letter respecting a naval engagement between the Spanish and English fleets, began to circulate the moment the English packet arrived, and was believed to have been brought by her, and as it was a matter of great consequence, if true, I lost no time in informing you of it. It is since known that it came from Philadelphia, and is disbelieved.

On Saturday last Mr. Bruce called upon me with two Nova Scotia men, who wanted to rent your House until next May. They had learnt your terms from him, and I found, wanted to obtain it still lower. They however concluded to give the sum you asked, on condition that the furniture should be removed by the first of October, as they expected to come into it by the middle of October, and wished to have shelves fixed in the lower front room for a store previous to their coming in. I desired Mr. Bruce to give you credit for the £27.10.0, and look to them for the payment of that Sum, which he will do.

He and Francis have been talking about some things which you put to the house, to wit, the Bell, the Board on which the flower pot was placed and the tubs for the Yard. Francis thinks these things should be paid for; but Mr. Bruce thinks they should not, and observes that custom has established it as a principle whenever any repair is made to a house by a tenant without a previous agreement with the owner, it of course belongs to the house. I will, Sir, thank you for directions on this head.

Sir John Temple called at the Office this day with Mr. Mac Donogh, the British Consul for the four Eastern States. He said he had been to Mr. Jay's, and was advised by him to leave Mr. Mac Donogh's commission with me, as possibly, his arrival being known by you and his visit expected, you might have left orders respecting his recognition. I told him I would take the commission, which I did, forward a copy of it to you, and let him know as early as I received it, the answer you might direct to be given. He said Mr. Mac Donogh would remain here until that time, altho' anxious to return to Boston. I now enclose a Copy of his Commission, and a copy of the act of Congress recognizing Mr. Miller, the last of which may be serviceable if you should think it expedient that Mr. Mac Donogh should be recognized, and the

Acts recognizing him forwarded to the States for which he is appointed, before you return from Monticello to Philadelphia. I have the honor to be with great respect Sir Your obliged and obedient Servt.,   HENRY REMSEN JUNR.

RC (DLC); endorsed as received 26 Sep. 1790 (at Monticello) and so recorded in SJL. On the erroneous intelligence in Remsen's LAST LETTER, 2 Sep. 1790, see note, TJ to Remsen, 7 Sep. 1790.

To William Short

DEAR SIR   Philadelphia Sep. 6. 1790.

I am here on my way to Virginia, to which place I set out to-morrow. The President left this this morning on his way to Mount Vernon. He engaged me some time ago to get him some wines from France, to wit 40. dozen of Champagne, 30 doz. of Sauterne, 20. dozen of Bordeaux de Segur, and 10. doz. of Frontignan, and he took a note of their prices in order to furnish me with a bill of exchange sufficient to cover the cost and charges. In the multiplicity of his business before his departure he has forgot to do this: and it remains that we do not permit him to be disappointed of his wine by this omission. But how to do it? For the amount of the whole I suppose will be 3000.ᵗᵗ and the being obliged to set up a house in New York, then to abandon it and remove here, has really put me out of condition to advance such a sum here. I think however it can be done, without incommoding you, by your drawing on the bankers in Amsterdam. On the President's return here (about the 1st. of December) bills shall be remitted you, and by using these for your own purposes instead of making new draughts for your salary on the bankers, all will stand right without any special mention in the public accounts. I will make any necessary explanations at the Treasury, should any be necessary.

I write for wines for my own use at the same time. These will amount to about 550. livres. I have sent out to seek for a bill of exchange to that amount. If it can be got to-day I will inclose it herein. If not, I will charge the person with whom I leave the present letter, not to send it off till he has got such a bill and to inclose one herewith, and forward a duplicate by some other opportunity. I leave the letter to Fenwick open, to the end that you may see the arrangements I take to leave you no other trouble than to forward it to him and let him know how he shall be furnished with money to pay for the wines. The bill for my part shall be made paiable to you.

The new constitution of this state has passed. The chair of government was to have been disputed between Morris and Mifflin. But the former has declined, and his friends set up Sinclair in opposition to Mifflin. I am, my dear Sir Your's affectionately,

TH: JEFFERSON

P.S. I am excessively anxious for the success of your mission to Amsterdam, that the business may be done, and so well done as to place you advantageously in the public view.

Sep. 7. The broker is come in and promised a good bill about a week hence. I therefore leave my letter and money in the hands of Mr. Brown (of Kentucke) who will receive the bill and forward that and the letter.

RC (ViW). PrC (DLC); lacks the postscript dated 7 Sep. The enclosed bill of exchange was issued by Pragers & Co., Philadelphia, 21 Sep. 1790, for 589.6^{lt} payable to Short and drawn on Tourton & Ravel, Paris, at sixty days sight (second and third of exchange—the first having been enclosed in the above by James Brown—were evidently forwarded to TJ and are in DLC: TJ Papers, 9: 9810, 9811).

To Stephen Cathalan, Jr.

DEAR SIR   Philadelphia Sep. 7. 1790.

Before this reaches you, you will have recieved two public letters from me, the one covering your commission as Vice-consul of the U.S. at Marseilles, the other containing some general instructions and explanations, and among other things that, the title of Vice-consul, does not render the office at all subordinate to the Consuls of other districts.

The object of the present is merely to enquire into the execution of the commission for sending olives and olive trees to Charleston. Of this I have heard nothing from you since I left France; nor any thing very particular from Charleston, the gentlemen from that state only saying to me in general that they have not heard that any were arrived. If they be not already sent to the amount formerly desired, I must beg of you, my dear Sir, to have it done in such season, and by such conveyance, as will promise the best success. The money for the purpose will be furnished by Mr. Short at Paris, and I feel myself bound in point of honour to have this object effectually fulfilled for the persons who have confided it's execution to me. Be so good as to inform me by a line (sent through Mr. Short) what is done, and what shall be done. Present me in the most friendly and respectful terms to your father and the ladies of the family, and accept assurances of the esteem with which I have the honour to be Dear Sir your most obedient & most humble servt.,   TH: JEFFERSON

PrC (DLC).

To Henry Remsen, Jr.

DEAR SIR   Philadelphia Sep. 7. 1790.

I find some difficulty in getting an office, and therefore leave it in charge with my landlord, Mr. Lieper to procure me one, convenient. When the papers are brought on therefore, you will only have to apply to him, and he will have provided one. He lives in Water street between Arch and Market streets.

There are at Berry & Rogers's in New York some small pocket inkpots of silver, with a silver pen to them, the whole not more than 4. or 5. inches long, and half or three quarters of an inch diameter in the thickest part. I saw one of them in possession of Mr. Nelson, who tells me he bough[t] it there and that there are others remaining. I will thank you to get me one of the smallest of them, and keep it till I see you. I am with great esteem Dr. Sir Your most obedt. servt.,   TH: JEFFERSON
P.S. Your favor, written a day or two after I left N. York is recieved. I am now setting out on my journey.

PrC (DLC).

The letter written A DAY OR TWO AFTER TJ left New York was one containing a false rumor that TJ did not bother to comment on; it was dated 2 Sep. 1790 and read in part: "The English packet has just arrived, and brought advice of a meeting and engagement between the English and Spanish fleets, wherein the latter lost four Ships, two being taken and two sunk.—I cannot be more particular, as the letters will not be delivered until tomorrow morning on account of her arrival so late in the evening. The post master says there are none for you" (RC in DLC, endorsed by TJ as received 6 Sep. 1790 and so recorded in SJL).

From C.W.F. Dumas

MONSIEUR   Lahaie 7e. 7bre. *1790.*

Je viens de recevoir les deux respectables vôtres, des 23 Juin et 13 Juillet derniers, comme aussi une dont notre illustre Président

m'a honoré en date du 30 Juin, sur un sujet qui regarde personnellement Son Excellence. Quoique abbattu et toujours martyr
d'une croix domestique, qui fait coup sur coup le malheur de ma
vieillesse, elles m'ont ranimé, consolé, et rendu des forces, pour
satisfaire à leur contenu. Leurs objets, pour être remplis, d'un côté
avec décence, et de l'autre surement et exactement, me firent partir
tout de suite pour Leide.—J'y ai remis la Lettre de Son Excellence
au Vice-Président de la Société hollandoise et poétique; et elle doit
être actuellement ouverte et lue en pleine Assemblée convoquée hier
extraordinairement pour cet effet.—Quant à la Gazette françoise
de Leide, voici la maniere simple, seule possible, et probablement
sûre, dont nous sommes convenus, Mr. Luzac et moi, de vous faire
parvenir son estimable Gazette. Le seul Correspondant à qui il
lui soit permis d'adresser, et qui distribue pour lui ses Gazettes
en Angleterre, c'est *Mr. Jn. Cooper, Commis du Département
Etranger des postes de S.M. Britannique à Londres*. Il a com-
mencé par ajouter dans le paquet qu'il lui expédie deux fois par
semaine un Exemplaire de sa Gazette, entouré comme tous les
autres (ne lui étant pas permis de faire autrement) d'une étroite
bande de papier sur laquelle est l'adresse *To Th. Jefferson Esqr.,
New York*; et dans une courte Lettre, il le charge de les faire
expédier chaque mois par le Paquebot qui va à New York. J'espère
ainsi d'apprendre en son temps, d'un côté par Mr. Luzac, que
l'Expédition est en train; et de l'autre par Votre Excellence, qu'Elle
est servie comme Elle le desire, pour le bien public et à sa satisfaction.

La communication que Votre Excellence a la bonté de me donner
du Poste éminent qu'elle a accepté de remplir est une consolation
pour moi plus grande que je ne puis l'exprimer.

Une autre faveur à laquelle je suis très-sensible, c'est les pre-
cieuses notions que Votre Excellence veut bien me donner sur la
maniere dont on doit envisager les fonds Américains externes et
internes. J'avois déjà, par instinct, placé tout le peu que j'ai pu
sauver, dans ceux de la Négotiation de 1787 et 1788, et je per-
sévererai certainement. J'ai fait parvenir ces memes notions dis-
cretement à nos Banquiers à Amsterdam, afin qu'ils soient prudens.

Je voudrois de tout mon coeur que mes paquets pussent parvenir en moins de temps, mais cela ne seroit possible que dans le
cas où l'on s'aviseroit en Amérique ou ici d'établir un Paquebot
régulier par mois. Faute de cela, je n'ai d'autre moyen que les
Vaisseaux marchands.

Le Congrès a la plus grande raison de ne pas s'ajourner trop longtemps dans ces conjectures critiques.

Deux évenemens importants viennent de changer visiblement la face des affaires, toujours critiques, de l'Europe:

1.° La paix subite entre la Russie et la Suede, sans admettre l'intervention d'aucune Puissance médiatrice. On croit la Russie déterminée à la faire de même avec les Turcs, leur rendant tout, sans l'intervention de Cours de Berlin et de Londres, contre lesquelles elle gardera apparemment une rancune qui pourra éclatter dans l'occasion.

2.° Le Décret de l'Assemblée de France, qui resserre plus que jamais l'Alliance avec l'Espagne. Il n'a fait nullement plaisir à la Cour de Londres qui, dit-on, s'étoit promis de forcer l'Espagne, par sa supériorité maritime, à lui faire payer les fraix de son armement (trois millions Sterling) et de la brouiller pour toujours avec la France, où la dite Cour n'avoit rien épargné pour empécher le Décret de passer.

Dans quelque temps, Monsieur, que ces deux Intelligences parviennent à la connoissance du Congrès, elles me paroissent mériter son attention.

Dieu bénisse les Etats-unis, leurs illustres Congrès, Président et Ministres. Ce sera jusqu'à mon dernier moment le voeu de mon coeur, plein de respect pour vous, et De Votre Excellence Le très-humble & très obéissant serviteur

C. W. F. Dumas

P.S. Je n'ai pu refuser de recevoir la lettre ci-jointe, du 10e. Août dernier, de Mr. Le Fevre de Montigny, Capitaine Ingénieur, et de promettre de la faire parvenir à la connoissance de Son Excellence le Président. L'Ecrivain est Patriote, et se plaint d'être chagriné, &c. Si ses talens peuvent être jugés utiles, comme il le desire, j'aurai la satisfaction d'avoir servi un homme en souffrance.

Quand il y aura un Consul, Agent ou Correspondant du Congrès à Londres, on pourra peut-être prendre des mesures pour lui envoyer, sans frais trop énormes, un de mes paquets par mois.

RC (DNA: RG 59, PCC No. 93); at head of text: "No. 67. A Son Excelle. Mr. Th. Jefferson Min. d'Et. & des Affes. Etr. en Congrès des Et. Un. d'Amerique. Dupl."; endorsed by TJ as received 30 Dec. 1790, but recorded in SJL under 28 Dec. FC (Dumas Letter Book, Rijksarchief, The Hague; photostats in DLC).

From Rayneval

Monsieur   Paris le 8. 7bre. 1790

J'ai été infiniment sensible à la lettre obligeante dont vous m'avez honoré. Vous devez être bien sûr que je suis dans ce pays-cy une des personnes qui vous regrettent le plus, mais qui, en même tems, vous voyent avec le plus de plaisir dans la place de confiance que vous occupez. Vos services et vos talents vous y ont appellés; et vous devez avoir éprouvé un sentiment bien doux en recevant une marque aussi éclatante de la justice de vos concitoyens. Je vous prie, Monsieur, de me conserver dans votre Souvenir. C'est un retour que vous devez aux sentimens d'attachement et de considération que je vous ai voüés, et avec lesquels j'ai l'honneur d'être, Monsieur, Votre très-humble et très-obéissant serviteur,

DE RAYNEVAL

RC (DLC); endorsed by TJ as received 12 Jan. 1791 and so recorded in SJL. Tr (DNA: RG 59, MLR); translation in Remsen's hand; endorsed in part: "sent to the President Jany. 14th. 1791." FC (DNA: RG 59, SDC); translation in clerk's hand.

From James Maury

Sir   Liverpool 9 Septr 1790

I am honored with your Letter of 15th June inclosing the Commission of Consul for this Port with which his Excellency the President has been pleased to honor me. For this flattering Mark of his Confidence I beg Leave, thro' you, Sir, most respectfully to offer my profound Acknowlegements. But as the powers appertaining to the Consuls of the United States have not been particularly defined to me, I request such farther Informations thereon as may be needful.—I have the Honor to be with great Respect & Esteem Sir your most obt St,

JAMES MAURY

Dupl (DNA: RG 59, CD); at foot of text: "The Honble Thos Jefferson Esqre Secretary of State to the United States"; endorsed by TJ as received 26 Nov. 1790 and so recorded in SJL. On verso Maury pasted a newspaper clipping quoting a dispatch in the *London Gazette* dated "Petersburgh August 17" announcing that on 14 Aug. 1790 preliminaries of peace and a suspension of arms between Russia and Sweden had been agreed upon, with ratifications to be discharged in six days. Maury placed the following note above this clipping: "The under is a true extract." RC (DNA: RG 59, CD); dated 8 Sep.; endorsed by TJ as received 3 Dec. 1790 and so recorded in SJL.

This, doubtless the first letter TJ had received from his early schoolmate since the Revolution, seems to indicate that Maury understood naturally enough that the Secretary of State desired authentic political information from consuls, hence the clipping attached to the duplicate.

From Henry Remsen, Jr.

DEAR SIR   New York Septemr. 9th. 1790

I had the honor of receiving your Letter of the 7th. instant this day, and shall immediately purchase one of the inkpots and pens you desire I would of Berry & Rogers.

The enclosed Letter from Mr. Dumas and the Gazettes I got from the Post Office. The packet that contained them was so large as to induce me to open it, and I found as I expected a large parcel of dutch Newspapers therein. These I have kept. I send the letter because it is of a later date than any received from him, altho' it is a duplicate; and the Gazettes on a presumption that they are of later dates than any you have perused. I also enclose Child's paper of this day on account of some intelligence it contains relative to the Spanish fleet's having sailed &c: Since my letter which covered a copy of Mr. McDonogh Commission, he has called and taken the original, but promises to present it to you whenever he is called upon to do it. He waits your answer. I have the honor to be with great respect Dr. Sir Your most obt. & obliged Servt.,

HENRY REMSEN JUNR.

RC (DLC); endorsed by TJ as received 26 Sep. 1790 (at Monticello) and so recorded in SJL. Enclosure: Dumas to TJ, 26 May 1790 (RC was received 2 Nov. 1790; this enclosure was the Dupl, not found).

From William Short

DEAR SIR   Paris Sepr. the 9th. 1790

It is not yet known here with what eye the British Minister views the late vote of the national assembly for augmenting their ships in commission. The preparations in England were already carried on with so much activity that no alteration seems to have taken place there. Lord Howe is now cruising with his fleet off the coast. It is supposed he will not be long out. The Spanish fleet has not yet returned into port, but it does not seem to be apprehended that it is the design of these two fleets to meet.

The Dutch fleet contrary to public expectation has returned to the Texel. Some say it is only to take in further provisions and then to join a British fleet and go into the Baltic. This however is only conjecture, and loses its probability as well from the season being so far advanced, as from the circumstance of a pacification having taken place between Russia and Sweden.—Preliminary articles were signed by an officer of each army (commissioned *ad hoc*) on the 14th. of last month. These articles are entirely on the principle of *status quo* at the beginning of the late war. It is not yet known what has been the leading motive of Sweden in making so sudden a peace. It is apprehended that it is without the participation of the British and Prussian cabinets.—The Porte had not been punctual in paying the promised stipend, so that the King of Sweden will have to bear the expences of a war begun and ended by treachery, and which has cost him near forty thousand subjects and embarassed his finances.

The question of paper money still continues to be discussed both in the national assembly and out of it. Nantes has declared in favor of them; several other commercial towns against them. The districts of Paris are now assembled in order to express their opinion also. It is not known what will be the result, but the public mind which has already vibrated seems now to be turning in favor of the paper system.

Should this paper emission take place, it will be for the purpose of paying off the *dette exigible*. Still it seems to me unavoidable that a great part of it will be diverted to supply immediate exigencies. I mean the debt that accrues every day, and which ought to be paid by the regular revenue. The taxes not being collected, government will be obliged to make use of the paper-money. This system is already begun. By Mr. Necker's report last May it appeared there would remain eleven millions in the treasury at the end of the year, but by a failure in the collection of the taxes the assembly was obliged a day or two ago to vote ten millions of paper money for momentary exigencies. It was then urged that there was not money in the treasury for the next days payments.

A general uneasiness seems now to pervade the minds of all parties, particularly those who surround the throne. Apprehensions of riot and disorder are entertained without any fixed reason. The conjectures of all float in this uncertainty and augment the alarms of each other. Many suppose a design in the party attached to the Duke of O——— to excite disorders in hopes of satisfying their ambitions by them. The incendiary papers increase every day in number, and force. All parties are attacked in them except the most popular corner of the assembly headed by Barnave and the LaMeths.—The Marquis de la fayette has sworn enemies in all the parties, owing to his having endeavoured to conciliate them all. Many of the gardes nationales have the popular sentiments which are supported by the faction in the assembly, and consequently see with an unfavorable eye, their general disposed to support subordination both in the army, and in the state, which appears to them contrary to those sentiments. He lately assembled deputies from the several battalions of the *Parisian gardes nationales*, in order to induce them to vote their thanks to M. de Bouillé and the gardes nationales who had acted under him at Nancy. To his astonishment these deputies seemed unwilling to do it, under an idea that the blood of citizens having been shed, it was proper to have further information. The deputies adjourned without coming to any resolution. They however assembled again yesterday and voted them thanks unanimously.—This shews that the Marquis has still a great deal of influence over them, but not so much as formerly. Every thing is done to destroy his confidence among them. Should this take place, it is impossible to say what would be the consequence, for it is evident that hitherto he and the gardes nationales have been the only barrier to the tumults and riots for which thousands in Paris seem now to be prepared.

A motion has been lately made in the assembly and carried for prosecuting the authors of the mob mentioned in my last, and for directing the municipality to preserve the public tranquillity. Nothing has since occurred to shew what effect will have been produced by this motion.

No person is talked of to fill Mr. Necker's place. It is possible that it will remain vacant. Mr. Lambert has always been comptroller general, and still continues so. The other ministers are yet in place, and nothing said about their going out.

Mr. Swann of Boston, whom you know, has made a contract with ministry for furnishing a certain quantity of ship-timber. He is now pressing a contract of a different nature. It is to furnish their fleets and troops in the West Indies with salted provisions. His offer is to supply them ten ₩ cent cheaper than their present price and to recieve in payment the debt due to France from the United States. The contractors or Regisseurs had refused his proposals. He has since made them known to the committee of finance, and he thinks they will take the matter up and force the

Regisseurs to contract with him.—I know nothing of this matter except from him, and I hope the subject will not be mentioned, if at all, to me before I shall be able to give some information of the manner in which Congress intend to realize their vote which you formerly communicated to me. Should Mr. Swann make such a contract as he speaks of it is much to be desired that he should be punctual in its fulfillment. He tells me that he shall be supported by several rich bankers of Paris. It will be an advantageous circumstance that our salted provisions should have this great experiment made on them as I have no doubt they will bear the comparison with those which are at present received from Ireland.

Nothing has been done by the committee of imposition since my last. Their reports on various subjects of taxation are ready, but the assembly has not yet found time to hear them. Their leading idea is to convert a great part of the revenue into one land tax, to be paid monthly. This will amount to far upwards of 300. millions. Many of the assembly are averse to this principle of taxation and have expressed their sentiments. Should they agree on the principle however a great difficulty still remains in proportioning this revenue among the different departments, without counting the same difficulty which will exist among the different districts of the same department and again among the different municipalities of the same district. This work if practicable must require a long time to be carried into execution, much more than can be admitted by the present situation of finances.—As to my own part it appears to me, that the system of administration adopted here is such that the taxes the most easily paid would not be collected under it; and that the taxes proposed are such as could not be collected under the best system of administration. It is not difficult to foresee a part of what this will lead to, but it may lead much farther than seems now to be apprehended. I beg you to accept assurances of the unalterable attachment with which I am, my dear Sir, your friend & servant,   W. SHORT

PrC (DLC: Short Papers); at head of text: "No. 42." Recorded in SJL as received 11 Jan. 1791. FC (DNA: RG 59, DD).

From William Short

DEAR SIR   Paris Sepr. the 9th. 1790

My last private was of the 22d. of August. I then hoped long before this to have recieved from Havre an account of the charges paid there for your effects so as to have given you a complete account of the pecuniary transactions between us. For what reason I know not that account has not been yet sent; I therefore return the memoires which are now in my hands, as vouchers for the cash paid Petit on your account and shall send them all together, as soon as I recieve that from Havre. My last letter from that place of the 29th. ulto. mentioned that all your effects had arrived there except the two carriages which had been embarked at Rouen on a different lighter. It was hoped then they would arrive in time to go with your other effects by the Henrietta, which was about to sail for Philadelphia. M. de la Motte wrote me that he had obtained permission of the custom house to embark these goods without landing them, immediately on board of the Henrietta, but that the mob had assembled and insisted on their being visited under pretext of their containing specie. As the municipalities are every where obedient to the mobs at present, several cases were unpacked, and no specie being found the rest were exempted from the search. He adds that no injury was done to them and nothing lost in this extra-fiscal visit: I suppose he will have written to you by the vessel which took your goods on board and given you an account of this circumstance. I infer from his letter that that vessel must have sailed ere this, but have not yet learned whether your carriages arrived in time to go by her.

I mentioned to you in my last how agreeably I had been sur-prized by Langeac who had accepted the congé although authorized to exact a continuance of the lease for three years from the date of the last renewal. The house rent due him has been paid first by the sale of your saddle horse 300.^{tt} soon after your departure and the rest by Mr. Grand out of the Algerine fund in his hands.

I have spoken with the Abbe Morellet agreeably to your desire on the business you mention. I fear nothing is to be hoped from him. He pleads the loss which the bookseller sustained in that business. He is now in the country but I will mention it to him again although I have no hopes of success, particularly as he pretends a kind of ignorance of the affair, or at least says he is not *au fait* of it.

Petrie is fully convinced of his error, and sees now that he had not paid the bill of exchange twice. M. de Ville has recieved the *balsamum Canadensa*. He insisted much on knowing the cost of it, but on my telling him that you intended it as a present he ex-pressed his gratitude in very obliging terms. The poor old Abbé

Chalu has had a kind of paralytic stroke which was near carrying him off but he is getting better.

Houdon has lately sent me a model in plaister of the vase you desired. I imagine you had desired a model on paper. It is impossible you could have desired to have sent to Florence the model in plaister as it would cost more than its worth. On the whole I must confess I do not recollect perfectly what you had desired on this subject, and therefore have thought it best not to do any thing in it until I recieve further orders from you. You will be able to judge whether I shall be at Paris or not. If I am, I will thank you to give me your instructions relative to this as well as any other commission you may wish to have executed here.

Charpentier has not yet finished the copying press but assures me it shall be done very soon. He was here a few days ago in order to ask an advance of two guineas which were necessary for the continuation of his work.

I have found it impossible to sell your horses as yet for any thing like a tolerable price, and repent now most sincerely having deviated from your instructions. I still hope however that your successor will be willing to give a better price for them. It was under that idea that I took on me to avoid their sale at that time, not doubting then that the moderate price then offered might be always commanded.

It is now three months since I have recieved your letters notifying your stay in America. From that time I have been in a state of anxiety and uneasiness which I fear my letters have too strongly expressed. It would have been a great relief to me to have heard from you from time to time. It would have been useful perhaps to have been informed of the different measures taken by Congress, but I imagine you have had no time to write, as I still persuade myself that if it had been possible you would have contributed to a pleasure of which your experience here must have made you know the full value. I await therefore with patience and resignation an event which three months habit has not taught me to view the uncertainty of, without real pain.—Since your letter of May the 27th. I have recieved only two short ones of July 1. and 8. merely to desire that your effects might be sent to Philadelphia. I am happy to have been able to have done in that respect what you desired.

The Newspapers have taught us that several consular appointments have been made, and that the Act for foreign intercourse was passed in the early part of July. I observe that the salaries of Chargés des affaires is augmented, and that that of Ministers remains the same.—I saw in the newspapers also that you had given it as your opinion that two ministers and two chargés des affaires would be necessary. As we have no reason here to suppose that any person will be sent to England we imagine that Paris, Spain, the Hague and Lisbon are the courts in view. But there are so few data to reason on respecting these subjects that it is painful when they force themselves involuntarily on the mind. As these nominations awaited only the passage of the bill and as this took place early in July, it is impossible now that it can be long before all uncertainty is removed.—Van Staphorst's correspondents write that Mr. Butler is talked of for Holland. Except that information no person in Europe has any idea of the persons in view at New-York, although it is certain that so long ago as April some were designed by the public at that place. I have frequently lost myself in conjectures on this and other subjects relative to it; which has given me occasion to reflect how much time and thought might be saved often by a little exact information.— I live in the hopes of hearing from you soon and fully on all these matters. This letter will go by the French packet. I beg you to accept assurances of the unalterable sentiments of attachment with which I am, my dear Sir, your friend & servant,

W. SHORT

RC (DLC); at head of text: *"Private"*; endorsed by TJ as received 11 Jan. 1791 and so recorded in SJL. PrC (DLC: Short Papers).

From William Goddard

SIR   Baltimore, Sept. 11, 1790

As the Charge of publishing the Acts of Congress, and the Proclamations of the Executive of the General Government, is committed to the Secretary of State, I take the Liberty of making an offer of the Maryland Journal, and Baltimore Advertiser, as a very useful Vehicle for the Promulgation of such Matters, it having an uncommonly extensive Circulation, in various States of the Union, especially in Virginia, Pennsylvania, and Maryland. Under a Persuasion that, in executing the Duties of your high office, you are actuated by a Zeal for the Interest of the Public, I have only to add, that if I shall have the Honour to be employed as a Printer, in the Service of your Department, the Trust shall be performed with Fidelity, and that my Charges shall be very moderate. I am, with Sentiments of profound Respect for your public & private Character, Sir, Your most obedt. Servt.,

WILLIAM GODDARD

RC (DNA: RG 59, PDL); endorsed by TJ as received 26 Sep. 1790 (at Monticello) and so recorded in SJL.

Goddard was one of the printers to whom Henry Remsen wrote the following letter at TJ's request, dated at New York 10 Sep. 1790: "I am directed by the Secretary of State of the United States to request that you will furnish his office with one copy of your newspaper, to commence on the first day of October next, and to be continued until otherwise ordered. You will be pleased to send them by Post under cover to the said Secretary at Philadelphia, and also to send your accounts at the periods you generally make them out, or quarterly, or half yearly, to some person there to receive the money for you" (FC in DNA: RG 59, PCC No. 120; names of recipients listed at foot of text, and at head of text is the following: "To Printers in the several states requesting a transmission of their papers"). In addition to Goddard, Remsen sent this letter to the following printers: John Melcher of the (Portsmouth) *New-Hampshire Gazette*; Benjamin Russell of the (Boston, Mass.) *Columbian Centinel*; John Carter of the *Providence* (R.I.) *Gazette*; [Barzillai] Hudson & [George] Goodwin of the (Hartford) *Connecticut Courant*; [Francis] Childs & [John] Swaine of the (N.Y.) *Daily Advertiser*; Shepard Kollock of the (Elizabethtown) *New-Jersey Journal*; John Fenno of the (Philadelphia) *Gazette of the United States*; Andrew Brown of the (Philadelphia) *Federal Gazette*; John Scull of the *Pittsburgh* (Pa.) *Gazette*; [Frederick] Craig & Co. of the (Wilmington) *Delaware Gazette*; Augustine Davis of the (Richmond) *Virginia Gazette, and General Advertiser*; John Bradford of the (Lexington) *Kentucky Gazette*; [Abraham] Hodge & [Henry] Wills of the (Edenton) *State Gazette of North-Carolina*; Mrs. Ann Timothy of the (Charleston) *State Gazette of South-Carolina*; and James & Nicholas Johnston of the (Savannah) *Georgia Gazette*.

From Thomas Lee Shippen

MY DEAR SIR   Alexandria Sept. 15. [i.e., 14] 1790

The prayers of my friends in your boat prevailed and I arrived at this place in an hour after I left you without the occurrence of any adverse accident. I am with my uncle who would be very happy if Mr. Madison and yourself could make it convenient to pass through Alexandria. I hope one of the letters which I have the pleasure of forwarding to you may contain such intelligence from Mr. Fitzhugh as may induce you to change your rout. I pray you Sir to offer my most respectful compliments to Mr. Madison and to believe that I am among your most attached and faithful servants,   TH: LEE SHIPPEN

RC (MHi); endorsed by TJ as received 14 Sep. 1790. The letters enclosed were probably those recorded in SJL as received the same day: from Wythe, 31 Aug. 1790, from William Fitzhugh, 5 Sep. 1790, from Thomas Mifflin, 29

Aug. 1790, and from Edward Telfair, governor of Georgia, 19 and 23 July 1790, and 5 Aug. 1790. Those from Mifflin and Telfair have not been found. Shippen erred in the date: he had parted from TJ the night of the 13th (see Document III, documents on the seat of government under 29 Aug 1790).

From Fulwar Skipwith

Sir   St. Pierre 18. Septemr 1790

On the 30th. Ulto. I did myself the pleasure to address your Excellency, expressing the hope I daily entertained of receiving the instructions necessary to my entering into the office of Consul for the United States at this Port &c. &c.; and likewise informing of the awkward situation in which I may stand with the Governor, in regard to the exequatur required by the 1st. Art. of the convention existing between his Most Christian Majesty and the U. States for the purpose of defining the functions of their Consuls; unless he should receive notice thereof from his Court. Heretofore, had I been possessed of instructions together with the exequatur, owing to an almost total suspension of police as well as government, I could not have been, and I fear shall not soon be, useful in my office.—The Citizens of this town with those of Fort-royal, forming what are called the patriotic party, having gained the military, except a company of grenadiers, possessed themselves in a turbulent manner of the fortifications, military stores &c. released the prisoners, who were confined by the General for having been instrumental in the late tumults, and induced him with most of the principal officers of Government to take refuge in a remote part of the Island. They have also taken upon themselves to annull the proceedings of and to suspend their colonial Assembly, instrumental as they had been in forming it, and authorized as it was by a decree of the national Assembly. Opposed to the patriotic are the aristocratic party, composed of the Governor, officers, grenadiers and color'd people together with the Planters, who endeavour to support the proceedings and constitution of their Assembly. The formation of this body seems to breed the chief and weighty bone of contention. They are chosen by the holders of lands and negroes only. The towns people possessed but in a small degree of either, think themselves unfairly represented; and have worked themselves and their opponents into the most violent and rancorous animosities. In so much that both are in arms, and without the opportune arrival of some interference from France, or the intervention of mediators from the adjacent Islands, there appears the strongest probability of the madest excesses; if not the ruin of the Island.—I remain in the pleasing hopes of hearing from your Excellency and with the greatest attachment Your Mo Ob Servant,

FULWAR SKIPWITH

RC (DNA: RG 59, CD); endorsed by TJ as received 22 Nov. 1790 and so recorded in SJL.

From Charles Cotesworth Pinckney

SIR   Charleston Sepr. 19. 1790.

The advantages which I am certain will accrue to my nephew Mr. Horrÿ from being introduced at Paris under the sanction of a name so greatly and deservedly esteemed there, will not permitt me to be satisfied with returning you my thanks through Mr. Izard for the letters I received under cover from him, but oblige me to trespass still further on your goodness in requesting you to beleive that the favor you have done me I shall always look upon as a high obligation.

I have taken the liberty of having this letter handed to you by another of my nephews, Mr: Henry Middleton, the Grandson of Mr: Henry Middleton with whom you served in the first Congress, and the son of Mr: Arthur Middleton with whom I think you served in a subsequent Congress. He is now on his travels through the Northern and Middle States for his improvement. Though I have not the pleasure of being personally acquainted with you, I feel that in requesting you to notice an amiable youth just entering into life I need not be very solicitous in making an apology. I have the honour to be with great respect Your much obliged & most obedient humble Servt.

CHARLES COTESWORTH PINCKNEY

RC (MHi); endorsed as received "2 July [1791?]," but not recorded in SJL.

To James Madison

DEAR SIR   Monticello Sep. 20. 1790.

Your servant now returns with many thanks for the aid of him and your horses. I was disappointed of meeting my family here:

however I am told they will arrive today. I wished to have seen Mr. Randolph, before the departure of your servant to know if he had found a horse for me; because if he has not I should determine to accept the offer of yours. I drove him about eight miles in the Phaeton, and he did as well as the awkwardness of so new a situation to him gave me right to expect. If Mr. Randolph should not have been succesful in his enquiries, I will send to you for the horse immediately. Notwithstanding your observing 'we should not differ about the price,' I know nobody with whom it is so difficult to settle a price, and with whom I should be so likely to differ. Witness the money disputes on our journey. As I would not chuse to trust to your setting a price therefore, I should propose your getting a Capt. Wood or some such good judge to do you justice. But of this more if I send for the horse. Adieu, my dear Sir. Your's affectionately,   TH: JEFFERSON

PrC (MHi).

On 23 Sep. 1790 TJ wrote to Madison: "Mr. Randolph arrived last night without having been able to get me a horse, or even to hear of one which he could approve of. Presuming you had made up your mind as to parting with yours, I take the liberty of sending for him. I should not hesitate to take him at your own price but that I apprehend you think him of less than his real value, and therefore propose that you should have him valued. If there be no urgency, I should propose to pay you the money not till our return to Philada., perhaps not till the receipt of our December quarter, as the arrival of my furniture from Paris, and commencing housekeeping will perhaps call for my previous resources. But this need make no difficulty.—We shall count on seeing you here about our next court and hope you will make some stay. The time and plan of our return may be then arranged. Adieu. Your's affectionately, Th: Jefferson" (RC in DLC: Madison Papers; PrC in MHi). Madison replied to this the next day: "I received yours of the 23 inst: by the bearer who now returns with the Horse. I will consult with some persons who are acquainted with him and let you know the price I set on him. The time and place of payment which you propose would suit me as well as immediate payment here: but I consider this credit as a necessary set off against advances which you will have made for me in France. If no obstacles not at present in view stand in the way, I shall have the pleasure of seeing Monticello a day or so before your next Court. My father sends the promised seed of the Mountain Cresses. Yours mo: affecty., Js. Madison Jr." (RC in DLC: Madison Papers; endorsed as received 24 Sep. 1790 and so recorded in SJL).

To William Ronald

SIR   Monticello Sep. 20. 1790.

Colo. Nicholas Lewis has communicated to me your letter of Aug. 1. on the subject of the purchase of my lands on the South side of James river opposite Elkisland, whereon you desire an answer as to the time of paiment, and the security. The object of selling the lands being to pay my part of a debt of Mr. Wayles's to

Farrell & Jones, any agreement you can make with their agent Mr. Hanson, so as that he may give me up any of my bonds in exchange for yours will perfectly answer my purpose. I shall remain here a month, unless any thing unforeseen should occasion me to be called away sooner. This is very possible, and will be certain should we hear of the actual commencement of hostilities in Europe. I mention this circumstance, as it would be more convenient for me to arrange this matter and make a conveyance while here. Indeed I could not frame the conveyance without reference to papers which remain here. Perhaps some other business may render it convenient to you to come to this part of the country, in which case I shall be glad to see you at my house. I am with great esteem Sir your most obedt. humble servt.,

TH: JEFFERSON

PrC (MHi).

From Sylvanus Bourne

SIR   Boston Septr 21st 1790.

Being absent from this place on a journey I was not honoured by the receipt of your last favor till yesterday.—I perfectly acquiesce in your relation of the circumstances attending my acceptance of the Consulate of Hispaniola while I recollect that at the time you observed it was very uncertain what arrangements Government might think fit to make relating to our Consuls abroad you gave it as your personal opinion that it was but reasonable that for services performed some rate of pay should be by Law established. The propriety of this will be (perhaps) as apparent in my District as in any of the Consular Line, it being not uncommon to have from 30 to 80 sail of Vessells in port at one time and in a place where impositions on our Countrymen are not unfrequent. Capt. Long (a Brother of Mr. Lear's) informed me a few days past that he had for a long time passed to and from Hispaniola and was confident from his acquaintance with every circumstance relating to the trade of that Island that my official Duty must employ very considerable part of my time. In this view of the Case I am persuaded of your assent to the propriety of such allowances as will amount to a reasonable satisfaction for services without burthening the Interests of Commerce. In this Idea and in confidence of having your support in maturing the bill now on the files of the Senate I shall proceed to make the arrangements of my departure with all convenient dispatch which will probably be in the first part of Novr. as my plans for a commercial establishment cannot be sooner ripened being that I wait the arrival of a person from Hispaniola on this account.

I shall punctually comply with your orders and requisitions on every occasion and while I endeavour to support the interests of our Countrymen within my District with that manly confidence which a consciousness of Right and Justice never fails to afford. I shall avoid every unnecessary application to the Government of the Island and in the mildest Language of remonstrances use my exertions to correct every abuse of the compact between the two Countries, and pursue every step which may tend to conciliate and cement an Union evidently founded on grounds of reciprocal advantage.

Fearful that some expressions of my last letter to you which was wrote in the moment of great disappointment may have been hasty and not sufficiently reflected on I have to ask the exercise of your wonted Candour and would urge this conviction upon your mind, that for any impropriety which I may [be] chargeable with, the pain of my own reflections operate as the severest Censure.

The constant intercourse from this Country to Hispaniola will afford you an early opportunity of transmitting me the Bill after it shall have passed which will essentially oblige him who has the honour to be in every sentiment of Respect Yr Obed Servt,

SILV : BOURNE

P.S. I would beg leave to ask whether some private Mode on American Registers may not be necessary in order to detect counterfeits.

RC (DLC: Washington Papers); endorsed by TJ as received 14 Oct. 1790 and so recorded in SJL.

From Benjamin Vaughan

DEAR SIR   London Septr. 21, 1790

The above letter from the keeper of the botanical garden at St. Vincent will shew you that measures have failed respecting the red dry rice from St. Vincent, but that they will be repeated and I hope with more success.—I have other accounts of this species of rice, which mention it to be growing; so that we may look upon it as in a good measure secured to our parts of the world.

Give me leave to suggest to you, as you have various opportunities for importing it from China, whether it may not be worth your while to naturalize the many useful species of bamboo known to the Chinese. You know that the analogy of your climate promises much in its favor.—If you could *afterwards* import a Chinese or two, to instruct your people in the application of it to use, it might be of much importance. I mention this last as a hint from Sir J. Banks, when conversing with him about the introduction of the Eastern bamboos into the Atlantic regions.

Let me now beg leave to thank you for your very interesting letter of June 24. I do not [think] that Europe at this moment furnishes any thing half so curious.—Dr. Herschell thinks the last (viz the 8th) Satellite of Saturn, which he had announced, will prove to be a luminous break in Saturn's ring, which of late has been seen edgeways. This is the whole that I know in philosophical matters though I attend my philosophical club constantly.

A curious phænomenon however has occurred in the literary world. Sir Wm. Jones has translated a play from an Indian author, who flourished a century before the Xn. Æra. It is called Sacontolæ or the fatal ring. It comes so close to European writing, that you might suppose it spurious; but our connoisseurs determine otherwise. For myself, I think it both singular and beautiful. I must confess, that I have never been able to learn at what æra the foundations were laid of those arts, sciences, good morals, remarkable manners, population, agriculture, and *free trade*, which have so long survived the succession of barbarian conquerors in India. If before the time of Alexander, it is wonderful, that we have obtained so few traces of them from the historians of that wanderer or through the Persians, or Romans. I will endeavor to send the book by this opportunity.

It may be proper for you to know upon the first authority from India, dated April 15, that Tipoo Saib having invaded the Rajah of Travancore's lines of 30 miles long (wretched in themselves and defended by rabble, though too strong for this chief to force), Lord Cornwallis has thought himself bound by interest and the late peace, to oppose Tippo. The Marathas and Nizam have readily joined, and the hair's and Tippoo's discontented subjects are equably reckoned upon, for attacking Tippoo; which from the late change in the Madras government, will probably be done with vigor, unless Tippo comes to terms.

The French go on as usual, except that the opposite party are making desperate pushes which seem to threaten nothing, as long the N. A. keeps up it's character.—I much fear a war, more against France than Spain.

Mr. Paine has nearly finished his bridge. I presume Mr. Rumsey has done the same by his boat, but he has had villainous workmen and finds the volume of stream arising from water much less than has usually been supposed, which will much abate from the success of his scheme. He is erecting a mill here. If. you see Mr. Jay, I will thank you to let him see this letter and tell him I will write by the packet. I have the honor to be with great esteem and regard, Dear sir, Your respectful humble servt.,

BENJN. VAUGHAN

I forwarded your letter to Mr. Short by the first post.

RC (DLC); written at the end of the received copy of a letter from Alexander Anderson to Vaughan; endorsed by TJ as received 6 Dec. 1790 and so recorded in SJL.

The ABOVE LETTER was that of Alexander Anderson, dated "Botanical Gardens Saint Vincent July 26th. 1790" and addressed to Vaughan: "I am honored with your note of 27th. March and sorry it confirms what I before supposed that General Washington had not recieved the Rice and other seeds I sent according to your desire. You may rest assured they were sent as soon as possible after I received your requisition for that intent. I sent several kinds of Rice, with some other seeds I conceived would prosper in the Southren Colonys with an offer of any other thing in my power. I am surprised how they should have been neglected. They were sent by way of Philadelphia. I shall endeavour to find out the Captain that took charge of them and interrogate him relative to them, and I shall not fail in sending them a second time, when I find a safe Oppertunity. I return you many thanks for your kind attentions at all times, particularly for the rice, which I have the pleasure to tell is already growing" (RC in DLC).

From John Carter

SIR   Providence, Sept. 24, 1790.

I have to acknowledge the Receipt of a Letter from Mr. Remsen, written by Direction of your Excellency. My grateful Thanks are due for this Mark of Attention, as well as for your Excellency's favourable Notice of my Name, in a late Letter to my worthy friend Mr. Howell.

Agreeably to Order, the Providence Gazette shall with great Pleasure be forwarded by Post, so long as the Publication thereof may go on: But labouring as I long have done under many Discouragements, particularly in the Countenance afforded and continued to an antifederal Competitor (who obtruded himself with a printing Apparatus sold by me, *under an express Stipulation that it should never be used here*) I have Contemplation to relinquish my typographical Concern, and adopt, if within the Compass of my Power, some other Line of Business, more adequate to the Support of a numerous Family. After a long printing Career, I shall reluctantly surrender to my said Competitor the Remains of a small Business, established with much Toil, Care and Expence; but should the Measure eventually take Place, your Excellency will be enabled to account for my Paper not arriving at your Office.

With the highest Consideration for your Excellency's Character and literary Attainments, and zealous Attachment to the Government in which you hold so distinguished a Station, I have the Honour to be, very respectfully, your Excellency's obedient and devoted Servant,

JNO. CARTER

RC (DNA: RG 59, PDL); endorsed as received 2 Nov. 1790 and so recorded in SJL.

From Stephen Cathalan, Sr.

SIR —   Marseilles the 25th. September 1790.

I Paid you my respects the 31th. ulto. and just now I receive a Letter from my Friends Messrs. Willing Morris & Swanwick of Philada. of the 23th. Last July, in which they say, "We Congratulate you on your appointment of American Consul at your Port under our new and respectable Government and are with esteem and regard yr. &c. &c."

That is the single advice I have yet received, but I can't doubt, that the appointments of Consuls in Europe may have been determined by your Government and Proclaimed in America, and that it is only to your Excellency that I owe that honorable Post; I beg you to accept my Gratefull thanks, and that I and my Son will employ all our zeal and efforts, to answer and deserve the Confidence that American Government and your Excellency have in me or in him.

I would wish however that being now at 75 years of age and not Speacking English, that the Commission would be in the name of my son, who is more active, and will however follow my advices, when any occasion will occur in that office, and hope you will have remembered that I asked your protection for him.

He is intimate Friend with the single house of this Place, who trades with algiers. It is highly considered by the Dey; Perhaps by that channel a Treaty could be made with united States; you know that with such Barbarians Powers, it is only money or Gifts which succeed; oppunings could be created if you desire it, and if you knew what Sum, united States would intend to Sacrifice for a Peace, which could opun the Mediterranean to American vessels; I have much at heart to give to America if Possible that Proof of my zeal for it's Service, and find that Marseilles is the best place for such a negotiation, and Mrs. Gisnon Brothers the Best agent, by whom I may Save Goodeal of money to America; meantime I may receive your official orders, I will tempt and sound the Grown.

All my Family and my Son present to your Excellency their best respects, as well as my Little daughter who rember of you very well. I am with respect Sir of your Excellency the most obedient humble & Devoted Servant, ESTIENNE CATHALAN, Sr.

I writte to M. Wm. Short at Paris to know if you still desire the olive trees.

RC (DNA: RG 59, CD); endorsed by TJ as received 12 Jan. 1791 and so recorded in SJL.

From Henry Remsen, Jr.

DR. SIR   New York September 25th. 1790

The enclosed Letter was this day handed to me by Mr. Jay, and is in answer to one he wrote to Mr. G. Morris the 15th. of December last forwarding a Packet for Mr. Chiappe. The Packet contained a triplicate of the Presidents Letter to the Emperor of the 1st: of that Month.

The Letters for you by the last french Packet I had the honor of forwarding a day or two ago, and at the same time put in the Post Office a Letter directed to the President in french which accompanied them.

It being represented to me by Francis, that the seven large cases of yours required hooping to prevent them from falling asunder, I got a Cooper to look at them, and he giving it as his Opinion that it was necessary, I had it done. I expect they will be put on board the Vessel with your other furniture, and that belonging to the Office which is to go by water, by the first or second of October.

The printing of the Treaties has been a tedious business and is not yet completed, but I hope they will be by the first of next Month. We had to read and correct some of the french and dutch proof-sheets five and six times, the Printers being quite ignorant of those languages.

Mr. MacDonogh has returned to Boston. He has requested me to write to him there, and to let him know, as soon as I receive your directions, what he is to do. I believe I mentioned in a former letter that I had returned to him his Commission after taking a second copy.

A few days after your departure, I told Okie that he could not be furnished with house room and fire wood in Philadelphia, and that he must look out for another place. He was at first much surprized, but acquiesced with a good grace and has behaved with great decency. He must have told some of his acquaintance that he meant to remain in New York; for there has been a number of applications for his place. George, the person employed since Spring in the Home-Office, is one of the applicants, and so is Ross, the young man who I saw at your house one morning. They are both married. George is well acquainted, he says, with Philadelphia; but the other not so much. I have told these two, and all the other applicants, that I could [do] nothing with respect to the place, not so much as recommend them; and that I did not know but that you had already filled it. I have the honor to be with the greatest Respect Dr. Sir Your obliged & most obt. Servant,

HENRY REMSEN JUNR.

RC (DLC); endorsed as received 14 Oct. 1790 and so recorded in SJL.

From Lucy Ludwell Paradise

DEAR SIR   London Sept. the 26th 1790.

I have been honoured by your very polite and friendly Letter of June the 23d on August the 31st 1790. It brings Me an Account of My Estates &c. in Virginia. I have received your first, and Answered it. In that Letter, I trouble you with my Grateful thanks. I now repeat the Same, and wish sincerely I had it in my power by some Means to convince Your Excellency of the sincerity of my heart. I beg you will not take up your precious time in writing a third Letter on that Subject. I am perfectly sensible of the zeal you have to serve Mr. Paradise and Myself, but be assured My dear Sir, *I have not the least wish to Make My appearance on the Great and fatiguen theatre of the World.* My wish is to live honestly, quiet, retired, without shew, and with all the Comforts of Life. The Person who wishes for a Publick Station ought first to know how to Make a tender affectionate Husband, Father, and Friend, and if such a person only knows the Name without the meaning, they little know their duty in a publick Life.

Many who think themselves calculated for a Minister were they to be put into such a station, instead of being respected might bring upon themselves the Laughter of the whole World, which would be no pleasing sight for their near Relations. Mr. Paradise has been out of London Six Week on a visit to one of his Learned Friends. He writes to Me, and says he is in perfect health. At his return to London I will shew him your Excellencies kind Letter. I have found London too dear a Place to live in; therefore, I have proposed to Mr. Paradise and Dr. Bancroft, for Us to go and Lodge and Board at Bath for a little time, as I find it is the Most certain Method to live within our Income. Dr. Bancroft is always the same tender, Sincere friend. Indeed, *I* owe him very Great Gratitude and shall, if I live, take one of his Daughters to live with Me. This I cannot do until all the Debts are paid. I have one favour to beg of your Excellency which is to have the goodness to be My Friend and protector and to write to *Me* Once a Year at least. For when some persons see *I am* protected by My Friends in America they will be affraid (altho' they will not say it) to use me unhandsomely for fear I should write. I earnestly beg of your Excellency to preserve Your health as it is of the greatest importance to our Country and to Me More then any American. I am happy to hear My Dear Mrs. Randolph has Married to your entire satisfaction. I hope Miss Jefferson will follow her example and that you will be blessed in the Winter of Life. Be pleased to present My affectionate Love to Mrs. Randolph and Miss Jefferson. I am with the greatest esteem Dear Sir Your Excellencies Most Grateful Humble Servant,

Lucy Paradise

Be pleased to send your Letters to Mr. Anderson.

P.S. I have hear that our good and great President is very Ill. God preserve his Life, but should any Accident happen to him I will Mourn as deep as for My Father, which is Six Months in Bombasin, Three Months in Black Silk and love Ribbons and the other Three in Black Silk and white Ribbons. Bishop Maddison brings this Letter.

RC (DLC); endorsed as received 15 Dec. 1790 and so recorded in SJL.

From John Rutledge, Jr.

Dr Sir   Philadelphia Septr. 26th. 1790

From the apprehension of Mr. Shorts writing to me, under cover to you, I take the liberty of troubling you with this letter, requesting you will address any you shall receive for me, to John Ross Esquire merchant of this City. I arrived here yesterday, from a tour I have been making thro' the eastern states. On this jaunt I found people very anxious to have conversations with a person who had lately been in france on the subject of the french revolution, of which, I found it very difficult to make them think well: even those who appeared to be the most philanthropic, thought unfavourably of the national assembly, and I was sorry to observe that many of our citizens, who pass for having intelligent and enlightened minds, possess much of the english political superstition which teaches, that for the good of the whole a few should have the inherent right to rule over the many, man being so contrived that he is unfit for the governing of himself. It is fortunate my dear Sir for this country, that you, and your associates, in 1775 and 6 held different opinions.

About a week before I left N. York the french packet arrived there. She had a long passage and brought no accounts we had not previously received by the way of england. I have seen in a french paper, which came in her, the decree of the National Assembly abolishing Titles, forbidding the use of livery &c. This law I had before seen in the english Prints, but believed it fabricated in london. I wish I may be wrong in thinking so, but the decree in question appears to me the most mischievous the assembly has passed. To use Lord Bottetours expression "I think it augures ill." It is an expostfacto law and of course a bad one. Hereditary titles are certainly property, and they ought, I think, to have been as sacred as any other part of a mans estate. If france thought it politic to destroy her Nobility it would have been well in her, I conceive, to have decree'd, that no title should in future be inherited, and no nobles created. The american Congress, appears to me, to have been more wise, than the N. Assembly, on the question of nobility; for it decree'd "there shall not be a nobility" but did not take away titles from those who had them. The Earl of Stirling was called, in all their public acts, Lord Stirling, Baron Steuben the same, and our Citizens who were Baronets continued to be called *Sirs*. The objections which I mention having to the abolition of Titles &c. have occur'd to me at first hearing of the law. I have not seen any letters from france which make mention of it. I long much to know the arguments used by those who voted for it, and as I before said, sincerely hope *I* may be wrong in thinking *they* have done wrong.—By the last ships from Europe we receive accounts of the swedish fleet having been entirely defeated by that of Russia, off Wibourg, on the fourth of July. The Swedes lost in this action seven ships of the line and four frigates. The Duke of Sudermania was wounded in the Shoulder. The rear Admiral Lejonachen [Leyonankar] made prisoner, with two thousand Seamen and soldiers, and the Baggage, which fell into the hands of the Russians, is valued at three millions of Dollars. From Prussia, we hear that the King had gone into Silesia where two very large armies were to rendezous: if he negotiates it will be sword in hand. From the Netherlands we learn the Austrian Troops had gained some advantages over the flemings, who, it seems, unless assisted by Prussia must ultimately be crushed. They appear to be more torn to pieces than ever by the feuds between the democratic party and the vilest kind of aristocracy, fortified by bigotry priestcraft and superstition. Mareschal Laudhon, the english prints mention, died the fifteenth of July: and the command of the imperial Army, they say, is given to mareschal Coloredo.

The accounts from England are that the press had ceased, and it was believed there would be no war. It is now probable that england will not have a war with Spain, but, I think, she must carry one on in the north. Her continental connexions appear to make it unavoidable and by the first ships from London I expect we shall hear of a british fleet having sailed for the Baltic. If this does not take place the king of Sweden must be ruined. I have received a letter from England saying, that the late elections in that country had gone much in favour of Opposition, which, it is thought, is strengthened by an addition of twenty members in england, and about half as many in Ireland. This, my correspondent tells me, has been owing to the great activity of the Dissenters.

My father and Mother, who are here on their way to south Carolina, unite in requesting you will accept their most respectful Compliments and I beg, Dr. Sir, that you will receive my sincere wishes [fo]r your always enjoying everything that can make life desirable. Your very much obliged friend and Servt.,

J. RUTLEDGE JUNIOR

RC (DLC); addressed: "The Honorable Thomas Jefferson Secretary of State Monticello in Albemarle County, Virginia—To go by the Richmond Post"; postmarked "FREE" and, within circle, "4 OC"; endorsed by TJ as received 25 Oct. 1790 and so recorded in SJL. On the same day TJ received Rutledge's letter from London of 12 May 1790.

From William Short

DEAR SIR   Paris Septr. 26. 1790.

I have recieved to-day within a few hours of each other your two letters of July 26. and Aug. 12.—I am sorry to find that my letters have all had such uncommonly long passages. I sent them for the most part to Havre, where they remained until the sailing of the first vessel. I avoided making use of the English packet though a more regular conveyance, because I thought it sufficient to have my letters opened in one post. I write this letter however to go by that conveyance, and as the post of tomorrow morning is the last which will be in time for it, I shall in a hurry crowd as much as I can into this letter, thinking it better to give you information in disorder than to let the opportunity slip.

The national assembly are deliberating to-day on the great question of paper money. They have been for a long time discussing it by intervals, and at length have determined that they will not quit it until it is decided. The decision will probably take place tomorrow. It will probably be a middle term in order to dissatisfy all parties as little as possible, viz. that the *dette exigible* which is now estimated at 13. instead of 18. hundred million, shall be paid one half in *assignats forcés*, a paper money without interest, and the other in a paper bearing interest recievable in the purchase of public lands, but not a legal tender. Besides they will be obliged to make a paper money of 200 millions more in order to pay the current expences of this year and to begin the next. During the course of this discussion several towns have sent their opinions on the subject, in many instances addresses came both for and against the assignats from the same town, in general however the opinions of the trading towns have been against them. Still parties run so high, and so much intrigue was made use of to obtain these addresses that each party in the assembly insists that the nation at large if properly consulted would desire them. The districts of Paris have shewn an almost unanimous wish for this paper-emission, and the mob who surround the assembly house, and fill the galleries shew almost as much ardor in favor of the assignats, as in the destruction of the bastille. They are made to believe that they will lower the price of bread, and augment the price of labour, that all those who are opposed to them are Aristocrats, and a variety of other such things. This criminal method of carrying a plan in the assembly by enlisting the mob in favor of it has been used on several occasions. Some of the provinces are already dissatisfied with the influence which this gives the city, and particularly the mob of Paris. Yesterday Dupont spoke very fully against the assignats. On coming out of the assembly he was pursued and surrounded by the mob. They had not gone further than injurious epithets, and menaces before the garde nationale came to his relief and took him out of their hands. As he has always been of the popular party, and is now in support of the opinion which is the most agreeable to the provinces on the question of the assignats, this will probably add to their jealousy of Paris influence.

This unsettled state of the public opinion as to the arrangement of the finances shews itself in a variety of shapes. Public credit stagnates or falls, the laws remain many of them without execution, even those who are destined for their execution form obstacles to it. The *corps administratifs* already shew a disposition to vye with the legislature. Several municipalities have omitted to execute the decrees of the assembly. Some have even protested against them and one department has joined lately in a protest against a decree for fixing the residence of one [of] the tribunals newly established.

I mentioned to you in a former letter the unexpected disposition shewn in the national guard of Paris relative to the voting of thanks to M. de Bouillé and those who fought under him at Nancy. Since then the municipality of Paris have had performed a funeral service for those who fell there. This service was in the champ de Mars. A deputation of the national assembly attended it, and the crowd was as great as the day of the federation. As the dead were considered the victims for the re-establishment of order and good government, the municipality thought themselves bound to give this proof of their desire to concur in whatever shewed a submission to the law. The necessity however of recurring to such proofs supposes a want of energy in the government which necessarily implies a state of anarchy.

An alarming proof of this state has lately been recieved from Brest. When the decrees of the assembly respecting the marine were read there to the sailors they refused to admit some parts of them. This occasioned some disorder which was soon after quieted. About the same time the Leopard a ship of war which had displaced its officers in the West-Indies and joined the assembly of St. Domingo, arrived at Brest with the whole assembly on board. The communication of the sailors at Brest with those on board of the Leopard soon created a spirit of insubordination. M. D'Albert de Rioms, the commander in chief attempting to impose a slight correction on one that misbehaved, was unable to exact obedience. He was insulted and even menaced with being drowned. They planted a gallows before the door of an officer that had displeased them, and were in short in a perfect state of revolt. He communicated these circumstances to the assembly, through the minister. Two commissioners are sent to Brest to enquire into the cause of these disorders.—Although it does not appear that the assembly on board of the Leopard had any connexion with the riot at Brest, still as their conduct at St. Domingo has given great displeasure to the national assembly, they are all *mandés à la barre* to give an account of their conduct. Whether they will come, or what will be the event I cannot say. During their passage they considered themselves as the Assembly of St. Domingo, and deliberated and decreed as usual. It is supposed, as they fled from St. Domingo to avoid falling into the hands of the Governor there, their plan was not to come to France, but that the crew had preferred this route and brought them here. The vessel was commanded by a M. Santo Domingo. I don't know who he is. The Captain of the Leopard has arrived also by another vessel. On the whole there is nothing yet clear in this business.

This situation of the French marine has probably had some influence on the negotiations between England and Spain. It was supposed that the decree of the national assembly for arming forty-five ships would have immediately broke them up. They were certainly suspended about that time; but they have been again renewed and it is generally thought now that they are nearly being concluded so as to prevent proceeding to hostilities. The terms will no doubt be advantageous to England either in a commercial or political view, or both. The fleets of both nations are now in port. The designs of Mr. Pitt have hitherto been clothed with a secrecy of which there are few examples in history. He has kept the government so long in its purely executive form that the usual issues of information seem now to be forgotten in that country. Their confidence in him is implicit, and the event will probably shew that it has been well placed. It has been however a deep, and might have turned out an hazardous game.

I mentioned to you in a former letter the sudden and unexpected peace between Russia and Sweden. It is known now that Prussia and England had counted on no peace being made without their intervention. The King of Sweden thought he had reasons to be dissatisfied both with the Porte and with them, and chose to have a peace by his own means rather than owe it to foreign powers.

The Austrian troops are marching towards the low countries, where every thing that can be imagined by fanati[ci]sm will be done to oppose them. Van der Noot has lately summoned to his standard immense numbers of these deluded people, to go on a secret expedition. All the companies are preceded by a crucifix, and a priest. The object of this crusade is not known.

Liege has named the Archbishop of Cambray, prince of Rohan, Regent with a supreme council, and has formed a kind of constitution. It is said I know not with what truth, that the Prince who has left them, is disposed to abandon his claims for a pension. In that case the new Regent will be made Prince.

The Ambassadors of France and Spain have both left Vienna under pretence of affairs and of health. It is said however by some on account of the two marriages about to make[1] place between the Princesses of Naples and the two Archdukes of Austria. The King and Queen of Naples are arrived or on their way to Vienna for that purpose. The Ambassador and Ambassadress of Naples have left this place to go and join their master, and the Imperial Ambassador is to go also to the Congress which will be held for the arrangement of the affairs in Brabant. The coronation of the Emperor will take place in October. There is no doubt it will be the King of Hungary.

It is said several of the German Princes will protest at the Diet against the decrees of the national assembly, which violate as they say, the treaties guaranteed by the Empire. Ternant has been sent to negotiate with them an indemnity for the losses they sustain by the suppression of the feudal system. He has returned and says they are well disposed, but wish previously to know the nature of the indemnity.

The committee of imposition have made their report on tobacco. The assembly ordered the impression. This was several days ago, but as yet it has not been printed and nothing has been since said on it. It will however be taken up very shortly and I fear will pass.

It is proposed that the cultivation should be free in France, and that the importation should be subjected to a national regie. I refer you for this matter to my No. 40. which you will recieve before this letter. I hope you will recieve safely also my Nos. 41 and 42. sent by the way of Havre. I have done and shall still do whatever I can to prevent the committees plan passing, but I fear it will be in vain, and the more so as I apprehend that there has been an undue influence used. Even the Economists are for this regie, and the most violent as they are the most unnatural supporters of it. They say it is a momentary necessity.

The depositions in the procedure of the Chatelet are printed. You know this affair was brought before the assembly on account of two of their members being implicated (the Duke of Orleans and Mirabeau). The committee of reports are to make their report the day after the question of the assignats shall be decided. It is known however that they report *qu'il n'y a pas lieu à l'accusation*, and indeed whoever reads the depositions is astonished that the Chatelet should have announced the procedure to the assembly in the manner they did. It is said Mirabeau means to attack the Procureur general for calumny. I shall send you these papers with others by the first conveyance.

The gun locks are not yet brought here. I have sent for them repeatedly and am promised them always very soon, but it seems they cannot be counted on with certainty. However I shall still insist. I mentioned to you the difficulty in a former letter.

Nothing further has been done in the business you mention in the fourth page of yours of July 26. I wish it was in my power to prevent it from languishing. But I really see no hopes of any thing being done through the chanel mentioned. I recieved lately a letter from those who suffer by it. They say that another mode has been tried by some persons in London authorized for that purpose as they suppose by *Congress*.[2] They say also that is, he who formerly wrote to you, that he himself has spoken on this business and that *the dey* agrees to take 17255 *algerine sequins for the fourteen who remain.*

This is all I know by any means relative to that affair.

Dupré is now engaged in engraving the medal you had ordered. As soon as it is finished your orders respecting it shall be executed.

The sending a consul to Martinique had been spoken of to me by de Moustiers. He observed he had seen it in a newspaper, but that it must be a mistake. I told him I only knew it from the newspaper also, but that it appeared to me the expression of the convention authorized it. He did not then think so, and we did not refer to it. I did not know what you say of the correspondence on that affair, which does not even admit of construction. I am glad to be acquainted with it.

De Moustiers is named for Berlin and goes there soon. I do not know whether he will have any successor immediately. The Viscount de Caraman desires the place and under the former order of things would have been sure of it. He is a very worthy, sensible, and well-disposed young man.—Ternant has been spoken of also and I think it more probable he will succeed.

I recieved by post from St. Valery in Normandy accompanying your letter of the 12th. of August, a copy of your report on weights and measures. I recieved at the same time the newspapers as low as the 14th. The two reports which you intended to send by Mr. Barrett for the Bishop of Autun and M. de Condorcet have not been received, nor do I learn that Barrett has arrived. The letter of the 26th. of July which you thought he would bring arrived by post under cover to Mr. Grand, he knows not from whom. I shall communicate the report I have recieved to the Bishop of Autun and M. de Condorcet. I am glad that the two standards are adapted to each other, being persuaded that uniformity in this circumstance will exceedingly accelerate human knowlege.

Colo. Blackden is going to Champagne in order to see the vintage. I shall put the commission for that place into his hands, and at the same time will speak to M. D'Orsaï on the subject if he should be in Paris. I think you may be satisfied that it will be well executed.

[What you tell me respecting my salary and the extra allowances is perfectly satisfactory. Every thing is allowed that should be, and it is well to know with precision what is intended on these occasions. There is certainly no crowned head in Europe who pays more handsomely the grade of chargé des affaires.

I saw by one of the newspapers recieved that Congress had adjourned, and not seeing that any diplomatic appointments had taken place, I am led to suppose they are deferred till the next session. I am just informed also by a letter from Mr. Morris that he has letters as low as the 14th. of August and nothing respecting this subject is mentioned by his correspondent. It leaves no doubt that nothing new had taken place in it. I hope however very shortly to have something certain from you respecting it. The unsettled state in which I have been for some time, has put it out of my power to take any arrangements for fixing myself, always supposing it possible I might the next day recieve intelligence that would render it unnecessary and even improper.][3] The adjournment having certainly taken place soon after the date of your last I may very shortly now expect to hear also from you on the subject which has been put into the hands of the executive and about which you say not an unnecessary moment shall be lost. It will produce a good effect here, as it will be a means of stating properly a matter which entirely misunderstood by numbers who having taken false ideas respecting it, will not give themselves time to examine it for better information. It will be the best answer also that can be given to some things of a disagreeable kind that are sometimes thrown out by private individuals. I wish it had been done long enough ago to have produced its effect here at present. The subject of the commercial and political connexions of this country with foreigners will probably be referred to a future legislature. They will be better acquainted with the United States before that time, and they will be better worth knowing also. It will then be the proper moment for fixing more permanently and more extensively their commercial intercourse. I have no doubt that they will then be easily induced to give up the plan respecting tobacco which is now proposed by the committee of imposition.

I mentioned to you in a former letter that Swann was making proposals respecting the American debt, backed by several bankers in Paris. The original plan was what I then mentioned to you. It seems it is now changed in order to purchase it with debts due by French government. Le Coulteux is the soul of this amendment. This circumstance as well as several others which have occurred since the probability of a peace, or rather since the negotiations between England and Spain have become serious, are new proofs of the attempts made on those who are supposed to have some influence on an operation, or an opportunity of being in the secret of affairs, and shews the danger there would be in trusting too much to those who have or are supposed to have a speculating turn.[4] I know that some calculations have been already formed on the business which will be soon to be carried on at Amsterdam, with a view to the person who it is thought by some will be employed in it, and although I am far from having any reason to believe or not believe that he has given any foundation for such calculations, still having been connected in various ways with these people, necessity gives them more facility in making their approaches. I have thought it my duty to mention this although there is no probability of its having any weight and no possibility of its arriving before the decision will have been finally taken.

I beg you to accept my best wishes and to be assured of the constant & sincere attachment of Dear Sir, your friend & servant,

W. SHORT

RC (DLC); at head of text: "*Private*"; with some words in code decoded interlineally by TJ; endorsed by TJ as received 29 Nov. 1790 and so recorded in SJL. PrC (DLC: Short Papers); without the deletion indicated in note 3, below.

¹ Thus in MS.

² This and other words in italics in the remainder of this paragraph are in code and TJ's interlinear decoding has been verified by the Editor, employing partially reconstructed key to Code No. 10.

³ The matter in brackets (supplied) has been encircled by pen in RC and each letter carefully cancelled (text in PrC not cancelled).

⁴ This sentence in RC has the following notation in the margin in TJ's hand: "Swan's Proposal."

From Christopher Gore

SIR   Boston Septr. 27. 1790.

On the last of August, I receiv'd your favor of the 12th of the same month, requesting information of such proceedings as had taken place, in the state of Massachusetts, since the treaty with Great Britain, which might be consider'd, by that nation, as infractions thereof; and likewise a complete collection of all the printed laws of this State.

None of the laws, enacted before the revolution, having been printed, since the year 1775, and the confusion of the times, from that period to 1781. has render'd a purchase of the laws, during those periods, very difficult; and occasion'd the delay, already taken place, in replying to your request. I have procur'd one volume of laws enacted, from the grant of Wm. and Mary's charter, to the year 1772. This volume is more complete, than any I know of elsewhere, and was obtain from a private gentleman, after fruitless endeavors to procure one at the common places of sale. I much doubt the success of my endeavors, to obtain the laws, between the periods of April 1775 and April 1781. The printer of the laws, during that time, can furnish me with only a few. I submit to you the propriety of obtaining all the printed laws, enacted within those periods, that can be purchased, and completing the set, by copies from the original rolls, in the office of the Secretary of the Commonwealth. The laws passed between 1772 and 1775 are few in number, and probably not attainable. The originals, which ought to have been in the office of the Secretary, were mostly destroyed before the present government possess'd itself, of the official records of the province, after the expulsion of the british from Massachusetts. Such as remain can be copied, if you judge it expedient. The laws passed since July 1787 to the last session you will receive by post.

Mr. Otis is so obliging as to take charge of that volume which contains the laws between 1630 and 1772. Beside the laws, which I have before referr'd to, the Government of Massachusetts has always been in the habit of making others, under the denomination of temporary acts, and likewise, resolves, which differ from acts merely in the formalities, of passing them, by the legislature. The objects of resolves, are, generally, tho' not always, of a personal nature. To procure them for the time past will be scarcely possible, but, if in your opinion, necessary to your office, I will chearfully endeavor to procure all that are attainable. The acts, called temporary, have been printed by themselves, and made perpetual, (in which case, they are with the volume of perpetual laws) as, on experiment, they prov'd beneficial. On the 10th of November 1784. the Legislature of this Commonwealth pass'd a resolve directing that judgment for interest, on debts due from citizens of America, to british subjects and absentees shoud be suspended. A copy of this resolve and one immediately suceeding it you have inclosed. From the time of passing this resolve to the 30th April 1787 the Judicial courts suspended rendering judgment for interest on such debts. By an act passed 29 Septr AD 1780 Entitled an act for carrying into execution a resolve of Congress of the 20th of March last, and for repealing certain clauses of an act, made in the year of our Lord one thousand seven hundred and seventy six, entitled "an act to prevent forging and altering bills of public credit, and for preventing the depreciation thereof, and for making the bills of credit of the United Colonies, and the bills of this government a tender in all payments; and for establishing a rule of depreciation" among other things it is enacted "that where any person has made a tender in bills of credit of this or the United States for the discharge of any debt, and the creditor has refused to receive the same, and shall hereafter bring his action for said debt, the judicial courts are empowered and directed, in all and every such case, that shall come before them to give judgment therein, for the nominal sum of the present current money of the United States, or a sum equal thereto in the bills of credit emitted by this government agreeably to an act of Congress of the eighteenth of March last, in case the tender was made previous to the 1st day of January AD 1777, but in case the tender was made at any time, since the first day of January 1777, or at any time to Executors, administrators, agents, or attornies or to any other person, acting in trust, the justices of the court before whom such cause may be, shall direct the same to be heard and finally determin'd by reference thereof, to indifferent persons, mutually chosen by the contending parties; and in case they or their attornies shall neglect or refuse to appoint such referees, the said justices are authorized to appoint three indifferent persons, freeholders within the county where such cause shall be tried, which said referees so chosen or appointed, shall hear and finally determine such cause, as, to them, shall appear just and equitable, taking into consideration all the circumstances thereof." On the 24 March AD 1784, the Legislature passed an act, entitled "An act for repealing two laws of this state, and for asserting the right of this free and sovereign Commonwealth, to expel such aliens as may be dangerous to the peace and good order of Government, and the 10th November 1784 An act entitled "An act in addition to an act made and pass'd the present year entitled an act for repealing two laws of this State and for asserting the right of this free and sovereign Commonwealth to expel such aliens as may be dangerous to the peace and good order of Government." There are clauses, in these laws, which may be deemed infractions of the treaty between the United States and Great Britain, and soon after the peace, one man, a refugee, was, conformably to the directions of the act of the 24 March AD 1784, committed to the common goal; and afterwards sent off by the order of the Governor, with the advice of Council. I know of no other proceedings on the statutes of the 24 March and 10th November AD 1784 that can be thought infractions of the treaty with Great Britain.

On the thirtieth day of April AD 1787 the Legislature passed an act Entitled, "An act for repealing any act or parts of acts heretofore passed by the Legislature of this Commonwealth, which may militate with, or infringe the treaty of peace, enter'd into by the United States of America and Great Britain. Since the passing of that act the Supreme Judicial Court of this Commonwealth has solemnly determined that interest was equally due as principal, on all debts due from citizens of America to British Subjects, or absentees, where, by the terms of the Contract, interest was payable thereon, and in all the judicial courts of the Commonwealth, judgment has been regularly and uniformly rendered for interest; as well as principal of debts due to british subjects in like manner as though they had been citizens of the United States, and, in the only case, which I know, that was committed to Referees, conformably to the act of the 29 Septr 1780. wherein an absentee was concern'd, a report was made by referees after the passing of the act of the 30th April AD 1787. An exception was taken to the rule of court ordering the cause to be submitted to referees, and to the report thereon, 'that it was contrary to the treaty of the United States with Great Britain, which exception was held valid, and the Court rejected the report, set aside the rule, and gave judgment for the principal sum and the interest thereon due according to the words of the Contract. I have endeavor'd to state, according to your request, all the acts of the Executive, Legislative, or Judicial, that may be considered as infractions of the treaty made with Great Britain. The act of April 1787, absolutely repealing all laws, that are contrary to the treaty, remov'd the foundation of any future infraction thereof by the Judicial or Executive. The Judicial acts that may be considered as infractions being rendered null by that act of the Legislature I did not consider it within your intention, that copies of those adjudications or others on the subject since April 1787 shoud be forwarded, but if you chuse either I will send them to you. With great respect I am Sir Your very obed servt.,

C. GORE

P.S. Octo. 20. 1790. I have detained the foregoing in hopes of procuring a set of the laws from 1775 to 1781. but have been unsuccessfull.

RC (DNA: RG 59, MLR); endorsed by TJ as received 22 Nov. 1790 and so recorded in SJL.

From Thomas Paine

DEAR SIR   London Sepr. 28th. 1790.

I enclose you a few Observations on the establishment of a Mint. I have not seen your report on that subject and therefore cannot tell how nearly our opinions run together, but as it is by thinking upon and talking Subjects over that we approach towards truth there may probably be something in the enclosed that may be of use.

As the establishment of a Mint combines a portion of Politics with a knowlege of the Arts and a variety of other Matters it is a subject I shall very much like to talk with you upon. I intend at all events to be in America in the Spring and it will please me much to arrive before you have gone thro' the arrangement. I am Dr. Sir with much esteem Your Obt. Hble. Servant,

THOMAS PAINE

As I do not know by what means this will arrive, or when it will go, I put nothing in it but the subject I write upon.

RC (DLC); endorsed by TJ as received 11 Feb. 1791 and so recorded in SJL.

TJ had not received Paine's essay when he informed Hamilton on 24 Jan. 1791 that he had read the latter's report on the establishment of a mint "with a great deal of satisfaction." Except for the reservation stated in that letter, there was no ground for feeling otherwise since in general Hamilton's recommendations harmonized with those TJ himself had advanced earlier (see TJ's notes on coinage, 1776 and 1784: Vol. 1: 511-8; Vol. 7: 150-202; Syrett, *Hamilton*, VII, 462-607, especially p. 467-8 where Hamilton's plan is compared with that of TJ). Copper coinage, however, was a controverted issue, partly because of the ease of passing debased or counterfeit specimens, as TJ had indicated in his comment on "Birmingham coppers" in his report of 1784. In his 1790 report on copper coinage TJ had suggested that billon might be used instead of copper for the larger coins, but Hamilton, following the lead of the London Mint, preferred to accept the handicap of weight in countering the threat of debasement and counterfeiting. Paine's ingenious solution to the problem of weight was characteristic and his advocacy of the use of waste copper also obviously appealed to TJ. The enabling legislation for establishing a mint on 3 Mch. 1791 reflected the division of opinion in the country over the issue, for the joint resolution passed the House of Representatives by the close vote of 25 to 21 (JHR, I, 402). TJ at that time was expecting Paine to come to America during the spring, hence the long delay in asking his permission to publish the above observations (TJ to Paine, 29 July 1791).

ENCLOSURE

Thoughts on the Establishment of a Mint in the United States
by Thomas Paine

The price of the machinery and the expence of labour are reserved to the conclusion. I proceed therefore to consider the Metals and the means of procuring them.

I begin with Copper.—This Metal is of too little value and of too much bulk, to answer the purposes of coin to any great extent: About ten or twenty thousand dollars worth of copper coin is, I believe, as much as can be circulated in America.

Copper may be had in America, cheaper than in any other part of the world, and in greater quantities than are necessary for coining. This copper comes from the West-Indies, it is the old boilers stills, and other utensils which being worn out, the Planters have no use for the old copper. They have not, as I am informed, the means of melting it up, or do not give themselves the trouble to do it, besides which there is a duty of 3d sterling per lb. on landing it in England.

Considerable quantities of this copper have, since the war, been bought in New-York, for 6d. per lb. York currency; but supposing ten pounds of it be bought for one dollar, it will consequently follow that ten pound weight of copper is only equal to about one ounce weight silver; if therefore one dollar worth of copper was to be divided into a hundred parts or cents, each cent would be above the weight and size of a silver dollar. Two opposite difficulties, therefore, present themselves with respect to a copper coinage; the one is, that to give the coins, or cents, the intrinsic value they ought to have by weight, they will be too heavy and bulky for the use they are intended for; the other is, that to make them light enough to be convenient, they will not have intrinsic value enough to pass, any more than half dollars would pass for dollars.

The proportionate or relative value of silver to gold, is about 16 to one; that is, 16 ounces of silver is about the value of one ounce of gold, but the relative value of copper to silver, is from 120 to 140 to 1, which makes them too remote to represent each other in the shape of coin convenient for the pocket. Nobody would think of carrying brass pound weights about him for coin, yet he must carry copper in that proportion.

The metal convenient for a coin under the silver coin, should not differ more in its value from silver than silver does from gold—and if it differed still less it would be better; but as the relative values now stand, the difference encreases where convenience requires it should decrease. But as no such a metal, which convenience requires, exists naturally, the question is whether it will answer to produce it by composition.

Of compositions, three methods present themselves—1st. Mixing silver and copper in fusion—2d. Plating the copper with silver—3d. Plugging the copper with silver. But against all these there are very capital objections.—Wherever there is a want of satisfaction there must necessarily be a want of confidence; and this must always take place in all compounded metals. There is also a decrease in the intrinsic value of metals when compounded; one shilling worth of silver compounded with one shilling worth of copper, the composition is not worth two shillings, or what the metals were worth before they were compounded, because they must again be separated to acquire their utmost value, and this only can be done at a refiner's. It is not what the coin cost to make, but what the coin is intrinsically worth when made; that only can give it currency in all cases. Plugging copper with silver is the least detrimental to the intrinsic value of the metals, because they are the easiest separated; but in all these cases the value of the silver put into the composition will be so predominant to the value of the copper, that it will be rather a base silver coin than a copper coin.

As therefore copper presents so many inconveniences arising from its great bulk and little value, and so small an object for establishing a mint (for people have learned the value of copper coin too well to take it as they formerly did) all the calculations for a mint must be made upon silver and gold, and whatever may be[1] done in copper to be considered only as incidental.

It is I think pretty evident that copper has become a coin not from the want or scarcity of silver (because the value of all the copper coin in any nation is but a trifle, and never considered in the estimation of national property) but because silver does not admit of being divided and sub-divided down into such small pieces as to contain only the value of a copper or a cent. It is this only which has induced a recourse to copper.

In England, the lowest silver coin is six-pence, which is equal to twelve coppers, and therefore the recource to coppers for change, or for the purchase of small articles under the value of six-pence is frequently recurring; but if in America we were to coin silver as low as the twentieth part of a dollar, which would be pieces of five cents, the occasion for coppers would be very much diminished, and such pieces would be nearly of the size of the French silver six sous. I think the policy is in favor of keeping as much silver coin as we can in the country; and this is one of my motives for excluding copper as much as possible.

Some denomination under the five cent pieces would still be necessary—but as the occasions would be diminished, a small quantity would be sufficient. It is *convenience* only that ought to be considered with respect to copper coinage, and not money or riches. It was going on this last idea instead of the first one that entangled the former Congress and the several States. They attempted to do what no other nation ever thought of doing, and which is impossible to do—that of exalting copper into national wealth. Nature has fixed its boundary and we must keep to it.

It is therefore something by which to divide the five cent silver pieces, that appears to me the only thing to be considered with respect to a copper coinage. This may be done either by coining copper cents of the size and intrinsic value they ought to be, which will prevent their being counterfeited, or depreciated, or to coin or stamp small copper pieces, as a sort of treasury notes, or notes of the mint, of the nominal value of one, two, and three cents, to be exchanged, if any person chuses to exchange them, at the treasury or the mint for silver. These will be more durable than paper tickets, and capable of being extended over the continent without the danger of wearing out; and people will not compare the value of them by the metal they contain, but by the obligation to exchange them for silver if required. To prevent their being counterfeited they should not be a tender for any thing above five cents, or more than five in any one payment; As they would be merely for the purpose of dividing the silver cents by, and not for the purpose of supplying the place of silver coin in large quantities, but the mint or the treasury should always exchange them to any amount, though the amount can never be much at any one time.

To give these notes the opportunity of getting into circulation no faster, nor in greater quantities than the occasions for them require, the mint should not issue them in payment, but have them in readiness for merchants, shop-keepers, &c. to fetch away by tale in exchange for silver or gold. This used to be the way the copper coinage at the tower of London got into circulation; Every shop-keeper knew where to go to get ten or twenty shillings worth.

Congress could sustain no inconvenience, nor run any risk in exchanging those pieces for silver whenever they should be presented, because the value of them in silver would be deposited when they were first taken away. The difference between coining cents of their full value by weight, which they must have if they are to depend on their own worth for a currency, and coining copper notes, whose value is to depend upon their being exchangeable for silver at the mint, is, that the first of these methods is more than double the expence of the last, and the convenience to the public not so great, nor the security so good. If twenty thousand dollars worth of nominal cents or notes were coined, the saving in metal and workmanship would be upwards of one-half, and Congress would have the nominal value of them realized in silver. This difference between the two methods is equal to the first year's expence in establishing a mint. To consider copper only as change, or as a medium by which to divide the silver coin, and to permit it to come out no faster than it shall be called for, will always prevent inconvenience in the copper coinage. The contract for 100,000 pounds (lawful) of copper coinage, is, I believe, ten times more than can be circulated, because it will only circulate as change. Of the profits which the contractors calculated upon, I send you a specimen upon six hundred weight of copper.

600 wt of West India copper in utensils, at 8d pr. ℔. York; or 6d lawful money			£15	0	0

Melting, Casting, and Plating.

Four hands at casting, 2/6	£0	10	0			
One hand at plating	0	3	0			
50 bushels coal	0	10	5			
Salt	0	1	0			
Molasses	0	1	0			
				1	5	5

Coining.

One man cleaning and boiling	0	2	6			
Four at the cutting mill 2/6	0	10	0			
Fifteen at stamping do.	1	17	6			
				2	10	0
Six shillings the dollar				£18 [1]5		5

Three English coppers new from the mint at the tower (London) weigh 1 ounce avoirdupoise—consequently 1 ℔. wt. copper coins 48 coppers, and 600 wt. coins 28,800, which at 108 to the dollar is £80 0 0. All these estimations are at 6s the dollar. From this may very easily be calculated the profits which the contractors expected to make upon £100,000. The expence of the machinery is to be added, as I have only stated the manual expence and materials.

Quitting this part of the subject, I come to make some considerations on the silver coin.

Opportunities for procuring silver and gold for coining do not present themselves like those for copper; but they undoubtedly would present themselves more frequently if a mint was established. As every nation puts some value upon its coin, the coin passes for more than the metal is worth—if, therefore, we are charged for the expence of making Spanish dollars, we had better make dollars for ourselves, provided we can procure the silver in bars. But until we have a mint the importation of silver will continue to be made in coin, because what can a merchant do with silver or gold in bars or ingots where there is no mint.

It therefore rests to know whether silver in bars or gold in ingots, or any other way not coin, can be procured cheaper than in coin, and what the difference is.

The most effectual method to acquire this knowledge and to procure silver in bars, is to establish a mint, and to deliver to every importer of bars, or other person, the nett produce in coin which his bars shall produce.

The price of silver in bars at the bullion-office in the bank (London) is 5s 1½—the price of silver in new Mexican dollars is 4s 11½—the difference is 2d. or the 27th part of a dollar. It is hardly to be supposed that we pay to the amount of this difference at the Havannah or elsewhere in receiving dollars instead of silver unmanufactured into coin—if we do, we pay above four times the price we can manufacture the coin for ourselves, provided we can procure the silver in that proportion.

Twenty-five men will be able to complete 4,000 dollars per day from the bars. A million of dollars, coined within the space of about a year and a half, at one cent per dollar, will pay all the expence of labor, and the price of machinery necessary for such an operation, after which the expence per dollar will diminish, provided the men are kept employed.

The following is given to me as a tolerable proportionate estimate of the expence of coining copper, silver and gold, into cents, dollars and half-joes;

The labor of 25 men will coin, per day, about . . 10,000 coppers,
      or   4,000 dollars,
      or   2,200 half-joes.

By this it appears that the expence of coining copper is about forty times greater than that of silver, and about two hundred times greater than that of gold. This furnishes an additional reason against copper coinage.

It may perhaps be asked, that if the importer of silver in bars is to receive the exact produce of his bars from the mint, in coin, where will be the advantage? I answer, that the advantage in the first instance will be to the importer, because he gets more dollars for his cargo than he would by receiving dollars at the place of sale, and this is his inducement to bring in bars. The advantage in the second instance, is to the whole country, because it makes a greater quantity of money than there would be by importing the silver in coin. If the difference is 1-27th in a dollar, and bars can be procured instead of Spanish dollars, the increase of silver money in the country would be as 112 is to 108.

There is another circumstance by which money would increase in the country if a mint were established, which is from the old silver plate which is now sent to England, and it is not improbable that some old silver plate might come from the West-Indies. But until there is a mint, we must remain ignorant of the resources by which silver and gold are to be obtained.

The whole apparatus of a mint can be made in America. The only thing necessary to import will be a small quantity of cast-steel, which is an article not made in America.

The following is a tolerable estimate of the expence of as much machinery as will be sufficient to begin with, as it can occasionally be employed in gold, silver, and copper,

1 coining mill	450 Dols.
2 cutting mills	180
1 plating mill for copper	270
1 do. for silver	180
1 do. for gold	180
1 sett of ingots, cast-steel, small tools, &c. . .	240
	1500

Coining is a new business in America. Those who have proposed contracts, knew, either of themselves, or from those who were to execute, what they were doing, but they supposed Congress to know nothing of the matter. Accident and a turn for mechanics have thrown me into a knowledge of their plans, and the profits they expected to make.

Whenever Congress goes into this business it will be best to do it on their own account. The experience will cost something, but it will be worth obtaining, and the cheapest way of obtaining it. The fact is, that the American coiners can afford to manufacture coppers and send them to England cheaper than the English coiners can send them to America. In England copper is about 10d or 10½ sterling, per ℔. but old copper from the West-Indies is not half that price. When copper coining first began in the New-England states, a person concerned in that business has since told me, that he sent his son to the West-Indies to see after copper—that in the possession of one person, at Providence, he found upwards of 50 tons, which was offered him at the rate of 15℔. for a dollar. When it is considered how great the exportation of copper utensils must annually be from England to the islands, and that they are a drug after they are worn out, and have no market for the old copper, but in America, it will be easy to account for the plans, schemes and proposed contracts that have been lately set on foot.

In contemplating the extent of a mint, I carry my mind a little further than the business of coining. The introduction of such a machinery as coining requires, will serve to bring forward those kind of arts which are connected with it, such as making buttons of various kinds. The mint may also be an Assay office for wrought plate, which will considerably contribute towards defraying the expence of the mint, at least it will be a convenient appendix to it—and the having an Assay office will promote the manufactory of plate in America, and prevent that branch of business going to England, which it now does from the want of that confidence in the purity of the metal which an Assay office would give. An Assay office is much wanted in Philadelphia. Before the war a bill was brought into the assembly to appoint an Assay master, but the Governor refused passing the bill unless he had the appointment of the person, and the matter dropt, and has not been since revived. But it ought to be connected with the mint, as the standard for metals comes properly into that department. The silver-smiths who bring the plate pay something for the stamp, and the office, as well for the seller as the buyer is a very necessary one.

Text from Philip Freneau's *National Gazette*, 17 Nov. 1791. The original MS, which TJ must have turned over to Freneau as copy, has not been found. It included some notes containing "facts relative to particular persons" which TJ omitted (TJ to Paine, 29 July 1791).

1 This word supplied, lacking in text.

From N. & J. Van Staphorst & Hubbard

Sir   Amsterdam 28 September 1790.

We had the honor to address you the 3. Instant and confident that a Business interesting the Commerce of your Country, is a sufficient apology for addressing you on the Subject, We inform you of difficulties having been started here against allowing public Sales of East India Goods imported by Individuals, on the ground of their not being accompanied with the Proofs required in an obsolete Ordinance of 1717., notwithstanding same has not been enforced for more than Half a century, during a constant and very extensive Practice to the contrary, which induced the few Persons who knew its Existence to deem it virtually repealed and without effect.

Upon a Petition stating these Facts corroberated by the Signed Opinions of the eminent Houses of Trade in this City, the States General it is true in spite of the opposition of our Burgomasters decided a large parcel of Teas from Ostend, should be sold by Public Auction, at same time however declaring that the Ordinance of 1717. should be renovated, which our Magistracy has availed itself of to dispute our Selling at Public Auction 34. chests china Silk we received from Philadelphia many months ago. But as we are in precisely the same State, as the House to whom the priviledge of so doing with their Teas was granted, we cannot doubt that our petition to the States General will meet same Fate and we trust to succeed likewise in obtaining permission to sell at Public Sale 1000. Chests Teas consigned to us ℔ the Brigt. Grange Capt. R. B. Gillchrist and 417 Chests we expect ℔ the Brigt. Eliza Capt. M. Cutter both from Newyork, as these Shipments were made to us before it was possible the News of the revival of the Ordinance of 1717. could reach America, and therefore cannot be pretended to have been made in contravention thereto.

It being probable however that in future the Proofs of East India Goods having been once sold conformable to the ordinance of 1717. will be demanded previous to allowing their Entry here, We inclose you Sir, that act, which Mr. R. J. van den Broek of Newyork is able to make a better translation of than we can procure here, that you may make the use of it, You will judge proper for the Information of the Merchants of the United States. We are respectfully, Sir! Your most obedient humble servants,

N. & J. Van Staphorst & Hubbard

RC (DNA: RG 59, PCC No. 145); at head of text: "(Copy)"; not recorded in SJL.

From C. W. F. Dumas

Monsieur   Lahaie 30e. 7br. 1790.

Après avoir eu soin, de la maniere la plus prompte possible, selon ma derniere du 7e. Court., de faire parvenir un Exemplaire de la Gazette françoise de Leide, par Mr. Luzac, même, et par son Correspondant *Mr. Cooper, Commis des Postes de S.M. Britannique à Londres*, sous l'adresse simple de *Ths. Jefferson Esqr. N.York*; j'ai pris tout de suite mes mesures pour en faire parvenir régulierement, par le même Paquebot, et d'une maniere encore plus sûre, un second Exemplaire à *Mess. Le Roi & Bajard à N. York*, qui recevront ordre d'Amsterdam de les faire parvenir immédiatement à Votre Excellence. De cette maniere, Monsieur, vous en recevrez deux extraordinaires par le Paquebot Anglois, outre les deux ordinaires par les Vaisseaux d'Amsterdam; et il n'y aura pas trop à 4 de cet estimable Papier, pour rouler entre les mains du Congrès, et pour en conserver la Collection bien complette.

Quant aux affaires de l'Europe, on n'en sait rien que du jour à la journée. Ce qui est sûr, c'est que la paix est faite entre la Russie et la Suede, *sans admission de Médiateurs*; et que la Russie a déclaré rondement, de n'en point vouloir admettre pour la sienne avec les Turcs. Il l'est pareillement, que la Pologne ne cedera pas Dantzick et Thorn au Roi de Pr[usse], comme il s'en étoit flatté. Il n'est pas certain qu'il veuille risquer une guerre avec la Russie, quelque mine qu'il en fasse. Les troupes Autrichiennes destinées à soumettre les Insurgens Belgiques, avancent lentement par l'Allemagne. En attendant ces fanatiques papimanes s'épuisent de plus en plus, abusés par leurs chefs. On ne sait pas encore à quoi les Anglois destinent leur Armement. On dit qu'ils répandent leur argent en France, *to do mischief*. Ils paroissent avoir tout récemment ou provoqué ou reçu un nouveau sujet de querelle au Golfe de Floride. Léopold ne paroît occupé que de son couronnement Impérial à Francfort, pour où il est en chemin; après, il se fera coeffer de sa Couronne d'Hongrie.—Ici l'on ne s'occupe que du mariage de la jeune Princesse avec l'héréditaire de Brunswick, pour lequel il y aura illumination forcée. Il n'y a rien à dire de plus où quelqûes-uns sont encore tout, entourés de satellites et valets, le Citoyen particulier virtuellement rien, et la nombreuse canaille, misérable au milieu de la Licence, surtout ici. La France seule s'occupe de choses vraiment importantes, spécialement de ses finances. Espérons de la bonne providence, que sa nouvelle Constitution consolidée pendant le reste de cette année, nous ouvrira enfin des scenes consolantes.

Un homme digne de foi m'a appris, qu'au mois de Mars dernier un Vaisseau étant arrivé de Baltimore au Texel, chargé de froment pour compte de Van Akeren, Marchand de Rotterdam, sa cargaison fut vendue ƒ40 d'hollde. le Last plus cher que celui de Zélande (le meilleur de ce pays), savoir ƒ320. le Last, tandis que le dernier se vendoit ƒ280. Le Last est de 28 sacs hollandois, dont deux faisant un sac Américain qui pese 186 ℔., ne pesent ensemble que 168 ℔. Ainsi le Last Américain pesoit 252 ℔. de plus que celui du meilleur froment d'ici. J'ai cru ceci digne d'être connu de Votre Excellence.

N.B. J'ai toujours dans l'idée, qu'un établissement de Paquebots *Américains* pour ce pays-ci pourroit être d'une très grande utilité, publique et particulière, aux Etats-Unis. Un chaque mois allant et un Venant pourroient suffire, comme actuellement celui des Anglois, qui savent bien ce qu'ils font, et sont par-là *les maîtres de votre correspondance.* Le Pouvoir exécutif pourroit en faire les fraix, et les retirer avec usure, par le Port des paquets, Lettres et Passagers, comme le Roi d'Angleterre fait des siens, entre autres de ceux qui deux fois par semaine vont et viennent entre Harwich et Hellevoetsluys. De cette maniere et le Citoyen, et le Ministere des Etats-Unis auroient au moins une voie *incontrôlable* de correspondance *réguliere* avec l'Europe.—Les Stations, ou points de départ et d'arrivée pour ces Paquebots, pourroient être N.York, Philadelphie et Baltimore en Amérique (qui pourroient partager entre eux les 12 mois de l'année convenablement); le Texel et Hellevoet-Sluys en Hollande. J'ai cru devoir communiquer cette idée à Votre Excellence, qui pourroit la communiquer à Son Excellence le Président; fermement persuadé que sa réalisation seroit plus utile, plus profitable et plus nécessaire que l'envoi et le séjour de Ministres coûteux ici, et quelque autre part, excepté la France, l'Espagne et l'Angleterre. Je suis avec le plus grand respect, De Votre Excellence Le très-humble, très-obéissant et fidele Serviteur, C W F Dumas

RC (DNA: RG 59, PCC No. 93); at head of text: "No. 68 A Son Excellence Mr. Ths. Jefferson, Minre. d'Etat & Secret. des Affes. Etr. des Et. Un. d'Amerique"; endorsed by TJ as received 15 Jan. 1791 and so recorded in SJL. FC (Dumas Letter Book, Rijksarchief, The Hague; photostats in DLC).

To William Short

Dear Sir   Monticello Sep. 30. 1790.

I wrote you last from Philadelphia. Your public letter of June 29. and private of June 14. and 29. are delivered to me here. My several letters, private, will have left me little to add on the subject of your stay in Europe. One circumstance only in your letters must be corrected, that is, your idea of my influence in the foreign affairs. You have forgotten your countrymen altogether, as well as the nature of our government, which renders it's heads too responsible to permit them to resign the direction of affairs to those under them. The public would not be satisfied with that kind of resignation, and be assured it does not exist, and consequently that your destination does not depend on me. I think it possible that it will be established into a maxim of the new government to discontinue it's foreign servants after a certain time of absence from their own country, because they lose in time that sufficient degree of intimacy with it's circumstances which alone can enable them to know and pursue it's interests. Seven years have been talked of. Be assured it is for your happiness and success to return. Every day increases your attachment to Europe and renders your future reconcilement to your own country more desperate: and you must run the career of public office here if you mean to stand on high and firm ground hereafter. Were you here now, you would be put into the Senate of Congress in the place of Grayson whose successor is to be chosen next month. (For the late appointment was only for the fragment of his time which remained.) There would scarcely be a dissenting voice, to your appointment. But it is too late for that. Monroe will be pressed into the service, really against his will. But, two years hence will come on another election in the place of R[ichard] H[enry] L[ee] who will unquestionably be dropped. If you were to be here a few months before I would forfeit every thing if you were not elected. It will be for 6. years, and is the most honorable and independent station in our government, one where you can peculiarly raise yourself in the public estimation. I cannot then but recommend it to you to have this in your view. I do not exactly see to what your late mission to Amsterdam may lead. Either to nothing, or something infirm, and by which you ought not to suffer yourself to be led on to the loss of an appointment here which will not recur for years, and never under such certainty. Your compeer in the neighboring kingdom is a proof of the necessity of refreshing his acquaintance with his own country, and will do wisely if he does as Bourgoin announced to you.

I know not what to do in the case of Tolozan and Sequeville. Indeed I can do nothing till I see the President. They must not lose their perquisite; it is a part of their livelihood. But I think their delicacy should yeild to the inflexibility of our constitution. Assure them of my friendly recollection of their attentions, and my resolution that some how or other they must accept the usual present. I will write further after having consulted the President, whom I shall not see however till December.—The house at Paris will certainly not be taken by the public for the use of their legation.

You will have seen that by the new arrangement, that article will be at their own charge. Very possibly, and very probably, my successor may take it. Be that as it may, I have nothing to do with it after the expiration of 6. months from the day of the notification. It is well known to M. de Langeac, and to M. Perrier the Notary that the notification I had given of determining the lease was to be void, and the lease to go on as if nothing had happened except as to the single circumstance of an abatement of the rent, which was therefore provided by a kind of marginal note, and no new lease. They may call it prorogation or what they please. No new commencement was meant.—Besides if it had been an absolutely new lease I was not obliged to keep it one day. I had exactly the same kind of lease, with the same condition from Gueraut for the house in Tete-bout. I entered it Oct. 16. 1784. and determined the lease March 10. 1786. by a notification given Sep. 10. 1785. Gueraut was sufficiently litigious, and desirous to continue the lease, but knew he could not. The objection too that it must be given up at no other time but the beginning of a term is contrary to the express letter of the lease. I gave up Gueraud's house the 10th. of March: and my notification to the Count de Langeac in Oct. 1788. was that his lease should finish Apr. 16. 1789. Both admitted my right to do so, and accepted the notification. If Langeac and his notary Perrier (for I trusted to his notary, because he had a candid appearance) have used words of a contrary import, it is one of those cheats against which the diplomatic indemnities were meant to be a protection. Foreign ministers are not bound to an acquaintance with the laws of the land. They are privileged by their ignorance of them. They are bound by the laws of natural justice only. These are in my favor, be the law of the land and it's forms what they will. I shall fulfil substantially my real agreement with the Count de Langeac and will certainly disregard the snares of formality in which they meant to take me. Give up the house at all events on the day six months from the notification.—I am really sorry Petit does not come. I am sure he will be disappointed in the expectation of employment from my successor. Besides that it will be some time in the next year before he can go, should he be a married man as all Americans are, his wife will not employ a maitre d'hotel who cannot speak English, if she employs one at all. I still wish him to come. If he will not, I think Madme. de Corny, when she reformed her house, parted with her Maitre d'hotel, and with great reluctance, and that she spoke of him to me in very high terms. I wish you would enquire about him, and barely sound him to see if he will come on moderate wages, and having his passage paid. But do not engage him till I write from Philadelphia where perhaps I may be able to get one.—Your brother did not come to New York. I know he was well when we last heard from Kentuckey. Remember me to all my friends, but most particularly those of the hotels de la Fayette, de la Rochefoucault, de Tessé, de Corny, the two Abbés, and all others as if named. I have only room left to assure you of the sincere esteem & attachment with which I am my dear sir your affectionate friend & servt.,

TH: JEFFERSON

RC (ViW); recorded in SJL as "private"; endorsed by Short as received 19 Dec. 1790. PrC (DLC).

From Francis Willis, Sr.

Virginia Sept 30th 1790

My dear Jeffersons extreme friendly letter dated the 18th of last April I received on the first of May and can assure him tho I was unsuccessfull in my application the receipt of his letter gave me great pleasure. The day I received it, I was unfortunately taken with that dreadfull complaint, fistula in ano, and have been the whole summer in great pain tho thank God I am at last releived and hope perfectly cur'd; I sincerely thank you for your wishes to serve me and am confindent they are sincere and hope when any new mode of Taxation takes place, which I doubt not must shortly be the case, you will then remember a real distress'd friend. I conceive we shall have a stamp Act or something like that. Perhaps you might in that line when it takes place get me some post for which I shall ever be thankfull and it will greatly assist my numerous family, and be a place I might remain at home and discharge my duty in, for I find my plan of removing to Wmburg. impracticable (desirable as it was for the education of my children) for I am so distress'd by a new securityship for my deceased acquaintance J. Dixon that I can scarce turn round. My whole misfortunes have originated by endeavouring to serve mankind. As to my friend Mr. Reynold I lament his not getting some little place for he is very clever with his pen and if he could have once got any place in that line his cleverness and great worth would have got him on. I can venture to say you can speak to no man from Virginia that will not give him an extreme good character. Had not your copying

clerks places of 800 Dll been fill'd up and you would have tryed him you would have been pleased with him and it would have made him an happy man. He has poor man within a few weeks met a severe loss that of his wife. Our friend Colo. Page soon replaced his loss at N. York and his Ladies Sister that is with him if I am not mistaken from appearances would have no objection to repairing hers by the same mode. God bless you & grant you every wish yr Sincere friend & Most Obdt. Sv., FRANCIS WILLIS SENR
Decr. 16.

I am just returned from Georgia and S. Carolina a trip of 1500 Miles after a person I am security for, and dread the consequences. I was sorry to find the said States so much out of humour with Congress. It seems as if our Government is not to be of such continuance as I could wish, which I expect will lessen our consequence in Europe and of course destroy the credit of the States.

RC (DLC: Washington Papers); endorsed by TJ as received 28 Dec. 1790 and so recorded in SJL.

On TJ's early relations with Willis, who had made his days as a law student difficult with his irresponsible pranks and with whom TJ had planned to make the journey to New York and Philadelphia in 1766, see Malone, *Jefferson*, I, 64, 98 (see also, TJ to Page, 4 May 1786, Page to TJ, 7 Mch. 1788).

From W. & J. Willink, N. & J. Van Staphorst & Hubbard

Amsterdam, 30 Sep. 1790. Acknowledging his letter of advice of 4 Aug. concerning the draft for "ƒ4036 which shall meet due protection, and be carried to the debit of the United-States, in Conformity with the permission received to that purpose from the Secretary of the Treasury.—The 21 Augst. Mr. Short valued on us ℔ ƒ4403.1 and advised that it was for the charges of packing your furniture, and articles purchased by your directions, which we have duly honored and charged to the debit of the United-States at the Agio of 1/4 ℔ Ct. with ƒ4414.1, not doubting but it will meet your approbation."

RC (DLC); in clerk's hand except for signatures; endorsed by TJ as received 10 Jan. 1791 and so recorded in SJL.

From Thomas Rodney

DR SIR   Delaware Septr: 1790.

Those who write to every body, in some Measure enti[t]le everybody to write to them. Under this privilige I take the liberty of addressing this letter to you, but you must not expect from others, and especially one who speaks only his Native Tongue, that Elegant language and beautiful Stile which carecterises your own writings.

The Revolution of America, by recognizing those rights which every Man is Entitled to by the laws of God and Nature, Seems to have broken off all those devious Tramels of Ignorance, prejudice and Superstition which have long depressed the Human Mind. Every door is now Open to the Sons of genius and Science to enquire after Truth. Hence we may expect the darkning clouds of error will vanish fast before the light of reason; and that the period is fast arriving when the Truth will enlighten the whole world.

In reading your writings I am often delighted with your Philosophical Sentiments; and was particularly pleased with the Justness of those relative to the Origin of Mankind. You Suppose the white, Red, and Black people to be different Species; the productions of different Climates. This is a subject of great importance and worthy the most profound Philosophical Enquiry; for nothing has Darkened and Obscured the True History of Mankind more than the common Opinion, that they all decended from one Original pair of Ancestors, to wit, Adam and Eve. This Opinion, erroniously founded on the testimony of Moses, has hitherto prevailed against the light of reason and the more certain view of Nature; for Nature Constantly Testifies that the Whites Originated in the Frigid, the Reds in the Temperate, and the Blacks in the Torrid Zones. And even the Testimony of Moses when fully understood will Shew us that Many More people Originated in the world at the same time with Adam and Eve: but to understand Moses right we must attend to the Chief Objects he had in view when he wrote his Antient history. These were—to shew the Israelites the great power wisdom and goodness of the Deity in the work of Creation—to shew them how their first Ancestors came into the world—to trace their decent from them—And to Shew them the Special care the Deity had Taken through a long Train of ages and Events to convey the True knowledge of his worship down to them, whom he had selected as his chosen people. Moses therefore does not Speak particularly of any other family but that of Adams, from whom they decended. Yet he frequently Shews us that there were others originated at or about the same time with Adam, and particularly a Species of Mankind of more than the Ordinary Size called Giants.

The following quotation without Troubling you with More, will be Sufficient to verify all that has been Alledged. "And it came to pass when Men began to Multiply on the face of the Earth, and daughters were born Unto them, That the Sons of God saw the daughters of Men, that they were fair, and they took them wives of all which they Chose. And there were Giants in the Earth in those days [to wit when Men began to Multiply] and after that when the Sons of God came in unto the daughters of Men, and they bare Children to them, the same became Mighty Men, Who were of Old Men of renown." Who were those Sons of God? Not the Angels, their nature renders them incapable of cohabiting with Women; and surely the Holy Men of that age would not be the first to sett the example of keeping Seralios of beautiful young women. It is very clear that Moses Means neither of these, but literally those very Men who came into the World at the Same time and in the Same Manner that Adam did; They were in Truth and in fact the Sons of God, because they had no other ancestor, and therefore were distinguished from the *Sons of Men* by being, Stiled the *Sons of God*. When these fathers of Mankind saw (perhaps in the third or fourth decent) that the daughters of Men were far more sprightly delicate and beautiful than the daughters of Nature, they became enamoured with them and Took as many of them as they Chose; and so much were they then reverenced and respected by their decendants that no One dare Say them nay.

The Children of these Marriages formed as it were a new race of Men, who considered themselves Superior to all others; and being Composed of the Strength and Vigor of their fathers, united with the beauty wit and sprightlyness of their Mothers, they became more Intelligent and interpizing than the rest of Mankind. Hence they Aspired to Rule and domination, and by their Superior Skill dexterity and prowess mastered the rest of Mankind; and therefore are Stiled by Moses "Mighty men who were of Old men of renown." The Hero of all these, as we learn from other writers, was the so much Celebrated Jubeter the Son of Saturn, who was a Son of Nature. This renowned Hero subdued the Giants and the rest of Mankind and parcelled the world into governments Among his brethren and children, he reigning as Emperor over the whole. Hence he became worshiped as a God; and in process of time was Accounted the Superior God and the father of all the Gods.

Tradition could not avoid conveying to posterity a wonderful account of these renowned Antideluvian Heroes; Hence Mankind after the flood run into the most extravigant and impious excess after this flatering kind of Idolatry.—And hence the poets have furnished the world with a wonderful account of the war between those renowned Heros and the Giants, Stiled by them the War of the Gods and Giants. But when these accounts are disrobed of their fabulous Ornaments we find they agree in Truth and Substance with the Story of Moses.

Both Moses and profane writers affirm the ixistance of Giants before as well as after the flood, and they are always Spoke of as a peculiar and extraordinary Species of Mankind. Several of this race remained in the land of Canaan long after the Israelites returned from Egypt and are discribed as being of Much greater Stature than the rest of Mankind and this Not Only Tends to prove the various origin of Mankind but in a Strong peice of Testimony against the universality of the flood; but the Object of this letter is Only to Shew that the Testimony of Moses agrees with the voice of Nature and light of reason as well as with profane writers respecting the Origin of Mankind. I will venture to Suppose enough is said to evince this; and if right, then that mighty cloud is removed which hath so long darked that most Interesting period of the world.

It may Seem Strange at first thought to Suppose that there is a better opertunity in the present age of examining into the Truth of remote Transactions, than in the ages nearer to them, yet this on reflection will be found True. It is but of late years that a general knowledge of the world, and the various Accounts of the different nations that have, and now inhabit it, have been brought into one point of view. And it is but very lately that the Human Mind has broke down those fixed Superstitious boundaries which prevented its expanding and reaping the benefits of that general knowledge which now flows to us through So Many different chanels. And our knowledge of the Universe as well as of the world is also greatly extended and our minds expanded by improvements which are daily disclosing a more perfect view of the planetary regions. Mankind long viewed the Sun Moon and Stars as merely formed for the benefit of this world, but it is now no longer a doubt with Philosophers but the Sun Moon and Stars are worlds like this, Inhabited with intelligent beings and other things as this is, and diferent from it perhaps only in Size and a different disposition of land and water so as to render each most Suitable to its Situation. Natural Philosophy is also greatly extending our knowledge of the things around us; the Origin, Genius and progress of Fossils, Plants and Animals, the power and operation of the Elements, the power and influence of the Planets &c. &c. is unfolding to us. But to enlarge on this Subject would carry me beyond the bounds and intention of this letter, therefore beg leave to conclude by Subscribing my self with great respect & Esteem Your most Obedient   TR

P.S. If this letter Should prove agreable, perhaps it may induce a further correspondence Tending to Elusterate the History of the rise and progress of mankind through the remote and dark ages of Antiquity, which Elusterations you will find made by a Mind free and unimbarrassed by any kind of prejudice, and only desirous of attaining the Truth by a fair investigation and comparison of the various Accounts handed down to us through different channels.

R.

RC (PHi); addressed: "Honble Thomas Jefferson Esqr. Secretary of the United States. Virginia ⅌ Post." Although sealed, addressed, and evidently intended for the post, this letter bears no postmark or other indication of having travelled through the mails or of having been received by TJ. It is not recorded in SJL and no reply to it has been found or is recorded in SJL. In view of these facts, the probability is that Rodney wrote, sealed, and addressed the letter but did not post it— hence that TJ never saw it.

To Elizabeth Chiswell Carter

DEAR MADAM   Monticello Oct. 1. 1790.

I am honoured with your letter of the 19th. Sep. and feel with great sensibility the events which have affected your circumstances. Assuredly I would do any thing in my power which might be useful to a family all the members of which are still very dear to me. I fear however that there is nothing in my position which can be rendered useful to your son at this moment. The office under my direction gives me the appointment of three clerks at 500. dollars a year, places of great drudgery, wherein no economy can save any thing, and no talents or merit give a prospect of rising. But I have said too much in saying that even these are in my gift; since they are at present held by gentlemen whom I found in them, whom my predecessor found in them, who in fact have exercised them for years and conducted themselves so unexceptionably in them, that nothing could justify the removing them to put others in. Nor would this I am sure be agreeable to you. I can do nothing more at present then but to assure you that should any thing occur hereafter I will keep in remembrance your anxieties for a son, and serve them with the zeal I retain for your family, assuring you that I am with unabated affection and attachment dear Madam, Your most obedient friend & servant,

TH: JEFFERSON

PrC (DLC); at foot of text: "Mrs. Elizabeth Carter of Ludlow."

Mrs. [Charles] Carter's letter of 19 Sep. 1790 from Fredericksburg read in part: "From your friendship and willingness always to oblige my mother I am induc'd to take the liberty of addressing you on a very interesting subject; had an opportunity offerd, when you honourd me with a Visit, it wou'd have given me the greatest satisfaction to have advis'd with you on the best method of advancing the future welfare of my Sons. By adverse fortune we are reduc'd in our circumstances, indeed, was it not for that best of friends Mr. Carter of Shirley we shou'd have been in real want, but, by his great bounty and the small advantage arising from the board of a few young Gentlemen we have been hitherto enabl'd to educate our Children; my eldest Son is just turnd of eighteen, and has often express'd a desire of being bound to any Gentleman whom his Father or myself woud approve, our first choice woud be yourself, might we presume to ask such a favour. He is of a placid disposition and quick apprehention, as free from Vice as any boy of his age can be, rather too diffident in company, writes a tolerable hand. . . . Shoud you honour me with an answer please to direct to Charles Carter of Ludlow to avoid mistakes" (RC in DLC: Applications for Office under Washington; endorsed by TJ as received 28 Sep. 1790 and so recorded in SJL). TJ's visit to the Carters evidently took place when he passed through Fredericksburg on 15-17 Sep. 1790.

From Robert R. Livingston

DR. SIR   ClerMont 1st. Octr. 1790

The hope I entertained of meeting you at New York when I vissited it in Sepr. has induced me to delay answering your polite favor, disappointed in this hope, I cannot deny myself the pleasure of informing you that I have made some experiments which satisfy me that the friction on a spindle or gudgeons[1] may, by the means I proposed, be reduced almost to nothing. As my trials were made with water (not having quicksilver at hand) I gave your objection the fairest chance since the base of the cylinder was necessarily larger as the medium was less dense. I find the fluid immediatly takes the direction of the cylinder and affords it so little obstruction that I do not know whether it might not be made to answer the purposes of a fly to a windmill.[2] I have an idea upon this subject which when I have reduced to practize I shall take liberty of communicating to you. When I first wrote to you upon the subject I had nothing farther in view than to diminish the friction on the wheel and spindle. But as a father who fondles his child daily thinks that he discovers new beauties in him, so I fancy I have discovered more important advantages in the plan I submitted to your consideration.[3] The principal force to be overcome in a mill is that of the stones upon each other and on the corn. This Martin computes at one third of the weight of the upper millstone. Yet the weight of the millstone so far as it acts by a perpendicular pressure on the grain is injurious, good flower being made by attrition and bad, or as the millers term it, dead flower by its pressure. When a mill is overloaded or the wheat not eaqualy dispersed it can only relieve itself by raising a stone weighing perhaps 1600 weight.[4] By reducing the weight to 100 ℔. and at the same time preserving the momentum of its original weight, I lessen the friction from 533 3/1 ℔ to 33 1/3 ℔. and at the same time make the flower by *attrition* only.[5] This circumstance taken with the one I first mentioned induces me to believe that much less water than is usually imployed may answer all the purposes of a grist mill, that the flower will be better and that great part of the trouble and expence of sharping the spindle and pecking the stones both of which will wear less will be saved.

Experience can allone determine what weight is necessary to the grinding of flower, and I am now only waiting for a workman to try it on one of my mills, and as it will be attended with less expence I shall prefer water to mercury in my first essay. Whether it succeeds or fails, I shall give myself the pleasure of communicating the result.

I thank you for the copy of your report on measures weights and coins. I had however received and read it before with great pleasure. The standard is happily chosen, and more particularly so if it should be adopted as the common measure of Europe. I do not know what greater accuracy will be required than that you propose. If however it should, as heat is always in our power, might not the thermometer be called in to your aid? On the subject of coins you have everything that can be wished by those who are pleased with the example of Europe, or the resolutions of Congress on this head. But I who consider the whole system as radically defective, while I admire your accuracy and ingenuity, wish to change it for my own. When I shall be fully satisfied under your hand that you have sufficient leisure to read my reveries on this subject I shall take pleasure in communicating them. I am Dr. Sir with the utmost respect & esteem, Your Most Obt: Hum: Servt.,

R R LIVINGSTON

RC (DLC); endorsed by TJ as received 15 Dec. 1790 and so recorded in SJL (being enclosed in Livingston's letter to TJ of 10 Dec. 1790). Dft (NHi); with a number of variations, some of which are noted below.

For other explanations by Livingston of his experiments, see his letters to TJ of 1 Aug. and 10 Dec. 1790. TJ's POLITE FAVOR was that of 8 Aug. 1790.

[1] Dft reads: "... on the end of a spindle or on gudgeons."

[2] Dft reads: "... whether it would not in a windmill if a large cylinder and a considerable quantity of mercury were used answer the purpose of a fly and correct the greatest fault of that machine by equalizing its motion."

[3] Dft reads: "... consideration as you will not feel the same parental partiality you will correct my error."

[4] Dft reads: "... weighing perhaps 1800."

[5] Dft reads: "... the friction on the face of the stones from 600 ℔. to 33⅓ ℔. and at the same time grind the flour merely by attrition."

To Henry Remsen, Jr.

DEAR SIR   Monticello Octob. 1. 1790.

I received on the 26th. your favors of the 6th. and 9th. Ult. I had not been apprised of Mr. Mc.Donogh's mission, and therefore could leave no directions about it. At present it seems to me impracticable that his recognition can take place till the President's return to Philadelphia. This however need not detain him personally from going to Boston if he can leave his original commission in the hands of some one to be exhibited and returned to him. I do not see that any inconvenience can arise from this or even a delay of his functions, which being merely voluntary as to the British subjects themselves, are as likely to meet their acquiescence before as after our recognition.

I thank you for your attention to the disposal of my house. I observe you name the sum of £27.10. The whole rent being £109-9 would be £9-2-5 a month. I believe I proposed to let it at half price, which would be £4-11-2½ a month, and for 7. months £31-18-5½. I do not mention this to make a difficulty if it has been settled at £27-10. but only to correct an error of calculation if it has been merely an error. I shall be glad to get any thing for the house. I wish Mr. Bruce would give me a discharge for that sum, or whatever sum they are to pay.—The little difficulties of Francis about bells, boards, tubs &c. are not worth a thought. Besides Mr. Bruce is right, in considering things fixed to the freehold by the tenant as becoming the property of the landlord.—I believe I shall be somewhat later in my return than I expected. Be pleased to forward the enclosed to Mr. Short. I am with great esteem Dr. Sir Your most obedt. humble servt.,　　　　　Th: Jefferson

RC (ViU); addressed: "Mr. Remsen Chief clerk of the Secretary of state's office New York"; franked by TJ; postmarked "RICHMOND Oct 4" and "FREE"; endorsed. PrC (DLC). Enclosure: TJ to Short, 30 Sep. 1790.

From William Short

Dear Sir　　　　　　　　　　Paris October the 3d. 1790

I am this moment informed of a conveyance for London, and forward you by it the newspapers as usual to which I beg leave to refer you for the present politics of Europe.—I inclose you also several letters which have been entrusted to me for you: among them are three from the American captives at Algiers. They will inform you of their present situation there, which you will find conformable to what I mentioned to you in my last of the 26th. ulto. sent by the English packet.

Since that the assembly have determined on an emission of paper money to the amount of 800,000,000.ᵗ exclusive of the 400,000,000.ᵗ already in circulation. It is not yet decided of what amount the bills shall be. The committee of finance are to make their report on this subject.

The report of the committee on the procedure of the Chatelet and the discussions which followed took up three days. The assembly yesterday confirmed the report "qu'il n'y a lieu à l'accusation contre Messieurs Mirabeau and D'Orleans." I send you the report inclosed together with the depositions in that affair. M. de Sillery one of the Duke of Orleans' friends informed the assembly that the Duke intended this morning to come and speak on the subject. This was after the decision taken. From what had been said by Mirabeau and by the Duke de Biron, it was supposed he meant to attack the Marquis de la fayette. I have this moment seen a person who came from the assembly. He tells me the Duke of Orleans made only a short speech promising that he would give a full account of his conduct that should satisfy the assembly and confound his enemies. He did not inculpate the Marquis de la fayette, who had gone to the assembly with an intention to answer him.

The deputies of the general assembly of St. Domingo, who had been *mandés à la barre*, appeared last evening. They complained of the abuses of power exercised by M. de Peynier, and of the massacre, as they style it, committed by M. Mauduit, but said nothing in justification of their conduct, which they seemed to think praiseworthy. Their orator was a very young man who spoke with a degree of vehemence and declamation that seemed to displease the assembly. The other deputies that appeared three days ago with the Captain of the Leopard, to accuse the general assembly, were received and heard with transport. The whole affair is referred to the colonial committee, contrary to the request made by the deputies yesterday evening of its being referred to a more numerous committee named ad hoc. The report of the committee will certainly be unfavorable to them, but to what degree I cannot say. They will at least be declared to have forfeited their seats as members of the assembly. The two parties in the national assembly unite in sentiment against them.

The assembly have not yet taken up the report on tobacco; the longer it can be put off the better. I have brought over a few members more to the opinion in favor of rendering this article free in commerce. One obstacle which I found with all of them, was my being an American. Ignorant themselves they were afraid to listen to a person whom they considered as interested. I endeavoured to persuade them that the interests of France and America were the same in this matter. But as their committee assure them they will have twelve millions in one way and nothing in the other, it is probable their report will be adopted, and particularly as they adhere to it with great obstinacy, and say it forms an essential part of their general plan of taxation. I shall leave nothing within my power untried, to obtain the free commerce of tobacco, but should I fail I hope you will be convinced that it is the fault of the present circumstances and not mine. I do not write to M. de Montmorin on this subject, because whatever is now communicated to the assembly by a minister is regarded with so evil and jealous an eye, as does more harm than good. The ministers therefore abstain from making any communication from which it is possible to dispense themselves.

I wait with impatience for the account which we must now soon receive of the dispositions of the Executive as to the French debt. Several people are now endeavouring to speculate on it; but nothing will be done I hope, until those accounts are recieved. Colo.

Swann supported by several rich houses here as he tells me, makes propositions for furnishing their troops and fleet with salted provisions, cheaper than they now get them from Ireland and to recieve the American debt in payment at par with specie. He was with me this morning to complain that the Bankers of the United States in Amsterdam, opposed his propositions by saying they would pay the cash only into the French treasury. I observed to him that I had no control over the actions and much less over the words of the Bankers. He proposes writing to the President and yourself on this subject. I rather think however that the government here will chuse to receive the cash in Amsterdam should it be offered to them. Swann is afraid to contract except for that debt, lest he should be paid in *assignats*. It is to be desired however that so extensive a market should be opened to our salted provisions. I have no doubt it will be easily effected as soon as this government is sufficiently organised to allow them to attend to their commerce. There will be then a favorable moment for making a treaty of commerce with this country, which I think the United States should not omit. The minds of people here are well disposed, and they will then be sufficiently enlightened also to see that the commercial interests of the two countries are not opposed to each other. Such a treaty should be confined to a few leading points only, to remove the obstacles which now exist and to secure the commerce against any apprehension of their return.

The last accounts from Brest communicated to the assembly yesterday by the minister of the marine, shew that the disorders which had had the appearance of subsiding there, have revived. It is apprehended that Spain had begun already not to count on succour from a marine subject to such movements, and that the negotiations were accordingly renewed with activity. A messenger from Madrid who lately passed through this place on his way to London, it is thought was the bearer of a result of importance, though it is affirmed that nothing definitive is yet concluded on. In the mean time the preparations in England go on as usual; and an account is now circulated which if true will perhaps precipitate a rupture. A British ship is said to have been searched on her passage from Jamacia, and the Captain confined for several hours and ill treated by the commanding Officer of a Spanish squadron. I refer you for further particulars to the English newspapers which you will receive before this letter, and from which the present account has been recieved by the public. I suppose it has foundation.

The Empress of Russia has given an haughty answer to the King of Prussia on the subject of a pacification with the Porte. She is far from adhering to the principle of the *status quo*, and insists on keeping Ockzakow and Akermann. In Poland the Prussian party loses ground daily on account of the demand of Dantzick and Thorn. This circumstance together with the unexpected peace concluded by Sweden, it is thought embarasses the court of Berlin a good deal. I mentioned to you in my last that the Count de Moustier was going to Berlin. Ternant is to succeed him, but his nomination is not yet publicly announced. It is probable it will not be for some time. I believe he is trying to be employed here, and in the mean time keeps the promise of the place to make use of in the case of nothing more agreeable being offered. It appears now that he has had this promise for some time.

I beg you to be persuaded of the sentiments of respect and attachment with which I have the honor to be dear Sir, your obedient servant,   W. Short

PrC (DLC: Short Papers); at head of text: "No. 43." FC (DNA: RG 59, DD). Recorded in SJL as received 12 Jan. 1791.

From William Short

Dear Sir   Paris Octob. 3. 1790

The papers inclosed besides the three letters from Algiers mentioned in my *No. 43.* of to-day, are two others addressed to me, one to the Marquis de la fayette, and the copy of one to Mr. Carmichael—a letter from Hilsborough which Baron Grimm recommends to you and begs you to obtain an answer for it and send it to him—one for Philadelphia to which Tronchin begs your attention, and three others for which no explanation is necessary.—There is also inclosed a list of plants or seeds which M. Barbancon begs you to put into the hands of the person you may suppose most likely to attend to them. I sent you a list some time ago for the Dutchess D'Enville which I am sure you will have procured for her with pleasure. The best way will be to consign them to M. de la Motte at Havre who will keep them until he gives notice here. Mde. D'Enville begs me to ask the favor of you to send her also some Irish potato seed.

I have not yet recieved the whole of your account from Havre, as the carriages though at length arrived there have not yet been shipped. The account for the other articles, the last of which were shipped on board of a vessel which sailed for Norfolk, has been recieved and paid. It amounted to 3023.ᵗᵗ 7. including 113.ᵗᵗ 11. for the shepherds dogs.

I have this moment recieved a letter from London which tells me that Mr. Barrett arrived there five days ago from Boston. That is all I know of it; he is coming immediately to Paris, so that I suppose I shall see him very soon. I dare not hope however that he brings any intelligence later than your letter of Aug. 12th., and yet I never was more anxious to know something decisive. As Congress adjourned on the 14th. and nothing was then done in the affair of appointments one would suppose that nothing could be done before the next session, and still that seems impossible when the business of Amsterdam and your communication to Congress respecting two ministers and two chargés des affaires are recollected.—On the whole after three, nearly four months passed in vague conjecture, I have not yet been able to arrive at a sufficient degree of certainty to make preparations either for leaving, or remaining at Paris. The surest mode would have been to have made the former, as it would have consisted for the most part in purchases that must be made sooner or later. But I know not why I have found it impossible to do it, for although cool reflexion founded on the cyphered parts of your letters of April 6. and 27. left me little doubt of what I had to expect, yet I was always pursued by a treacherous persuasion to believe the contrary. I have remained therefore in spite of myself in a state of fluctuation ever since I have recieved your letters. I desire to remain in Europe for several reasons which I have mentioned to you in my several letters; but I repeat it again because I feel that it is true. The strongest of these persuasions is a conviction that I could be useful here, and a desire to be so. It is not however for me to judge of this, and should it be thought otherwise, there is a circumstance I will mention now, because what you said to me before your departure leads to it. You asked me whether if a place in the department of foreign affairs somewhat like that of Reyneval's here should be created, and if they should inquire of you whether I would accept it, what answer you were to give. Since you are at the head of that department a place of the kind would be still more agreeable to me. I observed however that no such place was created by the law establishing the department and therefore I said nothing about it. Should the foreign correspondence however become so

[559]

extensive (as seems inevitable) as to render an assistant in that department necessary, and such an one be established as is in the treasury department, I should like it much. I would like better however being minister in Europe, or chargé des affaires either at Paris, London, or the Hague. I think I should prefer such a place to being chargé des affaires at Lisbon. I do not speak of Madrid because certainly Carmichael can be more useful there than any person that could be sent.

When I reflect on the freedom with which I write to you, and have hitherto written to you, on what concerns myself, I am sometimes alarmed by considering that in the course of future events it is possible my letters may fall into other hands. Unless they feel the force of the implicit confidence which I have been long accustomed to place in you and the unlimited frankness which you have always allowed me to use, I fear my letters will appear of an extraordinary kind. They would appear natural however I think to those who knew the sentiments with which your friendship has long ago inspired me.

The friends of your daughter here complain much of her having entirely forgotten them. They desire me to mention it to her. Accept my dear Sir, the best wishes of Your friend & servant,

W. SHORT

RC (DLC); at head of text: "*Private*"; endorsed by TJ as received 12 Jan. 1791 and so recorded in SJL. PrC (DLC: Short Papers).

From James Swan

SIR   Paris 3d. October 1790.

In the month of March last, I closed with the Minister of Marine, the Contract for Green Oak Timber, after having made the essay at Brest, which I had permission to make, before your departure from hence. It was found of an excellent quality, and very proper for the King's Service; and they being in want of Knees more than of streight timber, I fortunatly am permitted to make two thirds of the 100,000 french cubic feet ℔ ann. in such, which being of a larger price than the common timber, and Green Oak trees furnishing more of them than of any other species, renders it still more advantageous. Before 1 May next I am to furnish 35m. c.f. and for 6 years after 100m. feet yearly. I have been obliged to take in a french house as partners, which on many accounts was necessary, and I think you may be assured that the business will go on properly. I feel doubly interested that it should, not only because it is advantageous to my interest and consequently will enable me to do justice to my suspended creditors but because it is the first contract that has been established upon an essay made and approved; and may be the means of introducing a more intimate knowledge of other of our productions, especially since the same Contract gives me permission to make trial of Cedar plank and timber, and of Locust trunnells, which being approved, will also be Contracted for. Our white Oak and Elm, I am also to make essays of: the former from New York has been approved of at Toulon, and the officers of Marine now begin to think, that the sudden failure of the American ships was caused by having been constructed with bad season'd timber, and that the other trials which have been made were badly conducted, in as much as the worst of our oak was sent for a patern.

The happy change in the Constitution has rendered the Administrators of the different departments accountable, and consequently more tractable and reasonable than under the old: from hence no advantageous propositions dare be refused, without giving better arguments than used to be afforded, altho' yet, Commis have much weight in determining a bargain, and must be weighed.

Taking advantage of these happy changes and dispositions, I presented to the Regisseurs des Vivres de la Marine, about two Months ago, proposals to furnish the Marine and the Colonies with all the Salted Beef and Pork, Butter, fresh meat &ca., that they were obliged to take of Strangers, at 10 ℔ Cent below the price now given for such as should be delivered in the Islands, and at 4 ℔ Cent less, for such as should be needed in Europe; to find sufficient Surety in Paris to assure the Contract on my and my partners part; and to receive payment for none which should be rejected. They answered to these proposals, that they were certainly very tempting but by reason of the distance, of their being no person on their part to attend the inspection, and the incertainty to the service obliged them to decline them. I replied by obviating these forced objections, and at last finding an additional reason upon which I was satisfied they could not pass a negative, I offered to take my payment in orders upon the American Treasury, in part extinction of her debt to france.—This produced a short answer, that they were best able to judge of the

Service, and still declined. To shut the door against all future application or discussion, appear'd to me not consonant with the public interest, nor with that politeness and civility which I merited at their hands. For which reasons I concluded to make our correspondance known to the National assembly, and to pray them to order the Contract to be made, which the Regisseurs had refused me; for which purpose I drew up a Memorial stating the facts and drawing the benefits to France, and concluded by offering, after the debt of America should be thus absorbed in about 6 years, that after that, should the Contract be continued to us, we would engage to take half the furniture in Merchandizes, the Manufacture or produce of this Nation.—Every Member to whom I made these propositions known, was fully in Sentiment, that they were really advantageous to France, 1st because she would be supplied at a more reasonable rate, than by other powers, even to the amount of a clear gain of 3 million of livres at least; 2dy. because there was no necessity in this time of derangement, to provide finances for the Marine and Colonial supplies, to the amount of 6 millions a year, and 3dy. because it would introduce a ty[p]e of commerce between the two Countries, that otherways would not take place, and would insure a continuation of that Commerce, even to the value of 3 millions a Year in french Manufactures.—Having sounded many members, known the minds of a majority of the Committees of Commerce, Marine and finance, and being assur'd of every possible success, it was the concernd's duty to find the necessary Bondsmen, these we got in Le Couteulx, Pourra and other Bankers here: but as men could not in reason engage in such large sums, without knowing whether they could be assur'd in some time or other the payment out of the effects of the United States, Messrs. Vanstaphorsts & Hubbard were written to, who replied, that we know the Government of the U.S. are greatly averse to the transfer of any part of that Debt to individuals, as it might interfere with their intentions respecting it; a reason which in our opinion ought to dissuade any Citizens of America from pushing "*a matter that is injurious to the Credit* of their Country, and *after all would prove ruinous to the Speculators, from the disappointments they would experience in their view of procuring the Monies here,*" which answer has destroyed the whole plan, since no one would chuse to hazard such large Sums upon the repayment by Congress, since their Bankers, who are in possession of the means to satisfy the debt to france in part or whole, gives to understand, that Congress under any supposed or declared advantages will not promote a transfer of their debt, or when transfer'd will not pay the money for it.

Not doubting but that you will see the great benefits arising to America from such a Negociation, I dare presume to entreat you to propose to the President, and to the Secretary of the Treasury, that an Instruction be given to the Bankers, or Agent who may be sent to Holland, that the money due to France, should be paid into the Royal Treasury, or to the order of the Treasurer, or to the bearer of the bond of the U.S., (not entering into the business of the Contract) and which will give facility to the execution of that Exchange of produce, for the money proposed to be paid to the Government here. We cannot see by what means the honor or Credit of the U.S. can be in the smallest degree hazarded in the proposed transaction, which in the first instance, requires no discompt on the debt, (as has been the case in all former propositions respecting it) but on the contrary offers a premium of 10. and 4 ℔ Cent; and certainly it is a great object in our Commerce to have thus forced, a consumption of 6 million Livres a Year, which without such a Contract will not take place. Mr. Short will probably write on this business. I communicated to him every of our steps from day to day, and he entered from the first moment fully in to the views of the Contract, as being a very advantageous thing to the whole States, each partaking in some measure of the supplies, they being Rice, Green oak timber (for my Contract is included) Pitch and Tar, Tobacco, Corn, Flour, Wheat (these two last when demanded) Beef, Pork, Butter, Beans and pease, Cheese, Live oxen and sheep, Biscuit, White Oak and pine timber, Masts &c. &c. to the amount of 6 millions ℔ year.

The persons concern'd in the Contract, are, Messrs. Le Couteulx and two Bankers whom they may chuse (or in lieu of them a house in Amsterdam) Mr. Danl. Parker, Governier Morris (for himself and Robert) and myself.—This information I think necessary to give you.

Sometime ago, I caused to be forwarded from L'Orient some Copies of my Letters on the Commerce of the U.S. with france, with directions to my friends at Boston to forward you one, which I hope has got to hand, and which I pray you to do me the honor to accept.

When my affairs shall be all honorably paid at home—when the numerous correspondances with the several Consuls in france shall have wearied your department by the time they will take up, or when the Minister or *envoyie* here shall find it impossible to attend to the public affairs, and at the same time to the Consuls —then it may be necessary to establish one here to report that particular business, under the name of Consul, or Commercial Agent, or Secretary to the Consular department, or under any other name. In such cases I shall pray to be remembered, submiting always to those of superior abilities and qualifications. I am with perfect respect Sir Your mo. obed. huml. St.,

JAMS. SWAN

I should have written the President on this business, and the Secretary of the Treasury: but I presume it will come before both from you in due manner, or in the course of Office; and with Mr. Hamilton I have no Acquaintance.

I insisted the more obstinatly with the Regisseurs, because I produced Certificats from Nantes, Marseilles and Bordeaux, that our Beef and pork was superior to the Irish in that it was of as long conservation, was fatter and cheaper, and from the Inspector of the Prov[isio]ns for the Marine at Bordeaux, that he had bought American beef and that it had preserved good for two Years. Without these I should have been sent to make essays.

RC (DNA: RG 59, MLR); endorsed as received 7 Dec. 1790 and so recorded in SJL.

On Swan's interest in promoting trade between the United States and France, see TJ to Swan, 23 Mch. 1789. It is possible that he sent TJ about this time a copy of his *Causes qui se sont opposées aux progrès du commerce, entre la France, et les États-Unis de l'Amérique* (Paris, 1790); see Sowerby, No. 3608.

From Samuel Vaughan, Jr.

SIR   St. James's, Jamaica 4 Octr. 1790

My Father lately sent me a Note of your's requesting some seeds of the Mountain Rice. I am sorry I cannot accommodate you as You would wish, but I do what I can by sending you 40 Seeds by two different opportunities. Inclosed is 20 of them. In the Middle Parts of Hispaniola it is in great Plenty, and I had a Promise of 2 Barrs. A Scarcity of Provisions first, and then the Disturbances have disappointed me in my Expectations. If ever they are sent I shall amply supply you.

The Seeds I have at present, came from the Island of Timor in the East Indies, brought by the unfortunate Capt. Bligh. I had near 200 of them thro' my Brother from Sir Joseph Banks: I have given them in small Parcels to the Mountain settlers and have the pleasure to find it succeeds both with them and myself remarkably well.

I take the liberty of inclosing the Objects and Rules of an Agriculture Society just formed in the Mountains of this Parish. Meeting at each others houses, and the novelty of it enduced us at first to call it a Club. But its great and extensive benefit to the Mountain Settlements of this Country places it in the first mentioned Class. Any seeds Plants or Communications that you may have it in your power to communicate, will be very thankfully received.

I have often regretted that no Opportunity has given me the power of encreasing by a personal intercourse the pleasure and improvement I have derived from the Information you have given to the World. With every possible Respect I remain Dear Sir Your very obedt. Servt.,   SAMUEL VAUGHAN JUN.

RC (MiU-C); endorsed as received 22 Nov. 1790 and so recorded in SJL. Enclosure: Printed broadside, *The objects and rules of the Saint James's Mountain Club*, [St. James, Jamaica, 1790?], setting forth the purposes of a monthly dining club as follows: "To promote and improve the different Cultures that are at present in the Mountains, and to encourage attempts to introduce new ones.—Mutually to assist each with our advice, concealing nothing that experience or information may have furnished us with, that is likely to aid each other in our difficulties.—To improve the communications between each other, and to the more settled parts.—To encourage New Settlements in the Mountains, by every act a good neighbourship.—To encrease the sociability of the Mountain Settlers, for our mutual improvement and pleasure.—In short . . . to encourage a stricter attention to those duties that every man owes to his Neighbour and Fellow-Citizen, but which are the more requisite where a country is but thinly settled, and where the Settlements are new" (DLC).

On 3 Nov. 1790 Vaughan wrote TJ again enclosing "20 more seeds of the Mountain Rice," being "almost ashamed to send . . . so small a quantity," but referring TJ to the above letter for explanation (RC in MiU-C; endorsed by TJ as received 13 Dec. 1790 and so recorded in SJL). W. C. Ford's selection from the Bixby manuscripts (*Correspondence of Thomas Jefferson*, [Boston, 1916], p. 45), has an enclosure, not found, reading as follows: "Directions to be observed with the Mountain Rice—It is to be sown like Indian Corn, three Seeds in a Hole. In the East they do not cover the Holes with Earth but leave them exposed. If they are covered it should be very lightly. They should be sown in Spring as they do not bear the winter—or in a Hothouse. The Plants may be transplanted and seperated and planted at greater distances when young. Great Care must be taken to prevent Fowls getting at it when ripe. New Land is the best for it, but it succeeds here in Jamaica on Ridges and in Glades. It will not live under Water."

From Alexander Donald

I did myself the pleasure of addressing you by last Packet. And I am disapointed at not having been honoured with a few lines from you since I left America, but I have the pleasure of knowing from Mr. Short that he has received a letter from you dated 12th. August, he does not say any thing of your health, from which I flatter myself that you had gotten the better of your Head Ache.

I would do much injustice to my own feelings if I neglected mentioning to you, how much I consider myself obliged to Mr. Short. I had corresponded with him before I left Virga. upon his own business, for you must know that I held a large sum of his in Certificates which were put into my hands by Colo. H. Skipwith, and they are now in the hands of Mr. James Brown, my Agent at Richmond. Upon my arrival here I found that my House had a large quantity of Tobacco on hand, and that the sale of that article was very dull. I took the liberty of writing Mr. Short that he would do me a very particular favour by enquiring at some of the Gentlemen in the Tobacco department of the Farm if they were in want of any at this time. He accordingly waited on M. de la Hante, who told him that they were not in immediate want, and when he understood that I was an old Friend and acquaintance of yours, he was so good as say that he would always pay great attention to your recommendation, and would therefore inform Mr. Short whenever the Farm intended to purchase. You may recollect that you had the goodness to promise me a letter of introduction to one of the Gentlemen in the Tobacco department, it may have been to M. de la Hante, but be this as it may, you will oblige me greatly by sending me the letter as soon as you can, if it is not already on the way. When Mr. Short mentioned a Contract, M. de la Hante objected to this from the uncertainty of its being complied with on the Part of the Person who has the delivering of the Tobacco. In answer to this objection I have desired Mr. Short to say that I was willing and able to give an Undoubted Guarantee in Paris for Five Million or Ten Million of Livres Tournois, for the punctual and faithful discharge of my part of the Contract. If you will be so good as to give your opinion on this subject it must weigh greatly in my favour.—Without we can persuade the French to come to market either here or in America for a few thousand hhd., I do not see how the large crop made this year can be disposed off, for at this moment every market in Europe except France, is overstocked with it. I am much affraid that the demand for American wheat and flour will not be near so great as it was last winter, For the Crops in Europe this year have been very abundant. I pray that this Country may go to war with Spain. It will be a fine harvest for America if she remains neuter, as she will have all the carrying Trade, as well as the supplying of the West India Islands belonging to all the Belligerant Powers. It is the general opinion here that we will not go to War, but I am free to confess that I am of a contrary opinion. From the immense exertions made by this Country for Six months past and which are still continued with unremitted vigour, I cannot help thinking that war must be the result. We have now upwards of Sixty Sail of the Line ready for Sea at a days warning, and I am told that Spain is not far behind us. France cannot do much in her present situation unless Spain can supply her well with money.

It appears as if the Brabanters must again return under the Dominion of the House of Austria, indeed there cannot be a doubt about it. The revolution in France does not appear to me to be clearly fixed. The National Assembly appear to have lost in a great degree their Influence over the People, who seem to be much disatisfied, and in consequence, there has been several riots in different places, particularly in Nancy.—I am much inclined to think that the King must be vested with a larger share of Power than he has at present, or it will be very difficult if not impossible to restore Peace and good order, without much bloodshed.

Whether I am considered as a Proper Person to represent the Trade of America here, I shall be happy in every opportunity of promoting the Interest thereof, but as I said before, if I have that Honour, Salary will not be an object. It will give me much pleasure if I can serve you individually. I am with great consideration Dear Sir Your mo: obt. & obliged S[ervt.],　　A. DONALD

RC (DLC); endorsed as received 29 Nov. 1790 and so recorded in SJL.

Jefferson's Advertisement for Sale of Elk Hill

For Sale in Virginia

The lands called Elk-hill on James river and the Byrd creek, adjacent to Elk-island, in Goochland, containing 669 acres, in two parcels, separated from each other about 50 rod, through which interval a public road passes. The one parcel contains 307. acres, of which there are between 50. and 60. of the best James river lowgrounds, about 200 acres of highland of rich red loam with a very small mixture of sand, the residue a dark rich loam. There are no lands in Virginia, either high or low, richer than these.— The other parcel contains 362. acres. They are highlands, proper for grain, and well timbered.—On the former tract is a good dwelling house, of 4. rooms below, and two above; with convenient out-houses, on a very high and beautiful position, commanding a fine view of the Blue mountains, of James river for several miles, and of Elk island. It is in a thick seated neighborhood of independant farmers. There is also a small dwelling house on the latter tract. These buildings were in good repair within a few years past, but probably want some repairs at this time. There is a life right of a very antient person in 50. acres of the latter tract, being the most remote corner of it. These lands are 46. miles from Richmond, to which place there is navigation from the spot. The price is 6000. dollars, and the times of payment will be made very easy, allowing interest from the delivery of the lands, and giving good security. Capt. Henry Mullins, who lives adjoining to the lands, will shew them to any person wishing to purchase.

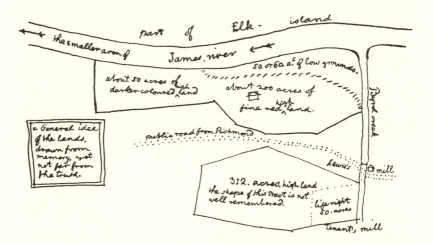

MS (MHi); undated, entirely in TJ's hand. It is possible that TJ drew this advertisement before he departed for Philadelphia in the spring of 1790. It must have been drawn after he received Robert Lewis' letter of 10 Jan. 1790, for in the memorandum listing the Elk Hill lands that he set down on that letter he appeared not to know whether the life tenant (Judith Smith) was still alive. The most that can be said with certainty is that it was written before 5 Oct. 1790. The caption may indicate that TJ intended to place the advertisement in a new York or Philadelphia newspaper. No allusion to it can be found in TJ's Account Book.

The Elk Hill lands became involved in litigation and TJ did not finally release them until 1797, though the determinative sale was made in 1793 (see Malone, *Jefferson*, I, 162, 442, 444, 356, 390, 445).

Agreement of Sale for Elk Hill

[5-13 Oct. 1790]

Articles of agreement entered into between William Ronald of the county of Powhatan of the one part and Thomas Jefferson of the county of Albemarle of the other part.

It is agreed that the said Thomas shall convey to the said William a good and indefeasible estate in fee-simple to his tract of land on the South-side James river opposite Elk-island together with the Little island, containing altogether by estimation one thousand and seventy six acres more or less, towit, 750. acres Skelton's patent, 200. acres Rob. Carter's patent, 113. acres Thomas Carter's patent, an entry of three acres, and the Little island patented for 10. acres: in consideration whereof the said William, his heirs, executors, administrators, shall pay to the said Thomas, his executors, administrators or assigns one thousand and seventy six pounds sterling money of Great Britain, with interest from the date of these presents, to wit five hundred and thirty eight pounds sterling with interest thereon from the date of these presents on or before the 1st. day of January one thousand seven hundred and ninety six, and the remaining five hundred and thirty eight pounds sterling with interest thereon also from the date hereof on or before the 1st. day of January one thousand seven hundred and ninety seven.

It is agreed that the said William shall give to the said Thomas two bonds to be executed by himself, one for each of the aforesaid paiments, and that he will as a security for the paiment of the first bond, mortgage to the said Thomas and his heirs six hundred acres of his land on Beaverdam in Goochland including the mill-seat, and being the lower part of the said tract: and that for the paiment of the last bond he will mortgage to the said Thomas and his heirs all the lands which the said Thomas has hereby covenanted to convey to him: and that all the bonds and deeds necessary for carrying these presents into full execution shall be executed on or before the last day of January next, at which time possession of the premisses shall be delivered to the said William.

And whereas Carter Henry Harrison or those claiming under him have claimed and cultivated a small part of Skelton's patent, it is expressly agreed that the warranty of the said Thomas shall not extend to that claim. But if, before the last day of paiment before named, it shall be found by the verdict of a jury definitively, in any suit against the said Carter or those claiming under him, that he or they are truly entitled to the said lands, then a credit shall be allowed on the last bond at the rate of twenty shillings sterling for every acre of the patent of the said Skelton so found in favor of the said Harrison or those claiming under him: but if not so found before that day, then no claim is ever to be made against the said Thomas or his heirs, executors or administrators on account of the lands so claimed.

In witness whereof the parties have hereto affixed their hands and seals this fifth day of October one thousand seven hundred and ninety. (Memorandum, that if the said William shall procure any of the bonds given by the said Thomas to William Jones of Bristol and shall deliver them up to the said Thomas, they shall be accepted in lieu of the security herein before specified, so far as they will go.)

Signed, sealed, and delivered   Wm. Ronald (L.S.)
in presence of   Th: Jefferson (L.S.)
    Jas. George.

I hereby acknolege and declare that the preceding is a true copy of an instrument of writing executed by Wm. Ronald and myself under our hands and seals on the day therein mentioned, at Ellis's ordinary in Goochland, and that being both on journeys in different directions, and not having time therefore to make out a duplicate, he confided to me the only original which was executed on my engagement to furnish him a true copy, which I hereby do, admitting these presents to be as good evidence of what is therein stipulated as if the original under our hands and seals were to be produced. In witness whereof I have hereto set my hand this 13th. day of October 1790.

PrC (MHi); entirely in TJ's hand.

TJ drew up this agreement to sell Elk Hill at Ellis' Ordinary on his return from his hurried trip to Richmond. He was at Tuckahoe on the third, where he not only persuaded Thomas Mann Randolph to sell Edgehill to his son but also collected £30 plus interest of £122 for a marquee that he had bought of David Ross and lent on 1 July 1782 to Col. Randolph, who had in turn lent it to Peyton Randolph and never got it back. On the 4th TJ was in Richmond attending to various affairs—he ordered two sets of the *Virginia Ga-*

zette, *and General Advertiser* for the Department of State, settled with the editor for copies of his map of Virginia that had been sold, bought a five-year-old horse got by Brimmer of an unknown dam, and that night was back at Tuckahoe. At Goochland Court House on the 5th he spent some time searching records, doubtless those pertaining to the title to the Cumberland lands, and the same day he made the above transaction. On the 6th he arrived back at Monticello (TJ to Eppes, 8 Oct. 1790; Account Book, 3-6 Oct. 1790; the horse was also named or known as Brimmer—see note, TJ to Fitzhugh, 24 Aug. 1790).

The following documents pertaining to the above transaction were generously made available to the Editor in 1960 by the late Forest H. Sweet: (1) original patent for 10 acres on LITTLE ISLAND, signed by Thomas Lee, president of the Council, and dated 1 June 1750. (2) Memorandum dated 24 May 1765 by which Robert Carter of Cumberland county, signing by mark, agreed to sell 313 acres to John Wayles for £75 (witnessed by Michael Smith, James Austin, and William Austin;

text in Wayles' hand). The tract involved here was made up of two parcels of 200 and 113 acres each (see note, Lewis to TJ, 10 Jan. 1790). (3) Abstract of deed from TJ and Lewis to Ronald, 17 Oct. 1790, reciting the chain of title to the total 1076 acres and also the terms of the mortgage covering them (in an unknown hand; at head of text: "recorded 23 May 1791"). (4) Survey of 1153 acres "part of Carter Henry Harrison's tract in Cumberland . . . survey'd [by Mayo Carrington] for Colonel Robert Carter Harrison March 1789," showing at the northeast corner opposite Little Island a part of the whole bearing this note: "Supposed to be in dispute with Jefferson 55 1/4 [acres]" (photocopies of all of the foregoing are in TJ Editorial Files). On TJ's comment on the tract in dispute, see note, Lewis to TJ, 10 Jan. 1790. Some idea of the increase of land values is indicated by the fact that the 313 acres purchased by Wayles for £75 were sold by TJ a quarter of a century later for over four times that sum. On the quality of the lands, see preceding advertisement.

From Ignatius Palyart

Philadelphia, 5 Oct. 1790. Has received a commission from the queen appointing him consul general to the United States for Portugal; asks instructions for having his appointment acknowledged.

RC (DNA: RG 59, CD); endorsed by TJ as received 2 Nov. 1790 and so recorded in SJL. An attested copy of the commission in Spanish, signed for

Queen Maria by the foreign minister, Luis Pinto de Souza, dated 12 June 1790, is also in RG 59, CD, accompanied by an English translation.

From James Brown

Richmond, 7 Oct. 1790. Enclosing account of items shipped. "No Fish as yet to be had, however the New England Vessells will be here in a short time when I will procure you some and send them by first Waggons."

RC (MHi); endorsed as received 12 Oct. 1790 and so recorded in SJL. Enclosure (MHi): "List of Sundries sent to Thomas Jefferson Esqr. by Waggon"—1 cask of Lisbon wine, 33½

gallons @ 6s.; 1 case of porter containing 6½ dozen bottles @ 14s. per dozen and another case @ 8s.; and a box containing six table cloths four by ten feet @ 24 s. each, 1 hand vise @

4s., 1 cheese weighing 14¼ lb. @ 1s. 6d. per pound; 1 "Bick Iron" weighing 33 ℔. @ 7s., 1 pair "Best Bed Blankets", £2 6s. 0d., 1 "White Iron Tea Vessel" @ 6s., "3 Loaves Single Refined English Sugar (no Double to be had)," weighing 33 ℔. @ 15s. per pound, 1 "Screw Plate" @ 13s., 12℔. chocolate @ 15s. per pound, 6 yards of "Diaper (No Huckabuck to be had)" @ 2s. 6d. per yard, the whole totalling £31 11s. 5 d. To this Brown added 10s. 6d. for the cask and the box containing the wine and porter, plus 1s. for cooperage and nails.

From Fredericksburg on 17 Sep. 1790 TJ had written Brown and adding one item omitted from his former order—"that is, half a gross of good porter. Should you not be able to get it good, I would then be glad of good ale. I am so far on my way to Monticello where I shall be glad to recieve it as soon as possible, that is to say by the first waggon which shall be passing Charlottesville" (RC in NN). At Monticello on 20 Sep. 1790 TJ met still other needs and ordered "by the first waggon passing thro' Charlottesville" six table-cloths "damask or diaper, 8 quarters wide and of any length above that. 1 pr. best and largest bed-blankets. A teakettle, rather large. White iron would be preferred. 3 loaves of double refined sugar, if any now: if not, then 3 loaves single. Cheese if any now. 12. lb. chocolate" (PrC in MHi). Brown acknowledged these orders on 24 Sep. 1790: "I shall be able to procure the Porter, Cheese and Sugar of this falls importation's in a few days. No Fish yet in Town. I will be glad to hear that the different articles sent pleases. I have just received a few Butts Lisbon of a Good quality . . . Tobacco 22/ Wheat 4/6d. 60 lb. If you have any late accounts of the Crops in Europe, I will esteem it a favor, your communicating them by next opportunity" (RC in MHi, endorsed by TJ as received 26 Sep. 1790 and so recorded in SJL). On 8 Oct. 1790 Brown wrote TJ: "I sent off the Sundry articles for you by a Waggon yesterday to the care of Col. Bell at Charlottesville or Mr. Lewis, where you will please apply" (RC in MHi, endorsed by TJ as received 14 Oct. 1790 and so recorded in SJL). From this it is evident that Brown's letter of the preceding day was in the nature of a manifest as well as an invoice and was carried by the wagoner. BICK: A cask (*English Dialect Dictionary*). HUCKABUCK: A stout linen fabric used for toweling (OED).—A letter from James Brown dated at Danville, 1 Oct. 1790, and recorded in SJL as received 20 Dec. 1790 has not been found.

From José Ignacio de Viar

DEAR SIR New York Octr. 7. 1790

I have the pleasure to send to you herein enclosed a letter which I have Received from the Governor of St. Augustine for you.

I suppose that the News it contains shall be very agreeable not only for you, but for all the people of this Country, according to what the Governor Mentions in his Letter to me, so I wish, you may so accord as to cause to be published it in the News papers and accuse to me the Receipt of it; Mean time I Remain with great Regard & esteem Your most humble & obt. servt.,

JOSEPH IGNATS. VIAR

RC (DNA: RG 59, NL); endorsed by TJ as received 25 Oct. 1790 and so recorded in SJL. The spelling that Viar gave to Monticello in the caption to his letter is interesting but perhaps not significant phonetically: "Honble. Thomas Jefferson Esrqe. at his Seat of Monteselo." Enclosure: Quesada to TJ, 18 Aug. 1790.

From Burrill Carnes

SIR   Phila. 7th. Octobr. 1790.

As my business in this City and in the State of Georgia render'd
it Impossible for me to leave America immediately after you did
me the honor to forward my Commission and Instructions, and
as you have been pleas'd to indulge me with leave of Absence till
early next Spring, I have now the Honour to Inform you that I
have appointed Mr. Leroux fils to discharge the duties of my Office
at Nantz par interim. I have also appointed M. Francis Baudin
Agent for the port of St. Martins Island of Ré and soon as I arrive
in France I shall make such other Appointments as will secure a
proper attention to all the ports of my District. I am under the
necessity however Sir to inform you that having extended my business in the Manufacturing line in this City, and in the Mercantile
line in Georgia beyond my intentions when I left France, I am
Obliged to Sollicit at this early period your permission to return
in the Course of next Year, when I must request that I may be
succeeded by some other person. My Brother Edwd. Carnes who
resides in this City will have the Honor to wait on you and if you
please will take charge of any orders you may do me the Honor
to favour me with. He has the Sole direction of our Manufactory.
It is a business we wish to extend and we both most humbly Solicit
your protection.

I have the Honor to be Most respectfully Sir Your Most Obedient
and most Humble Servt.,   BURRILL CARNES

RC (DNA: RG 59, CD); endorsed by TJ as received 30 Nov. 1790 and so
recorded in SJL.

From John Bondfield

SIR   Bordeaux 8. 8 bre. 1790

It is in common practise before an old Servant is dismist to
assign to him some mark of disapprobation or to thank him for
his past attentive Services, also to discharge the Sums due him, or
provide for him a decent retreat.

Publick Bodies are not to be supposed to know private chains
unless situated in a line to reflect lustre. This Letter being intended
as a private personal representation, particular circumstances,
which are indifferent to the Publick at large but consequential to
the individual will assign sufficient cause for the detail.

The American Army in 1775. under General Montgommery appeared before Quebec, then my residence, a Merchant in an extensive connection, having opposed before any hostilities the arbitrary measures of the British Gouvernment, the Colonial Administration, the Governer and Council, I was regarded as a dangerous Member. In 1774 I had made a Journey to New York and Philadelphia and had acquired some insight into the leading measures of America.

On the appearance of the Army before Quebec, I openly espoused the side of America, and the night that General, then Colonel Morgan crost the St. Laurence with his Riflemen being then at my Country Seat at Sillery, he immediately came to my house. I took an active part in the dispute, my return to Quebec was forbid, my affairs were left at discretion, and an Income of from 1500. to 1800 Pounds Sterling ₩ Annum that my Commercial connections procured me sacrificed; for to pursue the laudable reclamations of America against her Tyrants, abandoning every private consideration, after the miscarriage of General Montgomery's attempt against Quebec. I came over with a Mr. Price who had also taken an active part in favour of America to consult with the leading Members of the Revolution in Congress. I had the honor to be of different private Committees when at Philadelphia.—Mr. Price, by a resolve of Congress in April 1776. being appointed Commissary for the Army in Canada, Congress delivered to him the military Chest to make the necessary provision and we returned in May 1776 to Canada.

In our return through New York we had the honor of different Conferences with General Washington and General Lee and of being received Dining and Supping at their respective Tables at Lake George to receive from General Schuyler every attention and dispatcht by a private Boat in diligence across the Lakes.

At our return to Montreal we found the Commissioners that Congress had sent to Canada, with the American Army under the command of Arnold.

Mr. Price from causes that I do not attempt to expose in lieu of appropriating the Sums that Congress had put into his hands for the supplying of the Army, under pretense of his private advances, appropriated the whole to his private reimbursement, and abandoned thereby the American Army, the Commissioners and Commanders to every distress, the natural Consequence of such unprecedented and iniquitous proceeding and subjected thereby the Commissioners, and Commanders, and the American Army in general to many humiliating Scenes and alleviated the dispositions of many well intentioned Canadians.

The Commissioners and General Arnold exposed to me their situation and solicited my aid. The Army under General Thomas, retreating from Quebec were without Money, Credit, or means of subsistence. Unfortunately I at that time had only five hundred Pounds Sterling in Cash at my command, at the solicitation of the Commissioners and the General I sett off with my small stock (for Price would not advance one Sixpence) the General ordered a Boat to be immediately prepared and I sett off at midnight to go down the River, to give every succour in my Power. I found the Army marching up without Provision and dependant on Chance. I delivered my Letters to the General who received me as a most salutary Savior, desired my utmost Exertion to provide subsistence, sent with me to Three Rivers the Quarter Masters of the different Regiments, where I prepared Provisions of every Specie, and the Army that arrived the next day, halted, and refreshed themselves near fifteen days solely supported at my Expence, from whence we retreated to Sorel and there remained until General Thompson arrived with Colonel Sinclair. The Troops all this time had been supported by my Cash and Credit which continued until supplies arrived by General Sullivan.—My advances were honorably reimbursed by order from Congress, on the Treasury at Albany and I received a Letter of honorable mention of my services from Mr. R. Morris as President of the Secret Committee on the Report of the Honorable Commissioners and Officers of the Canadian Department.

The Campagne in Canada being ended, I repaired to Philadelphia. I there had the honor of receiving every mark of esteem from the members of Congress, with whom I had frequent occasions to co[n]fer.

My chain of Connections being destroyed, and looking forward not only for a future Subsistence, but also to render my services useful to the States, I determined in coming to France, the Language being to me familiar, and from a new change in measures, gave an opening for employing my experience usefully to myself and the party I had espoused.

I arrived in France in 1777. On my arrival at Bordeaux my Correspondence with the Commissioners at Paris immediately took place. In March 1778. I received from Mr. Wm. Lee at Paris the following Letter:

Mr. John Bondfield

    Sir

'As the Commercial Agency for the Secret Committee of Congress has devolved solely on me by the Death of Mr. Thomas Morris, and having a good opinion of your abilities, Industry, and Integrity, I am induced to request you will take upon yourself the management of any vessels, and the disposal of such Cargoes as may arrive in the Ports of Bordeaux, Bayonne, Rochelle and Rochefort, belonging to the said Committee, or in which they are interested or concerned, hereby authorising and improving[1] you to act in all such cases as fully as I could do if personally present always wishing you to attend closely to such instructions or advice as you may receive; with said vessels or Cargoes, whether addressed to me solely, or to Mr. Morris and myself jointly.

To facilitate your operations for the benefit of the Concerned, I have thought it advisable to inclose you a Certificate, also a Letter from the Chairman of the Secret Committee, Robert Morris Esqr. which will fully shew my authority, and consequently that under which you act.

I wish you to give the Committee the earliest advices of this arrangement and on all occasions, that you would advise them of your proceedings.

It will be proper to inform the American Commissioners at Paris when any property arrives in which the secret Committee are interested.

I have not the least doubt of your giving entire satisfaction in whatever is committed to your care, and wishing you both ease and Success in the management, I am with all due regard, Sir, Your most obedient and most humble Servant, Wm. Lee

    Commercial Agent for the Secret Committee of Congress'

From that day to this, I have ever acted as the agent for United States at this City.

My Conduct on my arrival had acquired to me in a short time same Consideration and Credit, which I had occasion to employ for the service of the States soon after my appointment. The present Vice President the Honble. John Adams being appointed a joint Commissioner arrived at this Port in the Boston, frigate. On his arrival, he immediately made his application to me. He is at present in Congress and I am satisfied will give an honorable report of the reception he met with, and of my then infant influence. The Boston arrived, required subsistence in provision, considerable advances to the Officers, great outfits and a general supply of Stores. My advances amounted to upwards of four thousand Pounds which the Commissioners reimburst me by giving me leave to draw on them at three months.

Thus I became in Europe as I had been in America of personal pecuniary support to the Public cause; I had been present at three engagements on the Continent, and in my passage to France had my part in an Engagement of two hours with a British Ship of superior force, that we took and brought the Prisoners to France who exceeded the double of our Ships Company after having mann'd the prize.

Mr. Gillon as Deputy from the State of Carolina after having exhausted his ingenuity to obtain a Loan, came to Bordeaux, to engage my influence, which I exerted so effectually as to obtain to him on the Credit of that State a Loan of twenty Thousand Pounds Sterling, that they still owe not having reimburst a Sixpence, notwithstanding every profession of assured punctuality, and I stand personally in advance upwards of Fifteen hundred Pounds Sterling, Funds thrown into Mr. Gillons hands, that I canot obtain any payment from the influence he holds in the Tribunal of that State.

An Armament under the Command of Captain Paul Jones in the *Bonhomme Richard* wanting Cannon, applyed to me to procure the supply, I gave orders, on the assurance of Captain Paul Jones of punctual reimbursement, to the Foundery, who under the directions of the said Captain cast the Cannon he wanted. I paid the founder Thirty two Thousand Livres, Captain Jones directed my Reimbursement on Monsieur Le Ray de Chaumont. He accepted my drafts paid twenty thousand Livres, the other twelve from the inability in Mr. de Chaumont remains protested, and I stand in advance for that Sum. I applied to Mr. Barclay Consul General, when in France who assured me of his in a liquidation of accompts that would take place relative to that Armement and Mr. de Chaumont. I am this day without any satisfaction and without any prospect from the inability of Mr. de Chaumont of being here reimbursed. Captain Paul Jones gave me a Certificate that these Cannon were sent afterwards to America ℘ the Alliance and made use of at the Siege of York Town and of singular Service in the

Capture of Cornwallis. It is not just my services which in this Circumstance proved in many cases useful, should lay a burthen on me of upwards of £12,000.ᵗᵗ Livres exclusive of Commission and Interest due thereon.

In 1778 In Concert with a Wm. Haywood who had came over from America we purchased, Armed, victualled, manned and Equipt compleatly four Ships from *300* to *700* Tons sent them to America with Cargoes part on our own accompt, and part on freight, the Commissioners shipt on board a considerable quantity of Military Stores that were landed safe in Virginia. The Honorable Arthur Lee as Agent for the State of Virginia shipt on Board in Military Stores 357 1/2 Tons, the freight was to have been paid in Europe amounting to £42900.ᵗᵗ The failure of Remittances from the States, deprived Mr. Lee of the means of paying that Debt which remains due to this Day, and with Interest amounts of £72000.ᵗᵗ Here is then an unjust burthen for Essential Services rendered.

In 1779, I sent over by different Vessels, supplies of Cloathing, many of which were captured, some got safe amongst others two parcels ⅌ the General Mercer, were delivered by my Correspondent to the Clothier General for the use of the Continental Army, as appears by the following Certificates.

'I do hereby Certify that the Goods contained in the within Bill of Parcels amounting to Forty three thousand, three hundred Sixty two Pounds 5/. were purchased by me of Mr. Mathew Irwin and received from him the 7th. february last, and that they have all been made up into Garments and delivered over to the Cloathier General for the use of the Continental Army and that the purchases were made by me in consequence of the orders of the honorable Board of War.

I made no particular stipulation with Mr. Irwin for the payment of the within Goods, further than a promise of payment so soon as the Board of war would enable me to do it, which I promised should be in a few Weeks, and I think two or three after the purchase was made, and it was mutually understood that the payment was to be made in Cash. Philadelphia 16th. May 1790. Signed SAMUEL CALDWELL.'

'The publick Credit at the time of Mr. Caldwells entering into the engagement being much impaired, we were applied to by him before he could purchase the Goods, and on the Credit of a Warrant we obtained from Congress (but which never was paid or could be procured) we gave Mr. Caldwell positive assurances that his engagements should be complied with notwithstanding the Scarcity of publick Money. Under these assurances the Merchants were induced to part with their Goods, without which the Troops to the Southward could not have moved. By order of the War Office the 16th. May 1780. To the Honorable The Treasury Board. Signed RICHARD PETERS.'

Here is a Debt of £43362.5/. Contracted in a time of most crying distress which remains undischarged to this Day, never having received a Single Sixpence nor Mr. Clymer impowered by me to make the needful reclamation, has not been able yet to Consolidate further injustice for essential Services.— To the above I can add innumerable others of equal effect on the Continent of America, which resulting from the exertion of an Individual, might claim at least if not recompense a barrier against Contempt and disesteem from the Body of the Representatives in favor of whom the events reflected.

Independant of what is above to Second to my utmost by my feeble endeavours what ever could serve to bring to Speedy conclusion the acknowledgement of the Independance of America, I set on foot in France by my Interest and influence (in taking shares) sundry Privateers, having at one time shares in not less than three or four and Twenty Sail in that line, in which I was far from being benefitted. Numbers of private adventures were set on foot thro my Interest, to Throw in wanted supplies to America.

During the War my House was the General Rendezvous of Americans, my Table and Purse was never shut to the Distrest. Seven Hundred and thirty is on my list that called on me during the five Years of the Contest, the greatest part distrest Prisoners. The Commissioners at Paris Reimbursed a part of my advances, say, all the Sums for which I took receipts, all the other Sums which were not trifling remained on my private list which I can advance without exceeding the Reality amounted to above two thousand Pounds. As a Proof permit me to quote a single Circumstance. Mr. Jay on his arrival in Spain, appointed Messieurs Le Normand & Co. to provide for the Distresst Americans that presented themselves at Cadiz, his advance in two months exceeded Six Thousand Livres. My Table cost me near five hundred Pounds Sterling ℔ Annum, during the said five years. Messrs. Adams,

Jay, Lawrence, Izard &c., Members or Ambassadors can appear in testimony, not from Ostentation that I plead these Circumstances. This Nation at that Day were captivated by appearances. The Interest of the Public created forced exertions. I supported chearfully the Burthen from conscientious certitude of my serving the cause. I pursued a line of Business, which tho' not always successful kept me in a State of Independance and I am without at this Day, not withstanding the heavy charges, and detentions above recited and others still more cruel of a private nature, without a single Creditor in France.

I here close my remonstrances, which are dictated not with a view to draw from you any pecuniary returns but to exhibit the injustice of a recent Act, which I attribute sooner to ignorance in the State of the Representation, than wilful intent to sully disinterested Conduct.

You have named Consuls in the different Residences in Europe. You have named to this City a Young Man, who I flatter myself will not degrade the nomination. But I cannot avoid observing that I had pretentions, and that I thought myself intitled to your Remembrance, when the States should form Solid Regulations.

I conducted the Bark in a Stormy Season and if I judge myself as I would judge others when at Anchor, would have been glad to have enjoy'd the fruits of my Labour. With Respectful Consideration I have the Honor to be Sir Your very humble Servant,

JOHN BONDFIELD

RC (DNA: RG 59, CD); in a clerk's hand, with date and signature in Bondfield's hand; endorsed by TJ as received 18 Dec. 1790 and so recorded in SJL.

In his letter of 14 Nov. 1788 TJ gave to John Jay a strong recommendation of Bondfield for a consular appointment: "He is well known in America; is of a higher degree of information than is usually to be found, and unexceptionable in every point of view. . . . He is likely to remain long at Bordeaux, and is so much respected that we cannot expect a better subject there." The son of George Mason subsequently applied to TJ in behalf of his partner, Joseph Fenwick, and TJ responded that he had already recommended Bondfield. When the elder Mason renewed the application early in 1790, reporting Bondfield to be in distressed circumstances, TJ replied that Fenwick was given the commission "according to your desire" (Mason to TJ, 16 Mch. 1790; TJ to Mason, 13 June 1790). The above is the last letter that TJ received from Bondfield, and there is no evidence that it was ever answered. The circumstances suggest that other factors must have intruded to influence the appointment, and among these the first that comes to mind is Mason's attitude in the Federal Convention of 1787 and in the Virginia ratifying Convention—an attitude that both Washington and TJ must have wished to placate.—For an abstract of Bondfield's testimony on the Canadian campaign, see Vol. 1: 453-4.

¹ Thus in MS: Lee must have written, or intended to write, "empowering."

To Francis Eppes

I was the other day as far as Richmond, but so circumscribed in time that it was impossible for me to turn either to right or left. I had but four days to go and return and do a good deal of business. The principal was to effect a purchase for my son in law of Edgehill from his father, which I did. He pays £2000 for the lands, stocks, 200 barrels of corn &c. They will now remain here. Another object was the sale of my Cumberland lands to W. Ronald, which I effected also. He gives me 20/ sterl. an acre, that is 1076£ sterl. with interest from the date. It provides for my last instalment with Hanson for the year 1797. and half of that of 1796. so as to reduce my matter with him to 6 instalments of £500. each. I shall next hope to sell Elk hill @ 40/ sterl an acre or 1338£ sterl. paiable in 1793.94.95.96. so as to leave only the instalments of 1791.92. and two thirds of 1793. unprovided for. My crop of this year will we hope pay the first, and therefore I shall trust to effecting those of 1792. 1793. by crops without further sales. This is my prospect as to Hanson. Ronald has secured me by mortgages on the Cumberld. lands and a moiety of his Beaverdam lands. I received at Annapolis (from a person whose name I have forgot) Hanbury's account against Mr. Wayles for £295-16-11 sterl. with interest from 1770. Oct. 31. I remember your mentioning this to us but have forgotten whether you supposed it could be paid out of the monies due to the estate. I therefore gave no other answer than that I would communicate it to you. I should be glad however to give such other answer as our prospects may justify. If we are to contribute for it time will be necessary.

I wish Mrs. Eppes and yourself could have taken a trip up. The shortness of my stay here (for I go within a fortnight or three weeks) does not permit me to see you at Eppington. I wished to know whether I could be useful to Jack in any way. I know there is nobody left at College to render his return there an object. Do you wish him still to pursue collegiate studies? The Princeton college is now on an excellent footing, and I would undertake to accompany him there and recommend him particularly. The Philadelphia college is also pretty good. If you liked that, he should live with me, and attend it. Do you wish him to proceed to the study of the law immediately? And where? If at Eppington, he shall have my books there and instructions what to read. If you would like to board him at Mr. Lewis's with two young students there, he shall have my books there, and Colo. Monroe will attend to him. If you would like he should read law in Philadelphia, he shall live with me and I will procure him books. Finally would you prefer his writing in my office? I think it the least for his benefit, as it would be a great deal of drudgery in merely copying. But if it should fall in with your views, he shall live with me and would be entitled to recieve 500. dollars a year from the public. Be so good as to chuse any of these propositions, and if any of them coincides with your views make free use of me in them, or any other way you can point out.

Mr. and Mrs. Skipwith I understand are with you. I should have been so with infinite pleasure had it been allowed me. Present me affectionately to them, to Mrs. Eppes and your young ones, and be assured of the sincere esteem and attachment of Dear Sir Your affectionate friend & servt.,   TH: JEFFERSON

PrC (ViU). The press copy is extremely blurred, but the text has been verified by comparison with a nineteenth-century transcript (ViU); for assistance in this verification the Editors are indebted to Mr. William H. Runge of the Alderman Library.

To John Key

SIR   Monticello Oct. 8. 1790.

I am now engaged in the settlement of my account with Inis[1] wherein I do not think he has credited my tobacco at just prices. As this was during the years you had the management of my affairs, I am obliged to trouble you to endeavor to search for any proofs you have of your contracts with him, or to recollect the contracts. I inclose you a list of the tobaccos and prices, as he credits them. Of 22893 delivered in 1784 he has credited 4167 @ 20/ and the rest @ 36/ tho' by the inclosed account he had at the time credited the whole @ 36/. But this account is not signed. I must therefore beg of you to state to me who gave you this account, for it is from you I had it, and in whose hand writing it is. This account will establish the price of the tobacco delivered in 1784. But I have no proof of the prices of those delivered in 1782 and 1783. For these I must depend on you. As I am now engaged in this settlement I will endeavor to see you in a day or two, by which time I hope you will have been able to make it out from your memory or papers. I will then also confer with you as to the form of proof. Should you pass this way before I have time to call on you, it will relieve me if you will be so good as to call as I am extremely pressed in time. I am Sir your most obedt. humble servt.,

TH: JEFFERSON

Tr (ViU); in an unidentified hand.

1 Thus in MS, a clerical error. The name should have been Ross (see TJ to Eppes, 10 Oct. 1790).

From Nathaniel Barrett

SIR   London October 10. 1790

I have the pleasure to inform you of my safe arrival at Cowes, from whence some business has called me to this City, and has detained me longer than I expected. I sent my Trunk in which were your dispatches by a particular friend and fellow passenger from Cowes to paris to my Son, and have directed him immediately on receiving it to deliver the Letters himself to Mr. Short.

The last Gazzette (which I take the Liberty of inclosing) contains a proclamation in favor of the Introduction of our Oils into this Kingdom in American or English Bottoms. The duties referr'd to the same as last paid.

Mr. Cutting Will hand you several papers which shew the great Difficulties attending the Impressments of our Seamen in the Kingdom, he has enterested himself much in this Business, and been the means of liberating several of his Countrymen.

Every vessell which arrives, is subjected to the Inconvenience of having her men taken out, and in many Instances conveyed out of the way of redress. I cannot but hope that Mr. Johnston when he enters on His office, will represent this Affair in such a Light to the Admiralty, that some Measures will be taken to prevent such Abuses in future.

I shall in a few days sett off for France and embrace every opportunity of communicating you any Intelligence which may occur, worthy of your Notice.

Mr. Parker with whom I am at present begs me to present his respectful Compliments to you. I have the honor to be Sir, Your most obedient & humble Servant

NAT BARRETT

RC (DNA: RG 59, CD); endorsed as received 3 Dec. 1790 and so recorded in SJL.

To Francis Eppes

DEAR SIR   Monticello Octob. 10. 1790.

In my other letter I forgot to ask information of you on the following subject. Mr. Ross sent me, thro' you, an account, partly in money, partly in tobacco. In this he has departed altogether from a former settlement, whereon I had given him a money and a tobacco bond for balances which I acknoleged. In this too he has undertaken to depart from an agreement with Key to allow 36/ for tobaccos delivered him by Key, and actually credited at 36/ in an account he rendered him which is in my possession. In his new account he credits these same tobaccos at 20/ and this on the ground of something which passed between you and him, at the sale at Elkhill. He says 'he there informed you of my tobacco debt, and that he expected the credit given should not operate to his prejudice and that the tobacco should be estimated at it's then value: that you thought this was reasonable and the price was then from 36/ to 30/.' And in this way he brings me in debt between four and five hundred pounds when otherwise he is over-paid on the face of his own accounts. I must beg the favor of you to recollect as exactly as you can what passed between you at Edgehill and to state it to me in writing, that I may know what it will be necessary for me to decide on. I am sorry to give you this trouble, but the occasion obliges me. I am Dear Sir Your affectionate friend & Servt.,   TH: JEFFERSON

PrC (CSmH).

From Maxey Ewell

SIR   Charlottesville October 10th 1790

Impressed with the highest reverence for your character, and convinced that it is always your wish to assist the distressed I feel a confidence that you will excuse the liberty I take in troubling you with this address.

Having not the most distant knowledge of Mr. Madison and acquainted with your intimacy, My request is that you Sir would condescent to lay my little affair before him and add your influence for his attention to it. If I ask too much, Sir, forgive and forget this intrusion on your time. If I do not the kindness of your assistance will be ever most gratefully remembered.

Having long served my country as a soldier, I was in the year 1781 appointed a commissary to the convention troops at Albemarle Barracks as assistant to Mr. John Allen who was the issuing commissary. In this post Sir did I serve within a few days of three years, and for these services Sir have I never received one single sixpence. Within the time appointed by Congress I lodged as I was informed was the right method the certificates of my services with Mr. Dunscomb. At the discolution of his office I applied to Mr. John Hopkins whom I was told was appointed to recieve all such paper from him. He told me he had mine but could then do nothing in the business. I have never Sir since that time been able to gather any information.

Urged by my duty to a wife and many children not far removed from absolute distress I have ventured to trouble you Sir with this application with the hope of your countenance.

Mr. Madison I do not know. This county claims Mr. Jefferson. Shall I hope that he will condescend to honor this business with his notice?—I will hope it till he tells me 'tis impertinent. With every sentiment of respect for his integrity and admiration of his superior abilities in his exertions for the good of his country I have the honor to be his devoted & obedient Servant,

MAXEY EWELL.

RC (DLC); addressed: "The Honorable Thomas Jefferson Monticello"; endorsed by TJ as received 16 Oct. 1790 and so recorded in SJL.

Ewell may have enclosed in the above his letter of 10 June 1788 to Jonathan Burwell asking him to let John Hopkins have his certificate of £157 14s 0d for his services as issuing commissary at Albemarle barracks in 1779-1780 (DLC; with endorsement by Hopkins, 4 Dec. 1790 to the effect that the certificates lodged in his office as commissioner of loans by Andrew Dunscomb, commissioner of accounts, had been forwarded to the Treasury "where alone application must be made").

From Fulwar Skipwith

SIR   St. Pierre 10. Octor. 1790

On the 30th. Ulto. I did myself the pleasure to address your Excellency, expressing the hope I entertained of receiving the instructions necessary to my entering into office, and likewise informing of the aukward situation in which I may stand in regard to the exequatur required by the 1st. art. of the convention existing between his M. C. Majesty and the U. States, should government here not receive official notice thereof from the court of France. Hitherto however, had I been possessed of instructions, together with the exequatur, I could have been but inactive in my office, and I fear cannot soon be otherways, owing to an almost total suspencion of police and government. To give your Excellency some idea of the true causes of the present unhappy state of this Island, I must look back to the time when the late revolution in the mother country took place, and of the then situation of the commercial and planting interests of Martinique. There has been for some time a law in force which prevents a debtor from seising on the lands and working negroes of his creditor, and only allows him the resource of attacking his Sugars or other produce. This leaves the merchant very much at the mercy of the planter he credits. The consequence is a debt of upwards of twenty millions of island livres due to St. Pierre upon so precarious a footing. This has created a deep rooted animosity between the merchants who demand and the planters who defer the payment. Fort-royal who has viewed the increase of her rival St. Pierre with an anxious and jealous eye sided with her opposers. When the accounts arrived from France of the great revolution which had taken place, the merchants of St. Pierre were enthusiastic in shewing their approbation of the national change. They waited on the Governor and forced him to take the cockade. This he did with a bad grace. All the military discoverd the same aversion, but saw the necessity of conforming. Those planters who had pretensions to nobility of birth, as well as some others who had not seemed to conform, but were generally supposed at bottom aristocrats, on the other hand St. Pierre was strongly attached to the revolution, and did not seem disposed to bear the least opposition. Such were the dispositions of the different parties when in March last two officers of the regiment of Martinique took out their national cockades and appeared in the Play house with white ones. This was instantly observed. The young citizens insisted on their replacing the national cockade. A dispute ensued. The next day fourteen of the officers of the regiment paraded the Streets in a threatning manner. A rendezvous was agreed on, and fourteen young citizens were to fight the fourteen officers. At the appointed time the concourse of spectators was great. The soldiers expecting their officers would be sacrificed became so exasperated as to present their musquets at the inhabitants, and were only prevented by their officers from firing. These Gentlemen seeing the whole town in arms against them withdrew their troops to fort-royal, where they were joined by many friends and found they might depend on the mulattos a body of 1200 or 1300 well armed and disciplined. The two officers who were the cause of the affair were seised by the popullace, their regimentals torn from their backs and otherwise severely handled. They were then ship'd for France. Volunteers from the neigbouring islands came to the assistance of St. Pierre on the first news of the transaction, stayed a few days and returned, leaving them much in the condition they found them. In about three weeks after St. Pierre apprehensive of an attac sent for the Volunteers who came over in greater numbers than before, upwards of 2000 'tis said, with the Baron de Clugny the governor of Guadalupe. All that his great abilities could accomplish was that the parties should wait the decission of France. About this time Monsr. Damas arrived and took M. Viominils place as general. Soon after some arrets of the national assembly likewise arrived concerning the regulation of the islands, which were far however from calming the minds of the citizens. St. Pierre did not like the mode of representation, nor did she wish to allow the legality of the then existing colonial assembly, which the arrets still permitted if it was agreeable to a majority. St. Pierre instead of permitting the majority to rule, withdrew her members. Such was the situation, when on the 3d. of June a massacre took place of 14 mullatoes 3 whites and 1 negroe, and upwards of 120 coloured men confined in jail. The cause of this unhappy affair does not seem to be satisfactorily ascertained, but it proved the weakness of the municipality who could not restrain such disgraceful enormities, and the total want of order. The colony alarmed and struck with horror at this transaction and glad to have so good a pretext to come against St. Pierre, requested the Governor to employ all his forces to reinstate order in that unhappy town. This he did on the 9th. of June, and altho the morning of that day seemed to threaten the destruction of the colony, yet the town was entered peacibly after the inhabitants had abandoned their posts. From circumstances it is very probable, and universally asserted here that the Municipality were in concert with the General, by preventing the inhabitants from firing and withdrawing the officers to throw them into confusion. In three or four days after the town was taken, the municipality was suspended and upwards 150 Inhabitants taken up and put on board a merchantman. Two thirds of them were soon after discharged, thirty or forty were reserved for trial as principals in the last massacre. The town assumed a different aspect, order was reinstated and commerce revived. The prisoners were tryed, but their fate was not determined on. Many suppose some would be made examples of and the rest sent to France. Opinions were various when on the 1st. September a very unexpected and a kind of counter revolution took place, which has hurried this unhappy Island on the brink of ruin. The two *basses compagnies*, the same two who presented at the inhabitants of St. Pierre, stationed at Fort Bourbon, it is said gained by the Prisoners and probably inflamed by wine, put three handkerchiefs together and hoisted them as a national colours on the ramparts. A party then descended and demanded the prisoners, whom they obtained and carried with them into the fort. All the overtures made by the general and the Municipality for an accomodation answered no purpose, and the General was forced to send to St. Pierre for the garrison to support his authority. These soldiers having been much caressed by the citizens left the town disposed to join, instead of opposing their brother soldiers. This they did immediately on their arrival. M. Damas therefore found himself obliged to fly from fort-royal, leaving the soldiers in possession of fort-bourbon, the strongest fortification in the windward Islands. He fled to a place called Grosmorne, where he has fortified himself with the colonial assembly, the greatest part of the officers belonging to the Martinique regiment, the Grenadiers who remained faithful to his orders, and the Mulattos. In addition to these forces, the General has the dangerous resource of arming the negroes if compelled by superiority of numbers. Some rencontres now took place with various success. The effect the accounts of this revolution had on the neighbouring french islands was the total derangement of the military, who came over without officers (some subalterns excepted) to assist the St. Pierre party which was now increased to about 900 or 1000 regulars and 1500 or 1600 citizens. On their arrival the town for many days exhibited a scene truely distressing. No discipline the soldiers entertained at the tables of the inhabitants. A monstrous grave was dug to bury aristocracy, in the afternoons generally when the wine operated most, they would force old men, pregnant women and all whom they suspected not to favour their measures, to dig at the grave and kiss the rope hanging over it. It would intrude too much on your Excellencys time to detail their excesses. This very confusion and madness as was foreseen by the considerate proved to be their misfortune. M. Chabrol the Colo. who had remained with his regiment and who was now appointed commander in chief of soldiers and citizens, used every exertion to conciliate the parties but to no purpose, and found himself absolutely obliged to lead the St. Pierre party against Gros-morne contrary to his advice. It has been conjectured that the Colo's chief view in remaining was to endeavour to bring back the troops to their duty. He marched with about 1100 in the morning of the 26th. Ulto. They had not advanced above five miles before, to their utter surprise they found one or two small parties of mulattos who fled before them untill they reached their main body, who were waiting to receive their enemies. Such was the want of order in this rencontre, that the column of Martinique broke at receiving the second fire and could not be rallied. The column of Guadalupe was then obliged to bear the Stress of the action, they fought better but suffered a great deal and were finally entirely routed. They lost their four pieces of Cannon, baggage, indeed every thing, and returned in confusion to fort-royal. The loss has been concealed as much as possible, 200 men at least it is however supposed must have been killed wounded and taken. This defeat which so much astonished the St. Pierre party who did not suppose such a thing possible, entirely changed their plan of operation from the most rapid offensive to the most cautious defensive. The commerce of this town entirely convulsed from being cut off from the country, and the City itself subject to continual alarms from the opposite party, added to this, the little discipline of the soldiery seems at present to render neither life or property safe. The troubles of the mother country has prevented her from paying that attention to her colonies which their situation has long required. An armament however is daily expected. Their arrival alone in my opinion can save the colony from ruin. This Island (as well as Guadalupe) is prodigiously fertile indeed, and their commerce with America infinitely greater than I had immagined. I am afraid the prolixty of my letter has tried your Excellency's patience, or I would attempt to give you a statement of the imports from America into the French windward islands, and their returns. This I will however take the liberty to do at another opportunity.

A very unnecessary, and a very injurious embargo has continued from the 21st. Ulto untill to day on the American flag. After numberless applications to and many evasive answers from the Council of the town the only supreme head at present acknowledged here, it was taken off, not however without their extracting a promise from me, which was given at the instance of the American Captains in port, that they should not after clearing out, enter into any other port of the Island; altho several had been opened by the colonial assembly and sanctioned by the governor.

I am as yet ignorant of the fate of the bill which was introduced last session of Congress respecting the emoluments of their Consuls, but flatter myself that some provision is made. The expence of living in the W. Indies with the strictest œconomy is greater than in most other countrys, and I think it will hereafter appear that the Consul in the W. Indies who does his duty will merit some compensation. With the sincerest attachment and Respect I remain your Excellency's mo. ob. & mo. H. Servant,

FULWAR SKIPWITH

RC (DNA: RG 59, CD); recorded in SJL as received 22 Nov. 1790.

From N. & J. Van Staphorst & Hubbard

SIR!   Amsterdam 11 October 1790.

We beg leave to introduce to your acquaintance the Bearer Mr. Joseph Ceracchi a Gentleman Native of Rome and an eminent Sculptor, requesting you to render him every Service and Civility in your Power, under our assurance of his being well worthy of them, and that you will thereby particularly oblige those who on similar and all other occasions are with great Regard & Respect Sir! your most obedt. humble Servts.,

N. & J. VAN STAPHORST & HUBBARD

RC (DLC); endorsed by TJ as received 2 Mch. 1791 and so recorded in SJL.

From William Temple Franklin

DEAR SIR   Philadelphia 13. Oct. 1790.

Since I had the Pleasure of seeing you here, I have received pressing Letters from my Friends both in England and France, to go over immediately with my Grandfathers Papers, in order to derive that Advantage from them, which they say, Delay would greatly diminish: this, together with some other private Business I have to transact in Europe, has determined me to embark as soon as possible.

My Reasons for wishing to have delay'd going till Spring, arose from my Desire of being in the Way if any foreign Appointments should take Place in the ensuing Session of Congress; but my Friends here are of Opinion, that my being absent, will in no Way impede my being Appointed, if it is intended. As however in such Case, Instances might occur, in which my Inclinations might without Impropriety be attended to, as to Situation; and as no doubt you will be consulted in Matters of this Nature; I shall here take the Liberty of suggesting my particular Wishes on this Head, relying on your Friendship to promote them, as far as may be consistent with Propriety. The highest of my Ambition is to be appointed to the Court of France. I have had it in View from the first of my being employ'd there in a Subordinate Public Capacity; and during my long Residence in that Country, endeavor'd to obtain such Knowledge and form such friendly connections as might, together with my being the Descendant of one who enjoy'd there so great a Reputation, render me a Suitable Person to be employ'd at that Court. The next Situation I should prefer, would be that of England, and after that Holland; as to other Courts, they would be nearly equal to me.—I hope my dear Sir, you will excuse the freedom of these Hints, as they are not address'd to you in your public Capacity, but as the Friend of my deceas'd Grandfather, and as one whose Patronage I shall ever be proud to acknowledge.

My Passage is taken in the Pigou, which will sail the latter end of this Month for London, and my Intention is to visit Paris in January, and if nothing further occurs, return hither in the Course of a Year.—If, while in Europe, I can render you any Service, I beg you will favor me with your Commands; and be assured that no one will feel a greater satisfaction in being either useful or agreable to you, than Dear Sir, Your truly affectionate and very humble Servant   W. T. Franklin

P.S. I shall leave the Dies of the Medals, with my cousin B. F. Bache, to be deposited in your Office when established here.— You will oblige me by sending to me the Manuscript you mentioned to have of my Grandfathers and by writing to N. York to direct the forwarding to me the 2 sheets of Mitchels Map, my Grandfather sent to you; the Remainder being incomplete without them

RC (DLC); endorsed by TJ as received 3 Nov. 1790 and so recorded in SJL.

From Francis Eppes

Dr. Sir.   Eppington October 14th. 1790

I am sorry your business when at Richmond was of sutch consequence as to prevent your calling. We were all desirous of seeing you particularly as it was out of our power to visit you, being at present confind by workmen who are reparing our houses added to this our horses are so worn down with wheat treading and other drudgery that they are unfit for so long a journey.

You have been very fortunate in the sale of your Cumberland land, the price is great, I wish you may be equally luckey in the sale of Elk Hill, it will make the balance due old Hanson a mear trifle. I expect to pay my first instalment out of my present crop, and shall this winter sell property to discharge the balance. I think it will not be amis to take time for the payment of Hanbury's debt, as its very uncertain when we shall receive the money due from Cary's Estate, and when we do in all probability it will be considerably curtail'd, in the article of interest. I am told the Chancelor has generally done so when it was possible. There is near a thousand pound due from Ruffin on which I have sent out an execution. However those matters are so tedious its impossible for me to say when it will be in hand. Ten thousand thanks for your kindness to Jack. I shou'd prefer his being in your Family to any other situation in the World. When his health will admit of it I will send him to you and after examining him you will be better able to Judge what he is fit for and whatever you think best will be my choice. I am much pleas'd to hear Mr. and Mrs. Randolph will be fix'd so much to their satisfaction and hope when leasure will admit of it they will visit. We shall take the first opportunity of seeing them in next summer. I am with best wishes to you all Dr Sir Your Friend & Servt.   Frans. Eppes

NB. I have been apply'd to in a very pointed manner by Mr. Dobson for your debt due him. I shall be glad to receive your directions on that head. The order on J. Banister Exr. has not produc'd one shilling indeed he has only promis'd to pay one hundred pounds out of the present crop and when that will be in hand is very uncertain.   FE

RC (MHi); endorsed by TJ as received 21 Oct. 1790 and so recorded in SJL. The same entry in SJL indicates that Eppes wrote again (or perhaps added a postscript) on 19 Oct., but this letter has not been found.

From David Humphreys

Sir London Octr. 14. 1790.

After a passage of five weeks, the four first of which were very tempestuous, I arrived in the Channel. In order to save time, and slip into London with the less probability of being noticed, I procured a boat from the shore to land me at Dover. From that place I took my passage in the Mail Coach, and arrived here at 6 O'Clock this morning. Having delivered the Dispatches to Mr. Johnson, and seen some other Americans, I thought it expedient to take the first moment to give you, with the notice of my arrival, such detached peices of political information as have been related to me.

The aspect of affairs on the Continent in general, and the complexion of the Negotiations in Spain, about the middle of Summer, induced the British Administration to believe, that, by their menaces and armaments, Peace would be preserved, and the honor of the nation not only saved, but even augmented in the judgment of the world. The Ministry seemed to have an overweening confidence in themselves. At that time Stocks rose rapidly, and nothing could exceed the exultation and pride of the nation. Since then considerable changes have taken place. The Spanish Government has gained time, by artfully protracting the negotiations, to learn where the efficient Power actually resides in France, and how that Power was disposed towards them. It now scarcely admits of a doubt that the national Assembly will yeild its assistance in a defensive War: that is, in case Britain should make the first attack. The Treaty of Peace between Russia and Sweden, of which I send you a Copy and which was effected by the superior address and prowess of the Empress, has changed the face of affairs in the North for the worse, with regard to Britain. The English had counted much in their calculations on the exhausted state of the two Empires, and the powerful combination, which was ready to assail them, while they were involved in the war with the Porte. The Empress of Russia, having warded off a part of the Storm from her Dominions, is enabled to turn it on her part with redoubled fury on the Turks. News has been received within a few days of a capital advantage obtained by her fleet over the enemy in the black Sea. And the Prince Potemkin, at the head of 100,000 men, is irresistible. These circumstances leave the Empress at liberty to afford her naval aid to the Spaniards, with whom it is believed she is strictly allied. It is also judged not improbable that Sweden and Denmark will do the same. So that of the boasted Allies of Britain, the Dutch is the only one capable of giving them any naval succour. The Dutch are slowly arming, under the influence of the Stadholder, contrary to the wishes of Amsterdam and a considerable Party. Six or eight of their ships have been in the channel but are returned to the Texel. They have twenty in commission. The English have seventy five, of which about forty are well manned. From the amazing quantity of supplies contracted for within a few days, and from all appearances, it is now thought, more than ever, that war is inevitable. On no other ground could the Minister be justified in incurring such an enormous expence. Three Messengers are now in Spain. The last of whom, many imagine, is gone with orders to recal the Minister. The Press still continues hot. I suppose Dr. Cutting, who was employed by some Masters of American vessels to assist them in obtaining the liberation of their men, has given you a Report of the difficulties and wrongs to which the American Seamen have been subjected in many instances.

Affairs in France remain in much the same situation they have been for some time past. The Duke of Orleans, and many of the considerable Refugees have returned home. A counter revolution has been much spoken of, and often predicted in this Country, and by the friends to the Aristocrats. But the affair of Nancy, in which the national Troops behaved with almost unexampled firmness as well as enthusiasm, through the course of a long and sharp action, gives occasion for a very different belief. The temper and feelings of 3 or 4,000,000, Citizens, who have arms in their hands, will not permit them to go back to their former government.

Leopold, who by consent of the Empress concluded a Truce with the Turks, has managed his policy with such dexterity as to have been unanimously elected Emperor, on the fourth of this month. He has gained some decided advantages over the Patriots of the Austrian Netherlands. But, in the mean time, a spirit of revolt, or at least of innovation, seems to have been insinuating itself into his hereditary Dominions. The part he will take in the general combinations is uncertain.

The King of Prussia has indeed a formidable Army on foot, but he can yeild no support to his English Allies, where they will, in case of war, have most occasion for it. He is said to be more addicted to women and pleasures than formerly. Consequently his reputation, even as a military man, is not so high as it was.

Poland appears to be still torne in peices by intestine factions, that which is now predominant, has thwarted the system of the King in several respects.

Thus are the affairs of nearly all Europe embroiled in an almost inexplicable manner. Nor has it perhaps ever been more difficult to form a true estimate of them. I shall endeavour to apply my undivided attention to the subject: and will hasten my departure for the Continent as much as possible. Previous to which, I will, without failure, write to you again. The vessel which carries this letter is to sail for New York tomorrow. The British Packet which left New York in the beginning of September, arrived four or five days before we did. I came into London entirely unobserved. Nor is there a person in the Hotel where I lodge, who knows even my name; or what part of the world I came from. With sentiments of the highest consideration, & esteem, I have the honor to be Sir Your Most obedient & Most humble Servant,

D. Humphreys.

RC (DNA: RG 59, DD); at head of text: "(No. 1.)"; on separate slip at foot of text: "The address of the Chr. de Pinto, in Portuguese, is: Ao Illmo. e Exmo. Snr. Luiz Pinto de Sousa Coutinho. Ministro e Secretario de Estado de S.M.F. dos Neocios Estrangeiros, e da Guerra. &c. &c. &c."; endorsed as received 11 Feb. 1790 and so recorded in SJL. FC (DNA: RG 59, DD).

From Henry Remsen, Jr.

Dr. Sir   New York October 14th. 1790

I had the honor of receiving your letter of the 1st. Inst. yesterday. The one enclosed for Mr. Short came too late for the french packet, which had sailed some days, but I shall send it under cover to Messrs. Willinks & Van Staphorsts, together with a parcel of Newspapers, by a vessel bound to Amsterdam which is advertised shortly to sail.

The people in bargaining for your house, said that they should not want to enter and live in it before the close of the present month or the beginning of the next, but that as several alterations must be made, particularly in the lower front room which was to be shelved for a store, it would be very convenient to them and the Landlord to have possession earlier. As I espected the vessel would be ready to sail for Philadelphia about the beginning of October, and was apprehensive no better offer would be made, I consented to the bargain which had been begun and partly concluded between them and the Landlord. By that bargain they were to pay half rent from the 1st. of November which is quarter-day. I enclose Mr. Bruce's Note respecting this affair given to me, agreeable to your request.

On the 1st. instant I presented the salary account for settlement and payment, and received all the money and distributed it according to practice, except 800 dollars belonging to you. The Treasurer's Order on the Bank of Philadelphia for this sum, and a statement of your quarterly account I have now the honor to enclose. I should have kept it 'till my arrival at Philadelphia and then lodged it in the Bank, did you not expect to stay longer in Virginia than you first proposed. The nature of the note is such that in case of its loss, no benefit can result to the finder, or loss to you. Mr. Meredith says he will renew it if necessary.

For the same reason I yesterday enclosed several letters and newspapers received since the 1st., and now forward some other papers, with the hope that they may come to hand before you depart from home. I thought of venturing the transmission of these papers even before the receipt of your last letter, as some of them were from Mr. Short addressed to you, and I knew they being the first might be important Letters. I have not heard any tidings of your servant and furniture from Paris.—Mr. Taylor has it in charge to do what is necessary should they get to Philadelphia before I do, and my father will with pleasure attend to them if they arrive here after my departure.

On the 2d. instant your furniture, Sir, and that of Francis, Mr. Taylor, and a Gentleman first Clerk in the Treasurer's Office, and also that part of the effects of the Office that was to go by water, were put on board of a Vessel bound for Philadelphia, which sailed two days after. Mr. Taylor went by land to receive them. He has written me a letter dated the 11th. mentioning the safe arrival of the vessel and her cargo, and that Mr. Leiper, who had not purchased the house adjoining yours, or hired that or any other, had then gone with him to view those you had looked at, and hired the one directly opposite yours for £70. It belong he says to a Widow Walker, and is three stories high with a garret, kitchen and stable. The freight of the Vessel is 106 dollars and 2/3, being the lowest sum that has been given, altho' somewhat higher than I expected to give. As far as I can judge by seeing every thing put on board, Your proportion will be near a fourth, including Francis's things; the proportion of the Office one half, and Taylor's and Anderson's rather more than a fourth, but the passages of Mathew, and Francis and his wife at 2 dollars each, is a separate charge.

That part of the effects of the Office that was to go by land, are boxed up and in readiness, and only wait for those belonging to the Treasury and other Departments to set out. The Secretary of the Treasury has made a Contract for transporting all those things to Philadelphia at 4/6 pr. hundred. They will go by water to Brunswick to avoid the risk of going to Sea, which they must have done if they had gone to Amboy, from thence to Trenton landing by land, and from thence to Philadelphia by water. He proposed this route, and his paying for the whole, to which I agreed. Mr. Blackwell and I shall attend our things. The Treasury Office will close on the 15th. when they will prepare for the Journey, and by the 20th. we shall be on the way.

I should have been in Philadelphia, Sir, when your things arrived, but found it impossible. I was to receive a sum of money from the Treasury to pay off the accounts against the Office, attend to the boxing of the cases that were to go by land, which chiefly appertained to the foreign Office, and also to the packing of the chests in the Hall (which were likewise to go by land) and the removal of them to the Office in broadway; for the Corporation had required the delivery of the two rooms we occupied in that building.—I flatter myself Mr. Taylor has paid proper attention to every thing I recommend to his care.

As I had received frequent enquiries from Mr. Mac Donogh, thro' his friends here after his return to Boston, respecting the steps he must take to be recognized, I wrote him a short letter informing him that the President and Secretary of State would be in Philadelphia about the Middle of November, and that it would be optional in him to exhibit his Commission personally, or by some of his friends; or if he preferred it, he might write to the Secrety. of State and enclose it, and his recognition would rest with them. I thought myself authorized to say this from your letter.

I have thought it my duty, Sir, to be thus minute. You have been long absent, and should know the exact situation of your office. I have also enclosed the Leyden Gazette, which I took from a large packet the seal of which I broke, that contained that and several parcels of dutch papers.—I have the honor to be with the greatest respect Dr Sir Your obliged & obedient Servant,

HENRY REMSEN JUNR.

RC (DLC); endorsed by TJ as received 2 Nov. 1790 and so recorded in SJL.

The letters that Remsen enclosed or forwarded the day before are evidently those also received on 2 Nov. 1790 and recorded in SJL: (1) Carter to TJ, 24 Sep. 1790. (2) Frederick Craig & Co. to TJ, Wilmington, 2 Oct. 1790 (not found). (3) Dumas to TJ, 26 May 1790. (4) Gilman to TJ, Exeter, 10 Sep. 1790. (5) Henry Knox to TJ, Boston, 27 Sep. 1790 (not found). (6) Lewis to TJ, 14 Sep. 1790. (7) John Neufville to TJ, Charleston, 22 Sep. 1790 (not found). (8) Palyart to TJ, 5 Oct. 1790. (9) Michael Roberts to TJ, New York, 7 Oct. 1790 (not found). (10) Short to TJ, 16 and 22 July 1790. (11) Skipwith to TJ, 30 Aug. 1790. (11) James Tilton to TJ, Dover, 25 Sep. 1790 (not found).

Remsen's receipt to TJ for his salary of $875, dated 7 Oct. 1790, with $75 deducted "to defray the expence of removing Mr. Jefferson's furniture to Philadelphia, is in DLC: TJ Papers, 57: 9846. That for FRANCIS AND HIS WIFE for a cabin in Thomas Thomson's sloop from New York to Philadelphia, and also for MATHEW (total $6) is in MHi.

From Noah Webster, Jr.

SIR   Hartford October 14th 1790.

The act of Congress, which secures to authors an exclusive right to their publications, requires that a copy of the works to be secured should be lodged in your office, within six months from the time of recording the same. On the 22d. of June last, I recorded the title of my "Grammatical Institute" and "Essays" with the Clerk of Connecticut District. Enclosed are two orders on my booksellers for a copy of my Essays to be appropriated as the act requires, and another copy, which please to accept for your private use. The reason of my enclosing two orders is, that I am not informed whether your office is *now* in N York or Philadelphia. If in N York, Mr. Allen will deliver the books to your servant; if in Philada. Mr. Dobson will do it.

A copy of the Institute will be forwarded as soon as an improved edition, now in the press, shall be finished; and if the six months should expire before that time, I flatter myself no advantage will be taken of a delay, occasioned merely by my wish to deposit, in your office, none but well printed copies.

You will observe, Sir, I have, in two places in the Essays, mentioned your name; and in one of them, with a view to confute your opinions on a political question. I hope, however, that your name and opinions are mentioned with that respect which is due to your superior rank and abilities, and which I certainly feel for both. I have the honor to be Sir with high respect your most obedient most humble Servt,   NOAH WEBSTER JUNR

RC (DLC); endorsed as received 20 Nov. 1790 and so recorded in SJL, but with the author there identified as "Webster Nathl."

To Maxey Ewell

SIR   Monticello Oct. 16. 1790.

I have communicated to Mr. Madison the subject of your letter. We are unable to say here exactly what is to be done. But Philadelphia is, as he supposes, the place where alone your business can be done. He therefore desires you will instruct Mr. Hopkins to forward your papers to him and he will put them into the necessary train. Perhaps you will be more secure if you obtain your papers from Mr. Hopkins yourself, see that they are all safe, and forward them yourself by post to Mr. Madison, at Philadelphia. I shall chearfully lend any aid I can in the business. [I am] with much esteem Sir Your most obedt. humble servt,

TH: JEFFERSON

PrC (MHi).

To James Lyle

DEAR SIR   Monticello Oct. 16. 1790.

We are not yet able to settle with Dr. Walker the sums he received from Mr. Mc.Caul for the estate. He has credited

1761. Mar. By Alexander Mc.Caul	£200-0-0
1764. Dec. 1. By cash of Alex. Mc.Caul	£220-0-0

but he has not credited the £200. received from him Aug. 31. 1766. (and not Aug. 26.[1] 1769. as I had mistated the date in my letter of Feb. 5. to you). He now imagines this £200. charged by you in Aug. 1766. is the same £200. he has credited in Mar. 1761. I am therefore to beg the favor of you to examine the accounts and inform us whether Doctor Walker appears there to have received all these three sums, or only two, and to ascertain the dates of his receipts, in fine to clear up this matter for us, which you alone can do. I am sorry to trouble you so much, but a credit of £200. in 1761. if now omitted would make £500. against us, with it's interest. As I have but a fortnight to stay I will beg the favor of you to be so good as to write to me on this subject immediately, and send your letter to the post office at Richmond. I am with great esteem Dear Sir Your friend & servt,

TH: JEFFERSON

PrC (CSmH).
1 Thus in MS (See TJ to Lyle, 5 Feb. 1790).

To John Nicholas, Sr.

DEAR SIR   Monticello Oct. 16. 1790.

We are not yet able to settle to the satisfaction of all parties the article of £200. omitted to be credited in Doctor Walker's account in August 1766. He supposes there may be some error of date. This renders it necessary for me to ask from you Kippen & co's account from which we were furnished with that credit. Your settlement with my brother seems to render that account not important to you. At any rate, if you will be so good as to spare it till we can settle this matter, it shall be as safe and as much subject to your orders in my hands as in your own, and shall be duly returned as soon as we can get this point out of the way. I stay here about a fortnight or three weeks longer and should be happy to recieve it during that time.

I am happy to hear that your health has got better, being at all times with great & sincere esteem Dear Sir Your affectionate friend and humble servt,   TH: JEFFERSON

PrC (CSmH).

To Richard Stith

DEAR SIR   Monticello Oct. 16. 1790.

I am here for two or three weeks more for the purpose of looking after my private affairs, and am much obliged to you for your kind attention to those in Bedford, manifested in your letter of July 10. which I have received only since I came here. The two entries for Mr. Wayles adjoining the Poplar forest I should be glad to have patented in my own name in one patent, including the two entries, but not including the Forest. The two small islands near the mouth of Judith's creek I would wish also to include together in one patent if it can be done. Any fees that may become due to you will be paid by Colo. Nicholas Lewis who will recieve the certificates from you and take care of them in my absence, as he does of my affairs in general. Should you fall in with him in his trips to Bedford, I recommend him to your acquaintance as a most excellent man. I am with great esteem Dear Sir Your most obedt. humble servt,

TH: JEFFERSON

PrC (MHi). Stith's letter of 10 July 1790, recorded in SJL as received 26 Sep. 1790, has not been found.

From Peter Delabigarre

SIR   Red Hook landing Octbr. 18th 1790.

Being an american and citizen of the state of New-York by purchasing a landed estate Here, I pray you to be so kind as to deliver to me a passeport to go to Angland and france where I am wanted to sell the remainder of my property there and Bring all Back in my adoptive country. I shall be very obliged to you to direct the said passeport to Messrs. John and Nich. Roosevelt, Meaden lane, N. York, as soon as possible; my passage Being taken on board of the British packet next to sail. I Remain with the Greatest Respect, Sir, Your most obedient & humble Servant,

PETER DELABIGARRE ESQR.

RC (DNA: RG 59, MLR); endorsed by TJ as received 22 Nov. 1790 and so recorded in SJL.

From C. W. F. Dumas

MONSIEUR   Lahaie 19e. Oct. 1790.

Je commence la présente aujourd'hui pendant l'illumination *ordonnée* à l'occasion du mariage de la jeune Princesse d'Orange avec le Prince héréditaire de Brunswick. C'est la cloture des réjouissances bruyantes qui durent depuis 8 jours, pendant lesquels la populace s'est donnée carrière.

Dans la nuit du 12 au 13, la valetaille mâle et femelle du Logement attenant des 3 villes de Gorcum, Schiedam et Schoonhoven, bien connu à Mr. Adams, cherchant querelle à mon valet en rue, le poursuivirent jusque dans le milieu et sur les montées de l'hôtel.— Prêt à me coucher, je descendis, et d'un ton impératif convenable, qui enfin leur en imposa, je parvins à les chasser. Le lendemain matin j'envoyai, par le même valet, remettre l'avertissement suivant en mains propres de deux Députés, qui le reçurent:

"Une interruption turbulente et indécente, qui eut lieu hier à 11 heures de la nuit dans l'intérieur de la maison des Etats-Unis d'Amérique, de la part de plusieurs gens du Logement voisin des trois villes de Gorcum, Schiedam et Schoonhoven, oblige le Soussigné, en présentant ses respects à Messieurs les Députés, de leur en donner connoissance, persuadé qu'ils désapprouveront le fait, et voudront bien en interdire la répétition insupportable.

Fait à Lahaie le 13e. Oct. 1790, au matiné

C W F DUMAS, Citoyen des Etats-Unis
D'Amérique, Membre de leur Académie
des Sciences et des Arts, &c."

Je suppose que l'interdiction a eu lieu. Si l'avanie se répétoit, je m'adresserois par avocat à la Cour de Justice, avec copie de mon Avertissement, jointe à la plainte.

J'ai tiré sur les Banquiers des Etats-Unis à Amsterdam ƒ297, montant de la Déclaration de mes Débours pour les 6 premiers mois de cette année, en leur transmettant une copie pour le Trésorier des Etats-Unis pareille à celle que j'ai jointe à l'original de cette Dépeche pour qu'elle passe sous les yeux de Votre Excellence.

Les Anglois font mine de vouloir tout de bon [la] guerre avec l'Espagne dans le Golfe de Mexique. Je suis loin de désirer que nos Etats y soient impliqués directement. Je crois néanmoins fermement qu'il n'est pas de leur intérêt de souffrir qu'on fasse là des conquêtes, ni qu'on s'empare de cette navigation-là. Je crois encore que ce sera une occasion de vous faire ouvrir de bonne grâce, et pour toujours, l'embouchure du Mississipi.—Je suis persuadé que ce n'est que dans l'intention de vous gêner et de vous en imposer en cas de telle guerre, qu'on vous retient les Forts que le Traité les oblige d'évacuer, notamment Niagara. Quant aux Espagnols, s'ils sont bien avisés, ils doivent naturellement, ce me semble, ne rien épargner pour avoir de leur côté vos Provisions et vos Armateurs, même de vos troupes volontaires à leur solde, et vos baies pour leurs Flottes et Vaisseaux de guerre, comme pour ceux de la France. De cette manière, le Commerce des autres seroit bientôt en souffrance et leur ambition frustrée. Si cette tirade politique ne paroissoit que radotage, qu'il soit pardonné à l'ardente pureté de mon Zèle qui ne vieillit pas.—Tel est pareillement le seul et unique principe de l'idée communiquée dans ma précédente touchant des Paquebots *Américains* à expédier régulièrement et directement en

Hollande. Je persiste à les penser nécessaires, utiles et profitables; et la dépendance où est *toute* Votre correspondance réguliere, politique et marchande, de la bonne foi, bon plaisir et vouloir des Anglois, dangereuse et pernicieuse. Je suis avec le plus respectueux dévouement, De Votre Excellence Le très-humble, très-obéissant & fidele serviteur,

C W F DUMAS

P.S. du 22e. Oct. J'ai eu le bonheur de me procurer le *founding Bill* du Congrès du 4 Août dernier. Cet Acte, et d'autres intelligences que j'avois déjà transmises à mon Ami L——— doit produire un article victorieux, que je l'ai requis d'insérer dans son papier, contre Ceux qui avoient débité ici, entre autres mensonges injurieux à notre excellente constitution et à notre crédit si bien établi, que le Congrès avoit réduit l'intérêt de la Dette liquidée de 6 à 4 p%.

RC (DNA: RG 59, PCC No. 93); at head of text: "No. 69 Dupl." Recorded in SJL as received 28 Dec. 1790.

From David Humphreys

SIR
London Octr. 20th. 1790.

In my first letter, I mentioned such circumstances of a political nature, relating to several of the principal Powers of Europe, as had then come to my knowledge. The facts, according to subsequent informations, were pretty justly stated. Leaving you to deduce such conclusions as your better judgment shall enable you to form, I proceed now to give you the sequel of intelligence which has resulted from my enquiries. As it is so difficult on the spot to know what to believe, I will name my authors, in some instances, that you may have the fairer opportunity of deciding the degree of credit is due to the reports: especially as you are generally acquainted with the persons themselves.

Nothing has yet happened to enable one to speak conclusively on the issue of the dispute between Spain and England. Still opinions are various, and sometimes appearances contradictory. Two days ago, a Messenger returned from Madrid, without bringing any thing satisfactory. Yesterday Stocks rose two pr Cent; and as Sir George Staunton told me, he heard in the City, without any ostensible reason, except that the British Messenger brought Dispatches to the Marquis del'Campo, and therefore the conclusion was adopted, that there must be some pacific understanding between the two nations. But, in fact, the stocks are affected in such an artificial manner and there is such gambling in them, that they remain no longer any criterion for forming a judgment whether there will be war or peace. A Company, in which Mr. Church is deeply concerned, have, according to report, speculated to an immense amount, insomuch that it is said he will gain or lose £50,000 by the event. He was with me a few days ago, and seemed rather to believe there will be a war. That, however, cannot be ascertained, even by persons the most interested to be informed, before the return of the Messenger who went to Madrid on the 3d. of this Month, and is expected back about the last of it. Nor is it probable that the men who are at the head of this government can form a judgment on good ground. They only know their own intentions; which are also to be apprehended by the measures they pursue. These have the most warlike appearance, and must now of necessity be continued. Under an idea that Spain would act on the present occasion in the same manner it did in the Falkland Island affair, the Ministry of this Country seem to have been hurried into embarrassments, which they had not fully foreseen, and from which they find it difficult to extricate themselves. The small importance of the object makes it believed by some that this was originally but a pretext for arming in order to avail themselves of the confusions in the North. If any thing of this kind was in contemplation, their views have been frustrated by an alteration of the state of affairs in that quarter. While Britain was disgusting, Spain was conciliating; and the apparent candour of the latter in offering to leave the determination of the right (upon the validity of existing Treaties) to any crowned Head in Europe, has had a tendency to interest other Powers in its favour.

At present, inconvenient, even pernicious as a war must be to this nation; and desirous of Peace as the Minister may in reality be, he has no choice—he must, after the declarations and preparations which have been made, proceed to hostilities, unless such concessions can be obtained as will satisfy the public expectation. For that purpose, it is reported he has, by the last Messenger, demanded three things to be explicitly allowed—the free Navigation of all Seas—the right of fishing in the Pacific Ocean—and of making establishments on any lands heretofore unoccupied.—Although this was related to me by a Person, likely to be better informed than most, as a truth he had through such an authentic channel as might be confided in, almost as much as if [it] was of an official kind; yet, I must avow, I believe this pretended ultimatum to be merely the offspring of conjecture, since it is acknowledged by all Parties, that the business of the Cabinet, has, at least, been conducted with great secrecy, during the course of the whole affair. Stockdale, the political Bookseller, however, informed me to-day, that he had just been assured by a person very high in office, that no war would happen.—The following facts are more obvious and speak a different language: the premium of insurance is at the war price: the preparations for war go on more vigorously than ever: on sunday last the Press Gangs took Watermen and Ferry-men, who had until then been exempted from impress: the three Battalions of Guards, detached for foreign Service, are getting in readiness to march on Monday next for Portsmouth, to which place their route, in three Columns, is designated: Transports are prepared for them to go on board: *Letters of Service* are just issued for raising 100 Companies of Infantry, of 100 men each: A friend of mine, an officer in the British Service, who called upon me yesterday, told me he had received his recruiting Orders, and was in treaty with a person to give ten Guineas for every Soldier he would inlist for him.—It is added, that the Colonels of Militia are ordered to be in readiness to assemble their Regiments at a short notice, if it shall become necessary, and that the Middlesex Militia have offered to do duty in place of the Guards. Doubtless every arrangement will be made for striking a strong blow in the onset, if the war shall take place. Parliament will pretty certainly meet in November.

During these transactions, the Ratification of the family Compact by the national Assembly of France, and the more recent order to have 15 Ships fitted for Sea in addition to the 30 which were in preparation, sufficiently shew their intentions, should matters proceed to extremity.

While the Powers of Europe are in such a political ferment, America is daily growing of more importance in their view. A report had prevailed in this place, that Spain has lately made some declaration, with respect to conceding to the United States the free Navigation of the Mississipi. I took considerable pains to trace it; and yesterday was told, Colo. Miranda had seen it in a letter to the Spanish Ambassador himself. My Informant received the intelligence from Miranda.

I learn from the Marq. de la Luzerne (to whom I brought a letter from the President) that the Compte de Moustiers is appointed Minister to Berlin. Upon asking him, who he thought would be appointed to replace that Minister in America, he seemed disposed to think, of the several persons who were Candidates, Colo. Ternant was the most likely to succeed.

Mr Paradise gave me, in conversation, to understand that he had seen the letter from the Secretary of foreign Affairs in Portugal to the Chevalier Freire, announcing (unofficially) his nomination as MINISTER RESIDENT, in the United States, and mentioning that the present *Portuguese Minister* at Rome, was immediately to repair in that Character to London. As a confirmation of this expectation, the Chevr. Freire (with whom I fell in company at dinner with the Marq. de la Luzerne) enquired of me "whether Mr. Jefferson had not heard of his appointment before I left America"?

The Administration here, it is also believed, have a serious intention to send a Minister forthwith to the United States. A Mr. Petre (a Gentleman who holds a newly created office in the Customs of this Port) said in my hearing, that the Duke of Leeds spoke to him on the subject, within a fortnight past, in such a positive manner as to make him suppose, it had been determined in Council. I know not whether there by any foundation for a rumour circulated here, that Sir John Temple has written for, and obtained permission to return to this Country on a visit.

I am perfectly ready to set out for the Continent. Unfortunately for me the Packet for Lisbon sailed from Falmouth about the time of my arrival in London, and will not sail again in less than a fortnight. There is no vessel here in immediate readiness to sail for that Port, or I should prefer going in that manner, notwithstanding the disagreeable navigation of the channel.—By taking passage in the Packet, one can hardly avoid getting into the News Papers, as I find they make it a practice to publish the names of all the Passengers. This is an inconvenience I wish very much to obviate. Although it was impossible to avoid being known by many persons I have met with; yet hitherto I have escaped public notice, and am considered merely in the light of a private traveller. I have the honor to be with perfect esteem & respect Sir Your most humble & Most obedient Servant, D. HUMPHREYS

RC (DNA: RG 59, DD); at head of text: "(No. 2)"; endorsed by TJ as received 10 Jan. 1791 and so recorded in SJL. FC (same).

From James Monroe

DEAR SIR   Richmond Octr. 20. 1790.

After the most mature reflection I have at length yielded to my inclinations to suffer my name to be mention'd for a public appointment. If it takes place, unless some unpleasant reflections on probable future events should press on me, it will contribute greatly to my own and the gratification of Mrs. M. as it will place us both with and nearer our friends. But to be candid there is not that certainty in the event we seem'd to suppose. Mr. Harvie, Mann Page, Walker and Govr. Harrison are in, or rather will be in, the nomination, and as some of them are active in their own behalf it is extremely doubtful how it will terminate. Colo. Lee and Mr. Marshall are for others. How a particular character of whom we spoke is dispos'd, I know not, but other circumstances have interven'd to make his inclination in my favor more questionable. There are but few men of any weight in the house and I really know none on whom I can rely with certainty. I have reason however to believe that with the body of the house I stand well. But the body, if well dispos'd, requires a head to keep it in a proper direction. I shall write further by the next opportunity and am sincerely yr friend & servant,   JAS. MONROE

RC (DLC); endorsed by TJ as received 27 Oct. 1790 and so recorded in SJL.

TJ had told Short on 30 Sep. 1790 that Monroe was to be "pressed into the service really against his will" to succeed William Grayson, who had died on 12 Mch. 1790. He was elected and took his seat on 6 Dec. 1790. The opposition of John Marshall indicates his alignment with the Federalists though TJ later noted that he had not come forth openly to this position.

From John Samuel Sherburne

SIR   Portsmouth October 20th 1790

My being absent on our fall Circuit at the time your circular letter arrived at the Post Office in this Town has hither prevented my paying that attention to your request, which I otherwise should have done. As the Clerk of our Superior Court is still on the Circuit I have not been able to examine his records for Adjudications on the points you mention, tho' I believe there have been but few if any in this State. On his return I will immediately attend Sir to that part of your request. I herewith have the honor to forward all the Laws of this State that are in print, which comprize all of a public nature that have been enacted for almost a Century past. Some of these being temporary have expired, and others of them have been repealed, should these not fully answer your wishes, I will procure from the Secretarys office all of an earlier date tho none such are now in force. Should it be in my power Sir on any future occasion to render the smallest aid in the Execution of the important duties of your Office, I hope you will honor me with your commands without any reserve. With the most perfect considerations I have the honor to be Sir Your Most Obdt. and very hum. Servt.,

JOHN SAMUEL SHERBURNE

RC (DNA: RG 59, MLR); endorsed by TJ as received 22 Nov. 1790 and so recorded in SJL.

From William Short

DEAR SIR   Paris Octob. 21. 1790.

Since my last the colonial committee have made their report on the disturbances of St. Domingo, and the conduct of the general assembly of that island.

The report was an historical series of the events which have taken place in that colony from the convocation of the States-general in France, together with the proposition of a decree in consequence of them. I refer you for the one and the other to the Nos. 285.286. of the Moniteur herewith sent.

The decree was immediately adopted in the manner that that of the 8th. of March last had been, viz: without allowing any member to speak on the subject, though several insisted with vehemence on being heard.

The reason of stifling all discussion on this subject, is, that it is known several members are of opinion that the assembly should fix several unsettled points respecting the free mulattoes, and the slave trade. The principles of the assembly and the sentiments of the islanders are in such direct opposition on this subject that the great majority are afraid to meet the question in the present critical situation of affairs.

It has been always represented here that of the three provincial assemblies, that of the north, which is much the most considerable, as well as several considerable parishes in the island were opposed to the general assembly, whom they accused of wishing to be separated from the mother country. The general assembly on the contrary insist that the most considerable and most respectable part of the island have implicit confidence in them, and that they never entertained any idea of independence.—These things however cannot be fully ascertained until further intelligence is had from S. Domingo.

Letters have arrived here within these few days which say that the disturbances there have been carried to such an height, since the departure of the general assembly, that the Governor has been obliged to leave the island and take refuge on board a ship of war. If so it may be apprehended that the late decree of the national assembly will not be well received there, and particularly as nothing was finally settled as to their commerce relative to provisions. The islanders know the influence that the trading towns have on this question and are persuaded the assembly will render the monopoly as strict as ever, so soon as they have nothing to fear from the resistance of the colonies. The principles of the assembly are fully known. The furthest they have any idea of going at present, is to agree that the ports of the islands shall be opened to foreigners whenever provisions rise above a stated price. They would not go even as far as this if they could venture to stop short of it. The report of the committee of impositions on tobacco remains as when I last wrote to you. The irregular manner of doing business in the assembly renders it impossible to say when this report will be taken up. The longer it is put off the less probable is its adoption. Indeed it would be lucky for their commerce with the United States if the subject in general could be postponed until a future legislature.— The present assembly are so fully occupied by subjects of a more pressing nature, that it is with infinite difficulty that any of its members can be brought to consider this fully. Their ignorance in matters of commerce in general is extreme, and [it cannot be dissembled that they[1] consider that with the United States of much less importance now than they will do in a short time hence. Some suppose us so much attached to England and to English manufactures, that every sacrifice which France could make to encourage commercial connexions with us, would be lost. They say that the experience of seven years has sufficed to shew this.—Others suppose that the commerce with the United States is a losing commerce. They are supported in this opinion by many of their merchants who tell them there is no instance of a French house having undertaken that commerce without having lost by it. It is easy to answer these arguments so as to satisfy individuals, and a short time will satisfy all. Still at present an unfavorable impression remains with many. When they are told that the Americans have continued to trade with England since the peace, because their articles of exportation were either subjected to a monopoly or to such shackles in France as prevented their coming here; that losses have been sustained in the American commerce by the failures which the peace brought on, and by the improper credit given to those who did not deserve it, by agents ill chosen, or by goods ill-assorted—when they are told that the exportations from America to Europe are annually upwards of ninety millions and of course that they are able to pay for that amount of European manufactures and productions, and that France can furnish the greater part of them on better or equal terms with England—that the United States furnish raw materials and receive in return only those which are manufactured—that the transportation of these articles has hitherto benefited the English, and might now benefit the Franch marine, they view the subject in a different light, and suppose it well worth attending to—they then come immediately to the necessity of a treaty of commerce as being the only means of securing the advantages to be expected from these connexions. They urge that laws which may be repealed from day to day, cannot be depended on; besides that there is no reciprocity in them. They quote the *arrêt du conseil* for the encouragement of American commerce, and our act of Congress on impost and tonnage. They complain bitterly on being placed on the same footing with the English —at the first session of the new Congress. The proceedings of the second are not yet known.

The desire of some of the members of the committee of commerce was to subject our articles imported into France, and our ships to the same duties and tonnage that we subjected theirs— a desire however not to discourage our commerce entirely. A hope that our system with respect to them would be changed, and a wish to have their tariff of duties on importation and exportation uniform for all, induced them to reject the idea. The report of the committee of commerce has been read in the assembly and ordered to be printed. You will receive it inclosed. The tariff is under press and shall be sent also as soon as it appears. How far it will be adopted I cannot say, but as the assembly feel the necessity of one being immediately established on the abolition of the internal barriers, it is much more than probable they will adopt it in the lump to save

time, although the members of the committee themselves agree
that it is very imperfect. They say time and experience alone can
shew what alterations should be made. Sacrifices have been mutually made by the different members of the committee, to each
other.

In what regards us, those who are graziers and those who are
interested with the Nantucket fishermen settled in France (of which
there are both in the committee) insist on heavy duties being laid
on salted meats and the productions of fisheries. They have succeeded in the committee and will probably succeed for the reasons
mentioned above, in the assembly. The low price of our salted
meats alarmed them; they were deaf to the advantages of procuring subsistance on the best terms possible to the poorer classes;
and the preference which should be given to the cultivation of corn
above grazing, on account of population. These arguments would
be good with a Minister whose duty it would be to examine the
subject in a general view as relative to the whole Kingdom, but are
of little avail when addressed to the owners of pasture grounds.[2]

There is little doubt therefore that the regulations made by the
present assembly respecting our commerce will not be such as we
could wish.][3] But it seems to me unquestionable that when the government here shall be organised, when we shall have attracted
their attention and their affection by having commenced the payment of the debt due them, and when they shall have considered
and felt the advantages as well commercial as political to be derived
from a close connexion with the United States, they will then be
ready to enter into such terms as we may chuse. The moment will
then be favorable also for stipulating definitively the conditions of
our admission to their islands. They will then perhaps consider it
as a political measure, although at present the mention of it by one
of their islanders is considered as criminal. It is essential however
that the representative of Congress here should be kept fully acquainted with their views on this subject.

The disorders in the fleet at Brest continuing, M. de Rioms the
commander in chief has resigned. The municipality had in a considerable measure contributed to the insurrection by an improper
and blind zeal. All parties there desire that Count D'Estaing should
take the command. It is uncertain however whether he will be sent,
as he has enemies in all parties here. Commissaries have been sent
to Brest in hopes of calming the disturbances and they write that
they have hopes of succeeding. The affair of Brest had been laid

before the assembly and referred to a committee. In the course of its examination several committees united and considering that want of energy in the government, arising from the Ministers being either unable or unwilling to support the new order of things, was one of the principal causes of present misfortunes, proposed to the assembly at the same time that they censured the conduct of the municipality of Brest, to address the King and to declare that the ministers had lost the confidence of the nation. Although all parties in the assembly censured the conduct of ministry, yet the proposition of the committee was rejected on the principle of its being destructive of the King's prerogative.

Before the question was put it was determined by a large majority that M. de Montmorin was not intended to be included. He was excepted by some because his department being foreign had nothing to do with the constitution, by others because he was friendly to it.

This was an unexpected circumstance, and the more so as his patriotism had been called into question in the assembly by the same members formerly who now supported him.

This change is attributed to two causes. 1. that M. de Montmorin has incurred the displeasure of the aristocratic party by communications which he had made to the *committee des recherches* concerning his apprehensions respecting the Prince de Condé and communicated to the assembly against his intention by that committee, and 2. because it was suspected the Queen wished to give that department to a person obnoxious to the popular party.

These circumstances will put M. de Montmorin in a disagreeable situation between the King and the national assembly. The other ministers must ere long be forced out of their places, and should he remain he will have the air of remaining against the King's consent, or at least without any proof of his approbation. On the whole every thing respecting the future organisation of the ministry is uncertain. The ministers all declare their desire to resign but it is known they will remain as long as it is possible. All hands declare they would on no consideration enter into the Ministry at this moment, and yet it is known that the committees were pushed on to the measure against ministry by those who desire to succeed them. The members of the assembly being excluded from the ministry by their decree are in general less disposed to change the present ministers than those who are out of the assembly and who desire their places.

In order to give some hopes that the assembly was approaching its end a motion was made some time ago for adding new members to the committee of constitution, who should present to the assembly such parts of the constitution as were finished, and such as remained still to be decreed, separating the laws already made and are *constitutionelles*, from those which are *reglementaires*. As these new members were taken from the most popular part of the assembly in general, it was hoped they would engage their friends to support and decree without delay such unfinished parts of the constitution as they should propose. The hopes of the constitution being thus soon finished and consequently the session of the present assembly, did not last long. Many days elapsed before the committee of constitution thus re-inforced had even a meeting: and the members who now compose it are of such opposite principles and so hostile to each other personally that they will probably never agree on any point among themselves.

Besides there are several questions which the members of the same party cannot agree about—as what points are constitutional and what merely legislative? whether the next legislature shall be considered as a convention? if not whether a term shall be fixed by this assembly for calling a convention? &c.

My own opinion has been for some time that a majority of the assembly have no desire to see the session ended. There are members of these sentiments in all parties for different, and frequently opposite reasons.

You will have observed by the variety of business and detail into which the assembly enter that there can be no term fixed to their business. They will be supported for some time yet by the majority of the people because they are considered as the only barrier to the designs of the Aristocrats, which the popular party here takes care to describe as dangerous—whereas in truth I believe the Aristocrats desire at present above all things, the establishment of a government, sufficiently strong to preserve order and tranquillity. In this they will sooner or later be supported by a great number of those who are now their enemies, and who will then see that the continuation of the present session is a continuation of anarchy.

Since the law for emitting a paper money the funds have risen very much, and the partisans of the plan plead this as a proof of its propriety. The true cause of the rise however is that the paper emission depreciating, and many of the *effets Royaux*, being rendered a tender in common with the assignats in the purchase of public lands, brings them both more nearly to a level and consequently raises the nominal value of stock, although public credit and public opinion as to the paper money remain the same.

The negotiations between Spain and England as well as their armaments still continue with great activity. Nobody can say what will be the result. It would seem impossible that Mr. Pitt could meet Parliament without having obtained for such expensive preparations, some advantages by negotiation, or having attempted something by arms. And yet the opinion of politicians seems to be that there will be no war between them. When Mr. Pitt first begun this business he had no apprehension of the peace between Sweden and Russia—and hopes of France being more averse to support the Court of Madrid. These circumstances render him much more averse to the war at present, but they render Spain also less disposed to make a sacrifice by negotiation. On the whole it seems highly probable that two if not all the three powers on the Baltic would join Spain and France in the case of a war. The animosity of the Empress of Russia towards the court of London on account of the late intrigues at Constantinople is well known. The frequent conferences between the Spanish Ambassador and Russian Minister here are remarked. At Court they seem to use affectation in taking each other a part in presence of the English Ambassador—so much shew however might induce one to question the reality if there were not other indications to fortify the suspicion.

In a conversation which I had lately with the Spanish Ambassador on the present situation of affairs he said in plain terms that he feared the disorders of Brest would have a bad effect for Spain, either in preventing success in the war, or in forcing them to a disadvantageous treaty. I thought he said this as if he meant to hold out an idea that Spain would make sacrifices rather than risk a war without being sure of being well supported by France. He said a few words also that had a distant allusion to the Mississipi, which was the point I was desirous of his coming to. It was occasioned by a paragraph in a newspaper here, an extract of a letter as it was said from New York, where the writer observes that the United States will certainly *'tirer le meilleur parti possible des querelles qui s'elevent entre l'Angleterre et l'Espagne.'*

He said he conceived it was manifestly for the interests of our two countries to be better acquainted with each other and be always united. I observed, after speaking in general terms on this subject, that there was a frankness and *loyauté* in the Spanish character which rendered them agreeable allies to all and particularly so to the Americans who being determined to act always as they had hitherto done, with fairness and candor desired to find the same qualities in those with whom they were connected. To this he replied—that frankness was well known to be the national character in Spain, and that besides, Spain was so situated that she had no interest to act otherwise—"duplicity said he suits only those nations who want to carry their manufactures to new markets, or extend their possessions. Spain has not manufactures sufficient for herself, of course she cannot fall under the first description. As to possessions she cannot want to extend to them. *On the contrary if she could dispose of a part of what she has so that they would not fall into the hands of enemies, it would be for her advantage.*" Our conversation was interrupted here by the Swedish Ambassador and Russian Minister who came up and turned it to other objects.

He had told me previously that the Emperor of Morocco was now making war on the Spanish possessions in his neighbourhood. He reprobated the conduct of those European nations, and particularly France, who rendered it necessary to pay a tribute to the piratical States instead of destroying their cruisers.

I forgot to mention what is considered by some as an indication of the continuance of peace and by others as a deception. The children of the English Ambassador and his horses are on their road here and will arrive to-morrow or next day. In opposition to this it is said that a part of the English fleet is immediately to sail with troops on board for the West-Indies. And its being known that the Parliament will assemble to proceed to business on the 25th. of Novr., which is six weeks sooner than was expected.

I received a letter very unexpectedly from Colo. Humphreys the day before yesterday. He tells me that he had that instant arrived in London and was to embark in the first vessel for Lisbon, without saying in what character. He wrote to inform me that he was charged with dispatches for me from the Secretary of the Treasury which he was going by his desire to deposit with Mr. Church. As I am told that Mr. Barritt is still in London and is coming on here soon, I hope he will bring them. I received also two days ago by the French packet your private letter of the 6th. of June. It is endorsed as having been put into the post-office the 8th. too late for the packet.

Du Moustier's successor is not yet publicly announced, but there is no doubt that it is Ternant. He has been promised the place two years ago. Some of the Americans here think that his appointment will be considered a slight in America. If so it will be without reason. Few people here are better supported by all the ministers than Ternant and besides the Marquis de la fayette is his friend. I think it possible that Ternant's ambition carries his expectation even higher and that he has some hopes of being employed in the administration here.

It is known that the Marquis de la fayette is endeavoring to form the new ministry which must necessarily soon be called, and that he supports Du Portail for the war department. He may succeed as to him perhaps, but he will certainly not name all the others. He might have done this twelve months ago, but he has lost much ground since that time by trying to please all parties, and by a want of decision in his conduct.

I send you the newspapers as usual and beg you to be assured of the sentiments of attachment with which I am, my dear Sir Your friend & Servant,   W. Short

P.S. October the 25th. Mr. St. Trys who is the bearer of this letter having been delayed several days longer than he expected gives me an opportunity of acknowledging the receipt of your letters by the French Packet of August the 26th and 31st. They were forwarded to me by a person from L'Orient, and arrived several days later than that of the 6th. of June which must have come by the same packet. He tells me that he has forwarded by the Messagerie the packets accompanying that letter. They have not yet arrived.

I have just received also by Mr. Barritt, the duplicate of your letter of July 26th. and that of August 10. He did not bring as I had hoped the letters from the Secretary of the treasury. He tells me he saw Mr. Church three or four days before he left London, and that he heard him tell Colo. Humphreys that he had forwarded my letters. To my astonishment however they have not yet arrived. Yet in consequence of your letter of Aug. 31. I am preparing to set out for Amsterdam as soon as I shall have received the letters of the Secretary of the treasury.

There are objects however depending here which interest the United States and require a very constant attention. I mean the reports of the committees of imposition and commerce, on tobacco and *traites*. [The proceedings of a large and tumultuous assembly are so irregular that one is obliged to be on a constant watch to prevent the individual members who are interested, from passing into a decree such things as the house do not consider of very great moment, or where there is no other individual particularly interested in its opposition. The importation of salted provisions and whale oil are in this class. You will see by the tariff inclosed that the committee proposes heavy duties on the former, and a prohibition of the latter, without any regard to the laws formerly made for the encouragement of our commerce. The Marquis de la fayette will do whatever he can to prevent these things passing, and I hope he will succeed. I have spoken to several of the members on this subject. They all agree on the necessity of putting the American commerce on a different footing. They talk of the propriety of reciprocity insured by a treaty and plead that favors hitherto granted to our commerce in France did not create similar dispositions in America. They say the Nantucket fishermen at L'Orient and Dunkirk have large quantities of oil on hand unsold, which proves they are competent to the supplies of the kingdom, and are buoyed up with the hopes that they will be joined by many others who will come to settle in France rather than go to the English possessions.][3] If these matters were to be treated with a minister capable of examining the subject in all its details, there is no doubt the result would be favorable to our wishes, and particularly with the million and an half of florins which are now at our disposal.

It is impossible however to say what will be the decision of an assembly like this. Its own members are always at a loss to know what decree will pass. It is impossible also to say when these reports will be taken up. There is every reason to suppose however that it will be ere long.

The Marquis de la fayette is so absolutely absorbed by his place, that it is indispensable to have a person here who may keep his attention from being diverted from such things as interest us. Amidst the multitude of letters which he receives and of which he reads only a small part, such as I should write from Amsterdam, would frequently remain unnoticed. This points out the propriety of my naming a Secretary. I shall consult with him so as to chuse a person to whom he will be most disposed to give access.

The laws respecting the commerce of the islands will not be settled until the assemblies which are to be formed there shall have expressed their sentiments. Of course the payment of the million and an half of florins cannot be postponed for it.—The principles of the assembly, with respect to that business seem to me unquestionably to be to restrict it as much as they dare to do. They will be determined in this not at all by the wishes of the colonies, but by the then situation of affairs, and the probability of success in using force. They plead the conduct of the general assembly of St. Domingo to shew that liberty of commerce and independence go hand in hand. There are other considerations also which will render it difficult to postpone the payment long.

The speculation which was proposed to Mr. Necker last year and not accepted by him for the reasons then mentioned are now renewing with the committee of finance. Some of the members of this committee are interested in it and promise to pass it through the house in a report from their committee. They will ground it on the delay on our part, and the propriety of the national assembly accepting an offer which may be counted on with certainty.—I have hitherto been instrumental in preventing this by telling them I would oppose it. Their plan came to my knowlege, because some of the parties interested thought it would be safest to consult me about it. If it were known that the order had arrived for payment, and there were still a delay, it would be impossible to prevent the speculation taking place. The order cannot be long unknown as it has been already communicated by the bankers in Amsterdam to Mr. Van Staphorst here, and who is interested in the speculation. It has been long known here that there were three millions of florins at Amsterdam subject to the order of Congress. This was communicated to Mr. Necker by the bankers; of course the present payment will be below their expectations. Still I will make the best of it.

The assembly passed a law some time ago for abolishing the *droits d'aubaine*. I do not recollect its expression sufficiently to say whether it extends to the islands, but I will immediately inform myself and act accordingly.

Should a war take place between Spain and England I think it highly probably the wishes of the United States would, at least in part, be accomplished. The sentiments of the Ambassador here would lead to this belief, as far as they may be judged of from the conversation mentioned above, which was however as you will have seen, a desultory one.

There was a report yesterday evening however which promised the continuation of a peace. It was said that on the return of the last express from Madrid stocks had risen 2½ pct. at London. I cannot yet say whether this is a report for speculating.—The papers inclosed in your letters of the 10th. of August, will be used or not, agreeably to your desire. Count D'Estaing told me four or five days ago that he had received through M. de Montmorin, an answer to his letter, from the President. That it was merely a letter of compliment, and that he would shew it to me. When I see him I will say what you have desired.

The Ministers have written a letter to the King which I inclose you together with his answer. M. de la Luzerne has since resigned and M. de Fleurieu has succeeded him. He has been a long time in that department and said to be very well acquainted with it.— The resignation of the other ministers is expected daily. I have the honor to be with sentiments of the most perfect attachment Dear Sir Your most obedient humble servant, W SHORT

FC (DNA: RG 59, DD); at head of text: "No. 44 W Short to the Secty of State." PrC of Extract (DLC); at head of text: "Extract of a Letter from William Short esquire Chargé des Affaires of the United States at the Court of France, to the Secretary of State, dated Paris October 21st. 1790"; in hand of George Taylor (see note 3 below). PrC (DLC: Short Papers). Recorded in SJL as received 27 Jan. 1791.
1 Extract reads: " . . . that the National Assembly consider their commerce with the United States," &c.
2 This sentence is omitted from Extract but without any indication of omission.
3 The matter embraced in two passages in square brackets (supplied) comprises the text of the Extract. There is no indication of omission or alteration as indicated in notes 1 and 2: the two passages are run together as if in a continuous text.

From Benjamin Vaughan

DEAR SIR   London, Oct. 21, 1790.

I am at a loss how to write to you about public affairs, unless negatively. We have no war, we have no peace. Our various European powers have neither principles that we can understand, nor passions that are avowed. We quarrel with Spain, and have German disagreements threatning us in which our court would mix by preference; and Spain disagrees with us, though hampered with the Moors. Prussia was yesterday the power dictating to Austria, and now Austria is the arbiter between Prussia and Russia. We have run great risques for Sweden and Prussia, and still neither are said to be contented with us. If we fight about Nootka sound, it will not be without a general persuasion that the object is not worth a war, which yet no one seeks to prevent.—I hope that this ridiculous scene of things will give strength to the future arguments for pacific systems. In the interim, it is not likely to exalt the opinion hitherto had of Mr. Pitt's talents, public views, and benevolent character.—As to France, I have every hope from the goodwill of the many to the revolution, notwithstanding the incidental impediments which they meet with. Their persistance, where their success is hitherto so imperfect, argues every thing to my mind, in favor of the stability of the revolution. They have much to do, much to change in what they have done, and must leave much undone till better times. Their army is coming back to its obedience, but their sailors will require much to satisfy them. I hope Spain will see this in so strong a light, as to become less tenacious, and consequently more favorable to peace. We are waiting their *answer*.[1]

Permit me now to suggest a *scheme*, for which I desire no patent at your office, it being an old invention; it being nothing more than that of the establishment of public games, prizes, and rewards, for the whole continent, at given periods of one or more years; to take in for actors and claimants, all residents and persons serving under you, as well as your citizens. The objects of the prizes and rewards, might respect agriculture, commerce, the arts, sciences, poetry, virtues exercised towards the state and individuals, &c., &c., We know the power of these things in elder times; men are still the same, and so also is the nature of free governments. You cannot have a better scene for action and representation than Philadelphia.—May I presume to ask it of you to consult with Mr Jay upon this subject, which I have also suggested to Count Mirabeau for the use of France knowing that it will be very popular at Paris, and very suitable to their champ de Mars, in many parts of it. I shall here conclude, fearful of making you more out of humor with me by farther nonsense.

Dr. Price took from me your pamphlet about weights and measures. I believe you are the first nation that ever produced statesmen who were natural philosophers. When I have read your remarks, I will take the liberty to return my opinion. In the meantime, I am, dear sir, with the highest esteem, your respectful & humble servt.,

BENJN. VAUGHAN

RC (DLC); endorsed by TJ as received 3 Jan. 1791 and so recorded in SJL.

[1] This sentence, crowded in at the end of the paragraph, was obviously added as an afterthought.

To James Currie

DEAR DOCTOR   Monticello Oct. 22. 1790.

The return of Mr. Randolph's servant affords me the first opportunity of informing you that I mentioned the subject you desired to the gentleman who was to call on me. He is intelligent and close, and has his suspicions always about him. I was obliged therefore to avoid any direct proposition or question, and only prepare him by declaring my opinion in such a way as to avoid suspicion. He has my testimony of the talents of the person proposed, and so given as to weigh with him, but I have no means of conjecturing the part he may take but his acquiescence in the correspondence between the character I gave and the idea he had formed from other information. Wishing you success in all your undertakings and health and happiness I am with great esteem Dr. Sir your friend & servt.,   TH: JEFFERSON

Tr (ViU).

On 13 Sep. 1790 Currie wrote TJ from Richmond: "I took the liberty of dropping you a line by Major Farley to N York some time ago: permit me now to welcome you to your native State and home. I should be glad to know whether you expect to be down here and when; if during your stay in Virginia you intend at all wishing to have the pleasure of some conversation with you and advice in some matter regarding myself. Your acquainting me as soon as convenient by a line, will much oblige me" (RC in DLC, endorsed by TJ as received 19 Sep. 1790 and so recorded in SJL). Currie's note by Major Farley has not been found and is not recorded in SJL. The GENTLEMAN to whom TJ spoke about Currie's subject has not been identified, but the matter may have related to that discussed in Currie's letters of 14 and 15 Mch. 1791.

From James Monroe

DEAR SIR   Richmond Octr. 22d. 1790.

I wrote you a few days past in great hurry by the Albemarle post which I presume has been received. You have been able to collect from that communication that my services will be offer'd for the Senate, unless upon the information of my friends it shall appear probable they will be rejected. I gave you there a detail of circumstances relative to that business, and can only now add that as far as I know it will equally suit their present situation; unless indeed the activity of some gentlemen professedly candidates for that station should have occasion'd a change: one additional competitor only excepted, Colo. Lee. You will observe that I only give you what I hear for I know nothing of myself. It is proposed by some to continue the present Gentleman until march. I have determined in great measure in case of my election to abandon my profession. You find my letters contain little foreign intelligence; that I engross the whole to myself. I may probably be up at the county court. I am with the greatest respect & esteem sincerely your friend and servant, JAS. MONROE

P.S. It is also said that Mr. Matthews the Speaker will be nominated and the chair has latterly been a step to other offices.

RC (DLC); endorsed by TJ as received 25 Oct. 1790 and so recorded in SJL.

To Thomas Mann Randolph, Jr.

DEAR SIR   Monticello Oct. 22. 1790.

When you shall have perused the inclosed, be so good as to stick a wafer in it and deliver it. It will explain it's own object, on which therefore I need add nothing. You are certainly right in deciding to relinquish the purchase if Colo. Randolph desires it. But I rather suppose he means nothing more than that he will not abide by the agreement if all the articles are insisted on. He mentions particularly that one could be given up, (that of the slaves.) I therefore suppose that if the others are moulded to his wish he will ratify it. If this should be his disposition, it might hurt him to have the purchase refused in that form. It is really so convenient a one that you cannot supply it's place. A plantation, ready stocked and in order for furnishing you every thing at once is a great object. Of Mr. Carter nothing but naked lands can be had. I am told too he will not sell any on the lower side of the mountain, and those above the mountain are not eligible at all. He asks 30/ and his lands not to compare to Edgehill. Besides this he is gone to Fredericksburg to remain. So that I think there is little prospect of buying of him, nor indeed do I know any other purchase that could be made. However if Colo. Randolph wishes to be absolutely off, it is best to let him off. Do in all this as you please, and excuse my interference which has been from the beginning with a view to promote your happiness and interest. I am with sincere attachment my dear Sir Yours affectionately,   TH: JEFFERSON

RC (DLC); addressed: "Thomas Mann Randolph junr. esqr. Richmond." PrC (CSmH).

To Thomas Mann Randolph

I understand with much pain that you are dissatisfied with the articles of agreement which, on behalf of your son, I entered into with you for the purchase of Edgehill. I do not write the present with a view to insist on those articles being enforced. Far from it. If you wish to rescind them, it is sufficient ground for me to wish the same: and I know that in this your son has but one mind with us. I write merely to justify this transaction by recalling to your memory what past. You know that in the ride we took on the day of the transaction, we had agreed all the articles except the sums and times of paiment and the quantity of corn to be delivered. Having a moment's leisure on our return to the house I committed to writing the things we were agreed in, leaving blanks for those abovementioned in which we had not yet agreed. I read the articles to you, gave you a copy into your hand, and I think you read it yourself. I insisted on 200. barrels of corn, you on 100; I on £1700. in paiments of £500, 600, and 600£. you on £2000. in payments of £500. 750. and 750£. Finding you would not abate in the sum, I agreed to it, but urged that the additional £300. should make a fourth paiment. You objected to it, but, as seemed to me, not very positively. I declared I would fill up the blanks for paiment with 500. 600. 600. and 300£ and that for the corn with 200. barrels. You still declared against it. But I so filled up the blanks before your face; you were sitting at the other end of the short table on which I did it, and within reading distance: and you signed before you rose from the table, which I considered to be meant as finally assenting. I mentioned these circumstances to your son on my return, and observed to him that if you should require to have these particulars altered back to what you had insisted on, it would be better to comply with your desire. He did not hesitate to say they should be arranged as you please. These particulars therefore can make no difficulty. You express objections to letting him take such of the slaves as he may chuse. There was no difference of meaning between us on this article. It is expressed exactly as we both agreed. He was to take such as he should chuse, only taking them in families, so as not to separate parent and child, or husband and wife. But I am sure he will modify this or relinquish it as you please. With respect to the lands adjacent to the 1600. acres, certainly there was never a thought or word between us to the contrary of their being included. I do not mean any which your contract with Mr. Harvie extended to. I knew that that contract being prior must prevail, and meant to bargain for the residue only. Recollect too, if you please, my Dear Sir, that there was no surprise or haste in this transaction. I proposed it to you in March at Richmond. I again proposed it in a letter from New York: and when I returned to Virginia, hearing that you had declared your intention of selling these lands, and that you had particularly expressed expectations that your son would be the purchaser, I went to Tuckahoe expressly to negotiate it, considering your mind as made up on the subject. I found it so, for you named your terms at once, and never relaxed to the sum. You said you had meant to ask that sum of any other purchaser, and that justice to your family, would not permit you to sell cheaper to him than to another. I concurred with you in the rectitude of this last sentiment. I recall these particulars to your recollection, my dear Sir, that you may do me justice in your own mind. As to the contract, be it off, if you wish it, no matter what the laws of the land are. Nature knows no laws between parent and child, but the will of the parent. If you desire to keep the land, your son decided in the first moment to comply with your desire. But if you are only dissatisfied with any particular articles, model the whole to your own mind. The sale being meant for a family purpose, you are a proper umpire between your son and your other children. If the contract can be adapted to your mind, I confess I have it much, very much at heart. It is impossible to find so convenient a settlement for them. They are antient lands of your family, had got out of it, but were purchased in again by you.—In any event I hope this will have no effect on your affection to your son. He has done nothing in it, but to declare the contract should be moulded to your will. Next to the desire of preserving your affections to him, which are of more consequence to his happiness than all the lands of the earth, I confess I am anxious that you should be sensible that I have done nothing improper on this occasion, for it could not be improper to urge terms which I thought reasonable. If this long letter is troublesome, ascribe it to my anxiety to preserve your esteem, and to the sincere attachment with which I am my dear sir your affectionate friend & servant,

Th: Jefferson

RC (MHi).

From Matthew McAllister

Sir   Savannah October 24th. 1790.

Occasional business in the Western parts of the State deprived me of the pleasure of receiving your Letter of the 12th. of August earlier than a few days ago. The purport of it requiring an examination into the records of the several departments of this Government will put it out of my power to make the collection so early as wished for. Indeed Sir, I fear there will not be a little difficulty in collecting the laws. It may appear strange, but so it is, that there are not more than four printed Copies of the Provincial laws in the State. A digest of all the statutes, both ancient and modern, has been undertaken by authority of the Legislature, but there is but little prospect of a completion this or next year. Many that passed during and since the war are not in print, manuscript copies are occasionally procured from the Secretary's office. You are pleased to suggest the necessity of a collection of all the *printed* laws and ordinances; this Sir will be impracticable at this time for the reason just offered. All the printed Acts passed since our Independancy, I flatter myself, I shall be able to procure and forward by the next packet, together with the proceedings relative to the Treaty. This business is likewise perplexed and will require my attendance at Augusta. A Gentleman in the Southern parts of the State has a printed copy of the laws before the war. Probably, as he has no immediate use for them, I may be able to get them. An application to that purpose has been made. Should it succeed, they shall be sent on, but if otherwise I know no alternative but to procure office copies, or copies from the printed volumes. Should the latter answer, they may be procured much sooner and with much less expence.

No time Sir shall be lost on my part in doing every thing in my power to procure the papers and to transmit them by the safest and earliest conveyance. In the mean time I should be happy to be informed whether, in case manuscript copies of such of the laws and ordinances as are not in print will answer, they must go as certified from the proper office, or whether copies taken from the printed volumes will do pro. tem. The first mode will be tedious and expensive. At the same time there may be a difference in other respects. I should likewise be glad to know if it will be necessary to send printed or other copies of any others than such as are now of force in the State. I have the honor to be with great respect Sir. Your most obedient & most Humble Servant,

MATT: MC.ALLISTER.

RC (DNA: RG 59, PCC No. 76); endorsed by TJ as received 3 Dec. 1790 and so recorded in SJL.

From Alexander Donald

MY DEAR SIR   London 25th. October 1790

Yesterday I had the Honour of receiving [you]r esteemed favour of the 29th. August. As you did not make any men[tio]n of your health therein, I am willing to believe and hope that you had gotten [b]etter of your Headachs.

I thank you sincerely for your [ki]ndly expressions towards Mr. Corbin Braxton, I am satisfied that if [you] have an opportunity of being serviceable to him, he will always be grateful [to you] and that you never will have reason to be ashamed of your choice. I have ob[serv]ed his conduct for some years past, and I never saw or heard anything improper [in] it. I do assure you Sir that I am more vexed at his disappointment than [at] my own, and I cannot but applaud the President's choice of Mr. Johnson.—I will [on]ly repeat what I said to you formerly, that it will make me very happy if ever it is in my power to be serviceable to the United States of America.

I have made myself pretty easy as to Mr. Heths conduct to Mr. B.—— Knowing Colo. Hamilton to be a man of Sence and Liberality, I was persuaded that upon reading the Papers which I sent to you, that he would see that Mr. B. had every reason to believe that Capt. Butler was an American Citizen. I depend greatly upon your known Friendship should any thing further be done in that business.

I have experienced much kindness and attention from Mr. Short, for which I consider myself greatly indebted to you. He has not been able to succeed in the business which I mentioned to him, but I consider myself under the same obligations to him as if he had. In a letter of the 27th. Sepr. he informs me that he had been with M. de la Hante, upon conversing with him upon the Tobacco business he found him averse to making any contract, but said, He would give an order for a Cargo (in the event of the Farm being continued) if that was found good, he would order more and soon.

Mr. Short writes me that Mr. de la Hante added that my having your confidence, would be an additional motive for dealing with me on terms of confidence.—From which you will see that your Friendship is likely to be of very material consequence to me in my future Life, and I promise you that I will conduct myself so as to merit a continuance of it, and to prevent any reflection upon your Judgement of Mankind.—If this M. de la Hante is the same Gentleman that you was so good as promise to give me a letter to when I had the pleasure of seeing you in Richmond, I will thank you for sending it to me at your convenience, or to any other Gentleman whom you think may be serviceable to me in this negotiation—Which to me is of more consequence than the one which has been so long pending between this Country and Spain. It is very strange that Preparations for War has been going on for Six months and are still continued with the utmost urgency by sea and land, yet so as many People are of opinion that there will not be war, as that there will. The Fact is, that the present Administration is so secret that the Publick have no sure ground to form an opinion upon. But I confess it astonishes me that [any] man who is not in the arcana of the Cabinet, and seeing such immence prepar[ations] for war going on, should entertain any doubt on the subject. I confess I wis[h for] War, because it will be of infinite service to America, Provided she does n[ot] take a part in it, and which I cannot suspect from the Wisdom of her present [administration] that she will do.

I really wish that you could make me serviceable to you here. I consider myself much in your debt, and I feel myself mo[re] uneasy under a Debt of Gratitude than any other.

I am with sincere esteem & respect My Dear Sir Your much obliged & faithful humb Servt,

A DONALD

RC (DLC); MS torn and some words editorially supplied; endorsed by TJ as received 10 Jan. 1791 and so recorded in SJL.

From David Humphreys

SIR   London Octr. 25th. 1790

The Russian Minister at this Court has received an authentic account from the Minister of his Nation at Vienna of the naval victory gained by the fleet of the Empress over that of the Porte.

Of the latter the Admiral's ship was destroyed, two smaller ships taken, and the rest very much shattered and obliged to fly. The English affect to say this event will protract the war, by making the imperious Sovereign of the Russias more difficult in agreeing upon terms with the Ottomans. The English are heartily mortified at her superiority in war and policy. A specimen of superiority in both was given, in reducing the Swedish army to the absolute want of bread for two days preceding the Treaty, in conducting the negotiation through a character whose known incapacity precluded him from suspicion, and in concluding it, before a Courier could arrive in England to bring advice that it was in agitation. Since which time, she has most munificently rewarded all who were concerned in that Army, by making Presents to the amount of 1,000,000 of Roubles. And in the rejoicings consequent on it, at Petersburg, the People were at once regaled with 2,400 Hogsheads of wine from the artificial fountains. I descend to these minute particulars only for the purpose of shewing, that she is not totally exhausted.

Leopold, since the Convention of Reichenbach, and his establishment on the imperial Throne, has given notice, that if Prussia shall engage in hostility against Russia, he is still obliged to assist the latter. A rupture between the Emperor and the King of Prussia is now much talked of. The affairs of the Patriots in the Austrian Netherlands seem to be declining very fast; while the Emperor is marching a strong Body of Troops against them: The troubles in Hungary having been in the interim somewhat appeased.

The King of Sweden is said to be extremely displeased with Great Britain for not having afforded him effectual aid. His navy consists, after the diminution of it by the late war, of only 28 Ships of the line. Some subjects of animosity exist between his Kingdom and that of Denmark. The Prince of Denmark is believed to be desirous of signalising himself for military talents, after the example of the Great King of Prussia. His genius, I suspect, is of a very different order. He delights, like a young man, in the pomp of war. He practices his manual exercise every day before a glass; insomuch that a gentleman who has seen the room in which he practices, mentioned to me that he had worn a place with the but of his firelock on the floor: he also manoeuvres paper men, in order to become expert in Tactics. These LITTLE traits of character require no comment: That nation is, however, pretty powerful at Sea, having 50 Sail of Ships of war, and a Body of 20,000 enrolled Seamen, who can be made use of, in an emergency.

All accounts still concur in reporting that the Spaniards are arming with the utmost assiduity. It is also currently reported here that a war has broke out between them and the Moors; they having taken a Moorish Galley and chaced another on shore.

A war certainly has commenced between Tippoo Saib and the English in India. A Gentleman of my acquaintance, a long time a prisoner of Tippoo, lately returned from India, related to me several facts concerning the war; and that Lord Cornwallis would remain in his government, on this account, contrary to his former intentions.

So far are the Ministers of this Country from suffering any re-laxation in their military preparations, that they have, since my last letter, issued orders for raising 50 more Companies, of 100 men each, making with the former 15,000 men. The Battalions of Guards, for foreign Service, were yesterday reviewed and com-pleted from the other Battalions. Their march is postponed until wednesday. One sees, in going through the City, at the shops of Mechanics, a great number of new travelling Trunks and haver-sacks with the names of the officers of the Guards painted on them: a fact, however trivial, which corroborates the belief in reports of their destination for service unusual to them.

Every thing in the Ordnance and Naval Departments has the face of preparation and hurry. No vessel arrives from any Port that is not entirely stript of its Crew by the Press Gangs. The 44 Gun Ships, which are intended for transports, are getting in readiness with more expedition than the rest of the fleet. A convoy is appointed to sail with the West India Trade on the 25th of next month. The maritime shew has become so great at Portsmouth as to attract vast multitudes to see it.

Stocks have fallen, since the 20th, to their ordinary level.

In the absence of Mr. G. Morris, I have not thought it prudent to converse with any man on the Dispositions of the Administra-tion of this Country, with respect to America. On the slightest observation, I found that neither a Treaty of Commerce, or the Delivery of the frontier Posts was ever mentioned. The reasons, which formerly operated with them on these subjects, probably still prevail. But, in truth, every other object has been totally disregarded, amidst the agitations that have been produced in men's minds by the dispute between Spain and this Country.

Mr Johnson's Commission as Consul of the Port of London is just recognised. I foresee he will have an amazing share of business and trouble in attempting to protect the American Seamen at this time. As Mr. Cutting, in his letters to you, has dwelt so fully and so pertinently on the difficulties which have attended the negotiation of this business hitherto, and has given you such authentic Documents to prove the unjust and irritating conduct practiced in particular instances; I will only add that I think his exertions in favor of his distressed Countrymen, entitle him to much credit from the Public, as well as to the sincerest thanks from the Individuals, who have been rescued from an abominable slavery by his means.

I fear, that in such a Port as London, so arduous a task will be imposed on the Consul, as must after a short time compel him to relinquish the office, unless he can in some way or another be compensated for his expences and trouble. The duties of the Consul at this Port will be widely different from, or, at least, vastly more troublesome than those of a Consul in any other, and I do not imagine the appointment will occasion any considerable encrease of commercial business, because every person who trades here has already his Correspondent or Agent, which is not the case in Ports where a new Commerce shall be undertaken. I make these observations entirely with out the knowledge of Mr. Johnson, and solely from the view in which the subject presents itself to my mind. It is true I have great personal obligations to him for his extreme attentions and politeness to me. By his assistance, I have found, in the Thames, a Brig bound to Lisbon, which is to sail the last of this week, and in which I have engaged my passage. With the highest sentiments of respect & esteem I have the honor to be, Sir Your Most obedient & Most devoted Servant,

D. Humphreys

RC (DNA: RG 59, DD); at head of text: "No. 3)"; endorsed by TJ as received 10 Jan. 1791 and so recorded in SJL. FC (same).

To David Ross

Dear Sir   Monticello Oct. 25. 1790.

I received at New York your letter inclosing your accounts, the result shewing a balance of between 4. and 500£ due from me on an account which I had been told (and, as was said, from yourself) was fully paid, shewed a necessity of examining into the subject.

I have made that examination here, where alone it could be made. Mr. Key, who delivered most of the tobaccos, has enabled me to establish them truly as to quantity and price, and Mr. Eppes has assured me by letter that nothing ever passed from him to you which could undo what Key or myself had done. On the Debtor side of the open account I re-establish money in the room of tobacco. I take the settlement and bonds of Sep. 1783. as conclusive as far as they went, and make supplementary accounts for all other articles. The result is that I owe you about 28,000 ℔ of tobacco and you owe me about £[42-7-6]. I inclose you a copy of my statement of the accounts, the preliminary explanations of which are so full that nothing need be added here. I have made them thus full, in hopes they may satisfy yourself, and if they should not, that then they may inform those who may have the settlement of this matter in my absence or any other case of accident. Mr. Key has established the information I recieve from him by oath at the foot of the original account [ren]dered him by Mr. Nicolson of their transactions. When you shall have considered this matter, I shall be glad to hear from you. I shall then be at Philadelphia, but can recieve and return communications by post. I wish a final and speedy settlement, being convinced no one will take the same trouble to understand and settle it which I will myself, and that no one desires more to do it in strict justice. Wishing to hear from you as soon as convenient I remain with great esteem Dear Sir Your most obedt. humble servt.,

TH: JEFFERSON

P.S. Be so good as to drop me a separate line immediately to Philadelphia, say whether Colo. T. M. Randolph's order on you for £42-7-6 be good. I inclose you a copy.

PrC (MHi).

From William Short

DEAR SIR   Paris Oct. 25. 1790

I have recieved within these two days your letters which came by the French Packet and those by Mr. Barrett. They are besides those mentioned in my No. 44. and postscript of to-day, of the following dates July 26. Aug. 25. and 31. Your commissions therein contained shall be punctually executed, and particularly you may assure Mr. Vernon should you see him that it will give me real pleasure to succeed in restoring his son to him. I will certainly use my utmost endeavours for it. I saw him lately at the Marquis de la fayette's, but know nothing more of him.

I am at a loss how to settle my account with Congress so as to shew the ballance due me on account of the depreciation which has for some time subsisted here and which obliges me to purchase specie at a loss. The different members of the corps diplomatique say they intend to charge this *agio* to their courts. But as the money of Congress is in Amsterdam I suppose they will settle it by their exchange with that place. I shall therefore draw off my account so as to shew the number of livres I received here and the number of florins which were paid for them at Amsterdam, and at the same time charge my salary in dollars so that Congress or the person named for settling my accounts may arrange it as they may judge proper. With respect to the account between you and me for cash paid to your Servants and other expences of a running nature of which I think I sent you a copy, they were paid in silver. My draughts were made on Amsterdam at the exchange of silver, so that the agio was included in the bill of exchange and thus paid to Mr. Grand to avoid the double trouble of purchasing it of those who sold it. The difference then however was very small. Upton was paid in the same manner for the boxes made by your order and which I have charged to you. M. de la Motte has not yet sent me the rest of your accounts for the carriages which he still has. I suppose he has detained it because he does not yet know what he shall pay for their embarkation. It was very unfortunate that they got separated from the other articles.—Petit has not yet sold the few trifling articles which still remain here and of which I sent you a list. He says he has hitherto found it impossible. I shall now sell your horses also, as I am to be so long absent from Paris. I shall be much mortified if they do not fetch what I was once offered for them. They are in perfect order, and are worth much more. Had I been to remain at Paris I should have been very glad to have paid a better price for them. I shall sell my Cabriolet horse also and expect to lose on him, as I know no person to whom I could trust him during three months, to keep him for his food.

I am sorry not to know what produced the sudden and unexpected change which took place between the 25th. and 31st. of August, and which occasions my going to pass three months at Amsterdam with the probability of performing the same journey once or twice in the interim. As far as your letters in cypher concern the person to be sent definitively to Paris it appears that no body was yet fixed on, but I observe you do not count on me as being even thought of, and of course I take it for granted that my name has never been put in the view of him who names. I readily concieve that it is a matter of much responsibility and one to which every body should be unwilling to expose themselves, and particularly for a person supposed to be intimately connected with us. How much one would chuse to commit himself in a case of this kind must depend on his own feelings, and no body certainly can complain of that tribunal. There are few things however which admit of a precise measure, and it is possible that a reserve which is perfectly justifiable might produce a different effect from what is intended. I will explain myself. I observe it is the opinion of all the Americans here (without mentioning that of the corps diplomatique and every body who speaks to me on the subject) that I shall be unquestionably appointed because say they Mr. Jefferson being at the head of the foreign department and having been in Europe his recommendation will be accepted without hesitation, and he will certainly recommend you strongly. With them I have no doubt that silence on your part would convey an idea that you do not wish. However you are not accountable for their errors. But if this should produce the same effect on the President, your known friendship for me by giving an unfavorable construction to your silence, may have a consequence that I am sure you do not wish. This consideration is suggested to me by your letters which shew me that you have never spoken of me to the President relative to this place. And when I for a moment suppose myself in his place, I feel that I should interpret the silence of a person in yours concerning one in mine by no means to the advantage of the latter. I know this is not your intention, and I am warranted in my supposition by all your letters and particularly that of *July 26 private*, as well as those you wrote in April last.—I cannot however flatter myself with the success with which you flatter me. Had I spent the last two or three years in America I should certainly have been less fit for this place than at present. And if I am now not thought of for it when the appointment is made either directly or indirectly by those to whom I am certainly better known than I can expect to be after some years residence in America, to the public at large, I can have no hopes that under other circumstances I should be thought more worthy of other places. What is still more; there are two ministers and two chargés des affaires to be named, and still you tell me 'to make up my mind on returning home' &c. If then situated as I am four other persons are to be sent out in preference to me, I may certainly suppose that it is time for me to resume an old favorite idea of mine, of returning to settle on a farm, probably in Kentuckey and living retired from public business, the rest of my life. I cannot however suppose that this is intended. I confess candidly I should feel myself mortified by such a preference being given to others, and should not consider it at all extraordinary that others should suppose (as they certainly would do) uncommon demerit on my part, since I should believe it myself.

I cannot however suppose that I should have been thus sent to Amsterdam, to go through the drudgery of learning a new lesson there, if running backwards and forwards between Paris and that place in such a season, if it were the intention of government to replace me immediately on the meeting of Congress. I cannot suppose it I say, because it strikes me as a real injustice, which I will never suppose in those from whom it comes. I do not speak of the injustice only in imposing the task mentioned above, if it were intended that another should come and reap the fruits of it, but of the situation in which it would place me. For instance having not yet recieved the letter of the Secretary of the treasury I do not know precisely what I am to do at Amsterdam, but your letter says it is to go "and possess myself of the ground." Supposing my functions to be those, and that I should be succeeded in this business at the end of that time, is there any body on earth who would not say that the first person was sent there to make a loan, not having been able to succeed, it was necessary to send a second, and this second will of course succeed in making the loans desired. My predicament will certainly in that case be an awkward one and such an one as few would chuse to be reduced to.—Still I count so much on the justice of our government to those whom they employ, that I confess I cannot apprehend any thing like this. Be it as it may I shall immediately go there and will use all the zeal of which I am master to possess myself of that business and shall be ready should it be thought proper to communicate what I may have learned to those who may be better entitled to the public confidence.—It is your mentioning nothing on this subject even confidentially, which raises those doubts in my mind. Otherwise I should have supposed it much more than probable that he who began would be allowed to finish this business. In that case however I should have added with real sincerity that I would wish to be joined by some other person. It would be better perhaps for the interests of Congress and certainly much more so for the tranquillity of my mind if employed. It is one of those commissions in which of all others perhaps, it is [. . .]¹ Pardon these details and believe me Yr. friend & servant,

W: SHORT

RC (DLC); at head of text: "*Private*"; endorsed by TJ as received 27 Jan. 1791 and so recorded in SJL.

¹ MS cropped, perhaps half a line missing.

From Madame d'Houdetot

Sannois Le 26. 8bre. 1790

Les Regrets que vous avés laissés En quittant la France sont Bien augmentés, Monsieur, depuis que nous avons perdû l'Esperance de Vous y Revoir. Les Consolations que je Recevois de Votre Bon Esprit m'y manquent infiniment. Les preuves que j'Espere de Votre Souvenir me seront une Ressource bien douce. Je Vous prie de Vouloir Bien Vous en occuper. Quelques fois j'ay Eû l'honneur de Vous Ecrire dans Votre Langue, ayant trouvé sous ma main un bon traducteur. Ce Moyen me manque Aujourdhuy. C'est dans ma langue que je puis seulement me Rapeller à Vous, Vous faire mon Compliment Bien Sincere du Mariage de Mademoiselle Votre fille, à qui je souhaite un Bonheur qui fera le Vôtre. Permettés moy de placer sous Votre protection speciale un jeune homme Dont la famille M'interesse infiniment. Plein de Bonnes Dispositions, à qui Vos avis et Votre Recommandation seront Egallement necessaires, il porte dans Votre paÿs Ce qui doit surtout y Reussir, L'amour du travail et l'intention d'une Bonne Conduite, dont son Caractere et Celuy de sa famille doit assurer. Les troubles de notre paÿs, en Derangeant toutes ses Esperances, l'ont Determiné au party qu'il prend. Il n'y a eu d'autre part que d'en souffrir et Chercher dans son travail et dans son Energie des Ressources que les Circonstances l'Empeschent de trouver icy. Je vous prie donc instament de vouloir Bien Luy procurer dans Le Vôtre tous les Moyens de Reussir qui seront en Votre pouvoir. Je le Regarderés comme un Service personel. Croyés que je n'aurais pas même tenté une Recommandation si la famille du jeune homme que je Vous Recommande n'etoit Digne à tous Egards de Vos Bontés. Permettés moy donc, Monsieur, de Le mettre sous Votre apuy et [de] Vous prier de Vouloir Bien Luy donner quelques Bons avis, plus precieux encore que tout le Reste, sur sa Conduite dans un paÿs inconnu, mais où le Merite personel et l'amour du travail ne peuvent Rester sans Recommandation. Veuillés Reçevoir, Monsieur, les assurances des Sentimens profonds et immuables que Vous m'avés inspirés. La Situation de notre paÿs n'Est encore ny heureuse ny tranquille. J'ay Bien peur que Cela ne soit Encore Long et que le Desordre ne fasse pas Encore place de sitôt à un Bien Estre qui puisse satisfaire Des Coeurs honestes et des Esprits Eclairés.

LALIVE D'HOUDETOT

RC (DLC); endorsed by TJ as received 18 Mch. 1791 and so recorded in SJL.

From Rigobert Bonne

MONSIEUR   De Paris le 27 Octobre 1790.

Je prends la liberté de vous envoyer deux exemplaires d'un petit ouvrage qui a pour titre *Principes sur les mesures*. Je vous prie d'en faire part à la société philosophique de Philadelphie, où toutes les sçiences humaines se trouvent réunies, ainsi que de la lettre que j'ai l'honneur de vous ecrire.

Ce petit ouvrage contient une mesure élémentaire qui paroît mériter attention; son origine très ancienne étoit oubliée, quoique son usage se soit propagé jusqu'à nous. Je présente ces Principes à notre assemblée Nationale qui paroît avoir indiqué pour mesure à l'Académie Royale des sciençes la longueur du pendule à secondes, ou une de ses fonctions. Mais l'Assemblée ne pouvoit pas connoître alors les fondemens stables de la mesure indiquée dans cet opuscule. Outre que la longueur du pendule à secondes est fondée sur le nombre conventionnel, 86400 secondes dans 24 heures, qui n'est pas universel, il paroît très difficile de fixer la longueur du pendule avec une certaine précision, ou de la retrouver pour la vérifier. Les differences considérables qui se trouvent dans les longueurs données par plusieurs savants le demontre assez. D'ailleurs le pendule équinoxial ne devroit-il pas être préféré à celui de 45 degrés de latitude? En cas toutefois que l'un ou l'autre puisse être choisi pour type des mesures.

La mesure elementaire que je propose dans ces Principes n'est point arbitraire, elle est fondée sur le mouvement des principaux astres et sur la longueur de l'Equateur terrestre. Son origine est très ancienne, car les Pieds les plus célèbres de l'Antiquité y sont tous enchaînés par des rapports simples. Les élemens inaltérables de cette mesure s'étoient perdus dans l'obscurité des siècles, je les ai rétablis avec précision. On se sert de cette mesure dans les plus grands états de l'Europe et de l'Asie, tels qu'en Perse, en Turquie, en Hongrie, en Russie, en Pologne, en quelques départemens de France, &c., et même le Pied de Londres en est à très peu près les six septièmes. Voilà déjà un grand pas de fait vers l'universalité de son usage. Et, dans l'intention d'unir tous les peuples par une même mesure, celle que je propose auroit en cela un grand avantage sur la longueur du pendule, qui n'est peut-être en usage nulle part.

Le Pied que je propose et que je nomme Equatorial paroît avoir toutes les qualités qu'on peut lui désirer: il est d'abord fondé dans la nature et a l'avantage de pouvoir être retrouvé facilement et dans tous les tems, il est très répandu, il est en outre contenu un nombre de fois fort commode dans le degré moyen du méridien; et, ce qui est unique et prouve son ancienneté, c'est qu'il fait retrouver par des rapports simples les principaux Pieds de l'Antiquité, comme le Pied Grec, le Pied Pythique, la coudée du Nilomètre, le Pied d'Egypte qui est la moitié de cette coudée, le Pied Alexandrin, le Pied Romain, le palme de Possidonius dans sa seconde mesure de la Terre, le Pied Philétéréen qui est précisément de la même longueur que celui qu'on a retrouvé ici, &c., &c. Et, tandis que des savans ont perdu, et perdent encore, un tems considérable à rechercher la longueur de ces Pieds, sans pouvoir toutefois la fixer avec précision, en produisant la mesure dont ils dependent, nous établissons leur longueur irrévocable de la manière la plus sûre et la plus exacte. Cela montre à quel degré cette mesure est précieuse et combien elle l'emporte sur la longueur du pendule, qui n'a pas à beaucoup près toutes ces propriétés et qu'on ne peut pas même trouver d'une manière précise. Cela vient en partie de ce que cette mesure dépend de très petits élémens, en comparaison du Pied Equatorial qui est conclu de très grandes quantités.

J'ai formé de ce Pied antique des mesures de longueurs plus grandes, comme des aunes, des brasses, des perches, &c. J'en ai déduit aussi les mesures de capacités en leur assignant la forme la plus avantageuse. J'en ai tiré enfin un mode de poids et de monnoies qui lui est également enchainé par les rapports les plus convenables. Ces differentes mesures sont tellement liées qu'avec une seule d'entr'elles on pourra toujours retrouver toutes les autres.

Je souhaite que cet ouvrage soit accueilli favorablement par la Société philosophique de Philadelphie, à laquelle aucun genre de connoissances n'est étranger ni indifferent. Et, si le changement des poids et mesures a lieu dans les Etats-unis, comme vous le laissez voir, Monsieur, je désirerois, par le sincère attachement que m'a inspiré le grand exemple de conquérir la liberté qu'a donné à l'univers le sage et courageux peuple de vos regions occidentales, je désirerois, dis-je, pouvoir y contribuer efficacement. Je suis avec un profond respect, Monsieur, Votre très humble et très obeissant serviteur   BONNE

RC (DLC); endorsed by TJ as received 18 Mch. 1791 and so recorded in SJL. Enclosure: Rigobert Bonne, *Principes sur les mesures en longueur et en capacité, sur les poids et les mon-* noies; *dépendant du mouvement des astres principaux et de la grandeur de la terre, ouvrage . . . presenté à l'Assemblée Nationale* (Paris, 1790). See Sowerby, No. 3764.

To the Governor of Georgia

SIR   Octob. 27. 1790.

I have just recieved a letter from the Governor of East Florida dated St. Augustine Aug. 18. 1790. wherein he notifies me that he has recieved the king's order not to permit, under any pretext, that persons held in slavery within the United states introduce themselves as free persons into the province of Florida. The dispositions which the Governor expresses on this, as he had done on a former occasion, to cultivate the friendship of the United states, give reason to hope he will carry this order into exact execution, and thus put an end to a grievance which had been a subject of complaint from the citizens of Georgia and of remonstrance from the general government to that of Spain. I have the honor to be with sentiments of the most perfect respect & esteem Your Excellency's most obedient & most humble servt.,   TH: JEFFERSON

RC (NNP); addressed: "His Excellency The Governor of Georgia"; franked; docketed in part: "Order taken 12 July 1791." FC (DNA: RG 59, PCC No. 120).

To José Ignacio de Viar

SIR   Monticello Octob. 27. 1790.

I am honoured here by the reciept of your favor of the 7th. instant, covering a letter to me from the Governor of East Florida wherein he informs me that he has recieved the King's orders not to permit, under any pretext, that persons sold in slavery in the United states introduce themselves, as free, into the province of East Florida. I am happy that this grievance, which had been a subject of great complaint from the citizens of Georgia, is to be removed, and that we have therein a proof as well of the general principles of justice which form the basis of his majesty's character and administration, as of his disposition to meet us in the cultivation of that mutual friendship and union of interests which would be the happiness of both countries, and is the sincere wish of ours. I have the honour to be with sentiments of the most perfect respect & esteem, Sir, Your most obedient and most humble servant,

TH: JEFFERSON

PrC (DLC). FC (DNA: RG 59, PCC No. 120).

From William Short

DEAR SIR   Paris Octob 27th. 1790

I wrote to you very fully on the 21st. and 25th. of this month, by M. de Trys who is gone to embark for America. In the latter I acknowleged the reciept of your several letters which arrived here almost at the same time although they came by different routes viz. those of Aug. 25. 26. 31. 31. by the French packet and those of July 26 pe[1] and a duplicate of the same date *pu.*[1] and Aug. 10. I mentioned at the same time that the letters from Mr. Hamilton by Colo. Humphreys had not yet been recieved. He wrote me on the 14th. of October that he was going to deposit them with Mr. Church agreeable to Mr. Hamilton's desire, and Mr. Barrett informs me that he heard Mr. Church say they had been forwarded. I begin to be uneasy at that not arriving as they must have left London before him.

This letter is to go by the English packet and of course will arrive probably before Mr. St. Trys who thinks it possible he may be obliged to wait at L'Orient for the French packet. I will therefore repeat here some parts of my letters by him. I mentioned there the troubles which had existed in the fleet at Brest. They were made the pretext of several of the committees of the assembly uniting in a report in which they propose that the assembly should declare that the ministers had lost the confidence of the nation. When the report was discussed, before being voted on, it was decided by an amendment that M. de Montmorin was not of the number of ministers designed by the assembly. The question of the adoption of the report being put, it was lost. Still it was evident that ministry would not be able to stand their ground against such a current. They wrote a letter (M. de Montmorin excepted) to the King, to offer their resignation. His answer contained flattering things for them all, with a desire that they would remain until he should make known his intentions to them. He accepted M. de la Luzerne's dismission on sunday last and named for his successor M. de Fleurieu, a man who has been long in the department of marine in different characters, and said to be well acquainted with it. There is no doubt the other ministers will resign from day to day. Their successors are not yet ascertained. Every body swears Nothing could induce him to accept a place in the ministry at this moment and yet no body refuses. The Comte de Segur was active in his endeavours to come into ministry, swearing all the time by himself and his friends, that it was the last place in the world he would accept under present circumstances. The exception in favor of M. de Montmorin destroys his pretensions. Du portail is much talked of for the war department, and what will surprize you Ternant is mentioned by some for the home department. I do not think however that he will succeed although he is well supported. The negotiations between England and Spain still continue. The report of the appearance of peace being continued, which circulated here a few days ago not being confirmed, it is probable it was groundless. The matter appears to every body here quite problematical. There are as many different opinions as there are politicians. No negotiation was ever carried on with more secrecy. The English Ambassador's children arrived here a few days ago. This is considered as a favorable symptom by many, and as a *ruse* by others.—Mr. Elliott left this place yesterday evening, and said he should return again in a very short time. He was lately minister for England at Copenhagen. His business here is I believe to treat with the diplomatick committee. You know that the assembly have named a committee for each department who exercise most of the ministerial functions.

The assembly recieved intelligence yesterday from the commissaries sent to Brest for the purpose of calming the disorders in the fleet there. They write that order is perfectly restored. This circumstance will probably have considerable influence in the negotiations now existing between England and Spain. It is certain the disorders at Brest had given very serious uneasiness to the Spanish Ambassador here, much more than even to the French themselves. It is possible however that the negotiations may have been too far advanced to admit of a change at present. I observe all parties seem sure that war or peace will have been decided on before the expiration of the month. The advanced season, and the approaching meeting of Parliament are the bases of this opinion.

I saw the Rapporteur of the committee yesterday who proposed the abolition of the *droits d'aubaine*. He told me his intention and that of the committee had been without question that it should extend to every part of the French dominions. On my mentioning to him that the term *France* was used in the decree, and that the construction hitherto put on it with respect to these *droits* excluded their foreign possessions, he told me he would immediately propose to the committee to have it explained, and that there was not the smallest doubt it would be done immediately. Still I should not be surprized if he found himself mistaken, as the dispositions towards the islands at present are exceedingly unfavorable on account of the proceedings of the assembly of St. Marc, and as a jealousy of their commercial connexions with foreigners will dispose them to preserve every regulation which tends to embarass these connexions. One may without hesitation however say that this cannot last long, and that a short time will induce this country (should its government become organised) to adopt what is prescribed by justice, hospitality, and interest.

I need not repeat here what I mentioned in my letter by M. de St. Trys that the papers contained in yours of Aug. 10. shall be made use of or not agreeably to your desire.

The Emperor of Morocco has declared war against the Spanish possessions of his coast. Hostilities have been commenced, and the Spaniards have taken several of his vessels of small force. His desire it is said is to be at war with Spain only on land, and to preserve peace at sea. This policy would suit most nations who have any thing to do with him and particularly us.

The reports of the committees of imposition and commerce, or at least such parts of them as were mentioned in my last have not been yet taken up and it is impossible to say when they will be. I think it highly probable that the prohibition mentioned in my last proposed by the latter, will not pass.

Count Du Moustier desired me to mention that he had written to the President and yourself, but had never received any answer.

He wished to know if his letters had been recieved. He expresses here in all places both publicly and privately the great advantages to be derived from opening a commercial intercourse with the United States—the necessity of doing it or of sacrificing all hopes of those of a political nature. He insists that the United States now are so different from what they were three years ago that they may be considered as entirely unknown to those who have not been there since that time. This is aimed against the Mis. de la f. He shewed me a very long letter he had written from New York in May 89. to Mr. Necker on the subject of commerce with the United States, together with his answer. The object of it was to point out the advantages of a close connexion with the United States and the means of obtaining it. Mr. Neckers answer shewed he entered fully into his sentiments but thought the then situation of France would prevent an immediate attention to that business and particularly would prevent the advances in cash which M. de Moustier proposed should be made.

The Minister[2] spoke to me to day on the subject contained in the fifth page of your letter of July 26. Upon giving the explanation you there mentioned he said he never understood it so and that he could not give an *exequatur*[1] for that place if one should be asked. I referred him to the correspondence on that subject which he said he would examine. I mentioned also the good effects with which such an appointment might be attended or rather the ill effects it might prevent. Our conversation ended there, as he was to examine the correspondence when we shall speak of it again.

M. de Bougainville is named to take the command of the fleet at Brest in the room of M. D'Albert de Rioms.—M. de la Luzerne has written a letter to the King in which he gives an account of the present situation of the marine, by which it appears that the ships capable of being put in commission are in a much greater number and much better order than had been supposed.

The *coins* of the medal you ordered some time ago are not yet finished. I am promised them now in a very short time and shall do what you desire respecting them.

The gun locks which you have so long waited for are at length sent by M. St. Trys. There is besides one for a soldiers musket, which the workman sends you as a model. The price of the six others is eight livres each.

The express which is to bring peace or war from Madrid is expected here with much impatience and anxiety. As he has been expected now for a day or two the delay begins to be considered as an unfavorable omen by those who desire peace.

I mentioned in my letter by M. St. Trys what an awkward *situation I was placed in* if the intention was *to send me to Amsterdam* merely to possess *myself* of the ground *and that* another was then to *be sent to make the loan.* It would inevitably be thought that *I had not been able to succeed* and that it has been necessary to send *another more [able]*[3] *in my place. My* situation would be the same as to this *place also as time will necessarily in[duce?]*[4] the Assembly *to change the system they are now disposed to adopt relative to some articles on which depends our commerce with them.*

I have quite lost sight of Pio since you left this place. He was recalled but refused to return to Italy, as he had reason to believe they meant to punish his democratical principles. He has become as I am told a meer fanatic for liberty, and lives in the district *des Cordeliers.* He is I believe also in the garde nationale. I have lately seen printed a deposition of his before the *committee des recherches,* in which he relates the conversations of M. de St. Priest at the Ambassador's table, to prove that he is an aristocrat and disposed to effect a counter revolution. Adieu my dear Sir and believe me with perfect sincerity, your friend & servant,

W SHORT

RC (DLC); at head of text: "*Private*"; endorsed by TJ as received 17 Jan. 1790 and so recorded in SJL, though there misdated as 27 Nov.

1 The abbreviations "pe" and "pu" refer respectively to Short's private and public letters.

2 This and subsequent words in italics are written in code and have been decoded by the Editors, employing a partially reconstructed key for Code No. 10. Short made some errors in en-coding which have been corrected. TJ began interlinear decoding of the letter and then ceased, realizing that he was employing the wrong key.

3 This word supplied. Since Short omitted the symbol for a whole word, it is plausible to assume that the one omitted was 534 [able] rather than the symbols for such a word as competent.

4 The syllable in brackets is conjectural.

To George Washington

SIR
Monticello Oct. 27. 1790.

I had intended to have set out about this time for Philadelphia, but the desire of having Mr. Madison's company, who cannot return for some days yet, and a belief that nothing important requires my presence at Philadelphia as yet, induce me to postpone my departure to the 8th. of the ensuing month, so that it will be about the 12th. before I can have the honor of waiting on you at Mount Vernon to take your commands. In the mean time the papers inclosed will communicate to you every thing which has occurred to me since I saw you, and worthy notice. Our affair with Algiers seems to call for some new decision: and something will be to be done with the new Emperor of Marocco. Mr. Madison and myself have endeavored to press on some members of the assembly the expediency of their undertaking to build ten good private dwelling houses a year, for ten years, in the new city, to be rented or sold for the benefit of the state. Should they do this, and Maryland as much, it will be one means of ensuri[ng] the removal of government thither. Candidates for the senate are said to be the Speaker, Colo. Harrison, Colo. H. Lee, and Mr. Walker: bu[t] it is the opinion of many that Colo. Monroe will be impressed into the service. He has agreed it seems, with a good deal of reluctance, to say he will serve if chosen. I have the honor to be with sentiments of the most perfect respect & attachment Sir, your most obedient & most humble servant, Th: Jefferson

[P.S. If you approve of the letters to Mr. Viar, and the Governor of Georgia, I must trouble you to throw them into the post-office.

A report of the substance of such letters, recieved since the 14th. of Sep. 1790. as the President might wish to have communicated to him.

Nathaniel Appleton. Boston Sep. 11. 1790.	accepting their
Jabez Bowen. Providence Sep. 15.	appointments as
Thomas Harwood. Annapolis Sep. 4.	Commissioners of
Thomas Smith. Phila. Aug. 27.	Loans.

Robert Morris. Brunswick. Sep. 2. Accepting commission of District judge.

Governr. Blount. Washington. Aug. 20. That he will set out on the 24th. for the ceded territory. Supposes he shall fix his residence not far from judge Campbell's, send letters for him to care of Govr. of Virga.

Dumas. May 26. Of course nothing new.

Moustier. Paris May 10. He does not know yet whether he is destined to return to America. If he did not fear the climate, which was always unfavorable to him, it is the mission he would like best.

Henry Remsen. N. York Sep. 6. That Mr. MacDonogh has presented his commission as British Consul for the four Eastern states.

The Governor of Florida. St. Augustine. Aug. 28. Acknowledging the receipt of mine of Aug. 12. and adds as follows. 'Having recieved the king's order to permit, on no account, that the slaves from the U.S. introduce themselves into this province (Florida) as free persons, I avail myself of the first occasion which presents itself to me to forward you notice of it. It seems to me useful, as well to preserve in part the interests of both parties, as that it may be a means of preventing wars, and finally shews that they are eradicating every where the remains of those laws which subsist to our shame.'

John B. Cutting. London. 1790. Aug. 11. and 12. The letters inclosed.

Gouverneur Morris. London. July 7. Letter inclosed.

Mr. Short. Paris. 1790.

May.	9.	No. 29.	Letter inclosed.
May.	11.	No. 30.	do.
May.	23.	No. 32.	do.
June.	14.	No. 33.	do.
June	25.	No. 34.	do.
June	29.	No. 35.	do.
July	7.	No. 36.	do.

RC (DNA: RG 59, MLR); at foot of text: "The President of the United States"; endorsed by Washington: "Thos. Jefferson Esq. 27th. Octr. 1790" with a list of Letters received." FC (DNA: RG 59, SDC). PrC (DLC: TJ Papers, 57: 9867 and 59: 10130-2)

From La Motte

MONSIEUR   Havre 28. octobre 1790.

Je n'ai recû qu'hier, timbrée de Paris, la Lettre que vous m'avés fait l'honneur de m'ecrire le 27. Juin. C'est un Espace de 4. mois qu'elle est restée en chemin, comme la mienne du 12. Xbre. qui ne vous est parvenuë que le 6. Avril. Il est bien malheureux que des lettres restent aussi longtems en chemin.

J'ai eû l'honneur de vous ecrire en vous envoyant vos meubles et de vous remercier de la Commission de Vice-Consul que vous voulés bien me confier; je vous prie d'en recevoir encore mes remerciments et de Compter sur mon Zèle à en bien remplir la tâche. La Commission ni les instructions ne me sont point encore parvenuës.

Nous avons toujours icy ceux de vos effets qui doivent aller

[645]

dırectement à Philadelphie. Lorsque j'aurai l'occasion de les em-
barquer, j'y joindrai quatre paniers de vin de Champagne que
M. Louis d'Aÿ m'annonce m'avoir expédiés pour vous. M. Short
nous a remboursé nos frais sur vos meubles et le Couts de ces
mêmes chiens dont vous me parlés et que je vous aı envoyés en
Janvier dernier par le brig Anglois Abigaïl, Cape. Harris, qui
alloit à New York, à l'adresse de Mrs. Adams Constable & Co.
Je juge qu'ils ne vous ont point été remis et j'en suis bien faché;
puissiés-vous seulement entretenir la race avec ceux dont vous
avés heureusement pris soin vous même.

L'Assemblée Nationale n'a encore rien décidé sur la ferme du
tabac, mais elle s'occupe en ce moment des impositions, et ce
chapitre-là sera incessamment mis sur le tapis. Elle doit maintenant
avoir réuni les avis de toutes les places de Commerce sur l'objet
du Tabac, et si Le Havre n'est pas favorable aux interets de
l'Amerique, il n'aura dependû ni de Mr. Short ni de moi de diriger
le rapport de nos representans du Commerce dans ces vuës là.

Je reçois au moment même, Monsieur, ma Commission et je
vais en solliciter l'*Exequatur* sans perte de temps, ayant deja
rencontré quelqu'Occasions où il auroit eté bien que je fusse installé.
J'attends encore les instructions d'après lesquelles je dois agir.
Mr. Short m'a dit que le Congrès s'en occupoit et je resterai impatient de les recevoir pour ne rien faire qui y soit contraire.

Le Navire qui vous portera la presente partira demain; je
comptois le charger des paquets de Mr. Short, mais il paroit qu'il
a pris une autre voye pour ce moment. Je serai par la suite en
etat de savoir et de lui dire à point nommé toutes les occasions
dont il pourra proffiter.

Je suis faché de n'avoir que très peu de papiers-nouvel[les] à
vous envoyer. Nous sommes plus que jamais dans la Crise de notre
incertitude sur la paix ou la guerre. Cependant les delais que
l'Angleterre apporte à Commencer des hostilités nous font croire
qu'elle n'a point un dessein bien arrêté d'entrer en guerre. Si les
preparatifs de toutes les puissances devoient être mis en oeuvre,
ce seroit assurement une guerre importante, et votre neutralité
seroit sans doute invoquée par plus d'une des parties belligerantes.

Permettés moi, Monsieur, de presenter mon homage à vos dames
et de me dire avec une parfaite consideration Monsieur Votre très
humble & très obeissant serviteur   DELAMOTTE

RC (DLC); endorsed by TJ as received 12 Mch. 1791 and so recorded in SJL.

From Pierpont Edwards

Sir   New Haven Octr. 28th. 1790

I do myself the honor to inclose you three Judgements of our Superior Court, in cases in which it has been contended, that the Judgements were an infraction of the treaty of peace. No. 1. Is a decree in Chancery, in which the Court determined, that no interest, during the war, was recoverable by a british subject upon a debt due from an american. No. 2. Is the case of a Refugee, in which the treaty was in vain urged against the Judgement which the Court gave. I was of Counsil for the Defendants in these two causes. No. 3. Is a case in some respects different from the other two. One of the Creditors and partners never Joined the enemy. I was of Counsil for the Defendant in this cause. I think this Judgement was wrong, even if the treaty is considered as having no effect upon questions of this kind.

I also send you a book, which contains the Laws of Connecticut, as revised and established in 1750, and all subsequent Laws to Octr. 1783 inclusive. In January 1784 the statutes were again revised. I have also contracted for a statute book, which contains the statutes of the Colony of Connecticut, as revised in 1782. I despair of finding a statute book containing the Laws antecedent to that revision.

I have found one or two books in the [hands] of gentleman who appreciate them very highly, which contain the statutes of the Colony of Connecticut, as revised in 1702, and the additional statutes for about twenty or twenty five years; but the holders could not be persuaded to part with them, insisting that I should endeavour to procure them from persons, in whose estimation, such monuments of legal antiquity would be less valuable. I will still keep the object in view, and endeavour to execute your commission in this respect also. I am with very great respect your most Obedient and very huml. servt.,

Pierpont Edwards

RC (DNA: RG 59, MLR); slightly mutilated so that one word is lost; endorsed by TJ as received 22 Nov. 1790 and so recorded in SJL.

From David Humphreys

While I am detained for the sailing of the vessel in which I am to go to Lisbon; I cannot do better, in my judgment, than to give you such farther facts, occurrences, or reports of the day, as may be in any degree interesting, in America, when compared with other accounts: though those I may have the honor to give should not be of much importance in themselves.—In my communications, I have generally distinguished things, which were derived from such authority as brought conviction of their veracity to my mind; circumstances, in support of which I named the immediate or remote Authors; and rumours of a more vague or doubtful nature. Here, from my knowledge of the Language and access to Sources of Intelligence, the materials, which (as it were) thrust themselves upon me from every quarter, are infinitely more abundant than I can expect to find them in any part of the Continent. This must be my apology for having written to you so frequently, in so short a time.

Parliament will meet on the 25th of next Month. It is composed, according to good calculations, of a rather greater number of adherents to Administration, than the last: although in the last, the majority was so decided as to enable [Ministry to] carry all their measures, even in the most critical junctures, when they were apparently on the point of losing their places, as must have been the case in the Regency business, had not the sudden recovery of the King prevented it. That crisis operated as an excellent touchstone to try the attachment of their *Supporters*. Still *Opposition* are preparing to commence the war of words against them, for their conduct in the Nootka-Sound dispute. Their demand of satisfaction previous to the settlement of the point of right; the Declaration; Counter-Declaration; procrastination before the ultimatum was brought in question; intermediate opportunity afforded to Spain for courting Alliances; and consequent leisure for Powers, hostilely inclined, to arm; will become subjects of animadversion. A Million was voted by the last Parliament to enable Government to make preparations to vindicate the honor of the Nation—More than double that sum must have been expended.— But, notwithstanding the enormous national Debt, and the heavy Burdens which the People at large are compelled to bear; yet the resource of credit and the influx of money, have crowded all the public and private

Banks with Specie, and embarrassed the great Money-holders to determine how to dispose of it. This may be [accounted] for from several causes. The Merchants of the United States, and the West India Islands have made large remittances, on account of the arrearages of their old Debts. Less capital can be employed in trade to the European Continent, by reason of the troubles there, than formerly. It is visible to every eye, that prodigious sums have been recently laid out in buildings and improvements. I believe nearly as many houses have been built in this City, within a year past, as the City of Philadelphia contains. This is the effect of a vast current which has run in favor of this Country, and stagnated here. But reasonable and well-informed men perceive, that this incidental surplusage of gold and silver would go but little way in supporting the expence of a war, at a distance. They say, that, flowing from the country in a direct stream, it would all be drained in two or three years: and that a war of that duration would be, beyond conception, ruinous to the nation. Other Classes, such as Merchants and decent citizens, who are zealous advocates (without much general knowledge) for the glory of Great Britain, warm themselves to a great degree of enthusiasm, by conversing on the subjects of its resources and prowess: especially in their blustering anticipations of capturing the *Dons* and the *Dollars*. Some of these appear to me to talk in this style [ra]ther because it is fashionable to talk [in] it, than because they credit their own observations; and even endeavour to persuade others what they do not believe themselves. It is thus that the bubble is not only kept up; but blown to still greater dimensions. Men, here, seem to have an interest as well as propensity to deceive one another. On the system and operation of the national credit I could not say any thing that would be new to you. It would be superfluous to observe, how it has arisen to its present wonderful height, partly by chance and partly by the sacred appropriation of funds to pay the interest of the debt; or how public and private Bank notes have encreased almost beyond the limits of credibility, how much the multiplied representation of property has facilitated the intercourse of business—or what serious disadvantages are to be expected hereafter from this immense paper circulation. It is evident there is a point (though often mistaken and hitherto unascertained) beyond which ability or credulity cannot go. Of little avail would all the artificial means which could be devised be, in keeping up the Stocks; if a superior hostile fleet should have the possession of the Channel, so that Bodies of Troops might be landed, with [impunity] in this Kingdom. Events of this kind, by no means [impossible], would shake the almost baseless fabric of credit to its very [Center].

Nothing new has occurred in this Kingdom, since [my] letter of the 25th, except the sailing of Admiral [Cornish], the day before yesterday, from Portsmouth, with four 74. two 64 Gun Ships, and a Frigate. The business of Government is conducted with so much secrecy, that it is not known whether he has gone on an expedition, or is to wait in the Channel to take transports or merchantmen under Convoy. When Lord Howe went out of Port some time ago, it was merely to try the Crews of the different Ships. Many of which now lye at a single anchor, completely ready for Service.

The precipitancy and extravagance of some of the monied Men, who have undertaken to raise independent Companies, have encreased the expences of raising Recruits to fifteen Guineas pr man. This circumstance, and the orders issued from the war office, a day or two since, making the Captains responsible for supplying the place of such Recruits as may desert, even after their arrival at the Rendezevous, but before the Companies shall be finally mustered, have occasioned thirty Captains to return their *Beating Orders.*

The King of Great Britain, whose health appears to be confirmed, has this day reviewed the Brigade of Guards, consisting of the 1st Battery of each of the three Regiments, destined for foreign Service. I was in a position to see them to good advantage. The crowd of Spectators was numerous beyond what I ever witnessed before in my life. The King [was] received with the greatest marks of loyalty, or, as one might truly say, with tokens of respect approaching to Idolatry. When Mr. Pit appeared a few of the Populace cried out "no Pit"—"no Pit"—"Fox forever"—But a more vociferous acclamation arising in his favor soon overcame the first cry: and he was attended out of the Park by a great number huzzaing, "Pit forever."

The Troops are composed of fine men, and are well-appointed. Their destination still a secret. In case of war, it will most likely be the post of enterprize and glory; though Gibralter has been much spoken of. Those who have concluded that they were to replace a part of the Garrison of Gibralter (intended for the West Indies) are probably erroneous in their conjectures; because the rank of the Officers of the Guards being higher in the Line of the Army than in their own Corps, would occasion both uneasiness and inconvenience, if they should be brought to do Garrison duty with the marching Regiments. Besides it is not probable Government would shut up in that honorable Prison (for such a narrow, dreary rock must be) so many Officers of the first families in the Kingdom, and Troops which one supposed to possess a more than common share of ardor for active Service. It is curious to remark the pride the People take in their *King and in his Troops*. As the Inhabitants of great Cities are commonly acquainted with nothing beyond the small space they have seen, and are the more ignorant in proportion to the greatness of those Cities, I have no doubt, that the greater part of the Spectators, believed these Troops in conjunction with those of their Prussian Ally, capable of carrying conquest wherever they shall go. Indeed it is not uncommon to hear men of respectability talk of this Nation and Prussia, as having dictated the Convention of Reichenbach, and being at this moment the Arbiters of Europe.

In my way from the Park I saw Mr. Church, who is much connected with great men in the *Opposition*, and a Member of Parliament himself. He still thinks there will be a war, and that the event cannot be kept in suspense after the return of the Messenger, who went to Madrid on the 3d of this month. Others holds a contrary language.

Mr. Grenville, who has been absent for a fortnight (at what place the Public knows not) is just returned to Town. It is asserted, in the News Papers, he has been at Paris. This is among the rumours, which, from the active character of the man, are probable enough; yet not to be relied upon. The absurdity and falsehood of many articles inserted in the Papers here, should teach us to doubt the truth of every thing we find in them. Two remarkable instances have [happened since my arrival. The one, an] account, universally credited for some days, that the Parliament of Toulouse had been massacred to a man—the other, that two Spanish armed vessels, which had been at Philadelphia and engaged hands to man them at an extravagant rate, were seen boarding an English ship in the Delaware; that this account was brought by a vessel lately arrived in Dublin, and confirmed by a Gentleman in Town who left America in July (the time when the affair was said to have happened). This appeared in the Ministerial Gazettes, and is uncontradicted.

Warm Debates have taken place, on the 20th of this month, in the National Assembly at Paris, on the question of requesting the King to remove his Ministers. An exception was finally made in the motion in favor of the Compte de Montmorin. Thus amended it was lost by a majority of about sixty. The reason assigned for bringing forward this business, was the dilatoriness of Administration in complying with the Order for fitting out a naval armament. That reason shews the National Assembly are in earnest in taking measures to support Spain. Great want of subordination exists among the Officers and Crews of the fleet at Brest. Some Resolutions have been passed for appointing Commissioners to assist in quieting disturbances there; for changing the white Flag for the national Colour; and for giving for the watch-word, instead of "vive le Roi"—"vive la Nation, la loi, et le Roi." The Compte D'Estaign is appointed to command the naval Armaments. The appointment is reported to be popular. There is a prospect that order will be re-established.

Official advice is said to be received here, that the French are, likewise, diligently employed in fitting for sea several Ships of war at Toulon.

Many terrible consequences have been foretold here as the inevitable result of a total failure of credit in France. Ruin has been predicted. A Counter revolution is still threatened, and the detail of its intended operations disclosed. The Politicians on this side of the Channel forget, in their speculations, how many men are actually armed and zealously attached to the success of the Revolution, because they are gainers by it; and how much property there is in that Nation. Since the *Assignats* were put in circulation there, the Exchange here has become rather more favorable to France, than it was before. The best informed Englishmen appear to believe, although this paper money may be pernicious in its consequence to Individuals and although it may operate as an unhandy machine in drawing forth the resources of the Country; yet, that, considering the foundation on which it is placed, must become a tolerably good substitute for Specie, [and] enable the Kingdom to make great exertions of strength. The Crops are said to have been very [good] in France this year.

A *report* prevails that the French Ministry, in consequence of the Proceedings of the National Assembly have, since the 20th, resigned.—I forbear to add others, as I know you will receive authentic, and, perhaps, earlier information from Mr Short.

I never was more impatient to leave any place, than I am to depart from this. The reasons for my reaching my ultimate destination grow every day more numerous and pressing. Hitherto I have not heard that any farther notice has been taken of me, than the frequent mention of my name at the New York Coffee House, with speculations on the cause of my coming here, at this time. I have as much as possible shunned all public Places and Coffee Houses, and shall consider myself peculiarly fortunate in departing without farther observations on myself or my business.

In the mean time, with every sentiment of consideration I tender the homage of the profound respect with which, I have the honor to be, Sir Your most obedient and very humble Servant,

D. HUMPHREYS

P.S. Octr. 29th. Since concluding this letter, the report of the resignation of the French Ministers gains credit.

RC (DNA: RG 59, DD); at head of text: "No. 4)"; endorsed by TJ as received 11 Feb. 1791 and so recorded in SJL; MS is torn and some words have been inserted from FC (same).

To James Brown

DEAR SIR   Monticello Oct. 29. 1790.

Your several favors of Aug. 30. Sep. 24. Oct. 7th. and 8th. have been duly received, together with the articles thereon noted to have been sent. The French brandy and the Lisbon wine both tapped by the waggoners, tho' the latter was in a double cask. They knocked out the head of the outer one. I will leave directions with Colo. Nicholas Lewis, who superintends my affairs, to make paiment of my account as soon as he can get money for the present crop. Probably it will be June or July first.

I have received information from France that the National Assembly, tho' disposed to suppress the Farms of tobacco do not think it safe to add that innovation to the many they have made at this moment. Their decree was not yet finally rendered but was to be soon. This assuring the Farmers general of their ground, and their stores of tobacco so low that early in the ensuing summer they will not have a single hhd. according to what they told me, they must soon come forward with a demand for 20. or 30,000 hhds. They cannot buy it however but after it shall have arrived in France, *directly* from the U.S. and in *French or American bottoms*. Such is their law on that subject, consequently individual merchants, French or American will have the purchases here. I set out for

Philadelphia the next week. I am Dear Sir with great esteem Your friend & servt., TH: JEFFERSON

Tr (DLC).

To Reuben Lindsay

DEAR SIR   Monticello Oct. 29. 1790.

On further examination of my papers, I find the inclosed as also a note in my memorandum book that Nov. 29. 1773 I recieved 50/ to act as arbitrator. Your letter to me suggests a possibility that our award may have been entered of record, and of course may be found there. But I cannot recall to my memory any part of the transaction with certainty. Perhaps these papers may enable you to give the particulars to Mr. Mercer so far as to enable him to recollect what passed. I am sorry that the infidelity of my own memory should render me so unable to serve justice on this occasion. I am with great and sincere esteem Dear Sir Your friend & servt.,   TH: JEFFERSON

PrC (ViU); badly blurred; at foot of text: "Colo. Lindsay."

From William Short

DEAR SIR   Paris Octob. 30. 1790

I wrote you the day before yesterday by the way of the English Packet. This will not arrive in time for that conveyance unless the English Ambassador should send off a courier for London this evening, in which case I shall ask the favor of him to forward it. It is merely to inform you and to beg you to inform the Secretary of the Treasury that I have recieved at length his letters of Aug. 29. and Sep. 1. They were sent to me last evening by M. de Montmorin; so that it appears Mr. Church had put them into the hands of the French Ambassador at London who must have forwarded them here. I know not why they were so long on the way, as Mr. Barrett who arrived here six days ago told me he heard Mr. Church say he had already forwarded them. The several papers which the letter of Sep. 1. mentioned containing, were recieved also inclosed. They were accompanied by a duplicate of your letter of Aug. 31. which I had previously recieved with several others by the way of the French Packet. I acknowleged their reciept in my two last of the 25th. and 27th. inst.

I will ask the favor of you also to mention to the Secretary of the Treasury that I shall write to him immediately on my arrival at the place of my destination. I am preparing to set out immediately, and shall go with much more pleasure since the uncertainty which I mentioned to you in my last letters as being disagreable, is now removed. I cannot help confessing that this gives me great hopes of another uncertainty of a more permanent nature being also removed in a manner agreeable to my wishes after December next.

No new circumstance has turned up in the negotiations between England and Spain that we know of, since my last. The return of the courier, who it is not doubted will decide of peace or war, is expected with much anxiety. His delay may proceed in some measure from the present indisposition of the King of Spain occasioned by a fall from his horse.

Baron de Blome never heard of the person you mention. He tells me he shall write immediately to inquire about him, and desired me to present you assurances of his attachment. This is frequently done also by your other acquaintance of the corps diplomatique here.

Should you see Mr. Vernon who will probably be anxious to hear about his son, I will thank you to mention to him that I have seen him and spoken with him about his return to America. He declares to me his real anxiety to be there and assures me he will set off in five or six days for Bordeaux and from thence by the first vessel that sails. Mr. Appleton who is his friend assures me he is in earnest. His father sent a bill of exchange of fifty pound sterling to enable him to leave Paris. By Mr. Appleton's advice I am to give him only the half of it here, and to inform him that the other half will be deposited with Mr. Fenwick at Bordeaux to pay his expenses there, and his passage, or a part of it.

I shall have a private conveyance for writing to you by a person who leaves this place in two days to embark at Havre for America. That will be the last letter that I shall write you before I leave Paris. I am with the most affectionate sentiments, your friend & servant,   W: SHORT

RC (DLC); at head of text: "*Private*"; endorsed by TJ as received 23 Jan. 1791 and so recorded in SJL.

Joseph Fenwick wrote TJ acknowledging his letter of 31 Aug. 1790 enclosing one from William Vernon of Newport about his son. He said that Short had seen young Vernon and reported that the latter would soon leave for Bordeaux and America, adding: "If Mr. Short can prevail on him to leave Paris and come as far as this, think there is no doubt but he may be induced to imbark for America, either by pursuation or stratagem. I shall willingly advance for any expences necessary to effect that purpose, and remembering your hint, avoid going any further" (Dupl., unsigned, in DNA: RG 59, CD, dated at Bordeaux, 4 Nov.

1790, endorsed by TJ as received 11 Aug. 1791; entry in SJL indicates that RC was received 15 Jan. 1791).

It was by Hamilton's instructions that Humphreys delivered his letters of 29 Aug. and 1 Sep. 1790 to John Barker Church. Barrett, who carried TJ's dispatches, could have carried these as well. The delay meant that possibly the British and certainly the French governments possessed the contents of these letters.

To Mary Jefferson Bolling

DEAR SISTER   Monticello Oct. 31. 1790

Being to set out for Philadelphia this week, I cannot take my departure without expressing to you my disappointment in having been unable to see you during my stay in the state. I was once obliged to go as far as Richmond, but my business here permitted only four days for that journey. I had hoped that a contract I had negotiated between Colo. T. M. R. and his son, had secured Edgehill as a settlement for the latter, but the father has since repented and wishes to be off which a son cannot refuse. We are yet to see what has been the motive. Mr. Randolph will now endeavor to buy some of Mr. Carter's land, most of which is for sale to pay his unfortunate concern with the Trents. In every event they will move here, perhaps for some years. The only advantage my present office offers is that of coming once a year to see my family and affairs. Perhaps the next year I may be able to pay you a visit. Present me affectionately to Mr. Bolling and your children, with wishes for their health and happiness. Accept the same for yourself from dear sister your affectionate brother,

TH: JEFFERSON

PrC (MHi).

To Francis Eppes

DEAR SIR   Monticello Oct. 31. 1790.

I set out for Philadelphia this week, and shall hope to recieve Jack there ere long. I shall not be housekeeping till I recieve my furniture from France. But that may be hourly expected, as it was to leave Paris the middle of July. I will write to you on my arrival at Philadelphia, or as so[on] after as I get my house ready, that Jack may come for[ward.] I hope you will let me know what course you would rather prefer for him.—As Mr. Ross sent his accounts thro' you, I trouble you to pass mine on to him. I leave them open for your perusal, and when perused, be so good as to stick a wafer in them, and send them to him by the first very safe hand. There is no article in my statement that is not solidly vouched. One only may perhaps be modified. That is the charge of 2883. ℔ tobacco for short credit. That object is so entangled that I am not able to satisfy myself about it. It may, if wrong, reduce the balance due from Ross to me, to about £200. which set off against the tobacco balance I owe him of 23,000 ℔. will make us even.— Pray Dobson to have mercy, and forbearance, and to push Mr. Bannister's representatives as much as possible. Mr. Dunbar assured me it should be the very first debt paid: and [it] would distress me extremely to find any other fund for the paiment of Mr. Dobson.—Tho' I believe that I might possibly make out Jones's debt by the sale of my Cumber[land] and Elkhill lands, and two or three more favourable crops, yet to relieve my mind, I think, on further consideration I shall sell 1000£ worth of negroes this time twelvemonth.—If tobacco is below 25/ this year, I determine to ship my Albemarle crop to James Maury. Our neighbors here ship to him every year, and he has never given them less than £15. to £19. for the tobacco made on our red land. He knows it's quality so well, that he buys a good deal here himself.—My Bedford tobacco fired so much that I fear it would not do to ship.—I do not think it possible the chancellor should touch the interest due us in Cary's bill. There is no circumstance, I think, which can give him foundation to do it.—Mr. and Mrs. Randolph join me in affections to yourself and family. They will be happy to see you at Monticello. I am dear Sir Your affectionate friend & servt.,

TH: JEFFERSON

P.S. I leave a charge with Mr. Lewis to remit you the amount of the bills (£ 19-6-10) which you have been so good as to pay for Polly. He will do it of the first proceeds of the crop.

PrC (CSmH).

To Elizabeth Wayles Eppes

DEAR MADAM   Monticello Oct. 31. 1790.

Being to set out for Philadelphia this week, I cannot take my departure without bidding you Adieu by letter. I had much wished it could have been in person, but my occupations here during my stay did not permit it. I had hoped that a contract I had procured between Colo. T.M.R. and his son had secured to the latter Edgehill for a settlement. But some subsequent motives have rendered the former so desirous of getting off the bargain, that a son cannot refuse to permit it. I suspect it is to gratify some other purchaser, which time will shew if true. At present I hardly expect Mr. Randolph will have it. If not, he will try to purchase of Mr. Carter who wishes to sell a great part of his land here to pay his debts. In any event Patsy will remain here. The solitude she will be in induces me to leave Polly with her this winter. In the spring I shall have her at Philadelphia if I can find a good situation for her there. I would not chuse to have her there after fourteen years of age.—As soon as I am fixed in Philadelphia, I shall be in hopes of receiving Jack. Load him on his departure with charges not to give his heart to any object he will find there. I know no such useless bauble in a house as a girl of mere city education. She would finish by fixing him there and ruining him. I will enforce on him your charges and all others which shall be for his good. Adieu my dear Madam Your's affectionately

                                                          TH: JEFFERSON

PrC (ViU).

From James Maury

Liverpool, 1 Nov. 1790. Wrote him on 9 Sep. and on 25 Oct. received TJ's letter of 26 Aug. Will pay particular attention to instructions and conform to them "as nearly as in my Power." For some months they had expected to be relieved of the suspense "relative to the War with Spain. But now the warlike preparations, already so great, continuing to augment, the prevailing Opinion of the Day seems better founded than any preceding that the Determination will be known within ten or fourteeen days. The Bounties to Seamen which were to have ceased the 31st Ulto. are continued two Months longer. —The abundant Crops of Wheat in this Country reduce the prices so that I have Reason to expect all the ports of the Kingdom will very shortly be shut against the Admission of all foreign wheat at the low

Duties.—Previous to the Aprehension of War with Spain, the American Bottoms had the preference in this port for carrying to the United States, but ever since that period they have enjoyed these Advantages almost exclusively."

RC (DNA: RG 59, CD); endorsed by TJ as received 17 Jan. 1791 and so recorded in SJL.

To Wilson Cary Nicholas

DEAR SIR   Monticello Nov. 1. 1790.

The bearer hereof Majr. Faire is the person whom Mr. Madison and myself mentioned as proposing to set up a glass manufactory. We had recommended James river to him. In passing thro' Culpeper however he had almost or even quite determined to fix there: induced principally by the offers of credit for their provisions, for the expence of first establishment being great, and their capital not so, they are obliged to attend to small advantages. I have re-impressed on him the advantages of James river, for navigation, cheapness of land, plenty of provision and persons as able to credit for provisions, and who will be as anxious to accommodate them as any in the state. Add to this a greater interest in the assembly from whom they are to ask privileges. Majr. Powell, who is with him, has lands in Culpeper and had offered some advantages to the establishment there. He is candid and acknowledges the superiority of James river in every point of view. I take the liberty of presenting him to your civilities, and the other, with his designs to your patronage, and am with great respect & esteem Dear Sir your most obedt. humble servt.,

TH: JEFFERSON

PrC (MHi).

From William Tatham

DEAR SIR   1st. Novr. Richmond

Colol. Monroe will afford me an Opertunity of sending a Power in the buisiness of my Map; and I allso take the liberty of sending one for Mr. Short, and one for Mr. Skipwith: leaving the Propriety of forwarding them to Your own choice.

Conscious how much the Public concerns must engage Your

Attention; I wish it to be understood that I am not solicitous to intrude my private buisiness on Your Time. Nevertheless I am anxious for Your Patronage, well knowing the advantage of Your approbation in forwarding a Work of such Magnitude and Public Utility.—If Mr. Jeffersons leisure, or situation, shou'd bring a Subscription in the Way of any Gentleman who might not otherwise meet with an opertunity my intentions will be answer'd. If not, or if wholy Neglected; no offence will be taken, or appology necessary.

Govr. Randolph did me the honor to convey a Line to Colo. Monroe, requesting The loan of my Sketch of The Holston Country to refresh my Memory of those parts.

Colol. M. did not think himself Authorised to lend in Your absence. If this can be spared or anything else that can be of Service in My Work, it will be thankfully receivd, and carefully return'd. All the Authorities You mentiond are in my possession, and many More equally Valuable.

I expect a Comittee of the House will be appointed to day for the purpose of inspection, and no time or pains shall be lost on my Part to render the Whole as Minute as possible.

I have done about Ten days Work on the Scale You reccomended; This will be a saleable one, but none less than the other can be renderd truely usefull in the *Great* World. I have the honor to be Dr Sir Yrs.   WM TATHAM

RC (MiU-C); endorsed by TJ as received 14 Dec. 1790 and so recorded in SJL.

Tatham's letter of 1 Nov. 1790 to the Speaker of the House of Delegates was referred that day to the committee on propositions and grievances. Henry Lee reported for the committee that Tatham's map of the southern part of the United States had been executed "in a very neat and correct manner," that it merited patronage, that his circular should receive attention, and that an appropriation in support of the undertaking should be made. The House agreed to the first three of these propositions but not to the last (JHD, Oct. sess., 1828 edn., p. 29, 48-9, 148).

To John Harvie, Jr.

DEAR SIR   Monticello Nov. 2. 1790.

Having had occasion to go to Richmond soon after my arrival here, I took with me the papers relative to the 490. as. of land, in hopes of seeing you there and settling that question. But you were gone to Caroline. Being now near my departure, I see no prospect of settling it before my return, the epoch of which is uncertain. I cannot help thinking but, were we to meet, we could convince one another: for both of us are capable of understanding the law, and neither would wish to oppose it. You cite the acts of assembly May 1779. c. 12. sect. 3. and 10. and Oct. 1779. c. 27. sect. 3. But be pleased to observe that of these it is only 1779. c. 12. sect. 3. which concerns our case, as relating to orders of council *not carried into execution by actual survey*: of which description mine was. Sect. 10. of the same act and sect. 3. of the October act relate only to orders of council *carried into execution by actual survey*. The law keeps these two descriptions perfectly separate and clear. It abolishes those *not surveyed* ipso facto, and totally: those *surveyed* it orders to be laid before the court of appeals to be decided on by them. I admit then that all orders of council, prior to 1779. *not surveyed*, were abolished by the act of May 1779. c. 12. sect. 3. and that mine was consequently completely abolished. [This general abolition was the basis of Mr. Mason's plan to get all the large grants out of the way, and he could not find a just discrimination between orders on the Eastern and Western waters, so as to condemn the latter only and leave the former subsisting. But so great was the clamour against abolishing orders of council on the Eastern waters against which there were no objections either of justice or policy, merely to countenance such an abolition on the Western waters where policy, either public or private, called for it, that the assembly in 1781. by their act c. 29. sect. 8. as completely re-established all orders of council, *on the Eastern waters*, not precluded from revival by entries or surveys made during their abolition. This revived my order of council so clearly, that I am at a loss to guess the objection to it.

Again, consider my right under the two entries of 1774 which were subsidiary to the order of council both as to title and quantity, for it was suggested there was more than 1000 acres. The act of ass. of May 1779, c.12. sect. 2. required the surveyors to survey *all entries on the Eastern waters* which had not been surveyed (of which description mine was) within 3. months, and declared that the party attending and complying with the regulations there specified, should be entitled to a grant. This term of 3. months was prolonged by subsequent acts till the assembly of 1781. impressed by the injustice of requiring surveyors to do in 3. months what was impossible to be done in many counties in 10. years, and by the public clamour against so wanton an ex post facto violation of private rights, by their same law c. 29. sect. 7. gave an indefinite time to their completion, only enjoining on the surveyors all practicable dispatch. Here then my entries, which from the 'failure of the surveyor, either wilful or involuntary,' as the act expresses it, had been in jeopardy, were placed again on just, reasonable, and safe ground. Neither before nor since this act was there ever a moment's failure on my part. I constantly pressed the surveyor to survey, which he postponed till he could have time to search out Colo. Randolph's line on which I was to bound. As soon as my back was turned, that is the next month ensuing my departure for Congress and Europe, he was induced by Mr. Marks, on what motives I have no opportunity of knowing, to survey 490 acres for him under a junior entry, and it was not till 5 years after that he would survey mine, and then he finds only 485. acres for me, tho' I was entitled to 1800 if there were so much. He sais in his justification in a letter to me of Jan. 10. 1790 that 'Mr. Marks assured him the land would be given up on my making it appear that my claim was prior.' He knew that it was prior, as well as Mr. Marks, but it was intended to effect by a juggle what could not be effected by law, and what the law will condemn now that it has been effected.]¹ On this view of my right then under the entries I cannot see an objection that can be raised. Yet, my dear Sir, if you can make any which are solid, I shall be ready to yeild to them. If we should stumble, in the course of our discussion, on any part of the law which we understand differently, we shall at least by discussion have brought the matter to it's true point, and that we will refer to the arbitration of any of the judges. You say my entries were not sufficiently special. Yet certainly they do apply exactly to the lands in question, and to no other spot of land on the globe. The order of council indeed mentions more of the landholders to whom these vacant lands were contiguous: but this was not necessary. It was never required to name all the contiguous landholders, nor any given proportion of them. Such an enumeration was mere surplusage, and the omission of a surplusage never vitiates. I have never seen Mr. Marks's entry. Perhaps that has not pretended to enumerate all the contiguous landholders. Can you take the trouble of writing to me at Philadelphia to see if we can agree ourselves whose is the right, or otherwise know the point on which it is to hang, that that may be ready for arbitration the first visit I make to this country?

My letters from thence may give you news. From this place you will expect none. I have only to add therefore assurances of the unalterable esteem with which I am Dear Sir Your affectionate friend & servt,

TH: JEFFERSON

PrC (MHi); extremely blurred, but text has been verified from a subsequent Tr (MHi) in TJ's hand (which varies as indicated below in note 1) and from a 19th-century Tr (ViU) in the hand of an amanuensis.

1 At this point in TJ's Tr the passage in brackets (supplied) is omitted. In its place is the following (including brackets): "[here followed in this letter a discussion of the effect of the acts. But as the whole substance of it is presented in a subsequent paper, and some additional considerations, the trouble of copying and reading this part of the letter may be saved. It proceeds thus]." On the tract in dispute, see TJ to Harvie, 11 Jan. 1790; see also TJ to Bryan, 6 Jan. 1790.

From David Humphreys

SIR   London Nov. 2nd. 1790

The vessel, in which I have engaged my passage, attempted to go down the river at the time appointed: but contrary winds have prevented, so that she cannot before this evening reach Gravesend. For which place I shall proceed immediately by land.

I have the honor to enclose a Paper containing a translation of the Correspondence between the King of France and his Ministers, consequent to the Proceedings of the National Assembly of the 20th of October; and which correspondence gave rise to the reports of their resignation, mentioned in my last.

Before I left this for the Continent, I intended to have stated some facts relative to the Commerce between the U.S. G. Britain, and particularly respecting the fishers of the latter. But my time has been so short, and my opportunities of gaining good information on these heads so few, that I dare not hazzard the imperfect remarks I had collected:—especially as Mr. Johnson, in his double capacity of Consul and Merchant, must be able to give you much clearer Statements, and more authentic Documents. I will only ask your indulgence for a few detached hints.—All articles which one purchases here by retail, I know by experience, are raised 25 pr Cent by the rumours of, and preparations for war. The favorable manner in which the expectation of war and the augmentation of the premium of Insurance affect the American Shipping, is very apparent. The value of some Commodities of the U.S. is likewise much enhanced by the trouble in the North of Europe; as for example, the demand for and price of pot and pearl ashes. In the year past, the Merchants of America have derived unusual emoluments from the rate of Exchange between that Country and this: and I was glad to find, a much smaller number of Bills (drawn in the midst of the high prices of wheat) have gone back protested, then could possibly have been expected.—The Irish are apprehensive that an Embargo will be laid on the exportation of salted Provisions; in which case, they foretell that the U.S. will supply those Markets where they have been accustomed to vend that Staple Article, and that, the U.S., having once taken the trade from Ireland, will forever keep possession of it, to the utter ruin of that devoted Country. Indeed, it appears to me, if our Countrymen could once gain the point, by Contract or otherwise, of supplying the French and other Navies with salted Provisions, they would not easily, or, by an ordinary competition, lose that advantage. Such a Market, well-opened, would be a great resource of wealth to the eastern and middle States. Some of which produce no other article, by any means, equal in its extent or value. Even the Western Settlements might hereafter profit by driving their Beef-Cattle to Sea-ports for exportation.

In general, I have said nothing of the Irish, because their Politics, notwithstanding the independent Spirit that reigns among individuals, follow exactly those of the English Cabinet.

The Prince de Ferstenbourg has arrived here as Ambassador Extraordinary from the Emperor to announce, in form, to this Court, the election and coronation of that Sovereign. And, as a ludicrous contrast, about the same time, Six Cherokee Chiefs arrived at the office of the Secretary of State; as Ambassadors from a Nation, which (according to the English printed annunciation) has 20,000 men in arms ready to assist G. Britain against Spain. Nor is this force all—they have 30,000 more capable of being called into immediate Service; besides Alliances with several other formidable Tribes, from which astonishing aid is expected. This account, preposterous as it is, which has run through all the Papers, is very well calculated for this meridian of political Ignorance; and you will readily recollect, is in the same style with the menaces of Russian auxiliars, who were to demolish the poor Americans at a blow, in the late war. These Indians (the same, I imagine, who were at Halifax when I left America) have come in a lucky time for themselves, to receive presents, and to be courted by great attentions. They were brought on shore at Portsmouth by the Admirals' Barge, and will be entertained in a very expensive manner. They are attended by one Bowles, who according to the best of my recollection, was sent from New Providence, two or three years ago, by Lord Dunmore with arms and horse-furniture for a Regiment, and with a few men to aid him in spiriting up the Savages bordering on the frontiers, to commit hostilities against the People of the U.S.—Governor Walton, at Augusta, last fall, put into my hand a letter from the Spanish Governor of the Floridas to the Executive of Georgia, giving a narrative in detail of the transactions and projects of this same Bowles. I think a Copy of that Communication is in the war office; and that Mr. Baldwin, a Representative in Congress from Georgia, can give farther accounts of this adventurer.

Of foreign News we have little that is important; if we except an uncredited whisper, that a Change has taken place in the Spanish Ministry.

In France some good friends to the Revolution begin to fear that the peccant humours of the State have arisen to such a height, that it will be necessary to let them off by bleeding, either in a civil or foreign war.—Much to be depricated as both sides of the alternative are, if either be inevitable, the latter is doubtless to be preferred. Here the Paragraphists and minor Politicians keep repeating projects of a Counter-revolution, and accounts of disorders committed there. But were the barriers of order in one Government broken down to make room for the substitution of those of another, in this Country, inconceivably greater enormities would be perpetrated. Revolution is a civil game there, to what it would be here. A Class of People here, and no inconsiderable one in point of numbers, is ripe for every scene of horrors. There are now upwards of 2000 Convicts ready for transportation to Botany-Bay. Yet the number of Desperadoes, and the instances of outrages against Society seem not to be diminished, by these means, or by the bad Subjects, who are engaged for the Navy and Army. Several intentional fires have lately happened in this Metropolis; and two days ago four Men were convicted of having been instrumental in them, for the sake of plunder. Here Man, from want, depravity and despair, wars against humanity. It seems to me, in passing the streets, eagerness and distrust are often painted on the countenances of the multitude. This is the Nation from whose morals and connections the U.S. are happily separated. —But in forming a general estimate of the degeneracy of character, I advert to very different Classes, and different circumstances, from those I have mentioned. It would take up too much time, as well as be foreign to my duty to enter into that discussion. With sentiments of the highest esteem & respect I have the honor to be Sir, Your most obedient & Most humble Servant,

D. HUMPHREYS.

RC (DNA: RG 59, DD); at head of text: "(No. 5)"; endorsed by TJ as received 4 Jan. 1791 and so recorded in SJL. FC (DNA: RG 59, DD).

Humphreys was correct in assuming that the Indians in London were the same as those that had appeared at Halifax. They were led by William Augustus Bowles (1763-1805), an unscrupulous adventurer who served in the Maryland Loyalist Regiment during the war, being cashiered at Pensacola in 1778 and then, having been reinstated, lived as a half-pay officer among the Creeks. Bowles' adventures and international intrigues are so hidden in the archives and in the murky depths of his own character that scholars are in doubt about his ultimate aim. He may have intended to establish an independent state or to throw his influence to Spain or to England. His main object probably was to serve himself first of all and to identify himself with whatever side promised to aid him in this, though there is no evidence that he was ever friendly toward the United States. In the present instance he took a small party of Creek and Cherokee Indians from the Bahamas in May 1789, intending, so he said, to go to England. In July 1790 he and his party turned up in Quebec, claiming that McGillivray had lost influence among the Indians, being suspected of holding a commission from the Spanish government, and that he himself had been deputed to convey an address to the crown. Bowles addressed himself to Dorchester, stating that the Indians were alarmed by recent actions of Spain, and that they held the Americans as their enemies. He also stated that the Creek and Cherokee tribes had enrolled some 20,000 fighting men, that his embassy to England would determine the manner in which the Indians would act in future, and that British "interest in that Country will be either entirely lost or permanently fixed" by the outcome. Clearly Bowles, after wandering around for a year, had leapt into action when the Nootka Sound crisis brought the possibility of war, though he told Dorchester he had come to Canada to offer his services after learning of a rumored attack by Americans on the western posts. Dorchester was skeptical and told Bowles that he could neither advise him to proceed to England nor to return home. He also pointed out very bluntly that the adventurer had "chosen to come [to Quebec] very much out of his way, without producing any Authority, and without assigning any satisfactory reason"; that if the attack had taken place when he heard the rumor in the Bahamas in 1789, the fate of the posts would have been decided before his arrival; that even if he had arrived in time, his presence in Canada could have been of no service either to Great Britain or "to the Nations, of whom he stiles himself the Representative"; and that if Dorchester had had any business to conduct with the Creek and Cherokee tribes, he possessed means of carrying it on and "could not by any means have employed Mr. Bowles for that purpose." He also told Bowles that "In London it would be thought very extraordinary that Six young Men should be sent to carry a Letter, that they should wander about so long, and so far out of the way." But in the end he advanced £100 to replenish their exhausted funds (Bowles to Dorchester, 7 July 1790; Dorchester to Bowles, without date, but ca. 10 July 1790; Bowles to Dorchester, 14 July 1790; Dorchester to Bowles, without date, but ca. 15 July 1790; Bowles to Dorchester, 16 July 1790, enclosing copy of address of Creek Indians to the king, 7 May 1789 and copy of address of Cherokee to the king, 6 May 1789; Bowles to Dorchester, 23 July 1790; and Dorchester to Bowles, undated, but ca. 24 July 1790, stating that he could interfere no further, that he and his followers would have to decide for themselves what to do; and that he was directing £100 to be given them as a mark of the king's friendly re- Grenville, 26 July 1790, PRO: CO gard—all enclosed in Dorchester to 42/68, f.279-81, received 3 Sep. 1790).

From Joshua Johnson

SIR   London 2nd. November 1790.

On the 14 Ultimo I had the Honor to receive the Commission of Appointment which the President of the United States had conferr'd on me together your letter of the 7 August by Coll. Humphreys; I beg you Sir, to assure the President of the gratitude and high sense I entertain of the distinguished favor conferred on me, and altho I feel myself very inadequate to the execution of the trust imposed on me, yet as an immediate exertion of it may be the means of relieving many of my Countrymen from the hands of the British Government, and prevent many more from being impress'd in their service, determined me to undertake the execution of the Office, trusting in your favorable representations and the generous constructions of my Country, on the rectitude of my intentions.—I presented my Commission at the Duke of Leeds's Office on the 20th. of last Month, and on the 22nd. obtained the King's declaration of approbation to the same, with directions to all his Officers &ca. to aid and assist me in the due exercise of the Functions appertaining thereto.

I am very sensible of the importance Political information is to you, and in this particular I dare not hope giving satisfaction: you who have been in Europe in a distinguished Character, know how difficult it is to obtain information that can be depended on without laying yourself out entirely for it, and spending considerable sums of money, this would be inconsistent with my pursuits and not justifiable to my Family; I will notwithstanding be watchfull in the attainment of every thing within my reach and transmit it you. The different Papers which you request, shall be regularly handed you, and a preference given to private conveyances, as being more secure and less expensive; All Letters received from, and for you, shall be regularly forwarded; and that by the first conveyance after their receipt.

I am striving to obtain the Account of the several Fisheries for the Year 1789, and also of the three past quarters in the present, as those documents must be obtain'd from the Clerks in the Public Office it will cost me Money, and I trust you will have no objection to refund it me out of the Funds of the Public.

Every respect and attention shall be paid to your directions regarding my applications to Government; firmness and moderation will undoubtedly do more than violence and I have received assurances of redress in all cases, from the Duke of Leeds's Office, when made with candor and supported with Justice.

I have opened an Account against the United States and charged them with the expences attending the recognizance of my Commission, to which I shall add Postage, Papers and what else may occur and render it you regularly once a Quarter to reimburse me for which, be pleased to direct a remittance for me in a Bill on London.

I note that a Bill has been brought into Congress, to define the duty of Consuls and to fix their Fees, and which had been rejected by the Senate, but which would be brought forward next Session. I trust that Congress will not be too confined, and that their liberality will be such as to enable me to continue the execution of the Office, the acceptance of which has involved me into a considerable expence, being obliged to remove from the Country to Town for the convenience of those who have business with me, and that I may be always at hand to release the men who are pressed, as well as give dispatch to Ships who want to enter, and clear, independent of which every application from other Consuls and Vice Consuls to Government must be made through me, and which with the extensive Business of this Port, will give me more employment than every other together: another situation it places me in, that of the Representative of my Country, (until a superior appointment takes place) and as such brings down on me an expence which I hope will not escape your Consideration. My recent appointment has not afforded me time to inform myself of the Practice of Consuls from other Nations so fully as I could wish, however so far as I have, I beg leave to submit them to you. In every case I find when a Consul grants a protection, he receives a Fee from the Person protected; Fees are likewise paid by the Masters of Vessells, at entrance and clearance, and in some instances there is a certain Sum collected to form a Fund for the relief of our Seamen who may be cast away, or otherwise distressed, and to place them in a situation to return and be useful to their Country, the Consul rendering you an Account quarterly of such receipts and expenditures; where such provision is not made, his humanity must supply the deficiency.—Your letter of instructions of the 26 August was delivered me the 22nd. Ultimo by

Mr. Knox, that shall be the rule of my conduct 'till I receive your further directions.

I shall at first find difficulties in getting the American Captains to conform in making their regular Reports, and Clearances, but unwearied industry shall be used to render the Account half Yearly, the most perfect possible. My endeavors shall not be wanted to discriminate who are the Proprietors of all Vessells sailing under American Colours, and who are not, as well as to prevent the transfer of Property covered by the Register granted in America, tho bona fide that of a Subject of another State. This I think might be remedied by Congress passing an Act, directing whenever a Sale of a Vessell was made that the Sellers and Buyers, should take a Certificate from the Consul resident ascertaining who the parties were, and in case of not producing the same on Entry in any of the American Ports, or other where an American Consul resides, to subject her to Seizure.

I shall from inclination as well as duty inform you of the preparations for War &c. in these Ports, as well as to guard the Merchants and others of any event that may affect Commerce and their Interest. I will not interfere with that of the appointment of any other Person, whether Consul or Vice Consul, but court a good understanding as the best means of promoting the Interest and welfare of my Country. As it was natural to suppose, I have already had applications from several who reside at different Ports, to appoint them under me; in some instances the service of my Country will require it, but I shall not take any steps, without first consulting with Mr. Maury and Mr. Aldjo, and agreeing with them on the propriety.

I have had several Complaints exhibited to me, by Commanders of American Vessells, against British Officers, for entering on board their Ships, and treating them with rough and indecent Language; when I can collect a State of Facts, on which I can ground a Memorial, I will present one to the Lords of the Admiralty, couched in very decent and firm language, and endeavor to secure their orders to their Officers, not to commit such outrages hereafter; then in case of similar complaints, I shall have a legal right to demand proper punishment. My appointment does not entitle me to Personal Political conference with the Duke of Leeds those which I have had with his Secretaries, warrant my saying that there appears every wish, and inclination, on the part of Government, to support a friendly and good understanding with the United States of America.

The opinions respecting War are various, tho' the preparations are immense and extravagantly expensive, I cannot pretend to form any decisive opinion on the Subject, but from the best information I have obtain'd, I draw this conclusion that the Minister will ward off Hostilities, and on the meeting of Parliament, state his conduct to them, and rest a War or a continuance of Peace on their decision, and by which means secure himself from the censure of the Nation.

It has occurred to me that granting Protections to individuals, they may make use of them to the prejudice of the Navigation, and Commerce of our Country, by entering in the Service of those, who will pay the highest Wages, the English now give Three pounds five shillings Sterling ℔ Month, while the Americans only give thirty Six Shillings. To remedy this evil I have determined to grant one general Protection to all American Subjects, on board each Ship, and that on the back of their Shipping Articles; this will confine them to their duty and engagements and promote the success and demand for our Ships, notwithstanding when Seamen, the Subjects of America have come to Europe in English, or other Vessells, and can give me a satisfactory proof, that they are the Subjects of the United States, I shall give them protection, recommending at the same time their serving their Country.

I have had some conversation with the Duke of Leeds's Secretary Mr. Auste on the Subject of what constitutes an American Subject, and that of an English one; his answer was that the similarity of manners, language &c. put it out of the power of Government to discriminate, and nothing but a Treaty of Alliance or a Treaty of Commerce could define, and which he had sanguine hopes of seeing take place; but for my better regulation, I should be glad that you would issue orders to every Naval Officer, to see that proper affidavits were deliver'd the Captains of Ships, at the time of clearance and to transmit me from under the Seal of the United States, that such Officers were empowered to administer the Oath, and take affidavit; such Certificates have been transmitted by the Naval Officer of New York, but for want of the Seal of the United States, certifying that such power had been invested in him, those certificates have been rejected, and not respected by the Admiralty as sufficient proof.

I am much in want of the Laws of the first and Second Session of Congress, and shall esteem your sending them to me (with any other Public Act or information) a favor, if Congress does not allow their Servants such Papers, please to deduct the cost from my Quarterly expenditures. I have by the Two Brothers Captn. Ceely, bound to New York, sent you the Court Gazette from the 14th. Ultimo up to this day: Woodfalls Register from the 14th last Month up to this day; I have also sent you two Pamphlets, the one wrote by Mr. E. Burke, the other by M. de Calonne they are esteemed curious and which I offer as my apology for sending to you; it is probable you may wish to recieve any other new publication from this, should you, you will be pleased only to say so, and they shall be forwarded you. I will do myself the Honor to write you by the British Packet on Wednesday. In the mean time I have the Honor to be with great Respect & Esteem Sir &c.

JOSHUA JOHNSON

RC (DNA: RG 59, CD); in clerk's hand, except for signature. Tr (same). Recorded in SJL as received 17 Jan. 1791 and also a duplicate received 11 Feb. 1791. Enclosures: (1) Charles Alexandre de Calonne, *De l'etat de la France, present et a venir* (London, 1790). A copy sent by William Temple Franklin to John Adams is in DLC, bearing this notation: "Mr. Adams is desired after perusing this Work to lend it to Mr. Jefferson and Mr. Secy. Hamilton. W.T.F." (Sowerby, No. 2543). (2) Edmund Burke, *Reflections on the Revolution in France* (published in London only on 1 Nov. 1790).

From William Short

DEAR SIR   Paris Nov. 2. 1790

It was not my intention to have written to you again from this place except by a person who is setting out for Philadelphia by the way of Havre; but the arrival of the long expected courier from Madrid induces me to send a few lines by the English post, merely to inform you that the negotiations at Madrid have ended in the conservation of peace.—This comes by the English messenger who in passing through [this] place yesterday evening brought dispatches as well to the Spanish as the English Ambassador. The former immediately went to M. de Montmorin's and made him the communication. It does not appear that the messenger was charged with the definitive articles. All that was communicated officially was that peace would not be interrupted.—It is said that the English have obtained the privilege of forming an establishment north of Nootka sound. This however I do not know with certainty, nor anything else of the result of the negotiation except that war will not take place between England and Spain.—I mentioned in my last that I had received the letter of the Secretary of the treasury together with yours of Aug. 31.—I have the honor to be with sentiments of the most perfect attachment, Sir, your most obedient humble servant, W: SHORT

PrC (DLC: Short Papers); at head of text: "*No. 45.*" Tr (DNA: RG 59, DD). Recorded in SJL as received 9 Feb. 1790.

To Meriwether Smith

DEAR SIR   Monticello Nov. 2. 1790.

Your letter of Feb. 4. was duly recieved, and the one it inclosed was forwarded to Mr. Short. That this was not announced to you was owing to a succession of untoward circumstances. I found on my arrival at New York a mass of business which had been accumulating for me. This employed me night and day till I was attacked by a headach which rendered me incapable of business for a month or six weeks, which again occasioned a new accumulation and this was followed by the recess of government. I am happy that your letter of Sep. 27th. which came to hand to-day, finds me here two or three days before my departure for Philadelphia, and at leisure to assure you that tho' I was unable to tell you so, yet your letter to Mr. Short was taken care of, and to add assurances of the esteem & attachment with which I have the honor to be Dr. Sir Your most obedt. & most humble servt, TH: JEFFERSON

PrC (MHi).

Smith's letter to TJ of SEP. 27TH inquiring about his of 4 Feb. 1790 covering a letter to William Short "on important Business" was forwarded to TJ at Monticello by Remsen (RC in DLC; endorsed by TJ as received 2 Nov. 1792 and so recorded in SJL).

To Garland Carr

DEAR SIR   Monticello Nov. 3. 1790.

I inclose you some papers on the matters in dispute with Mr. and Mrs. Riddick. There is a copy of the answer I shall put in, which I communicate that the executors may not place the matter on any ground inconsistent therewith. When these papers shall have been communicated to them, be so good as to put them into the hands of the lawyer you shall employ to defend the interests of Sam

Carr in aid of Mr. Ronald. Colo. Monroe would be the most convenient if he should not be sent to Congress. Mr. Anderson and Mr. Ronald have a copy of these opinions and answer of mine.

The attorney to be employed will decide what he will do in the separate suit for waste, on which subject I state some short notes only, being just on my departure and without leisure to satisfy myself on that question. I had rather a little risk should be run, if the action of waste would stand any chance, because of the superiority of the redress. I am Dear Sir Your friend & servt.,

Th: Jefferson

PrC (CSmH).

From Joshua Johnson

Sir   London 3 November 1790

The foregoing is the Copy of what I had the honor to write you on the 2 Instant, by the two Brothers Capt. Ceely, via New York, and to which I beg reference; nothing of any material consequence has since occurred; the Armaments going on as before described. The arrival of six Cherokee Indians engrosses public speculation and various are the conjectures, but the most probable is that their visit is to procure some presents from Government. Mr. Maury has transmitted me his Commission which I presented at the Duke of Leeds's Office, on Saturday, and received an assurance, that it should be recognized, and returned me in a few days; the next Gazette I suppose will announce the Kings approbation. I was informed at the Duke of Leeds's Office that some objections were made to the recognizance of Mr. Aldjo's Commission; I asked if it was on account of his being a British Subject, when they said it was not, but on account of Cowes, not being one of the regulated Ports of Trade; I observed to them that I conceived that could be no objection; that Cowes was one of the Ports which Tobacco was permitted to be landed in, and reshipped off; this seemed to remove the difficulty, but as there has not appeared any notification of the Kings approval, I am fearfull he will not be permitted to act. I will know the Minister's intention in a few days, and transmit it to you; Colo. Humphreys has taken his passage for Lisbon in one of the Traders: he leaves London this day. I will write you by the next conveyance, in the mean time, I have the honor to be, with the most perfect respect & esteem, Sir, Your most ob. & most humble Servt.,   JOSHUA JOHNSON

RC (DNA: RG 59, CD). FC (same). Recorded in SJL as received 12 Mch. 1791.

To James Lyle

DEAR SIR   Monticello November 3. 1790.

I have duly recieved your favor of the 23d. Ult. and wish I could have permitted your trouble on the subject to end there. But the sum is become too important by near 30. years interest to be left in doubt. Doctr. Walker does not question his receipt of such a sum in 1761. or 1762. His entries prove it beyond doubt and his recollection also probably. He only supposes that McCaul failed to charge the estate with it till 5. years after, to wit, Aug. 31. 1766. and that the £200. charged to him in 1766. (for which he finds no entry in his books) is the same which he in fact recieved in 1761. 1762. Since writing to you, I have turned to Mr. Harvie's books and find an account settled between him and Mr. McCaul in the following words.

Mr. Alexr. McCaul Dr.

			£
1762. Aug. 13.	To ballance of his account from folio 39.		245- 3- 1¾
1763.	To 17. hhds. tobacco Wt. 22044 22/6		247-19-10
	To 10. hhds. do. 9999 [i.e. 1999] 20/		99-19- 9
	22. casks.		3- 6- 0
			596- 8- 8¾
Aug. 3.	To ballance of the above account.		301- 8- 0¼

Contra.   Cr.

			£
1762. Dec. 25.	By cash paid pr. orders from Thomas Walker		199-18- 1
1763.	By do. paid Thurmond pr. orders from John Nicholas		12-
Aug. 3.	By sundry goods had of him as pr. account rendered to this day		83- 2- 7½
	By ballance due to the estate as pr. *settlement*		301- 8- ¼
			596- 8- 8¾

Thus you will percieve that this article (which was truly of £199-18-1. and not £200. as loosely entered by Dr. Walker) has been acknowleged and *settled* by Mr. McCaul himself as appears by the testimony of Mr. Harvie. It seems not to have been cash paid into Dr. Walker's own hands; but drawn out by orders in favor of others, which perhaps have been transferred circuitously thro' several hands so as to disguise them from your detection.

Another proof from Mr. Harvie's book is the account he has stated against Dr. Walker, in which this article stands as follows. '1762. To cash *in account* with Mr. McCaul £199-18-1.' Had Dr. Walker any account with Mr. McCaul at that time and does that throw any light on the subject?

I have no apprehension but that your books will establish the payment of £200. in Aug. 31. 1766. in date as well as sum: and there would never have been a doubt of the £199-18-1 of 1761. 1762. against the evidence of Mr. Harvie and admission of Doctr. Walker, but from your not being able to trace it in Mr. McCaul's accounts. I must therefore give you the trouble of employing some person to copy the whole accounts of my father's estate from his death till Mr. Harvie turned over the business to Mr. Nicholas, which was I believe in 1764. Of the transactions subsequent to this event you gave an account to Mr. Nicholas. As all the dealings of the estate were with Kippen & co. their account complete is essential to the settlement of the affairs of the estate. The expence of copying this earlier part of the account, which I now ask, shall be mine. Once possessed of the account fully, I trust I shall be able to decypher these payments. I can get no account of Mr. Harvie's papers or they might have saved all this trouble.

But there is another kind of evidence I think you must possess. As Dr. Walker seems to have drawn this money in 1761. 1762. by orders, those orders must have been taken in, and put away with the vouchers of the account. If you can find these, it will put the matter out of doubt. If any one or two vouchers can be found, it should establish the whole. Do, my dear Sir, take the trouble to have them sought out, as a sum of near £500. which this becomes now, is too serious a thing to lose for want of proof.[1]

I thought that my mother's balance had been included in my account which I settled with you and gave bonds for. I am now so near my departure for Philadelphia that it is impossible for me to open two such bundles as that and my account of the administration of her estate. I will examine into it the next visit I pay here and then write to you.

Be so good as to forward the account asked, to me at Philadelphia by post, together with any further information you can give me.

I shall write you again either from here or there on the subject of my payment of next July. I am with great esteem Dear Sir Your most obedt. humble servt,   TH: JEFFERSON

PrC (MHi).

¹ At this point TJ heavily deleted a sentence which appears to read as follows: "Indeed if I were to suffer this [our affair . . .]."

To Francis Walker

DEAR SIR   Monticello Nov. 3. 1790.

I have paid due attention to the memorandum you were so good as to put into my hands. Since I recieved it, it occurred to me that as Mr. Harvie was a very exact accountant his accounts would probably throw light on the transaction of 1761. I have turned to his book, and in fact find that in the account he stated between Dr. Walker and my father's estate he has charged Doctr. Walker '1762. To cash *in account* with Mr. McCaul £199-18-1.' and in the account he has stated between Mr. McCaul and my father's estate he credits McCaul '1762. Dec. 25. By cash paid pr. orders from Thomas Walker £199-18-1.' and this account appears to have been settled with McCaul, and a balance acknowledged due to the estate of £301-8-0½. I have no doubt but that Dr. Walker's rough memorandum book will confirm and explain this paiment of £199-18-1 in 1761. or 1762. according to Mr. Harvie's and his own account, and consider it as perfectly established, tho as yet Mr. Lyle has not been able to decypher it in the entries of McCaul's account against the estate. I have written to him for a copy of the whole account, and trust I shall be able to trace it.

With respect to the £200. Aug. 31. 1766. Mr. Lyle is clear and positive. He says in a letter to me that it is impossible that that can have been the same with the charges of either 1761. or 1764. and I suppose the books of Kippen & co. will establish this payment also.

As I cannot expect to recieve the account I have asked from Mr. Lyle till some time hence, and I am now near my departure, it will not be possible to settle this question till my next visit to Albemarle. My confidence unlimited in the justice of Dr. Walker, and consciousness of my own wishes for nothing more, induce me to have no doubt we shall settle it to mutual satisfaction as soon as all the evidence necessary can be had.

As I have never actually meddled with the administration of[1] Mr. Carr's estate, I am desirous of still avoiding it in any instance, that I may have no administration account to settle as to his estate. I have therefore put the account against him which you gave me, into Peter Carr's hands, who will either settle it himself, or get it done by the most convenient executor. Indeed there is nothing to settle but to reduce the credit of £200. to £100. and ascertain the dates of the two articles on which the interest depends. I am with great esteem & attachment Dear Sir Your most obedt & most humble servt,   TH: JEFFERSON

RC (DLC: Rives Papers); addressed: "Francis Walker esquire Castlehill Albemarle." PrC (ViU); incomplete (see note).

[1] PrC ends at this point.

Preliminary indexes will be issued periodically for groups of volumes. Indexes covering Vols. 1-6 and 7-12 have been published. A comprehensive index of persons, places, subjects, etc., arranged in a single consolidated sequence, will be issued at the conclusion of the series.

THE PAPERS OF THOMAS JEFFERSON is composed in Monticello, a type specially designed by the Mergenthaler Linotype Company for this series. Monticello is based on a type design originally developed by Binny & Ronaldson, the first successful typefounding company in America. It is considered historically appropriate here because it was used extensively in American printing during the last thirty years of Jefferson's life, 1796 to 1826; and because Jefferson himself expressed cordial approval of Binny & Ronaldson types.

❖

DESIGNED BY P. J. CONKWRIGHT